ADVANCES IN OCCUPATIONAL ERGONOMICS AND SAFETY 1997

Proceedings of the Annual International Occupational Ergonomics
and Safety Conference held in Washington, D. C., U.S.A.,
June 1–4 1997

Edited by
BIMAN DAS
Department of Industrial Engineering
Dalhousie University
Halifax, Nova Scotia, Canada

and

WALDEMAR KARWOWSKI
Center for Industrial Engineering
University of Louisville
Louisville, KY, U.S.A.

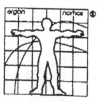

International Society
for Occupational
Ergonomics and Safety

IOS
Press

Ohmsha

ISBN 90 5199 349 8 (IOS Press)
ISBN 4 274 90174 2 C3050 (Ohmsha)

Printed on acid-free paper.

Publisher
IOS Press
Van Diemenstraat 94
1013 CN Amsterdam
Netherlands

Distributor in the UK and Ireland
IOS Press/Lavis Marketing
73 Lime Walk
Headington
Oxford OX3 7AD
England

Distributor in Germany
IOS Press
Spandauer Strasse 2
D–10178 Berlin
Germany

Distributor in the USA and Canada
IOS Press, Inc.
P.O. Box 10558
Burke, VA 22009–0558
USA

Distributor in Japan
Ohmsha Ltd.
3–1 Kanda Nishiki-cho
Chiyoda-ku
Tokyo 101
Japan

LEGAL NOTICE
The publisher is not responsible for the use that might be made of the following information.

PRINTED IN THE UNITED STATES OF AMERICA

Preface

Over the last decade the *Annual International Occupational Ergonomics and Safety Conference* sponsored by the *International Society for Occupational Ergonomics and safety (ISOES)* has truly become an important yearly forum, where international researchers and industrial practitioners can meet and focus their attention to current issues and problems of occupational ergonomics and safety. Although the conference participants come from various discipline areas, they all have a common objective to create productive, healthy and safe workplaces. Proceedings of this conference provide a wide range of research topics and variety of industrial applications that should prove to be a valuable source of knowledge and information to all concerned with occupational ergonomics and safety.

The *Advances in Occupational Ergonomics and safety II* volume contains one hundred and thirty-nine papers, authored by two hundred and seventy-five researchers and practitioners around the world. The papers are arranged under main topical areas (by sections) and further subdivided into relevant chapters . Overall, the volume contains six sections and twenty chapters. We wish to convey our sincere thanks to all the authors for their contributions.

Special thanks are extended to Mr. Bijon Das and Ms. Cindi Hardiman for their help in the preparation of this volume. The cooperation of Dr. Einar H. Fredriksson and Ms. Margaret Brown, IOS Press (Publishers) is duly acknowledged.

Finally, we are indeed grateful to our families for their understanding and support of our professional efforts.

June 1, 1997
Halifax, Nova Scotia, Canada &
Louisville, Kentucky, USA

Biman Das and
Waldemar Karwowski
Editors

Dedication

This volume is dedicated to our families:

Diane, Anjali and Bijon Das

Bernardette, Mateusz and Jessica Karwowski

CONTENTS

2. Occupational Risk and Cost Assessment

3. Work Assessment Techniques

4. Education and Training in Ergonomics

II.   ERGONOMICS PRODUCT AND PROCESS DESIGN

5.   Ergonomics Analysis and Design

6.   Product Design and Ergonomics

7. Ergonomics in Design

III.   PHYSICAL ERGONOMICS

8. Occupational Biomechanics

9. Manual Materials Handling

10. Human Strength and Measurement

14. Cumulative Trauma Disorders

V. INFORMATION, COMMUNICATIONS AND PERFORMANCE ERGONOMICS

15. Human Computer Interaction

19. Work Environment

AUTHOR INDEX

CONFERENCE ADDRESSES

Advances in Occupational Ergonomics and Safety II
Edited by Biman Das and Waldemar Karwowski
IOS Press and Ohmsha, 1997

The Economics of Ergonomics

Hal W. HENDRICK

Error Analysis, Inc., 7100 E. Crestline Avenue, Englewood, CO, 80111 USA

Abstract. A lack of managerial exposure to the discipline, and to what can be accomplished through sound ergonomics application, is cited as a major reason for organizations not giving greater attention to the use of ergonomics. To help remedy this situation, a series of case studies which resulted in both improved health and safety and substantial documented cost benefits is presented.

1. Introduction

Human factors/ergonomics professionals have long recognized the tremendous potential of their discipline for improving the health, safety and comfort of persons, and both human and system productivity. Indeed, through the application of human-system interface technology, ergonomics has the *potential* to truly make a difference in the quality of life for virtually all persons on this globe.

In light of this potential, why is it, then, that more organizations, with their strong need to obtain employee commitment, reduce expenses, and increase productivity, are not giving greater attention to the use of ergonomics. Although various reasons could be cited, a major one often is a lack of managerial exposure to the discipline of ergonomics. Of particular note, managers often are not aware of the cost benefits that often result from effective use of ergonomics in occupational settings. Put simply, when there is a true managerial commitment to effectively applying ergonomics to the design or modification of work systems and environments, not only are improvements in health and safety possible, but considerable cost benefits usually can be realized as well. To demonstrate this point, what follows are documented case examples from a variety of industries, in the United States and elsewhere, that have been collected by my predecessor as HFES President, Tom Eggemeier, and myself for the Human Factors and Ergonomics Society. The Society's goal is to make these, and the other cases collected, widely available for the purpose of increasing public awareness of the benefits of ergonomics.

2. Case Examples

2.1. Forestry Industry

The first set of examples deal with forestry. A coordinated series of joint projects were undertaken by the Forest Engineering Technology Department of the University of Stellenbosch and Ergotech - the only true ergonomics consulting firm in South Africa - to improve safety and productivity in the South African forestry industry.

Leg protectors. In one project, an anthropometric survey was conducted of the very heterogeneous work force to provide the basic data for redesigning leg protectors for foresters. The South African Forestry Industry is populated with a wide variety of ethnic groups, having widely varying anthropometric measurements. The original protector, obtained from Brazil, was modified to ergonomically improve the types of fastening and anthropometric dimensions, as well as to incorporate improved materials. Included in the ergonomic design modification process was an extensive series of usability tests over a six month period. Then, in a well designed field test, this ergonomically modified leg protector was introduced in a eucalyptus plantation for use by persons responsible for ax/hatchet debranching. Among the 300 laborers, an average of ten injuries per day was occurring with an average sick leave of five days per injury. During the one year period of the test, not one single ax/hatchet leg injury occurred, resulting not only in the considerable savings in human pain and suffering, but also in a direct net cost savings to the company of $250,000. Use of the leg protectors throughout the South African hardwood forestry industry is conservatively calculated to save $4 million annually. [1]

Tractor-trailer design. A second study involved ergonomically improving the seating and visibility of 23 tractor-trailer forwarding units of a logging company with an investment of $300 per unit. This resulted in a better operating position for loading , improved vision, and improved operator comfort. As a result, downtimes caused by accident damage to hydraulic hoses, fittings, etc. went down by $2,000 per year per unit; and daily hardwood extraction was increased by one load per day per vehicle. All toll, for a total investment of $6,900, a savings of $65,000 per year was achieved - a 1 to 9.4 cost benefit ratio. [1]

Other Projects. Other innovations by this same collaborative effort between Stellenbosch University, Ergotec, and various forestry companies have included (a) the development of a unique light-weight, environmentally friendly pipe type of timber chute for more efficiently and safely transporting logs down slopes, (b) redesign of three-wheeled hydrostatic loaders to reduce both excessive whole-body vibration and noise, (c) classifying different terrain conditions - including ground slope, roughness, and other conditions - and determining the most effective tree harvesting system (method and equipment) for each, and (d) developing ergonomic check lists and work environment surveys tailored to the forest industry. All of these are expected to result in significant cost savings, as well as greater employee satisfaction and improved quality of work life. [1]

This series of ergonomics applications provides a good example of what ergonomics can potentially contribute to *any* given industry when there is a true collaborative effort.

2.2. Materials Handling Systems

One group that does a somewhat better job of documenting the costs and benefits of their ergonomic interventions than many ergonomists is the faculty of the Department of Human Work Sciences at Lulea University of Technology in Sweden. The following examples are from the Department's Division of Environment Technology's work with steel mills. The basic approach to ergonomic analysis and redesign in these projects was to involve employee representatives with the Lulea faculty. For each project, the economic "pay off" period was calculated jointly with the company's management. (personal communication)

Steel pipes and rods handling & stock-keeping system. A semi-automatic materials handling and stock keeping system for steel pipes and rods was ergonomically redesigned. The old system had an unacceptably high noise level and rejection rate. The redesign reduced the noise level in the area from 96 dba to 78 dba, increased production by 10%, dropped rejection from 2.5% to 1%, and paid back the redesign and development costs in approximately 18 months. After that, it was all profit.

Tube manufacturing handling & storage system. In a tube manufacturing facility, a tube handling and storage system had an unacceptably high noise level, high rejection rate from damage, required heavy lifting, had inefficient product organization and a poor safety record. Ergonomic redesign eliminated stock damage, improved stock organization, reduced lifting forces to an acceptable level, reduced the noise level by 20 dba; and has, to date, resulted in zero accidents, and in a productivity increase with a payback period of only 15 months.

Forge shop manipulator. In a forge shop, the old manipulator was replaced with a new one, having an ergonomically designed cabin and over-all better work place design. In comparison with the old manipulator, whole body vibration was reduced, noise was reduced by 18 dba, operator sick leave dropped from 8% to 2%, productivity improved, and maintenance costs dropped by 80%.

2.3. Workstation Redesign

Fine assembly work stations. Typical work stations at a major electronics assembly plant result in poor postures and resultant work-related musculoskeletal disorders. Valrie Venda of the University of Manitoba has designed a new type of fine assembly work station which utilizes a TV Camera and Monitor. Not only does the TV camera provide a greatly enlarged image of the assembly work, but enables the worker to maintain a better posture and more dynamic motion. Based on extensive comparative testing of the old and new work stations, a 15% higher productivity rate is obtained with the new one. Venda reports that the average value of products assembled per worker per shift at these types of workstations varies between $15,000 and $20,000. Thus, the additional value produced by one worker per day using the new work station will be $2,250 to $3,000 per day. Although it is too early to say precisely, Venda predicts the new work stations eventually will decrease occupational injuries for these jobs by about 20% (Valrie Venda, personal communication).

Workstation tools: Poultry de-boning knife. A conventional de-boning knife in use at a poultry packaging plant did a poor job of de-boning and resulted in a high incident rate of carpal tunnel syndrome, tendinitis, and tenosynovitis. A new, ergonomically designed pistol-shaped knife was introduced by ergonomist Ian Chong, Principal of Ergonomics, Inc. of Seattle Washington. Less pain and happier cutting crews were reported almost immediately. Upper extremity work-related musculoskeletal disorders were greatly reduced, line speeds increased by two percent to six percent, profits increased because of more efficient de-boning; and, over a five year period, $500,000 was saved in worker's compensation premiums (Ian Chong, personal communication). This is a good example of how a simple, often inexpensive ergonomic solution can sometimes have a very high cost-benefit payoff.

2.4. Reducing Work-Related Musculoskeletal Disorders

AT&T Global. AT&T Global Information Solutions in San Diego employees 800 people and manufactures large mainframe computers. Following analyses of their OSHA 200 logs, the company identified three types of frequent injuries: lifting, fastening, and keyboarding. The company next conducted extensive work site analyses to identify ergonomic deficiencies. As a result, the company made extensive ergonomic workstation improvements and provided proper lifting training for all employees. In the first year following the changes, worker's compensation losses dropped more than 75%, from $400,000 to $94,000. In a second round of changes, conveyor systems were replaced with small, individual scissors-lift platforms, and heavy pneumatic drivers with lighter electric ones; this was followed by moving from an assembly line process to one where each worker builds an entire cabinet, with the ability to readily shift from standing to sitting. A further reduction in worker's compensation losses to $12,000 resulted. In terms of lost workdays due to injury, in 1990 there were 298; in both 1993 and 1994 there were none. All toll, these ergonomic changes have reduced worker's compensation costs at AT&T Global over the 1990-1994 period by

$1.48 million. The added costs for these ergonomic improvements represent only a small fraction of these savings. [2]

Red Wing Shoes. Beginning in 1985 with (a) the initiation of a safety awareness program which includes basic machine setup and operation, safety principles and body mechanics, CTD's, and monthly safety meetings, (b) a stretching, exercise and conditioning program, (c) the hiring of an ergonomics advisor, and (d) specialized training on ergonomics and workstation setup for machine maintenance workers and industrial engineers, the Red Wing Shoe Company of Red Wing, Minnesota made a commitment to reducing WMSD's via ergonomics. The company purchased adjustable ergonomic chairs for all seated operators and anti fatigue mats for all standing jobs, instituted Continuous Flow Manufacturing, which included operators working in groups, cross training and job rotation, ergonomically redesigned selected machines and workstations for flexibility and elimination of awkward postures, and greater ease of operation, and modified production processes to reduce cumulative trauma strain. As a result of these various ergonomic interventions, workers compensation insurance premiums dropped by 70% from 1989 to 1995, for a savings of $3.1 million. During this same period, the number of OSHA reportable lost time injury days dropped from a ratio of 75 for 100 employees working a year, to 19. The success of this program is attributed to upper management's support, employee education and training, and having everyone responsible for coordinating ergonomics. [3]

Reducing WMSDs via ergonomics training. In 1992, Bill Brough of Washington Ergonomics conducted a one day seminar for cross disciplinary teams of engineers, human resource management personnel, and safety/ergonomics committee members from seven manufacturing companies insured by Tokyo Marine and Fire Insurance Company, Ltd.. The seminar taught the basic principles of ergonomics and provided the materials to implement a participatory ergonomics process. The training focused on techniques for involving the workers in evaluating present workplace conditions and making cost effective improvements. The class materials provided the tools for establishing a baseline, setting improvement goals, and measuring results. In six of the companies, the seminar data and materials were used by the teams to implement a participatory ergonomics program with the workers, and received both funding from management and support from labor. The seventh company did *not* participate in the implementation of the training. Follow-up support was provided by a Senior Loss Control Consultant for Tokyo Marine. For the six companies that *did* participate, reported strain type injuries dropped progressively from 131 in the six months prior to the training to 42 for the six month period ending 18 months later. The cost of these injuries for the six months prior was $688,344. for the six month period ending 18 months later, the injury costs had dropped to $72,600, for a net savings over 18 months of $1,348,748, using the six months prior as the baseline. Worker involvement reportedly created enthusiasm and encouraged each individual to assume responsibility for the program's success. According to Bill Brough, the reduction of injuries resulted from a commitment to continuous improvement and was obtained by many small changes, not a major singular event. For the one company that did not participate in implementing the training, the number of reported strain injuries was 12 for the six months prior to training, and 10, 16, and 25 respectively for the next three six months periods. In short, things got worse rather than better. Coupled with both management's and labor's active support, Tokyo Marine traces these reductions in strain type injuries for the six participating companies directly back to Bill Brough's participatory ergonomics training program and related materials. This is a good example of what can happen when you couple collaborative management-labor commitment with professional ergonomics. (Bill Brough, personal communication and supporting documentation).

Deer and Company. One of the best known successful industrial safety ergonomics programs is that at Deere and Company. In 1979, Deere recognized that traditional interventions like employee lift training and conservative medical management were, by them-selves, insufficient to reduce injuries. So the company began to use ergonomic principles to redesign and reduce physical stresses of the job. Eventually, ergonomics coordinators were appointed in all of Deere's U.S. and Canadian factories, foundries and distribution centers. These coordinators, chosen from the industrial engineering and safety departments, were trained in ergonomics. Today, job evaluations and analyses are done in-house by both part-time ergonomics coordinators and wage-employee ergonomics teams and committees. The company has developed its own ergonomics check lists and surveys. The program involves extensive employee participation. Since 1979, Deere has recorded an 83% reduction in back injuries, and by 1984 had reduced workers' compensation costs by 32%. According to Gary Lovestead, each year, literally hundreds to thousands of ergonomics improvements are implemented; and today, ergonomics is built into Deere's operating culture. [4]

Union Pacific. In the early 80's, the Palestine Car Shop near Dallas, Texas had the worst safety statistics of the Union Pacific Railroad's shop operations. Of particular note was the high incidence of back injuries. The University of Michigan Center for Ergonomics computer model for back compression was modified and expanded for easy application to the railroad environment, and packaged by the Association of American Railroads. The AAR-Back Model was introduced at the Palistine Car Shop to identify job tasks that ex-ceeded acceptable back compression values, and equipment supporting various jobs requir-ing lifting was redesigned. In addition, a commercial back injury training program, "Pro-Back", was adopted and every employee was taught how to bend and lift safely. Finally, management attitude and priorities about safety were conveyed through weekly meetings with safety captains from each work area, and quarterly "town hall" meetings with all shop employees. From 1985 to 1988, the total incidents of injuries went from 33 to 12; back in-cidents from 13 to 0; Lost days from 579 to 0; restricted days from 194 to 40 (all from mi-nor, non-back injuries), and absenteeism from 4 percent to 1 percent. Number of cars re-paired per year went from 1,564 in 1985 to 2,900 in 1988, an increase in dollar value of $3.96 million. Union Pacific calculates the cost-benefit ratio as approximately 1 to 10. [5]

2.5 Macroergonomics

Petroleum distribution company. Several years ago, Andy Imada of the University of Southern California began a macroergonomic analysis and intervention program to improve safety and health in a major petroleum distribution company. The key components of this intervention included an organizational assessment that generated a strategic plan for im-proving safety, equipment changes to improve working conditions and enhance safety, and three macroergonomic classes of action items. These items included improving employee involvement, communication, and integrating safety into the broader organizational culture. The program utilized a participatory ergonomics approach involving all levels of the divi-sion's management and supervision, terminal and filling station personnel, and the truck drivers. Over the course of several years, many aspects of the system's organizational de-sign and management structure and processes were examined from a macroergonomics per-spective and, in some cases, modified. Employee initiated ergonomic modifications were made to some of the equipment, new employee-designed safety training methods and structures were implemented, and employees were given a greater role in selecting new tools and equipment related to their jobs. Two years after initial installation of the program, industrial injuries had been reduced by 54%, motor vehicle accidents by 51%, off-the-job injuries by 84%, and lost work days by 94%. By four years later, further reductions oc-curred for all but off-the-job injuries, which climbed back 15%. [6]

The company's Area Manager of Operations reports that he continues to save one-half of one percent of the petroleum delivery costs every year as a direct result of the macroergonomics intervention program - a net savings of approximately $60,000 per year for the past three years, or $180,000 - and expects this savings to continue. Imada reports that perhaps the greatest reason for these *sustained* improvements has been the successful installation of safety as part of the organization's culture. (Imada, personal communication)

L L Bean. Rooney, Morency, and Herrick [7] have reported on the use of macroergonomics as an approach and methodology for introducing total quality management (TQM) at the L. L. Bean corporation. Using methods similar to those described above for Imada's intervention, but with TQM as the primary objective, over a 70% reduction in lost time accidents and injuries was achieved within a two year period in both the production and distribution divisions of the company. Other benefits, such as greater employee satisfaction and improvements in additional quality measures also were achieved. Given the present emphasis in many organizations on implementing ISO 9000, these results take on an even greater significance.

3. Conclusion

The above are but a sample of the variety of ergonomic interventions which the human factors/ergonomics profession is capable of providing to not only improve the human condition, but the bottom line as well. From my 35 years of observation and experience, only rarely are truly good ergonomic interventions *not* beneficial in terms of the criteria that are used by managers in evaluating the allocation of their resources.

As many of the above cases also illustrate, ergonomics offers a wonderful common ground for labor and management collaboration; for invariably, both can benefit - managers, in terms of reduced costs and improved productivity, employees in terms of improved safety, health, comfort, usability of tools and equipment, including software, and improved quality of work life. Of course, both groups benefit from the increased competitiveness and related increased likelihood of long-term organizational survival that ultimately is afforded.

Acknowledgments

Reprinted with adoptions from, and additions to the author's 1996 HFES Presidential Address: The Ergonomics of Economics is the Economics of Ergonomics, *Proceedings of the Human Factors and Ergonomics Society 40th Annual Meeting,* Human Factors and Ergonomics Society, Santa Monica, CA, with permission.

References

[1] W. Warkotsch, Ergonomic Research in South African Forestry. *Suid-Afrikaanse Bosbou Tydskrif, 171* (1994) 53-62.

[2] Center for Workplace Health Information, An Ergonomics Honor Roll: Case Studies of Results-Oriented Programs, AT&T Global, *CTD News Special Report: Best Ergonomic Practices* (1995) 4-6.

[3] Center for Workplace Health Information, An Ergonomics Honor Roll: Case Studies of Results-Oriented Programs, Red Wing Shoes, *CTD News Special Report: Best Ergonomic Practices* (1955) 2-3.

[4] Center for Workplace Health Information, An Ergo Process That Runs Like A Deer, *CTD News, 8* (1995) 6-10.

[5] American Association of Railroads, Research Pays Off: Preventing Back Injuries, AAR Program Adopted at Union Pacific, *TR News, 140* (1989) 16-17.

[6] M. Nagamachi and A. S. Imada, A Macroergonomic Approach for Improving Safety and Work Design. *Proceedings of the 36th Annual Meeting of the Human Factors and Ergonomics Society,* Human Factors and Ergonomics Society, Santa Monica, CA, 1992, pp. 859-861.

[7] E. F. Rooney, R. R. Morency, and D. R. Herrick, Macroergonomics and Total Quality Management at L. L. Bean, In N. R. Neilson and K. Jorgansen (eds.), *Advances in Industrial Ergonomics and Safety V,* Taylor & Francis, London, 1993, pp. 493-498.

Advances in Occupational Ergonomics and Safety II
Edited by Biman Das and Waldemar Karwowski
IOS Press and Ohmsha, 1997

System of Occupational Health & Safety Management in Conditions of Poland's Economic Renewal and Entrepreneurship

Leszek M. PACHOLSKI

Labour Protection Council, Parliament of the Republic of Poland;
ul Wiejska 6/8, 00-902 Warsaw, Poland

Abstract. The observed *restructure disproportion* consisting in the occurrence of biggest socio-economical losses associated with occupational health and safety during the period of the fastest progress in economic development of countries realizing programs of entrepreneurship and economic renewal is a general regularity, only seemingly constituted a case concerning Polish conditions of economic renewal. It appears that it is possible to restrict the bove mentioned social and economic losses by effective implementation of systemic solutions presented in this article which comprise three areas: economic stimulation, legislation and management.

1. Introduction

Available literature data from countries which achieved significant economical progress in recent decades indicate that the period of the most rapid economical growth (characterized by the highest increase of total gross domestic product) is coincidental with the highest socio-economical losses connected with occupational health and safety.

This regularity, further referred to as *restructure disproportion*, appears to be corroborated also by the current period of economical renewal and entrepreneurship in Poland.

In the last three years, there has been an unequivocal progress in economical growth in Poland. Its most important parameters are:

a. real-term growth of the gross national product (GNP) by over 20%, of which 7% growth was recorded in 1996,

b. threefold drop in the rate of inflation to 18. 5% in 1996, in the case of the price index of industrial production, the drop amounted to about 10%,

c. almost 40% increase of investment expenditures, of which 18% occurred in 1996,

d. improvement of competitiveness of economy by realization of foreign investments on the cumulative sum of 14 billion US$, of which 5 billion occurred in 1996.

Furthermore, for Poles, last year (1996) resulted in: creation of nearly half a million new jobs, 4. 2% increase of real wages, the lowest for five years budget deficit at the level of approximately 2. 4% of the GNP as well as a drop in the public debt in relation to GNP to below 53%. Also last year Poland became a full member of the prestigious organization - OECD.

Unfortunately, good condition of Polish economy is accompanied by negative phenomena in the field of occupational health and safety. Annually, nearly a 10% increase in the number of victims of occupational accidents is recorded (despite a few percentage drop in the number of most severe accidents). A particularly apparent increase of indexes of incidence of occupational accidents occurs in the dynamically developing sector of private companies. An equally disturbing growing tendency, during the past three years of transformation of Polish economy, has been recorded in the incidence indexes of occupational diseases.

2. Causes of restructure disproportions

The influence of processes of economical renewal and entrepreneurship on the state of labour conditions in Poland today seems to vary and depends on such factors as: the economical condition of an enterprise before renewal, knowledge and managerial qualifications of the management and supervision, habits and customs taken over from the enterprise from the period preceding the period of renewal, development perspectives of the company. In those companies which were economically sound and well managed before privatization, occupational health and safety standards are, as a rule, satisfactory. A positive effect of transformation processes in the area of entrepreneurship and economical renewal can be observed in companies with foreign capital in which a significant influx of investment resources made it possible to introduce new technologies which effectively improved the state of occupational health and safety. However, numerous irregularities in the area of occupational ergonomics and safety occur in enterprises characterized by bad financial situation and low level of management which were privatized by way of bankruptcy.

The scale of contraventions of labour law, including occupational health and safety regulations, is strongly affected by the lack of equilibrium between the degree of organization, on the one hand, and the appeal to employers and employees, on the other. In the public sector enterprises trade unions retained their dominant role, whereas in private companies employers are dominant at almost total absence of trade unions. Social control of labour conditions remains in retreat and the activity of social partners (trade unions) is quite insufficient. Employee organizations remain unprepared to fulfill their role of a coordinator and organizer of undertakings which would lead to improvement of occupational health and safety standards.

In conclusion, is should be stated that many negative phenomena in the field of occupational health and safety result from the lack of systemic solutions comprising, management, law and economy.

3. Aim and subject of the system renewal

The aim and subject of the system renewal in the field of occupational health and safety can be defined as: *anthropocentrically orientated rationalization of management of human resources in labour processes*. These resources comprise physical, intellectual, spiritual and social condition of the worker as the subject of occupational health and safety.

A systemic approach allows to include into the category of labour subject all participants of the system, i.e.: *employees, employers and the state*. Hence, we can talk about a tri-elemental subject within the system of occupational health and safety.

Any rationalization of resources must take into considerations the following three problems: *economical, formal / legal and organizational*. Naturally, these problems also comprise questions of evaluation criteria of the state, institutional solutions and issues connected with personnel qualifications.

It should be emphasized that *instrumentally* (economy, law, management) and *institutionally* (organizational structures) treated system of occupational health and safety constitutes a unity, in a cybernetic sense, which is relatively detached. It means that the system is functionally determined by such peripheral areas as: level of technology and management, state of ergological knowledge and perception, civilization and mental preconceptions, social and political culture, legislative effectiveness, property relations etc.

Implementation of new systemic solutions concerning occupational health and safety is a process. One of the characteristic features of all processes is that they take time and, in a long-term perspective, any attempt to apply *action approach* procedures can only inhibit progress. Therefore, the essential issue of the occupational health and safety system must address the *implementation mode of a complex of mutually consistent economical, legal and organizational solutions which would stimulate occupational health and safety behaviour of employers, employees and the state in accordance with international conventions.*

Current attempts to create such strategies encounter two types of resistance. The first of them, based on particularism, often on lack of education, perceives changes of mechanisms as threats to petrified organizational structures. It is also based on cliquish centralization and dominance of phraseology over professionalism. The second type of resistance is associated with a lack of social awareness of the existence of division of tasks and obligations in the field of occupational health and safety between the state, employers and employees.

4. Economical stimulators

At first sight, activation of economical stimulators of the occupational health and safety system appears to belong to the domain of the state. However, the economical game goes on among all the participants of the tri-elemental subject. In this situation, it would not be fair to talk even about a one-sided initiative when all the three partners are interested in concrete rational and irrational consequences of the assumed stimulation rules. Let us analyze some selected details of this game, as exemplified by the following four mechanisms:

a. *The subsystem of employers' payments* for postponement of administrative decision concerning breaching of acceptable norms and standards should be based on the responsibility of employers to perform specified measurements of harmful factors. In case of non-compliance, the employer would be obliged to undertake appropriate actions to reduce concentrations of harmful agents to the level of current norms. The process of reaching the level recommended by current norms should not exceed the time specified by the safety supervisor. During this period of time, the employer would have a special responsibility to increase his care over employees' life and health by e.g.: shortening of working time, increased rotation of the staff or individual protective measures. The system of payments should be designed so as to encourage a given enterprise to invest money into the removal of the threat. The decision imposing the payment should be an administrative decision with a possibility of its change by an organ of a higher rank and with the right of appeal against it to an administrative court. It is essential to work out a catalog of payments and to make it public so that employers can perform appropriate economic calculations. Payments paid by individual 'economic subjects' should supply a *labour protection fund*. The fund should additionally be supplied from fines and other payments of repressive character imposed on employers. The objective of the fund ought to be the support of all initiatives aiming at improvement of labour safety and conditions. The fund board should, therefore, grant low-interest and partially amortized loans to those who fulfill the statutory goals of the fund. The fund board (which should be made of representatives of employers and employees) should periodically present settlement of its results to a "state strategic institution of the system". Since the fund would play an important role in the area of accident prevention, its statute should provide possibility of additional supply from prevention funds of insurance institutions.

b. *Insurance system* - of both employers (property and indemnity insurance) and employees (accident and social insurance) - should have certain common elements which would be independent of insurance institution. Risk assessment should be carried out taking into consideration specificity of branch, accident incidence in a given group of enterprises, state of safety in a given company. The insurer should, therefore, diversify the insurance premium in cases of increased hazard. The system of social insurance - both compulsory and voluntary - should vary the premium not only in relation to the income of the insured but also to the level of risk. When assessing the degree of risk in a given enterprise, the insuring institution should have the right to seek the advice of the so *called Central Office of State Administration of the System.* Within individual types of insurance, it should be possible to diversify the insurance premium for a given subject, for example, at the request of the above mentioned Office, both with regards to reducing it (if the economic subject implements measures aiming at improvement of labour conditions) or punitive increase the premium. At economic transformations, the insurance system should act as a stimulator of desirable behaviour of employers.

c. The fiscal policy of the state should allow for the development *of a subsystem of tax concessions* for subjects investing in improvement of labour conditions. These concessions should be granted to individual firms by an organ of tax police (or its equivalent) on condition that they realize specified tasks. The subsystem of tax concessions should constitute a sufficiently stable solution so as to allow employers to plan several years ahead.

d. The above mentioned subsystem of tax concessions should cooperate *with a subsystem of preferential bank loans* stimulating improvement of labour conditions. Loans granted to economic subjects for realization of specific tasks should have more attractive interest rates in comparison with others, while banks granting such credits should have the difference in the cost of interest rates reimbursed from budgetary sources. The credit policy of banks in this respect should be supervised by the above mentioned *Central Office of State Administration of the System* which would be responsible for the reimbursement within resources allocated from the state budget.

5. Legislation

Creation of legal regulations is primarily the domain of the state. The organs which are responsible for legislation is the parliament as well as highest administrative state organs which issue appropriate executive regulations to bills. There is an urgent need to pass new formal regulations of the occupational health and safety system adjusted to modern requirements. Assuming as the point of departure the existing Labour Code, it is essential to elaborate and implement, as the result of cooperation of the strategic institution of the system with all administrative units of the system, the entire package of legal regulations and norms which would allow implementation and operation of the occupational health and safety system. The main requirement to be fulfilled by this new legislation should be: coherence and transparency. Therefore, it would be necessary: to clearly distinguish general and specific regulations, to separate clearly the object range of normative acts (overlapping of directives issued by different organs), to establish appropriate hierarchy of normative acts and do everything not to abuse them.

In order to accomplish the specified tasks, a certain amount of planning is needed to prepare and issue the required regulations. This can be achieved when all responsibilities connected with the realization of the occupational health and safety task are controlled by one organ. Such an organ, tentatively called *Strategic Institution of the System*, should assist parliamentarians in the process of preparation of the bill on labour protection system. This bill could constitute the basis for further legislative work of lower order concerning: economic mechanisms, operation of the system institutions, standards and norms as well as education, promotion and scientific backup.

The legislative-formal aspect only seemingly appears to be the domain of only one of the participants of the tri-elemental subject in the occupational health and safety system. In practice, both the parliamentary representation of employers and employees organizations as well as their representatives supporting *Strategic Institution of the System* (for example, sitting on the board of this institution) can actively, albeit indirectly, participate in the process of legislation and improvement of the assessment criteria of labour conditions.

6. Management and managers

Generation of the policy within the area of occupational health and safety system ought to be supervised and stimulated by an independent, state strategic organ. Such an organ would be responsible for the management of the entire occupational health and safety system by formulating objectives, stimulation, ensuring resources and initiating legislative solutions. The *Strategic Institution of the System*, by way of supervision of the occupational health and safety fund, could effectively promote undertakings or solutions for occupational health and safety. Earlier in this article another state institution was mentioned under the name of *Central Office of State Administration of the System*. Such an office would be responsible for the following four tasks: diagnosis of the state of labour conditions with the aim to assess the level of hazards and delivering the decision concerning their elimination, supervising scientific research, education and promotion in the field of occupational health and safety, support of legislative processes and improvement of evaluation criteria of the state of labour conditions, adjustment - to regional conditions - of international norms and standards in the field of occupational health and safety.

The existence of both of these institutions seems indispensable, irrespective of functioning of other structures such as: the coordinator of all government activities or industrial health service.

It is obvious that the remaining two participants of the tri-elemental economic subject, i. e.: employers and employees, within their association structures, should distinguish appropriate professional units - both independent and cooperating with the state partner - on two levels: central and local.

It should be stressed here that for all the three partners making the tri-elemental subject the most important issue is that of professional staff qualifications employed in the area of occupational health and safety. This means a dramatic change in the extent of utilization of information technologies in the currently applied system of status diagnosis and corrective and conceptual decision taking.

Processing of information by computers as well as their transmission in computer networks will result in the fact that time and distance separating people will practically disappear. This, in turn, will lead to the *centralization of the control function* in management systems accompanied by a simultaneous *decentralization of the process of decision taking*. According to modern requirements, management structures based on autonomous centers of decision taking should, on the one hand, be characterized by high flexibility faced with dynamically changing environment and, on the other, by complete integration. This means that managers from the medium level of management disappear from traditional structures as their communicative-coordination functions are being taken over by computer systems.

However, there is no doubt that inevitably, also in the field of occupational health and safety, times of efficient managers are approaching, specialists combining high professional qualifications with thorough knowledge of planning methods and techniques as well as principles governing organization dynamics and finances supported by capabilities of rapid analysis of new situations and negotiating qualifications. Managers responsible for the occupational health and safety system will be required to possess such features of character as: smart intelligence, activity, strong will and motivation for professional success, honesty and integrity as well as high degree of responsibility, confidence in their subordinates and openness for their initiative and ideas, flexibility and eloquence, constant drive to the development of subordinates and himself.

Without professional managerial personnel in all the three partners of the tri-elemental economic subject, i.e. in state institutions, employers' associations and trade unions, it is impossible to speak about rationalization in the management of human resources in labour processes which constitutes a significant component of present entrepreneurship and economic renewal.

7. Conclusions

The above presented concept of management system of occupational health and safety only seemingly constitutes a case concerning Polish conditions of economic renewal. The observed *restructure disproportion* consisting in the occurrence of biggest socio-economical losses associated with occupational health and safety during the period of the fastest progress in economic development of countries realizing programs of entrepreneurship and economic renewal is a general regularity

It appears that it is possible to restrict the above mentioned social and economic losses by effective implementation of systemic solutions presented in this article which comprise three areas: economic stimulation, legislation and management.

Successive countries, which are only at the beginning of their road of fast progress in economic development, can easily draw positive conclusions from the case of the so called *restructure disproportion* accompanying the development of the countries of Far East (in years 1955 - 1970) and Central Europe (in 1990s).

Avoidance of this *disproportion* poses a serious challenge for current processes of entrepreneurship and economic renewal. The problems associated with occupational health and safety constitute part of category of resource management. Its rational restructuring may increase manyfold, through additional social and economic effect, traditional *product* of classical enterpreneurship and economic renewal.

I. ERGONOMICS METHODS AND TECHNIQUES

1. Ergonomics Methodology
2. Occupational Risk and Cost Assessment
3. Work Assessment Techniques
4. Education and Training in Ergonomics

1. Ergonomics Methodology

Advances in Occupational Ergonomics and Safety II
Edited by Biman Das and Waldemar Karwowski
IOS Press and Ohmsha, 1997

Objective method of assessing hand efficiency for the needs of ergonomics and rehabilitation

Ewa Nowak

Institute of Industrial Design, Department of Ergonomics Research
ul. Świętojerska 5/7, 00-236 WARSAW, POLAND
Tel.: 31-09-03, Fax: 31-64-78 (Institute), 666-83-47 (home)

1. Objective

The aim of this paper is to present an objective method of hand efficiency assessment. This method can be used for assessing hand efficiency both of a healthy hand and an impaired one, showing dysfunction in movement.

2. Assumptions

One of the basic functions of the man's hand, i.e. performing function, being at the same time, from the ergonomic point of view, one of the most important effectors operating in the man-machine system was used while developing the method. Clenching capabilities of the hand constitute this function. From among several hand grips mentioned [2, 3, 4, 5, 6] a grip defined (by majority of authors) as the cylindrical grip was chosen for investigations. This kind of grip appears as first during ontogenesis, for a newborn child has already an unconditional gripping reflex. At the same time this grip is used most often in everyday life. It is also used most willingly during the rehabilitation process. This results also from the fact that a deformed hand is placed most easily in the form of a cylinder [4].

Considering the above it was assumed that the assessment of the hand efficiency would be done basing on the measurement of clenching a cylindrical handle. On the basis of the above assumptions a prototype testing equipment has been developed.

3. Measuring stand

The stand is meant for performing measurements and for quantitative assessment of hand efficiency. It can also act as a:
- testing apparatus that defines the actual state of hand efficiency,
- rehabilitation device for hand practice,
- device for assessing rehabilitation progress
  a) referring to the initial position before rehabilitation,
  b) referring to standards developed by the Institute of Industrial Design.

The measurement consists in clenching a cylindrical handle, which is a part of a hydraulic system. Changes in pressure obtained are recorded as a numerical value and coded in the central unit of PC. Figure 1 shows a drawing of the measuring stand.

The cylindrical handle was adjusted to the diameter of each child's individual grip.

The subject investigated can follow the result of the measurement, that is additionally presented on the monitor in the form of a diagram. This can motivate obtaining better results e.g. during rehabilitation exercises operating as a natural feedback. For the needs of children rehabilitation a special computer programme has been developed, that assists the rehabilitation process by means of playing.

4. Subject

Two groups of children aged 6-10 were investigated. First group embraced healthy population and amounted to 300 persons, including 150 boys and 150 girls. The group consisted of children from families of the highest living standard, characterized by the highest development index in Poland [7, 8].

The results of this group of children investigation served as the basis to develop data for the needs of design as well as standards (bases of reference) for the needs of rehabilitation.

Second group embraced children with hand dysfunction. 26 children suffering from rheumatism, treated in the Rheumatological Hospital, were investigated. This group investigation was of piloting character. On its basis it was determined how the efficiency of children with hand dysfunction differs from this of healthy children, the method of investigation was verified and the extent of the method suitability for the needs of rehabilitation was defined.

5. Results and Analyses

The investigation results were developed in the form of mean values (x), standard deviations (S.D.) and percentiles. Table 1 includes the measurement of clenching a cylindrical handle. It was assumed that for rehabilitation needs the measurement of clenching a cylindrical handle as an index of hand efficiency is significant. The values of this measurement for the healthy children served as the bases of reference - standards for the needs of rehabilitation. These standards were determined in relation to three characteristics: age, stature and body mass. (These characteristics have the highest coefficients of correlation with the measurement of clenching.)

The standards developed in this way make it possible for a person conducting rehabilitation to assess the hand efficiency of a child in relation to three independent characteristics. This can be the age or the measurement of stature as well as body mass. For each one of these characteristics individual classes comprising boundary values (minimum, maximum) of the clenching measurement were determined. Minimum was defined by the value of the 5th percentile, and maximum by the value of the 95th percentile.

These values are the directions for a person conducting rehabilitation, as far as they inform him (or her) of the limits of a child's "efficiency" and the upper limit towards which he should aim at during rehabilitation process [9]. Figure 2 presents a theoretical example of a rehabilitation process of a child carried on systematically for several months. Having known initial values (the beginning of rehabilitation) and final values one can assess in a quantitative way rehabilitation progress.

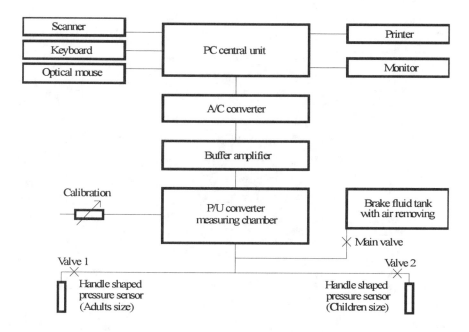

Figure 1. Schematic diagram of measuring stand for estimation of hand capabilities

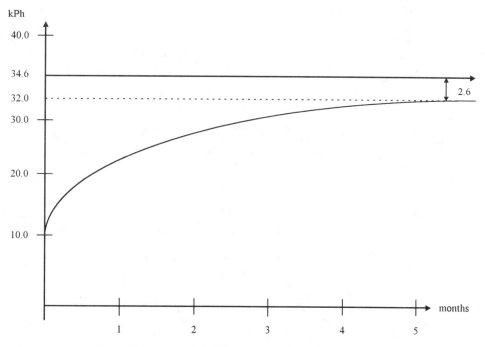

Figure 2. Example of rehabilitacion process in relation to the age of eight years

Table 1. Measurement of clenching a cylindrical handle

Measurement of cylindrical grip clenching								
Age	Sex	Left hand				Right hand			
		x̄	S.D.	min	max	x̄	S.D.	min	max
6	boys	30.61	8.39	18.02	43.19	31.60	10.01	16.59	46.61
	girls	29.37	5.62	20.94	37.80	27.73	6.64	17.76	37.69
	total	29.99	7.17	19.24	40.74	29.66	8.71	16.60	42.73
7	boys	36.70	7.11	26.04	47.37	34.16	7.45	22.98	45.34
	girls	30.61	6.68	20.59	40.62	30.81	9.55	16.49	45.13
	total	33.66	7.54	22.34	44.97	32.49	8.73	19.40	45.57
8	boys	41.33	5.53	33.03	49.62	44.96	6.93	34.56	55.35
	girls	36.08	4.73	28.99	43.17	37.28	7.18	26.51	48.05
	total	38.70	5.77	30.04	47.37	41.12	8.03	29.07	53.17
9	boys	45.83	10.05	30.75	60.90	47.73	10.07	32.62	62.84
	girls	41.17	6.52	31.39	50.95	43.12	10.28	27.71	58.54
	total	43.50	8.78	30.33	56.67	45.43	10.43	29.78	61.08
10	boys	56.47	7.76	44.84	68.11	56.45	8.15	44.22	68.68
	girls	47.71	7.85	35.94	59.48	47.63	9.40	33.53	61.73
	total	52.09	8.95	38.67	65.51	52.04	9.84	37.28	66.80

6. Conclusions

1. Measurement of clenching a cylindrical handle was assumed as a criterion for quantitative assessment of hand dysfunction.

2. The method presented can be applied to the quantitative assessment of the rehabilitation process of an individual subject.

3. The method presented requires verification and future studies to test its usability as far as rehabilitation needs of other groups of disables are concerned (e.g. aftter mechanical injuries).

Reference

[1] S.Kumar, Rehabilitation: An ergonomic dimension, *International Journal of Industrial Ergonomics* 2 (1992) 97-108.

[2] R.Kadefords and others, An approach to Ergonomics evaluation of hand tools, *Applied Ergonomics* 24 (1993) 203-211.

[3] Z.Nadolski, Tensiometric study on the impaired hand usefulness (in Polish), PZWL,   Warsaw, 1997.

[4] M.Musur, Functional tests of rheumatic hands (in Polish), *Reumatologia*, vol. XIII, 4 (1975) 135-146.

[5] E.Nowak, Trial of hand grips classification (in Polish), *Prace i Materiały IWP*, Warsaw, 1984.

[6] D.Scott and S.Marcus, Hand impairment assessment: some suggestions, *Applied Ergonomics* 22 (1991) 263-269.

[7] I.Charzewski, Social conditioning of physical development of children in Warsaw (in Polish), *Studia i Monografie AWF*, Warsaw, 1984.

[8] E.Nowak, Physical development of children and the young from the centre of Warsaw, *Annals of Human Biology* 4 (1994) 401-408.

[9] E.Nowak, Determination of the spatial reach area of the arms for workplace design purposes, *Ergonomics* 7 (1978) 493-507.

[10] E.Nowak, Practical application of anthropometric research in rehabilitation, *International Journal of Industrial Ergonomics* 9 (1992) 109-115.

Advances in Occupational Ergonomics and Safety II
Edited by Biman Das and Waldemar Karwowski
IOS Press and Ohmsha, 1997

Proposal for Ergonomics Manufacturing Design Process Guide

Robert L. Getty, Randall B. Aust

Lockheed Martin Tactical Aircraft Systems, P.O. Box 748, Fort Worth, Texas

Abstract. A guide is proposed that addresses engineering methodology and
focuses on the design process rather than the design criteria as most
standards/guidelines do. For manufacturing processes to meet ergonomic
criteria, all involved with determining the manufacturing product, processes,
technology, materials, tools, fixtures and vendor support need to have a
reference or standard that will delineate ergonomics guidelines.

1. Introduction

Manufacturing design processes for complex systems, like advanced fighter aircraft,
require a special emphasis on human interactions to technical fabrication and assembly
functions. The role of the human is being refined as manufacturing processes become
more sophisticated. The design of tools, fixtures, fabrication and assembly procedures are
just a few of the areas that need support to capitalize on the capabilities of the human
component in the manufacturing process. The use of a design guide that provides useful
information about how to infuse human performance information into manufacturing
design is a sensible approach to achieving efficient, cost-effective manufacturing
processes.

An ergonomics manufacturing guide should focus on the design processes as the key to
exploiting human capabilities while minimizing exposure to human limitations, such as,
for example, cumulative trauma. Areas to be addressed should include the product design,
technology determination, tooling and fixture selection, sequencing of processes and the
planning for each process. These characteristics will be applicable to design for
manufacturability, assembly, and producibility. We will discuss the need for early input of
ergonomics criteria, the benefits of addressing the human interaction in the manufacturing
design process, the essential aspects of the suggested design methodology, and the value of
this process using metrics that describe how well ergonomics criteria are incorporated into
the design of manufacturing processes.

Most human factors/ergonomics standards contain design-to specifications (refer to, for
example, the American National Standard for Human Factors Engineering of Visual
Display Terminal Workstations (ANSI/HFS 100-1988) and Ergonomics Guidelines for the
Design, Installation and Use of Machine Tools (ANSI B11 TR 1-1933)). In contrast, the
proposed design process guide will contain methods and rationale for incorporating
ergonomics into a manufacturing design process. Function allocation must be described to
assist in comparing the best match between skills and requirements in the man-machine
systems that exist in manufacturing environments. Task analysis will be covered in the
manufacturing context to include production plans, technology, materials, rates and
layouts. Methodology should be emphasized, but the standard would include reference

material such as tables of values, decision models, and checklists. Definitions and an annotated bibliography would complete the manufacturing design guide.

2. The Goals of Early Involvement to Achieve Integrated Product Design

Traditionally, the human factor is considered in design activities based on a role in the operation and maintenance of a system. This consideration begins early in the design process where preliminary and detailed system requirements are defined. While system operation and maintenance considerations are important, the manufacturer can benefit also by adding consideration for human interaction to the manufacturing design process. Significant costs are often incurred when complex system designs must be altered to accommodate manufacturing problems. Unraveling and rework of an integrated system design requires significant effort and time. A reduction in the number and magnitude of manufacturing problems is the primary goal of emphasizing manufacturing processes earlier in a system design life cycle.

Design integration of manufacturing processes requires input from individuals actively involved in manufacturing. Design processes as early as research and development (R&D) must be aware of the manufacturing commitment of uninterrupted output and the anxiety caused by retraining of skills, new status and communication patterns.[1] Consequently, manufacturing people must be involved in technology development. In order to achieve producibility and productivity, designers must be aware of all the elements of the manufacturing processes and effectively utilize all resources and talents.[2]

3. Human Interaction Considerations

The human-system interaction must be considered when designs are developed. Without awareness of human capabilities, the impact of the human role is not sufficiently evaluated. Designers underestimate variability and its importance in industry.[3] Ergonomists should, in addition to contributing their knowledge, "create design situations which enable the use of operators' and designers' knowledge and their confrontation in order to establish forecasts of future work situations concerning health and efficiency criteria in order to transform them" (Ref. 3, p. 1666). The focus of this "confrontation" should be work activity and not technology. Some work activity topics include: succession of operations, processing of information by the operator, physical strain (efforts, posture) and exposures to environmental factors. These discussions would lead to the evaluation of processes in terms of health and efficiency. This, in turn, would lead to modification and improvement.

Failing to account for ergonomics is antagonistic to the business goals of productivity, quality and safety. Any change that takes ergonomics into account will cost money but should lead to reduced injury and cost, as well as improve efficiency.[4] Ideally, there should be ways of predicting benefits and developing and implementing workable recommendations, but the cause and effect of poor design are not always apparent. Alexander states, "One must learn to distinguish between value and the ability to measure. In some cases, the value is there but it is just not worth much to develop the quantitative measures necessary to prove it" (Ref. 4, p. 4). Those involved in reviewing causes for quality defects, missed production rates or dissatisfied customers can relate to a need to fix the obvious cause rather than spending extensive amount of time pondering all the possible causes.

When determining the area that ergonomics or human engineering covers, the focus may only address a single element such as the physical aspects. Ergonomic principles cover *all* aspects of human skills. Alexander[4] explains that industrial ergonomics problems should be characterized according to the type of body system that is affected. These body systems include: (1) Physical Size: Anthropometric, (2) Endurance: Cardiovascular, (3) Strength: Biomechanical, (4) Manipulative: Kinesiology, (5) Environmental: External, and (6) Cognitive: Thought. These systems should be considered as human engineering principles to be followed, not soft, optional choices that are less important than other factors. Once ergonomic precepts are made part of the design process, a new awareness of human capabilities and limitations emerges and the desired outcome of the processes can be achieved.

4. Methodology Applied to Design

The methods followed during the design process are more important than the use of specific guidelines and checklist. Although guidelines may help visualize the human-system interaction, the activities of function analysis, function allocation, workload analysis, task analysis and job design will lead to the optimal design. Ergonomics principles must be integrated with: (a) all functions of the manufacturing process, (b) the design of new manufacturing processes during product design, (c) the process analysis techniques to improve manufacturing processes, (d) the root-cause analysis of workmanship defects, (e) the purchase of tools and equipment for facilities, plant maintenance and factory workers, and (f) the improvement of the office environment throughout the company. The primary goal will be to enhance the work place environment and improve productivity, quality and minimize potential for injury.

Selection of the correct assignment to the human:machine system is based on comparing task requirements to human capabilities or to technology. Where physical demands are excessive, technology will be considered to address these high demands. Computer strengths are speed of calculations and memory. Humans excel in decision making and physical control in highly variable settings. References from literature that make these comparisons may be included in the appendices of a manufacturing guide. The analyses described will come from human factors engineering references. Throughout these analyses, the roles of the human and the system will be assessed. A design engineer will make initial function and task allocations to a human, the system, or both based on capabilities and limitations. When function or task assignment requires more evaluation, then specialists with more extensive background in ergonomics engineering can assist in the design process.

Following the initial design decisions, validation occurs. The time for validation will be determined by the impact of the design on the human element and the risk potential of an incorrect human:machine system selection. When either the human risks or the costs of machine design change are high, early validation is justified. This may include a simulation of the process or the human-system interaction. In low risk situations, validation may occur during early stages of implementing manufacturing plans and processes.

5. Value Added to Design Processes

Performance metrics show the value added as one progresses through the phases of system design, manufacturing development, and implementation. The following delineate the benefits to industry from the consideration of human-system interaction in manufacturing processes with metrics that can be used to verify the success of a design.

a. Include ergonomic principles in the *development of new processes before they reach the factory floor*. Metric: reduced engineering changes early in the manufacturing or "make-it-work" changes.

b. *Lower overall costs of tooling, fixtures and processes* due to reduced rework. Metric: lower tool change orders

c. *Reduced schedules* due to better match with human skills by integrating ergonomics methods with management of cost, quality and schedule. Metric: on-schedule and in-station work flow.

d. A *continually evolving simplification of physical demands that improves productivity and quality* is consistent with continuous improvement. Metric: improving trends for productivity and quality.

e. Provide ergonomic inputs to design of processes to attain *increased productivity and quality at less cost.* Metric: improved productivity.

f. *Quality improvements* through reduction of rework due to human error. Metric: Decreasing quality defects requiring rework.

g. Physical demands data become available for the *supervision of exposure to the work hazards.* Metric: Reduced lost time due to fatigue and injury.

h. *Return-to-Work* (RTW) gains by an ergonomic focus by pulling together the elements that must be integrated. Metric: Reduced lost work days.

i. *Individuals* are able to understand the various factors that expose them to cumulative trauma and *have a role in reducing their exposure*. Metric: fewer cumulative trauma incidences.

j. Physical description of the tasks can be used to *improve medical treatment.* Metric: lower workers' compensation costs.

6. Conclusion

Due to the potential for many individuals involved in design of manufacturing processes, some guidance must be made available to ensure early considerations of ergonomics. Some of the ergonomics principles are intuitive and easily understood, but are essential to maximize the design of the human: machine system in manufacturing processes. Guidance that will differentiate between ergonomic design tasks that can be performed by design engineers with little ergonomic background or those that require ergonomic experts is the intent of this proposal for a manufacturing ergonomics standard.

References

[1] Steele, L. W. (1989). *Managing Technology*, McGraw-Hill.

[2] Stephanou, S. E. And Spiegl, F. (1992). *The Manufacturing Challenge: From Concepts to Production*, Van Nostrand Reinhold.

[3] Garrigou, A. (1991). The role of the ergonomist in the case of workers' participation in the design of complex industrial installations, In *Proceedings of the 11th Congress of IEA*, Taylor & Francis, London.

[4] Alexander, D. C. (1986). *The Practice and Management of Industrial Ergonomics*, Prentice-Hall

Advances in Occupational Ergonomics and Safety II
Edited by Biman Das and Waldemar Karwowski
IOS Press and Ohmsha, 1997

Program for Workplace Investigation in Accordance with the Austrian Act on Occupational Health and Safety

Christoph JUNGWIRTH

*IBE - Institute for vocational and adult educational research at Linz University,
Raimundstr. 17, 4020 Linz, Austria*

Abstract:
The new Austrian Act on Occupational Health and Safety obliges
enterprises to investigate their workplaces regularly. For this purpose
the Institute for vocational and adult educational research at Linz
University developed a program for workplace investigation in offices
and workshops with the necessary empirical tests and uses it in
participatory workdesign projects.

1. Introduction

The new Austrian Act on Occupational Health and Safety forces employers to investigate
the risks and strains at workplaces („workplace investigation"). To support enterprises in
fulfilling this obligation the IBE - Institute for vocational and adult educational research at
Linz University - developed a program for workplace investigation in workshops and
offices.

This article discusses the above mentioned act, describes the program and its
development and gives an example of ist application.

2. The Austrian Act on Occupational Safety

The Austrian Act on Occupational Health and Safety, which has been in force since 1995,
originates from European Union regulations [1] which lay down a comprehensive list of
employers´ responsibilities for the safety of the employees. The act stresses the importance
of preventive measures [2] in the area of ergonomics and safety to reduce risks and strains
at work and tries to change the attitude towards safety and health in enterprises. This
approach includes new obligations to Austrian employers:

Occupational safety and health service (including a safety-engineer and a occupational
physician) is now compulsory in all enterprises. For small enterprises interim regulations
have been grant. Until 1st of January 2000, however every enterprise has to establish a
safety and health service (or has to use an external one). The extent of the service a firm has
to provide depends on the number of employees. The safety-engineer has to advise and
support employer and employees within all areas of safety- and health-management, e.g. the
prevention of accidents, workdesign, ergonomics and planning new workplaces or work-

processes. An occupational physician has the same duties and is also responsible for the organization of first aid and the integration of persons with disabilities in an enterprise.

Every enterprise with more than ten workers has to nominate a so called „Sicherheitsvertrauensperson" (safety officer) who can be seen as a member of the works council with special functions in the area of occupational safety and health.

All employers are forced to prepare and run regular (at least every year) safety and health instructions for their employees.

The most important innovation of the act is that an investigation of workplaces has to be carried out in each firms. Employers have to analyze the workplaces or work-processes and must investigate risks or strains. Subsequently measures, which are able to avoid or reduce risks and strains, have to be defined, carried out and documented.

It can be expected that these new regulations will improve safety and health in Austrian enterprises because, for the first time, all employers have to carry out a systematic investigation of risks and strains within their firms. Nevertheless two deficits of this act have to be discussed.

(1) Although the European Union prescribes the same occupational safety and health standards for private enterprises and civil service, the Austrian act excludes employees in the civil service.

(2) The above mentioned act focuses on safety engineering, prevention of accidents and reduction of physical strain. Psychosocial strains, strains which result from deficits in the organization of work or psychic problems we can find in service jobs, especially in personal service jobs (i.e. nursing, ...) are not regulated by this law. Therefore it can be argued that the Austrian act only partially meets the comprehensive view of occupational health and safety intended by the basic regulations of the European Union.

3. Program for workplace investigation and its theoretical framework

The developed program for workplace investigation consists of five modules. *Module 1* is a checklist with 64 items concerning risks in the whole enterprise (and not individual workplaces). *Module 2* is a checklist (111 items) to guide and support the investigation of manual and machinery workplaces in workshops. The checklist in *module 3* consists of 80 items and can be used at office workplaces, especially where computers are used.

Module 4 is a form in which all detected risks and strains and the agreed measures can be documented. This document can be used as a guide for improving health and safety in the analyzed enterprise.

Module 5 is a short checklist and a documentation pattern which helps to establish an information system and a risk management concerning used dangerous chemicals.

These five modules are offered in paper form and as computer solutions which can be used with standard word processing software. The users are not forced to buy and learn special software.

The developed checklists are based upon a comprehensive view of workdesign which includes four dimensions. They can be seen as an extension of Volpert [3]:

- *working tasks* (tasks, work-content, demands, stresses);
- *tools, workplace and work environment* (ergonomics, safety);
- *organization and cooperation* (organization of the production, social relationships);
- *qualification* (vocational rehabilitation, occupational training, personnel development.

Newer concepts stressing the individual development of employees are included [4]. These approaches go back to the discussion about the end of labour division and the extension of occupational tasks [5]. In short terms: the mental and physical growth of persons has to be seen in a strong interaction with their work. In such a view the important determinants are work-content, latitudes of action, latitudes within decisions concerning planning and possibilities to influence workplace-design. For all these determinants points of attachment can be found in the described dimensions of work design.

Not only does the program comply with the demands of the Austrian act on occupational health and safety, but it alos includes the above mentioned theories.

Therefore every checklist used in module 1, 2 or 3 includes items out of the following areas: (1) tasks; (2) strains and risk resulting from the workplace-design; (3) design of used tools (including energy and electrical supply); (4) work environment; (5) dangerous chemicals and their influence on employees; (6) psychosocial and mental strains; (7) organization and communication.

4. Program development

The program development focused on the creation of the checklists used in modules 1, 2 and 3 (see figure 1).

The first step was to gather necessary items to cover all possible risks and strains. This was done by analyzing the Austrian act including the appropriate decrees and ergonomics standard literature in German [6,7,8].

The so generated items were arranged into thematic groups and than into checklists. Together with documentation patterns these lists were used to create the five modules which are discribed above.

Figure 1: Development of the program for workplace investigation

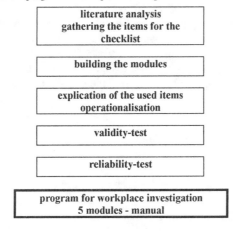

During the „explication" and „operationalisation" all items used in the checklists were defined in words which are understood by practicians in workshops or offices (no scientific expressions). The generated definitions were completed with (1) indications of how risks or strains, which are represented by an item, can be analyzed and measured; (2) information on how these risks and strains can be avoided or reduced; and (3) where detailed information can be found (e.g. in acts, decrees, standard specifications or literature). All this was arranged into a manual for the program.

The validity was tested in four steps to detect whether the checklists covered all pertinent risks and strains: (1) the checklists were discussed with practicians in enterprises; (2) were tested by a group of safety engineers and (3) discussed with members of the occupational health and safety authority; (4) 33 office-workplaces, 68 different manual- and a variety of 50 machinery workplaces in workshops were analyzed. These test showed the validity of the program for office-workplaces and manual- or machinery-workplaces in workshops but not for personal service (e.g. nursing), building sites and chemical industry.

To perform the reliability test a group of 6 safety engineers were asked to read the manual and to investigate 5 different workplaces. All the engineers suggested the same measures to improve the design of the workplace. Thus the reliability of the checklists can be assumed.[1]

5. Application

During the last year this program for workplace investigation was applied at about 1.450 workplaces in 14 enterprises. Most of the workplace improvements were suggested in the area of ergonomics, followed by safety engineering and recommendations to optimize the organization of work. In 6 enterprises the program was used within participatory workdesign projects. These are performed in 6 steps: (1) In a meeting the employees get information concerning the project activities. (2) In every division of the firm working groups with both members of the supervisory staff and workers are established. The working groups are moderated by a labor scientist. These groups are instructed to apply the program for workplace investigation, have to analyze the workplaces with the given checklists, document the investigation results and suggest solutions to improve occupational safety and ergonomics. (3) The recommendations are given to the management whose responsibility is to decide about the realization. (4) The working groups have to implement the approved innovations and (5) evaluate the effects of the measures.

This practice shows that the program, when it is used within participatory projects, does not only lead to suggestions which are able to improve the occupational safety and ergonomics in a firm - but it also helps to train the employees in these areas in a practice-orientated manner.

References

[1]   European Union, Rahmenrichtlinie 89/391/EWG.

[2]   ArbeitnehmerInnenschutzgesetz (Austrian Act on Occupational Health and Safety), §7.

[3]   Volpert W., Arbeitsinformation - der Kooperationsbereich von Information und Arbeitswissenschaft, Zeitschrift für Arbeitswissenschaft 1993(2), pp. 65-68.

[4]   Schubert H.J., Zink K.J., Handlungsanleitung Persönlichkeitsförderliche Arbeitsgestaltung in Werkstätten für Behinderte, University Kaiserslautern, 1991.

[5]   Rohmert W., Möglichkeiten menschengerechter Arbeitsgestaltung. In *Menschen-gerechte Gestaltung der Arbeit* by Fürstenberg F. (ed.), Mannheim, 1988, p. 39.

[6]   Bullinger H.J., Ergonomie, Stuttgart, 1994.

[7]   Hettinger Th. et. al. (ed.), Kompendium Arbeitswissenschaft, Ludwigshafen, 1993.

[8]   Cooper C.L. et.al. (ed.) Creating Healthy Work organizations, Chichester, 1994.

---

[1] Further reliability tests with more test persons and at more workplaces are planned.

Advances in Occupational Ergonomics and Safety II
Edited by Biman Das and Waldemar Karwowski
IOS Press and Ohmsha, 1997

Fiberglass extension ladder carrying in difficult conditions: evaluating alternate work methods

Daniel Imbeau[1], Yves Montpetit[2], and James D. Allan[2]

[1]*Industrial Engineering Department, Université du Québec, Trois-Rivières (Qc), Canada*

[2]*Bell Canada, Montréal (Qc), Canada*

A research program aimed at reducing the risks involved in handling the fiberglass extension ladders in the work of telephone technicians was started 2 years ago. An analysis of accident results indicated that carrying the ladder in combination with environmental conditions (e.g., wind, tree branches, uneven terrain) was associated with an important number of severe injuries to the back. A first field study designed to obtain detailed information on the current ladder handling methods of telephone technicians in actual work conditions indicated that the ladder carrying method in current use has many drawbacks which make it hazardous in the presence of several environmental conditions. An experiment aimed at comparing three new methods of carrying the ladder with the usual method was then conducted. This experiment showed the potential superiority of one of the new methods over the usual method in specific work conditions. Following this study, a field trial involving the participation of 29 technicians was conducted to better evaluate and compare the new method to that in current use. The trial showed that the new method has strong advantages in some conditions.

1.0 Introduction

Straight ladder carrying is a frequent manual materials handling task that has yet to be addressed in depth in the literature. Every day across North-America, thousands of telephone, cable TV, power utility, and construction workers handle fiberglass extension ladders in difficult environmental conditions as part of their work. According to the manual materials handling literature, such portable ladders which weigh between 26 and 30 kg-f and range in length between 3.7 and 4.3 m (folded) are heavy, bulky, and are handled in conditions that increase the risk of injury [1, 2, 3].

1.1 An observational study

A recent study [4] designed to obtain detailed information on the current ladder handling methods of telephone technicians in actual work conditions indicated that a large majority of the ladder handling accidents in telephone technicians employed by a large telephone company in Canada were associated with ladder carrying operations. These accidents typically result in severe overexertion injuries particularly to the back. In this study, 42 experienced telephone technicians handled their fiberglass extension ladder on seven sites that were judged to be representative of actual work conditions by a joint employer-union committee. Each technician was asked to unload his ladder from the truck he uses in his daily work, to carry the ladder to the installation site, to raise it, and then to perform the reverse maneuver back to the truck. He was asked to use the usual work methods. After completion of the handling activities, each technician was interviewed about the various aspects of the maneuver he had just completed and on the usual work methods. In total, 49 runs were completed and videotaped. An equal number of interviews were conducted on the sites.

The results indicated that the ladder carrying method commonly used by telephone technicians presents several drawbacks when considered in combination with the environmental conditions in which the ladder is typically carried (e.g., wet conditions, sloping terrain, wind, overhead obstacles, uneven terrain, etc.). For instance, the method provides poor stability of the ladder which is carried on the shoulder, it provides precarious balance when attitude of the ladder is changed on the shoulder (e.g. when climbing a slope), it is difficult to balance the ladder comfortably on the shoulder, and with this method the ladder is more prone to catch in wind or hit overhead obstacles. The method currently used by telephone technicians has been in use for more than fifty years and is still the most widely used portable ladder carrying method in North America. An alternate method of carrying long and heavy ladders that would diminish if not eliminate most of these drawbacks would likely contribute to reduce the number of injuries associated with ladder carrying. Such an outcome would be highly desirable given the large number of workers who do carry this type of ladder using the same method in the same environmental conditions in their daily work and given the fact that the ladder cannot be eliminated form their work in the short term.

This study also indicated that the telephone technicians usually carry a ladder that is longer than actually required in a majority of their interventions. This excess ladder length and weight increases the risk of an overexertion injury.

Based on worker opinions and basic biomechanics principles, the authors [4] identified three alternate methods that could realistically be used in the work context of many workers and which might prove safer than the ladder carrying method in current wide use.

1.2 An experimental study

The three alternate ladder carrying methods were then compared with the usual method in two studies [5]. The first study was conducted in actual work conditions while the other took place in the laboratory. Twenty one telephone technicians participated in the field study while seven participated in the laboratory study together with three subjects having no prior experience with ladder handling. In the field study, the technicians were asked to carry their ladder with each of the four carrying methods. After completion of each carrying task, the technician rated the method he had just tried on seven subjective measures. Technicians' heart rate was monitored during the complete experiment. In the laboratory study, a similar protocol was used with the difference that the carrying tasks were longer since oxygen uptake was also measured. All telephone technicians had no prior knowledge or practice with the three alternate carrying methods tested: they had experience only with the carrying method they use in their daily work.

The results of the field study showed that carrying a fiberglass extension ladder on the shoulder with the arm "through-the-rungs" imposed the least strain on the cardiovascular system and this method was judged better than or at least equivalent to the carrying method in current use. The results of the laboratory experiment were consistent with those of the field study. The other two methods tested yielded a performance that was inferior to that of the method currently used by telephone technicians in both the field and laboratory studies. The results further showed that the study performed in actual work conditions had better validity than the study performed in the laboratory.

Given the encouraging results of both the observational and the experimental studies, a field trial in which the new method would be tested was designed and conducted.

2.0 Methods

2.1 Subjects

Twenty nine experienced telephone technicians separated into two groups (15 in the province of Québec and 14 in the province of Ontario) participated in the field trial. Age and experience ranged from 27 to 51 years (mean = 40, SD = 6.8) and from 2 to 30 years (mean = 17, SD = 7.0), respectively. Each group included the three technician job categories: installation and repair technicians -I&R- (9 in Québec and 7 in Ontario), cable maintenance technicians -CR- (3 in Québec and 4 in Ontario), and splicers/linemen -SL- (3 in each group). One of the I&R technicians was a woman. This distribution was commensurate with that of the job categories within the telephone company. Four ladders types were used: 20-foot, 24-foot, 26-foot used by I&R technicians and 28-foot used by some I&R and most CR and SL.

2.2 Procedure

Each participant was given a three-hour training session by groups of 7 or 8 technicians. The training session first consisted of a presentation regarding ladder carrying methods and results from the observational and experimental studies. Then, each participant was given a hands-on training on two new ladder carrying methods. In the hands-on part the participant would familiarize him/herself with the new methods and would carry the ladder on a sloped terrain to better compare the new methods with the one used in the daily work.

At the end of the training session, each participant was given twenty questionnaire sheets and asked to fill-up one sheet each time the ladder was carried during the trial period which lasted 2 months. The questionnaire, was aimed at collecting data on the type of ladder used, type of truck, and the environmental conditions in which the maneuver had been performed. Also, the questionnaire sheet required the technician to rate the carrying maneuver on convenience and ease of use of the method, stability or balance while carrying the ladder, satisfaction, comfort, and perceived safety using five-point rating scales (1 = very poor, 5 = very good). The questionnaire also included an area for comments. The technicians were asked to try the new methods as often as possible together with the usual one.

Two weeks after the beginning of the trial, a follow-up visit was paid to each participant by the trainer and a union representative. This was a "show-me" session to ensure the new methods were correctly used. At the end of the trial period, an interview was conducted with each participant to gather their final feedback on the new ladder carrying methods.

2.3 New ladder carrying methods

The new ladder carrying methods were the "through-the-rungs" method (TR) and the "modified" method (M). In the first one, the ladder is supported at its mid-lengths by the shoulder and carried close to the horizontal (aft part is slightly higher than rear part); one of the railings of the ladder sits on the shoulder while the other one is propped against the trunk near waist level, thereby providing excellent ladder stability. In the "modified" method, the ladder is carried in much the same way with the exception that it sits completely on the shoulder (i.e., the railing nearest to the ground is on the shoulder while the other is above head level). With this method, the left hand must be used to prevent the ladder from tipping and falling to the side. The "modified" method has the advantage of easy loading/unloading of the ladder on/from the shoulder since the ladder is much higher with respect to the ground.

3.0 Results and discussion

A total of 206 questionnaire sheets were returned, of which 17 had to be rejected because of incomplete information. A total of 189 sheets were thus analyzed. Table 1 presents the advantages and disadvantages reported by the technicians for both the TR and the M methods.

Globally, the usual method and the M method received equivalent ratings which were, however, higher than those of the TR method ($P < 0.02$ for all measures), all ladder lengths considered. This result is understandable since practice level is much higher with the usual method and transfer of practice is much easier for the M method which resembles in many respects, the usual method. Although the ratings were lower for the TR method, the lowest average rating was 3.5 for this method which is almost "good". An analysis of variance on each measure revealed that the rating depended on ladder length. For all measures, the same interaction profile as shown in Figure 1 could be observed with minor differences among the measures. This interaction was significant at the 0.05 level for all five measures.

The TR method was rated lower than the other methods with the 26 and 28-foot ladders because; 1- they are difficult to raise directly from the shoulder with the TR method owing to their increased length (this is true for shorter workers), and 2- they are heavier and thus cause more discomfort on the shoulder with the TR method; with the TR method, the weight is supported mostly by the acromion instead of the deltoid muscle [5]. The comfort problem can be easily corrected though, by installing a small shoulder pad on the inside of the ladder railing. When considering only the shorter and lighter 20 and 24-foot ladders, the TR method fared equally or better than the M method (e.g., Figure 1).

Table 1: Advantages and disadvantages of the TR and M methods

Advantages of the method	
TR method	M method
•Better stability because of lower center of gravity	•Better weight distribution on shoulder than usual method
•Comfortable to carry long distances	•Easy to carry ladder and to raise
•Free head movement and excellent visibility	•Useful to go over obstacles such as fence
•Very good to go under overhead obstacles	•Good for crossing ditches
•Not hitting of obstacles	•Easy to get rid of ladder in case of loss of balance
•Easy to balance on shoulder regardless of arm length	•Comfortable on shoulder
•Easy to unload	
Disadvantages of the method	
TR method	M method
•Difficult to raise (particularly with 28-foot ladder)	•Catches more in wind than TR method
•Shoulder/hip pain	•Not as stable as TR method
•Difficult to balance a 26-foot ladder	•Visibility and head movement restricted
•More difficult to maneuver in narrow passages and going around corners	

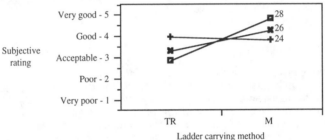

Figure 1: Interaction profile obtained for all measures.

Most technicians reported that having the choice among three ladder carrying methods from then on, represented an advantage from a safety and convenience point of view, since they were now able to select the best method depending on the environmental conditions, ladder length, body shape and strength, individual preferences and experience.

4.0 Conclusions

The field trial led to the following conclusions:
• The M method was very successful and appears best for longer and heavier ladders.
• The TR method was very successful for shorter and lighter ladders. This method presents strong advantages over the other methods particularly where obstacles are present [5].
• The trial clearly showed that a choice of methods should be made available to the technicians: one method just can fit all when it comes to ladder carrying.

5.0 References

[1] A. Mital, A.S. Nicholson, and M.M. Ayoub, A guide to manual materials handling.ISBN: 0-85066-801-8. Taylor and Francis, London, 1993.
[2] S.H. Snook and V.M. Ciriello, The design of manual handling tasks: revised tables of maximum acceptable weights and forces. Ergonomics, 34, 9, (1991) 1197-1213.
[3] T.R. Waters, V. Putz-Anderson, A. Garg, and L.J. Fine, Revised NIOSH equation for the design and evaluation of manual lifting tasks. Ergonomics, 36(7), (1993) 749-776.
[4] D. Imbeau, Y. Montpetit, L. Desjardins, P.F Riel, and J.D. Allan. Handling of fiberglass extension ladders in the work of telephone technicians. International Journal of Industrial Ergonomics (in press).
[5] D. Imbeau, L. Desjardins, Y. Montpetit, P.F. Riel, and J.D. Allan, Comparison of four methods for carrying a fiberglass extension ladder. International Journal of Industrial Ergonomics (in press).

Advances in Occupational Ergonomics and Safety II
Edited by Biman Das and Waldemar Karwowski
IOS Press and Ohmsha, 1997

Development and Implementation of Information Technology for the Psychophysiological Valuation and Forecasting of the Efficiency and Safety of Operators' Work

Alexander BUROV,
National Research Institute for Design, Department of Ergonomics;
30 Dmitrievskaya Str., 252054. Kyiv. Ukraine
Yuri CHETVERNYA,
Infocenter ALIAS Ltd Infocenter ALIAS Ltd. Post Box 3, 254214. Kyiv. Ukraine

Abstract. The development of the methodology and applied systems of psychophysiological maintenance of operator's fitness to work during all stages of his professional biography in the electricity production and distribution industry in order to reduce human errors and to raise his efficiency. To solve this problem they were developed systems of industrial purpose: (a) for a psychophysiological initial professional selection, (b) for a periodical check, (c) for a daily check. Each system permits to evaluate the reliability and efficiency of work of operator, as well as to construct the prognosis of changes of these parameters pursuant in relation to the period of his professional biography.

1. Introduction

The technic development is accompanied by the transmission to human more and more number of managing functions permiting to him ever more shun from a labour instruments and to be transformed from a fulfilled into a control unit of the production system. Such transformation of the human role results in the replacement of physical labour by a mental, reducing the necessity of manual work and appropriate consumptions of energy. However thus the psyche load of a human grows considerably, who has to decide tasks of valuations and forecasting of the work efficiency of an equipment and of other people.

This modern problem requires and a modern way its decision. Because the most functions of operators are the functions of control, the adequate means of his check are information technologies of tests, analysis and prognostication.

Theoretical analysis and analysis of the actual data shows that the psychophysiological opportunities of human are a base, which permits to operator to realize his knowledges and skills. If the psychophysiological base does not correspond requirements of trade, such discrepancy in critical situation can prevent to operator to manage with professional duties and to result in accident or failure.

2. Information technologies of the psychophysiological maintenance of the operators' work

Professional fitness to work of the operator (and his psychophysiological professionally important qualities) has the several components:
- professional knowledge (skills),
- conformity of psychophysiological features of an individual to requirements of trade,
- conditions of health,
- socio-psychological ones.

The methodological feature of our approach is the development of interactive display systems for psychophysiological maintenance of operators fitness to work enabling to evaluate not only some of human professionally important psychophysiological qualities, but also of his general characteristic of fitness to work as the system as a whole. The psychophysiological information recording, which concerns the human state, should be accumulated and to be integrated within specialized systems on all stages of human professional biography:
- psychophysiological professional selection (recommendations oftraining individualization);
- periodic psychophysiological check of operator including the monitoring of professional ageing rate;
- daily (preshift) check of professional fitness to work in "regular" operationes;
- daily (intrashift) check of professional fitness to work in extreme operationes (start-up and shutdown, changing, high complexity and responsibility etc.);
- functional rehabilitation (psychophysiological correction of the operator functional state);
- support of training process directly included in means of training;
- professionally important psychophysiological qualities training and correction with specialized psychological simulators.

3. Applied systems

As applied systems they were developed systems of industrial purpose:
- (a) for a psychophysiological initial professional selection,
- (b) for a periodical check,
- (c) for a daily check.

These systems allow to do a monitoring of operator's psychophysiological professionally important qualities during all stadies of his professional biography. All systems are intended for a work in real-life industrial settings, can be made multy-systems with automated trainer systems, do not require additional staff from experts of medical and psychological services. It permits to user to have the objective information about his state and forecast of its change, to analyze reason of deviation from norm, if it is, and to make the appropriate decision about condition correction.

Each of systems permits to evaluate the reliability and efficiency of operator's work, as well as to construct the prognosis of changes of these parameters pursuant in relation to the period of his professional biography. The results of valuation and prognosis permit to make arrangements not to admit of unreliable operator to work or to increase his reliability and fitness to work, as the duly and exact information concerning to significances of these parameters of operator permits to operate reliability of a human as an element of a socio-technical system and to accept the preventive measures for accident precautions.

System for the psychophysiological initial professional selection

The efficiency of operator's work depends not only from his professional knowledges and working conditions, but also from conformity of psychophysiological features of person to requirements of trade. About 70 % of accidents on energetics' enterprises of Ukraine happens on this reason. As the results of preliminary researches have shown the following structure of tests for determinations of professional fitness group of operator is optimum: structure of person, structure of intelligence, undividual's psychodynamical features, bent for either kinds of mental activity.

The most informationable parameters of efficiency of tests performance are included in model of a "standard operator" enabling to conduct the psychophysiological prediction of the group of the professional fitness of a candidate in operators. Such methodical approach to the professional selection was confirmed by results received on data of inspection more than 500 operators of thermoelectric power stations and more 200 operators of hydroelectric power stations and power systems.

System for the periodical check

The periodical check, which can be conducted once a year, is intended for a valuation of changes of psychophysiological professionally important qualities slowly varying, that permits to evaluate when the operator needs some rehabilitation steps or when it is necessary to him to be prepared to leave his trade, if the irreversible age-related changes came. With this purpose the system of valuation of rate of operators' professional ageing is used.

The system of valuation of rates of professional ageing is intended for use during annual routine inspection of staff of enterprise. The results of valuation of staff's professional age are presented as an integrated age value, which is calculated by the chosen model, as well as " age profile ", which is a vectorial diagram of main parameters determining biological and professional age of human.

They are two possible ways to use the calculated marks:
(a) determination of a moment for beginning of a special training of operator,
(b) forecasting of possible operator's leaving his profession.

System for a daily check

From our data, it is clear that the dynamics of mental activity (and particularly of its biorhythmical structure) play a central role in the analysis of operator's fit-ness to work and maintenance of functional state.   Biorythmical structure of task performance at simulation of operator's activity is a correlate of human psychophysiological condition, on the one hand, and his professional serviceability - on the other one. Hence, it can be used as an objective predictor of the professional operators' fitness to work, which is more steady and exact than professional knowledge and medical parameters. Variations in the operational effectiveness of a particular operator can be expressed in terms of deviations of currently obtained indixes from his 'norm'. Further refinement of the evaluation can be obtained by taking normal shifts in the 'norm' into account.

It has been developed an individual-based approach to evaluation of operational efficiency and psychophysiological state, allowing to establish individual 'norms' development of objective methods for the evaluation of the operators' current psychophysiological state, development of organisation-technical methods for formal application of the results of the evaluation .

This development may be a practical and valid method which can be employed in various applied environments to evaluate operator efficiency. Application of this method may be expected to be helpful in improving and sustaining operator performance and to prevent errors and accidents, and may thereby contribute to enhanced safety and operational reliability of power plants, complex processing industries, and so on.

Applied research, employing the system in a thermal power plant, has evaluated the validity of the predictions concerning operator effectiveness by correlating the prediction indexes with expert ratings of operator effectiveness, as well as with operational output measures (f.e., fuel burn-out) during a one-year period among 38 power plant operators. Preliminary findings suggest that the approach may be useful in prediction of operator's efficiency.

System for the functional rehabilitation

Means and methods of functional rehabilitation should restore the functional abilities, which could decrease as a result of professional work. Such methods can include the various excercises and measures for recovery of health, as well as a complete store of phisio- and psychotherapeutic means. Rehabilitation process should apply the individual methods of valuation of psychophysiological status with the purpose of determinations of individual procedures for recovery and their efficiency control. This can be achieved by results of testing (f.e., with the systems of daily check) with account of individual-typological features of particular person, which were fixed by systems of (1) and/or (2) type.

Thus, result of data processing of operator inspection on each stage is the psychophysiological professionally important qualities set, which is recorded in data bank. The opportunity of maintenance of uniform information psychophysio-logical passport of operator is created. The particular individual passport (individual data bank of psychophysiological and medical-biological information) can be transmitted together with attestation documents to the operator.

The experience of use of such systems for operators of power industry (5 power plants in Russia and Ukraine) has shown the quite high efficiency of this approach (by objective and subjective parameters).

Advances in Occupational Ergonomics and Safety II
Edited by Biman Das and Waldemar Karwowski
IOS Press and Ohmsha, 1997

THE APPROPRIATENESS OF A CURRENTLY EMPLOYED INDUSTRIAL STRENGTH TESTING TECHNIQUE

M. Kolich[1], G.W. Marino[2], and S.M. Taboun[1]

University of Windsor
[1]*Department of Industrial and Manufacturing Systems Engineering*
[2]*Department of Kinesiology*
Windsor, Ontario, Canada

An investigation was carried out to determine whether hand-grip strength can be used to predict two specific types of manual material handling strength. A total of twenty-four subjects participated in a study which involved pushing and pulling in optimal configurations. Body posture was adjusted to individual body dimensions to facilitate application to other subject populations. Peak pushing and pulling forces were recorded and compared to grip strength values. Prediction equations were developed using a stepwise regression analysis. The results indicate that grip strength can be used to predict pushing but not pulling strength. Further research is recommended with respect to the appropriateness of using grip strength to predict manual materials handling tasks capabilities.

INTRODUCTION

Today's media has made much of the escalating costs associated with workplace injuries due to manual material handling (MMH). To deal with this problem, there appears to be a world-wide trend away from prescribing rigid weight limits and training workers in 'correct' MMH techniques, to an approach that requires manual handling risk identification, assessment and control (Worksafe Australia, 1990; European Communities Commission, 1990; NIOSH, 1983). This new approach is dependent on effective risk assessment to enable appropriate control decisions.

Part of effective risk assessment involves selecting the strongest workers and matching them to the MMH tasks that require the greatest strength. Strength testing is invaluable in this regard. Industries have attempted to combat the escalating costs of workers' compensation by using strength testing techniques to predict the likelihood of injury. In other words, employers are interested in methods that allow the strength capabilities of workers to be matched to various physical jobs. The premise being that a successful match limits the risk of injury.

Objectives: Since no reports of studies evaluating the appropriateness of currently employed industrial strength testing techniques could be found, the aim of this paper is to examine the validity of employing a common strength testing technique to match workers to MMH jobs. More specifically, the objective is to determine whether hand-grip strength can be used to predict maximum pushing and pulling forces. Ultimately, this study hopes to improve worker selection and placement procedures thereby effectively reducing the risk of injury due to MMH.

METHOD

Design: A repeated measures design was employed. Each subject was measured on each of eight variables. They were: sex, age, standing height, shoulder height, body weight, peak pushing force in an optimal posture, peak pulling force in an optimal posture, and grip

37

strength. For modelling purposes, male subjects were assigned a 1 while female subjects were assigned a 0.

Subjects: Twelve male and twelve female University of Windsor graduate and undergraduate students volunteered for the experiment. All subjects had no previous or current disorder that may have predisposed them to injury or affected their performance and were free of medication that may have altered their injury risk. Subjects were fully informed of the risks inherent in the testing procedure and were instructed as to the intent of the study. In addition, the subjects were all briefed on and familiarized with the tasks to be performed. The mean age of the subjects was 22.7 years (SD = 2.8 years). The subjects' mean standing height was 176.7 cm (SD = 10.3 cm) and mean shoulder height was 148.6 cm (SD = 9.1 cm). The mean body weight was 75.7 kg (SD = 14.7 kg).

Equipment: The strength testing apparatus, which was obtained from the Prototype Design & Fabrication Company, consisted of a vertical post assembly bolted to a high traction platform which had a tape measure secured to it. Mounted to the vertical post was a bar that could be adjusted for height by locking a pin into the appropriate pin-hole. This vertical post was calibrated in centimetres. At the end of the bar was a rotating head that locked into five positions. Attached to the rotating head was a load cell, which was connected to a force monitor and an 18 inch tote pan handle. The force monitor measured peak and average forces in pounds. In addition, grip strength was assessed using a standard hand-grip dynamometer made by the Lafayette Instrument Company.

Procedure: Much of the following methodology is drawn form the work of Ayoub and McDaniel (1974). In order for the pushing and pulling posture to be fixed for each subject, the height of the subject was removed as a variable by choosing the bar heights (BH) and foot distances (FD) as a percentage of shoulder height. Shoulder height was measured from the floor to the acromion process. Bar height was easily adjusted because the vertical post was calibrated. Since the forces exerted by the subject on the handle are transmitted through the body to the floor, the FD was defined as the distance from the vertical plane of the handle to the lateral malleolus of the back leg (in the case of pushing) or the near leg (in the case of pulling). The basic body postures chosen for this study are considered to be representative of generalized pushing and pulling situations.

For pushing purposes the BH was adjusted so that the hands applied the forces at 70% of the subject's shoulder height above the floor (approximately chest height), while the rear foot was placed at 100% of shoulder height away from the plane of force application. For pulling, however, the hands applied the forces at a BH of 40% of shoulder height above the floor, while the front foot was at a distance of -10% of shoulder height from the plane of force application.

Each subject completed two trials in each posture, for a total of four trials. Following a demonstration of the task to be performed, each subject was instructed to exert maximum force. The previously described force monitor was set to accept a trial only after the voluntary exertion was maintained for five seconds. Subjects were provided a 30 second rest period between successive trials. This was deemed appropriate due to the relatively small number of measurements taken. If the force monitor's error light went on, subjects were asked to repeat the trial after a 30 second rest. Peak forces were recorded in all trials and converted to kilograms. In each posture, the average of the two trials was used for the ensuing analysis. The fact that BH and FD were adjusted to individual body dimensions, rather than given to absolute measures should facilitate application to other subject populations.

To assess grip strength, the dynamometer was placed comfortably in the hand to be tested (dominant hand). The subject assumed a slightly bent forward position, with the hand to be tested out in front of the body. The hand and arm were free of the body, not touching anything. The subject was allowed to slightly bend his/her arm. The test involved an all-out gripping effort for 2-3 seconds. No swinging or pumping of the arm was allowed. Two trials were taken. The score was the average of the two trials in kilograms.

RESULTS

A stepwise regression analysis was done to arrive at equations to predict peak pushing and pulling forces in optimal postures. In both cases, six variables were selected as candidates to enter the two separate equations. The variables considered were: sex, age, standing height, shoulder height, body weight, and grip strength. These variables were chosen because they are all relatively easy and inexpensive to assess. These are important criteria when it comes to industrial strength testing. The thresholds for both leaving and entering the equation were determined by probability values. The probability threshold to enter the equation was .05 and the probability threshold to leave the equation was also .05.

When the criterion was peak pushing force, the only predictor variable to enter the equation was grip strength. The r value of was +.851 which was significant at the .00001 level. This relationship is given in equation (1), where Y was the predicted peak pushing force and X was the actual grip strength. The standard error of estimate when predicting peak pushing force from grip strength was determined to be 11.2. When the criterion was peak pulling force, the only predictor variable to enter the equation was body weight. The multiple r value was +.790. This value was significant at the .00003 level. This relationship is given in equation, where Y was the predicted peak pulling force and X was the actual body weight. Under these circumstances, the standard error of estimate was 16.1. The relationships are:

$$Y = 1.235058 + 1.2629X \qquad (1)$$
$$Y = -46.44727 + 1.373546X \qquad (2)$$

To validate these results, an additional sample, comprised of three males and three females, was tested. Once again, these six subjects were volunteers obtained from the student body at the University of Windsor. The testing protocol followed was identical to the one outlined in the experimental design section of this paper. The mean age for this sample was 21.3 years (SD = 2.2 years). The mean standing height was 172.7 cm (SD = 8.9 cm). The mean shoulder height was 144.3 cm (SD = 7.9 cm). The mean body weight was 76.5 kg (SD = 12.9 kg). Independent groups t-tests were used to test for differences between the means of the two samples. The results are as follows: $t(28) = +1.136$, $p > .05$ (for age), $t(28) = +0.861$, $p > .05$ (for standing height); $t(28) = +1.042$, $p > .05$ (for shoulder height); $t(28) = -0.120$, $p > .05$ (for body weight). Since there were no statistically significant differences found, the samples can be considered identical. Using the previously outlined equations, peak pushing and pulling forces were predicted for the six extra subjects. Correlation coefficients were obtained between the actual and predicted peak forces. The cross-validated r value for peak pushing force was determined to be +.830. This value was compared to the actual multiple r value (+.851). The difference is only .021. The cross-validated r value for peak pulling force was +.659. Given that the original multiple r value was +.790, the difference is .131.

DISCUSSION

The present study demonstrates that grip strength can be used to predict peak pushing forces. However, when the objective was the prediction of peak pulling forces, grip strength did not provide a statistically significant improvement to the multiple r value obtained through a stepwise regression analysis. Therefore, grip strength should not be used to predict the peak pulling forces required in industrial jobs.

Based on the small differences discovered between the actual and cross-validated r values, the regression equations presented in this paper are not to be taken lightly. They can be used as powerful predictors of peak pushing and pulling forces in similar samples. There is however one caveat; pushing and pulling tasks should be arranged so that workers of all sizes can take on optimal postures. In essence, this calls for complete adjustability. MMH equipment, like carts and dollies, should be designed with handles that can be adjusted to 70% of shoulder height above the ground (for pushing) and 40% of shoulder height above the ground (for pulling). This is an especially important consideration if the loads to be pushed or pulled require maximum or near maximum force exertion. In addition, to be proactive in the treatment of injuries related to pushing and pulling, workers should be trained as to what body configurations are optimal (with respect to handle height and foot distance). In this way, the proposed adjustability feature would not be wasted.

While it is true that many MMH jobs involve combinations of pushing, pulling, lifting, lowering, and carrying, most recommendations on how to assess combination tasks are based on the assumption that the risk of a combination task can be assessed adequately by assessing the components of the task separately. Although some researchers are beginning to suggest further research into the validity of this assumption, risk assessment is still conducted based on the aforementioned premise. Therefore, if, as an example, the most critical single task of a combination MMH job is pushing, then performance can be adequately predicted, for a given worker, based on grip strength. Thus equation (1) can be used to match the strongest workers to the jobs requiring the greatest pushing strength, thereby reducing the risk of injury. If the most critical single task happens to involve pulling, then MMH performance can best be predicted using body weight [equation(2)] and not grip strength . However, if a MMH task is truly a combination task (ie. one in which a single critical task cannot be identified), then neither of the two equations presented may be appropriate.

Future research is required to determine if grip strength can be used to predict other forms of MMH strength like lifting, lowering, and carrying. Until these types of studies are conducted, published, and validated the use of grip strength as a general indicator of industrial strength will continue to be justifiably questioned. In addition, it would be useful for researchers in this area to arrive at a consensus as to the best way to predict the strength of true combination tasks.

CONCLUDING REMARKS

This study was deemed essential for four reasons. Firstly, injuries attributable to MMH are now, and will continue to be, prevalent in many industries. Secondly, the research literature was found to be lacking with regard to the appropriateness of currently employed industrial strength testing techniques (of any type). Thirdly, a better understanding of the appropriateness of industrial strength testing practices can only help ergonomic practitioners improve worker selection and placement procedures which would, it is believed, combat the rapidly escalating costs associated with workers' compensation claims. Finally, the overall benefit of this type of study is the provision of a safer, healthier, and more efficient workforce.

REFERENCES

[1]   Ayoub, M.M. and McDaniel, J.W. (1974). Effect of operator stance on pushing and pulling tasks. *AIIE Tr.*, *6*, 185-195.
[2]   European Communities Commission (1990). *Manual Handling Directive* (90/269/EEC). Brussels: European Communities Commission.
[3]   National Institute for Occupational Safety and Health (1983). *A Work Practices Guide for Manual Lifting*. Akron, OH: American Industrial Hygiene Association.
[4]   Worksafe Australia (1990). *National Standard for Manual Handling and National Code of Practice for Manual Handling*. Canberra: Australian Government Publishing Service.

Advances in Occupational Ergonomics and Safety II
Edited by Biman Das and Waldemar Karwowski
IOS Press and Ohmsha, 1997

A METHODOLOGY OF OFFICE LAYOUT AND BUILDING LAYOUT FOR HUMAN PERFORMANCE

Chae-Bogk Kim †, Soo Chan Park ǂ and Jin Ho Kim ǂ

† Department of Technology Education, Korea National University of Education
Cheongwon-Kun, Chungbuk, Korea, 363-791
ǂ Ergonomics Laboratory, Korea Research Institute of Standards and Science
Daedeok Science Town, Taejon, Korea, 305-600

Abstract

This paper investigates workspace design, determination of furniture specification, and office layout for better office environment as well as human performance. Task analysis and evaluation are performed to determine the specification of furniture. According to the task characteristics, departments are grouped into four types. Then, the number of workers, the dimension of equipments as well as the amount of documents are surveyed to decide building layout. Moreover activity relationships among departments are investigated. With cut tree approach and eigenvector approaches, the constructed relationship charts are used to obtain several alternative office layouts. These layouts are provided to decision makers.

1. Introduction

In recent years, office environment has received a great attention by human factor researchers because office is designed to satisfy various workers' needs. For better office environment, the design of workspace, specification of furniture and office layout are essential. Task analysis and evaluation are useful tool to design workspace and to determine the specification of furniture. In order to determine office layout, activity relationships as well as amount of documents and equipments are important factors.

Such a better design problem of office environment is emerged when departments at Korea National Housing Corporation (KNHC) moves to a new intelligent building. KNHC, located in Seoul, is one of the best housing corporation in Korea. KNHC consists of 7 sectors, 28 divisions, 102 departments, and over 1300 employees. This study deals with the design of office layout and the determination of furniture specification given building space and the number of workers.

2. Methodology

Task analysis and evaluation are performed to define the characteristics of workers in each department. Then, we group 4 types of workers according to task characteristics: administration, accounting, drawing and research.

2.1. Workspace design

In order to design workspace, we experiment on maximum working area and normal working area[1] on the desk. Desk is divided into three sections: main working area, computer working area and assistant working area. Figure 1 shows these working areas. Since the width of maximum working area and normal working area are considered as 1m 60cm and 1m 10cm, respectively by the anthropometry of Korean adults[2], we try to assign the width of maximum working area to main desk and assign the width of normal working area to computer working area and assistant working area. Also, the depth of maximum working area and normal working area are 70cm and 50cm, respectively. Therefore, we assign the depth of maximum working area to main desk and assistant table.

For the workers in drawing departments, we assign extra width to main desk because of the size of drawing sheet as well as discussion area. Figure 2 shows three types of furniture specifications for administration and research group, accounting group, and drawing group.

2.2. Office layout

Given the number of workers in each department as well as division of KNHC, we investigate the amount of documents and dimensions of equipments in order to determine space requirements for departments and divisions. The width of aisle is allocated at least 1m for easy movement. According to task types, space requirement for each department is estimated.   Then, we survey activity relationships between departments as well as divisions for building layout.   The obtained relationship charts are simplified for easy analysis by eigenvector method [3] and cut tree method [4]. Figure 3 shows examples of analyzed results by two methods.

For the zoning operation of each division, obtained results by two methods are used. Since there are fixed areas for specific departments and rooms, information of fixed areas is useful clue for zoning operation.   Several alternative zoning layouts are presented to KNHC and one of alternatives is selected by KNHC.   Figure 4 represents example of zoning result. After zoning operation, office layout operation is performed. Desks, chairs, equipments, drawers, shelves, etc. are allocated.   For each aisle, at least 1m width is allocated.   Figure 5 represents example of office layout result.

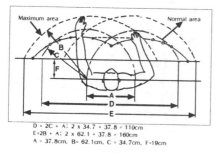

D = 2C + A: 2 x 34.7 + 37.8 = 110cm
E = 2B + A: 2 x 62.1 + 37.8 = 160cm
A = 37.8cm, B= 62.1cm, C = 34.7cm, F=19cm

Figure 1. Dimension of working area

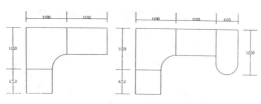

(a) administration, research,   (b) Drawing group
   accounting group
Figure 2. Furniture Specification for users' group

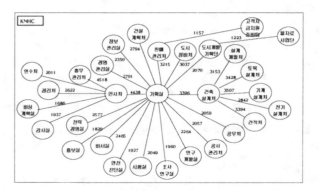

Figure 3. Example of relationship charts

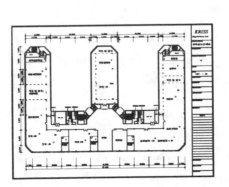

Figure 4. Example of zoning layoutt

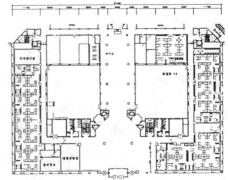

Figure 5. Example of office layout

3. Conclusion

For the better office environment as well as human performance, this paper presents a methodology to design workspace, determination of furniture specification and design office layout. Maximum working area and normal working area are investigated and the obtained results are applied to the determination of furniture specification as well as workspace design. In order to obtain office layout, space requirements for departments and divisions are estimated based on the number of workers, amount of documents and dimensions of equipments.   Then, eigenvector and cut tree methods are employed to obtain office layout by using activity relationships between departments and divisions.   KNHC (management as well as employees) is   satisfied by the provided office layout.

REFERENCE

[1] Mark S. Sanders and Ernest J. McCormick, Human Factors in Enf\gineering and Design.   McGraw Hill, 1987, pp. 343-346.

[2] C. J. KIM et al., National Anthropometric Survey of Korea 1992. KRISS-92-144-IR, 1992.

[3] Zvi Drezner, A heuristic procedure for the layout of a large number of facilities, *Management Science* 33 (1987) 907-915.

[4] Benoit Montreuil and H. D. Ratliff, Utilizing cut trees as design skeletons for facility layout, IIE Transactions (1989) 136-143.

2. Occupational Risk and Cost Assessment

Advances in Occupational Ergonomics and Safety II
Edited by Biman Das and Waldemar Karwowski
IOS Press and Ohmsha, 1997

Development of Potential Injury Risk Cost for the CAFER Model

Isaac Barsky   and   Sourin Dutta
Workplace Basics   *Dept. Of Industrial &Mfg. Systems Engg.*
La Salle   *University of Windsor*
Ont., Canada   *Windsor,Ont., Canada*

The paper reports on the analysis of injury data drawn from a cross-section of automotive parts manufacturers in South-Western Ontario, to establish a table of costs categorized according to anatomical location, gender and age grouping. This attempt at grouping costs by gender and age groups is the first step towards establishing benchmarks for use in proactive assessment of product and process designs using CAFER.

1. Introduction

The Cost Assessment For Ergonomic Risk (CAFER) model attempts to determine a cost (in dollars or minutes) of injury expense suffered by a worker, and attributable directly to a product or process which has been designed in such a manner that the risk of injury is present . The model described in a recent publication by Barsky and Dutta [1], requires that a cross-functional team identify all tasks which may present an injury risk for the worker, the type of injury possible and the area of the anatomy which may be affected. In applying this model to the assessment of a product or process design which may lead to a potential injury, it is necessary to estimate the severity of this injury in terms of its corresponding dollar value. It is assumed that these estimated costs will need to be established for different types of industries, through the analysis of empirical data. However, there is reason to assume, based on data previously collected by the authors [2], that these costs may be affected in a significant way by age groups and by gender differences. This paper reports on an analysis of these data sets to establish whether any significant differences do exist and establishes a table of costs, categorized according to: anatomical location, gender and age grouping.

2. Objectives

The objectives of the investigation undertaken by the authors were:
1. To develop a table of cost data, to be used in the CAFER analysis model.
2. To determine whether there is a significant difference between costs associated with injuries incurred by males vs. Females.
3. To determine whether costs should be separated by age group categories.

This attempt at grouping costs by gender and age group is the first step towards establishing benchmarks for use in the proactive assessment of product and process designs using CAFER.

3. Methodology

The data being considered for use in CAFER was obtained by the authors from local automotive parts manufacturing and assembly companies in South-Western Ontario. This data, portions of which are profiled in [1] included 1,949 individual injuries recorded over a three-year period, and was organized by the date and shift on which each injury occurred, the gender and age of the injured person, the part of the anatomy affected and the total cost corresponding to the injury. The following procedure was used in analyzing the data:

1. The raw data was normalized or adjusted for differences in population for each company by using a factor equivalent to the ratio of the injured population to the total number of employees in that company.
2. The normalized data for each company was then pooled to establish a total weighted average cost and grouped by anatomical categories.
3. The total weighted cost was then grouped according to male and female populations and age groups, working in the companies providing the data. The finalized data was presented as injury cost in dollars per 10 workers, for ease of calculations.
4. A statistical analysis was then conducted to determine whether the separation of the costs by gender and age group was valid.

4. Analysis And Results

The data in Table 1 is a summary of the adjusted injury costs to be used in the CAFER application and is only valid for the manufacturing industries in the South-Western Ontario region, although, the application may be extended to other manufacturing industries and regions. When the data was developed and a graph constructed (as shown in Figure 1), it became evident that there existed a marked difference between the costs associated with the male population and those associated with the female population. In order to establish the significance of this variance, a number of statistical tests were conducted on the data sets. The results of these tests are shown in Table 2.

The summary in Table 2 indicates that in all tests conducted, the average weighted cost of injury incurred by males, are significantly higher than those for females. However, similar analyses conducted on age group categories (test data not shown), demonstrated a similar, but insufficiently conclusive effect. These results were not included here due to space limitations. The work reported here is preliminary and more data is being collected to verify these results and extend them to the CAFER type analysis of workplaces.

TABLE 1

INJURY COSTS /10 WORKERS

ORGANIZED BY ANATOMICAL CATEGORY

ANATOMY GROUP OR CATEGORY	MALES COST OF INJURIES BY AGE GROUP		FEMALES COST OF INJURIES BY AGE GROUP		TOTAL COST MALES ($)	TOTAL COST FEMALES ($)
	0 - 39	40-70	0 - 39	40-70		
ABDOMINAL	136.22	116.13	1.16	11.09	252.36	12.24
FOOT	58.98	109.50	70.31	18.20	168.48	88.52
CHEST	31.36	76.32	0.50	0.66	107.69	1.16
FINGER	242.52	224.06	99.09	175.52	466.58	274.61
LOWER ARM	301.07	335.92	262.42	239.67	636.99	502.09
GROIN AREA	0.34	2.95	2.48	0.17	3.28	2.65
HAND/WRIST	395.67	336.59	310.07	124.94	732.26	435.01
HEAD/FACE	64.11	147.18	5.77	93.55	211.29	99.32
HIP/BACK	1285.78	778.29	397.20	815.47	2064.07	1212.66
LOWER LEG	250.67	254.43	89.67	170.28	505.10	259.94
MULTIPLE	217.99	177.54	46.94	97.40	395.53	144.34
OTHER	65.26	53.62	104.41	0.00	118.88	104.41
UNDETERM.	155.23	536.26	107.56	336.73	691.49	444.29
UPPER ARM	561.12	676.99	562.83	371.11	1238.12	933.94

FIGURE 1

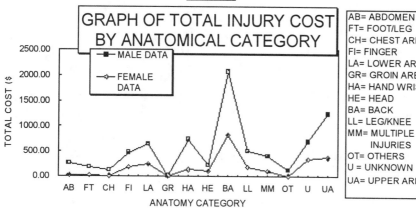

GRAPH OF TOTAL INJURY COST BY ANATOMICAL CATEGORY

AB= ABDOMEN
FT= FOOT/LEG
CH= CHEST AREA
FI= FINGER
LA= LOWER ARM
GR= GROIN AREA
HA= HAND WRIST
HE= HEAD
BA= BACK
LL= LEG/KNEE
MM= MULTIPLE
        INJURIES
OT= OTHERS
U = UNKNOWN
UA= UPPER ARM

TABLE 2

STATISTICAL TESTS CONDUCTED ON TABLE 1 DATA

PARAMETERS	PAIRED SIGN TEST	MANN - WHITNEY RANKED U TEST	PAIRED t TEST
Hypothesis H0:	P= 0.5	Mu(m) = Mu(F)	Mu (diff.)=0
Sigma	0.072	59.4	164.39
Pbar	0.821	-------------	-------------
U	-------------	684	-------------
t	-------------	-------------	3.47
Reject UL	0.642	494.42	-------------
t (0.05, 27)	-------------	-------------	2.052
Decision	Reject H0	Reject H0	Reject H0

5. Concluding Remarks

It is noted from Table 2, that injuries appear to be more probable and more costly, among male rather than female employees. Dieterly[3] reported that male employees have a significantly higher risk of potential injuries. Furthermore, it has been reported by Mital [4], that in general males are willing to lift more weight than females, which may contribute to a higher incidence of back and upper torso injuries. He also observed that experience on the job, which compensates for any physiological changes due to aging, may be one possible explanation for the relative lack of age group dominance with respect to injury propensity.

6. References

[1] Barsky, I. & Dutta, S.P., Cost Assessment For Ergonomic Risk (CAFER), accepted for publication, International Journal of Industrial Ergonomics.

[2] Dutta, S.P., & Barsky, I., Age, Shift work and Industrial Accidents - A Longitudinal Study, In, Kumar,S.(ed.) Advances in Industrial Ergonomics and Safety IV, Taylor & Francis, 1992, pp 113- 120.

[3] Dieterly, D.L., Multiple Injury Employee: Problem or Acceptable Consequence, In, A.C. Bittner and P.C. Champney (eds.), Advances in Industrial Ergonomics and Safety VII, Taylor & Francis, 1995, pp 915 - 923.

[4] Mital, A. Maximum Weights of Lift Acceptable to Male and Female Industrial Workers For Extended Work Shifts, *Ergonomics*, 27, 1984, 1115 - 1126.

Advances in Occupational Ergonomics and Safety II
Edited by Biman Das and Waldemar Karwowski
IOS Press and Ohmsha, 1997

Anthropometric Disparity:
Why Things Don't Fit

James F. Annis
Annis Consulting
Yellow Springs, OH 45387, U.S.A.

Abstract. Ergonomists, engineers, and others that frequently use anthropometric data in design, typically must rely on statistical values in textbooks, technical manuals, or ones buried in computer models. Frequently used are means, standard deviations, and percentile values but these only give the user information about the variability of a single dimension and say nothing about the variability of one dimension in relation to another. Almost all ergonomic problems are multivariate in nature; therefore, in order to give the designer a different look at human variability, this article presents data showing the range and incidence of disparate values for dimensions used in design. Using groups of men and women selected with height and weight near the ends of the distribution in a major anthropometric database, the minimum and maximum values found at opposite ends of the distribution are presented for combinations of workspace, torso lengths and circumferences, and segmental dimensions. An example of a special application. is also presented.

1. Introduction

Sometimes workplaces and *'ergonomically designed'* products appear to be constructed using the concept that, if a person's size is 50th percentile in one area of their body, the same person is 50th percentile in all areas. The fallacy of the 'average man' concept was demonstrated using modern applied anthropometry almost 40 years ago [1]. The error of the concept was re-confirmed by this author using the most recent database containing workspace dimensions [2]. Almost all anthropometric problems in ergonomics are multivariate in nature, yet ergonomists are often forced to look at statistical values for one variable at a time, since the most widely available summary statistics, e.g., mean, standard deviation, and percentile values, are univariate. Typical problems facing the designer involve the need to know the interrelationship of several variables. For example, in a group of men that are all 1778 mm (70 inches) tall, the ergonomist may need to know the range of variability of reaching distance or popliteal height within the group. Also, in a sample of small women whose height and weight are both equivalent to 10th percentile in their population, one may ask, what are the maximum percentile values found in other dimensions in these individuals. Although the relative frequency is not high, some physically small individuals may possess some dimensions ranging above the 90th percentile. Similarly, in a group of large persons, a number of individuals will be found that run below the 10th percentile for certain variables important to workplace layout. The incidence rates associated with such disparate combinations is not necessarily high, but such variability confronts all design decisions.

The main objective herein is to give the ergonomist and/or safety engineer a look at the magnitude of individual variability by showing through the use simple statistics the disparity extant in selected applied dimensions. Such information is hard to find since one must have access to raw data files in order to examine the range and incidence of disparate values for combinations of dimensions. Finally, the analyses presented below demonstrate the importance of adjustability in ergonomic design.

2. Workspace Dimensions

Anthropometric dimensions that are most frequently needed by the industrial ergonomist are those used to layout workspace. For reasons that are politically complex in the U.S., workspace dimensions have rarely been collected on large, nationwide samples of civilians. The most recent major survey which included workspace dimensions on civilian men and women in the U.S. was completed in 1962 [3]. These data are now 35 years old and because of the possibility of secular change factors they may no longer reflect the true body size and shape of the workforce. Therefore, in all of the analyses presented below, I have used anthropometry from a major survey of military personnel which was completed in 1988 (ANSUR) [4]. The ANSUR survey included 132 basic dimensions (plus demographics, special 3-D head/face dimensions, etc.) on over 5500 men and 3400 women of the U.S. Army. Both sexes were measured concurrently and using exactly the same procedures and the same measurement team. This survey provides the best, currently available database in applied anthropometry in the U.S. The dimensional values in these databases have been strictly edited so that analyses, such as presented here, do not include extraneous outliers. Because of selective criteria used by the military it is known that such samples are truncated at the ends of the distribution for some variables when compared to random samples of civilians. For example, men shorter than 60 inches (1524 mm) or taller than 80 inches (2032 mm) are exempt from service. Men and women in the military must now meet weight/height standards, hence soldiers tend to be more muscular and less obese than civilians. As with most military samples, ANSUR tends to include few individuals over 50 years of age. For these reasons these data present the 'best' rather than the 'worst' case when looking at disparate values. That is, the variability described below is not doubt less than would be seen in the civilian workforce of most nations. The general principle however will apply to all populations.

In the search for disparate values in workspace dimensions, men and women possessing Stature and Weight values equalling either 10th percentile or less (SMALL) or 90th percentile or more (LARGE) were pulled from their respective database files. Stature and Weight were selected as the control variables, because this pair does the best job of explaining variance across a group of dimensions. The samples of men (SMALL, n=180; LARGE, n=156) and the samples of women (SMALL, n=186; LARGE, n=112) were then examined individually using SPSS software to determine the maximum and minimum values for a series of 20 workspace dimensions. Next, the maximum value associated with each dimension for the SMALL samples (MAX10) and the minimum value associated with workspace dimension for the LARGE samples (MIN90) were converted percentile values based upon their respective values in the full ANSUR populations. The resulting values for the men and women of both size groups are presented in Table 1. The SMALL women showed higher percentile values than did the SMALL men for 14 of the 20 dimensions with an mean percentile value of 64.2 versus 60.0. The largest male-female difference in percentiles observed were found with Abdominal Extension Height, Cervicale Height, Hip Breadth, Popliteal Height, Thumbtip Reach, and Sitting Height. It was no surprise to find that the dimensions with the most disparate percentiles were those that have a low multiple correlation coefficient with height and weight.

For the LARGE men and women the picture is somewhat reversed. That is, MIN90 for men tend to show the lower values (13 of 20 cases). The lowest percentile observed averaged 40.6 and 45,5 for males and females respectively. In both SMALL and LARGE men and women, the most nebulous variable to design for is Elbow Rest Height. These data suggest that the potential problems areas to look for, particularly seated workplace design, are the following:

SMALL female- Elbow Rest Ht., Forearm-Forearm, Hip Brdth., and ThighClearance

SMALL male--- Abdominal Extension, Elbow Rest Ht., and Forearm-Forearm

LARGE female - Acromial Ht., Elbow Rest Ht., and Popliteal Ht.
LARGE male--- Abdominal Extension, Acromial Ht., Cervicale Ht., Eye Ht.,
    Forearm-Forearm, Thigh Clearance, and Sitting Ht.

In areas of the body suggested by these dimensions, a greater amount of adjustabilty is needed.

Table 1. Disparity for Selected Workspace Dimensions in Females and Males when Height (Ht.) and Weight (Wt.) are Controlled at 10th and 90th Percentile Levels.
(expressed as percentile values at opposite extreme)

Dimension	Max% when Ht & Wt = 10%		Max% when Ht & Wt = 90%	
	Females	Males	Females	Males
Abdominal Ext Ht	70	83	25	21
Acromial Ht, Sit*	73	64	27	12
Buttock-Knee L	50	46	63	66
Buttock-Popliteal L	61	64	35	42
Cervicale Ht, Sit	55	69	35	20
Elbow Rest Ht*	99	97	3	1
Eye Ht, Sitting	61	63	34	16
Forearm-Forearm*	93	82	47	18
Forearm-Hand L	73	65	42	55
Gluteal Furrow Ht	63	60	62	61
Hip Brdth, Sit	75	61	39	60
Knee Ht, Sit	50	32	70	66
OH Fingertip Reach	37	34	73	77
OH Fingertip Rch,Sit	32	37	72	47
Popliteal Ht	66	52	30	61
Thigh Clearance*	80	71	35	20
Thumbtip Reach	74	60	55	44
Functional Leg L	54	39	76	75
Shoulder-Elbow L	65	54	46	35
Sitting Ht	53	66	40	14

*Suggestive of lower correlation with height and weight

3. Body Segmental Relationships

Today engineers and ergonomists often use computerized models of humans to assist them in designing a machine or laying out a workstation. In most cases the source of the anthropometry and biomechanical data applied in such models is unknown to the user. The linkage system of the some human analogs may be based upon the sum of individual body segment percentile values. The error introduced by this practice has been described [2],[5],[6]. Regardless of whether a given model provides a number of percentile representations or is able to compute a continuum of body sizes by multiple regression, little attention is paid to the potential for or the magnitude of disparity between body segments that occurs some people. Using the full ANSUR databases, a series of three individual segment lengths comprising the torso and four combined/multiple segment lengths were computed for intercomparison. The anthropometric definitions for the seven segments were as follows:

1. Pelvis ---- Vertical distance from the tip of the greater trochanter of the femur (Trochanterion landmark) to the top of the hip bone (Iliocristale landmark).

2. Lower Torso- Vertical distance from Iliocristale to Waist at the navel (Omphalion).
3. Upper Torso- Vertical distance from the Waist to the tip of the spinous process
    of the 7th cervical vertebra (Cervicale landmark).
4. Arm-Hand (total)-- Distance from the shoulder (Acromion landmark) to the tip of
    the middle finger (Dactylion 3).
5. Leg (total)--------- Vertical distance from the Trochanterion landmark to the
    floor.
6. Torso Height (total) - (Pelvis+Lower Torso+Upper Torso).
7. Torso Front (total)- Vertical distance from the Trochanterion landmark to the top
    of the sternum (Suprasternale landmark).

The disparity of the various segments using the MAX10 and MIN90 method discussed above are summarized for the upper aspect of the body in Table 2 and the lower body in Table 3. Not all of the possible combinations are presented. Possibly because of the complex, multi-dimensional character of segments, the MAX10 and the MIN90 percentiles represented are frequently nearer the opposite extreme of the distribution than seen with the more simple workspace dimensions. For example, short individuals that have a Torso Height equal to 10th

Table 2. Disparity in Male (M) and Female (F) Combined Upper Body Segments when Compared Near the Ends of the Distribution

Controlled Segment	Compared Segment	Extreme Percentile M	F
Total Torso Height = 10th%tile or less	Arm-Hand	98th	92nd
	Pelvis	73rd*	92nd
	Lower Torso	99th	99th
	Upper Torso	69th*	77th*
	Torso Front	96th	72nd*
	Leg	99th	96th
Total Torso Height = 90th%tile or more	Arm-Hand	12th	6th
	Pelvis	7th	27th*
	Lower Torso	1st	1st
	Upper Torso	13th	16th
	Torso Front	23rd*	11th
	Leg	3rd	3rd
Arm-Hand = 10th%tile or less	Total Torso	85th*	98th
	Pelvis	96th	93rd
	Lower Torso	99th	99th
	Upper Torso	97th	99th
	Torso Front	96th	99th
	Leg	45th*	48th*
Arm-Hand = 90th%tile or more	Total Torso	2nd	7th
	Pelvis	1st	1st
	Lower Torso	1st	1st
	Upper Torso	3rd	5th
	Torso Front	1st	3rd
	Leg	55th*	45th*

* Higher level of correlation indicated between segments

percentile or less may have an Arm-Hand length MAX10 value as high as the 92nd or 98th percentile. People with longer torsos tend to have low MIN90 values only for the Lower Torso and Leg segments while for the other segments have disparate values ranging from 6th to 27th percentile levels for women and from 7th to 23rd percentile levels for men. MAX10 and MIN90 values for the Pelvis and the Leg segments run near the opposite extremes in all cases. However, in Table 3 the data indicate that women with short pelvises tend to also have short torsos while men with long pelvises tend to have long torsos, while the opposite is not the case. Other interesting findings are indicated on the tables by the asterisks. It is not too surprising that the two segments showing the highest level of interrelationship or the least disparate values are the Arm-Hand and Leg segments. This is demonstrated in both Table 2 and Table 3 when one or the other is the controlled segment.

4. Lengths and Circumferences of the Torso

A MAX10-MIN90 analysis was also performed on ANSUR men only for combinations of torso dimensions considered to be useful for design, as well as the sizing of clothing. The four principal torso circumferences (Shoulder, Chest, Waist. and Buttock) were examined in relation to four torso lengths (Waist-Back, Waist-Front, Cervicale-Iliocristale, and Shoulder Length). With few exceptions the MAX10 and the MIN90 values were either greater than 95th

Table 3. Disparity in Male (M) and Female (F) Lower Body Segments when Compared Near the Ends of the Distribution

Controlled Segment	Compared Segment	Extreme Percentile	
		M	**F**
Pelvis = 10th%tile	Total Torso	92nd	77th*
or less	Lower Torso	99th	99th
	Upper Torso	99th	99th
	Torso Front	99th	99th
	Arm-Hand	99th	99th
	Leg	99th	99th
Pelvis = 90th%tile	Total Torso	40th*	7th
or more	Lower Torso	1st	1st
	Upper Torso	3rd	2nd
	Torso Front	3rd	1st
	Arm-Hand	2nd	1st
	Leg	2nd	1st
Leg = 10th%tile	Total Torso	97th	99th
or less	Pelvis	97th	99th
	Lower Torso	98th	99th
	Upper Torso	97th	98th
	Torso Front	97th	99th
	Arm-Hand	55th*	61st*
Leg = 90th%tile	Total Torso	2nd	1st
	Pelvis	1st	1st
	Lower Torso	1st	1st
	Upper Torso	2nd	2nd
	Torso Front	2nd	1st
	Arm-Hand	51st*	45th*

* Higher level of correlation indicated

percentile or less than 1st percentile, respectively. For example, for 180 men with a small Shoulder Circumference individuals were found with MAX10 values ranging from 91st to 97th percentile levels for torso lengths. Similarly, for the men with large shoulders, MIN90 values were found that were below 1st percentile for all four length dimensions. Of the matrix of 32 cells in the analysis (4 circumferences x 4 lengths x 2 conditions) no individuals having MAX10 values greater that 90th percentile were found in 2 cases: Waist and Buttock Circumference (10%tile or less) versus Waist-Front Length (both %tile levels). Also, no men with a large Waist or Buttock Circumference were found in relation to short Waist-Front Lengths. In the matrix of the 16 cells required for the comparison of the four circumferences only, the incidence rate for men with MAX10 values above the 50th percentile level were less than 1% in all cases. The highest incidence was for the Shoulder Circumference-Waist Circumference pair where the rate was 0.8% of the sample. The MAX10 incidence rates for the length comparison were somewhat higher overall, but less than 1% in all cells of the matrix.

The fraction of individuals in a population with dimensions at opposite extremes is fortunately usually small for most combinations of dimensions. In the analysis above, no individuuals were found in 4 of 32 cells (12.5%) that had test dimensions within 10% of the opposite extreme. The number of individuals in the remaining cells ranged from 1 (0.6% of sample) to 16 (8.9%). The latter percentage would represent a significant proportion of individuals that would be difficult to fit. Of the tested dimensions, Shoulder Length versus all four circumferences shows the greatest potential for misfit. Although not designed to differentiate the amount or frequency of disparate relationships, the correlation coefficient reflects the likelihood of such cases happening. In this case, Shoulder Length shows the lowest r values of the four length versus the three of four circumferences

5. A Special Application

Disparate values can have application in design where one is interested in being sure that the target workstation or product can accommodate the likely 'worst case'. An example of this type of application formed part of the development of a hi-tech load bearing system in which the buyer wanted to be sure that the innermost edges of the shoulder straps would not cut into the lateral aspect of the user's neck (trapezius muscle). The best way to accomplish this goal is to do a search for disparate values for the critical variables. In this particular case, since the needed dimensions were not immediately available in the ANSUR database, a new dimension to provide the distance across the base of the neck had to be computed from those currently available. The dimensions used were Shoulder Length, Biacromial Breadth, and the angle of Shoulder Slope (in degrees). Shoulder Length, which is the surface distance from a lateral neck landmark to the acromion landmark, is usually only measured on the right side, so bilateral symmetry had to be assumed. The direct horizontal distance between the right and left acromia was measured (Biacromial Breadth), however, the distance across the base of the neck was not measured. A new dimension - Neck Base Breadth, was computed via the relationship: [Biacromial Breadth - 2(cosO x Shoulder Length)]; where the angle O equals the shoulder slope in degrees. Since the design limit would be established by individuals with a combination of a wide neck base and a short shoulder length, search for such individuals in the database was completed. A summary of the data from the analysis is presented in Table 4. Using only the data for the 180 men with a Neck Base Breadth ranging from 90th percentile up to the maximum, individuals were found that had Shoulder Lengths equalling 5th percentile or less in 15 of the 18, one millimeter brackets with subjects. If, indeed, the objective is to have a shoulder strap width that is not likely to impinge on the neck of anyone, the design limit has to be set well below the 1st percentile value of Shoulder Length. The solution appears to be obvious, however without the supporting data it is doubtful if such a design would actually be specified.

**Table 4. Disparate Shoulder Length-Neck Base Breadth Combinations
for Men with Wide Necks**

Percentile Bracket	No.Subj. (#)	Neck Base Breadth (mm)	Min.Shoulder Length (mm)	(%tile)
90th to 94th	17	118	126	<2nd
	14	119	132	<5th
	12	120	127	<2nd
	12	121	118	<1st
	19	122	125	>1st
	11	123	125	>1st
95th to 99th	13	124	124	1st
	7	125	131	4th
	9	126	123	<1st
	6	127	138	13th
	9	128	128	2nd
	6	129	121	<1st
	3	130	126	>1st
	3	131	133	>5th
	5	132	117	<1st
	0	133	-	-
	3	134	138	13th
	1	135	146	35th
99th to Max	30	136-157	114	<1st

References

[1] Daniels, G.S., The 'Average Man', Technical Note WCRD 53-7, Wright Air Development Center, Wright-Patterson Air Force Base, Ohio, 1952.

[2] Annis, J.F. and J.T. McConville, Applications of Anthropometric Data in Sizing and Design, Advances in Industrial Ergonomics and Safety II, Biman Das editor, Taylor & Francis, London, 1990, pp. 309-314.

[3] Stoudt, H.W., A. Damon, R. McFarland, and J.Roberts, Weight, Height, and Selected Body Dimensions of Adults. United States 1960-62, *Public Health Service Publication No 1000*, Series 11, No. 8, Government Printing Office, Washington. D.C., 1965.

[4] Gordon, C.C. *et al.,* 1988 Anthropometric Survey of U.S. Army Personnel: Methods and Summary Statistics, NATICK/TR-89/044, United States Army Natick Research, Development and Engineering Center, Natick, MA, 1989.

[5] McConville, J.T. and E. Churchill, Statistical Concepts in Design, Technical Report, AMRL-TR-76-29, Aerospace Medical Research Laboratory, Wright-Patterson Air Force Base, Ohio, 1976.

[6] Robinette, K. and J.T. McConville, An Alternative to Percentile Models, *Society of Automotive Engineers, Inc.,* 810217, Warrendale PA, 1981.

Advances in Occupational Ergonomics and Safety II
Edited by Biman Das and Waldemar Karwowski
IOS Press and Ohmsha, 1997

Risk and Strain of Organism at Founded Metallic Parts Cleaning

Hilda HERMAN and Ileana GRIGORIU

Institute of Hygiene, Public Health, Health Services and Management
Dr.Leonte Street 1-3, Bucharest, Romania

Abstract. Study carried out at cleaning founded cast iron parts by pneumatic hammer in machine building industry. Research methods included: work analysis; environment characterisation; measurement of vibrations produced by the pneumatic hammer and transmitted to the body; dynamic investigation of some organism's indicators; morbidity analysis. The work is manual - mechanised. The manual maintaining of the pneumatic hammer determines an important postural strain, tiresome for the organism. The physical effort is high - the energy expenditure of 3.7-7 kcal/min and the heart rate of 98-132 beats/min. The hammer running and the cleaning generate noise and respectively, dust which exceed the TLVs. The acceleration of vibrations transmitted to the body exceeds the TLV at the lower frequencies. There are conditions for mechanical accidents. Prophylactic technical, organizatory, personal protective and medical measures have been established.

1. Introduction

The cleaning of founded metallic parts by the pneumatic hammer is a manual-mechanised work. The "man-machine" system of this technology seems to be simply, but there are many problems in its frame regarding the human organism. For this reason we have studied the working conditions at cleaning founded cast iron parts by pneumatic hammer in machine building industry, for evidencing the strain and the risk of organism and establishing prophylactic measures.

2. Methods

Research methods included:
- Equipment and work analysis; working environment characterisation: microclimate, lighting, noise, air dust concentration.
- Organism's physical effort assessment by energy expenditure (Douglas-Haldane technique) - EE, and heart rate (HR) investigation per operations and body's positions in 20 workers.
- Measurement of vibrations produced by the pneumatic hammer (on the handle and chisel) and of the vibrations transmitted to the body (on the dorsal hand face and ossa carpi zone, elbow - ulna head, shoulder - acromion, first cervical vertebra) in 20 subjects. There were measured the acceleration (cm/s^2) and the amplitude (mm) by Bruel & Kjaer apparatus.
- Investigation of some hand indicators influenced by vibrations, at the work start and end, in 80 workers: skin temperature by thermocouple on the dorsal face of the third finger (second

phalange zone), vibratory sensibility (acceleration) on the dorsal face of the third finger (third phalange zone) at the frequency from 20 to 500 Hz obtained from a vibration excitator supplied by a vibration oscillator (Bruel & Kjaer apparatuses).
- Fatigue investigation by determining the reaction time (RT) at visual and auditory stimuli, the hand force by dynamometer, the rhythm and precision of movements by tremormeter in 54 workers.
- Morbidity analysis in a period of 5 years for 120 cleaning workers.

3. Results and Discussion

The work carried on in great halls with windows and skylights, placed near the foundry. The microclimate is influenced by the meteorological conditions. In the hall there are places for cleaning and circulation ways. The ventilation was natural and mechanical. The temperature was higher in summer, above 20 degrees Celsius with the air humidity of 40-60% and lower in winter, of 14-18 degrees Celsius with the air humidity of 50-90%. The air speed was 0.1-1 m/s. The lighting was natural, artificial or mixed depending on the season, hour, workplace emplacement, sky state. For the cleaning activity there is necessary an illumination of 300 lx. The many shadows made by the great parts decrease the illumination. The noise is produced by the running of the pneumatic hammer and other equipment. The acoustic level and the air dust (including particles of casting material and of metal) concentration exceeded the TLV.
The activity is manual-mechanised. There is a close relation between the hammer and the worker, with reciprocal influence. The worker maintains the hammer with the two hands: the right applied to the handle, the left applied to the chisel, assuring the work direction of the tool. The hammer weight and the force of the compressed hammer air are taken over by the hand applied to the handle. The hammer weight is great (6-15 kg) and because of this the worker's effort is important to maintain the hammer in the most adequate position determining a permanent forced contraction of the upper limb muscles. The body's position is various and forced, depending on the form, dimension and emplacement of the part, the chisel dimension, the work space. The muscular contraction is static, more much tiresome for the organism than the dynamic contraction. The orthostatism is the basic posture and the most strained are the muscles of the shank, thigh, back and nape, which are in a permanent tension. The hammer maintaining produces static contraction of other muscles too, of the forearm, arm and scapular-humeral girdle. There are many vicious positions (figure 1): orthostatism with the trunk right or bent to various degrees, crouched, knelt, extension or flexion of upper and/or lower limbs. When the height of the cleaning surface is at the abdomen level (high parts placed on the ground, low parts placed on cleaning tables) there is a standing position with the trunk right or bent and the upper limbs are in flexion (position 1). When the cleaning surface is higher, at the thorax level, the hammer is maintained and directed in horizontal or oblique up direction, therefore against the gravity force (position 2). The difficulty of this position is greater increasing the static and forced muscular contraction of the upper and lower limbs; the lower limbs have to assure a good basis for maintaining the body's equilibrium. At the low parts placed on the ground the hammer is directed down and the trunk bent is of 20-90 degrees, according to the part height and the lower limbs are in flexion or extension (positions 3-8). At the cleaning of very low surfaces, the position is crouched, with the lower limbs in flexion and frequently the hammer leant on the thigh. In this condition the worker may adopt also the knelt position with the trunk right or bent fore as the hammer is maintained horizontally or down (positions 9 and 10). In limited space (inside part), the position is crouched or sitting with the lower limbs in complete flexion (positions 11 and 12). The EE was 3,6-7 kcal/min and the HR was 98-132 beats/min, depending on the part characteristics. Results showed that the effort increases when the trunk bent is greater. When the bent increased from 20 to 70 degrees, the EE was higher with 8% and the HR with 15% (with 16

beats/min). The most stressing positions are the orthostatism on the part with the trunk bent fore to 90 degrees (position 8) and the orthostatism with the hammer maintained horizontally or up (position 2). The lowest effort is at the position with the trunk right and the hammer directed down - position 3 (EE of 3.67 kcal/min, HR of 100 beats/min). The emplacement of the low parts on tables may reduce the trunk bent and therefore the organism's postural strain and effort. The work rhythm influences the level strain too. A high rhythm increases the effort, therefore the EE and HR values.

The neuropsychic charge is especially sensorial (visual, auditory, tactile, vibratory), but also of the concentrated and distributive attention to keep the hammer running, to follow the surface cleaning, to prevent injury and accident.

The hammer running generates vibrations. At the handle, depending on the frequency, the vibration acceleration was 2800-12000 cm/s^2 and the displacement was 0.45-0.00007 mm. The lowest values correspond to the lower frequencies, which may produce the vibration disease. The static contraction of the upper limb muscles favours the transmission of the vibration from the hammer to worker's body by the hand. But the vibration may be transmitted also to other zones on which the hammer may be leant on directly during the cleaning (thigh, thorax, shoulder). The vibration acceleration exceeded the TLV at the frequencies of 31.5 and 63 Hz on the dorsal hand face and on the elbow (418-300 cm/s^2 on the right hand, 470-418 cm/s^2 on the left hand). On the shoulder and cervical vertebrae the TLV has been exceeded only at 31.5 Hz (37-75 cm/s^2). The vibration displacement was under the TLV (0.035 mm and lower). Therefore the body's tissues reduce the vibration intensity. During the cleaning inside part, the part vibration is transmitted to the zones of the body in contact direct with the part walls. The vibrations of low frequencies (2-20 Hz) produce bone injury (metacarpus, carpus, distal epiphysis of radius and ulna) and osteoarthrosis injury (especially the upper limb and spine articulations). The vibrations of 30-100 Hz produce vascular hand troubles - the vibration disease (Raynaud's phenomenon). The cold favours the vibration action on the blood vessels: the low temperature (11-15 degrees Celsius) of the compressed hammer air with great speed (7-8 m/s), the lower temperature of the working environment and of the metallic part surface in winter.

The hand skin temperature increased at the work end because of the blood circulation increase as effect of the muscular work: in winter from 23 degrees Celsius before work to 25 degrees Celsius at the work end, in summer from 25 to 31 degrees Celsius. The vibratory sensibility was higher at the work end than before work for the right hand in most subjects, but for the left hand it decreased in most subjects at the work end because the chisel vibration has a greater intensity. The hand force increased in most subjects during work as effect of blood circulation increase by work influence: from 45 kgf to 47 kgf in the right hand, from 42 to 48 kgf in the left hand.

The visual and auditory RT decreased at the work end. The tremormeter test showed also better results at the work end than before work: decrease of test duration, of number and duration of errors. Therefore the work determines an activation state of the organism, who performs better the two tests, evidencing apparently the absence of the neuropsychic fatigue, because the studied work is firstly a physical muscular work.

There are conditions which favour production of accidents: manual handling of parts and pneumatic hammers, fall of parts and tools, projection of metallic fragments or founded materials (especially to the eye), fall of the workers because of forced and vicious positions, of slip, agglomeration of parts at the workplaces, lighting deficiencies. The microtraumatisms were frequent, especially ocular particles and sores of hands and foot. The morbidity showed higher frequency of acute respiratory ways infections, respiratory virosis and angina, that may be favoured by the dust and the lower winter temperature in the work hall.

Other frequent diseases were: digestive diseases, skin infections favoured probably by the dust and the microtraumatisms, lumbosciatica neuralgia favoured by the forced and vicious work positions and materials handling. The most workers had a seniority at this activity under 5 years that may explain why the morbidity does not contain vibration and pneumoconiosis diseases and they were between 20 and 50 years old (most from 25 to 40 years).

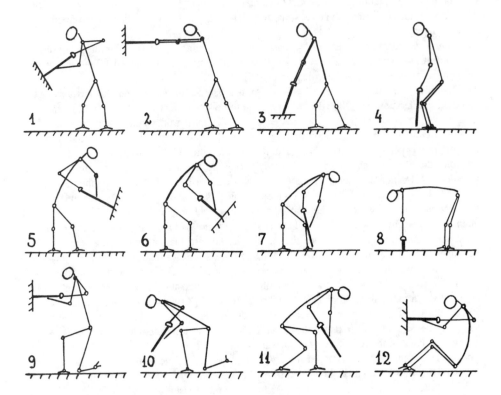

Figure 1. Representative positions of the human body during cleaning the founded metallic parts.

4. Conclusions

At the cleaning of founded metallic parts by the pneumatic hammer there are various unfavourable factors and risks for the human organism: dynamic and static muscular effort (especially postural), noise, vibrations, dust, accident conditions. Complex interventions are necessary to improve the working conditions and prevent the accidents and some diseases, regarding: the microclimate and the lighting, the organisation of the workplaces, the realisation and use of cleaning tables with ventilation for dust absorption, the decrease of noise and vibrations generated by the pneumatic hammer, the use of protective gloves against the vibrations and the low temperature, the prophylactic medical supervision and the sanitary education of the workers.

Advances in Occupational Ergonomics and Safety II
Edited by Biman Das and Waldemar Karwowski
IOS Press and Ohmsha, 1997

Human performance and strain at control of electric power system running

Hilda HERMAN, Andriana CONTULESCU, Greta NITA and Nuti DELIU
*Institute of Hygiene, Public Health, Health Services and Management,
Dr.Leonte Street 1-3, 76256 Bucharest, Romania*

Abstract. Study carried out in activity of central and district electric power dispatchers for evidencing and assessing the organism's strain and establishing measures to optimise the working conditions. Research methods included: work analysis; equipment and environment characterisation; dynamic investigation of some physiological, psychological and hormonal indicators in 45 dispatchers. The work carries on in sitting position and the effort is low. The neuropsychic charge predominates: sensorial and mental, for receiving and transmitting correctly the great number of information by computer and telecommunication, taking decisions, co-ordinating actions in the power system. The great responsibility to prevent the incidents and damages in the system determines a permanent emotional state increasing the neuropsychic strain. At the work end the performance of investigated ·:.dicators decreased in most subjects reflecting organism's fatigue and disactivation. Technical, organisatory and medical measures to prevent the dispatchers' overstrain are necessary.

1. Introduction

The installations and the equipment which produce, transport, distribute and use the electric power must run in conditions of efficiency and safety. Therefore the unitary control of the electric power system (PS) has a great importance for its good running and it is realised by central and district dispatchers. The activity carries on continually in alternating work shifts with various changes. Although the PS is automatized and informatized the dispatcher remains the central actor of PS and conditions its good running. For this reason we have studied the working conditions and tasks of the dispatchers and the strain of their organism with a view to evidence the strain causes and establish measures to prevent the overstrain and optimise the activity.

The ergonomic and medical literature shows studies regarding the activity and the working conditions in power plants, that produce the electric power [1, 2, 3] and here are not studies on the PS control. But there are many studies on work at video display terminals, used by the dispatcher in his activity and of course on neuropsychic charge in other activities.

2. Methods

Researches carried out in the real conditions of the work including [4, 5, 6]:
- Work analysis, by direct observation, by photographing the work day. 73 work analysis have been made.

- Building, equipment and work furniture characterisation, by direct observation of emplacement and form, by measuring dimensions and distances.
- Characterisation of working environment: microclimate, lighting, noise.
- Assessment of organism`s strain by dynamic investigation during work shift of 6 hours (11-16 hours, 16-22 hours) in 45 dispatchers (17 central, 28 district), of the following parameters: heart rate (HR), blood pressure, critical fusion flicker (CFF), visual acuity to near with performance elements (time and mistakes at optotype reading - "Optotype" test), visual perception speed and memory of short duration (tachystoscopy), palpebral blink frequency, reaction time (RT) to visual and auditory stimuli, performance at Weston test (with interrupted Landolt rings). The optotype and tachystoscopy tests and RT were investigated at the video terminal by a special program [6].
- Dosing on urinary excretion of catecholamines (adrenaline, noradrenaline) in 24 subjects (17 central and 7 district dispatchers).
- Measurement of skin temperature on central (forehead, sternum) and peripherical (nose top, hand finger, foot) zones and also thermal sensation investigation.
- Subjective symptomatology investigation by a questionnaire in the 45 dispatchers and by self-rating regarding the organism`s capacity and state at the work start and end.
Results have been calculated statistically: arithmetical mean, standard deviation, mean of differences between the values of work end and start, Student test (t), statistical significance (p), percentage of subjects with changes of values at the work end.

2. Results and Discussion

The task of dispatchers is to assure the running of PS in good conditions: to follow and supervise the running of installations and equipment, to co-ordinate the running conditions and the operations made in PS, to prevent and liquidate the incidents and the damages.
The activity carries on according to the regulations and the instructions of this domain, to the knowledge and experience of dispatchers, to the great number of information received and transmitted during the work by means of telecommunication (telephone, radio) and informational devices (computer). The dispatcher must know permanently the situation of the PS. The information which have been collected and analysed automatically are transmitted to the dispatchers by the computer and are displayed on the cathodic screen - numbers, diagrams, schemata of various colours according to their significance. The information have a great importance and represent the basis of the operative control of PS; the dispatchers analyse the information and take the necessary decisions. The information become functional thanks to dispatchers` activity. The activity carries on sitting in front of the cathodic screens and the command table on which there are the necessary equipment and materials: telephonic central and posts, cathodic screens and keyboards of videoterminals connected with the automatic calculating equipment, evidence registers, documents. Across the table, in front of dispatchers, there are other cathodic screens of greater dimensions. The work rooms (command rooms) are great and have large windows at the two extremities. The equipment and the work furniture (command table, chairs) are disposed in the room middle in its lengthways. The ventilation is realised by conditioned air, which assures a comfortable microclimate. The air temperature of 20-23 degrees Celsius and the air speed of 0.1 m/s assure the thermal comfort for this sedentary work. The lighting is natural, artificial or mixed according to the season, hour, sky state. Fluorescent tubular lamps placed on the ceiling assure the artificial lighting. There are differences of luminance between the work surfaces, especially between the cathodic screen and the work table surface, and also reflections of the light sources (windows, lamps) on the screen which may produce blindness. The noise is generated by the telephonic discussions and circuits, by the street traffic. The maximum admissible acoustic level in dispatchers` activity is 50 dB(A).

The dispatchers receive and transmit a very great number of information by telecommunication and teleinformation way. They must watch the screens permanently (distance eye-screen of 1-3 m) for surprising the changes, the deviations and taking the best measures in PS. Watching the screens is a basic activity of dispatchers, even during the telephonic discussion. Therefore the best conditions for the correct visual and auditory receiving of information, for correct transmission of information in PS must be assured. The receiving of information is conditioned by the participation of dispatchers' concentrated and distributive attention. Hence there is an intense strain of attention and of course of other superior nervous functions. The vigilance is present permanently because the moment and the place of a change appearance in PS are aleatory. Each information received by the dispatcher has a proper significance which must be understood by dispatcher who is not a simple collector and transmitter of information. The dispatcher must analyse and interpret the information in relation with the concrete situation, on the basis of his training and experience, of his stored knowledge. Thus the dispatcher takes decisions that are transmitted in PS for applying. The decision must be taken fast as result of many hypothesises analysed by dispatcher [7]. It is the mental, intellectual stage of the neuropsychic strain which may be solved by dispatchers with participation of technical thinking, memory, analysis and synthesis processes; it is the cognition process of dispatcher's neuropsychic activity. Dispatchers' responsibility for his work is very great. The dispatcher does not make a mistake because each mistake may have grave technical and even human consequences in PS, in other domains. The efficient achievement of the tasks by the dispatcher is depending on many factors: information presentation, work furniture characteristics, environmental factors, work organisation, work duration and regimen, functional and health state of human organism, professional training and experience. Deficiencies of these factors increase the strain of organism. The dispatcher's work is stressing because of its content and it is not possible to change this content which defines even the profession. It is possible to influence only the favourable or unfavourable factors for the organism, enumerated higher. Therefore these factors must be known and applied for designing the dispatching workplaces, for correcting the running workplaces.

It results that the neuropsychic strain is predominant. The sensorial charge is visual, auditory and tactile for receiving and transmitting the information by computer and telecommunication. The mental charge is determined by the participation of attention, memory and technical thinking in work for obtaining and treating correctly the information, for taking correct decisions. The great responsibility to assure the good running of PS and to prevent the incidents and damages produces a permanent state of emotional tension. The dispatcher must stay permanently in his workplace, he must reply to all signals which appear in the informational systems. The organism's strain increases during the incidents or damages. The physical effort is low; it is determined only by the sitting position and the movements of the upper limbs, especially of the hands for acting the informational devices and writing. At the work end the HR decreased in all subjects, from 74-91 beats/min at work start, to 70-85 beats/min at work end. Noradrenaline decreased during work in 85% of central dispatchers ($p<0.005$ and 0.05) and in 62% of district dispatchers. Adrenaline decreased in 79% of central dispatchers ($p<0.05$) and in 62% of district dispatchers. The decrease of HR and urinary catecholamines shows a fatigue state, a disactivation state, generated by the neuropsychic charge and the sedentary character of activity without motor discharge. Performance of neuropsychic indicators decreased at the work end in most or all subjects: decrease of CFF (in 78-82% of subjects, $p<0.005$ and 0.05), of exactitude coefficient at visual perception test (in 73% of subjects, $p<0.02$); increase of visual (in all subjects, $p<0.003$ and 0.002) and auditory (in 73-92% of subjects, $p<0.01$ and 0.02) RT, of reading time at optotype (in 85-100% of subjects, $p<0.001$ and 0.004), of blink frequency (in 91 and 72 % of subjects, $p<0.006$ and 0.009); the exactitude coefficient at Weston test decreased in 44-46% of subjects. These changes reflect organism's fatigue. Similar results have been obtained in the videoterminal operators of calculating centers [4, 5]. In critical situation the HR and urinary catecholamines increase and show the organism's alert.

The questionnaire showed an important number of plaints (in 48-88% of subjects) which may be the subjective manifestations of dispatchers` fatigue. The principal plaints were: ocular and visual troubles (photophobia, ocular smarting and ache, sheding tears and others on the first place, torpor and drowsiness, nervousness, headache, difficulty of attention concentration and others). The subjective manifestations of the fatigue during work may appear between after 2 hours (29% of subjects) and 5-6 hours (41% of subjects) from the work start. Some complaints (drowsiness, headache, nervousness, torpor) may remain after the work shift end from 1 to 5 hours. The self-rating showed at the work start the predominance of the tonic state and good humour in most subjects (64-93%), but at the work end these manifestations have decreased (present in only 30-70% of subjects) in favour of fatigue manifestations.

4. Conclusions

Results of study show the great neurosychic strain of the PS dispatchers. The work content is the principal cause of this strain, but other factors (technical, environmental, organizatory) may increase the dispatchers` strain. Ergonomic and medical measures are necessary for preventing the overstrain of organism, contributing to assure the performance and the good state of the human organism and also the good running of the PS, regarding: the emplacement and the characteristics of the building, the working environment and furniture, the technical informational system, the work duration, the organisation of the work shifts, the professional training, the dispatchers` free time for assuring an active rest in free air, the medical prophylactic supervision, the professional, medical and psychological orientation and selection.

References

[1] Deno *et al.*, Electrostatic effect of overhead transmission lines and stations. Transmission line reference book, 345 KV and above, 2nd Edition Palo Alto, CA, Electric Power Research Institute, 1082.

[2] R. Iacheta *et al.*, The information system for health surveillance of the workers developed at ENEL SPA. In: Resumes du 24eme Congres de la Comission Internationale de la Sante au Travail, Nice 1993, pp.228.

[3] Siv. Torqvist *et al.*, Health risk during work with production and distribution of electricity: a prospective study. In: Resumes du 24eme Congres de la Comission Internationale du Travail, Nice, 1993, pp.262.

[4] Hila Herman *et al.*, Study on strain of videoterminal operators, *Igiena*, 4 (1986) 271-289 (in Romanian).

[5] Hilda Herman *et al.*, Study of visual strain in informational activities, *Romanian Journal of Occupational Health*, 1 (1991) 1-19.

[6] Hilda Herman, Investigation of some indicators of organism during work by means of the videoterminal, *Romanian Journal of Occupational Health*, 3 (1995) 696-699.

[7] G. Iosif, Making the diagnosis of incidents by the operators in the thermic centrals, *Journal of Psychology*, 1 (1972) 102-112 (in Romanian).

Advances in Occupational Ergonomics and Safety II
Edited by Biman Das and Waldemar Karowski
IOS Press and Ohmsha, 1997

Factors affecting
the classes of causal explanations
by industrial safety specialists

Kathryn Woodcock, Ph.D., P.Eng.
Assistant Professor, Industrial and Manufacturing Engineering
Rochester Institute of Technology, Rochester NY 14623
KLWEIE@RIT.EDU http://www.rit.edu/~klweie

Alison Smiley, Ph.D.
University of Toronto & Human Factors North Inc.
118 Baldwin St., Toronto ON M5T 1L6

Causal explanations determine how industry acts to prevent accident recurrence.
Little is known about industrial accident cause-finding practices. Sixteen practicing
safety specialists performed three common tasks: walkthrough accounts of subjects'
own experiences, non-interactive exercises and interactive simulated investigations
to elicit schemas. Analysis examined the relation of individual differences in
knowledge sources and organizational factors to the causal concepts retrieved and
the process of reasoning. Particular interest was taken in influences on the retrieval
and use of worker-related causal factors and management or design-related causal
factors.

No evidence was observed of overattribution to worker-centered
explanations, nor did the investigation approaches resemble attribution judgements.
The predominance of management/design causal explanations does reflect current
explanatory fashions, although the self-serving bias is the one that best describes
the observed effects. Status and to a lesser degree operations values and operations
pressures influenced the proportion of factors retrieved as well as the class of
factors used for starting and concluding investigations.

1 Introduction

Causal explanations determine how industry acts to prevent accident recurrence. A previous
paper [1] discussed the complexity of the concept of 'bias' as applied to the understanding
of causal explanations. Little is known about industrial accident cause-finding practices.
Consequently, whether these practices are 'biased' is a matter of speculation. The present
study aimed to examine causal reasoning among a sample of actual practitioners, using a
variety of knowledge elicitation tasks.

2 Method

Sixteen subjects were recruited from a local chapter of practitioners. All subjects had
completed self-report questionnaires describing their educational and continuing education
backgrounds, their work history and current position, as well as several questions about

work beliefs. As the interviews were conducted at a central research site, a sample of convenience was required, introducing a self-selection factor. However, the sample reflected a range of characteristics both in the observed independent variables (experience, education, status, etc.) and in other characteristics.

All subjects performed the same tasks. First, they recounted a couple of investigations they had experienced, in the chronological order of their own information acquisition. Secondly, six accident descriptions were provided, and subjects were asked to state the information they would initially seek if asked to determine the cause. Third, they performed two interactive simulated investigations. Subjects were provided with the initial 'accident report'. Additional facts and observations were provided on request. The researcher impersonated any character in the accident story that the subject wished to question. The additional information was standardized across subjects by reference to a hidden 'story tree'. There were no limits imposed on hypothesis revision and closure. Subjects could ask as few or as many questions as they wished and could take as long as they needed.

'World view' statements were also obtained from subjects, asking them generally to state why accidents occur in the workplace. These world views dictated three classes into which factors were grouped: worker-centered, management/design-centered, and fatalistic.

The data were reduced through a process of open coding of the verbatim interview transcripts (recorded by a certified real-time court reporter). Coded factors were tabulated in the same classes as the world views. A large proportion remained ambiguous; although the subject may have had an unambiguous intent, their way of stating their thoughts was not clearly worker-related or management-related. Analysis examined the relation of knowledge factors (education, experience, peer interaction) and organizational factors (status, satisfaction, powerlessness, operations values) to the concepts retrieved and the process of reasoning. Particular interest was taken in influences on the retrieval and use of worker-related causal factors and management or design-related causal factors.

This paper reports only on the factors influencing the predominant classes of causal explanations. Other variables measured included the total number of factors elicited from each subject with the standard set of experimental material, and the revision of hypotheses during the simulated investigations. These will not be reported here.

3 Results

The method of interview was well accepted by the practitioners. Only one indicated that his approach to the simulated investigation differed from his usual practice, specifically that he would usually investigate much less thoroughly. Others indicated that they approached it essentially the same way as they would in the field. (Verification of this impression was achieved by comparing data from the simulated investigations with the data provided in reports of past experiences, but an independent source of actual investigation was not sought.)

3.1 Over-attribution to worker-centered causes?

The number of different codes considered in each exercise was significantly greater than 1 ($p<.001$) describing causal reasoning that differs from attributional thinking. The ratio of references to the two types of codes (worker-centered to management/design-centered) was computed for each subject. The mean ratio was 0.68 worker-centered codes per management/design-centered code. However, there was extreme variation among subjects. The ratio ranged from 0.31 through 1.29, signifying that some subjects generated predominantly management-centered explanations while others generated many more worker-centered explanations. The 95% confidence interval from 0.56–0.79 clearly lies on the side of management or design-centered causal explanations predominating.

The tendency to start with worker-centered factors also differed widely among subjects. Individual subjects started with a worker-centered line of inquiry in anywhere from 0% to 71% of their exercises. However, both initial codes and conclusions were significantly more likely to refer to management/design factors than to worker-centered factors ($p<.001$ and $p<.05$ respectively). These findings are contrary to the expectation of "overattribution" to worker-centered causes. Rather, the results seem to support the observation that management and design oriented explanations for accidents are currently more 'fashionable' than blaming the injured worker [2].

In addition, worker-related factors comprised less than half of all codes generated from all the transcripts taken together. Overall, there was no indication that "overattribution" to worker-related explanations occurred.

3.2   What increases consideration of worker-centered explanations?

Correlational methods obviously do not permit establishment of causality. The observations made here pertain to association between the subject characteristics and the explanations they used. An increase in the *proportion* of worker-centered explanations mentioned by a subject was associated with higher job status. Holding the top safety job in the organization (as indicated by the subject's self-reported title and superior's title) increased the proportion of worker-centered explanations among factors considered. Of all the interpersonal variables and combinations, status alone was the best predictor of ratio of factors mentioned ($B=0.52$. $R^2=.20$, $p=.08$). Among the factors which did *not* appear to be correlated with the ratio of worker-centered to management/design-centered factors were experience, safety education, and practitioner-group activity, operations values, satisfaction with recognition, indications of perceived powerlessness, 'world view' of accident causation, or perceived role in the investigation context.

Expression of operations values, in responses to the questionnaire, and length of work experience, along with status, combine to predict the likelihood of *beginning* an investigation with an worker-centered explanation ($R^2=54.6\%$, $F_{3,12}=4.8$, $p=.02$). Status, length of work experience, and expressions of powerlessness (in questionnaire responses) combined to predict the likelihood of *concluding* at a worker-centered explanation ($R^2=61.3\%$, $F_{3,11}=5.81$, $p=.012$).

These results suggest that practitioners who identify with management tend to favour worker-centered explanations over management or design centered explanations, and both begin and end investigations with these preferences. The preferences are not apparently conscious, however: world views were not associated with either start or conclusion class. Rather than supporting a cognitive error explanation such as overattribution, the results appear to describe a self-serving bias that is quite rational within the "corporate survival" environment.

World view, or the explanation given by the subject for the causes of accidents in general, *was* significantly correlated with the operations pressures reported by the subject ($r=.52$, $p=.04$; a worker-centered world view was associated with greater operations pressures). Operations pressures were considered to be responsibility for compensation claims management (keep claims costs under control) and the company's use of compensation cost as a measure of safety program effectiveness. These pressures would tend to make worker-centered explanations more attractive, since a worker-centered explanation might relieve the company of responsibility for the injury claim.

3.3 Mechanisms

As already mentioned, it appears improbable that a cognitive attribution error accounts for biases in causal reasoning among practitioners.

World view was not associated with either starting point class or the ratio of worker to management factors. However, world view did correlate with the class of the conclusion ($r=.55$, $p=.03$) suggesting that there may be some confirmation bias, or self-fulfilling prophecy involved with causal reasoning.

A self-serving bias explains the observations better than alternative mechanisms considered. The prominent role of status in regressions for class ratio, starting point, and end point seems to support the idea of incompatibility between a management role and management-centered causal explanations. Self-serving bias was also consistent with results obtained for search length and hypothesis revision, results not fully reported here.

4 Discussion

No evidence of the fundamental attribution error was observed, nor did the investigation approaches resemble attribution judgements. Generating and using management/design causal explanations more than worker-oriented explanations does reflect current explanatory fashions, although the self-serving bias is the one that best describes the observed effects.

Safety specialists are conscious of the values of company operations and their accident investigations show its effects. Holding the top safety position and responsibility for managing workers compensation are associated with increased affinity to worker-oriented explanations and investigation characteristics that favour them.

Other variables observed in the study included the number of factors elicited using standardized materials, and length of causal search and number of hypotheses generated in the interactive exercises. Those variables, which cannot be discussed here, also showed similar effects of status and operations values.

5 Further study

The greatest concern about the data obtained is the high proportion of factors mentioned which were not unambiguously classifiable by the researchers [3]. There is no reason to suspect that the factors which seem to be ambiguous were intended by their users to refer significantly more often to one class over the other, but resolving this ambiguity is a primary objective. Referring the elicited collection of causal schemas to classification by a larger sample of practitioners would be a desirable next step.

6 References

[1]Woodcock, K. (1995) Bias in real-world accident cause-finding. *Advances in Industrial Ergonomics and Safety* Bittner, A.C. & Champney, P. (Eds.) London: Taylor & Francis

[2]Rasmussen, J. 1993 Diagnostic reasoning in action. *IEEE Transactions on Systems, Man, and Cybernetics* **23**(4):981-992

[3] Woodcock, K. & Smiley, A.M. (1996) Causal explanation knowledge base of occupational safety practitioners. *Proceedings of the Human Factors Association of Canada.* Mississauga, Ontario: HFAC

Advances in Occupational Ergonomics and Safety II
Edited by Biman Das and Waldemar Karwowski
IOS Press and Ohmsha, 1997

Lockheed Martin Corporate Ergonomics Initiative

Robert L. Getty[A], Andrew J. Marcotte[B]
[A]*Lockheed Martin Tactical Aircraft Systems, P.O. Box 748, Fort Worth, TX*
[B]*The Joyce Institute a Unit of Arthur D. Little, 313 N. Palisades, Signal Mountain, TN*

Abstract. Workers' experiencing cumulative trauma, led the Lockheed Martin Corporation (LMCO) to form an Ergonomics Task Force (ETF). The goal will be to initially identify the areas of concern and then to evolve ergonomics to become part of process design The plan is straight forward: Identify the problem. Assess current ergonomics efforts. Partner with a well-known ergonomics consultant to assist in developing corporate policy and training. Participation of representatives throughout the corporation was a first step. This is a major task considering the complexity of the corporation. There are approximately 200,000 people in LMCO. Six sectors have been established that comprise the different specialties of Aeronautics, Energy & Environment, Space & Strategic Missiles, Electronics, Information & Technology Services, and Tactical Systems.

1. Introduction

The key themes of the LMCO ergonomics initiative are diversity, culture and macroergonomics. The corporation has been evolving since the introduction of aerospace technology. Throughout aerospace history mergers of similar interest have created large organizations. LMCO has gone a step beyond this arena of similar interest and has combined diverse processes and products into one complex organization. Each of the six sectors focus on similar industries, but at the same time are comprised of companies that have diverse products. The corporation has diverse cultures, since some entities have had single individuals as founders. Others have been developed to meet specific government initiatives. The cultures of the specific locations of each company's origins may have influenced the existing collection of cultures. Macroergonomics with the focus on the human, technological and environmental systems is portrayed dramatically. The 200,000 people reflect the diversity of the country. The numerous technologies require a myriad of processes and expertise. The shrinking public funds for the LMCO products and the more sensitive concerns of interaction with natural resources depict a continually changing environment.

This paper will expound on the policy development process and show the structure of the corporate ergonomics effort. The partnership with the various sectors and the development of the awareness training will be discussed. The magnitude of the corporation and the different types of industries represented are the major challenges, which definitely put this effort into the macroergonomics realm. In addition the corporation's history of mergers and acquisitions has brought together companies that have had different cultural development. The diversity presents both a potential for difficulty as well as strengths to draw from. With the current focus on ergonomics, every company in the corporation has been in the process of forming its approach to the application of ergonomics. Now these individual initiatives will be combined and LMCO will gain insight from the current experiences and each company will be able to leverage the successes by sharing lessons learned. Thus the cooperation of all the companies and sectors within LMCO are realizing the benefits of a collective effort.

The LMCO ergonomics initiative clearly portrays a unique portrayal of a corporate ergonomics effort in contrast to corporations that have similar product, manufacturing and organizational structure. Bringing together the diverse products and processes will be a challenge to determine the appropriate level for managing the ergonomics emphasis. The Corporate level may well be the facilitator with the sectors bringing together the common processes. Although processes are similar within sectors, products are different between companies. The company level may the appropriate level for ergonomics to integrate with the design of processes.

2. Policy Development Process

The structure of LMCO clearly requires a unified policy that is flexible to the different product and process focus of the six sectors. The first priority was to establish the need for this major initiative. In general terms, a preliminary sampling of 1994 corporate workers' compensation costs indicated that sixty to seventy percent of the costs could be linked to cumulative trauma chronic exposures. This was a major incentive for initiating the program with the strong endorsement of corporate senior management.

The purpose for forming the ergonomics task force was to assist in reducing days away case injuries and associated costs. With the diversity in the corporation, each sector and company must take over the ownership and management of ergonomics within their organizations. The roles of the Corporate Environmental Safety and Health (CESH) and the ETF are to provide guidance and a resource nucleus to assist the individual efforts throughout the organizations.

The CESH requested each company solicit those who would be able to participate in the ETF. Once this list was compiled a conference call was held to "kick off" the effort. Participants were called on individually to discuss their ideas and expectations concerning the ETF. A sampling of common themes expressed included:

- Company success is dependent on management support and buy-in to the program. One challenge is to demonstrate to management the cost benefit of implementing ergonomics programs.
- Company level management support could be facilitated by corporate policy, procedures or other leveraging methods addressing ergonomics.
- Communication of best practices and success stories would be very helpful.
- Cross-functional training and awareness is a key to a successful ergonomics program whereby:
    - engineers design process to minimize ergonomic hazards.
    - employees recognize and take actions to fix ergonomic hazards.
    - managers understand the benefits (including increased productivity of proactive ergonomics.
- The ETF should establish clear objectives.

A discussion on the structure of the ETF concluded that a tiered approach would be most effective. The corporate level ETF will consist of one representative from each sector.

These representatives will assist corporate in developing policy, guidance, communications (web site), model programs and identifying best practices. The second tier would be led by these sector representatives and would eventually involve one representative from each operating company in the sector. The issues for sector ETFs would include: leveraging programs, training and awareness programs, best practices, research, measures, cross talk, and integration with the business.

A meeting was called of the six sector representatives with CESH, and the consultant representative. The ergonomic consultant had to meet strong qualifications such as experience in program development, a Certified Professional Ergonomist, demonstrated success and experience in training and manufacturing environments. This meeting began the process of developing policy of the LMCO ergonomics initiative. The goal at the beginning for the ETF is to move beyond the safety orientation and into the design of processes in order to gain full benefit of ergonomics to productivity and quality. The ETF was challenged to work together, share ideas and give success stories. Success stories will validate the benefits of ergonomics and help gain buy-in by those outside the Safety and Health departments. They will also illustrate the benefits of ergonomics to productivity, quality and as a method to achieve more affordable manufacturing. It was emphasized that the challenging goal of significantly reducing lost work day cases will require more buy-in by those controlling facilities, manufacturing and designing processes to prevent exposure levels to cumulative trauma. The focus of the meeting was to provide input to the development and preparation of the corporate policy for review by early 1997.

Sector efforts will be to determine methods of helping each sector meet the goals. These efforts may be to discuss ways of orienting cross-functional sector level management to the benefits of ergonomics that may flow down to company levels. The primary focus will be to convey how ergonomics will be a tool to improve all company processes and also achieve Health and Safety goals.

3. LMCO Ergonomics Policy Highlights

OSHA and NIOSH ergonomics documents have been referred to for general structure. The LMCO ergonomics policy will be in the form of a guidance document. The development will involve visiting various LMCO companies as an internal benchmarking process. Since a number of companies have initiated ergonomics programs, the intent is to improve and learn from those rather than creating any conflict to successful efforts. Some areas that were emphasized are covered here:

Hazard Identification/Worksite Analysis
A cross-functional team consisting of Safety and Health, Facilities, Manufacturing, Medical, Finance, Engineering and Management will be recommended to oversee, prioritize and provide resources for the ergonomics program. Prioritization of identified hazards will focus on meeting the significant challenges with sufficient resources as aggressively as possible.

Hazard Prevention and Control
Although the primary intent is to reduce ergonomics hazards in order to minimize the potential for cumulative trauma injury, the simultaneous improvement of product quality or manufacturing system performance should be encouraged.

Training

The purpose of training is to ensure that those individuals who have impact on the way jobs are designed and performed are able to integrate ergonomics into the process. Core ergonomics issues will be discussed in all training courses. However, time requirements and training objectives will be specific to site needs and responsibilities.

Medical Management

The focus for ergonomics is for medical to liaison with ergonomics for job analysis and modification following identification of symptoms. This process is an extension of other work related medical activity.

Program Review and Measurement of Results

Reviewing and assessing the results of the ergonomics effort will provide feedback that will ensure success and provide the data for continuous improvement of the program. Additional measures beyond standard safety and health measures might include, manufacturing costs, product or process quality and demonstrated return-on-investments.

4. Maximizing the Benefits of the Corporate Diversity

Due to the cultural and history differences within the LMCO, an evolution of the ergonomics initiative will occur. This evolutionary process parallels the ergonomics processes of function analysis, function allocation, workload analysis, task analysis and job design. This parallel is drawn, since with the high diversity in LMCO, an early requirement is to determine the activity that is currently in progress. Then an assessment must be made of where the strengths and weaknesses of the various and diverse programs are. Determination of the areas where improvement is needed will be made by each of the sectors and companies. As these activities occur there will be more awareness of areas within the corporation that can serve as resources.

The utilization of internet resources will enhance the progress of the LMCO ergonomics efforts. Presently, there is a CESH home web page. Here the successes identified within the corporation are shared. LMCO has subscribed to the ErgoWeb System developed at the University of Utah. This will provide further references and resources. The tools within ErgoWeb can be used to train management and various engineering specialties. ErgoWeb can also provide design and evaluation tools. LMCO has vast internet web resources. Individuals in each company can contact others in the corporation either by electronic mail or through web mail. Success stories, reports of procedures, ergonomic improvements, lessons learned can all be shared through the various internet resources.

5. Conclusion

Although LMCO is a diverse corporation with many companies focused on different products, ergonomics will be applied to all processes that involve the human-machine system. This effort supports corporate goals for high quality, cost effective products as well as the goal of providing a safe, healthy work environment for all employees. By sharing the ergonomics expertise throughout the corporation the collective effort will enable each sector and company to realize the benefits of applying ergonomics sooner than if each group was working on their own.

Advances in Occupational Ergonomics and Safety II
Edited by Biman Das and Waldemar Karwowski
IOS Press and Ohmsha, 1997

Avoiding Musculoskeletal Injuries Through Design and Application of Industrial Engineering Methodology in an Automotive Brakes Manufacturing Plant

Arvind S. Ramakrishnan [+]
Ursula Wright
Anil Mital [*]

Ergonomics and Engineering Controls Research Laboratory [*]
Industrial Engineering
University of Cincinnati
Cincinnati, OH 45221-0116, U.S.A.

System Resources Corporation [+]
5218 Atlantic Avenue, 3rd Floor,
Mays Landing, NJ 08330, U.S.A.

ABSTRACT

An ergonomic evaluation was performed in the assembly and machining areas of an automotive brake manufacturing facility. Many of the operators in these areas suffered from repetitive strain injuries and back pain due to the nature of the task they performed.
Assessment of the assembly and machining areas identified the following:
1. Highly repetitive (wrist intensive) activities involving excessive application of forces.
2. Abnormal body posture necessitated by the workplace design prior to the intervention.
3. Unnecessary body motions due to inadequate designs and inconvenient placement of equipment, components and tools.
4. Abnormally high pace of operation, while performing machining area activities.
5. Lack of ergonomic and safety training programs for the operators.
Industrial engineering techniques like micro motion analysis, and time study were used to examine the problems. Recommendations were provided based on the findings, aimed at reducing injuries and making the facility more safe to work.

1. Introduction

A myriad of research have been conducted to study musculoskeletal injuries at workplace. Musculoskeletal injuries includes any bodily injuries to muscles and bones like cumulative trauma disorder (CTD), lower back injuries etc. Each study has lead to a variety of recommendations. This demonstrates that the best solutions in every case is specific to that particular case. In general, poor work postures have been attributed as a leading cause of musculoskeletal strains [1]. Conditions of poor work postures differ considerably from those found in medium sized and large companies. Work practices involving high precision activities and sustained static loads have also been found to cause musculoskeletal disorders [2]. Musculoskeletal injuries like lower back pains and CTD are common in today's industries. Back pain causes 40% of all recorded absences from work [3]. In 1990, the Bureau of Labor Statistics figures show that 56% of all workers compensation claims were due to CTD. Tendinities and wrist injuries are the most prevalent causes of CTD [4]. Apart from bodily pain these injuries cause, medical bills incurred by the government and the industry are also very high. It has been estimated that the US spends about $56 billion a year on lost wages, compensation, and medical treatment for back injuries. The estimate increases with decrease in productivity [5]. These figures indicate the importance of industrial engineering intervention to reduce musculoskeletal injuries.

A local automotive brake manufacturing company reported increasing number of work related injuries. The company is involved in the manufacturing and assembly of automobile brakes. Three main components of a brake are the housing, bracket, and the piston. The company manufactures these components on its machine lines. Five machine lines are utilized for the manufacture of bracket and housing, and one line for the pistons. The manufactured components are given an in-house chemical treatment. The components are then assembled into brakes in the assembly area and stacked in cardboard boxes to be shipped to the customers.

2. Problem Areas

This section discusses the problems identified in the assembly and machine line areas.

2.1 Assembly Area

The operators handled various brake parts like the housing, brackets, pistons, brushes, etc. In the assembly area, each of these parts were assembled to make up the brake and stacked into cardboard boxes in three levels. During the entire process of assembling a brake, three operators in three stations handled the brakes in series. The third operator stacked the brakes into the package boxes.

The entire process of assembly involved highly wrist intensive activities. Each of the three assembly stations were observed. The wrist motions were observed using micro-motion analysis. Micro-motion analysis involves video taping the entire process and observing each motion over successive cycles using frame by frame video advance. Wrist motions were categorized into flexion, extension, radial deviation and ulnar deviation. The number of wrist motions for each category were counted per cycle for every assembly station. Total number of wrist motions for each operator for an entire day (8 hours) were computed.

The third station operator handles each brake last and stacks them in boxes. Each brake on an average weighs 15 pounds. The operator had to bend over to stack the brakes in the lowest level (ground level) of the cardboard carton. This forced the operator to assume abnormal body posture which could lead to back problems.

Pneumatic guns were used to tighten nuts which secured the housing to the bracket. These guns were placed in holders at the hip level of the operator. Every time the operator had to use the guns he/she had to make extra body motions to get it. Control panels were located near the second station projecting into the path of the operator. The operator had to make abnormal body motions to avoid the panel.

The first station operator was in-charge for securing excluders, made of rubber, in the housing and the pistons in the housing. A tool was used to secure the excluders to the

housing. This involved the use of excessive force with the tool not aiding the process.
Further, this tool necessitated extra wrist motions in order to perform the operation.

2.2 Machining Area

Each machining area was divided into housing and brackets machining. Even
though seven operators were assigned to a machining area, only five operators performed
the operations on an average. Two operators handled the bracket machining and three
handled the housing machining. The entire operation was performed by automatic
machines timed to maximize production. Each operator had to remove a part from one
machine and install it on the next machine then proceed on to the succeeding machines.

The pace of performing the operations were evaluated using MTM standards and
time study techniques. Pace of movement of the operators between machines and the pace
of removing and installing parts in machines were observed. Environmental conditions
like floor conditions and heat were considered during the evaluation.

2.3 Training

Many operators were suffering from physical problems like cumulative trauma
disorder and back pain. They had no formal training on ergonomic work practices. They
were provided training on how to perform each operation but none on how to do the
operation ergonomically.

3. Solutions

This section deals with the recommendations provided to mitigate the problems
discussed above.

3.1 Assembly Area

The cardboard carton was redesigned as shown in Figure 1. The design allowed for
the sides of the corrugated box to be folded for easy access to each of the three levels of
packaging. This design was recommended along with a hydraulic lift table which made
sure that the operator did not have to bend over to stack the finished brakes. The
specifications for the hydraulic lift tables made sure that the operator stacked the brakes at
a constant level. The recommended design ensured that the operator did not have to
assume abnormal body posture.

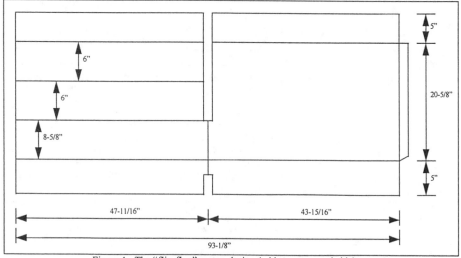

Figure 1. The "flip-flop" carton design (with a corrugated side)

The frequency of wrist motions differed from station to station in the assembly area and from the machine lines. A job rotation scheme was designed to optimize the wrist motion so that no single operator had a very high frequency of wrist motions. Operators were rotated between each station of the assembly lines and the machining lines.

Figure 2. Pneumatic gun from a spring coil.

A retractable spring coil was designed to hang the pneumatic guns from the top of the assembly area (Figure 2). With this setup the operator had to reach for the guns without having to make unnecessary wrist and body motions. This further reduced the number of wrist motions. The control panels were moved back so that it was not on the straight path of the operator.

A fixture was designed with a long handle to help secure the excluder to the brake housing. The long handle helped increasing the moment and thus decreasing the force necessary to perform the operation.

3.2 Machining Area

The pace of performing each operation in the machining lines were computed according to MTM standards. On an average the actual pace of operations on the housing line were 26% more than the prescribed pace. An additional operator was recommended to the housing line machining area to ensure that the pace remained within prescribed limits. Even though this was a high cost recommendation, the gain on the longer run arising from an under manned line was more. Recommendations were also made to change the floor mats more frequently to prevent slipping.

3.3 Training

The operators and management were given training on ergonomic principles. Training sessions showed the operators the correct body postures for each operation and the operators were told the importance of having a correct posture while performing their tasks. Immediate results from the recommendations could not be reported as is the case with most ergonomic recommendations.

4. References

[1] L. Waltari et al., Ergonomics in Small Workplaces with Special References to Occupational Health Services, Scandinavian Journal of Work Environmental Health, Vol. 5, Supplement 2, (1979) 24-29.
[2] E. Milerad, and M. O. Ericson, Effects of Precision and Force Demands, Grip Diameter, and Arm Support during Manual Work: an Electromyographic Study, Ergonomics, Vol. 37, No. 2, (1994) 255-264.
[3] M. A. McReynolds, Managing the High Cost of Back Injury, Journal of Occupational Health and Safety, Vol. 61, No. 4 (1992) 58-64.
[4] T. Votel, CTDs and Management's Role in Preventing them, Supervision, Vol. 53, No. 11, (1992) 14-16.
[5] Back Injury Prevention in Health Care requires Training Techniques, Exercise, Journal of Occupational Health and Safety, Vol. 63, No. 6, (1994) 66-72.

3. Work Assessment Techniques

Advances in Occupational Ergonomics and Safety II
Edited by Biman Das and Waldemar Karwowski
IOS Press and Ohmsha, 1997

Ergonomic Tools for Evaluating Manual Material Handling Jobs

Thomas R. WATERS, Vern PUTZ-ANDERSON, and Sherry BARON
National Institute for Occupational Safety and Health
4676 Columbia Parkway, Cincinnati, Ohio 45226 USA

Abstract

Assessment of the physical demands of potentially hazardous manual material handling (MMH) activities is fundamental to the prevention of occupationally-related low back pain (LBP), a problem costing the nation billions of dollars annually. Although there are a variety of ergonomic assessment methods available for assessing MMH activities, there is a lack of practical information to assist users in choosing the most appropriate assessment methods for a particular job. The purpose of this paper is to review currently available assessment methods and to present the results of a case study of a physically-demanding repetitive manual lifting job in two grocery warehouses. The case study will provide a framework for a comparison of the methods.

Introduction

Work-related musculoskeletal disorders (WRMSDs) of the arms, shoulders, and low back resulting from excessive manual material handling (MMH) are a significant occupational problem. Back injuries alone cost the nation millions of dollars annually and result in numerous lost work days. For this reason, there is a renewed interest in developing and evaluating practical and valid tools for assessing the physical demands of manual material handling that can be used to identify high risk jobs.

The purpose of this paper is to review a number of methods available for assessing manual material handling (MMH) jobs, and to present a case study of an analysis of a physically demanding manual lifting activity in a dry grocery warehouse that will serve as an example for discussion purposes.

Assessment Methods

Current assessment tools range in complexity from simple checklists and equations to complex risk assessment models. These tools are designed to provide quantitative estimates of the biomechanical and physiological demands associated with a particular MMH job. These estimates can then be used to help develop interventions for jobs considered hazardous.

A partial list of some of the more common tools include: (1) the Revised NIOSH Lifting Equation (NLE); (2) the University of Michigan 3D Static Strength Prediction Program (3DSSPP); (3) the Oxylog portable oxygen consumption meter (O2); (4) the Polar portable heart rate monitor (HR); (5) the University of Michigan Energy Expenditure Prediction Program (EEPP); (6) the Chattanooga Corp. Lumbar Motion Monitor (LMM); (7) The Ohio State University Risk Assessment Model (OSU); and, (8) the Snook and Ciriello psychophysical approach for assessing manual lifting demands [1]. For the most part, these tools are based on the biomechancal, physiological, and psychophysical capacity data published in the literature for the industrial working population.

Case Study Methods

Data needed to apply the various assessment methods were collected for the job of "grocery selector" at two dry grocery warehouses. The job of grocery selector involves repetitive lifting of cases or bags of grocery items from supply pallets to an electrically-driven pallet jack that moves along the aisles of the warehouse. The selection or "picking order" is dictated by a computer-generated list that contains the items and locations (aisle and slot numbers) for the order. An order typically consists of two full pallets stacked to a height of 70 to 90 inches. The workload, a term denoting the amount of weight lifted per minute when an order is selected, was determined for six typical orders by stopwatch and from the picking list.

In addition to the data collected for the ergonomic assessment tools, a questionnaire was administered to selectors to determine their perceptions of physical workload and symptoms of musculoskeletal disorders. Additionally, Bureau of Labor Statistics Log of Occupational Injury and Illnesses (OSHA 200 Logs) for the two worksites were reviewed to determine the extent of recorded injuries and lost time due to injury for workers employed in these jobs. Previous reports have summarized the findings, conclusions, and suggestions for manual lifting in grocery warehouses obtained from these two studies [2, 3, 4, 5].

In the first warehouse, the job of 'grocery selector' was analyzed with the Revised NIOSH Lifting Equation (NLE), the University of Michigan 3D Static Strength Prediction Program (3DSSPP), an Oxylog portable oxygen consumption meter (O2), a portable heart rate monitor (HR), the University of Michigan Energy Expenditure Prediction Program (EEPP), the Chattanooga Corp. Lumbar Motion Monitor (LMM) and The Ohio State University Risk Assessment Model (OSU). In the second warehouse, the job of 'grocery selector' was analyzed with the same tools as in the first warehouse, with the exception that the 3DSSPP and the EEPP methods were replaced with the Snook and Ciriello [1] psychophysical method for assessing manual lifting (SNOOK). Details of the assessment methods are presented elsewhere [6].

Results

Table 1 provides a summary of the workload for each of the three participants studied in each of two warehouses. Workload was assessed by the number cases handled, the weight of the cases and the handling time. The physiological effects of the workloads were assessed by actual and estimated measures of energy expenditure and working heart rate. The results from each assessment method are summarized in Table 2. Specifically, the LI from the NLE as computed on the six workers studied in the two warehouses ranged from 2.7 to as high as 9.1. The latter figure suggests a risk that is nine times greater than what is recognized as an acceptable level of risk of low back injury for the majority of workers. Moreover according to Snook's and Ciriello's tables, the average lift in either warehouse would be "acceptable" to less that 10% of working males. Similarly, energy expenditure values ranged from 2.6 to 7.3 kcal/min; working heart rate between 106 and 142. The correlation between workload and pulse rate was high, as expected, $r^2=.80$. A more detailed presentation of the results are presented elsewhere [6].

Table 1
Summary of Workload and Physiological Responses for Participants in Warehouses 1 and 2.

Variable	Participant					
	1	2	3	4	5	6
Total Cases/order	167	138	101	168	120	116
Total Weight/order (lbs)	2198	4220	3862	4750	2522	1894
Allowed Time/order (min)	34.9	36.7	25.8	51	38	43
Weight/min (lbs/min)	63	115	150	114	75	48
Performance Index[1] (%)	116	116	143	122	113	106
Working Metabolic Rate (kcal/min)	5.5	5.8	7.3	6.3	4.0	2.6
Working Heart Rate (beats/min)	130	106	140	140	142	138
Predicted Metabolic Rate (kcal/min)	6.0	5.0	7.6	-	-	-

Table 2
Summary of Assessment Results

Assessment Method	Response Variable	Result
NLE	Recommended Weight Limit (RWL) and Lifting Index (LI)	RWL for 15 jobs between 4.5 and 10.4 lbs; LI values between 2.7 and 9.1.
3DSSPP	Disc Compression Force (DCF) and minimum percent male capable	DCF for 5 lifts between 662 lbs and 930 lbs, minimum male capability between 1% and 70 %
LMM	Tri-axial position, velocity, and acceleration about the L1/S1 joint	Sagittal position, velocity and acceleration greatest for lifts below 30 inches.
OSU Risk Models [7] and [8] versions)	Probability of High Risk Group membership	Probability of high risk group membership between 41% and 97%.
O2/HR	Heart rate, work pulse, and energy expenditure from oxygen consumption (energy expenditure equal to liters O2 x 5 kcal/min)	Energy expenditure between 2.6 and 7.3 kcal/min; working heart rate between 106 and 142 beats/min; and, work pulse between 18 and 35 beats/min
EEPP	Predicted energy expenditure	Predicted energy expenditure between 5.0 and 7.6 kcal/min for three selected orders
SNOOK Psychophysical	Comparison of weights lifted to population capability database	Average lift in either warehouse would be acceptable to less than 10% of industrial male

---

[1]. Performance Index = (allowed time per order/actual time per order) * 100.

Discussion
It is clear from the results of the analyses that all of the assessment methods indicated that the job of order selector is a high risk job for low back disorders. These findings are supported by the medical data, which indicate that in the years 1987 to 1992, between 17% and 40% of grocery selectors had an OSHA recordable back injury each year at the two warehouses we investigated. Although there are a number of similarities between the various assessment methods, there are also significant differences. Each method has a unique set of strengths and weaknesses. None of the existing methods appear to be well suited to work environments where the loads and postures are constantly changing.

In addition to issues of scientific validity, there are a number of practical concerns that will determine which assessment tool is appropriate for a particular situation. These may include issues such as ease of use, degree of training required, and usefulness of results. A method may be scientifically valid, but have little practical value because the results are not useful to the job designer. Also, economic issues, such as the cost of the equipment needed to obtain the measurements, the amount of time and effort required to collect and analyze the data, and the costs of work disruption may be important determinants in choosing an approach. In all likelihood, these issues will have different levels of importance, depending upon the needs of the analyst.

REFERENCES

[1] Snook SH and Ciriello VM The design of manual handling tasks: revised tables of maximum acceptable weights and forces. *Ergonomics*, 34(9): (1991) 1197-1213.

[2] NIOSH *Big Bear grocery warehouse: Columbus, Ohio.* U.S. Department of Health and Human Services, Center for Disease Control and Prevention, National Institute for Occupational Safety and Health. HETA Report No. 91-405-2340, 1993. Cincinnati, Ohio.

[3] Waters TR Workplace factors and trunk motion in grocery assembler tasks. Proceedings of the Human Factors and Ergonomics Society 37th Annual Meeting, 1993, *Human Factors and Ergonomics Society.* 654-658. Santa Monica, CA.

[4] Baron S, Putz-Anderson V., Waters T, and Hanley K (1995) Musculoskeletal disorders among grocery warehouse workers. *Proceedings of the Sixth FIOSH-NIOSH Joint Symposium on Occupational Safety and Health.* pp 146-150. (1995) Finnish Institute of Occupational Safety and Health. Helsinki, Finland.

[5] Waters T, Putz-Anderson V, and Baron S. *Kroger grocery warehouse: Nashville, Tennessee.* U.S. Department of Health and Human Services, Center for Disease Control and Prevention, National Institute for Occupational Safety and Health. HETA Report No. 93-0920-2548, 1995. Cincinnati, Ohio

[6] Waters T, Putz-Anderson V. and Baron S. Methods for Assessing the Physical Demands of Manual Lifting: A Review and Case Study from Warehousing, 1997. In review.

[7] Marras WS, Lavender SA, Leurgans SE, Ranjulu SL, Allread GW, Fathallah FA, and Ferguson SA. The role of dynamic three-dimensional trunk motion in occupationally-related low back disorders. Spine, 18(5) (1993):617-628.

[8] Marras WS, Lavender SA, Leurgans SE, Fatahallah FA, Ferguson SA, Allread WG, and Rajulu SL Biomechanical risk factors for occupationally related low back disorders. Ergonomics, 38(2) (1995):377-410.

Advances in Occupational Ergonomics and Safety II
Edited by Biman Das and Waldemar Karwowski
IOS Press and Ohmsha, 1997

Development of a Risk Factor Analysis Model For Predicting Postural Instability at Workplace

Angshuman Bagchee, Amit Bhattacharya, Paul A. Succop, and Chwan-Fu Lai,

Dept of Environmental Health, University of Cincinnati, Cincinnati, OH 45267-0056.

Falls at the workplace are often preceded by a momentary loss of balance that may be attributed to several risk factors related to the workplace and the worker. Based on the multiple regression analysis performed on 52 industrial workers in a laboratory-based study, a risk factor analysis model was developed to evaluate the potential for postural instability. Based on the regression model, a windows-based application has been developed with simplified user-interface for entering the risk factors associated with any particular task. It shows the relative level of postural stability for a combination of risk factors and allows graphical display of what-if analyses. The model illustrates the possible use of laboratory-based statistical models to actual worksite analysis in determining the risk factors that would have a significant impact in reducing postural imbalance and preventing fall-related injuries.

Introduction

Falls have been found to be a significant contributor in causing fatal and non-fatal injury, especially in the construction industry, including lumbar spine injury, fracture of bones, and disability [1]. A number of fall risk factors exist at the workplace, and a combination of one or more of these risk factors may be responsible for momentary loss of balance leading to an accidents resulting from a fall or near-fall situation. Several extrinsic and intrinsic factors may influence a worker's ability to maintain postural upright stability during task performance. Extrinsic factors may include availability of peripheral vision, environmental lighting, surface condition and slipperiness. Intrinsic factors would involve the worker's physical ability, age, and other physiological factors such as neuromuscular coordination that influence postural balance maintenance [2]. Fatigue resulting from prolonged physical exertion and respiratory loading may suppress the ability of the nervous system to regulate the upright balance efficiently.

The relative role of each individual risk factors in influencing the workers' postural stability is poorly understood. A first step would be the identification of the risk factors influencing a worker's postural stability at the workplace and designing a laboratory-based study to quantify the role of these risk factors. The results from the laboratory-based study should then be able to provide us with the necessary tools for evaluating a task at the workplace based on the risk factors associated with that particular task. The present study aimed at identifying some of the risk factors associated with postural instability in industrial falls and evaluated the effect of these risk factors under laboratory conditions. Postural instability was quantified through sway area, sway length, and non-dimensional indices of postural stability representing the proximity and spread of the center of pressure (CP) to the functional stability boundary (FSB) of the subject, formed by the outline of his/her base of support. Based on the results, a mathematical model was developed to predict the postural stability outcome measures depending on the level of the individual risk factors associated with any given industrial task.

Methods

A total of 52 industrial workers (age = 37.4±8.9 years range 21.1 - 52.2 years; 50% male) participated in this study [3]. The study consisted of four experimental conditions 1. Surface slipperiness - Dry (coefficient of friction, COF = 0.6), and Slippery (COF = 0.3); 2. Environmental Lighting - Good (> 70 footcandles), and Poor (< 0.2 footcandles); 3. Peripheral Vision - Unblocked and Blocked; and 4. Standing Surface - Firm, and Compliant (aluminum plate over a 10.2 cm thick foam). The subjects performed four different tasks under each of these conditions. These tasks were: 1. Stationary: Subjects stood upright for 30 s; 2. Bending - Subjects stood still for 12 s, then bent down at the torso to touch the knees and maintained this posture for 5s, and regained their upright posture for remaining 13 s; 3. Sudden Loading - Subjects stood still for 30 s, while a weight of 2.3 kg was suddenly released from a height of 30.5 cm into a hand-held basket (weighing 170 g) at the elbow level at a randomly determined time; 4. Reach - Subjects stood still for 5s, then reached forward/upward to retrieve a 2.3 kg weight from functional upward/forward reach distance and deposit it to a shelf at maximal forward reach at elbow height, repeating the cycle four times.

The subjects performed these tasks under three different workloads - 0, 40, and 100 watts, administered on an ergometer. The ground reaction forces and moments were collected to calculate the movement of the CP under the feet. The subject's feet position were traced to obtain the FSB [2,4]. The dependent variables included the sway area and sway length from the projection of the subject's CP on the horizontal plane during the task. Three non-dimensional indices of IPSB, SAR, and WRTI, based on the proximity and the spread of the CP to the subject's FSB, were also used for outcome measures [4]. Further details of the study and the interpretation of the outcome variables can be found in Bhattacharya, et al. [3].

Results

The values of the estimated increase in the dependent measures of sway parameters were obtained from multivariate analysis of the results, and are indicated in table 1. Further details of the analysis may be found in Bhattacharya, et al. [3]. The values from table 1 were then utilized in constructing a Windows-based computer application software for use in estimating the magnitude of postural instability increase associated with a task where a worker is exposed to fall risk factors. The program is able to present a graphical interface with the following input - (i) measured baseline sway parameter of the worker for stationary standing (baseline sway parameter) and (ii) identification of the risk factors under which the worker has to perform the task at his/her workplace. The program then automatically evaluates the percent increase in the various sway parameters, and graphically represents the same for visual interpretation. The mathematical model, based on values from table 1, calculates the increase in the baseline sway parameters as follows:

For a task, with risk factors $r_1, r_2,...., r_j,....., r_n$,

$$(\text{Sway parameter}_i) = (\text{baseline sway parameter}_i)(1+ a_1/100)(1+ a_2/100)..(1+a_j/100)..(1+a_n/100),$$

where a_j represents the percent increase corresponding to risk factor j for sway parameter$_i$ from table 1. The software also allows what-if analysis, whereby the risk factors can be manipulated to reduce the sway parameters as close to the baseline sway, thereby allowing the identification and prioritization of the risk factors contributing most to the postural instability associated with the task.

Discussion

The mathematical model and the computer software developed present an effective evaluation tool for identifying tasks which may cause undue postural instability at the workplace. The model considers both environmental and individual factors in predicting the increase in the postural instability. A higher value of sway area, sway length, SAR, WRTI, and a lower value of IPSB implies greater danger of postural instability. Although it is not clear at this stage, how much absolute values of these parameters will be associated with loss of momentary loss of balance leading to a fall, it allows the comparison of tasks and facilitates in prioritizing the risk factors responsible for postural instability. Larger number of subjects are required for establishing acceptable limits of the sway parameters.

Table 1. Estimated percent increase in the sway parameters due to environmental and inter-individual effects [3].

Main Effects		Sway Area	Sway Length	IPSB	SAR	WRTI
Task	Bending	425.91	140.92	-36.10	633.33	39.13
	Reach	671.55	244.81	-65.12	1300.00	321.74
	Loading	147.42	48.96	-44.55	333.33	26.09
Dim Light		16.29	12.58	-3.83	15.38	0.00
Compliant Surface		10.81	6.16	-31.69	7.14	100.00
Gender: Male		5.56	5.71	6.40	-13.33	-23.53
Peripheral vision: Obstructed		5.66	3.87	-0.69	7.14	0.00
Workload	40 W	3.88	2.15	-1.35	0.00	4.65
	100 W	2.73	5.00	-3.84	0.00	6.98
Age	29-37	-3.05	1.60	-2.18	-6.67	45.71
	37-45	-8.23	-1.89	-13.94	-6.67	57.14
	> 45	3.16	7.64	-5.01	-6.67	11.43
Surface: Oily		-3.39	-1.47	6.15	0.00	-12.50

References

1.   D. P. Manning and I. M. Ayers, Disability Resulting from Underfoot First Events, J. Occupational Accidents, (1987): 37-39.

2.   A. Bagchee, A. Bhattacharya, and R. Emerich, Method for Estimating Fall Potential in Clinical, Occupational, and Environmental Exposure Cases, J. Biomechanics, 26(3). (1993): 305.

3.   A. Bhattacharya, P. Succop, S. Chiou, C. Lai, A. Bagchee, Effect of Task, Environmental Factors on Workers' Postural Balance. Submitted for review. 1997.

4.   A. Bagchee, A. Bhattacharya, and P. Succop, Postural Stability Assessment during Task Performance, accepted for publication in Occupation Ergonomics, 1997.

Advances in Occupational Ergonomics and Safety II
Edited by Biman Das and Waldemar Karwowski
IOS Press and Ohmsha, 1997

ASSESSMENT TOOLS FOR ANALYZING CARPENTRY TASKS

Amit Bhattacharya
Biomechanics-Eg onomics Reseagch Labogatogies
Depagtment of Envigonmental Health; M.L. #056
Univegsity of Cincinnati Medical School
Cincinnati, OH 45267-0056

The strategy to analyze carpentry jobs involved three major steps. The first step involved learning and educating ourselves about the carpentry jobs through several focus group meetings consisting of experienced carpenters and visiting local carpenters' apprenticeship training school. The second step involved obtaining preliminary information about the presence of ergonomic risk factors and "soft-sign" symptoms by conducting ergonomic walkthrough assessments and body discomfort and psychophysical assessments by carpenters at construction sites. The third step involved ergonomic exposure assessment of journeymen through posture loading measurements made on carpenters. The posture loading assessments were made with a custom developed ergonomic dosimeter which quantified time dependent changes in postures of the arm, back and the kneeling activities. In summary, for the characterization of carpentry tasks the following assessment tools were developed, validated and used on carpenters at construction site: ergonomic walkthrough checklist, self-reported symptom survey questionnaire, and an ergonomic dosimeter.

1. Introduction

The carpenters are involved in several aspects of construction projects which expose them to ergonomic risk factors such as awkward postures, repetitive tasks and excessive use of force. In a recently completed NIOSH sponsored study, Atterbury et. al [1] showed preliminary evidence of association between ergonomic risk factors and the development of hand wrist CTD. For the last 5 years we have been involved in the development, validation and use of ergonomic tools for characterizing one type of construction job i.e. carpentry tasks at the construction sites. While the general guidelines of traditional job analysis can be applied to carpentry tasks, specific strategies and methods need to be modified/developed to better characterize carpentry tasks. This is necessary because unlike traditional jobs such as those in manufacturing, the carpentry tasks are highly variable from day to day, significantly influenced by the environmental factors, significantly influenced by the changing workplace layout on a daily basis, influenced by the need to work with the schedules of other specialties and contract deadlines and generally unstructured and have a long cycle time. Therefore, the ergonomic data collection period has to be long enough to capture all the significant variations of the carpentry tasks. The job evaluation strategy for carpentry task was carried out in three steps which are explained in the following.

2.   Carpenters-Focus Group

The major purpose of forming focus groups consisting of experienced carpenters representing various specialties was to obtain their "expert" opinion to help identify problem/high risk tasks within job specialties [2]. Each focus group consisted of about 5 experienced carpenters. The secondary purpose was to obtain information about job sequence, task requirements within job specialty, work practice methods, selection criteria for materials and equipment and intervention ideas. In the following, a summary of major findings from the focus group is presented: There are eight carpentry specialties represented by the local carpenters' union, ceiling, drywall, formwork, flooring, piledriving, scaffolding, welding, and finishing (included framing, fixture and cabinetry). Among the eight specialties, the focus group members ranked formwork, drywall and ceiling work as the top three specialties which they considered as most physically demanding. In the following task components of formwork, drywall and ceiling specialties which in the opinion of the "expert" carpenters were most physically demanding, are listed: Formwork: preparing the form, placing the form, climbing form, stripping the form, placing and climbing the form, and preparing and placing the form; Drywall: Lifting and carrying drywall, hanging drywall, securing drywall, lift/carry/hang/secure drywall, and stud installation; Ceiling: hanger wire installation; unloading material from truck, grid installation/wire twisting and installation of drywall ceiling.

3.   A Pilot Study of Ergonomic Walkthrough Observation and Body-part Discomfort Evaluation of Carpentry Tasks

The purpose of this phase of the study was to determine the ergonomic risk factors of cumulative trauma disorders (CTD) associated with the carpentry tasks. For this purpose, a checklist of ergonomic walkthrough surveys was developed. This checklist allowed identification of awkward postures of 5 body segments, Neck-shoulder, Hips-legs, Back, Elbow and wrist. [3] The checklist contains various pictures depicting different postures of 5 body segments which carpenters may use throughout their workday. Each picture was given weighting of 1 to 5 which represented biomechanically least to most stressful posture. The checklist was also designed to obtain approximate time period each of the most awkward postures maintained. Also, the checklist was designed to obtain repetitiveness information regarding torso and lower extremity motions. The checklists were completed at the worksites and video of the task performance was also collected to assist in validating the postures and repetitiveness scores in the checklist. The specialties of carpentry observed during the site visits were dry wall (n=6), formwork (n=7), ceilings (n=8), finish work (n=6), pile-driving (n=5), welding (n=3) and scaffolding (n=2).

The self-reported body-discomfort [4] survey as well as BORG's perceived exertion scale were administered at the end of the work day. For this purpose, 46 carpenters were studied from different construction sites representing eight specialties of carpentry such as dry wall, concrete form, finish work, pile driving, ceiling, fixtures, welding and scaffolding [5]. Eighty-three percent of carpenters reported that they had experienced pain in the past year. The results from body part discomfort analysis showed that mid- to lower back and knees were chosen more often than any other body parts as having the most discomfort. Seventy-six percent of carpenters chose a Borg's scale measuring perceived physical exertion of 13 ("somewhat hard work") or higher.

Based on the preliminary evaluation of checklist data from all eight specialties and rank ordering information from the Focus Group, we focused our attention on evaluating the posture and repetition risk factors associated with the three specialties, i.e. formwork, drywall and ceiling [3]. For these three specialties, 21 carpenters were observed at 17 construction sites. Based upon combined score of postures from formwork, drywall and ceiling, the most stressful postures were used by the neck/shoulder region followed by the elbow and the back regions. The formwork produced the most stressful postures for the hips/legs, back and elbows. The lower extremity (kneeling and squatting) repetitiveness of the formwork and the drywall were significantly higher than that for the ceiling tasks.

4. Detailed Ergonomic Evaluation

The ergonomic exposure assessment of journeymen was divided into two components: Ergonomic Posture Loading aspects and Physiological aspects. These data were collected at construction sites on three specialties: drywall, ceiling and formwork. In this article we will mainly discuss the tool developed for collecting ergonomic posture loading. For the ergonomic posture loading evaluation an ergonomic dosimeter was designed and developed to meet the following criteria: measure arm and torso angles simultaneously, measure kneeling activities, store frequency of postures maintained and kneeling events for a prolonged period (at least 4 hours), lightweight and non-interfering with job performance, and transmit data to a laptop computer at the field site. The sensors chosen for the postural angle detection (measured with respect to the gravitational vertical) were wafer-thin (less than the diameter of a quarter) angle detectors generally used in the aerospace industry. The knee sensor was a Force Sensing Resistor (FSR) which responds to kneeling pressure and is designed to count number of kneels once a "real" (as opposed to slight bending of knee during walking) kneeling event has occurred. All the sensors send their signals to a portable microprocessor box for analog/digital conversion and storage. All the sensors and wiring are rugged and concealed inside the "work-coverall" thereby keeping the carpenter totally free to carry out his task uninterrupted without any interference. The posture data collected are categorized according to ergonomic classification system for "neutral (safe): -20 to < 20", "Low risk: 20 to < 45", "Medium risk: 45 to < 90", "High risk: 90 to < 135 and "Very high risk: >135".

5. References

[1]   Atterbury M. R. Et. al., "Nested case-control study of hand and wrist work-related musculoskeletal disorders in carpenters" Amer. J. Of Industrial Medicine 3: 695-701, 1996.

[2]   Warren, J, Bhattacharya A, Lemasters, G, Applegate, H and Stinson R. "Focus Groups: An aid for ergonomic assessments of carpentry tasks" Presented at the American Industrial Hygiene Association Conference, Kansas City, MO., May 20-26, 1995.

[3]   Bhattacharya, A., Greathouse, Warren J, L., Lemasters, G., Dimov, M, Applegate, H. and Stinson, R., "An Ergonomic walkthrough Observation of Carpentry Tasks: A Pilot

Study." **Applied Occupational and Environmental Hygiene Journal (In Press)**

[4]   Sauter, S.; Schleifer, L.; and Knutson, S., Work posture, work station design, and musculoskeletal discomfort in a VDT data entry task, Human Factors, 33(2), 151-167, (1991).

[5]   Greathouse, L., Bhattacharya, A., Lemasters, G., Applegate, H. and Stinson, R. "Ergonomic risk factors associated with carpentry tasks" American Industrial Hygiene Conference, New Orleans, LA, May 15-21, 1993.

ACKNOWLEDGMENT

This study was sponsored by a cooperative agreement contract (NIOSH #U60/CCU506171-01) awarded to the Greater Cincinnati Occupational Health Center (GCOHC), Cincinnati, OH.

Advances in Occupational Ergonomics and Safety II
Edited by Biman Das and Waldemar Karwowski
IOS Press and Ohmsha, 1997

Assessment of Muscular Activities in Industry

Ashraf M. Genaidy and Doran M. Christensen
Industrial Engineering, University of Cincinnati, Cincinnati OH 45221-0116, USA

Abstract. In recent years, the demands of work have dramatically changed due to advances in technologies and global competition. Today, the worker is expected to perform varied levels and types of demands. Although work demands consist of combined physical, mental and environmental loads, this paper presents a framework for the analysis of physical loads.

1. Background

Work demands should be assessed at the job and task levels. Within this context, a *job* is defined as all the work carried out by an employee or a group of employees in the completion of their prescribed duties and grouped together under one title or definition and a *task* describes a distinct part of a job for convenience of analysis purposes. As such, a job may consist of one or more tasks.

Some jobs may consist of the same tasks, day-in and day-out. Other jobs require performance of different tasks on different days, weeks and months (figure 1). Accordingly, job demands should be expressed daily, weekly, monthly, and/or yearly.

To allow flexibility in analysis, task demands can be characterized by task contents and task context. Task contents consist of *physical demands* (physical activities and related work factors required for job performance) and *mental demands* (mental activities and related work factors required for job performance). Task context is comprised of *environmental demands* (physical environment and organizational environment conditions which can create additional demands for job performance; *e.g.*: noise, lighting, relations at work).

The same task in a given job can be performed in various locations. As such, task contents are the same, however, task context may be different. It is also possible that the same task may require varied levels of task contents at different times.

In the analysis of work demands, it is assumed that the evaluation process is performed for the so-called "normative" person. "Normative" is usually derived from an overall average, and normative persons are assumed to possess the abilities, tolerance limits, training and education required for specific work. The concept of a normative person is similar to that utilized in the field of motion and time study, and may be known as a *representative worker*. This class of worker is "a person whose skill and performance is the average of a group under consideration", and is not necessarily a *qualified worker*. A qualified worker, on the other hand, is one who is accepted as having the necessary physical attributes, who possesses the required cognitive demands and education, and has the required skill and knowledge to carry out the work in hand to satisfactory standards of safety, quantity and quality.

In many applications, however, there is always a need to tailor the evaluation of work demands for a specific person or a group of persons characterized by certain human factors. If this is the case, then *personal demands* must be assessed (personal factors such as strength, endurance, education, experience, and skill levels required for performing the job).

2. Framework for Analysis of Muscular Activities in Industry

The complex muscular demands encountered in industry can be described in terms of two general classes of muscular work: *overall body* and *extremity-postural*. Overall body work is any physical activity which requires the use of the extremities and some action of the trunk. Extremity-postural work requires the use of the upper and/or lower extremities with the body in a fixed or dynamic position (*e.g.*: seated, walking).

Figure 2 presents a framework for the hierarchical assessment of muscular work in industry. This type of assessment must be able to analyze three types of human abilities:

1) Endurance is a major concern for continuous work. Admittedly, repetition and duration become very important factors in the evaluation of continuous physical tasks.
2) Strength governs the ability to perform infrequent work. Maximum load handled or force exerted is the most influential factor in this situation.
3) Range of motion and constrained postures resulting in prolonged static effort are determinants of static postural load. The angular deviation of a body part from neutral positions coupled with the time spent in that position has been considered as an indicator of static postural load.

Two approaches can be used to put the above mentioned framework into practice. The first approach can be based on a "not-so-smart" system similar to the checklist methods. The second approach can employ a "smart" system which makes use of advanced techniques such as neural networks and fuzzy logic.

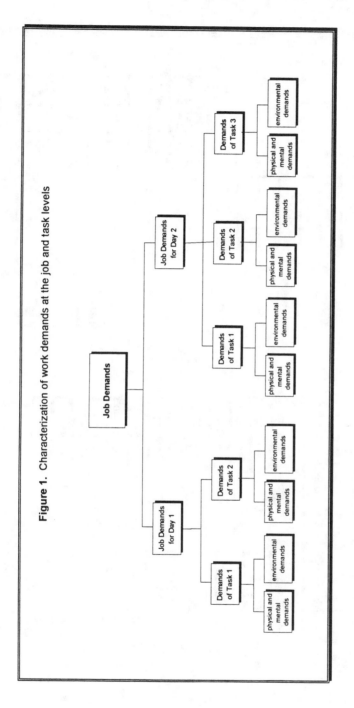

Figure 1. Characterization of work demands at the job and task levels

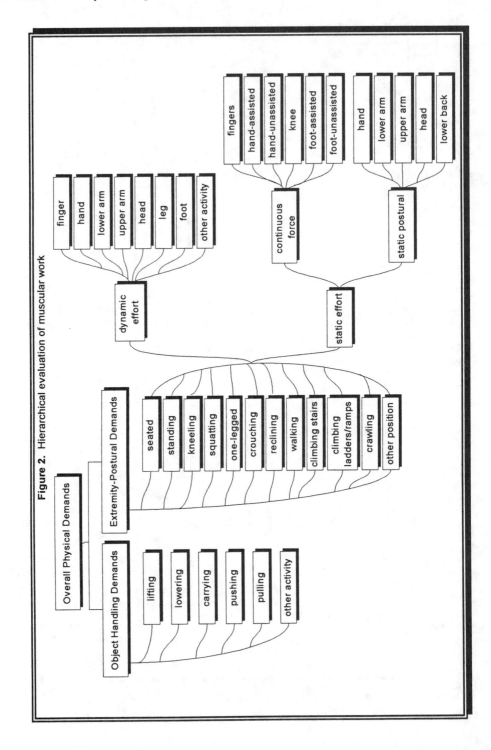

Figure 2. Hierarchical evaluation of muscular work

Advances in Occupational Ergonomics and Safety II
Edited by Biman Das and Waldemar Karwowski
IOS Press and Ohmsha, 1997

Use of an Electromagnetic System for Assessment of Lumbar Loading

Albert WJ, Day JS, Murdoch DJ, Dumas GA, Wheeler RW and Stevenson JM
Ergonomics Research Group Queen's University, Kingston, Ontario Canada

Abstract

An alternative method to video- and optoelectric-based motion analysis systems is presented for assessment of lumbar loading in an industrial setting. It benefits from its accuracy in tracking three-dimensional motion, portability and cost. The signal distortion caused by metal and restriction to tracking four body landmarks are potential limitations to address and a method for modelling the upper body is presented. In this lifting study, the Fastrak electromagnetic system has been demonstrated to be a useful tool in collecting position and orientation of body landmarks in an industrial setting for use in determining trunk motions and lumbar moments.

1. Introduction

The determination of lumbar loads during symmetric lifts was one aspect of the Queen's-DuPont Longitudinal Back Pain Study, which has been ongoing since the fall of 1994. The aim of the study is to determine the potential risk factors to LBP, as such the moments generated at the lumbar level is a primary question to be addressed. The co-ordination and velocity of motion, of and between, the segments is also of concern to determine the motion signature of different lifting patterns and pathologies.

Data collection was conducted on-site at the DuPont (Kingston site) nylon manufacturing plant. The tracking of the three-dimensional (3D) motion was accomplished using the Polhemus Fastrak magnetic motion system. The Fastrak utilizes a transmitter (source) to produce a low frequency field which can be detected by an electronics unit to determine the position and orientation of up to four sensors in three dimensions as described in Raab et al. [1]. Kinesiologic application of such magnetic tracking devices have been investigated [2] and applied to the shoulder motion [3] and spine kinematics [4].

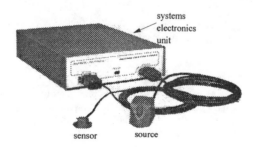

Figure 1: The components of an electromagnetic motion system

Video and opto-electric systems are used almost exclusively to collect kinematic data for lifting studies. However, these two systems have some limitations. Although multiple camera systems are capable of collecting 3D coordinate data, the simple lifting movements of the arm and shoulder can combine to cause difficulties such as hidden markers and marker collision. Sufficient space is also required to obtain large video images for analysis of the entire task. As well, use of video recording on site is a sensitive issue with many companies. Opto-electric equipment suffers from some of the same limitations as video systems and is expensive.

The Fastrak system is portable, relatively inexpensive and can accurately track 3D motion within a specified range. However, to date, electromagnetic tracking devices have not been employed in the collection of data for use in a link segment model. One reason is due to its restriction to the collection of data from only four body landmarks. A second limitation is its sensitivity to a metallic environment, typical of many manufacturing plants. Overcoming these limitations has been an integral component of this back pain study. This paper addresses the calibration procedure only briefly and refers the reader to previous work [5, 6, 7]. The main focus will be to present the development of a 2D link segment model for the calculation of lumbar loads, using the four Fastrak sensors.

2. Calibration of Fastrak Data

The floor of the plant was metal reinforced and there was metal ducting at a height of 2.5 m. This configuration led to distortions in the signal which were stronger near the floor and ceiling. The space for the lifting tests was calibrated using a 1.2m x 1.8m x 1.8m calibration frame with the source mounted mid-way at one side. A cube housing a sensor and levels was placed at set displacements of 20cm on a plexiglass sheet within this frame (Figure 2a). The plexiglass sheet was moved through nine positions along the base of the frame and the process repeated, in order to calibrate the above volume. The main distortion occurred as a result of magnetic field weakness due primarily to distance from the source and proximity to the floor or ceiling as can be seen in figure 2b. Since the distortions are known a correction algorithm was developed [Murdoch] in order to calibrate the position and orientation data. A view of the frame after correction for distortion is shown in figure 2c. For more in-depth discussions on the calibration and evaluation of the Fastrak the reader is referred to previous work done by this group [6,7].

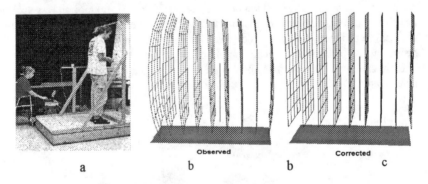

Figure 2 : A volume 1.2m x 1.8m x 1.8m was calibrated by moving the plexiglass with holes of known distances and a jig of known orientation along the platform. A) shows the calibration frame with the plexiglass in one of the nine positions; b) graphical display of the volume before and c) after the correction algorithm was applied.

3. Application to Lumbar Load Determination

3.1 Methods

The participants consisted of 150 employees from DuPont (Kingston site), who lifted 7,000 kg per day in 4-12 kg increments. A box lift was performed by each subject to simulate demands experienced in the plant. The task required the box to be lifted, in the sagittal plane, from the floor and placed on a shelf 15 cm below shoulder height.

3.2 Model Development

The 2D model for the DuPont study was defined by sensors placed as follows: 1) wrist; 2) T1 spinous process 3) L1 spinous process and 4) L5/S1 spinous process interspace (figure 3). The sensors at each of the spinous processes provided information on the motion at the thoracic, lumbar and sacral levels, respectively. The wrist sensor was used to define the forearm and the location of the box. Although this model provides sufficient information for modeling the trunk segments, it seems to suffer from a lack of available sensors to fully define the upper arm and shoulder region. The rationale for not placing a sensor on the shoulder to define the upper arm and trunk segments was the result of Wheeler's [6] validation research.

Wheeler [6] investigated the effects of shoulder joint translation on moment calculation at the level of L5/S1. The four Fastrak sensors were placed as follows: 1) distal end of the radius; b) L5/S1 spinous process interspace; c) T1 spinous process and d) lateral edge of the acromion. The sensor on the acromion was used to determine the location of the shoulder joint. To evaluate lumbar moments and the effect of shoulder translation on these moments, three 2D link segment models were developed using the constraints of the Fastrak system (figure 4). The proximal end of the trunk segment was considered to be the L5/S1 disc centre and the distal end was different for each model. In the first model, the distal end of the trunk was T1 and the shoulder was estimated from the acromion sensor. The second model, the shoulder was assumed to be a fixed hinge joint and trunk orientation was represented by a line joining the L5/S1 to the shoulder joint. The third model used a shoulder estimation point as the distal end of the trunk, which was a fixed distance from the T1 sensor as determined from the average of the data set. The upper arm was attached to the trunk at the shoulder point via a massless segment.

There were no significant differences found between the three shoulder models when compared on L5/S1 moment calculation. There was a mean difference of less than 6 Nm in all cases. Therefore, the role of shoulder joint translation (relative to T1) was seen to play a minor role in determining peak L5/S1 moments and the use of the a shoulder estimation point was justified.

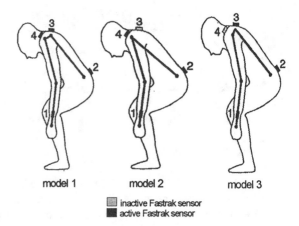

model 1   model 2   model 3

inactive Fastrak sensor
active Fastrak sensor

Figure 3: Fastrak sensor placement   Figure 4. Trunk definitions for the three 2D
models DuPont study model   with different trunk definitions

4. Conclusions

The Fastrak motion tracking system was shown to be a useful tool in collecting kinematic data. A 2D link segment model was developed and its configuration validated for use in analyzing lifting tasks. The system was used in the back pain study and the kinematic data is being analyzed to determine motion pattern and loads of different lifting patterns and pathologies.

Acknowledgements

This project was funded jointly by the Natural Science and Engineering Research Council - Collaborative Research Development Grant (#661-001/95), the University Research Incentive Fund (QU27-005) and DuPont Canada (Kingston) Inc.

References

1. Raab F.H., Blood E.B., Steiner, T.O. and Jones, H.R. (1979). Magnetic position and orientation tracking system. **IEEE Trans. Aerospace Elector Syst**. AES15, 709-718.
2. An K.N., Jacobsen, M.C., Berglund, L.J. and Chao, E.Y.S. (1988). Application of a magnetic tracking device to kinesiologic studies. **J. Biomechanics**, 21:613-620.
3. Johnson, G.R. and Anderson, J.M. (1990). Measurement of three-dimensional shoulder movement by an electromagnetic sensor. **Clin. Biomech.**, 5:131-136.
4. Pearcy, M.J. and Hindle, R.J. (1989). New method for non-invasive three-dimensional measurement of human back movement. **Clin. Biomech.**, 4:73-79.
5. Milne A.D., Chess, D.G., Johnson J.A., and King, J.W. (1996). Accuracy of an electromagnetic tracking device: A study of the optimal operating range and metal interference.
6. Day J.S., Dumas G.A. and Murdoch, D.J. (1996). Evaluation of the Polhemus Fastrak for the collection of biomechanical kinematic data. Proceedings, Ninth Biennial Conference, Canadian Society of Biomechanics, 338-339.
7. Murdoch D.J. (1996). Calibration of an oriented measurement system. Proceedings 24th Annual Meeting of the Statistical Society of Canada, Ottawa, Ontario, Canada.
8. Wheeler R.W. (1994) Investigation of the effect of shoulder joint translation on lumbar moments for two-dimensional modelling strategies. Unpublished Masters Thesis, Queen's University, Kingston, Ontario, Canada.

Advances in Occupational Ergonomics and Safety II
Edited by Biman Das and Waldemar Karwowski
IOS Press and Ohmsha, 1997

ERGONOMIC REVIEW OF OFFICE WORKSTATIONS

M. Kolich and S.M. Taboun

University of Windsor
Department of Industrial and Manufacturing Systems Engineering
Windsor, Ontario, Canada

This paper provides a comprehensive ergonomic evaluation of the various offices, computer rooms, and individual workstations, used by 30 Canadian government employees working at three different locations. In order to arrive at a reasonable approach to reducing the incidence of complaints, the first step involved the collection of accurate and detailed information concerning the nature, frequency, seriousness, and possible causes of the problems. This was accomplished in two ways. Firstly, data were obtained through the administration of a specially developed questionnaire. Secondly, data were collected by systematically measuring and observing the work areas in question. The recommendations outlined are essential to healthy office environments.

INTRODUCTION

In today's environment, social, economic, and technological pressures force employers to put increased emphasis on employee performance. To this end, computers have played a tremendous role. In most cases, organizations struggle to find enough money to buy the computers. As a result, proper furniture and accessories are frequently not included in the budget. This fact, coupled with poor utilization and arrangement of existing equipment, can lead to many health-related problems.

The ill effects of computer work are cumulative and, therefore, tend to come on slowly. Often the computer work is not recognized as the source of the problem. Two of the most common problems related to computer work are musculoskeletal injuries and visual discomfort. The occupational causes of these problems have been recognized and studied in the past. Unfortunately, the number of complaints associated with computer use is increasing at an alarming rate; leading to a renewal of interest. Part of this new-found concern can be attributed to the sheer magnitude of people working with computers (Arndt, 1983). In view of the accelerating trend towards office automation and information processing, the current number is certainly going to increase.

Objective

The objective of this particular investigation was to provide a comprehensive ergonomic evaluation of the various offices, computer rooms, and individual workstations used by employees of the Canadian government.

METHODOLOGY

Based on much of the literature reviewed, it is evident that complaints and medical complications related to working in office environments do occur. The first step involved in arriving at a reasonable approach to reducing the incidence of complaints is the collection of accurate and detailed information concerning the nature, frequency, seriousness, and possible causes of problems. For the purposes of this investigation, this included (1) information obtained directly from the employees and (2) information obtained by examining workstation characteristics.

Data were collected directly from the operators via a specially developed questionnaire. This questionnaire was divided into two sections. The first section was designed to gather information related to the types of visual and musculoskeletal problems experienced. Through this section various problem areas were identified and qualified accordingly. This was accomplished by asking each employee to indicate whether the problem, considering only the past twelve months, was experienced daily, occasionally, seldom, or never. The five problem areas were vision, neck and shoulders, back, arms and hands, and lower extremities. Associated with each of these five problem areas were questions that evaluated employee workstation comfort. These questions were formulated from research conducted by a number of reputable scientists (Fahrbach and Chapman, 1990; Grandjean, 1987; and Sauter et al., 1991).

The second section of the questionnaire gauged employee opinions. Here, employees were asked to rate different parameters regarding the design of their own workstations using the following four point scale:

No Bother / No Problem	[0]
Seldom Bothersome	[1]
Occasionally Bothersome	[2]
Constantly Bothersome	[3]

Next, the workstation, as a whole, was rated as either excellent, good, fair, or poor. Finally, employees were asked to make recommendations as to what they felt should be changed with respect to their own particular workstations. This final question was included because it is considered good practice to solicit employees' opinions with regards to matters that affect them.

A great deal of information concerning problems and potential solutions was also gathered by systematically examining the existing workstations. Listed below are the types of data collected using this method:

(i)   Workstation dimensions and adjustability
(ii)   Types of office furniture, chairs, equipment, etc.
(iii)   Available workspace
(iv)   Workstation arrangement

Subjects

For this study, a total of 30 Canadian government employees, all of whom requested that their workstations be ergonomically evaluated, acted as subjects. These employees worked at three different office locations scattered around southwestern Ontario. Although the subjects were not selected at random, they can be considered, to a certain extent, a representative sample.

In terms of demographics, 23 of the 30 office employees were female. A total of 26 office employees considered themselves VDT operators, that is, in their estimation they spent a considerable amount of their working day in front of a VDT. It was also found that 12 office employees used a typewriter for at least a small part of their working day.

DISCUSSION OF RESULTS

Many of the recommendations made in this section are based on the office workers' responses on all parts of the questionnaire. In many cases the problems experienced were directly related to the employees' responses to the various questions. Also involved in this discussion is a comparison of the recommended working postures, types of equipment, and workstation arrangements with those currently present in the office employees' actual settings.

The most important result of the entire questionnaire was that 50% of the office employees rated their workstation as "poor", while 0% rated it as "excellent". This result provides a true indication of what the office employees in this study thought of their particular workstations.

In other words, the general consensus among the office workers was that their situation could be improved in some way. The most common recommendation made was to improve the air quality and/or temperature. Many office workers (i.e. 15) felt that the air was dirty, dusty, dry and stuffy or that the temperature was never at a comfortable level (i.e it was either too cold or too hot). The second most common recommendation, expressed by 14 of the employees surveyed, dealt with a need for some type of furniture. The suggestions included foot rests, wrist pads, document holders or stands, task lamps, adjustable height VDT tables, adjustable chairs, and plexiglass for improved manoeuvrability of chairs over carpeted floors. Thirteen office workers recommended more space. The suggestions ranged from more desk-top space to more general office space. The next most popular recommendation, conveyed by 12 office workers, dealt with some aspect of lighting. Some office workers felt it was too bright, others felt it was too dull, and still others expressed a concern about glare and/or reflections. Finally, nine office workers found their working environment to be too noisy and consequently distracting.

There are a number of things that can be done to alleviate the eye problems experienced by the office workers in this study. To deal with the problem of glare it is preferable to reduce or eliminate light at the source. If this is not possible there are several options that should be considered. Firstly, anti-glare screens can be provided. Secondly, a hood can be placed on the monitor. This would help to diminish some of the glare and/or reflections. Thirdly, it is well known that flat screens are better at reducing glare and/or reflections than curved screens.

In this context, the best way to decrease the incidence of itchy, tired, dry and/or sore eyes would be to provide office workers with access to task lamps. This type of light is used to supplement the general sources of light in the workplace. Researchers have shown that task lamps do reduce eye strain when the surrounding lighting is not bright enough to perform non-VDT tasks. They are also useful in illuminating source documents.

An easy and effective way to reduce neck, shoulder, and eye problems is to provide an adjustable document holder or stand. Based on discussions with the VDT operators in this study, it is obvious that the document holder or stand should be large enough to accommodate all sizes of source documents. This is important because these VDT operators frequently work with very large files. With respect to the operator, the benefits of an adjustable document holder or stand are obtained only when it is positioned, in terms of height and distance, exactly like the monitor.

To lessen the effects of arm and hand problems, particularly carpal tunnel syndrome and tenosynovitis, wrist pads may be provided. There are currently two types available: sponge and firm. There are no clear cut advantages to either of the two types. For this reason workers should be provided the opportunity to try both types of wrist pads, for a period of time, and then make a selection based on their individual preferences. However, there are some important considerations that need to be addressed. For example, wrist pads should be used intermittently when the operator pauses during typing. They should not be used constantly as a crutch while typing.

Some operators may prefer a forearm rest. There are many advantages to forearm rests. A forearm rest is designed to support the weight of the arms which decreases the muscular tension in the neck and shoulder regions. Freed of their responsibility to support the weight of the arms, the larger muscles of the shoulder are now able to assist the operator in getting his/her hands/fingers to the keys. Therefore, instead of hyperextending or hyperflexing to reach the upper row of keys, the wrist is easily maintained in a neutral position. This helps to decrease hand pain and pain around the elbow. In terms of disadvantages, there is a risk of undue pressure on the soft tissue of the forearm.

From an ergonomics perspective, the examination of the various workstations indicated that, for most of the office employees, the available furniture was adequate. Although many of the computer workstations were adjustable and mobile they lacked a surface space, which was required, in many cases, for storage of various working materials and source documents. More modern office furniture, equipped with many of the necessary ergonomic features that reduce some of the physical stress created by office work, can be purchased (this suggestion will, most likely, be implemented).

In terms of workspace arrangement and space requirements, a mixture of results were found in the three office locations. Many of the offices surveyed where adequate in terms of the minimum space requirements and proper arrangements. However, a few of the work areas were found to be inadequate due to existing structural constraints. It is possible to overcome this problem by adopting the landscaped office concept. Since new office furniture is being acquired, it may be a good idea to consider this concept during the planning and subsequent arrangement of the new workspaces. If properly planned, the landscaped office can provide employees with some additional privacy which was found to be lacking in the current office environments. Obviously, some of the offices and meeting areas may remain totally open because of specific administrative requirements.

Typewriter use has decreased drastically over the years. At the offices in question, although virtually every employee had a typewriter, it was only used for labels and other minor typing jobs. This fact was clearly outlined in the questionnaire survey results. Therefore, to free-up the space these typewriters were occupying, it may be reasonable to place a few typewriters on the adjustable and mobile computer workstations which were found to be plentiful. These typewriters can then be kept in a centralized location and borrowed when needed. Otherwise, it may be possible to use computerized sticker labels and forms to further reduce or even eliminate the need for typewriters.

CONCLUDING REMARKS

There are many different products on the market which may help eliminate problems. The claim by manufacturers that their equipment is adjustable or ergonomically designed should not, however, be the sole criterion for selection. Tables and desks will vary in terms of range and ease of adjustment, available workspace, leg room, quality, and cost. Chairs will vary in terms of adjustability, ease of adjustment, type of backrest, size of seat pan, angle of backrest, durability, maintenance, fabric, cost, and most importantly, comfort. Selection should be based upon the data collected concerning visual and musculoskeletal problems, equipment problems, observations, and task requirements. For this reason, the problem solving methodology employed in this particular study is considered fundamental to the modern organization. In summary, presented here is a powerful tool for increasing productivity, improving equipment utilization, reducing human effort, and addressing the goals of the organization on many fronts.

REFERENCES

[1]   Arndt, R. (1983). Working posture and musculoskeletal problems of video display terminal operators - Review and reappraisal. *American Industrial Hygiene Association Journal, 44*(6), 437-446.

[2[Fahrbach, P.A. & Chapman, L.J. (1990). VDT work duration and musculoskeletal discomfort. *AAOHN Journal, 38*(1), 32-36.

[3]   Grandjean, E. (1987). Design of VDT workstations. In G. Salvendy (Ed.), *Handbook of Human Factors* (pp. 1359-1397). Purdue University.

[4]   Sauter, S.L., Schleifer, L.M., & Knutson, S.J. (1991). Work posture, workstation design, and musculoskeletal discomfort in a VDT data entry task. *Human Factors, 33*(2), 151-167.

Advances in Occupational Ergonomics and Safety II
Edited by Biman Das and Waldemar Karwowski
IOS Press and Ohmsha, 1997

Trends and Inconsistencies Among Studies in Self-estimation of Body Weight and Height

Sheik N. Imrhan, Ph.D., P.E.
Department of Industrial and Manufacturing Systems Engineering
The University of Texas at Arlington
Box 19017, Arlington, TX 76013

Victorine Imrhan, Ph.D., R.D.
Department of Nutrition and Food Science
Texas Woman's University, Denton, TX

This paper reviews the results of published studies in self-estimation of height and body weight. While the studies differed considerably in sample sizes and characteristics, they all showed relatively small mean errors of estimation indicating only weak tendencies for people to overestimate or underestimate. The association between errors of estimation and associated factors are discussed, with the focus on areas of agreements and inconsistencies. For ergonomics studies, self-estimates can replace actual measurements.

1. Introduction

Standing height (stature) and body weight are two of the most widely used anthropometric measurements in scientific work. Their uses across different disciplines have been outlined in [1]. Imrhan et al. [1] has also provided evidence to show that self-estimation of height and weight are accurate enough to be substituted for measured values in ergonomic studies. Several other studies have been performed before [1] and contradictions exist in the direction (overall overestimation or underestimation) in which biasing factors (e.g. age, education, etc.) act during self-estimation.

2. Methods

Data from the published studies dealing with self-estimates of height or weight have been compared across studies to determine the influence of biasing factors. Unfortunately accuracy, from mean absolute errors, could not be compared since only one study [1] published absolute errors.

3. Results

The comparison of results across studies will use mean percentage errors of estimation. In general, people show a tendency toward overall underestimation of weight and overestimation of height but there are distinct differences among some subgroups within samples, especially body weight subgroups.

Height has been overestimated more than underestimated in all studies, with the greatest mean error being 3.0 cm and the least being 0.47 cm. Weight was underestimated more than it was overestimated in all except two studies -- the males in [2] and [3]. The greatest mean error (ME) of weight self-estimation was 4.0 kg and the least 0.28 kg. Most of the underestimation was due to the severely overweight and obese persons. The least mean errors for both weight and height were found in a study of college students [1].

The overall mean error in individual studies tend to obscure important differences in population subgroups. These studies show that the generally held view that heavier people underestimate weight and lighter people overestimate it is not true in all cases. Certain studies support this view [3,4,5,6], but others have found that lighter females do not overestimate weight [2,7,8,9,10,11]. In, some lighter females actually underestimated weight [7,8,9,10].

The degree to which people underestimate weight depends on their true body weight. Thus, as true weight increases, the error of underestimation increases, especially among overweight persons [3, 4, 5, 6, 7 in students, 8, 9, 10, 11, 12, 13, 14, 15,16, 17]. This trend seems to be stronger in females than males, among both adults [8, 10] and children in different age groups -- high school senior females [2] and 6th grade children [13]. There are a couple of exceptions to this trend: Tell et al. [11] who found that women in the heaviest group had the smallest mean error (overall underestimation) than women in other weight groups, the reason being their sample characteristics; and the 4 obese subjects in [12] did not differ in their weight estimation from the other 46. One must note that these observations are based on average errors and, as stated in [11], a few people may overestimate when an average for the group indicates underestimation, and vice-versa. Dwyer et al. [2] has shown that adolescent males overestimate weight and adolescent females underestimate it.

The association between people's height and their weight estimation is not clear. Studies [13, 14, 16] show results that are contradictory.

People's true heights have been found to be related to self-estimation of height. In general, tall people tend to underestimate their height and short people tend to overestimate it but, across studies, errors of height estimation seem to follow different trends with actual height. The results show that errors increase with [4, 6, 9], decrease with (4, 8, 9, 10 in women) or are unrelated to actual height (10 in men, 13, 14 among Danish subjects, 15].

Robinson and Wright [18] found that younger men tend underestimate weight while older men and women overestimated it, but Jalkanen et al. [5] found that both younger and older men underestimated it. Overestimation of weight by older people may be related to the fact that weight declines after a certain age and older people may be stating weight at a younger age. Most studies reported no strong relationship between age and error of weight estimation [6, 8 in men, 14, 15, 16], but a few found that errors either decreased with age [3, 9, 10, 16] or increased with age [5 in women, 8 in women]. However, trends are confounded by degree of overweight such that young severely overweight people may underestimate weight to a greater extent than older people [3].

People tend to report themselves taller that they are, except older people [18]. The reasons may be different in different age groups. While younger people may overestimate because of a desire to be taller, older people tend to underestimate because they may be unaware of their loss in height with age. The relationship between age and error of height estimation differs across studies. There seems to be more evidence that error of height reporting increases as age increases [6, 8 among women, 9, 10, 15 among professionals, 18]. But Buckle [15 among college students] and Rowland [16] found no significant association.

Some studies have found a difference in the accuracy of weight estimation between the sexes [2, 7 among students, 8, 10, 13, 19] with males showing lesser underestimation than females for adults, adolescents and young children. Other studies, such as Wing et al. [11] among 18-89 year old health fair attendees, Stewart [16] and DelPrete [6] have found no difference in mean error between the sexes.   In the studies that found a sex difference, women tend to underestimate weight and overestimate height more than men. Adolescent girls seem to want to weigh lighter than their true weight, and boys, except the obese ones, want to weigh more than their true weight [2].

The association between level of education and errors in estimation is confusing for both height and weight. For weight underestimation, errors have been found to decrease as education level increases [16 in females, 17 in females], increase as education level increases [5 in females, 8 in males and females, 9 in males, 10 in males], or have no significant relationship with education level [5 in males, 17 in males). For height estimation, two trends have been found: errors decrease as education level increases [9 in males and females], and errors have no significant association [10 in females].

Tell et al. [11], DelPrete [6], and Imrhan et al. [1] found that those who weigh more frequently tend to underestimate weight less than others, but Imrhan et al. [1] did not find greater accuracy of weight estimation (smaller mean absolute error) among college students who weighed more frequently. Tell et al. [11] also found that those who weighed more recently within 14 days of their self reports made significantly smaller errors of estimation than others; Imrhan et al. [1] found smaller but non-significant errors of weight estimation for those who weighed more recently; and Murphy et al. [20] found no relationship. However, Imrhan et al. [1] found that both weight and height were estimated more accurately (smaller mean absolute error) by those who self-measured themselves more recently than others. They also found that when people knew that they would be measured later they estimated height and weight more accurately than when they didn't know that they would be measured.

Some researchers [5, 8, 11, 13] have suggested that a systematic error of estimation occurs if people are accustomed to self-weighing with little or no clothing. One study [5] found that men and women with low family incomes were more likely to underestimate weight than those with high family incomes. It is also possible that the duration between estimation and measurement could have had an effect on the magnitude or direction of errors but, unfortunately, this has not been tested in any of the studies. Stewart [10] expressed the opinion that it is possible for more accurate estimates to be obtained from face-to-face interview instead of self-administered questionnaires. Only one study [14] compared self-estimates of people of different cultures, races or nationalities. They found that, among applicants for medical insurance, Danes estimated weight less accurately than Americans.

4. Reference

[1]   S. N. Imrhan, V. Imrhan and C. Hart, Can Self-estimates of Body Weight and Height be Used in Place of Measurements for College Students, Ergonomics, 39(12), 1996, 1445-1453.

[2]   J.T. Dwyer, J.L. Feldman, C.C. Seltzer, J. Mayer,   Adolescent Attitudes Towards Weight and Appearance. *Journal of Nutrition Education*, 1 (1969), 14-19.

[3]   M.L. Rowland, 1990, Self-reported Weight and Height, *American Journal of Clinical Nutrition*, 54 (1990), 1125-1133.

[4]   P. Schlichting, P.F. Hoilund-Carlsen, and F. Quaade, Comparison of Self-reported Height and Weight with Controlled Height and Weight in Women and Men, *International Journal of Obesity*, 1981, 67-76.

[5]   L. Jalkanen, J. Tuomilehto, A. Tanskanen, and P. Puska,   Accuracy of Self-reported Body Weight Compared to Measured Body Weight, *Scandinavian Journal of Social Medicine*, 15 (1987), 191-198.

[6]   L.R. DelPrete, M. Caldwell, C. English, S. Banspach, and C. LeFebvre,   Self-reported and Measured Heights of Participants in Community-based Weight Loss Programs. *Journal of the American Dietetic Association*, 92(12), 1992, 1483-1486.

[7]   R.R. Wing, L.H. Epstein, D.J. Ossip, and R.E. LaPorte, Reliability and Validity of Self-report and Observers' Estimates of Relative Weight, *Addictive Behaviors*, 4 (1979), 133-140.

[8]   P. Pirie, D., Jacobs, R.W. Jeffery, and P. Hannan, Distortion in Self-reported Height and Weight Data, *Journal of the American Dietetic Association*, 78 (1981), 601-606.

[9]   M. Palta, R.J., Prineas, R. Berman, and P. Hannan, Comparison of Self-reported and Measured Height and Weight. *American Journal of Epidemiology*, 115 (2), 1982, 223-230.

[10]   A.L. Stewart, The Reliability and Validity of Self reported Weight and Height. *Journal of Chronic Disability*, 35 (1982), 295-309.

[11]   G.S. Tell, R.W. Jeffery, F.M. Kramer, and M.K. Snell, Can Self-reported Body Weight be Used to Evaluate Long-term Follow-up of a Weight-loss program? *Journal of the American Dietetic Association*, 87 (1987), 1198-1201.

[12]   H.C. Charney, M. Goodman, B. McBride, Lyon and R. Pratt, Childhood Antecedents of Adult Obesity. Do Chubby Infants Become Obese Adults? *New England Journal of Medicine*, 295(1), 1976, 6-9.

[13]   B. Shannon, H. Smickalas-Wright, and M.Q. Wang, Inaccuracies in Self-reported Weights and Heights of a Sample of Sixth-grade Children, *Journal of the American Dietetic Association*, 91(6), 1991, 675-678.

[14]   Stunkard, A.J. and J.M. Albaum, The Accuracy of Self-reported Weights, *The American Journal of Chemical Nutrition*, 34 (1981), 1593-1599.

[15]   Buckle, Self-reported Anthropometry, *Ergonomics*, 28(11), 1985, 1575-1577.

[16]   A. W. Stewart, R.T. Jackson, M.A. Ford and R. Beaglehole,   Underestimation of Relative Weight by Use of Self-reported Height and Weight. *American Journal of Epidemiology*, 125 (1), 1987, 122-126.

[17]   M.L.Rowland, Reporting Bias in Height and Weight Data. *Statistical Bulletin, Metropolitan Life Insurance Co.*, 70(2), 1989, 2-11.

[18]   L.A. Robinson, and B.T. Wright, Comparison of Stated and Measured Patient Heights and Weights, *American Journal of Hospital Pharmacy*, 39 (1982), 882-885.

[19]   R.L. Huenemann, L.R. Shapiro, M.C. Hampton, B.W. Mitchell, and A.R. Behnke, A Longitudinal Study of Gross Body Composition and Body Conformation and Their Association with Food and Activity in a Teenage Population: Views of Teen-age Subjects. *American Journal of Clinical Nutrition*, 18 (1966), 325-338.

[20]   J.K. Murphy, B.K. Bruce, and D.A. Wiliamson, A Comparison of Measured and Self-reported Weights in a 4-year Follow-up in Spouse Involvement in Obesity Treatment. *Behavioral Therapy*, 16 (1985), 524-530.

5. Conclusions

Though the various studies on self-estimation of height and weight show areas of contradictions, certain important generalizations are valid. However, one should be cautious in accepting the findings from single self-estimation studies because of idiosyncrasies.

4. Education and Training in Ergonomics

Advances in Occupational Ergonomics and Safety II
Edited by Biman Das and Waldemar Karwowski
IOS Press and Ohmsha, 1997

COMPUTER-AIDED HUMAN MODELLING FROM TRAINING THRU TO INDUSTRIAL APPLICATION

Ewa GÓRSKA

Institute of Organization for Production Systems, Warsaw University of Technology,
ul. Narbutta 85, 02-524 Warsaw, Poland

Prof. Ronald LIPPMANN

IST GmbH Gernsheim, Waldstraße 13, D-68649 Groß-Rohrheim

Abstract: The fact the many young engineers do not have the necessary experience in using modern construction methods is not the only complaint of construction managers. They are particularly disappointed that in mechanical engineering and in product and industrial design at German and Polish universities computer-aided ergonomic methods are hardly taught and practised. But from future industrial employees in particular one expects support in the areas which were not yet in the curriculum when their older colleagues were trained. It is really amazing to find that the universities which offer these progressive ergonomie methods as a compulsory subject can be counted on the fingers of one hand.

1. Introduction

A characteristic feature of ergonomics is its complex approach to solving theoretical and practical issues related to the man-technology system. It is impossible, even for a team of specialists, to consider all the factors and mutual interactions between variables and objects unless their work is in the form of a dialogue with a large and fast computer system.

Therefore a new quality of man's activity, as regards the solution of ergonomic problems, consists in an effective dialogue conducted between a designer and a computer.

Moreover, a computer-aided design helps us to carry out research and ergonomic evaluations which cannot be conducted by means of traditional methods.

Computer systems enable us to:

- display anthropometric dimensions on a display screen with regard to the population, sex, build type, etc.,
- simulate such movements of a mannequin which reflect the biomechanics of a human body with best possible probability,
- generate the visual field and angular grid depending on the vision geometry of a selected mannequin,
- to establish the quality and correctness of spatial relations through proper positioning of the entire model and its individual elements,
- assess the correctness of the adjustment scope of the technical elements (levers, seats) depending on the body posture at work,
- present the maximum force and boundary load during lifting and hoisting in relation to the path, time and frequency of heavy load moving,

- generate sets that describe the position of individual parts of a human body in the course of designing simulations of working positions,
- to remember particular arrangements in an adequate database,
- transfer a verified model of a workstation to the professional CAD system in order to make technical drawings based on this model,
- create a library in which all the data that concern the analyses can be accumulated and used again in solving similar problems.

Moreover, the system is expected to provide universal methods and software so that they can be adopted for various categories of computers and constantly changing CAD systems.

Below please find a more detailed description of a professional computer software known as ANTHROPOS, which is more and more widely applied in German design offices. The software has been installed in the Laboratory of Ergonomics and Work Environment Design at the Institute for Organization of Production Systems, Warsaw University of Technology.

2. The ANTHROPOS software

The ANTHROPOS software package is just one more application of 3D-CAD software known as CAD-KEY and it can be used on such computers as PC 80386 or 80486 equipped with 8 MB RAM as well as on computers IRIS 4D25/35 and SUN stations.

A user can choose between four levels of difficulty:
- easy (LIGHT),
- standard (STANDARD),
- practical (PRAXIS),
- professional (PROFI),

and for ergonomic design in automobiles one can possibly use a special package SAE (Society of Automotive Engineer Standard).

Owing to an excellent communication between databases to CAD software and ANTHROPOS software, a user is free to decide whether he is going to work only with a model or whether he wants to place his model in a work environment he simulates himself by means of CAD system (or transferred from another system by means of such adjusting systems as for example DXF).

Simple objects that are generated in professional CAD systems are transposed to ANTHROPOS. Inside the software and using individual elements, one can construct models of complex workstations.

A special program generates kinematic models of human body with preset real dimensions or in centile units.

An adequate mannequin can be used to verify individual elements of a simulated workplace, distribution and arrangement of control devices, the field of vision, the height and shape of the working field, position of a human body at work.

Therefore it is important to define sets of points that belong to particular walls or planes of reference and that are used as co-ordinates of connections for single or all effectors simultaneously.

They are an important starting point (apart from data input) leading to a complex animation, e.g. animation of reaching a destination point, reaction animation, movements performed by the entire body which can be used in any sequence when controlled by means of a menu.

3. Animation of reaching the destination point

In animation of reaching the destination point it is important that the kinematic chain (e.g. a hand and forearm) with regard to turning, stretching and bending of a limb should stay in accordance with the point on the object. The kinematic chain may take various positions in the space. By controlling the position of a hand, we search for the best point to accomplish the formulated task. Using a set of additional commands we can make the model's hand grab an object.

4. Reaction animation

Reaction animation is performed with a prolonged kinematic chain, e.g. a hand, an arm, a spine. Within this program movements can be made with the participation of all effectors and with regard to the vision geometry and gravity of a standing figure.

In the case of a deep bend and a simultaneous lifting of a definite weight when the gravity centre moves beyond the base plane, the model is automatically set in a position which maintains equilibrium.

5. Animation of positioning the entire figure

This part of software positions and moves the entire figure (all effectors, vision geometry) in relation to constant points and planes of reference over the whole work cycle.

In the course of movements, the system automatically corrects the overall animation of the figure for various populations at work

At the end of each animation we can print out synthetic data along with the animated model and its environment.

6. Sequence registration

The PROFI module allows us to divide the record of 3D animation into any number of sequences. Each phase presents the scope of movements performed by limbs, which can be measured on a plane or in space.

5. Additional information

Apart from the above referenced steps, it is desirable that a list of anthropmetric and biomechanical data should be printed out.

Using a special modelling editor and using his own data, a user can introduce a new form, adapt it to standard models and join it to the system.

An experienced user of CAD is able to use this method after a three-day training, a beginner will probably need twice as much time.

Both the software and the design methods are being constantly improved.

Internationally the aforementioned software is used to assess the construction of machines and various devices. It is also used in design of workplaces and also in science.

1. Model animation

In accordance with international anthropometric data bases ANTHROPOS develops 3D models which can be loaded using a type selection box. Men and women from 10 nationalities and 20 regions of the world aged from 3 to 64 and in 5 standard sizes (percentiles) are available for selection and combination. In addition to the disproportionalities sitting giant and sitting dwarf with normal, short or long arms, variants of somato-types can be generated using a 9x9 matrix.

And since in spite of this great number of human types, products and workplaces must also be tested and designed for particular individuals, if necessary also for people with special disabilities, a USER type editor is available for generating special models with data-base support; these can be used exactly like standard models in the course of further analysis. Workplace analyses with models whose limbs have been amputated or with models representing spastic disabilities, obese people and dwarfs, have on many occasions been successfully carried out with comprehensive detailed redesign recommendations.

Movement of the human body is extremely complicated and variable. In order to be able to imitate it by means of mathematics alone, six different but mutually related animation techniques are available in ANTHROPOS: auto-animation, manual animation, complex animation, sequence animation, parametric animation, restriction animation.

All animations can be combined in accordance with the requirements in each case and the efficiency and quality of the analysis thus improved. This also applies to the special settings to be used in animations; these are amongst other things the various hand shapes. A comprehensive redefine function, with which goal points for the kinematic chains are read in automatically singly or in gather mode at the current position of the model or the figures are set to an anthropometric basic posture at the global co-ordinates 0/0/0, complete the rational application of the various animation techniques.

Using the ergonomic analysis with ANTHROPOS system user can work creatively every day without loss of time. It is to be hoped that industry in future will generally use computer-aided systems.

6. Conclusions

Research and works on the development of ergonomic computer-aided design systems aim at increasing their "intelligence". The point is to enrich the system and/or its environment with proper algorithms and methods of ergonomic design, additional databases, methods of work analysis, elements of biomechanical analysis.

Scientists are also interested in a possibility of a contactless recording of 3D situations of the human body in the work process and in measuring the kinematics of a machine along with biomechanics of a man.

They are planning to develop a computer system that will be able to produce expertise and ergonomic consultations automatically.

Obviously it difficult to mention all the possible development directions of the system, especially when the permanent development of hardware and software opens new perspectives and new possibilities.

Advances in Occupational Ergonomics and Safety II
Edited by Biman Das and Waldemar Karwowski
IOS Press and Ohmsha, 1997

Ergonomics Training:
Bridging the Gap Between Employee
Knowledge of Basic Ergonomics and Job
Specific Risk Factors

Michael Parker, P.E.
Microwave Instruments Division
Hewlett-Packard Company
1212 Valley House Dr.
Rohnert Park, CA 94928

Abstract: This paper reports the results of an internal benchmark investigation of the effectiveness of ergonomics training programs in electronics manufacturing environments and introduces a new model for ergonomics training developed for Hewlett-Packard's Microwave Instruments Division. The new ergonomics training model combines the traditional classroom training in basic ergonomics with additional training in job specific risk factors. The new training model also uses a persuasion model to further encourage employees to take action to reduce the ergonomic risk factors in their environments.

1. Introduction

The reduction of occupational illnesses and injuries is a major business objective at Hewlett-Packard. In order to achieve reduction in ergonomic related occupational injuries, Hewlett-Packard has implemented a three phased approach which consists of encouraging employee involvement and responsibility for ergonomics, using management leadership and accountability, and designing safe work environments. For this approach to be successful, Hewlett-Packard recognizes the need to achieve excellence in each of these key areas. However, surveys of our work force at the Microwave Instruments Division show that our current approach to encouraging employee involvement and responsibility in our ergonomics program is falling short of our goals. Post training surveys of basic ergonomics training class participants show that their general knowledge of ergonomics is consistently rated as medium to high on a five point scale. However, their specific knowledge of job specific ergonomic risk factors is evenly distributed across the five point scale, with an equal number of training participants reporting a low level of knowledge of job specific risk factors to those reporting a high level of knowledge. Additional questions which queried how the employees used the basic ergonomics training class to improve their work environment also confirmed this result. The fact that our current basic ergonomics training program is inconsistently promoting a high level of understanding of job specific risk factors is seen as a major obstacle to achieving an injury free work environment.

2. Benchmarked Training Programs

An internal benchmark investigation was initiated to determine whether other Hewlett-Packard operations were experiencing similar problems with their basic ergonomics training programs and to determine whether any operations had implemented significantly superior programs. Three different basic ergonomics training programs within Hewlett-Packard were chosen for the benchmark investigation. The training program coordinator at each of the organizations was contacted and queried as to what there ergonomics training program was intended to achieve and how they felt that this was being achieved. Additionally, statistics were sought to compare the effectiveness of each of the training programs. Unfortunately, a lack of adequate statistics supporting the comparison of the effectiveness of the training programs was found. As a result, a series of interviews and focused questionnaires were conducted to fill the void in training program statistics.

In general, the basic ergonomics training program at Hewlett-Packard's Microwave Instruments Division was found to be very similar to the internally benchmarked programs. All of the training coordinators believed that the ultimate goal of the training programs were to persuade employees to take action to reduce the ergonomic risk factors in their work (and home) environments. These programs all provided training in basic ergonomics, with two of the three classes additionally focusing on basic physiology of the upper extremities. Each program also explained the causes of work-related pain and discomfort, as well as limited recommendations or "best practices" to avoid ergonomic risk factors on the job. However, due to the fact that these programs are targeted to a wide audience, only one of the three programs specifically focused on helping the operator translate the general ergonomics training they receive into the specific ergonomic issues associated with their jobs. A summary of the training packages benchmarked is shown in Table 1.

Table 1: Training Program Summary

Training Program	Training Goals	Training Components	Duration	Training Frequency	Results
No. 1	Awareness and recognition of ergonomic risk factors	Ergonomics Overview; Explanation of Risk Factors; Video Tape; Explanation of Job Specific Risk Factors	3 hours	2 years initially, 1 year subsequent training	Basic Ergonomics Understanding: Med - Hi Job Specific Risk Factor Identification: Med Actions Taken to Reduce Ergonomic Risks: Med
No. 2	Awareness and recognition of ergonomic risk factors	Business Overview Video Tape	45 minutes	N.A.	Basic Ergonomics Understanding: Low Job Specific Risk Factor Identification: Low Actions Taken to Reduce Ergonomic Risks: Low
No. 3	Awareness and recognition of ergonomic risk factors	Ergonomics Overview, Video Tape, Explanation of Risk Factors	2 hours	2 years	Basic Ergonomics Understanding: Med Job Specific Risk Factor Identification: Med Actions Taken to Reduce Ergonomic Risks: Low

3. Benchmark Comparison Model

As noted in Table 1, all of the training programs had similar goals and used similar methods. However, in general, the longer classes which covered more materials and helped the employees link their daily activities to ergonomic risk factors scored higher. However, the comments from the employees, trainers, and training coordinators suggested a further element that was initially not measured. This element is the focus on achieving the primary purpose of the ergonomics training programs: to persuade the employees to take an active role in identifying and eliminating ergonomic risk factors in their environment (both personal and physical). The overall emphasis on persuasion suggests that a persuasion model may be the most appropriate to compare the programs.

Cialdini [2] offers a persuasion model to compare the programs against. According to Cialdini, the six basic categories which can be used to persuade an individual to take action are consistency, reciprocation, social proof, authority, liking, and scarcity. Cialdini explains that each of these categories is governed by a fundamental psychological principle that directs human behavior. It is this fundamental psychological principle that gives each of these persuasion categories their strength. The six persuasion categories are described below in Table 2 and each of the three training programs are compared to this model in Table 3.

Table 2: Persuasion Model

Persuasion Category	Potential Application to Ergonomics Training
Commitment and Consistency: The rule of consistency states that once we have made a choice or taken a stand, we will encounter personal and interpersonal pressures to behave consistently with that commitment.	Training encourages employees to make a commitment to their personal ergonomics (e.g. action plan, public statement, etc.)
Reciprocity: The rule of reciprocity states that we should try to repay, in kind, what another person has provided us. By virtue of the reciprocity rule, we are obligated to repay a favor, gift or the like.	Training applies reciprocity rule (e.g. complete a personal workstation assessment, etc.)
Social Proof: The principle of social proof states that one means we use to determine what is correct is to find out what other people think is correct, especially if these people are acting on their beliefs.	Training uses social proof via explanation of the widespread nature of ergonomics, examples of people that have made positive changes to their work environment, etc.
Liking: The rule of liking is that we most prefer to say yes to the requests of someone we know, like, and is similar to us.	Trainers are likable. Trainers include people that are similar to the trainees.
Authority: The rule of authority states that there is a deep-seated sense of authority within all of us.	Authority figures used to present materials (e.g. Physicians, Physical Therapists, Engineers)
Scarcity: The scarcity principle states that opportunities seem more valuable to us when their availability is limited.	Training focuses on the potentially damaging consequences of not applying ergonomic principles.

Table 3: Training Program Comparison Via Persuasion Elements

Training Program	Persuasion Model Elements					
	Commitment / Consistency	Reciprocity	Social Proof	Likability	Authority	Scarcity
No. 1	N/A	Participants asked to fill out a personal risk identification survey upon return to work	Examples given from outside industries and some inside the factory	Instructor approachable	Classes taught by external Physical Therapist	Emphasis on the potentially damaging consequences of CTDs
No. 2	N/A	N/A	Examples given from dissimilar industries	Instructor approachable	Classes taught by Company Health & Safety Liaison	Limited emphasis on damaging effects of CTDs
No. 3	N/A	N/A	Limited examples given from inside the factory	Supervisor had similar back-ground to class.	Classes taught by Company Supervisor	Emphasis on the potentially damaging consequences of CTDs

4. Results and Discussion

The comparison of the programs in Table 3 more clearly explains why training program No. 1 most effectively persuaded employees to take action to reduce the ergonomic risk factors in their work environment. Notably, training program No. 1 used five of the six elements of Cialdini's persuasion model, including the use of reciprocity. Additionally, training program No. 1 used the elements of the persuasion model is used more effectively. For example, trainng program No. 1 used a higher authority figure than the other training programs. The impact of this difference was readily apparent to the class participants who noted that the use of the external physical therapist to teach the class positively influenced the message they received versus the use of a company supervisor or health and safety liaison.

The strong correlation between the effectiveness of the three training programs and the persuasion model suggests that future training programs can also be enhanced by further using the model. Future work on improving the effectiveness of basic ergonomics training at Microwave Instruments Division will focus on extending the use of this model to further promote employee involvement and responsibility in ergonomics.

References

[1] R. Raborn, S. Ulin, and T. Armstrong, Initiating Ergonomics Activities In Smal Companies. In: Advances in Occupational Ergonomics and Safety I (2 Vol.) 1996, pp. 925 - 930.
[2] R. Cialdini. Influence: The Psychology of Persuasion. 1984. Quill, New York.
[3] Eastman Kodak Company. Ergonomic Design for People at Work, Vol. 2. 1986. Van Nostrand Reinhold, New York.
[4] T. Krause. Employee-Driven Systems for Safe Behavior. 1995. Van Nostrand Reinhold, New York.
[5] M. Helander. A Guide to the Ergonomics of Manufacturing. 1995. Taylor & Francis, London.

Advances in Occupational Ergonomics and Safety II
Edited by Biman Das and Waldemar Karwowski
IOS Press and Ohmsha, 1997

Long-Term Training Effects On The Implementation Of A Legislated Safety System

J. SAARI, G. THÉRIAULT, S. BÉDARD, M. FERRON, V. DUFORT, J. HRYNIEWIECKI

Joint Departments of Epidemiology and Biostatistics

and Occupational Health, McGill University, 1130 Pine Avenue, Montréal, Canada H3A 1A3

Abstract. This is a longitudinal study exploring the long-term impact of various training strategies on conformity to the new Workplace Hazardous Materials Information System (WHMIS) introduced in Canada in the late eighties. Fifty six companies in the transportation equipment and machinery manufacturing sectors in Quebec participated in this study. Companies were divided into two main groups based on strategies chosen for employee training: (1) external safety association experts used for training of all employees, or (2) safety experts used to train selected employees, who would then train the remaining employees and serve as internal experts. A further fourteen companies who had not used the sectorial association for training at the time of the sample selection were used as a comparison group. About six months after the initial implementation of WHMIS, a random sample of employees representing 14 job titles was selected to answer a short questionnaire on WHMIS and general workplace health and safety. Three years later, the companies were revisited and an equivalent questionnaire was applied to selected workers. Short term results showed WHMIS knowledge to be best in companies with all employees trained by an external expert. However, the long-term results showed that WHMIS knowledge in companies with internal trainers improved while WHMIS knowledge in companies with external experts declined.

1. Introduction

How does a company optimize results when implementing new safety systems? Hiring external experts can quickly bring knowledge to a company. The learning curve needed to get internal experts up to par with external experts may compromise the immediate benefits to companies. However, the day-to-day presence of an internal expert can provide continued support for workers and the long-term benefits of internal experts may outweigh the initial success of using external experts for one-shot training.

In the mid 1980's, the Canadian federal government made efforts to improve working conditions through the introduction of a new workplace right-to-know regulation commonly referred to as WHMIS - (Workplace Hazardous Materials Information System). This legislation addressed the safer use of hazardous materials in the workplace through improved information on handling, use and hazards of these materials.

The three basic components of the system were: (1) uniform labeling of containers, (2) ready availability of detailed information in the form of Material Safety Data Sheets (MSDS), and (3) employee training focusing on hazardous materials used in the workplace. A study on the short-term implementation of WHMIS employee training was conducted six months after initial training [1,2]. All companies in the transportation equipment and machinery manufacturing sectors in Quebec were eligible to be included in this study.

The results of this first study indicated that companies using external experts for employee training had the best WHMIS knowledge. Employees in companies where internal trainers were used knew somewhat less about hazardous materials. However, both groups outperformed companies which had either not trained any employees or had not completed employee training.

It was hypothesized that this situation could change over time. Since companies with internal trainers had a knowledgeable person continuously available, worker training could continue. Eventually, worker knowledge of hazardous materials in companies with resident experts may equal or even surpass knowledge in companies where external experts were used. The second evaluation round was conducted three years after the initial training to test this hypothesis. This report describes some of the results of the long-term analysis.

2. Material and methods

Fifty-six companies agreed to participate in the second evaluation round. Twenty-four companies dropped out for reasons such as bankruptcy, considerable downsizing, or outright refusal. Among these companies, there were two main groups, using different strategies, chosen for employee training: (1) external sectorial association experts (SAE) used for training of all employees (13 establishments), or (2) internal experts trained by SAE, who would then train the remaining employees (16 establishments). A further fourteen companies who had not used the sectorial association for training at the time of the sample selection were used as a comparison group.

About six months after the initial implementation of WHMIS, visits were made to each participating company to assess WHMIS conformity. A sample of employees representing 14 job titles was selected to answer a short questionnaire on WHMIS and general workplace health and safety. Three years later, the companies were revisited. A new knowledge test was given to a similar sample of employees. The knowledge test consisted of both WHMIS specific questions and general questions related to hazardous materials. The three year questionnaire was designed to correspond to the 6 month questionnaire and was piloted before its use. Test questions were designed to be reasonably difficult.

3. Results

Figure 1 shows the main results. The companies that used external experts from the safety association to train all the employees clearly performed best in the short-term (six months after training). Comparison companies showed the poorest results in terms of WHMIS knowledge. Knowledge three years after initial training showed substantially different results. Companies that used internal experts performed much better than companies that relied on external experts.

Table 1 shows the results for WHMIS specific and for general questions in the second evaluation round (three years after initial training). All groups performed equally well on general questions. The differences between groups come from a different performance in WHMIS specific questions. This indicates that WHMIS specific activities obviously have been more effective in "internal expert" companies.

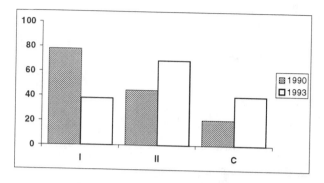

Figure 1. Percentage of plants above the average success rate for WHMIS specific questions.

Table 1. Performance on different types of questions by implementation group. The numbers indicate the percentage of companies above the average result in all 56 establishments studied.

	External experts	Internal experts	Comparison group
WHMIS specific questions	38	69	40
General questions	63	77	60

4. Discussion

Short-term training results clearly favored external experts. However, the other components of WHMIS, such as labeling, and Materials Safety Data Sheet, were equally good in both groups. These results would support the assumption that the companies choosing different methods of training were otherwise similar to each other and only differed in areas which would be directly influence by different training approaches.

The second evaluation, three years later, showed a maturation effect in companies with internal trainers. These companies probably benefited from the fact that a resource person was continuously present in the workplace. External experts are usually available for only a limited time. That seemed to be the case even in this situation where the external experts (SAE) continued to be available to the companies but were not present to the extent that the internal experts would have been.

Internal experts have several advantages over external experts. In addition to being available continuously, they know the local conditions and people and can therefore better initiate improvements. Internal consultants can also be a "driving force". They are, most likely, actively interested in safety and continually monitor developments.

Reference

[1] J. Saari, S. Bédard, V. Dufort, J. Hryniewiecki, and G. Thériault, Efficacy Of Training Procedures In Implementing A Legislated Safety Programme, *Applied Ergonomics* 24(1994) 116-118.

[2] J. Saari, S. Bédard, V. Dufort, J. Hryniewiecki, and G. Thériault, Successful Training Strategies To Implement A Workplace Hazardous Materials Information System, *Journal of Occupational Medicine* 36(1994) 569-574.

Advances in Occupational Ergonomics and Safety II
Edited by Biman Das and Waldemar Karwowski
IOS Press and Ohmsha, 1997

Interactive Computer-Based Training Tutorial for Adult Learners

Maria Demetriou, Hector Him, A. K. Gramopadhye, and Delbert Kimbler
Department of Industrial Engineering, Clemson University, Clemson, S. C. 29634-0920

Abstract—Computer-based training is an effective way to address the unique characteristics of adult learners. In an industrial setting, an adult learner is an individual "employed by an organization, at any level, engaged in any type of learning activity within that organization [1]." This paper reports the development efforts of a computer-based Commercial Driver's License Tutorial in addressing adult training issues.

1.1 Adult learners vs Traditional learners

Several elements distinguish adult learners from traditional learners. Adult learners, for example, are selective in their learning, and often need to feel a direct need to learn what is being taught [2]. Additionally adult learners need more control over their own learning [3]. This can be partially attributed to the fact that adult learners have been out of the school setting longer than younger learners and may fear failing in the learning process. Finally, adult learners generally take longer to process information, and require more active participation than their younger counterparts [4].

1.2 Computer-Based Training

Advances in programmed instruction and the development of newer computer systems has enabled computer-based training (CBT) to be considered as a viable addition to training programs. Training effectiveness, performance standardization across learners, and standardization of instructional content and delivery are only a few reasons for employing CBT. In an industrial setting, cost and time saving, ease of modification and ease of distribution are additional advantages [5]. The increasing availability of multimedia resources provides a wonderful opportunity to expand the use of CBT in industrial settings. In this paper, an example is presented which demonstrates how computer-based training addresses many of the adult learner issues.

2. The Commercial Driver's License Training Software

The Commercial Driver's License Training (CDLT) software was developed for a major corporation. This tool is intended to be an instructional aid in the training of drivers for the commercial driver's license.

This software assumes limited familiarity with the mouse and the windows operating environment. Since the interactive nature of the software underlies most of its benefits, it was essential that the interface used acts as a guide rather than a barrier. For this reason, a "Navigation Tutorial" has been included for those individuals with limited computer exposure. This tutorial is divided into two parts: a general section on how to maneuver using the mouse; and a more detailed, software-specific section. The later section is presented as a brief simulation in order to familiarize the user with the specific components of the software.

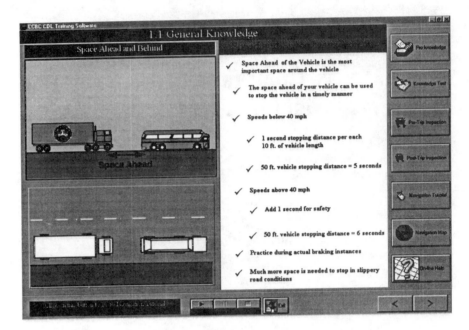

Figure 1. A typical information screen

2.1 Interface Design Issues

The development of the training program followed the classic training program development methodology [6]. The cycle of design, test, measure and redesign was repeated several times in the development process. Special attention was given throughout the development of this software to ensure that the deadly temptation of creeping featurism was avoided [7]. For this product to be useful as a training aid, it was essential that overly complex, features be avoided so that users would not be easily distracted from learning.

Many of the recommendations applicable to design of interfaces for CBT were taken into consideration in the development of this product [8]. The typical information presenting screen in this software is divided into three main areas, and combines audio, pictorial and text based information (Figure 1). The primary information appears in bullet form on the right half of the screen. As each bullet appears on the screen, it is accompanied by a more descriptive audio comment. A pictorial representation of the primary information is shown in the panel on the top left side of the screen. This picture is updated as each bullet appears. A panel at the lower left side of the screen provides supporting information which will help the user understand the material better. This information is either in the form of pictures or text.

Audio controls are located in the bottom center of each screen. The user can utilize these controls to pause, stop and play the audio. The update of text and pictures on the screen will also stop when the pause or stop button is clicked. Clicking on the arrow button enables the user to progress to the next screen.

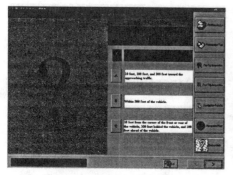

Figure 2. Typical Test Screen

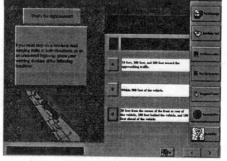

Figure 3. Answer Screen

2.2 Training Approach

The goal of any training program should be to impact the performance level of the individuals being trained. To ensure an impact on performance level, the basic knowledge, skills and abilities required for the task were addressed. In this effort, two main sources were used: the CDL Manual distributed by the state highway department, and the human resource manager of the sponsor company. The first provided exhaustive documentation of all knowledge, skills, and abilities, while the later was able to provide insight of the unique requirements of the company demanding additional attention.

Each topic of the CDL Training module is followed by some multiple choice review questions on the material just covered (Figure 2). The user's response is evaluated by the program itself and feedback is provided immediately. If the answer chosen is incorrect, a message appears indicating the same. The user can make another choice. When the correct answer is chosen, a label appears on the left side of the screen indicating why that answer is correct. The label may be in the form of text or an image (Figure 3). These embedded questions serve two purposes: first, to see if they user has understood the material presented; and secondly they help reinforce the material just covered.

A user has the option of going through all of the topics covered in a single session or during multiple sessions. This software will help the user trace the path taken by maintaining a record of the topics already covered. The order in which the topics are covered can be determined by the user.

3. Conclusions

The purpose of this effort was to develop a CBT program which can be effectively used by adults. In doing so, several adult learning issues were addressed. The Commercial Driver's License Tutorial serves as an example of how CBT addresses many of these issues in an industrial environment. The interactive nature of this product underlies most of its benefits. First, the user must interact with the tutorial in order to continue, therefore emphasizing the active mode of learning. The tutorial also minimizes resources without endangering training outcomes. From the organizational perspective, this efficiency should in the long-run translate to cost-savings (i.e. increasing student throughput). Additionally, computer-based training provides consistency. This is contrasted by traditional courses whose outcomes may be different based on modifications made by the instructor. Finally, such a device increases the control of the user: each person is able to work at their own pace as well as control the order in which they learn each module. The results of usability tests and knowledge tests will be reported as part of a larger paper.

4. Aknowledgements

We would like to thank the Department of Industrial Engineering, Clemson University for the use of their facilities in conducting this research. We would also like to acknowledge the support of Daniel Jebaraj, Davis Jebaraj, Scott Koenig, Lee Nichols, Dan Stanton and Sri Soundararajan. This research was funded from a grant from Coca Cola Bottling Consolidated to Dr. Anand Gramopadhye.

5. References

[1] Fisher, Sheldon. The adult learner. In: William R Tracey (Ed.), Human resources management and development handbook. New York: American Management Association (1985) pp. 1395-1403.

[2] Knowles, Malcom S. Adult learning. In: Robert L. Craig (Ed.) Training and development handbook. New York: McGraw-Hill (1987) pp. 168-179.

[3] Knowles, 1987.

[4] Sterns, H., and Doverspike, D. Training and developing the older worker: Implications for human resource management. In: H. Dennis (Ed.), Fourteen steps to managing an aging workforce. New York: Lexington (1988) pp. 97-110.

[5] Babbit, B., Pieper, W., Semple C., and Swanson, D. Effectiveness and efficiency of computer-based training: Recent research findings. Proc. Human Factors Society—29th Annual Meeting, (1985) pp. 198-201.

[6] Gramopadhye, A. K., Drury, C.G., Prabhu, P. Training Strategies for Visual Inspection (To appear in the International Journal of Human Factors in Manufacturing). (1997)

[7] Norman, Donald A. The Design of Everyday Things. New York: Doubleday (1988) pp. 172-174.

[8] Chabay, R.W., and Sherwood, B.A. A practical guide for the creation of educational software. In: J.H. Larkin and R.W. Chabay (Eds.), Computer-assisted instruction and intelligent tutoring systems: Shared goals and complementary approaches. Hillsdale, N.J.: Erlbaum. (1992) pp. 151-186.

6. Biographies

Maria Demetriou holds an International Master of Business Administration (IMBA) degree from the University of South Carolina with a concentration in Human Resources. She is currently pursuing her Ph.D. in the Department of Industrial Engineering, Clemson University and has special interest in training.

Hector Him received an M.S. in Industrial and System Engineering from University of Florida, and B.S. in Electromechanical Engineering from La Universidad Tecnologica de Panama, and has special interest in computer applications in industry. He is currently pursuing his Ph.D. in Industrial Engineering.

Dr. Anand Gramopadhye is Assistant Professor of Industrial Engineering at Clemson University. His research interests are focused in modeling humans in quality and process control systems, human factors in manufacturing and training.

Dr. Delbert Kimbler is Professor and Chair of the Department of Industrial Engineering, Clemson University. His research interests are focused in quality engineering, distance learning, and computer applications for the internet.

Advances in Occupational Ergonomics and Safety II
Edited by Biman Das and Waldemar Karwowski
IOS Press and Ohmsha, 1997

Harnessing the Power of Virtual Reality
for Ergonomics Education

Edward L. Harden, Lesia L. Crumpton, Ph.D., and Brian K. Smith
Department of Industrial Engineering
P.O. Drawer 9542
Mississippi State University
Mississippi State, MS 39762
(601) 325-8952 office
(601) 325-7618 facsimile
elh2@ra.msstate.edu
crumpton@engr.msstate.edu
bks5@ra.msstate.edu

Abstract. As an instruction tool, Virtual Reality (VR) can be used to present
ergonomic concepts and demonstrate ergonomic analysis techniques. As an
evaluation tool VR can be used to access students' mastery of ergonomic
concepts and their ability to identify ergonomic problems within virtual
environments. Also, the use of this technology will enable instructors to present
ergonomic concepts within the physical context that they appear. Thus, students
should obtain a more comprehensive understanding of relevant ergonomic
issues. This paper explores the possibilities of using VR as an instruction and
evaluation tool within an Ergonomics curriculum. Results from this research
study were used to quantify benefits attributed to incorporating Virtual Reality in
the classroom. Also, improvements on the overall quality of classroom
instruction were assessed.

1.0 INTRODUCTION

Virtual Reality (VR) technology is continuing to capture the attention of computer
users worldwide. VR applications include scientific visualization, model prototyping,
industrial design, manufacturing, marketing, telerobotics, telecommunications, training,
and education. In fields as diverse as engineering, medicine, and architecture, Virtual
Reality is making inroads into the way problems are presented, understood, and solved.

Although significant technological contributions in the area of Virtual Reality have
been developed at research institutions, VR is in its infancy stage as a tool for educating
students. In fact, recently, companies have been using VR in an educational capacity as a
training tool for their employees. For example, Motorola found VR to be a very promising
tool for training their employees to operate robotics assembly lines.
Results from their study indicate that "virtually" trained employees performed as well as
or better than those trained on the actual machinery. For Motorola, the use of VR has
made it possible for employees to receive "hands on" training while greatly reducing the

costs of training due to the elimination of the physical training machinery [1].

Many of the features which make VR a desirable tool for training also contribute to it's attractiveness as an tool for use in higher education, especially within athe technical disciplines. The ability to rapidly prototype, and incorporate aspects of simulation are especially useful in these areas. Also, VR's ability to represent three-dimensional objects and spaces makes it an excellent tool for the development and validation of designs. Furthermore, features such as visualization and maneuverability, make this an excellent medium for presenting information in ways which are impossible in the physical realm. According to Dede, Salzman, and Loftin state, "through using multisensory immersion in virtual realities customized for education, we believe that complex, abstract material now considered to difficult for many students—and taught even to advanced learners only at the college level—could be mastered by most students in middle school and high school,"[2].

2.0 WHY USE VR IN ERGONOMICS CURRICULUM?

Many of the concepts put forth within the Ergonomics curriculum naturally lend themselves to representation within the virtual medium. This is because successful comprehension of these concepts is heavily dependent on the ability to visualize them. Students should benefit from concepts such as proper workstation design, workspace layout, noise level, and illumination being presented in a manner more indicative of their real world counterparts. In addition to enhancing the presentation of these concepts, VR should also prove useful when evaluating student comprehension of ergonomic concepts, principles, and practices. Thus, it is the purpose of the study to explore the proficiency of Virtual Reality as a tool for instruction and ergonomic evaluation.

To meet the goals of this project, two independent studies were conducted. The first study focused accessing the use of VR as an evaluation tool, while the second focused on measuring the use of VR as a classroom instruction tool.

3.0 STUDY 1: VIRTUAL REALITY AS AN EVALUATION TOOL

In this study, ten undergraduate students enrolled in the Ergonomics class were chosen to participate. Students had previously received classroom instruction on the topics of work area and workstation design. A computer generated virtual packing task was developed to allow students to perform an ergonomic evaluation of the work environment. In this virtual environment cereal boxes proceeded down the conveyor and were grabbed by the operator and placed into a larger packing box. Within this environment, there were a number of areas that did not conform to proper workstation and work area design guidelines. Thus, the goal for students was to play the part of an Ergonomist – to explore the environment and identify the areas of improper work area and workstation design. There were two main modules for this experiment. In the first module, while exploring the environment, students were asked to list areas where the environment conformed and failed to conform to ergonomic principles of a safe work area. This module of the study was performed to identify whether or not students could go into an environment and perform the job of an ergonomist. In the second module of this study, students were asked to answer questions concerning specific ergonomic problems within the environment. The purpose of the second module of the study was to identify if the students were aware of the relevant ergonomic concepts. Finally, students were asked to complete a subjective questionnaire rating their virtual experience.

3.1 Results

During data collection, student performance was evaluated based on the percentage of areas correctly identified as conforming and those nonconforming to ergonomic design principles. Six major areas of nonconformity, and one area of conformity, were to be identified, some of which included: incorrect workstation height, inadequate knee clearance, and lack of adjustability. On average participants correctly identified 18.6% , or less than one out of seven, of the areas of concern.

During data collection methods in the second module of this study, students were asked to respond to specific questions about each of the areas of concern identified in the first module of the study. The questions were similar to the following: "Is the workstation height correct?" On average, for the second module of the experiment, participants correctly identified the problems (or lack of problems) in 54.3 % , or almost four out of seven, of the areas of concern. The analysis of variance of all scores reveals that students showed significant improvement in identifying ergonomic problem areas of the environment when asked specifically about possible problem areas. These results would seem to indicate that although the students have some understanding of the relevant ergonomic guidelines, they are less able to apply them without being given a leading question.

4.0 VIRTUAL REALITY AS AN INSTRUCTIONAL TOOL

In this portion of the research, a virtual environment was used to illustrate concepts of using the NIOSH lifting guideline. A comparison was made between the resulting performance of students taught using traditional methods (including handouts, overhead projector slides, and a chalkboard) and students instructed through the use of VR. A virtual representation was created based a sample lifting task. The twenty-two students of the Ergonomics class were divided into two groups, with one group receiving instruction in a virtual setting, and the other in the traditional setting. Using similar case study scenarios, both groups were exposed to instruction for approximately thirty minutes. For the VR group, the virtual environment was projected using a multi-media data projection system. While the professor lectured, an assistant followed along guiding the group through the virtual lifting task. Following each lecture session, students were asked to evaluate an actual lifting task performed in the laboratory. While an operator performed the lifting task, participants measured and calculated the values for each of the NIOSH equations. While the participants were performing the task, observers recorded information on the types of errors made. After completing the evaluation, participants completed a questionnaire which asked them to subjectively rate their opinion of the training technique by identifying areas of difficulty with the guideline, rating their perceived understanding of each of the multipliers, and rating the effectiveness of their respective teaching methods.

4.1 Results

Data collected from the evaluation, was divided into two major categories, the measurement of relevant factors of the lifting task, and the calculation of each multiplier. Within each of these categories, information for each of NIOSH's multipliers was recorded at the origin of the lift, and at the destination. Correctly measured or calculated values were given value of 1, while incorrect values were given a value of 0. Overall, for multipliers in both categories, VR instructed students were 79.8% accurate in using the NIOSH guideline, compared to 56.4% for students instructed with traditional methods. An analysis of variance indicates that at the 0.05 alpha level of significance, this difference is statistically significant.

Analysis of this data reveals a number of unique distinctions between the two groups. The VR instructed students displayed errors which where more similar in nature than the traditional group. For example, for the VR group, all errors in calculating the horizontal multiplier were a result of starting or ending the measurement from the wrong horizontal point. For the traditional group errors included these and also measuring diagonal distances. Another distinction between the two groups is revealed in comparing average performance data of the multipliers to the average perceived comprehension values. For four of the multipliers, the group trained using VR, on average, perceived that they had a greater understanding of how to take these measurements than the traditional group. Based on the mean accuracy of performance, the VR group averaged higher performance than did the traditional group.

5.0 DISCUSSION

The results from these two studies indicate that Virtual Reality is a viable tool to enhance the quality of Ergonomics education. Because much of Ergonomics deals with the design and layout of environments, VR seems ideal for prototyping possible design solutions in representative settings generated by computer environments. As an instruction tool, VR has the potential to present concepts in a manner which is more realistic and representative of actual work scenarios than present instructional methods. As an evaluation tool, Virtual Reality offers instructors the opportunity to test student's ability to apply concepts discussed in the classroom. Accurate ergonomic evaluation is possible because VR offers the ability to represent settings which are as complex and diverse as those in the real world. Thus the student has at their fingertips the potential to tap an endless resource for training and experience.

REFERENCES

[1] N. Adams, Lessons from the Virtual World, *Training* June (1995), 45-48.

[2] C. Dede, M. Salzman, and R. Loftin, ScienceSpace: Virtual Realities for Learning Complex and Abstract Scientific Concepts, Proceedings of VRAIS '96. ISBN: 0-8186-7295-1, IEEE Computer Society Press, Los Alamitos, (1996).

5. Ergonomics Analysis and Design

Advances in Occupational Ergonomics and Safety II
Edited by Biman Das and Waldemar Karwowski
IOS Press and Ohmsha, 1997

OUTBREAKS OF HUMAN FACTORS/ERGONOMICS (HF/E) PROBLEMS: DÉJÀ VU ALL OVER AGAIN

Alvah C. Bittner Jr.
Battelle ASE & HFTC
Seattle, WA 98105

Stephen J. Morrissey
State of Oregon, OSHA
Portland, OR 97219

Allen T. Bramwell
The Bramwell Group
American Fork, UT 84003

Frank J. Winn Jr.
East Carolina University
Greenville, NC 27858

ABSTRACT
Outbreaks of poor human factors/ergonomics (HF/E) design and practice are discussed with respect to their causes and avoidance. HF/E outbreaks are suggested to be traceable to one or more of the following: 1) misreliance of designers and developers on intuitively appealing algorithms for design and development; 2) ignoring lessons-learned when hardware technology is rapid, and 3) the rapid growth and diversification of the HF/E profession. We propose three recommendations for preventing future outbreaks.

1. INTRODUCTION

Outbreaks of poor human factors/ergonomics (HF/E) design and practice often occur that parallel those seen years or decades earlier. These repeated occurrences, and associated feelings of having repeatedly been there before, have been informally characterized as *déjà vu all over again*. Diverse examples of these HF/E failures that range from the micro to macro include:

- *Computer key-board related repetitive-strain injuries (RSI) outbreak during the last decade* -- the same types of problems were largely understood and addressed with respect to adjustment of the computer workplace and keyboards by HF/E practitioners more almost 20 years ago (e.g., Miller and Suther, 1981). Cameron and Moroney (1994), in the context of keyboard musical instruments, point to analogous problems and solutions that reach back to the turn of this century.
- *Devolving performance of tools and systems with increasing options* -- the time to prepare basic documentation using later-generations of word processing tools, for example, has been seen to increase because of the increased requirements for key and mouse strokes to (de)select from among increasing numbers of options. Similar performance devolvements were seen three decades ago when subjective user information was also used to determine features (versus objective performance assessments).
- *Clumsy systems automation* -- systems continue to be designed that reduce operator workload (OWL) during low-workload periods (when not needed), but greatly

increase OWL during problematical or emergency conditions (when needed). This paradoxical misdesign was recognized more that a decade ago, in the context of nuclear power plants (NPPs) and in aviation, but occurrences continue despite clear warnings and design guidance being given.

These, and a diversity of other cycles of outbreaks prompted a search for (1) patterns in the HF/E outbreaks and (2) potential interventions to avoid future outbreaks. The following sections delineate (1) our method and findings regarding the patterns of cyclic outbreaks and (2) discuss potential interventions to avoid the future occurrence of HF/E outbreaks.

2. METHOD AND RESULTS

An evaluation was conducted of more than three-dozen critical incidents involving HF/E that appeared to represent repeated outbreaks of the same conceptual type. Successively condensing HF/E outbreaks with similar etiologies (causal factors), we ultimately identified three basic patterns: 1) misreliance of designers and developers on intuitively appealing algorithms for design and development; 2) ignoring lessons-learned when changes in technology are rapid, and 3) the rapid growth and diversification of the HF/E profession. These are discussed in subsequent sections.

2.1. MISRELIANCE ON INTUITIVE ALGORITHMS

Designers frequently employ intuitively-appealing design algorithms and simplification strategies to expedite or simplify their design process. Reflecting a kind of *bounded rationality* as identified in other decision making situations (Simon, 1959, p. 273ff; Slovic, Lichtenstein & Fischhoff, 1988, 716ff) such algorithms and strategies are employed by the designer to overcome his/her cognitive, resource, and experience limitations by construction of simplified models of problems. Difficulties can then arise when simplified models collide against real world requirements.

One problematic, intuitive approach we often observed was for designers to progressively work toward a design (e.g., equipment, system, or facility) that would be optimal if they, the designer(s), were to *personally use it.* The advantage of this approach, of course, is that the designer minimizes the need for obtaining information regarding other potential users -- all information lies within the designer as user.   Of course, the disadvantage of the approach is that only the designer, or those sufficiently close in critical details, are adequately accommodated.

Devolving of computer-based tools and systems, as mentioned above, appears to be largely the result of misreliance of on intuitively appealing design approaches. In part, this appears to be due to the reemergence of the above discussed designer-centered approach. This more often appears to be due to another plague of *over-reliance on user subjective data* similar to that seen three decades ago (i.e., failures to consider performance).

2.2 IGNORING LESSONS-LEARNED

The degree that lessons-learned are ignored appears directly related to the speed that technology and products are changing. Based on considerations of ignored lessons-learned and rapid and emerging technology/product changes, there are several plausible explanations of why this is the case:

- *New technology product developers and distributors are increasingly disinterested in the details of lessons-learned with preceding technology as the rate of change increases.*
- *Technology developers and distributors increasingly fail to see the relationship between their developments and previous developments in other domains with increasing technology change.*

Interestingly, these explanations could be taken to suggest that technology developers are increasingly overloaded as the pace of change is increasing. Hence, designers increasingly appear to adopt a *shedding strategy* (Lysaght et al., 1989), i.e., "ignore all that is not immediately expediting the design process." This shedding strategy consequently attempts, in a less functional way, to address the same information processing overload as the earlier discussed use of *bounded rationality* (where the designer employs simplified models to address design problems).

2.3 RAPID GROWTH AND DIVERSIFICATION OF HF/E

The rapid growth and diversification of the HF/E has led to an influx of younger professionals with increasingly narrow focuses and often few analytical tools or skills that are not aimed at their narrow focus (Bittner, 1994). Too often, these younger professionals also appear largely ignorant of the problems delineated above as well as of the nature and scope of the HF/E profession.   Perhaps, these younger professionals are experiencing technological growth problems similar to those facing developers of rapidly changing technology, but this ignorance also points to basic problems in *how and what we train*. Unfortunately, this may also reflect on the ignorance of their academic mentors for why else would they not provided at least a sensitization to such issues?

3. PREVENTING HF/E PROBLEM OUTBREAKS

The first step in preventing outbreaks of poor HF/E design and practice would be to understand their origins or causes. Towards this end, we have identified three sources for these causes. However, we believe that further efforts will be necessary, as our understanding of the causes of HF/E outbreaks is almost certainly incomplete (as etiological understanding is an emerging process). Likewise, we believe that focused efforts will be required to promote emerging understandings of outbreak origins and causes. Our first step toward understanding outbreak etiology hopefully will open discussions and efforts toward understanding the causes of the outbreaks of poor HF/E design and practice.

The second step in preventing outbreaks is to break the cycle of their causes. This would appear to require a three part effort:

- *Sensitizing HF/E practitioners and educators regarding the etiology of outbreaks of poor HF/E design and practices* -- this might serve to partially prevent their occurrence or at least permit recognition of such outbreaks as they are occurring.
- *Educating HF/E practitioners and educators regarding formal means to avoid or ameliorate the causes of HF/E outbreaks* -- there are a number of often simple methods and approaches to address the various types of outbreaks (e.g., evaluating performance as well as subjective responses). Educating HF/E practitioners regarding such simple methods could begin the process of education regarding means to avoid or ameliorate the causes of outbreaks of poor HF/E design and practice.

- *Encouraging educators and students to explore, and be functionally aware of the breadth of the HF/E profession, its methodologies and histories.*

Breaking the cycle outbreaks of poor HF/E design and practice will take some effort, but the steps appear clear, and means for accomplishing these within possibility.

4. ACKNOWLEDGMENTS

The authors would like to acknowledge David Meister who made the original comment about "having seen this before" with respect to HF/E problems that became the initiative for the efforts that lead to this report.

5. REFERENCES

Bittner, A.C., Jr. (1994). Future of HF T&E [Human Factors Testing & Evaluation]. *Proceedings of the Human Factors and Ergonomics Society 38th Annual Meeting* (pp. 1077-1078). Santa Monica CA: Human Factors and Ergonomics Society.

Cameron, J.A. & Moroney, W.F. (1994). A systems approach to computer keyboard usage for continuous text transcription. In: F. Agazadeh (ed.), *Advances in industrial Ergonomics and Safety IV* (pp. 467-474).

Lysaght, R.J., Hill, S.G., Dick, A.O., Plamondon, B.D., Linton, P.M., Wierwille, W.W., Zaklad, A.L., Bittner, A.C., Jr. & Wherry, R.J. (1989). *Operator workload (OWL) assessment program for the Army: Comprehensive review and evaluation of operator workload methodologies* (ARI Technical Report 851). Alexandria, VA: U.S. Army Research Institute. (NTIS AD A212 879)

Miller, I., and T.W. Suther, III (1981). Preferred height and angle settings of crt and keyboard for a display station input task. *Proceedings of the Human Factors Society-25th Annual Meeting, 492-496.*

Simon, H.A. (1959). Theories of decision making in economics and behavioral science. *American Economic Review, 49,* 253-283.

Slovic, P., Lichtenstein, S. & Fischhoff, B. (1988). Decision Making. In: *Steven's Handbook of Experimental Psychology* (Vol.2, pp. 673-738). New York, NY: Wiley & Sons.

Advances in Occupational Ergonomics and Safety II
Edited by Biman Das and Waldemar Karwowski
IOS Press and Ohmsha, 1997

BRAIN IMAGING AND HUMAN PERFORMANCE: FATIGUE AND OCCUPATIONAL EXPOSURE APPLICATIONS

R.K. Mahurin[1,3], A.C. Bittner[1,2], and N.J. Heyer[2]
[1]*Battelle Seattle Research Center*
4000 N.E. 41st Street, Seattle, WA 98015, USA
[2]*University of Washington, Department of Environmental Health*
[3]*University of Washington, Department of Psychiatry*

ABSTRACT

Recent advances in brain imaging and computational modeling provide powerful new techniques for human factors/ergonomics (HF/E) investigations. Noninvasive measurement of brain activity in normal subjects can be obtained during the performance of specific cognitive tasks measuring memory, attention, language, skilled movement, and perception. Meta-analysis of brain imaging studies has yielded associations between regional brain activity and performance of specific cognitive activities and psychological states. Taken together, integrated maps of mental function (*cognitive space*) and regional cerebral metabolism (*brain space*) can be used to attack specific ergonomics and safety problems. Using brain imaging and performance data, we have begun to establish a pattern of resting-state networks in brain activity. These patterns are associated with specific cognitive capabilities and reflect sleep loss, fatigue, and the influence of environmental variables.

1. Introduction

Transient sleep loss has been shown to produce reliable decrements in human performance. These include short-term memory loss, decreased vigilance, diminished attention, impairments in reasoning ability, and decrements in choice reaction time and complex motor skills. Affective (mood) changes include increased irritability, depression, frustration and discouragement, together with decreased motivation and lessened interest in the environment [1,2].

These effects on mood and cognition suggest involvement of specific brain regions. However, few neuroimaging studies have been conducted directly examining this relationship. One previous study, however, did compare brain activity before and after sleep deprivation [3]. Findings included a small overall reduction in brain activity (glucose metabolic rate). However, significant regional reductions were noted in frontal regions of the brain relative to more posterior regions. Poor performance on a concurrently administered continuous attention task also was significantly correlated with reductions in frontal brain activity.

The present study examines the relationship between resting-state brain imaging (positron emission tomography (PET) of regional blood flow (rCBF), transient sleep loss, emotional state, and cognitive performance in normal subjects. We hypothesized there would be significant associations between self-reported sleep loss, attention and memory abilities, and regions of the brain know to subserve these functions. This study illustrates the potential of brain imaging for future studies of sleep loss, as well as circadian rhythms, fatigue, and other HF/E applications as discussed in the Conclusions.

2. Methods

Subjects, imaging techniques, cognitive testing and sleep values are described in the following sections[1].

2.1 Subjects. Subjects consisted of 19 healthy volunteers, 20 to 55 years of age. 15 subjects were male, 4 were female. All subjects were free from history or presence of neurologic or psychiatric disease.

2.2 Imaging Technique. PET scans using an ^{15}O tracer were acquired over a 40-second acquisition period, with values averaged over three repeated scans. Subjects were instructed to lie in the scanner with their eyes closed, and remain in a resting state throughout. Blood flow values were normalized to right and left hemisphere global mean values. Centers of regions of interest (ROIs) were translated to a standard three-dimensional coordinate space [4] for cross-group averaging. 31 ROIs were examined for the right and left hemispheres, with standard levels of statistical significance ($p < .05$) adjusted for multiple comparisons.

2.3 Cognitive Testing. Cognitive and mood testing was performed prior to the PET scans. All subjects were assessed with the *NeuroCog Assessment Battery*. *NeuroCog* is a computer-administered test battery that provides a comprehensive assessment of a subject's health, psychological state and cognitive abilities. The full battery of scales and tests requires one hour for completion. Output from *NeuroCog* consists of raw and normative scores from all tests, including *health history, self-report scales, motor and psychomotor speed, decision speed, attention, visual perception, verbal memory, visual memory, vocabulary*, and *reasoning*. Additional indices are calculated for factor-derived clusters assessing *Initiation, Inhibition, Laterality, Information Processing Speed, Motor Consistency*, and *Validity of Performance*.

2.4 Sleep Values. Self-reported sleep values were collected via analog scales in *NeuroCog*. Subjects were asked questions regarding the number of hours they "typically" slept (ST) and the number of hours they had slept "last night" (SLN). Sleep change (ΔS) was calculated by subtracting the typical hours of sleep minus the hours of sleep the night before (i.e., ST-SLN). Thus, a negative ΔS reflects transient sleep loss on the night before the scan.

3. Results

Specific *NeuroCog* tests selected for attention, memory and reaction time were correlated with activity of *a priori* identified brain regions. Additional correlations were

---

[1] The following method and results were previously presented at the Society for Neuroscience Annual Meeting in Washington D.C., November, 1996 -- Mahurin, R.K., Liotti, M., Mayberg, H.S., Zamarripa, F., McGinnis, S.M., & Fox, P. *A positron emission tomography study of transient sleep reduction, limbic activity and attentional control.*

conducted between ΔS and these pre-defined regions of brain activity. This analysis revealed significant *positive* correlations between reduced sleep and rCBF in paralimbic cortical and limbic subcortical regions, including brainstem, mesial-temporal, and frontal areas. Significant *negative* correlations were found between sleep reduction and rCBF in neocortical regions, including cingulate, parietal, occipital, and superior temporal (Table 1).

Increase	*Decrease*
Supplementary Motor Area (BA 6)	Occipital (BA 19)
Hippocampal region (BA 28/35/56)	Cingulate (BA 23/31)
Superior Cerebellum	
Medial Thalamus	
Midbrain	

Increase	*Decrease*
Anxiety	Attention & Continuous Performance
Depression	Verbal & Visual Recall
Irritability	Simple & Choice Reaction Time

Table 1. Summary of the effects of sleep loss on specific brain regions, cognition and emotional regulation.

Sleep reduction was significantly associated with negative scores on several *NeuroCog* mood scales, including depression, anxiety, and irritability. Sleep reduction also was significantly associated with increased false alarms on the *NeuroCog* continuous response attentional test, and approached significance for verbal short-term memory and reaction time tests (Figure 1).

Normal Condition: Cortex inhibits subcortical regions

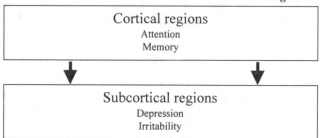

Sleep Loss Condition: Cortex loses ability to inhibit subcortical regions

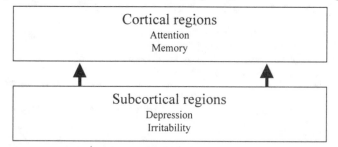

Figure 1. Brain and behavioral interactions for normal and abnormal sleep conditions.

4. Conclusions

4.1 Summary. The current data indicate that transient sleep loss is associated with relative *increases* in resting-state subcortical-limbic brain activity, *decreases* in resting-state neocortical activity, release of dysphoric emotions, and impaired response control. The pattern of changes in brain functioning and cognitive performance suggests that sleep loss depresses cortical mechanisms that normally control attention and information processing. Such changes will also serve to reduce the capacity of the cortex to inhibit emotional reactivity of lower brain centers. These changes have detrimental effects on human performance, and can affect safety and efficiency in moderate to high demand workplace settings.

4.2 Future Directions. Brain imaging can offer new insights into the effects of environmental insults to the central nervous system and occupational performance. It is assumed, and the earlier sleep data indicate, that decreases in cognitive performance have direct correlates with the integrity of underlying brain mechanisms. Based on previous drug studies, it is anticipated that noninvasive brain imaging will provide a means of assessing effects of heavy metals, pesticides, and solvents. The level of toxic exposure required for detectable influence remains to be established for each toxic substance and concentration. However, network modeling of brain systems already has been used to generate hypotheses on the cognitive effects of neurotrauma and low-level environmental exposure [5].

Brain imaging techniques appear ready to be successfully applied to HF/E and safety problems. With continued decreases in brain imaging costs, this feasibility will increasingly make possible systematic studies of work-related changes in performance. With integration of disciplines, results from experimental imaging studies can be applied to the human performance occupational domain. This particularly is true for assessment of the capability of an individual to rapidly and appropriately respond to emergency and other non-routine or unexpected events. Direct use of brain imaging also has the potential of being an effective tool for evaluating effects of, and recovery from, work-related medical insults such as traumatic brain injury. However, some questions of sensitivity, specificity, and generalizability must be considered before the techniques of brain imaging can be applied with full confidence to the variety of human safety problems. The full extent that relative changes in brain function are associated with changes in performance and behavioral potential remains to be established in future investigations.

References

[1] M. Bonnet *et al.*, Sleep Deprivation. In: M. Kryger, T. Roth & W. Dement. (eds.), Principles and Practice of Sleep Medicine, 2nd ed., Saunders, Philadelphia, 1991.
[2] J. Freidmann, *et al.*, Performance and Mood During and After Gradual Sleep Reduction, *Psychophysiology* 14 (1977) 245-250.
[3] J. Wu *et al.*, The Effect of Sleep Deprivation on Cerebral Glucose Metabolic Rate in Normal Humans Assessed with Positron Emission Tomography, *Sleep* 14 (1991) 155-162.
[4] J. Talairach, & P. Tournoux, Co-planar Stereotaxic Atlas of the Human Brain. Georg Thiem Verlag, New York, 1987.
[5] R. Mahurin *et al.*, Object-Oriented Modeling of Neurocognitive Subsystems: A Reformulation of Test-Based Reasoning. Proceedings of the 163rd Annual Meeting of the American Association of the Advancement of Science (1997) A-93.

Advances in Occupational Ergonomics and Safety II
Edited by Biman Das and Waldemar Karwowski
IOS Press and Ohmsha, 1997

A Study of Ergonomic Design Knowledge Required in Industrial Product Design Curriculum

Feng-Huo Sheu
Department of Industrial Design
National Yunlin Institute of Technology
Touliu, Yunlin, Taiwan 640

Abstract

In order to meet the social and environmental changes, the academic and professional world as well as governmental officials have put many efforts in the promotion of industrial design education in Taiwan. This study conducted an investigation of ergonomics related knowledge required in product design. Methodologically, this study adopted in-depth interview, content analysis, panel discussion of ergonomics specialists and questionnaire to accomplish the specific objectives of this study. Firstly, it is necessary to identify design tasks required ergonomics design knowledge during product development. Secondly, the study aims at developing knowledge items and their framework according to professional needs. The ultimate goal is to construct an integral body of knowledge to improve the course content for educating future designers who will be able to originate humanized design concept in practice. In reviewing the statistical data, there are four kinds of knowledge ,namely physical, psychological, environmental and cultural, used during product design activities. Most professional designers believe that the ergonomic knowledge items in psychological aspect are quite important. In physical aspect, anthropometry data of civilian population are vital in preliminary design stage. It is also suggested that case study method and hands on experiences are required for teaching and learning of ergonomics knowledge in industrial design education. The research findings provide feasible content changes for ergonomics course required in industrial design.

1. INTRODUCTION

Industrial design education concepts and curricula have undergone little changes since its introduction to Taiwan's higher education system in late fifties. However, the manufacturing industries in Taiwan over the last three decades, have progressed dynamically. In recent years, restructuring has become a necessity in domestic industries due to rapid social changes, fast economic growth and growing competition in the international market. Domestic industries are facing greater challenges than ever before in the export-depended economy. To meet these challenges, governmental efforts are striving to upgrade the quality of industrial product and improve design manpower. In particular, the design education concepts face dramatic impact due to techno-social changes. In order to provide well-qualified designer to industries, it is necessary to have up-dated design education concepts to meet the challenge.

Although ergonomics has received extensive attention in the field of system engineering[1]. It was not until 1984 that the National Science Council of Executive Yuan in Taiwan established an ergonomic group to promote the application of ergonomic concepts to various professions [2]. In 1986, the Ministry of Education (MOE) in Taiwan included ergonomics as a required subject of study in industrial design curriculum[3]. Generally, industrial product designer has been trained in Taiwan at two different levels, namely engineering colleges within university (degree level) and junior colleges (diploma level). Both degree and diploma level are under the auspices of MOE of the Republic of China. Design education under the ROC's construction plan, is one of the most important tasks to implement. The main objective of educating various designers at college level is to meet the growing demand of design manpower for industries and global economic environment. For three decades, anthropometry has been regarded as the primary ergonomic knowledge applicable to industrial design[4]. The restricted application of ergonomics to industrial design course resulted in educating designers who are not fully capable of solving humanistic design problems. The main objective of this study is thus to explore the required ergonomic knowledge suitable for improving design course content in order to produce capable professional designers to meet the demand for domestic R&D requirements in the particular industrial settings in Taiwan.

2. METHODS

2.1 In-depth interview

Thirty professional designers whose working experiences ranged from 5 years to 21 years with a mean of 12.5 years were selected for in-depth interview. The designers were geographically sampled from the northern, central and southern region of Taiwan. The main task of each in-depth interview was to collect information concerning design tasks that required ergonomic design knowledge in every product development process.

2.2 Questionnaire Survey

A questionnaire survey was performed among different practicing product designers. The questionnaire was administered as a tool to collect information regarding the importance of each ergonomic knowledge and it's items. The questions corresponded to three design phases as concluded by in-depth interviews and the knowledge structure as discussed by Spiro [5] were categorized into four aspects. Each question was evaluated according to every respondent's working experiences toward the relative importance of adopting ergonomic knowledge in successfully carrying out design tasks. Relevant knowledge items were rated from "extremely important" to "not important at all". Seventy three professional designers selected from the China Industrial Designers' Association completed the questionnaire. The questionnaire included two parts. The first part included questions in relation to design tasks requiring ergonomic knowledge at three design phases. Questions in second portion were measures of relative importance of knowledge in every one of the knowledge aspects. They included items about "how important each ergonomic knowledge item the subjects felt when completing design tasks". Every question was scaled on a five-interval scale, with 2 ndicating extremely important, 0 indicating no opinion and -2 indicating not important at ll.

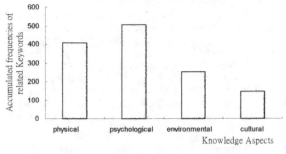

Figure 1. Related Keywords frequencies in knowledge Aspects

TABLE 1. Summary of ANOVA on Design Tasks for each phases

Variable	MS	df	f value
Design Research	57568.49	3	8398.934***
Design Development	79299.12	5	10517.18***
Design Evaluation	87822.24	5	10336.19***

f value for Design Tasks
*** P<0.0001

3. RESULTS AND DISCUSSIONS

All information gathered from professional designers' in-depth interviews were subjected to content analysis. Relevant keywords and phrases in regard to ergonomic concepts were extracted for questionnaire design. Figure 1 shows the accumulated frequencies of related keywords in relation to physical, psychological, environmental and cultural aspects in design phases.

3.1 Design Tasks

Information collected from structured questionnaires, were analyzed and compared. Separate ANOVAs were performed on the degree of importance of three different design phases--design research, design development and design evaluation. The results were summarized in Table 1. As the statistics revealed, tasks required ergonomic knowledge at design research phase are highly significant. The Duncan's multiple range test for tasks showed that knowledge concerning product users' study and operational analysis require more ergonomic knowledge than trend analysis and design motive. During the design development phase, ANOVAs on the importance of ergonomic knowledge on tasks also indicate highly significant. Tasks such as conceptual design, idea development and form development are required more ergonomic knowledge than product dimensioning, and minor operation variations. The knowledge items for modelling tasks are not as important as those of other tasks in design development. The ANOVAs on design tasks at evaluation phase also indicated significant difference. Duncan's test showed that product graphics, detail control design and colour scheme required more ergonomic knowledge than form and functional evaluation as well as alternative evaluations. Among three phases, they required varying level of knowledge for completing those subtasks (f(2,72))=4.45, Pr< 0.003). Duncan's test distinguished the phase of design research and evaluation from that of design development.

3.2 Ergonomic Knowledge required in Product Design

Four ergonomic knowledge categories were identified. They comprised physical, psychological, environmental and cultural aspects. The results of statistical analysis for knowledge of physical aspects show that six knowledge items are highly significant; (f(5,72))=3890.562 Pr<0.0001). Posture studies, functional reach and safety are more important than anthropometric differences, physical capabilities and biomechanics. Results of statistical analysis for psychological aspects also indicated that seven knowledge items are widely applied in product design and they are highly significant (f(6,72)=9958.942 Pr<0.0001). Items such as cognitive processes, gestalt psychology and visual process are identified as the most important items. Aesthetic concepts are more important than auditory and cutaneous processes. The Anova for knowledge items of environmental aspects showed significant differences for the overall processes (f(4,72)=3629.149, Pr<0.0001).The related knowledge units were then grouped into two groups. Considerations of social setting and space configuration are more important than those of sound, noise, temperature and humidity. Anova for required items of cultural aspects also revealed highly significant differences for typical product design process $(f(4,72)=4305.195, Pr<0.0001)$. Duncan's range test grouped the related knowledge items into three categories. Lifestyle study and users behaviour, as well as trait study are more important than other knowledge items. Geological differences are more important than ethnic differences in defining users' valuation. In summary, twenty three knowledge items belong to four ergonomic related knowledge categories were found. Further analysis of variance for professional designers effects on the importance rating of knowledge content were conducted. Results showed that only "working experience" of designers indicated significant differences $(f(4,72)=4.45, Pr<0.0030)$. Inferences of this results typified that opinion of practicing designers toward the varying degree of importance of applying ergonomic knowledge in product design are quite coherent and consistent. Practicing designers educated at different stages of industrial design professional development did reflect differing thoughts on humanizing design concept.

4. CONCLUSION

The major objective of this study was to investigate the ergonomic related knowledge required in the profession of industrial product design . Four knowledge categories had been identified. They were knowledge of physical, psychological, environmental and cultural aspects. Twenty three knowledge items applicable in design and development process were also concluded. Since the subjects had been selected from the China Industrial Designers' Association and practiced different types of product design for at least five years, their insightful opinions on the ergonomic knowledge will hopefully provide a basis for restructuring better ergonomic design course for educating domestic young designers to meet the particular industrial settings in Taiwan.

ACKNOWLEDGMENT

The author would like to express his appreciation and gratitude to the National Science Council of the Republic of Chian for financial support (research project code number: NSC 85-2511-S-224-001). The research assistants of J.C. Chen and K.S. Liu of NYIT are also greatly appreciated.

REFERENCES

[1] Woodson. Wesley E., Human Factors Design Handbook. McGraw-Hill Book Co., New York, 1981,pp.1-17.

[2] Hsu, S.H.,Pen, Y. and Wu, S. P. Ergonomics/Human Factors. ISBN:957-9001-05-06. Yang-Ji Publishing Co., Taipei, 1991, pp.1-16.

[3] Technical and Vocational Educational Department, Ministry of Education, Curricula Structure and Equipment Requirements for the Department of Industrial Design. Cheng-Chong Book Co., Taipei, pp.123-128.

[4] Lee, Y. L. Introduction to Ergonomics. Liu-Hou Publishing Co., Taipei, 1980,pp.5-28.

[5] Spiro, R. J., Coulson, R., Feltovich, P. & Anderson, D., Cognitive Flexibility Theory: Advanced Knowledge Acquisition in ill-structure Domains. Proceeding of the Annual Conference of the Cognitive Science Society, Hillsolate, Lawrence Erlbum, New Jersey, p.375.

Advances in Occupational Ergonomics and Safety II
Edited by Biman Das and Waldemar Karwowski
IOS Press and Ohmsha, 1997

Virtual Reality Based System for Accessibility and Ergonomic Analyses of Floor Assembly Jigs

Venkat N. RAJAN, Jeffrey E. FERNANDEZ, and Kadir SIVASUBRAMANIAN
Department of Industrial and Manufacturing Engineering
Wichita State University
Wichita, Kansas 67260-0035, USA

Abstract. Floor assembly jigs (FAJs) are used to create large subassemblies in the aircraft industry. The design involves tool frame generation and locator and clamp placement to ensure that the assembly components are held properly with respect to each other to meet the required tolerances. The tool designer also has to analyze the design to ensure that the assembly process does not pose interference and accessibility problems. The current approach is dependent on the experience of the tool designer and the limited visualization possible on commercial CAD systems. This leads to extensive redesign when loading/unloading, accessibility, and ergonomic related problems are detected on the physical prototype. In this research, an integrated CAD-based assembly tool design and analysis environment is being developed. A CAD model of the tool design is imported into a Virtual Reality (VR) based visualization system for loading/unloading, accessibility, and ergonomic analyses. The VR system allows combined evaluation of alternate tool designs and assembly sequences. In this paper, an overview of the design and analysis environment is presented.

1. Introduction

Assembly of components is an important and common activity in the manufacture of complex products. The assembly activity in aircraft manufacturing affects to a significant extent the quality, the nature of the end product, and the productivity of the entire process. Manufacturing breaks are used to define parts of aircraft sections like the fuselage, wing sections, upper tail cone, and lower tail cone that are assembled separately and then joined together. Floor assembly jigs (FAJ) are used extensively to manually create these larger subassemblies. These assembly jigs are generally of large dimensions and their designs are complex.

The tool design activity initially involves the generation of the tool frame. This is based on the general requirements of the subassembly to be created. Then locators and clamps are designed to ensure that assembly components are held properly, and assembly processes can be performed. The FAJ should allow orientation, alignment, and joining operations to be performed such that required tolerances are met. Current tool design methods are based on the experience of the designer, coupled with the limited visualization and experiential design capabilities provided by commercial CAD systems.

Problems that arise as a result of deficient or improper design of these assembly tools usually result in expensive redesign efforts. A host of associated problems also arise, including interference, accessibility, and loss of accuracy. Conventional CAD and animation systems usually fail to account for the actual behavioral and geometrical constraints of material, equipment, and people. Interference refers to the unintended obstruction caused by the presence of structural components of tooling in the assembly trajectory of components, subassemblies, and hand tools. Accessibility problems also arise when assembly workers are forced to adopt ergonomically stressful postures when assembling components to the assembly jig. The effects of awkward postures are accompanied and/or aggravated by other risks of injury, including muscular overexertion.

Repetitive strain injuries of the upper limbs and back persist as shown by the high number of reported workplace illnesses and injuries. Research clearly shows a relationship between awkward postures and the risk of injury [1, 2, 3]. Muscle-loading requirements of the forearm flexors have been found to change with posture [4], implying that certain postures are more favorable than others in keeping muscle exertion within safe limits. The automobile industry is leading the effort to take advantage of virtual reality (VR) technology in addressing ergonomic issues [5]. Virtual environments (VE) are now used to evaluate and rectify ergonomics-related problems in manufacturing before the building of physical prototypes.

Systems available today do not allow the designer to concurrently model the assembly task and perform several tool design iterations, based on ergonomic concerns including accessibility, before committing physical resources to the task. Temporal collocation of manufacturing/ assembly related problems and design would help identify problems before erecting expensive equipment or tooling. Therefore, there is a need for a system that is capable of allowing interference and accessibility analysis along with real-time CAD based visualization capabilities.

The objective for this research is to develop a VR based system to enable interactive analysis and evaluation of assembly tooling for interference and ergonomics. This paper describes the overall research framework from which this system has evolved. It also presents an overview of the assembly tool design and analysis environment.

2. Overall Research Effort

The prototype implementation of a system for integrating assembly design, planning, and analysis with ergonomics, using VR as a medium is currently under development. Work done as part of the Product Realization and Intelligent Systems for Manufacture (PRISM) and the Ergonomics groups at WSU forms the basis for this effort. Figure 1 represents this structure.

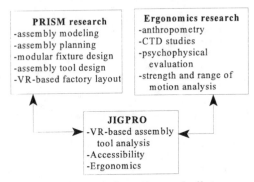

Figure 1. Structure of overall research effort

The PRISM research is integrated with the JIGPRO system in three ways: The assembly modeling research has resulted in the development of assembly representations and constraint propagation and verification methodologies [7]. The prototype assembly modeling system is directly interfaced with the JIGPRO system to provide the assembly model. The modular fixturing research [8] has resulted in the development of methodologies for geometric design and analysis of fixturing setups. These methodologies form the basis for the assembly tool design system that provides feasible jig designs to the JIGPRO environment. Virtual reality has been used to design factory layouts [9]. This knowledge is applied to the assembly tool evaluation process to create the JIGPRO system.

Ergonomics research has been focused in various areas, such as psychophysics, cumulative trauma disorders, and anthropometry evaluation [10]. The effects of various ergonomic risk factors such as force, posture, duration, and repetition on human capacity have been extensively studied. Psychophysical studies have revealed that deviated wrist postures affects maximum acceptable frequency of upper extremity exertions in some aircraft assembly tasks [11]. The JIGPRO system is designed to integrate this knowledge to evaluate the ergonomic aspects of a given FAJ.

3. Methodology and Implementation

Currently available systems allow certain limited analyses of assembly jigs and permit the analysis of simple designs. More attention needs to be given to features that would enable designers to actually mock typical assembly tasks on a given tool, manipulate and 'operate' hand tools as in manual assembly and determine the characteristics of the tooling with regard to interference and ergonomics. For interference analysis, the system derives its behavior from assembly modeling and assembly tool design considerations. In accessibility analysis ergonomic principles are used to determine the appropriateness of postures and work surface heights. Figure 2 shows the architecture of the JIGPRO system.

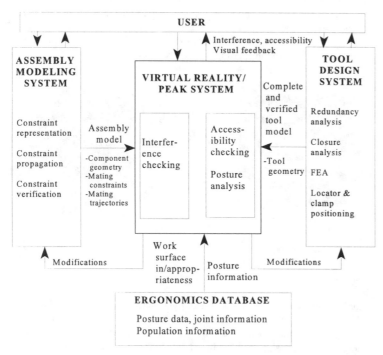

Figure 2.   Architecture of the JIGPRO system

The VE, being the central integrating environment, is interfaced with each of the peripheral systems and serves as the medium by which intelligent human input can be incorporated into the design process. The interface with the tool design system provides a complete and verified tool model. Assembly modeling information is ported to the VE via a file that contains the specification of mating constraints and assembly mating trajectories. This information is used in the VR to warn the user of interference and disallow component placement when these constraints are violated. The ergonomics module contributes posture and anthropometry information. The interface with the ergonomics system enables the user to evaluate the tool from the perspective of work surface heights, upper extremity posture of the user during the assembly task, and work envelopes. The VR system then gives feedback to the various interfacing modules for the modification of the workplace configuration, assembly model, and fixture design.

In the prototype JIGPRO implementation, users can load in a Pro/Engineer CAD model of an assembly tool into the VR implemented using the WorldToolKit VR modeling software. The design can be examined from all directions for a preliminary idea of assembly locations and distances. A component can be loaded into the environment and moved towards its assembly location. Once the object is in a predetermined region near the point of assembly, it automatically moves along the fine motion trajectory and reaches its mating location.

The motion of a user's hand during the assembly of a component is captured by the system as a series of points in 3D space. The overall assembly motion trajectory can be divided into two parts. The gross motion trajectory is generated by the user in the VE. It represents the gross movement of the user's hand when transferring a component from the bin to its general location on the assembly tool. The fine motion trajectory information is obtained from the assembly model and serves to automatically locate the component in its final position. It requires the user's hand to bring the component only along a certain predetermined path, and helps overcome the fine placement limitations of VR systems. A Bezier curve is fitted to the gross trajectory points to generate a smooth assembly trajectory as shown in Figure 3. This path can be saved for further analysis. Such a saved path can be played back and the user's hand constrained to follow this predefined trajectory towards the mating location of a given component as shown in Figure 4. The arm and hand motions of the user during virtual assembly are videotaped. This sequence is analyzed for angles between body segments and hence the upper extremity postures of the user, on the Peak motion measurement system. The output of this analysis serves as feedback to indicate areas of improvement in the ergonomics of the assembly process.

Figure 3. Assembly trajectory generation   Figure 4. Using a predefined trajectory

4. Concluding Remarks

A virtual reality based system for accessibility and ergonomic analysis of assembly tooling is being developed as part of a larger effort in assembly modeling, tool design, and ergonomics. The information obtained from the virtual assembly experience is used to provide feedback to the assembly modeling and tool design modules based on interference and accessibility problems so as to reduce ergonomics related problems. Future research will involve experimentation with the system using actual floor assembly jig CAD models. Force and torque sensing capability will also be added to simulate real-life situations.

References

[1]   R. S. Bridger, Introduction to Ergonomics, McGraw-Hill, New York, NY, 1995.
[2]   T. J. Armstrong, *et al.*, A conceptual model for work-related neck and upper-limb musculoskeletal disorder, *Scandinavian Journal of Work, Environment, and Health* **19** (1993) 915-933.
[3]   E. R. Tichauer, Ergonomic aspects of biomechanics. In: Industrial Environment - Its Evaluation and Control, NIOSH, Washington, D. C., (1973).
[4]   A. E. Moore, *et al.*, Quantifying exposure in occupational manual tasks with cumulative trauma disorder potential, *Ergonomics* **34** (1991), 1433-1453.
[5]   Automotive News, Virtual humanity helps boost quality, cut costs, Crain Communications, May 6, 1996.
[6]   H. I. Connacher, *et al.*, Virtual Assembly Design Environment, Proceedings of the 1995 Computers in Engineering Conference, Boston, MA, (1995).
[7]   K. W. Lyons, *et al.*, Representations and methodologies for assembly modeling, NIST Internal Report, (1997).
[8]   V. N. Rajan, *et al.*, Correct and complete algorithms for geometric analysis and design of modular fixturing setups, Accepted for publication in the *Transactions of the NAMRI/SME*, (1997).
[9]   V. N. Rajan, *et al.*, Virtual environment for design and analysis of factory layouts, To be presented at the 1997 SME General Corporate and Regional Aviation Meeting and Exposition, Wichita, KS. (1997).
[10]   J. E. Fernandez, Ergonomics in the Workplace, *Facilities* **13** (1995) (4), MCB University Press.
[11]   J. E. Fernandez, *et al.*, The psychophysical approach in upper extremities work, Contemporary Ergonomics, Taylor & Francis, (1995).

Advances in Occupational Ergonomics and Safety II
Edited by Biman Das and Waldemar Karwowski
IOS Press and Ohmsha, 1997

Problems of Occupational Safety in Small Business

Jerzy LEWANDOWSKI
Technical University of Łódź, Piotrkowska 266, 90-361 Łódź, Poland
Warsaw University of Technology, Narbutta 85, 02-524 Warsaw, Poland

Abstract. The work presents problems of occupational safety in Polish small business. Analysis of accidents and factors influencing occupational safety was made. In the final section directions of activities were pointed out to improve occupational safety in Polish small business.

1. Introduction

Every employer should be obliged to possess knowledge referring to the effective occupational safety and prevention against accidents. Disregarding this duty is one of the reasons which results in the fact that Poland is characterised by one of the highest rates of accidents at work and occupational diseases. The number of accidents at work (ca. 100. 000 annually) and occupational diseases (ca. 12.000 annually) proves the low degree of safety. Statistic data concerning the accidents in the years 1990-93 are presented in Table 1.

Table 1. Accidents at work in the years 1990-93.

Year	The general number of accidents	Deadly accidents	Accidents resulting in severe injuries
1990	108 274	850	5 507
1991	116 066	781	4 925
1992	102 944	644	3 380
1993	103 073	655	2 711

The importance of the problem of accidents at work results not only from the costs of treatment and compensation but also the costs of losses linked with disturbance in the production process.

Research proves that in many countries of the world the costs of accidents at work are as high as 1 - 4% of the national product. The importance of the problem gave rise to the scientific research works aiming at establishing in Poland occupational safety management system. Especially unfavourable is the dynamics of growth of accident impendence in small business.

2. Analysis of accidents in enterprises

Accidents at work, due to their number and the consequences for health and economy, still remain an important problem. The analysis of accident impendence has proved a considerable influence of technical and organisational factors on occupational safety. Research has proved that accident impendence is largely influenced by (while operating on technical objects):

- lacking instructions and technical documentation,
- lacking shields which hinder injuries,
- improper construction of technical objects which impedes occupational safety
- lacking certificates allowing the usage of the technical object,
- constructional changes in technical objects which are not in conformance with occupational safety rules and regulations.

The analysis of accident impendence has proved an interesting phenomenon regarding occupational safety while using technical objects. A decreasing number of accident impendence caused by technical objects usage can be observed if the number of employees in the firm grows.

Analysing the rate of accident impendence caused by technical objects usage one can say that the largest percentage of impendence is observed in small business (ca. 40 - 80%) with no more than 10 employees. This rate in enterprises with more than 50 employees is only 10 - 25%. One can assume that this fact results mainly from the wish of the owners to maximise the income at the cost of lowered quota for occupational safety.

The analysis of accident impendence has also proved a considerable influence of organisational factors on occupational safety. Research has proved the growing number of accidents caused by improper organisation of work and work stands. This fact has partly resulted from the system transformation in Poland.

According to world research works, work organisation, widely understood, is one of the most important elements in every system of occupational safety and work protection. According to some researchers, organisational factors are the direct and indirect cause of accidents - 80-90% of all accidents.

The research has also proved a relatively low level of work organisation in Polish production firms. It is particularly the case with medium-size and small business. For example, a large number (60-80%) of work stands did not have properly described technological procedures. Research has proved a considerable percentage (ca. 40%) of accident impendence resulting from disorder and faulty organisation of work stands.

Detailed analysis of organisational factors referred to (among others):
- work stands
- work methods
- communication points (transportation and travels of employees)

For example, the percentage of work stands with the surface not conforming to the standards was 82% in small business with less than 10 employees and 54% in enterprises with more than 50 employees.

In case of work methods, the percentage of work stands lacking technological procedures was 63 % in small business with less than 10 employees and 74% in enterprises with more than 50 employees.

The percentage of places with bad condition of roads and paths of access was 16% in small business with less than 10 employees and 30% in enterprises with more than 50 employees.

In enterprises a general lack of preventive systems of occupational safety evaluation was noted, ex: quality auditors. The growing role of occupational safety in business is largely dependent on preparation and conformance to the appropriate technological procedures and the quality assertion system. However, it requires a certain degree of knowledge on the part of employers which is a factor encouraging activities aiming at improvement of occupational safety with regard to work organisation.

The standing rules in Poland do not form economic motivation to undertake actions decreasing accident impendence. Employers pay permanent insurance shares (45% of the salary) . It makes it more difficult to stimulate genuine interest of employers in the issues of occupational safety. Undertaking promotional activities encouraging employers' interest in occupational safety has become an essential problem. Therefore, research has been made on the average knowledge about occupational safety on the part of business owners and managers. The results prove that employers in Poland have very little knowledge about work organisation with reference to occupational safety. After the political-economic transformation in Poland after 1989 many people became employers overnight, often without proper professional preparation. It strongly influences the problems of occupational safety in their business.

One of the conditions of improving occupational safety in small business where the owner organises and is responsible for the safety system himself/ herself is organising informative courses about the above mentioned issues as well as preparation of appropriate didactic materials. It is regarded that introduction of safety systems should be promoted among small business owners and be based on quality assertion system (according to ISO standards 9000) as it will best guarantee improvement of occupational safety.

3. Summary

The results presented in the paper refer to the complex research subject which aims at introduction in Poland of the occupational safety management system. Long-term activities undertaken by the institutions responsible for protection and occupational safety should be relevant to the following issues:

- legal and economic stimuli should encourage small business owners to invest in work protection and occupational safety,
- organisation of training for small business owners with the aim of distributing information about work protection and occupational safety and the legal responsibility for the work conditions,
- distribution of literature about work protection and occupational safety in small business.

Reference

[1] J. Lewandowski, C. Kowalczyk, Z. Sobczak: Analysis of technical and organisational factors with regard to occupational safety. Materials for the II International Conference - Economic Organisations Management. Łódź, 1995.

[2] J. Lewandowski, C. Kowalczyk, Z. Sobczak: Analysis of occupational safety in small business. Materials for the IIIrd International Conference - Science and the Quality of Life, Vilnius, 1994.

[3] J. Lewandowski: Ergonomy - Materials for tutorials and design, Edition MARCUS, Łódź, 1995.

Advances in Occupational Ergonomics and Safety II
Edited by Biman Das and Waldemar Karwowski
IOS Press and Ohmsha, 1997

Methods of Improvement
of Ergonomics Solutions

Jerzy LEWANDOWSKI

Technical University of Łódź, Piotrkowska 266, 90-361 Łódź, Poland
Warsaw University of Technology, Narbutta 85, 02-524 Warsaw, Poland

Abstract. The paper gives fundamental principles of methods of improvement of ergonomics solutions. The process of ergonomics in design will be presented. This process concerns the following problems: requirements of customer, material, technology, human-being, legislation and equipment in the hardware and software. The proposal of the system of computer-aided ergonomic calculations will be presented. This system refers to the following systems: data base, statistic analysis of data, analysis of mathematical relations, reliability of the system: human being - technical object - environment , optimisation methods of ergonomic solutions, data and results presentation. Some results of the ergonomic research and solutions concerning some elements of machines and workplace will be shown.

1. Introduction

Quality is the main factor in competitiveness among enterprises. An enterprise, if it intends to be successful must approach the issue of quality in a complex manner. Complexity should refer to quality in micro and macro scale, and in particular:

- product and service quality which fulfil customers requirements,
- quality of factors linked with ergonomic design of work stands, occupational and process safety as well as environment protection

Accomplishment of the above objectives requires a continuous search for methods offering ergonomic solutions in a complex approach. The activities understood in this manner guarantee the „quality of life" which refers to product users and all those who are employed in the production process.

2. Ergonominess of products and work stands

Taking into account the definition of quality, which says that the quality is fulfilment of customer requirements, we can assume that ergominess of product is one of the most important, in some cases the most important, quality criterion. Therefore, we can assume that each of the products possesses ergonomic quality of a defined level. In such an understanding, ergonominess is depicted as a number of features of the object which influence the appropriation of its functions, construction, shape and appearance to the psychophysical and anatomic features of man who uses this object.

Preference for the ergonomic quality by the users of the technique proves the growth of the development of the society because the accepted level of technique humanisation may be treated as a measure of the civilisation development. If the activities which aim at improvement of ergonominess of the objects are undertaken at the early stages of product design, high ergonomic level of this object can be achieved.

Product improvement should refer to all its features, also ergonomic: functionality and safety of exploitation, aesthetic features, etc.

Ergonomy also refers to work stand organisation and work environment of the workers. Work stand organisation and work environment should refer to:

- the sphere of man
- the sphere of work

In analysing the sphere of man the following factors influencing ergonominess of work stands can be distinguished: qualifications, experience, discipline, technical culture, motivations, etc.

In analysing the sphere of work the following factors can be distinguished:

- work stand equipment (machines and equipment, technological equipment, work space, etc.)
- material work environment (microclimate, lightening, air pollution, noise, etc.)
- work organisation (duration, breaks, planning system, etc.)

Apart from issues presented above, product safety and occupational safety is of great importance. Occupational safety and its management is particularly important with regard to the procedure:

- the programme of safe work organisation
- practical realisation of the programme of the safe work organisation (organisational and technical preparation, people, monitoring, etc.)
- safety auditor

3. Methods of ergonomic product improvement

Improvement of the level of ergonomic solutions should be undertaken in the product design phase. The ergonomically appropriate product design process should refer to two spheres:

- designer with high quality equipment (hardware and software)
- customer requirements concerning production, technology, psychophysical and anthropomorphic features of the future users, legislation concerning production and sales on the given markets.

Methods of optimalisation of ergonomic solutions are particularly important in the design procedure. Their application requires an appropriate computer-aided system. Such a system, according to the author, should include the following sub-systems:

- subsystem - ergonomic data basis
- subsystem - statistic analysis
- subsystem - mathematical relations
- subsystem - reliability of the system: human being - technical object - environment
- subsystem - methods of optimalisation of ergonomic solutions
- subsystem - presentation of data and results of solutions

Each of the subsystems is made of modules. For example, the subsystem of optimalisation of ergonomic solutions involves the following modules:

- analytical methods of search for solutions
- heuristic methods
- multicriteria optimalisation

4. Results of ergonomic solutions examination

The search for ergonomic solutions was presented on the example of paper machines. The specific construction and the huge size of these objects require inconvenient positions during repair works which impend with accidents. Various height of the specific elements of the machine which have to be repaired or checked more often compel the workers to cover larger distances and carry tools and supplementary materials. Basing on the observations done during the research the position of the workers who do the repair work, the classification was made and a schedule(histogram) was depicted which illustrates in percentage various positions of the workers during the reparatory works.

Static and dynamic loads of the workers doing reparairs of the rolls of paper machines were analysed. Also influence of important factors on ergonominess of reparairs while replacement of the rolls in paper machine was analysed. The function of multiple regression was used here. Taking into consideration the possibility of improvement of ergonominess of reparairs through constructional advancement several solutions were analysed. One of them referred to the appropriate bearing of the felt -guiding roll which largely diminishes the disassembly time when it's being replaced due to some kind of defect.

To increase ergonominess of repair by shortening its duration and eliminating unfavourable static loads of workers a method of guiding-roll replacement was worked out basing on auxiliary equipment. It is forecasted that the time of replacement will reduce from 6-8 hours to 2-3 hours. The method and the equipment were patented.

5. Summary

The issues presented in the work linked with search for optimal ergonomic solutions are the research-subject carried out by the author and his team as part of the programme of research and Ph.D. theses.

The final effect should be the procedure analysis of ergonomic solutions design of products and work stands. Moreover, the final effect will also be the working out of the system of computer-aided ergonomic calculation.

Reference

[1] J. Lewandowski, Ergonomy - Materials for classes and design, MARCUS Edition, Łódź 1995.
[2] J. Lewandowski, Quantitative Assessment of Ergonominess of Paper Machine's Repair Work, Taylor & Francis Ltd, London and Washington, 1993.

Advances in Occupational Ergonomics and Safety II
Edited by Biman Das and Waldemar Karwowski
IOS Press and Ohmsha, 1997

Stabilometric Studies of Men in Standing and Sitting Work Positions

Elżbieta Chlebicka and Edward Ziobro

Institute of Industrial Engineering and Management, Technical University of Wroclaw,

50 -370 Wroclaw, Poland

Abstract. The stabilometric studies of men have been performed by means of a stabilometer. The stabilometr operates in conjunction with an extensometer bridge enabling static and dynamic measurements of changes in human body pressure on a force platform. A total of 20 men were examined in free standing and sitting positions and also in two selected work positions. In the work positions, the men examined perfomed tasks on a computer. The stabilograms obtained present the shifting of the point of application of resultant force on the force platform. Analysis of stabilograms was conducted by means of the autocorrelation function and periodogram.

1. Introduction

Stabilometric studies on keeping the human body in equilibrium might be applied in many fields; among others, in neurology, biomechanics, rehabilitation and ergonomics. Biomechanicians attention was focused mainly on the standing position [1,2]. Ergonomists are interested in stabilometric studies at both standing and sitting positions and, above all, on performing various working duties [4]. The objective of this work was to conduct stabilometric studies of men mainly in working positions as computer operators and also, for comparison, at free standing and sitting positions.

2. Methods

Studies were carried out by means of a stabilometer, i.e. an instrument used for measuring changes in the pressure force of human bodies by means of the force platform. This unit collaborates with any extensometric bridge, thus making possible computerized recording of measurements. In general, 20 men aged from 20 to 21 were examined in four positions, including two working positions. In working positions the subjects performed operations on a computer keyboard positioned on the table edge 73 cm high. Each subject was exposed to a series of four stabilometric measurements in the following positions: 1) free standing, 2) working standing, 3) free sitting and 4) working sitting. The signal was recorded after 60 seconds from starting work and the recording procedure lasted 20 seconds. Stabilograms were analyzed by means of the autocorrelation function and periodogram [3]. The autocorrelation function $R_x(\tau)$ is defined by the formula:

$$R_x(\tau) = \lim_{T_s \to \infty} \frac{1}{T_s} \int_0^{T_s} x(t) \cdot x(t+t)\, dt \quad dla \quad 0 \le t \le T_s$$

The autocorrelation function makes it possible to assess differentiation of the non-stationary condition of the stabilogram and the correlation degree of the pressure forces for two time sequences. On the plots presented here the bar height on the ordinate axis is equivalent to the value of the autocorrelation coefficient (these values may vary from -1 to +1). The values of delays are shown on the abscissae (its measure is the number of samples, a delay by one minute is equivalent to 0.05 s). Dotted lines on the plotted autocorrelation functions denote a double value of the standard error. Using the periodogram function, the sums of squared coefficients with harmonic cosine and sine components. This function is defined by the formula:

$$y(f_i) = \frac{N}{2}\left(a_i^2 + b_i^2\right)$$

where a_i, b_i are Fourier coefficients and f_i are frequencies ($f_i = i / N$, $i = 1,2........,N$). The f_1 frequency is a fundamental frequency while the f_2, f_3 frequencies are its multiples. The signal which is characterized by high intensity has also high values of the periodogram function while the lower intensity signal has lower values of the periodogram function.

3. Results

In the free standing position (1) we are dealing with a considerable change in the autocorrelation coefficients from -0.4 to 0.7. This indicates irregular changes in the pressure force exerted on the substrate by the subject.

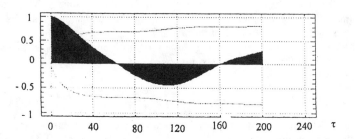

Figure 1. Autocorrelation functions for the free standing position

While using a computer keyboard in the standing position the autocorrelation coefficients are found to decrease considerably from -0.3 to 0.3, the frequency of changes from the negative to positive relationship and vice versa being much higher (it occurs every 4 seconds).

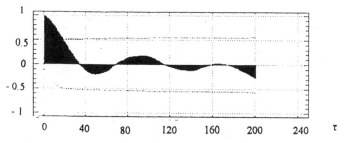

Figure. 2. Autocorrelation functions for the working standing position.

In the free sitting position (3) the value of autocorrelation coefficients are changed from -0.3 to 0.6. Changes in the coefficient occur at a much slower rate and transition from positive to negative values occurs every 10 seconds.

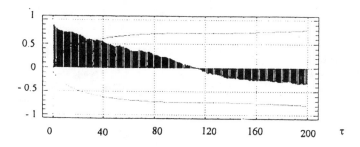

Figure.3. Autocorrelation functions for the free sitting position.

When operating a keyboard in the sitting position, the signals are found to vary rapidly. A common quality of the autocorrelation function plots is their rapid reaching of values close to zero. Then constant deflections occur which result from controlling the body position. Since a large portion of subjects' attention is focused on the job being performed, deflections occur at a higher rate than those in persons in free sitting positions.

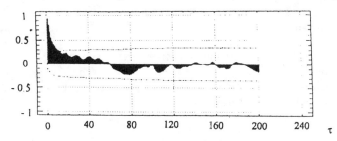

Figure.4. Autocorrelation functions for the working sitting position

Equally interesting results of studies were obtained by using the periodogram function. It appeared that when working with a keyboard in sitting position, the size and number of harmonics is evidently larger in free positions. Similar, some what weaker differences appear in periodograms of free standing and working positions.

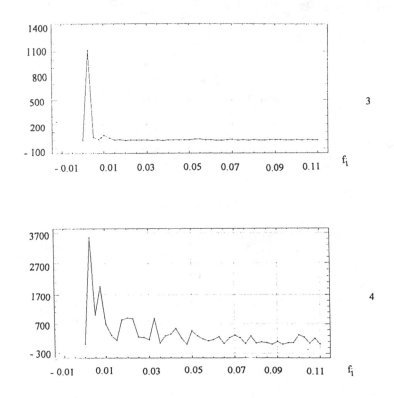

Figure. 5. Periodogram function for free (3) and working (4) sitting positions.

4.Conclusions

The measurements and calculations performed show that the recorded stabilograms, described by autocorrelation and periodogram functions reveal differences on typing on the computer keyboard as compared to the free sitting position. Similar some what weaker differences both in autocorrelation coefficients as well in size and number of harmonics were found for the standing position. Such an analysis of variations resulting from specific working operations maybe suitable in ergonomic evaluation of loads resulting from the body posture.

References

[1] M. Golema, Stabilność pozycji stojącej. Studia i Monografie AWF, z. 17, Wrocław 1987.
[2] W.S.Gurfinkel et al., Regulacja pozy czełowieka . Moskwa 1965.
[3] E. Ozimek, Podstawy teoretyczne analizy widmowej sygnałów.PWN,Warszawa- Poznań,1985.
[4] K.M.G. Noaman,I.A. Ahmed, E. Ziobro,Komputerowe poszukiwanie optymalnych pozycji roboczych. XIII Biomechanics, AWF, Poznań, 1996.
[5] A.J.Spaepen, M.Vranken, E.J.Willems, Comparison of the movements of the center of gravity and of the center of pressure in stabilometric studies. Agressologie, 18, 2, 1977.

6. Product Design and Ergonomics

Advances in Occupational Ergonomics and Safety II
Edited by Biman Das and Waldemar Karwowski
IOS Press and Ohmsha, 1997

Micropipettes:
An Ergonomic Product Evaluation

David D. Wood MSIE, AEP, Robert O. Andres PhD, CPE, and Nancy E. Laurie, MS, AEP
Ergonomic Engineering, Inc., Pelham, MA.

Abstract

A new American pipette manufacturer redesigned their micropipettes, incorporating several modifications intended to improve the ergonomics of the device. A fatiguing experiment is reported here. Six healthy college students with at least 1 year of lab experience using pipettes participated. 384 samples were performed in one hour (with each pipette) and subject discomfort, subject fatigue (power and pinch strength decrements), and subject satisfaction data were collected.

The user satisfaction survey revealed that users were most satisfied with the New American pipette, with the German (old model) and the Finnish pipettes running a close second and third, respectively. These three were close enough that there was no significant statistical difference, however, the New American pipette was significantly preferred over the Unique American, the German (new model), and the French models. The New American had significantly less pinch force decrement (caused less fatigue) than both the German (old model) and the French models. The New American caused significantly less discomfort in hand and wrist than the French model.

1.0 Introduction

Biotechnology is a rapidly growing industry; each year there is research leading to more diagnostic tests requiring more laboratory technicians to use pipettes. Ergonomists can consider the pipette to be a thumb actuated in-line hand tool. Often the pipette's plunger has 2 or 3 stops. The first stop requires the lowest force and draws or ejects the fluid sample. By increasing the force the worker can clean the sample by going to the "blow" stop because it uses air to force out any remaining liquid from the tip. The last task is to change the tip, to prevent contamination in the next condition of samples. Some pipettes have a separate tip eject button (which can require a very low force) while other pipettes use a third, even higher force stop, in the single plunger. The thumb force needed to depress the plunger varies from approximately 0.5 kilograms to nearly 5 kilograms. Of course the risk of musculoskeletal disorders related to pipetting depends on the work rate (samples per worker per day). Bjorsten, Ambly and Jansson [1], in a nested cohort case control study of hospital lab technicians, found that using a pipette for more than 300 hours per year was associated with an increased risk of hand and shoulder ailments.

A New American pipette company requested a series of ergonomic evaluations of their single volume-individual sample pipette. The investigation included a fatigue experiment and an electromyography experiment (this paper only reports the fatigue experiement). Initially, a subjective evaluation of the New American pipette and a French Model pipette was performed. The investigators believed from their evaluation that the plunger force for the New American pipette was too high and recommended that it be lowered for both the first and blow stops. The forces were changed by New American pipette company from 1.35 kg to .45 kg for the first stop and 3.2 kg to 1.5 kg for the blow stop.

2.0 Methods

Three men and 3 women with at least 1 year of experience in pipetting were recruited from the biological sciences departments at the University of Massachusetts at Amherst. The subjects received verbal and written descriptions of the experiment and gave their informed consent in writing. A Physical Activity Readiness Questionnaire (PAR-Q) was used to identify any potential confounding injuries. Only injury free subjects were allowed to participate. Subjects were compensated at a rate of $10 per hour. Sessions were separated by at least 24 and not more than 72 hours.

2.1 Methods-Protocol

Before the first session, subjects were informed about the protocol: how to pipette, how their strength would be tested, and how to use the Borg 10 point Rating of Perceived Exertion scale to rate their discomfort. A balanced order was used (there were 6 models: New American, Unique American (different companies), French, Finnish, and German new and old (same company)) with each subject receiving a different presentation of pipettes.

Prior to beginning a one hour fatiguing session of 384 samples subjects were required to firmly grip a rubber ball 20 times (warm-up). Their maximal grip strengths (power and pinch) were tested twice with a minute rest between trials.

During the fatiguing sessions subjects inserted the end of the pipette into a tip while the tip was held in the tip storage box, drew a sample, ejected the sample (down to the 2nd or "blow" stop), drew another sample, ejected the sample and then ejected the tip. Tips were in boxes of 96 and subjects used 2 boxes during the one hour fatigue experiment. Therefore, a total of 384 samples were performed during each session. Subjects were asked to work at their own pace, but they were told that they must complete one box in 30 minutes. They were required to rest if they finished the first box in less than 30 minutes.

Immediately after the second box was completed, the subject's grip strength was tested and then they stated their discomfort levels using the Borg scale. After the strength and discomfort measures were completed, subjects filled out a user satisfaction survey.

2.2 Methods-Measures

Borg states that the 10 point scale is better than his 21 point scale for subjective ratings of aches and pains [2]. Borg's 10 point scale was used to quantify each subject's perceived discomfort in 3 separate body parts: (1) thumb (including the muscle at the base of the thumb), (2) hand (minus the thumb) and wrist, and (3) the finger flexors in the forearm.

A Chatillon spring gauge (model CAT 719-10) with zero to 5 kilogram range was used to directly measure the forces required to use each pipette. Three trials for each action (first stop, second stop, and eject tip) for each pipette were collected and averaged. These forces were summed because each user would perform all three actions during the use of a pipette. Thus, the sum reveals the overall force required to use each pipette.

Pre- and post-experiment strength for both pinch and power grips were collected during the fatigue experiment. A Lafayette instruments power grip dynamometer was used with the handles set at 3 cm apart and a Jamar pinch dynamometer registered pinch forces.

Subjects were told to gradually build up their strength in one second and then hold the maximal effort for 2 more seconds. Only one trial was performed after the completion of the hour fatiguing session, to ensure that subjects could accurately remember their discomfort levels, which were ascertained immediately after the strength measures were collected. The strength decrement was calculated as the largest pre-experiment strength measure for that session minus the post-experiment value. If the post-experiment strength measure was larger than the pre-experiment strength, then zero was entered as the decrement for analysis purposes.

A 0 to 10 point user satisfaction survey was developed to gather data about ten aspects of a pipette. A score of zero indicated very dissatisfied and score of 10 indicated very satisfied. Subjects were asked to rate how their day had been going before each session, their overall satisfaction and their satisfaction with the following specific items: Weight, Handle diameter, Handle texture, Handle compliance, Position of the plunger, Position of the tip eject button, Force to go to the first stop, Force to go to second stop, Force to eject the tip, Finger overhang position and overall design.

Repeated measures (within subjects) Analysis of Variance (ANOVA) was used to test for differences between pipettes. A 0.05 alpha level of significance was used.

3.0 Results

3.1 Results-direct measurement of plunger forces

The New American had the lowest direct measurement of plunger forces or summation score while the French Model had the largest summation score (see Table 1). Note that the Unique American does not have a second stop and the scores for the first were used.

Table 1. Direct measurement of forces (kg) required to use each pipette.

Pipette	1st stop	Blow stop	Tip eject	Sum
German Model (New)	1.05	2.87	2.12	6.044
New American	0.48	1.54	0.73	2.750
Finnish Model	0.83	2.67	0.83	4.317
German Model (Old)	0.71	1.45	3.62	5.781
French Model	0.89	4.65	1.13	6.672
Unique American	0.95	0.95	1.24	3.106

3.2 Results-Satisfaction Survey

The 11 scores were summed, with 110 being the highest possible score. Subjects gave low scores to the German (new), Unique American and French models and high summed scores to the German (old), Finnish, and the New American. The differences between the New American and German(old), French and Unique American were significant (see Table 2 for means and p values).

Table 2. Post-hoc non-orthgonal contrasts for satisfaction survey total score.

Pipette	Mean	Comparison to New American (P value)
German Model (New)	67.83	0.008
Unique American	76.83	0.037
French Model	69.66	0.007
German Model (Old)	94.17	ns
Finnish Model	91.33	ns
New American	96.83	

where: ns = not significantly different

3.3 Result-Strength Decrements

Subjects were asked to grip and pinch as hard as possible before and after each 1 hour fatiguing session. The pinch grip differences between the New American, German (old), and French were significant (see Table 3 for means and p values), while the power grip differences were not significant.

Table 3. Post-hoc non-orthgonal contrasts for strength decrements.

Pipette	Mean Decrement (kg)		Comparison to New American (P value)	
	Power	Pinch	Power	Pinch
German Model (New)	4.50	2.12	ns	ns (0.056)
Unique American	2.30	1.17	ns	ns
French Model	3.00	2.18	ns	0.010
German Model (Old)	1.71	1.45	ns	0.037
Finnish Model	2.46	0.97	ns	ns
New American	2.17	0.52		

where: ns = not significantly different

3.4 Result-Ratings of Discomfort

Subjects were asked to use Borg's 10 point scale to rate their discomfort after each 1 hour fatiguing session. There were no significant differences between the New American and other pipettes for the thumb and forearm (see Table 4 for means and P values). The New American created significantly less hand discomfort than the French model.

Table 4. Means for Borg discomfort ratings and P values.

Pipette	Mean Borg score			Comparison to New American (P value)		
	Thumb	Hand	Forearm	Thumb	Hand	Forearm
German Model (New)	2.58	2.08	1.58	ns	ns	ns
Unique American	0.62	1.67	1.08	ns	ns	ns
French Model	2.08	3.33	0.83	ns	0.048	ns
German Model (Old)	2.80	1.50	1.00	ns	ns	ns
Finnish Model	1.42	1.92	1.20	ns	ns	ns
New American	1.50	1.25	0.92			

4.0 Discussion

Increased fatigue, discomfort, and decreased user satisfaction have all been associated with increased incidence of work-related musculoskeletal disorders. Intensively used products need to be designed and built to minimize discomfort and fatigue. The information gained in this investigation can be used to identify sources of fatigue and discomfort during pipetting and identify designs which minimize these factors.

The New American pipette has many good qualities (low plunger force, optimal diameter and soft handle texture). Within the limitations of our experimental design, the New American was ergonomically superior to the French Model and new German Model models used in this study. After this investigation, the New American pipette manufacturer incorporated one recommended change to significantly improve the design of the pipette used in this experiment. The finger over-hang (which normally covers the radial aspect of the proximal phalanx of the index finger) was made much larger to prevent users from dropping the pipette. After this study was completed the new model with the larger finger over-hang was tested similarly. Future research may test improved plunger characteristics including surface area size and shape.

References

[1] Bjorkstein, M.G., B. Almby and E.S. Jansson, Hand and Shoulder ailments among laboratory technicians using modern plunger-operated pipettes, Applied Ergonomics, 1994 25(2) 88-94

[2] Borg, G. Psychophysical bases of percieved exertion. Medicine and Science in Sports and Exercise, 1982 14 377-381

Advances in Occupational Ergonomics and Safety II
Edited by Biman Das and Waldemar Karwowski
IOS Press and Ohmsha, 1997

An Ergonomics Evaluation of a Hospital Meal Cart

Biman DAS[*], Julia WIMPEE[+] and Bijon DAS[*]
[*] *Biman Das and Associates Consultants in Industrial Ergonomics*
Bedford, Nova Scotia B4A 2V2, Canada
[+] *Aladdin Synergetics Incorporated*
Advanced Meal Systems
Nashville, Tennessee 37224, U.S.A.

A worker survey was conducted through questionnaires to obtain operator ratings of design and other factors and postural discomfort ratings for the body regions. This was done to assess employee comfort, ease of use and health issues involved. The operators encountered difficulty in setting the cart in motion, seeing over the cart and stopping the cart while in motion. The handle height was of some concern to the operators. The operators expressed postural discomfort in the shoulder, neck, back, lower back, knee and leg and ankle and foot. The female operators had consistently higher postural discomfort than the male operators. There was a significant difference in postural discomfort between the male and female operators in terms of lower back.

1. Introduction

The hospital meal cart operators move the cart from the kitchen (ground floor) to various floors and serve hot meals: breakfast, lunch and dinner, to patients on meal trays. The operation of a hospital meal cart involves pushing and pulling actions along with bending and lifting while handling meal trays. While designing a hospital meal cart consideration should be given to the problems dealing with manual materials handling and in particular pushing and pulling activities. It is necessary to evaluate the design and operation of a hospital meal cart from an ergonomics viewpoint to minimize operator discomfort and resulting injury. For the evaluation of equipment, tasks and workstations, discomfort analyses have been shown to be advantageous [1,2,3].

Worker survey through questionnaires are often used to evaluate the design characteristics, physical fatigue and postural discomfort. This input would be useful in the modification of existing equipment design through the application of ergonomics principles and data. A worker survey was conducted with the following objectives in mind: (1) the general operator rating of various meal cart designs and other factors, (2) the current level of physical fatigue induced by the job to the operators, and (3) the changes in postural discomfort in specific anatomical regions.

2. Method

The conventional meal cart operators participated in an ergonomics study to measure via questionnaire the effect of the cart design and other factors related to employee comfort, health and safety, and ease of use. A total of 24 operators, 11 male and 13 female were surveyed in this study.

For the purpose of this study, a preliminary analysis was conducted to identify design problems of the conventional hospital meal cart from an ergonomics viewpoint (Figure 1). The specific problems identified were: maneuverability of the cart, handle height and placement, eye height above the cart, ease of stopping the cart and pushing/pulling the cart. Two separate questionnaires were developed and administered to the hospital meal cart workers. The questionnaires included: (1) hospital meal cart worker survey I had eleven questions on a Likert type 5-point scale that dealt with design and other factors, and (2) hospital meal cart worker survey II that dealt with postural discomfort in specific body regions on both sides of the body. The questionnaires were administered near the end of the shift. For worker survey I the operator ratings (frequency) of design and other factors are presented under: (1) general, (2) handle height, (3) stopping force, (4) emergency and parking brakes, and (5) tiredness. For worker survey II the postural discomfort questionnaire provides a diagram of the human body which has been divided into 22 body regions equally split between a right and left half. The data were analyzed separately for the male and female.

3. Results

3.1 Operator responses (scores) obtained for the design and other factors

For males, the mean scores for "stopping force" and "parking brake" were 3.0 and 3.2, respectively. Stated otherwise, the stopping force requirement and the need for the parking brake were of concern to the male operator. The mean score for the tiredness factor was 2.4. In other words, the male operators felt some tiredness at the end of the work shift. The other factors had mean scores between 1.8 and 2.1. Consequently, the extent of concern for the factors was less.

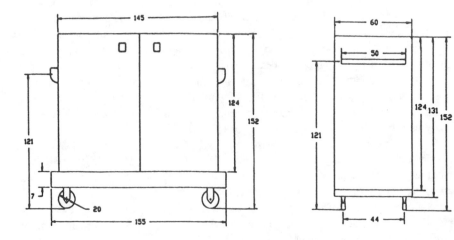

Figure 1. Front and side elevations of the conventional hospital meal cart. All dimensions in centimeters.

For females, the mean scores were consistently higher than the scores obtained for the male operators, except one factor, "handling trays". The results are expected, since female operators in general have two-thirds of the strength of male operators. The female mean scores for "stopping force" and "parking brake" were the highest or 3.5. For the "tiredness factor", the mean score was 3.3. Consequently, the female operators felt more tired at the end of the work shift compared to the male operators (mean score, 2.4). The mean score for the factor, "seeing over the cart" was 3.0. Hence this factor was a concern for the female operator. The factors, "cart in motion", "turning cart", "handle height/pushing", "handle height/pulling", and "emergency hand brake", had mean scores of 2.6, 2.4, 2.6 and 2.8, respectively. Stated otherwise these factors were of some concern to the female operators. The "handling of trays" and "handling of doors" had mean scores of 1.6 and 2.0, respectively, so these factors were of less concern to the operators.

An analysis of variance (ANOVA) test performed for the male and female responses to the design and other factors, revealed that there was significant ($p<0.05$) difference between male and female operators in the perception of the factors "cart in motion" and "seeing over the cart". Stated otherwise, the female operators perception of difficulty in getting the cart in motion and seeing over the cart was significantly greater than the male operators. Highly significant ($p<0.01$) difference between male and female operators was found in terms of their perception of tiredness at the end of the work shift.

3.2 Discomfort scale rating scores for the body regions

For the male operator, the back, lower back, and ankle and foot in the left region had postural discomfort scores of 1.6, 1.6 and 1.4, respectively. Stated otherwise the male operators felt postural discomfort in these areas more than the other areas. In the right region, the postural discomfort score in the shoulder was 1.8. The operators tend to pull the cart forward using only the right hand. This could be the reason for the postural discomfort in the right shoulder. Apparently, the male operators did not feel any postural discomfort in other regions.

The female operators consistently had higher postural discomfort scores than the male operators. In the left region, the postural discomfort scores for the shoulder, neck, back, lower back, knee and thigh, and ankle and foot were 1.7, 1.5, 2.7, 3.5, 1.7 and 2.1, respectively. The results revealed that the female operators encountered considerable discomfort in the back and lower back. For the right region, the postural discomfort scores for the shoulder, neck, back, lower back, knee and foot, and ankle and foot were 1.9, 1.7, 3.1, 3.6, 1.6 and 1.9, respectively. For the right region, the maximum postural discomfort was felt in the back and lower back. Similar results were found for the left region.

An analysis of variance (ANOVA) test was performed to determine the difference, if any, between the male and female responses (scores) to postural discomfort. The results revealed that there was a significant difference in the responses to postural discomfort between the male and female operators in terms of left and right lower back and right neck. Stated otherwise, the female operators felt significantly greater discomfort than the male operators in the left and right lower back and the right back. No significant difference was found in postural discomfort between male and female operators for the left back.

4. Conclusions

In summary, from this investigation the following conclusions are made:

1. A conventional hospital meal cart worker survey was conducted through questionnaires to obtain: (1) operator ratings of design and other factors and (2) postural discomfort ratings for the body regions.
2. The operators encountered difficulty in setting the cart in motion, seeing over the cart (especially female), turning the cart and stopping the cart while in motion. The handle height was of some concern to the operators. The subjects agreed or strongly agreed to the usefulness of an emergency hand brake. Some (female) subjects felt tired to a large or great extent at the end of the work shift.
3. There was a significant difference between male and female operators in their perception of the factors "cart in motion", "seeing over the cart" and "tiredness".
4. The male operators expressed postural discomfort in the back, lower back and ankle and foot in the left region and shoulder in the right region. The female operators encountered postural discomfort in the shoulder, back, knee and leg, ankle and foot in both the left and right regions. The female operators had consistently higher postural discomfort than the male operators.
5. There was significant difference in postural discomfort between the male and female operators in terms of left and right lower back and right back.

References

[1] V. Bhatnager, C.G. Drury, and S.G. Schiro, Posture, postural discomfort, and performance, *Human Factors* 27(2), 1985, 189-199.
[2] E.N. Corlett and R.P. Bishop, A technique for assessing postural discomfort, *Ergonomics* 19(2), 1976, 175-182.
[3] R.W. Schoenmarklin and W.S. Marras, Effects of handle and work orientation on hammering: II. Muscle fatigue and subjective ratings of body discomfort, *Human Factors* (31)4, 1989, 413-420.

Advances in Occupational Ergonomics and Safety II
Edited by Biman Das and Waldemar Karwowski
IOS Press and Ohmsha, 1997

Redesign of a Hospital Meal Cart: An Ergonomics Approach

Biman DAS[*], Julia WIMPEE[+] and Bijon DAS[*]
[*] *Biman Das and Associates*
Consultants in Industrial Ergonomics
Bedford, Nova Scotia B4A 2V2, Canada
[+] *Aladdin Synergetics Incorporated*
Advanced Meal Systems
Nashville, Tennessee 37224, U.S.A.

A prototype hospital meal cart was designed by incorporating ergonomics principles and data. Recommendations were made with regard to the: (1) use of plastic material for the construction of the cart, (2) provision of four swivel wheels at each and of the corner of the cart along with two fixed wheels in the middle and use of wheel ball bearings for improved maneuverability, (3) proper placement of cart handles and handle diameter, (4) reduction of cart height, (5) provision of emergency hand brake, (6) provision of individually (electrically) heated plates for soup and main meal, (7) provision of thick air tight plastic doors, and (8) reduction of the meal tray size. To minimize postural discomfort, the cart should be pushed forward using both hands. The need for training operators to follow the proper work method was highlighted.

1. Introduction

The hospital meal carts are used to deliver hot meals, breakfast, lunch and dinner, on trays to the patients in a multi-floor hospital building. The conventional hospital meal carts are equipped to deliver 24 trays. They are moved manually through the use of elevators by one or two operators and generally two operators serve the meals on trays to the patients. Considerable pushing and pulling forces are involved in moving the hospital meal carts. Also bending and lifting are required in handling the meal trays. To date no formal study has been conducted to evaluate the design and operation of a hospital meal cart from an ergonomics viewpoint.

An equipment design objective is to ensure that the majority of the population of the intended user group can be accommodated comfortably, without any harmful posture. Improperly designed equipment results in inadequate posture and this in turn causes static efforts [1,2]. The objective of this investigation was to recommend modifications to the conventional hospital meal cart for the purpose of designing a prototype hospital meal cart based on ergonomic/anthropometric principles and data.

2. Conventional Hospital Meal Cart Design

Several ergonomics design and operational problems that resulted in postural discomfort were identified from a conventional hospital meal cart worker survey [3]. Considerable pushing and pulling forces are involved in moving the hospital meal carts. Also bending and lifting are required in handling the meal trays. These factors were identified in the survey along with other equipment design problems including: cart maneuverability, handle height and placement, vision or eye height above the cart, opening and closing of cart doors, and ease of stopping the cart.

For the purpose of this investigation, push, pull and turning forces (initial) on tile and carpet floors were determined for the conventional hospital meal cart. This was done to ensure that the force requirements were within the permissible limits and would not cause any health hazards and in particular low back pain. The push, pull and turning forces of the conventional hospital meal cart was determined using a hand dynamometer.

2.1 Determination of push, pull and turning forces

The push forces of the meal cart with 24 trays and food for the tile floor was 6.3 kg, and the corresponding value for the carpet floor was 12.2 kg. The turning force of the meal cart with 24 trays and food for the tile floor was 20.2 kg, and the corresponding value for the carpet floor was 22.7 kg. The turning push forces of the meal cart on both tile and carpet exceeded the acceptable initial push force of 17.5 kg for the 5th percentile female for one push in 5 minutes, which is usually performed by the workers [4]. At present the meal cart is moved forward by pulling with only one hand. The cart is moved by one operator or sometimes by two operators.

2.2 Identification of design problems

The conventional meal cart was analyzed and several design problems were identified:
1. *Maneuverability of the cart.* The front two wheels of the conventional meal cart do not turn laterally [3]. This does not allow general maneuverability of the cart and in particular contributes to an increased turning radius. The additional force requirement to maneuver the cart can be a source of twisting and turning injuries especially in the low back region.
2. *Cart handle height and placement.* The horizontal, cylindrical handle is placed on both ends of the cart at a height of 121 cm form the floor. The placement of the handle does not allow a comfortable posture for a small (5th percentile female) or a large (95th percentile male) person. Furthermore, adequate spacing is not provided between the handle and the cart surface, especially for a person with a large or thick palm.
3. *Vision above the cart.* The present height of 152 cm from the floor level exceeds the permissible eye height of a small person (5th percentile female). Thus a small operator must stretch or assume an awkward posture to see above the cart. This can be a potential source of accident hazard.
4. *Ease of stopping the cart.* There is no provision of emergency brakes to stop the cart. If the operator has to make a panic stop, considerable energy is required which is a potential source of back injury.
5. *Provision of hot meals.* To keep the meal and soup hot, stainless steel covers are used. The metallic covers have poor heat insulation properties. With the present design it is not possible to keep the meals hot for a considerable period of time.
6. *Size of the meal tray.* The size of the meal tray is 38 x 51 cm. There is considerable unutilized space on the tray. It is possible to reduce the size of the tray without causing any inconvenience to the patient. This will obviously reduce the size of the meal cart.
7. *Pushing versus pulling the cart.* Presently the cart is moved by one operator or sometimes by two operators. They pull the cart using one hand. This is a source of neck and back injury and puts considerable stress on the trunk.

3. Redesigned/Prototype Hospital Meal Cart

The proposed design changes based on ergonomics principles and data are stated below:

1. Maneuverability of the cart. The redesigned prototype hospital meal cart would be constructed with durable plastic. This will reduce weight and thus enhance maneuverability and enhance aesthetic values. It is advisable to have the four swivel wheels at each corner of the cart with the addition of two fixed wheels in the middle of the cart (Figure 1). This would not only reduce the force required to turn the cart but also decrease turning radius. Presumably the bearing used in the meal cart is a sleeve bearing. If it is changed to ball bearing, further reduction in initial push force is possible.

2. Cart handle height and placement. The handle should be placed at a height between 94 and 115.4 cm from the floor [1,2]. The two handles should be placed 47.8 cm apart, based on the average value between 95th percentile male (51.7 cm) and female (43.8 cm) elbow-to-elbow widths. The handle shape can be cylindrical and the diameter of the handle should be based on hand anthropometry. A handle diameter of 3.2 cm is recommended. The handle material can be made of hard rubber or synthetic material. Since the cart is often moved by two operators, two handles could be provided on the sides of the cart. It is possible to provide a seven degree bias to the handle from the vertical away from the cart, so that the orientation of the handle is in line with the forearm. This will minimize or eliminate the possibility of carpel tunnel syndrome of the hand.

3. Vision above the cart. The cart height should be reduced to 143.6 cm or less based on the 5th percentile female, eye height (slump posture). A worker survey questionnaire revealed that about half of the operators had moderate to extreme difficulty in seeing over the cart [3]. This would allow proper vision and promote an improved posture and minimize traffic hazards.

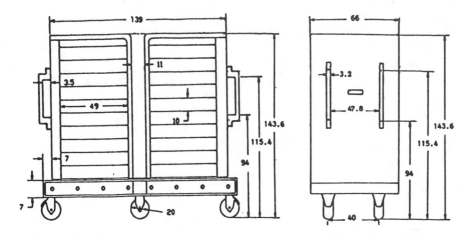

Figure 1.   Front and side elevations of the redesigned/prototype hospital meal cart.   All dimensions in centimeters.

4. Ease of stopping the cart. It is desirable to install emergency brakes for panic stops especially when the cart is loaded with full meal trays. An emergency hand brake can be installed between the cart handles for easy access.

5. Provision of hot meals. It is possible to provide individually (electrically) heated plates for the soup and the main meal. This is an innovative idea for serving hot meals at all times to the patients of the hospital. By using insulated Tupperware covers as opposed to conventional metallic covers, improved heat insulation would be provided. Furthermore it would reduce the weight of the covers. The provision of airtight or solid transparent plastic doors will conserve heat energy and keep the meals hot and improve the aesthetic value.

6. Size of meal tray. The size of the meal tray should be reduced to 33 x 47 cm. A compact meal tray will prevent the crockery and cutlery from sliding on the tray.

7. Pushing versus pulling the cart. To realize optimum benefit the cart must be pushed using both hands.

4. Conclusions

In summary, the following conclusions and recommendations are made:

1. Use of plastic material would reduce the weight of the hospital meal cart. This will reduce initial push/pull force requirements and enhance maneuverability.

2. The provision of four swivel wheels at each corner of the cart along with two fixed wheels in the middle of the cart would reduce the turning force and decrease the turning radius. Further reduction in initial push force is possible by changing the conventional sleeve bearing to ball bearing for the wheels.

3. The proposed cart would meet the initial push force requirements based on (1) and (2).

4. The cart handles should be placed between 94 and 115.4 cm from the floor and the two handles should be placed 47.8 cm apart. A cart handle diameter of 3.2 cm is recommended.

5. The height of the cart should be reduced to 143.6 cm or less (preferably 140 cm) from the floor to provide better vision especially for the small person (5th percentile female).

6. Provide individually (electrically) heated plates for the soup and main meal.

7. Provide thick air-tight transparent plastic doors. This will conserve heat energy and keep the meals hot and improve the aesthetic value.

8. Provide an emergency hand brake and locate it between the cart handles for easy access.

9. Reduce the size of the meal tray from 38 x 51 cm to 33 x 47 cm.

10. To obtain optimum benefit, the cart must be pushed using both hands. The meal trays on the lower level of the cart should be handled using a kinetic lift to minimize lower back pain.

11. The operators should be trained to follow the proper work method.

References

[1] B. Das and R.M. Grady, Industrial workplace layout design: An application of engineering anthropometry, *Ergonomics*, 26(5), 1983, 433-447.
[2] B. Das and A.K. Sengupta, Industrial workstation design: A systematic ergonomics approach, *Applied Ergonomics*, 27(3), 1996, 157-163.
[3] B. Das, J. Wimpee, and B.Das, An ergonomic evaluation of a hospital meal cart. *Proceeding of the Annual International Occupational and Safety Conference*, Washington, D.C., U.S.A., June 1-4, 1997.
[4] S.H. Snook and V.M. Ciriello, The design of manual handling tasks: Revised tables of maximum acceptable weights and forces. *Ergonomics*, 34(9), 1991, 1197-1213.

Advances in Occupational Ergonomics and Safety II
Edited by Biman Das and Waldemar Karwowski
IOS Press and Ohmsha, 1997

Ergonomic Seat With Viscoelastic Foam Reduces Shock on Underground Mobile Equipment

Alan Mayton and Sean Gallagher
*National Institute for Occupational Safety and Health,
Pittsburgh Research Center
P. O. Box 18070, Pittsburgh, PA 15236*

Ron Merkel
*Roush Anatrol
11916 Market Street
Livonia, MI 46150*

Operators of underground mobile equipment, particularly shuttle cars, are often exposed to significant levels of whole-body vibration (WBV) and shock. The Human Factors group at the NIOSH - Pittsburgh Research Center has investigated the use of viscoelastic foam to reduce shock for the equipment operator and improve seats on mine shuttle cars. In-mine data were recorded on a JOY 21SC shuttle car for the original seat and an ergonomic version with viscoelastic foam. A review of the data shows improved isolation across the driver/seat pad interface. For the full-load case, the ergonomic seat decreased transmissibility and isolated the shuttle car operator down to 15 Hz. Additional testing of the foam materials with the development and use of a lumped-parameter analytical model showed different composites of the foam materials can reduce the isolation frequency to below 5 Hz. This paper describes the underground mine trials and the testing done to evaluate properties of the viscoelastic foams. The paper also discusses the development of an analytical model using the data from underground trials and the foam testing.

1. Introduction

Studies sponsored by the U. S. Bureau of Mines (USBM) have reported that as many as one-third of the equipment operators in underground coal mines may be exposed to adverse levels of whole-body vibration (WBV) (Remington et al., 1984). Shuttle cars are identified as a primary source of this adverse exposure. The operator experiences WBV and shock when the shuttle car travels over rough mine floor marked by bumps, ruts, and potholes. In low-coal mines (< 1.25 m or 50 in), restricted space makes seat suspension systems difficult to use in isolating operators from WBV and shock. Miners log 25 million hours of work annually in these mines.

Interviews with underground mobile equipment operators revealed complaints mostly about shocks or jolts they received when operating shuttle cars. Hence, the feedback from equipment operators made the case for research to reduce shock. Specifically, this research focuses on a more ergonomically designed seat and on identifying how well various types and thicknesses of viscoelastic foams reduce the shock experienced by shuttle car operators.

2. Underground Mine Trials

Researchers at the Pittsburgh Research Center (PRC) modified the original seat (Figure 1) in a JOY 21SC shuttle car used at an eastern Kentucky mine. The coal seam at this mine is .889 m (35 in) thick with an operating height of approximately 1.09 m (43 in). Owing to the low mining height, operators must adopt a reclining posture to operate the shuttle car. From observing and talking with the shuttle car operators, it became obvious that the original seat provided little adjustability or lower back support. Modifications to the original seat resulted in a more ergonomically designed version with an easily adjustable lumbar support, fore-aft seat pan movement, and viscoelastic foam padding (Figure 2). The padding included six layers, each .013 m (½ in) in thickness, of the following order from top to bottom: EXTRA-SOFT, PUDGEE, BLUE, YELLOW,

Figure 1 - Original seat.   Figure 2 - Ergonomic version of original seat.

SOFT, and GREEN. The BLUE, YELLOW, and GREEN layers are CONFOR medium-density, open-celled polyurethane foams from E-A-R Specialty Composites Corporation, Newark, DE. The remaining materials are manufactured by Dynamic Systems, Inc., Leicester, NC. EXTRA-SOFT and SOFT are SUN-MATE polyurethane foams with organic composition of more than 50% plant derivatives. SUN-MATE PUDGEE is unique among the materials as a viscoelastic gel-foam with a soft dough-like consistency. Data were recorded for a typical shock with the shuttle car operating empty and with a full load. In terms of transmissibility across the driver/seat pad interface, the ergonomic design shows considerably improved isolation for the full load case. Below 15 Hz, transmission increases across the seat due to the improvement in isolation frequency. The design objective was to lower the isolation frequency and improve the damping characteristics of the seat so an increase in transmissibility is minimized.

Although the seating foam composite above provided substantially improved isolation for the shuttle car operator, PRC researchers were interested in further reducing the isolation frequency. Consequently, additional testing of the viscoelastic foams was arranged with a company specializing in noise and vibration engineering, Roush Anatrol.

3. Material Property Evaluation

Using the forced oscillation technique, investigators at Roush Anatrol evaluated the six foams above plus SUN-MATE MED-SOFT. This method was used to quantify the influence of static preload, dynamic strain amplitude, and temperature on the modulus of elasticity and damping properties of the foams. With the forced oscillation method, a sinusoidal displacement (strain) was applied to the specimen as the resulting force (stress) and input displacement were measured. The forced oscillation device appears in Figure 3.

Each specimen, .013 m (1/2 in) in diameter and .013 m (1/2 in) long, was tested at three temperatures, 4.4 °C (40° F), 21.1° C (70° F), and 37.8 °C (100° F). Test temperatures were selected from actual readings and knowledge of the mine environment.

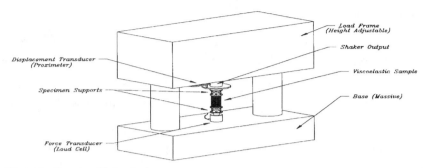

Figure 3 - Forced oscillation device.

The chamber temperature was held constant at these temperatures for testing at pre-strain levels of 0%, 10%, and 45%,. For each temperature, data was recorded at discrete frequencies from 1 to 100 Hz in steps of 25 Hz. The input strain was controlled to provide the prescribed dynamic strain levels of .1%, 1%, and 2%. Force and displacement data during the first several oscillations were collected in the time (versus frequency) domain. This was necessary to avoid changes in foam properties due to internal heating of the foam over repeated cycling.

The dynamic properties of the material were calculated using the amplitudes of the force and displacement responses with phase angle in the following equations:

$$E_1 = [K] \, F_f \, (h \, / \, S_e) \, \cos\delta$$
$$E_2 = E_1 \tan\delta$$
$$\text{Damping} = \tan\delta = E_2 \, / \, E_1$$

Where, $[K]$ = stiffness modulus (N/m) - measured, δ = loss angle (degrees) - measured, h = height of test piece (m), S_e = excited surface area on test piece (m^2), S_1 = lateral surface area of test piece (m^2), F_f = corrective factor, test piece geometry dependent, and $F_f = 1 \, / \, (1 + 2 \, (S_e \, / \, S_1)^2)$.

4. Analytical Model

The isolation system provided by the foam was analyzed dynamically using a lumped-parameter, analytical model. The dynamic interaction of the vehicle, isolation system, and driver was simulated with the model using a seven degree of freedom spring-mass-damper system. Six material layers with variable material thickness were included in the model.

The ergonomic seat was chosen as the baseline seat in the model because of its known material configuration and properties. Modulus of elasticity and damping values were applied to the analytical model for 10% pre-strain on each material. The entire depth of the material was assigned a temperature of 21.1° C (70° F) for the assumed typical day. Several designs were also evaluated with a material temperature of 4.4° C (40° F) to look at the suitability of the configuration to colder environments.

A shock input, taken from in-mine data recordings, was applied analytically to the system to determine the driver's response for each material configuration. Responses were generated at the driver/seat interface (seat accelerometer location) and at the driver's torso. The responses were then compared to the experimentally measured, modified seat response and to the analytically predicted driver response. An analytical transfer function between the input force and the torso was also generated to show the isolation frequency and the amplification at resonance. Accordingly, investigators optimized the seat material configuration using an iterative process.

5. Analytical Model Results

For isolating the shuttle car operator, EXTRA-SOFT, SOFT, and PUDGEE foams exhibited characteristics that make them the best of the materials evaluated. At 4.4° C (40° F) and 21.1° C (70° F), the SOFT and EXTRA-SOFT have lower modulus of elasticity values than the YELLOW, with EXTRA-SOFT the lowest. The SOFT and EXTRA-SOFT are relatively stable with temperature and have similar damping properties. Across the temperature range tested, PUDGEE shows less than an order of magnitude change in modulus of elasticity. Across the frequency span and temperature range, the damping properties of PUDGEE are also fairly uniform . Moreover, PUDGEE has the lowest modulus of elasticity values of the seven foams tested. PUDGEE'S higher damping than the EXTRA-SOFT could, however, restrict its ability to expand from a compressed state during a jolt or shock.

The EXTRA-SOFT and PUDGEE composite was evaluated as Case #2. This provided the maximum depth of a low modulus foam as well as one that maintains its stiffness and damping properties over the expected operating temperature range. The isolation characteristics of the seat are improved to approximately 4 Hz. A small amplification in the 3 Hz region appears due to the lowering of the driver/seat resonance.

Five inches of EXTRA-SOFT constituted Case #6. For a low-coal application, this design represents nearly the maximum amount of seat padding that might be used. The design also employs the best single material in terms of low modulus of elasticity, low and consistent damping, and low temperature sensitivity. This foam configuration provides analytical isolation frequency of 5 Hz.

6. Conclusions

The shuttle car seat design that shows the best isolation properties corresponds to foam configurations of Case #2 or #6. Either of these selections maximizes the isolation performance of the seat in the limited space available. The analytical model provides a usable tool to design and optimize shock and vibration isolation systems for use on a variety of seating configurations in underground mines. It will greatly aid investigators at the NIOSH - PRC in providing mining companies and manufacturers with guidelines for the construction of ergonomically designed seats to reduce the shock exposure of underground mobile equipment operators.

7. Acknowledgments

The authors thank J. R. Bartels, J. P. DuCarme, R. L. Unger, and R. S. Fowkes for their contributions in the design and construction of the ergonomic seat.

References

[1] Remington, P.J., D.A. Andersen, and M.N. Alakel. Assessment of whole body vibration levels of coal miners. Volume II: Whole-body vibration exposure of underground coal mining machine operators (contract JO308045, Bolt, Beranek, and Newman, Inc.), U.S. Bureau of Mines OFR 1B-87, Mar. 1984, 114 pp.; NTIS PB 87-144-119.

Advances in Occupational Ergonomics and Safety II
Edited by Biman Das and Waldemar Karwowski
IOS Press and Ohmsha, 1997

Design and Evaluation of an Ergonomic Hand-Held Scraper

Feng-Huo Sheu and *Chia-Lung Chang

*Department of Industrial Design and *Mechanical Engineering*

National Yunlin Institute of Technology, Touliu, Yunlin, Taiwan 640

Abstract

This study aims at designing a "user friendly" scraper based on the ergonomic design concept. It included two phases of investigation. In phase one, a list of criteria for tool operations were developed and a new improved design alternative was accomplished through design development. The new design was then adopted for further performance evaluation in the second phase. Two types of scraper, a traditional one and the new design, were studied. Twelve subjects were asked to simulated tool operations with three angles of working conditions (horizontal, 45-degree slant, and vertical working surfaces). The experimental investigation was conducted by making direct strain gauge measurement on the neck of the tool. Force exertions were studied by the data collected. Results showed that tool design can be effectively developed with ergonomics in mind and an improved design was confirmed. The significant improvement in performance was then evaluated in terms of force exertions when operating hand tool by various working postures. The study concluded that both objective and subjective evaluation verified merits of new design. It is therefore necessary to adopt ergonomic concept in hand tool design.

1. INTRODUCTION

One of the most serious occupational concerns today is the occurrence of cumulative trauma disorders (CTDs) resulting from awkward, repetitive working postures, poorly designed tools and inadequate job design. Based on findings by Taylor 1982 [1], Renold, et al., 1982 [2], Suggestal.[3], Dupuis and Jansen 1981[4], various hand-held tools are sometimes hazardous to operators and may cause adverse effects on tool users. One of the primary tools used by many maintenance workers is the hand-held scrapers. Since there seems to be a need of investigation pertaining to the effects of hand-held scraper design characteristics on operation and discomfort, this study centered on the ergonomic aspect of human-tool interface design as applied to this ubiquitous tool. There are a number of sources [5][6] that recommended principles and criteria for the design and use of hand tools. The proper design of hand tools requires many considerations, such as the application of technical, physiological, anatomic, anthropometric as well as hygienic considerations. A general review of good hand tool ergonomic design principles recommends the use of special designed tools when they are economically feasible and more efficient, tool should be designed to maintain a straight wrist, avoid repetitive finger actions, avoid tissue compression stress, design for safe operation and consider left-handers and women.

A detailed study of the design characteristics of hand-held scrapers revealed that few ergonomic design principles have been observed and applied to this tool. The operator's hand postures are forced to adapt to the conventional straight handle configuration that causes ulnar wrist deviations, forearm pronations during tool operation. Such postures can result in many effects such as low job efficiency, reduced work quality, increased local muscle fatigue, loss grip strength and finally hand-wrist discomfort.

Sound ergonomic principles should be applied to this tool design in order to eliminated those adverse effects. In observations of scraper operations with current design, the tool does not provide an appropriate interface between operator and tool itself.

The primary objective of this research therefore was to optimize a new tool based on ergonomics. The work included: (1) Determining what ergonomic design criteria should be observed for scraper; (2) Developing an improved scraper based on the results of objective (1); and (3) Evaluating the design in comparison to a conventional scraper at three working conditions.

2. METHODS

2.1 Phase I: Design Development

As a rule, it takes a combination of strategies to protect tool operators effectively from possible injuries, to ease operator's local muscle fatigue, and to improve job efficiency. In general, the best strategy is improved   by design. If no alternative in design is possible, then an appropriate selection of tool and procedures for use should follow. According to ergonomics design principles, human-tool relationships cannot be optimized without special consideration of the operator's interface with the tool itself. Strain caused by improper postures should be effectively reduced and comfort should be achieved, if tool design can be improved. The primary purpose of phase I was to develop the appropriate hand-arm postures suitable for operation of the scrapers and evaluate alternative designs using styrofoam mockups. Based on the aforementioned considerations, six different ideas sketching on paper were generated and presented to three research and design personnels at a local hand tool manufacturing company and six prospective tool users. Three ideas on paper were selected for making styrofoam mockups for three dimensional concept evaluations. Review of the comments from field survey of prospective users, were analized. A unified scraper idea had been improved, detailed and developed consistently into a complete concept. A working prototype (Figure 1) then was made possible for phase II evaluation. As shown in Fig. 1, the left one is the traditional scraper, the right one is the alternative design.

Fig 1. Two types of scraper   Fig 2. Experimental set-up

2.2 Phase II: Performance Evaluation

In order to evaluate the new design effects on tool operation, tool simulations were required for performance evaluation. The study was conducted in the applied mechanics lab. on NYIT, Taiwan. In the study, each participant was asked to simulate three working operations at three different working conditions. The participants in this study were twelve male students from NYIT with a mean height of 175.9cm. Their ages ranged from 21 to 26 years with a mean of 22.7 years. Before the actual experiment, participants were given an initial instruction, describing the details of the experiment.

A standard anthropometric kit was used to obtain stature and other anthropometric data, and an experimental plateform were constructed for determining maximum voluntary force exertions transfering to the neck of tool under each experimental conditions. Figure 2 displays the experimental settings. Foil strain gages (CEA-13-062-uw-350, Measurements Group) were bonded to the tools at neck area to measure the bending moments at each location. The gages were calibrated directly for these moments and hand forces by appropriate static loadings. The forces were calculated from the calibration. The strain gage amplifier (2120A, Measurements Group) transmitted data via an analogue/digit converter (model 2000, Measurements Group) direct onto a PC; data was stored for subsequent statistical analysis. The design of the experiment was a repeated measures type in which the twelve participants work with two working prototypes in different randomly determined orders to block out any ordering confounding variables such as fatigue and conditioning. In this design the assumption was made that the participants were distributed as a random varible and tool were fix categories. Prior to the beginning of the experiment, each participant was given an explaination of the experiment. After the explaination an opportunity was given to ask questions concerning the purpose and procedures of the study. After the information period, the participant was asked to performed warm up exercise designed to stretch hand, forearm muscle groups to avoid strains. At this point the participant was ready to begin simulating tasks. First few trials were considered practices to become accustomed to the tool and working technique. The next three trials were used for data collection. Participants were asked to complete a tool evaluation form after completing the tasks. Data from the experiment were later used for statistical analysis to determine which design formed a better choice.

3. RESULTS AND DISCUSSIONS

3.1 Phase I. Alternative Designs

Based on a preliminary investigation of user activities in field, of users working postures and on users opinion survey in different workplaces, it was decided that the design should: (1) offer sufficient space for keeping best fit between object and tool blade; (2) enable users to apply power grip for most working requirements; (3) avoid radial deviation and ulnar deviation of wrist; (4) allow for simultaneous control of tool orientation via a larger, shaped handle offering concurrent response to working surface; (5)require efficient downward push forces transmitting to the tool blade and pull forces for operations; (6) comply with both right-handers' and left-handers' working needs; (7) have safety design considerations; (8) avoid tissue compression; (9) have high aesthetic appeal.

Three ideas on paper were selected for making styrofoam mockups for three dimensional concept evaluations. Review of the comments from field survey of prospective users, were analyzed. A unified scraper idea had been improved, detailed and developed consistently into a complete concept. A working prototype was then made possible for phase II evaluation.

3.2 Phase II Design Evaluations

Objective Evaluation: Effects of new design on force exertions.
Data collected from strain gauge measurements were analyzed. On the whole, results of statistical analyses showed significant ergonomic design effects on tool. Anova on average force exertions ($f(1,23)=44.9028$,Pr<0.0001) and peak value analyses ($f(1,23)=25.649$,Pr<0.0001) revealed significant differences. This result indicated design did improve the performance of tool. Detail examination of data showed the interactions existed between tools and working conditions. Further analyses showed average force on tool under horizontal ($f(1,23)=5.1434$,Pr<0.0035) and vertical ($f(1,23)=140.3359$, Pr<0.0001) conditions were significant. However, statistical data did not result any significant differences on average force under 45 degree working condition. Conclusively, in addition to the working angels, the significant ergonomic design effects on the performance of tool is evaluated.

Subjective evaluations: Both hand-wrist discomfort survey and preference rating were collected as subjective evaluation data. For an overall discomfort analysis, all discomfort ratings on hand-wrist from operating tools were accumulated to obtain an overall discomfort ratings. Results of hand-wrist discomfort survey data analysis indicated that there were significant differences in operating scrapers ($F(1,11)=9.36$, $Pr<0.0051$). New ergonomic design was rated at an average of 3.27 which was significantly lower than the traditional design with an average of 5.81. Preference rating was provided after completing all experimental sessions. Results showed that the ergonomic design scraper was regarded as the prefer choice. Eight participants out of twelve favored new design. Two subjects prefer the traditional scraper and the other two subjects prefered neither the new design nor the traditional one.

4. CONCLUSION

The intent of the present study is to design and evaluate an ergonomic hand-held scraper. A list of criteria for scraper was carefully investigated and provided the basis for generating new ideas. The succeeding ideas on paper and three mockups had been carefully evaluated. A final prototype was made possible by refining detail comments from prospective users for performance evaluations.

The conclusion that can be derived from performance evaluation of alternative design is simply that the traditional tool can be better optimized to reduce operator's effort and therefore possibly to reduce the immediate muscle fatigue of upper extremities. Results of subjective evaluations corresponded to that of objective evaluations. In summary, there is evidence to support that the ergonomic design can provide physical, postural and comfort improvements in the operation of hand-held scraper.

ACKNOWLEDGMENT

This work was supported in part by the National Science Council of R.O.C. under contract no. NSC-84-2512-S-224-001. The authors would like to express their thanks herewith. The assistance of graduate student K.S. Liu of NYIT is also gratefully appreciated.

REFERENCES

[1]Taylor,W. and Brammer,A.J. Vibration Effects on the Hand Arm in Industry: in Vibration Effects in the Hand Arm in Industry, Wiley   Interscience, New York,1982,pp.

[2]1-12.Renald, D. and Wasserman D., Vibration Acceleration Measured on Pneumatic Tools in Chipping and Grinding Operation, Proceeding of Hand-arm Vibration Symposium, Toronto,Canada,1982,pp.225-238.

[3]Suggs,C.W. and Hanks,J.M. Vibration of Power Tool Handles. In: Proceedings of Hand-Arm Vibration Symposium. Toronto: Canada. 1982,pp.245-251.

[4]Dupuis,H. and Jansen, G, Immediate Effects of Vibration Transmitted to the Hand. Man Under Vibration Suffering and Protection, Elsevier Scientific Publishing Co., New York,1981, pp.76-96

[5]Huchingson, R. New Horizons for Human Factors in Design. ISBN: 0-07 030815 2. McGraw-Hill Book Co., New York,1980 pp.322-332.

[6]Mabey,M.H.,Rushworth, A.M., Graves, R. J. And Colliers. S.G., Development of Ergonomic Criteria for Power Hand Tool. In: D.J. Osbourne (ed.), Procdings of the Ergonomics Society's Annual Conference, Taylor & Francis, London, 1985, pp. 117-123.

Advances in Occupational Ergonomics and Safety II
Edited by Biman Das and Waldemar Karwowski
IOS Press and Ohmsha, 1997

ERGONOMIC EVALUATION OF THREE DIFFERENT-HANDLED HAMMERS

Mark Stuart[1] and Peregrin Spielholz[2]

[1] SHARP, Washington State Department of Labor and Industries,
Olympia, Washington 98504-4330

[2] University of Washington, Department of Environmental Health, Box 357234,
Seattle, Washington 98195-7234

Three different-handled carpentry framing hammers: steel, fiberglas and wood shank, were evaluated in an effort to determine if one material transmits less physical stress than another. It was also of interest to determine if there were other design factors which explain why carpenters have such strong opinions concerning the use of these three different types of handles. Performance data of speed, number of strokes and miss-hits did not show any significant difference between the hammers ($p > 0.05$). No significant differences were found either for reported body area discomfort ratings or median frequency electromyography (EMG) recordings of the flexor digitorum profundus ($p > 0.05$). These findings suggest that individual preferences may be a function of vibration transmission, which was not measured, or may not be related to physical stress.

1.0 INTRODUCTION

Previous studies of work-related musculoskeletal disorders have primarily focused on office, service and manufacturing environments. However, recent studies suggest that musculoskeletal injuries are much higher in the construction trades [1-3]. The injuries resulting from work in this sector can have a profound effect on the length and quality of working life for many carpenters as well as other trades.

The frequent use of handtools and associated activities has been reported as significantly contributing to lost-time injuries [4, 5]. Axelsson and Fang [6] determined that handheld machines or tools were the "primary external factor" in 18% of all construction accidents in Sweden. Additionally, the right wrist is one of the most frequently reported areas of body discomfort in construction workers [3, 7].

Spielholz and Wiker [8] determined from work sampling that hammering was the most frequently performed activity (18% of the day) for union carpenters during their most common types of construction work. Anecdotal information obtained from union carpenters and members of a focus group on ergonomics in carpentry suggested that there may be a difference in stress transmitted to the hand and arm by different types of shank materials.

Previous studies of hammers have primarily focused on the handle geometry [9-13]. However, no studies were found which addressed the more common issues faced by construction workers such as which off-the-shelf different-shank-material hammers will be the most comfortable and produce the highest quality work. Therefore, the objectives of this study were to determine if there were subjective preference, performance and physiological differences between the use of three commonly used off-the-shelf hammers with different shank material handles.

2.0 METHOD

2.1 Subjects

Nine apprentice carpenters (8 males and 1 female) volunteered to participate in the study. Respondents had worked in carpentry for an average of seven years with a range between 2 to 15 years.

2.2 Apparatus

2.2.1 Hammers. Three hammers of different shank materials with 20 ounce heads were purchased "off-the-shelf." A fiberglas shank model by Stanley, a steel shank hammer by Stanley and a wood shank Vaughan hammer were used.

2.2.2 Questionnaires. A general background questionnaire was administered before the study with an approved consent form. A discomfort rating questionnaire was constructed using horizontal visual analog scales for each of nine body regions. A subjective questionnaire was designed to obtain scaled ratings of preference, handle comfort and amount of impact. A rank-ordering of the hammers was performed after the final trial and free response questions were administered relating what the participant liked or disliked about the hammers.

2.2.3 Electromyography (EMG). EMG data were recorded from surface electrodes placed over the flexor digitorum profundus. A Mega ME 3000 data recording system was used on-line with a portable computer. Mega EMG data analysis software was used to calculate median frequencies for each pre-trial and post-trial EMG measurement.

2.2.4 Fixture. A standard carpenter apprentice testing fixture was used for the trials. Fifty 12-penny nails were hammered into a 2 X 4 board placed in a horizontal orientation at a height of 30 inches.

2.3 Procedures

The hammering trials were administered using a Latin Square design. Participants performed the hammering task separately using each of the three different hammers in counterbalanced order to control for order effects.

The participants were instructed to hammer 50 nails, contained in their tool belt, as quickly as they could while still striking accurately. Subjective rating questionnaires were completed for each hammer immediately following the trial. Discomfort rating scales were completed before and after each hammering trial.

EMG recording of a 3 second maximum voluntary contraction (MVC) and a 50% MVC were recorded immediately before and after each trial. Participants were given approximately one minute of rest between trials.

3.0 RESULTS

Statistical analysis of the task performance data using a repeated measures analysis of variance did not yield significant differences between the three different hammers ($p > 0.05$), although participants using the steel shank handle hammered faster with fewer strokes and miss-hit nails. This result may be due to the steel shank hammer's shorter length handle compared to the other two hammers.

There were no statistically significant differences revealed with any of the body-area discomfort data ($p > 0.05$). It was also found that there were no muscle fatigue differences after analyzing the EMG median frequency data ($p > 0.05$).

Analysis of the hammer rank-ordering data indicated that participants did not always rank the type of hammer he or she normally used on the job as the most preferred in this study.

4.0 DISCUSSION

Data analysis revealed that most participants were not fatigued as a result of the hammering task performed in this experiment. This conclusion is based on an analysis of participants' EMG median frequency data. Most participants displayed an increase in EMG median frequency from the pre-trial measurements to the post-trial measurements. If the hammering task used was longer in duration so that participants displayed electromyographic evidence of muscle fatigue, there may have been empirical data to support construction worker preference for different-handled hammers. A possible solution is to only measure fatigue if one works at 40% MVC for the whole day [14].

Anecdotal information indicated that the carpenters' hammer-purchase decisions were not always based on the quality of the hammer nor the hammer's handle. It was learned that purchases are sometimes made based on a hammer's durability and the manufacturer's warranty. Some carpenters prefer wood-handled hammers because they think there is greater vibration attenuation, but these hammers are often not purchased because wood-handled hammers break more often.

5.0 CONCLUSIONS

The types of data collected in this study have not helped explain the strong preferences among carpenters for certain materialed-handles. Some researchers believe this is determined somewhat by the vibration attenuating characteristics of the different materials, such as wood. Further research to describe the biomechanics of hammering and vibration-transmission characteristics of different handles is needed to better understand the issues associated with optimal hammer design.

6.0 ACKNOWLEDGMENTS

This study was completed under a grant from the National Institute for Occupational Safety and Health (NIOSH). In addition, the authors would like to thank the United Brotherhood of Carpenters and Western Washington general contractors for their participation and contributions to the research.

7.0 REFERENCES

1. Holmstrom, E.B., Lindell, J. and Moritz, U., Low Back and Neck/Shoulder Pain in Construction Workers: Occupational Workload and Psychosocial Risk Factors, Part 1: Relationship to Low Back Pain, *Spine* **17**(6) (1992) 663-671.
2. Holmstrom, E.B., Lindell, J. and Moritz, U., Low Back and Neck/Shoulder Pain in Construction Workers: Occupational Workload and Psychosocial Risk Factors, Part 2: Relationship to Neck and Shoulder Pain, *Spine* **17**(6) (1992) 672-677.
3. Eastern Iowa Construction Alliance/University of Iowa Joint Project on Reduction of Work-Related Injuries and Illnesses Through Ergonomic Intervention, *Final Report, Phase I*, 1991 (unpublished report).
4. Aghazadeh, F. and Mital, A., Injuries Due to Handtools: Results of a Questionnaire, *Applied Ergonomics*, **18**(4) (1987) 273-278.
5. Marras, W. S., Bobick, T. G., Lavender, S. A., Rockwell, T. H. and Lundquist, R. L., Risks of Hand Tool Injury in US Underground Mining from 1978 through 1982, Part I: Coal Mining, *Journal of Safety Research*, **19**(2) (1988) 71-85.
6. Axelsson and Fang, *Accidents with Hand-held Machines and Tools in Construction Work* (in Swedish). Report TRITA-AOG-0032. Royal Institute of Technology, Stockholm, Sweden, 1985.
7. Cook, T.M., and Zimmerman, C.L., A Symptom and Job Factor Survey of Unionized Construction Workers. In Kumar, S.(ed.), *Advances in Industrial Ergonomics and Safety IV*, Taylor and Francis, 1992.
8. Spielholz, P. and Wiker, S. F., Assessing Ergonomic Hazards in Unstructured Work Using Work Sampling Techniques: An Application in Construction of Concrete Formwork. In Bittner, A. and Champney, P. (eds.), *Advances in Industrial Safety and Ergonomics VII*, Bristol, PA: Taylor and Francis, 1995, pp. 75-80.
9. Schoenmarklin, R. W., The Effect of Angled Hammers on Wrist Motion, *Proceedings of the Human Factors Society 32nd Annual Meeting*, 1988.
10. Konz, S., Bent Hammer Handles, *Human Factors*, **28**(3) (1986) 317-323.
11. Knowlton, R. G. and Gilbert, J. C., Ulnar Deviation and Short-term Strength Reductions as Affected by a Curve-Handled Ripping Hammer and a Conventional Claw Hammer, *Ergonomics*, **26**(2) (1983) 173-179.
12. Shoenmarklin, R. W. and Marras, W. S., Effects of Handle Angle and Work Orientation on Hammering: I. Wrist Motion and Hammering Performance, *Human Factors*, **31**(4) (1989) 397-411.
13. Shoenmarklin, R. W. and Marras, W. S., Effects of Handle Angle and Work Orientation on Hammering: II. Muscle Fatigue and Subjective Ratings of Body Discomfort, *Human Factors*, **31**(4) (1989) 413-420.
14. National Institute for Occupational Safety and Health, *Selected Topics in Surface Electromyography for Use in the Occupational Setting: Expert Perspectives*, DHHS (NIOSH) Publication No. 91-100, 1992.

Advances in Occupational Ergonomics and Safety II
Edited by Biman Das and Waldemar Karwowski
IOS Press and Ohmsha, 1997

Design and Validation of Measurement Systems for Load Carriage

[1]J.M. Stevenson, [1]S.A. Reid, [2]J.T. Bryant, [1]J.B. Doan, R. DePencier, [2]G. Saunders, [2]D.Siu,
[1]Ergonomics Research Group, [2]Clinical Mechanics Group
Queen's University, Kingston, Ontario, Canada K7L 3N6

Abstract

An evaluation protocol for assessment of load carriage systems was developed consisting of human input on comfort, features and fit, and a standardized measurement system using a computer-controlled Load Carriage (LC Sim) Simulator. The purpose of this study was to validate the measurement systems used in the LC Sim under static and dynamic conditions. Independent measurement strategies were formed for the LC Sim output measures: a) shoulder strap and waist belt tension, b) shoulder strap, waist belt and lumbar pad pressure and c) relative displacement of the pack. Results indicated that the shoulder and waist belt transducers were stable over time. In dynamic tests, the maximum STD within a test was 0.9 N, across tests was 2.3 N with less that 4% decay over 1200 cycles. The TEKSCAN™ Pressure System under static conditions was more stable in average pressure and contact area than peak pressures. The SEM for average pressures was .5 kPa to 1.3 kPa, peak values were less stable with a SEM of 3.7 kPa to 12.6 kPa and decreased in magnitude over time. FASTRAK™ assessment of relative displacement between the pack and the person was validated with an OPTOTRAK™ system. Results showed the pack/person relative position had a 0.65 mm RMS error.

1. Introduction

In October 1994 a research team was contracted by the Defence and Civil Institute for Environmental Medicine, (DCIEM) to develop a comprehensive measurement system for the evaluation of current and future designs of personal load carriage systems (PLCS). The objectives of the measurement system were to develop an accurate assessment strategy for load carriage systems that was rapid and cost effective. There are two facets to the assessment strategy; human input with regard to comfort, features and fit, and standardized performance measurements which are established using a programmable pneumatic Load Carriage Simulator and a torsional stiffness testing system. The purpose of this study was to validate these standardized performance measurements using independent measurement strategies.

2. Method

The LC Simulator consists of a scaled model of the human torso which cycled through the vertical displacement of a walking cadence of three kilometres per hour using computer-controlled pneumatic actuators. The mannikin was instrumented to determine the relative motion the pack using 3D FASTRAK™ electromagnetic sensors. Transducers were designed to measure strap forces, and a TEKSCAN™ pressure sensor system was used to assess contact pressures between the pack suspension elements and the torso.

2.1   Strap Force Transducer Testing

Static: The strap force transducers were strain gauge based in a full bridge configuration. For the static test, transducers were positioned vertically and the bridge was zeroed under no load. Repeat measures were taken at time equal 0, 1 and 3 minutes. This was repeated under the following hanging loads: 44.5 N, 89.0 N, 133.2 N and 177.5 N. Each load condition was repeated 4 times.

Dynamic: Four independent trials were performed following the LC Sim standard protocol for a level walking test. The strap forces were examined for repeatability between trials and for variation during each 20 minute dynamic test. Strap forces were sampled for 10 seconds at 55 hz, at time 10, 300, 600, 900 and 1200 seconds.

Results

Table 1   Strap Force Results: Dynamic Test

Time (s)	Mean Shoulder Strap Force (N)				Mean Waist Belt Force (N)			
	1	2	3	4	1	2	3	4
Avg(N)	41.9	46.2	44.0	45.9	27.6	32.8	34.4	32.3
STD(N)	3.1	0.1	0.2	0.3	0.9	0.9	0.6	0.4
4 Trial Avg (N)	44.5				4 Trial Avg (N)	31.8		
4 Trial STD (N)	2.3				4 Trial STD (N)	2.6		

2.2   Pressure Sensing System Testing

Static: Pressure sensors were affixed to the simulator torso in predefined contact areas, and checked for a zero pressure value in a no load condition. Load carriage systems (LCS's) were centrally packed with 245.3 N. The LCS was loaded onto the LC Sim and the torso was leaned forward to balance the reaction moments at the base. Waist belt and shoulder straps were set to a fixed value. Pressure recordings at contact sites on the shoulder, waist, and lower lumbar area were taken.

Dynamic: The LCS was set up with pack C as described above. Four trials were performed using the LC Sim standard protocol for a level walking test. Contact pressure was recorded for

10 seconds at 55 hz, at time 10, 300, 600, 900 and 1200 seconds. Pressure distribution (peak, average, and contact area) was examined for repeatability and variation between static and dynamic testing.

Results

Table 2   Comparison of Static to Dynamic Contact Pressure Measurement

Pack D Pressure Results		Static (n=3)		Dynamic (n=4)	
		Pressure (kPa)	Area (m²)	Pressure (kPa)	Area (m²)
Shoulder	Avg	6.3	0.003	15.2	0.005
	Peak	12.5	0.003	24.0	0.005
Waist	Avg	8.2	0.004	2.1	0.005
	Peak	23.6	0.004	10.5	0.005
Lumbar	Avg	8.7	0.006	8.6	0.011
	Peak	17.2	0.006	20.8	0.011

Table 3   Dynamic Pressure Results for 4 Independent Trials

Pressure Results (kPa)	Shoulder		Waist		Lumbar	
	Avg	Peak	Avg	Peak	Avg	Peak
Mean	11.6	41.5	6.6	12.4	9.4	19.9
Variance	6.6	159.4	1	13.5	3.7	21.3
Std Deviation	2.6	12.6	1	3.7	1.9	4.6
Std. Error (SE)	1.3	6.3	.5	1.8	1	2.3
n for SE <2.0 kPa with 95% confidence level	2	40	1	4	1	6

2.3   Motion Measurement System Testing

The relative displacement of the pack with respect to the torso of the person is the parameter used to evaluate the laxity of a LC suspension system. An OPTOTRAK™ system (accuracy ±0.1 mm) was used simultaneously with a FASTRAK™ system to validate relative displacement measurements.

Results

Table 4   Relative Displacement of LCS with Respect to Torso (mm)

	FASTRAK™	OPTOTRAK™
Max.	2.99	2.82
Min.	-2.35	-3.28
Peak to Peak	5.34	6.10

RMS Error of FASTRAK ™ data: 0.65 mm

3. Conclusions

After individual calibration, strap force transducers were highly linear ($R^2 > .9995$), with a small error (2.7 N) and were stable over time. Under dynamic testing, maximum STD within tests was 0.9 N and across tests was 2.3 N with less that 4% decay over 2100 cycles.

The TEKSCAN™ Pressure Sensor System under static conditions was more stable in Pavg. and contact area than peak pressures, with peak pressure magnitude sensitive to stress raisers (i.e. seams). During simulated walking, SEM for Pavg. was 0.5 kPa to 1.3 kPa depending on location and pack characteristics. Peak values were less stable (SEM of 3.7 kPa to 12.6 kPa), dropped in magnitude over time, and were better suited to identifying high pressure points.

The FASTRAK™ assessment of relative displacement between the pack and the person was validated with the OPTOTRACK™ system under static and dynamic conditions.   The pack/person relative positions had a 0.65 mm RMS error in all test conditions.

The results of testing show that the current measurement systems are a valid means of quantifying characteristics of load carriage designs. Comparison of static and dynamic test results indicates that static testing does not adequately predict dynamic performance.

4. References

1.   Datta, S.R. & Ramanathan, N.L. (1970) Ergonomic comparison of seven modes of carrying loads on the horizontal plane. *Ergonomics*, **13(2)**, 269-278.

2.   Devita, P., Hong, D., & Hammill, J. (1991) Effects of assymetric load carrying on the biomechanics of walking. *Journal of Biomechanics*, **24(12)**, 1119-1129.

3.   Goel, K.V., Weinstein, J.N., & Patwardhan, A.G. (1995). *Biomechanics of the Spine: Clinical and Surgical Perspective*. CRC Press.

4.   Winsmann, F.R., & Goldman, R.F. (1976). Methods for evaluation of load carriage systems. *Perceptual and Motor Skills*, **43**, 1211-1218.

Advances in Occupational Ergonomics and Safety II
Edited by Biman Das and Waldemar Karwowski
IOS Press and Ohmsha, 1997

Human factors testing of load carriage designs

[1] J.B. Doan, [1]J.M. Stevenson, [2]J.T. Bryant, [1]J.M. Deakin
[1]Ergonomics Research Group, [2]Clinical Mechanics Group
Queen's University, Kingston, Ontario, Canada K7L 3N6

This study was performed to obtain subjective response for evaluation
of five different military load carriage systems (LCS). It is part of a
larger study which is aimed at the development of standardized load
carriage evaluation for the Canadian Forces (Stevenson et al., 1995).
Twenty eight experienced military subjects were assigned four of the
LCS over the course of four consecutive trials. In each trial, subjects
completed a march of 5.0 km over level ground as well as five activity
stations (AS) in full marching order. Each lap of the march (1.0 km)
was followed by one of these AS, presented to subjects in random
order. Subject responses were elicited immediately following each
AS. Subjects also completed a secondary set of AS and evaluated
battle order capabilities. Ratings were highest for LCS with short
back length and internal frame while battle order testing favoured
designs with a reduced profile, particularly in the anterior waist area.

1.0 Introduction

Military operations often involve the movement of personnel and equipment into areas which
are difficult to access and inhospitable. The ability to maintain a supply of food and protection, as
well as establishing shelter and communications, is critical to the survival of the soldier in these
circumstances. For this reason, the personal load carriage system (LCS), or 'rucksack', has long
been used to transport military and personal items into battle (Renbourn, 1954). The cost of this
portability is discomfort and potential injury for soldiers who carry large loads or carry loads
improperly. Injuries due to load carriage such as skin pressure sores, restricted blood flow to arms,
muscle fatigue, and reduced functional ability have been well documented (Datta and Ramanathan,
1971; Winsmann and Goldman, 1976; Legg and Mahanty, 1985; Balogun et al., 1986; Holewijn,
1990; Holewijn and Lotens, 1992). However, research into the capabilities of various LCS in
preventing these injuries and maintaining a high level of comfort for the soldier has not focused on
the design of the pack, but on the location of the load.

The purpose of this research was to develop a methodology for subjective analysis of five
different LCS, and to relate these subjective rankings to LCS design. This research is one component
of a project to design standardized LCS testing, and to use this testing to develop LCS equipment
for the Canadian Forces (CF).

2.0   Method

Subjects - Testing was performed on twenty-eight male CF subjects (25.3 +/- 2.0 years, 179.6 +/- 7.6 cm height, 83.2 +/- 8.8 kg weight). Subjects were all infantry soldiers from the same CF unit and as such were equally familiar with the rigours of load carriage as a military operation. All subjects were informed of the nature of the testing and they gave their consent to participate in the study.

Load Carriage Systems - The LCS tested were selected from existing military systems. All LCS were filled to maximum dimensions with rigid foam. This foam contained the load for each pack (27.5 +/- 1.0 kg) and kept this load in a consistent position. All battle orders were filled with a standard operational load.

Marching Order Testing - LCS were assigned to all subjects in an incomplete block design. Figure 1 is a flowchart outlining the path of one LCS marching order trial. Subject start times were staggered, allowing for the recording of elapsed time and aural temperature when subjects returned to the testing centre. AS, as described in Table 1, were randomly assigned for all subjects, and questionnaires were completed following each station. After the fifth march lap, subjects attempted a series of investigator led static tasks (ST1) in an effort to evaluate any reduction in range of motion imposed by the LCS. Following ST1, subjects completed a marching order summary questionnaire.

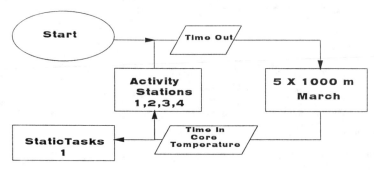

Figure 1 - Path for LCS marching order trial.

Table 1 - Marching order activity stations.

Activity Station	Station Name	Description
1	Bent Balance Beam	- 10 m balance beam, 9 cm wide w/ 65 degree directional changes
	Boulder Hop	- 7 stones, 25 cm in diameter, w/ 90 degree directional changes
2	Straight Balance Beam	- 10 m balance beam, 9 cm wide
3	Fence Climb	- scale and descend 1.2 m fence
	Agility Run	- 10 pairs pylons (0.75 m apart) in slalom course over 10 m
4	Side Slope Walk	- 7.5 m long w/ 26 degree side slope angle
	Forward Ramp Climb	- 4.5 m long w/ 21 degree angle of elevation

Battle Order Testing - Following ST1, subjects doffed their marching order and attempted to complete a second series of AS (Table 2). These AS were designed to evaluate access restrictions through closed spaces based on the geometric profile of the battle order. Battle order, in this study either belt or vest design, is integrated with marching order and is used to contain the personal equipment a soldier requires to exist independently for 24 hours. Subjects completed subjective questionnaires rating their ability to complete these AS in the respective battle orders.

Table 2 - Battle order activity stations.

Activity Station	Station Name	Description
1	Vertical Mousehole	- 0.5 m x 0.5 m vertical tunnel, 2.25 m in height
2	Horizontal Mousehole	- 0.5 m x 0.5 x horizontal tunnel, 2.0 m in length
3	Leopard Crawl	- 6.0 m in length, with overhead obstacles at a height of 0.5 m
4	Over and Under	- under 0.5 m barrier, over 1.2 m fence, under 0.5 m barrier
		- 0.5 m distance between obstacles

3.0   Results

All responses were selected from the following numerical scale: a score of 1 was 'totally unacceptable' and a score of 6 was 'totally acceptable' (Shek, 1995). Average system scores greater than 5 (*) were considered superior while scores of 3.5 or less (grey) were considered to be inferior. *Marching Order Testing* - Table 3 contains the results from the trial summary for the LCS marching orders. System B, an internal frame model with a short back length, had average or superior ratings in all categories. The smaller design of this system located it higher on the back, increasing the mobility performance but also excessively loading the shoulders.

Table 3 - Summary ratings for marching order testing.

	A	B	C	D	E
Acceptability	4.1	5.5 *	3.1	2.9	4.0
Integration	3.6	4.8	2.7	2.6	4.1
Mobility	4.3	5.2 *	3.0	2.9	3.8
Physical Comfort	4.1	4.5	2.4	2.4	3.1
Thermal Comfort	4.8	5.0 *	3.0	3.2	4.0

This can be contrasted with systems C and D, external frame models with increased back length and bottom slung valises, which had inferior scores in all aspects.

Battle Order Testing - Battle orders with a minimum amount of kit at the front waist level (BW, LCV) exhibited superior scores for all tasks, except thermal comfort (Table 4). BW, a yoke style webbing made of mesh, also had a superior score for thermal comfort. The larger profile of system CW and the flimsy connection between webbing and components led to low ratings for this system.

Table 4 - Summary ratings for battle order testing.

	AW	BW	C,D,EW	LCV
Acceptability	4.3	5.1 *	4.1	5.1 *
Durability	4.9	5.1 *	3.4	4.9
Mobility	4.8	5.0 *	4.1	5.1 *
Physical Comfort	4.4	5.3 *	3.8	4.9
Thermal Comfort	4.5	5.1 *	4.3	3.8

4.0   References

1.   Balogun, JA., Robertson, RJ., Goss, FL., Edwards, MA., Cox, RC., and KF. Metz. (1986). Metabolic and perceptual responses while carrying external loads on the head and by yoke. *Ergonomics*, **29(12)**, 1623-1635.

2.   Datta, SR., and NL. Ramanathan. (1970). Ergonomic comparison of seven modes of carrying loads on the horizontal plane. *Ergonomics*, **13(2)**, 269-278.

3.   Holewijn, M. (1990). Physiological strain due to load carrying. *European Journal of Applied Physiology*, **59**, 237- 245.

4.   Holewijn, M., and WA. Lotens. (1992). The influence of backpack design on physical performance. *Ergonomics*, **35(2)**, 149-157.

5.   Legg, SJ., and A. Mahanty. (1985). Comparison of five modes of carrying a load close to the trunk. *Ergonomics*, **28(12)**, 1653-1660.

6.   Renbourn, ET. (1954). The knapsack and pack. *Journal of the Royal Army Medical Corps*, **99(5)**, 1-200.

7.   Shek, Y. *Subjective ratings of webbing and rucksack*. Report #3753-1, January 1995, DCIEM.

8.   Stevenson, JM., Bryant, JT., dePencier, RD., Pelot, RP., and JG. Reid. *Research and development of an advanced personal load carriage system*. Report for DCIEM, September 1995, Queen's University.

9.   Winsmann, FR., and RF. Goldman. (1976). Methods for evaluation of load carriage systems. *Perceptual and Motor Skills*, **43**, 1211-1218.

Acknowledgements

Support for this project has been provided by the Canadian Forces' Defence and Civil Institute of Environmental Medicine (DCIEM). In particular, the assistance of Dr. Ken Ackles, Major Linda Bossi, and Captain Steve Kroone has been greatly appreciated. Subjects for pilot and full testing were provided by CFB Petawawa (1st Canadian Light Infantry Battalion), CFB Kingston (1st Canadian Signals Regiment), and CFB Gagetown (2nd Royal Canadian Regiment).

Advances in Occupational Ergonomics and Safety II
Edited by Biman Das and Waldemar Karwowski
IOS Press and Ohmsha, 1997

Impact of the use of welding guns equipped with a fume extraction nozzle on muscular activation, psychophysical perception, and quality of welded joints

Yves BEAUCHAMP.[1], Denis MARCHAND[2], Michel GALOPIN, [1] and Nicole GOYER[3]

[1] *École de technologie supérieure, Mechanical Engineering Department, Montréal, CANADA*
[2] *Université du Québec à Montréal, Kinanthropology Department, Montréal, CANADA*
[3] *Institut de recherche en santé et sécurité du travail, Montréal, CANADA*

1. Introduction

MIG-type welding guns equipped with a fume extraction nozzle are commercially available but seldom used. According to welders, the main reasons for this situation are: the strenuousness involved (discomfort, heaviness of the gun, difficulty of handling at some angles) and the poor quality of welding. We conducted a study in order to assess the impact of fume extraction nozzles of GMAW[1] (MIG/MAG) welding guns on the muscular activation of the major muscles involved during welding, the welders' psychophysical perception, and the quality of the joints made in various positions.

2. Methodology

Design of experiment

Experimental evaluations concerning the use of five (5) different GMAW guns (see table 1 for specifications) were conducted in real working conditions (welding of a T-joint) in the welding laboratory of the École de technologie supérieure. The following independent variables were used:

Welding guns (5):   - BERNARDair (with fume extraction nozzle)
                 - BERNARD
                 - BINZELair (with fume extraction nozzle)
                 - BINZEL
                 - AIRMIG (with fume extraction nozzle)
Welding positions (3): - horizontal (2G)
                 - vertical (3G)
                 - ceiling (4G)

For the experimental trials, we used a full factorial design in a 5 x 3 x 2 form, i.e., five (5) welding guns, three (3) welding positions, and two (2) trials per participant. In total, 300 trials were conducted with a group of 10 participating welders, i.e., 30 trials per welder. The following dependent variables were used:

- Percentage of use (PMU) of the five muscles in the upper limbs most called upon during the welding activity;

---

[1] GMAW: Gas Metal Arc Welding; MIG: Metal Inert Gas; MAG: Metal Active Gas.

- Subjective assessment of the ease of handling of the welding gun, discomfort, and impact of the gun on the welding; and
- Quality of the resulting joint.

Table 1. Welding gun characteristics

Welding gun	Gooseneck angle (θ)	Dimension (cm)			Grip circumference (cm)	Position	Moment (N-m) [1]	Weight (kg) [2]	Handle characteristics
		a	b	c					
AirMig	125	11.0	22.0	28.0	13.0	2G	1.075	1.25	Oval et
						3G	null	1.38	curved
						4G	-0.825	1.47	
Bernard	135	12.1	25.0	33.0	12.0	2G	1.755	1.47	
						3G	1.102	1.57	Round
						4G	-0.754	1.66	
Bernardair	130	13.2	27.1	36.0	13.2	2G	2.263	2.08	
						3G	1.081	2.37	Round
						4G	-0.511	2.50	
Binzel	130	11.3	28.0	34.1	12.4	2G	0.697	1.1	Rectangular
						3G	0.526	1.2	and rounded
						4G	-0.395	1.27	
Binzelair	135	13.0	25.1	35.0	12.3	2G	1.684	1.4	Rectangular
						3G	1.559	1.53	and rounded
						4G	-0.621	1.62	

1) Moment required to maintain the welding gun in the desired position (2G, 3G ou 4G) with an angle of 45° between the nozzle and the welded joint . The moment has been measured from the center of the handle.

2) The weight includes the weight of the welding gun and the hose. Since the length of the hose varies in different positions, therefore, the weight of the gun/hose ensemble also varies.

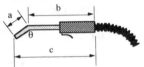

Experienced welders welded the angle of a T-joint (this type of work represents almost two thirds of the welding in the industry) in three different positions: horizontal (2G), vertical (3G) and ceiling (4G). A test bench was designed specifically for the rapid change of welding positions between each trial.

Subjects

Ten (10) experienced welders participated in the study. Subjects were between 30 and 53 (mean = 38.1 years old; std.dev. = 7.7 years old) and had between 3 and 35 years of experience as welders. They were all volunteers, and were paid for their participation.

General procedure

With each of the five welding guns in question, workers were asked to weld the angle of a T-joint from three positions: horizontal (2G), vertical (3G), and ceiling (4G). Workers completed two trials for each of the test conditions. In total, each worker completed 30 trials including a repetition of 15 different test conditions. At each first trial, a worker welded a joint with one of the welding guns, from one of the three preestablished positions. At the second trial, the worker went through the same motions, but did not actually weld a new joint. Welding guns' electric arcs create electromagnetic fields that transform EMG signals necessary to measure muscular activity. It was therefore necessary to measure the quality of the weld at the first trial, and the level of muscular activity at the second trial. Welding guns and positions were assigned to each worker at random.

After each trial, workers' psychophysical conditions were evaluated by means of a questionnaire. A rest period was given between trials. Workers each required approximately three (3) hours to complete thirty (30) tests. At the end of the experiment, each worker was asked to undertake further welding within the format of a semi-directed interview, so that his comments could be noted. Also, EMG signals were processed with the help of a specialized computer programme.

Finally, we evaluated the quality of the 300 joints welded throughout the course of the study. Quality was measured on the basis of appearance, geometry, and sturdiness. For this, we asked an expert welder to evaluate joints on a analogic visual scale from "poor" to "excellent" quality weldings. Joints were marked in such a way that the evaluator could not know which welding guns had been used, or from which positions. In addition, joints were evaluated at random.

Welding Conditions and Fume Control Setting

Each experiment was carried out following the same methodology. For fillets, S6 soft steel welding wire (HB28), 1.2 mm in diameter was used. The gas shield was an Ar-10% CO_2 mixture (Mig-Or). T-joints were made of ASTM A36 hot-rolled steel. Fume control was set according to welding expert's advice, and remained the same for all trials. We wish to mention that the relationship between fume control and the quality of joints was not considered, as this question was not part of our mandate.

3. Statistical Analyses

An analysis of variance (ANOVA) was undertaken on the 300 tests. ANOVA was applied to each of the variables studied: workers' subjective assessment of the manageability of welding guns, discomfort experienced, and influence of the type of gun used on the welding; percentage of muscular use (PMU) in those five upper-body muscles most used in welding; the quality of welded joints as evaluated by the expert welder. The level of significance was set at 5% ($p < 0.05$) to identify effective variables.

4. Results

With respect to most explanatory variables, BERNARDair and BINZELair welding guns were rated as performing less impressively than those guns of the same brand not fitted with a fume extraction nozzle (BERNARD and BINZEL). Welders perceive BERNARDair and BINZELair welding guns as being distinctly less manageable and comfortable than counterparts of the same brand. Welders generally agree that the addition of fume extraction nozzles makes these welding guns too heavy and comparatively less flexible. In turn, these guns are more difficult to manage, particularly the BERNARDair gun when used in vertical and ceiling positions (3G and 4G, respectively). When the BERNARDair gun is used in these positions, the long supinator shows a notably higher average PMU, in part because the fume extraction nozzle makes the gun heavier.

Welders report that the relatively large fume extraction nozzles on the BERNARDair and BINZELair guns tend to hinder a welder's view of his work. However, welders insist that BERNARDair and BINZELair guns are adequate for work in the horizontal position (2G). Be that as it may, our evaluation reveals a higher PMU in the anterior cubital when welding is undertaken from position 2G. (The anterior cubital is responsible for adduction and flexion of the wrist, and flexion of the elbow.) This result can be explained by moments where higher levels of force were measured when operating these two guns from the horizontal position (2G).

It is interesting to note that the AIRMIG welding gun, though fitted with a fume extraction nozzle, shows a better performance in both the psychophysical and electromyographical evaluations. All in all, the AIRMIG gun places second, just after the BINZEL welding gun (no fume extraction nozzle), which has the least weight of any guns. The BINZEL gun is characterized by its lighter weight, its shorter handle, and the slightly narrower angle of its gooseneck (125 degrees). The latter factor is responsible for a null moment in the vertical welding position (3G). Welders maintain that this gun is very handy and lightweight. Returning again to the AIRMIG, welders report that suction of the AIRMIG's fume extraction nozzle is noisier than that of either the BERNARDair or BINZELair guns. (Note: We did not measure actual noise levels.) When work is undertaken from the ceiling position (4G), we note that the anterior deltoid works harder with the AIRMIG than it does with any of the other welding guns. The anterior deltoid is responsible for flexion of the shoulder. The increase in PMU of this muscle is a function of the narrower gooseneck's angle: What is an advantage for vertical welding (3G) is a disadvantage for ceiling welding (4G).

Our analyses show that the main drawbacks concerning the use of welding guns equipped with an extraction nozzle are due to: the increased weight of the gun, the excessive rigidity of the hose, and the impact of a specific gooseneck angle when welding in various positions. The welders in our study preferred the AIRMIG gun mainly because it is light, has a shorter handle and a more flexible hose, all of these making the gun easier to handle. The psychophysical and electromyographic evaluations confirm that these features give the AIRMIG a clear advantage over other guns. However, according to our observations, none of these guns is ideal for all welding positions. Although a gun with a contracted (i.e., narrower angle) gooseneck is preferable for vertical welding, it can be a disadvantage for ceiling welding (4G). Ideally, a welding gun equipped with a fume extraction nozzle should present the following features: an adjustable gooseneck, a handle that is slightly shorter than that of the AIRMIG, and a gun/hose ensemble that is both lightweight and flexible. To conclude, the design of the AIRMIG nozzle is good, but its efficiency for extracting welding fumes has not, to our knowledge, been evaluated.

Acknowledgements

The authors of this study wish to thank Messrs. **Martin Brosseau**, professional researcher for the Occupational Safety Research Team (ÉREST) of the École de technologie supérieure; **Stéphane Patenaude**, graduate student in kinanthropology at the Université du Québec à Montréal; and **Marc-André Gouin**, technician at the École de technologie supérieure, for their active participation in the planning and realization of laboratory trials. The authors are also very grateful to the welders who participated in the study. Finally, the authors wish to thank the Institut de recherche en santé et en sécurité du travail (IRSST) for its financial support.

Advances in Occupational Ergonomics and Safety II
Edited by Biman Das and Waldemar Karwowski
IOS Press and Ohmsha, 1997

Increasing Usability of Voice Activated Dialing Systems

Nancy E. Laurie, MS, AEP,*† Robert O. Andres, Ph.D, CPE† and Donald Fisher, Ph.D.*
† *Ergonomic Engineering, Inc. 20 Gulf Rd. Pelham, MA 01002*
* *University of Massachusetts Amherst, MA 01002*

Research suggests that cellular phone use while driving increases the risk of an auto accident by a factor of 4. Additionally, it has yet to be shown that hands-free phones (such as those which use voice activated dialing systems (VADS)) provide any added safety benefit over manual phones. Since it has been shown that driving performance is degraded during complex conversations especially under demanding driving conditions it makes sense to design the VADS interface to be as intuitive and simple to navigate as possible in order to reduce the risk of an accident. This paper presents the results of an investigation of a commercially available voice activated dialing system under simulated driving conditions and provides recommendations for improvement of its call flows and user interface design. Considering the call flow findings, we conclude that the voice phone book metaphor provides an adequate mental map which helps users navigate the menu hierarchy with some minor exceptions. With regards to the user interface design findings, we conclude that any VADS could be improved by following the principles of conversational speech such as avoiding repetition and being flexible in its handling of interruptions.

1. Introduction

Consumer statistics report an increase of 1,685% from 1986 to 1995 in the number of cellular phone subscribers; current estimates are around 34 million users [1]. Because of its convenience cellular phones are often used while operating motor vehicles. Cellular phones allow the time spent driving between worksites or the home and office to be productive where once it was considered wasted. Unfortunately, a by-product of the cellular phone boom may be an increase in automobile accidents associated with car phone use [2]. A study by Redelmeier and Tibshirani [2] suggests that using a cellular phone while driving may increase ones risk of getting into an accident 4 fold.

Simultaneous driving and conducting a conversation via cellular phone requires divided attention. If the cellular phone conversation or interaction with a voice activated dialing service becomes too complex attention will be diverted from the road to the phone in order to perform the required task. This can lead to automobile accidents. Improving the user interface design and call flow structures can decrease overall system complexity and increase user satisfaction. It was our purpose to evaluate a commercially available voice activated dialing system and make recommendations for its improvement.

The VADS simulated in this study consists of a main level menu with the commands: DIAL, DIRECTORY, NAME and HELP. DIAL is the command which allows the user to dial a telephone number. DIRECTORY is used as the metaphor for a voice phone book to which you can ADD, DELETE and LIST names and numbers. Within the LIST command is the opportunity to CHANGE a number associated with a name on your list. NAME is replaced by a person's name who is in your directory and is the command used for contacting that person. Finally, the command word HELP is used to access directory assistance, customer service and tutorial options.

2. Methodology

The methodology has already been presented in Laurie, Andres and Fisher [3]. Therefore, only a brief overview will be presented here.

2.1. Experimental Design

The experiment was a two factor design (instruction set x accuracy level) with repeated measures on accuracy level. The instruction set was either brief or extended. The only difference between the instruction sets was the addition of an interactive example in which the VADS required the user to repeat themselves three times before being understood.

Two levels of voice recognition accuracy (50% and 83%) were presented to the subjects. Accuracy was determined by the number of repetitions required of the user to complete a task. In the 50% accuracy condition there were three frustration levels that could be assigned to a task (least, intermediate and most frustrating). The 83% accuracy condition consisted of the least and most frustrating levels presented in the 50% accuracy condition.

Testing consisted of seven different tasks including: contacting a person who is/is not on your list; add/delete a person to/from your list; change a telephone number on your list; review the entire contents (or just an individual) on your list and contact directory assistance or customer service. Each task was presented a total of six times during each session for a total of 42 trials. The trials were blocked into groups of 7 so that each task was presented once per block. The trial order was randomly assigned in each block and the frustration level per trial was balanced across blocks such that accuracy levels remained at either 83% or 50% per task over the entire session.

Sixteen subjects, ranging in age from 19-31 years, were randomly divided into two instruction set groups (4 males and 4 females per group). Each subject participated in two sessions, one at each accuracy level. These primary tasks were performed while driving in a simulator on a 12 mile deserted stretch of highway. Dependent measures included 11 questions on a satisfaction survey. The questions covered each of the options offered by the VADS and the overall VADS package. Subjects were also allowed to write suggestions they had to improve the system.

2.2. Procedure

During the first session subjects were asked to fill out an informed consent document and a pre-screening questionnaire. Immediately following, the subject was allowed to familiarize themselves with the equipment. Once done, the subject was told that they had just logged into the VADS for the first time and that they would be given the system tutorial. Depending on which experimental group they belonged to, the subject either received the extended or brief tutorial. During testing the experimenter would ask the subject to perform a task such as "Contact Rob, his name is not in your list". The subject was then given a main level prompt by the WoZ. The subject had to decide which menu option was correct and respond accordingly. After all 42 trials were completed the subject completed a user satisfaction survey. The second session was identical procedurally to the first with the exclusion of the tutorial and pre-session paperwork.

3. Results & Recommendations

The most common mistakes made by participants can be related to problems with the call flow structure or the user interface design. Call flow structure is defined as the natural or logical placement of commands or items and the logical progression of steps or prompts within each command flow. The call flow structure of this particular VADS follows the metaphor of a voice phone book and the commands used are actions surrounding the phone book. User interface design on the other hand is defined as the interaction between the user and the VADS.

Mistakes commonly made due to call flow structure were locating the CHANGE command and not immediately realizing that customer service and directory assistance were two separate services and both were located in the HELP function. Currently the CHANGE function is located in the DIRECTORY menu under the option LIST. It is embedded within LIST and can only be accessed if the user lists one name (see following example). Since the change command was not mentioned explicitly in the tutorial, subjects had to work their way through the different menus to find it. Because of the randomization of tasks within each block of 7 it was very possible that a subject may not be required to LIST the number associated with one name until after they were required to CHANGE the number associated with a name on their list. Once the subject was exposed to listing one number they usually remembered that a phone number could be changed from there. However, some subjects required 2 or 3 exposures before they stopped trying to change a phone number by adding or deleting it.

The obvious solution to alleviate this call flow problem is to move the CHANGE function out of LIST and make it an option at the DIRECTORY level. For example, the prompt at the DIRECTORY level would be changed to "Say ADD, DELETE, LIST or CHANGE".

The second most common call flow mistake was expecting to find customer service or directory assistance in the user's directory. This mistake can be explained if one looks at the metaphor being used. Even though these items provide the user with help they are names and therefore fit very well into the directory metaphor because they could be put on a user's list. A simple solution at the user level would be to simply add customer service and directory assistance to the user's list. This does not however remove the call flow confusion. Perhaps a better solution is have those two options "factory installed" into the customer's directory thus allowing for the HELP command to refer to system tutorial options only.

As participants learned the system they would occasionally give the wrong command and enter a call flow that they didn't want to be in. Once they realized their mistake they had no quick and graceful way to back up to the main menu and try again. Adding either a verbal or manual key press to return to the main menu would surely reduce user frustration.

There are four different areas of user interface design problems which manifested themselves through commonly made mistakes. The first is simulating conversational speech with the VADS. Users sometimes made the mistake of saying "Dial Sally" instead of just "Sally". This problem is easily justified. It is very intuitive to say "Dial Sally" instead of "Sally" because this is more common in daily speech and it explicitly conveys the requested information. Yankelovich et al. [4] stated one of the major user interface design challenges of speech-only applications is simulating conversation. In order to do this more effectively a goal of the VADS system should be to accept synonyms of command words and implicit user responses, in essence to be more flexible.

The second problem arises when the system expects confirmation in the form of yes or no before it will act. Often the user will be confused by a system re-prompt and respond with their initial request such as directory or help instead of "no". This is the direct result of the inconsistency of the VADS in its use of the yes/no prompt. For example, dialog in only some of the call flows prompt the user with "please respond yes or no". Some subjects felt that the system should always prompt when it expects a yes or no response. This would reduce the number of errors experienced.

The third area of user interface design concerns the "speak over". This occurs when the user interrupts the VADS prompt with an early reply. This type of error can prove very frustrating. We observed that most participants became fully familiar with the VADS options and navigation by the middle of the first session due to the highly repetitive nature of the experimental session. During the second half of the first session and the entire second session the participants were more likely to interrupt the VADS because they could successfully anticipate the VADS prompts. Some users suggested being able to "speak over the instructions", "jump ahead" of the menu options or perform multiple options simultaneously. The prompt level should be a function of the user's proficiency and experience level with the system. We recommend the system have the ability to automatically adjust the prompt level and reduce the level of prompting as the user becomes more experienced and proficient.

The final user interface concern to be discussed is the repetition of VADS prompts. Inherent to the experimental design the errors encountered were rejection errors and substitution errors. Prompt repetition is used to diminish both these types of errors. An example of a rejection error would be the user providing a number and the system responding "repeat the number or use the keypad". Likewise, an example of a substitution error would be if a user requested HELP and the system responded "did you say Herbert?". We found that users became frustrated with increased VADS repetition which would avoid rejection errors during the low accuracy condition but at times wanted additional confirmation when data error checking was being performed. We suggest that data verification should be done implicitly such as "the number for so and so is ..." and any destruction of data such as deleting a person from your directory should be done only after explicit verification.

4. Conclusions

Simultaneous driving and conducting a conversation via cellular phone requires divided attention. If the cellular phone conversation or interaction with a voice activated dialing service becomes too complex attention will be diverted from the road to the phone in order to perform the required task. This can lead to automobile accidents. Improving the user interface design and call flow structures can decrease overall system complexity and increase user satisfaction. It was our purpose to evaluate a commercially available voice activated dialing system and make recommendations for its improvement. Considering the call flow findings, we conclude that the voice phone book metaphor provides an adequate mental map which helps users navigate the menu hierarchy. With the exception of the location of the CHANGE command and location of customer service and directory assistance, menu navigation appears intuitive.

With regards to the user interface design findings, we conclude that any VADS could be improved by following the principles of conversational speech such as avoiding repetition and being flexible in its handling of interruptions. VADS will generally be successful if they provide brief, informative prompts, allow users to change their level of expertise (and hence prompt length), and balance the time costs associated with reducing rejection (more prompt repetition) and substitution errors (more data verification).

References

[1]   Cellular Telecommunications Industry, U.S. wireless industry survey results: more than 9.6 million customers added in 1995, News Release, Washington, D.C., March 25, 1996, pp. 5.
[2]   D. Redelmeier and R. Tibshirani, Association between cellular-telephone calls and motor vehicle collisions. The New England Journal of Medicine, 336(7):453-458, 1997.
[3]   N. E. Laurie, R. Andres and D. Fisher, The Role of Instruction Sets in Operator Satisfaction While Using a Voice Activated Dialing System. In: L. Straker & C. Pollock (Eds.) Virtual Proceedings of CybErg 1996, The First International Cyberspace Conference on Ergonomics. URL http://www.curtin.edu.au/conference/cyberg. Curtin University of Technology, 1996.
[4]   A. Yankelovich, G. Levow, and M. Marx, Designing SpeachActs: Issues in speech user interfaces. ACM CHI '95 Conference Proceedings, Denver, CO, May 7-11, 1995, pp. 369-376.

7. Ergonomics in Design

Advances in Occupational Ergonomics and Safety II
Edited by Biman Das and Waldemar Karwowski
IOS Press and Ohmsha, 1997

Design Support with Ergonomic Guidelines

Mark L. NOWACK, Paul A. RODGERS, Chris T. CHARLTON, Ken M. WALLACE
Engineering Design Centre, University of Cambridge,
Department of Engineering, Trumpington Street,
Cambridge CB2 1PZ, UNITED KINGDOM

Abstract

The paper describes the Cambridge Engineering Design Database (CEDD) - a design tool developed to support designers in the early stages of the design process. CEDD is a development of a database of over 3,500 engineering design guidelines, created by researchers in the Cambridge Engineering Design Centre.

Design guidelines are context-sensitive heuristic rules based on actual design practice and serve as a repository of general design knowledge. Guidelines assist the designer by highlighting issues to address or by recommending specific design actions to take. The context of the design problem determines the appropriateness of applying a given guideline. By explicitly presenting rationale for a guideline, the designer is better able to determine its appropriateness for the current situation.

A useful characteristic of design guidelines is their ability to link different design areas such as a product's form and appearance, manufacturing, and human factors / ergonomics. By exploiting this capability, CEDD can increase the breadth of issues addressed by a designer in the early stages of the design process. Addressing life cycle issues early in the design process can significantly reduce product development costs, lead-times and the incidences of design oversights.

CEDD supports consideration of rationale by providing a variety of links between guidelines. It also provides links to other forms of design knowledge such as case examples and definitions. CEDD employs a flexible, extensible, and context-sensitive system that learns about and suggests links between guidelines, making the guideline collection easy to construct and use.

CEDD has been populated with guidelines collected from case studies, experts, and engineering design, manufacturing, and ergonomics literature. The use of CEDD for design support in engineering design tasks with ergonomic considerations is demonstrated with an example in the paper.

1. Introduction

Designers tend to rely primarily on their skills and experiences during the early stages of design [1]. This may significantly hinder the potential for design success, particularly when dealing with unfamiliar or very complex design problems. Additionally, investment costs involved in new product design and development increase greatly as the design process proceeds. That is, costs during the early stages of design, where many major decisions are made, tend to be low, whereas costs involved during the latter stages of the process are much higher, but with fewer opportunities for change [2]. There is a need, therefore, to capture and supply design knowledge and information in an effective and efficient manner that will support the designer in these early stages [3]. The CEDD guideline support tool has been developed for this purpose. It supports decision making and problem solving and is intended to fulfil three primary roles:

(i) as a pointer to design resources (e.g. information sources, design tools);
(ii) to help structure the design process;
(iii) to provide guidance on artefact configuration.

2. Design Guideline Methodology

To help provide proper information at the appropriate time in the design process, a structured approach to the collection, organisation and utilisation of guidelines is used. The basic element, a *Design Guideline*, is a recommendation for a context-sensitive course of action to address a specific design issue. A design guideline has four main parts:

(i) issue(s) addressed - the goal or objective;
(ii) links to design context - conditions for applying the guideline;
(iii) action recommendations - recommended courses of action;
(iv) rationale - why this is a good idea such as expected consequences.

These parts are incorporated into a guideline network containing issues, actions, consequences, subjects, and relational links. These links provide the means for the guidelines to relate to other guidelines, more general principles, and various types of other design information and tools. A useful set of links includes:

similar action	how/why	definition
alternative	related issue	example
requirement	impact	design tool

These links are based upon a simple model of design progression and provide the means to exploit guidelines in the early stages of design. In this stage, broad knowledge is required to avoid design oversights [4] and this is provided by the links.

3. The Guidelines Tool (CEDD)

CEDD is a graphical front-end for a relational database implementing the guideline and link scheme, together with extra information in the form of definitions, examples, and links to other tools as shown in Figure 1. CEDD also provides the search system.

There are two main access routes to relevant guidelines: users may follow links from the current guideline; or they may search the database with the associative search system. By exploiting the co-occurrence of words in guidelines, the system is able to propose words which might be similar to the user's query. After selection by the user, these extra words are used both to refine the current search and to improve the search accuracy over time. In this way, users are able to 'tailor' their own personalised CEDD version. The user window with both the search list and link list is shown in Figure 2.

The link structure is relatively easy for the user to maintain. As a guideline is entered, CEDD suggests other guidelines which appear to be similar. This may result in guidelines being merged, or a link being made between them. Alternatively, the user may explicitly search for guidelines to link to. This seems to be a useful way to capture expert knowledge as some types of related information may not necessarily be found by a similarity-based retrieval system, especially if they concern different subjects (such as different "Design for X" methods). Expert knowledge is required to identify these links.

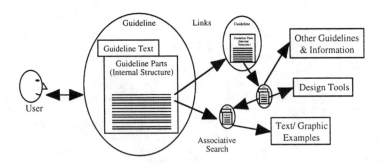

Figure 1. Guideline Structure

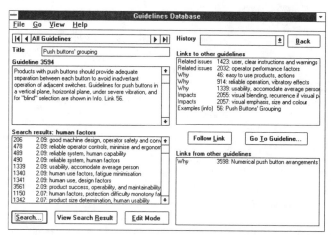

Figure 2. Main CEDD User Window

Links with non-ergonomic guidelines are key in providing ergonomic guideline support to a designer during the early design stages. This allows a designer to be alerted to ergonomic issues associated with a design concept. A recent ergonomic guideline entry trial produced a set of guidelines with the characteristics noted in Table 1. The high number of links to other ergonomic guidelines is an indication that the set is well integrated into the existing database. The four links to non-ergonomic guidelines is low when compared to other sets of guidelines which address life-cycle issues. One approach used to provide more external links is to study a product, or a designer at work to identify further useful links [5]. The example in the next section provides such an opportunity.

Guideline Summary	Count
number of guidelines in set	9
number of examples in set	7
number of design tools in set	0
links within set	4
links to non-ergonomic guidelines	4
links to other ergonomic guidelines	29

Table 1. Ergonomic Guideline Collection Summary

4. Case Study: Ergonomic Guidelines in Mobile Phone Design

This section describes the use of the CEDD design tool in an example involving the design of a 'new' mobile (cellular) telephone. In the early stages of design, the designer will usually have a design "brief" or a vague statement of needs from the client or manufacturer. From this brief, the designer explores ideas and develops a more refined statement of the problem. The brief here was to *"...increase UK market share by designing a 'new' cellular mobile phone that will appeal to the 18 to 35 age range..."*.

Previous research [6] has identified two basic styles of using design guidelines: interactively as the design is developed, or by generating a concept design and then critiquing it. The designer, in this case, adopted the latter approach. That is, the designer sketched out an idea for a phone and then proceeded to assess the concept against relevant information contained in CEDD (see Figure 3).

During the 65 minutes focused on critiquing the ergonomic aspects of the design, 71 guidelines and three examples were visited as a result of a single search on "human factors". A number of guidelines were visited several times as the network of guidelines was navigated for a total of 234 "visits".

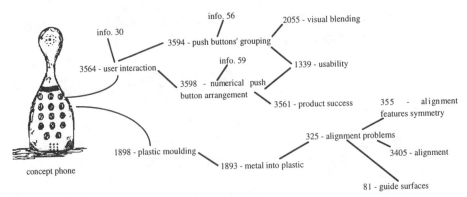

Figure 3: Phone Example Search "Hits"

An example of an ergonomic issue addressed by CEDD is shown in Figure 3 where links from a general ergonomic guideline (3564) led to issues about the spacing of push buttons. This was a concern given the small size of the phone. Information link 56 provided a table of suggested size ranges and confirmed that the proposed button size and spacing was indeed small but not totally unacceptable.

From the initial search and by following links, a number of other areas were visited, such as manufacturing methods, materials, etc. This is not suprising as ergonomic considerations place constraints on shape that directly impact manufacture. For example, guideline 325 raised general issues concerning assembly of mass-produced products. Not being overly familiar with the area, the designer followed links to a number of more detailed guidelines. Problems assembling slightly asymmetric parts were noted in guideline 355. At that point another engineer more experienced in the area was consulted on the issue to determine that in this case it should not be a problem.

5. Conclusions and Future Work

The paper has described the new Cambridge Engineering Design Database (CEDD) design tool which has been developed to support designers during the early stages of the design process. Development of the link suggestion scheme and search system is continuing. Laboratory and field trials are ongoing as is the collection of new guidelines.

References

[1] N. Cross, Engineering Design Methods: Strategies for Product Design. John Wiley & Sons, Chichester, UK, (Second Edition), 1994.
[2] B. Hollins and S. Pugh, Successful Product Design: What to Do and When. Butterworth & Co., London, UK, 1990.
[3] R. Marsh, Capture and Utilisation of Experience in Engineering Design. PhD Thesis, Cambridge University, 1997.
[4] Z. Yao, Constraint Management for Engineering Design. Phd Thesis, Cambridge University, 1996.
[5] C. Charlton, M. Nowack, K. Wallace, Engineering Design Guideline Support Scheme. ICED 97, Tampere, Finland, 1997.
[6] A. Ackers, The Guidelines Database. MSc Thesis, University of Delft, The Netherlands, 1994.

Acknowledgements

The authors gratefully acknowledge the financial support of the United Kingdom Engineering and Physical Sciences Research Council and the United States Air Force for this project.

Advances in Occupational Ergonomics and Safety II
Edited by Biman Das and Waldemar Karwowski
IOS Press and Ohmsha, 1997

Selecting handtools - guidelines for the prevention of upper limb disorders

R.J. Feeney, O. Bobjer, C. Jansson

Ergonomi Design Gruppen AB, Box 14021, S-161 14 Bromma, Sweden

Robert Feeney Associates, Somerset House, 26 Frederick Street, Loughborough LE11 3BJ, UK

AB Sandvik Bahco, S-745 82 Enköping, Sweden

Introduction

These guidelines are concerned with the prevention of upper limb disorders (ULDs) which may be caused or exacerbated by work activities involving the use of handtools [1].

Work related upper limb disorders of the hands, arm and shoulders are not new, they have always been prevalent in some types of jobs including sewing, assembly work, and in the preparing of meat carcasses. They are now perhaps more prevalent because of the intensity of work undertaken and because of the number of people involved in work of a repetitive nature.

Upper limb disorders often occur as a result of activities where high force, repetition, and pressure on the skin surface. Many such actions are commonplace in work activities and often occur when using handtools. In industry today, the use of handtools is not confined to any particular sector and includes the electronics industries, motor vehicles assembly industry, the meat industry and industries where keyboard operators are employed.

Legal requirements

The legal requirements in most industrialised countries pust a general duty on employers to ensure, as far as is practicable, the health, safety and welfare at work of all their employees and also upon manufacturers, designers, suppliers and importers of machines and equipment. The UK Health and Safety at Work etc. Act of 1974 is one such example of this [2].

Although their are no known specific legal requirements with regard to the design and use of handtools, other industrial laws make some provision in this respect. These include those laws dealing with the provision of safe plant and machinery and systems of work, safe use and handling of articles and provision of information and training which are particularly relevant to handtool use and the way they are designed.

Symptoms

Although many symptoms are associated with ULDs, the most notable are pain, restriction of joint movement and soft tissue swelling. In the early stages there may be little or no visible sign of bruising or swollen joints. In some conditions the sense of touch and manual dexterity may be reduced.

Because the onset of symptoms is often gradual, a person's response to pain and restricted mobility may result in an adaptation to the way in which work is performed. There may then be involvement of other parts of the limb and a complex symptom pattern may result with the risk of a permanent disability.

A classification

No generally agreed framework exists to classify adequately the range of ULDs. They vary enormously in what causes them, what the underlying disease mechanisms are, their severity and outcome as far as the individual is concerned. A classification put forward by the UK Health and Safety Executive [3] was as follows :

a) inflammation or trauma of the tendon, muscle-tendon junction or surrounding tissue, particularly the tendon sheath. Such inflammatory conditions in and around the tendon are for the most part of a temporary nature but in some individuals may become chronic

b) inflammation of tissue of the hand caused by constant bruising or friction of the palm (a similar condition may occur in the elbow or knee). Collectively these are known as the 'beat conditions'

c) compression of the peripheral nerves serving the upper limb, particularly the hand. Many of these conditions, such as carpal tunnel syndrome, may arise spontaneously in the general population and may be aggravated by work conditions

d) temporary fatigue, stiffness or soreness of the muscles comparable to that following unaccustomed exertion but where no permanent pathological condition results.

This is not a definitive or precise list. The conditions are not mutually exclusive and some individuals exhibit several variants simultaneously.

Commonly used terms

When the hand and arm exerts high forces or is subjected to repetitive motions or when it is subjected to point pressure on the skin, several problems can arise :

- the sheath can become dry causing friction and inflammation (tendonitis)
- the sheath can also be flooded with synovial fluid causing ganglionic cysts
- carpal tunnel syndrome is caused by pressure on the median nerve when inflamed tendon sheaths swell. When the wrist is angled the tendons are squashed into a smaller space and friction dramatically increases causing inflammation.
- pressure on the hand surface can result in compression or entrapment of the nerves or tendon sheaths just below the surface of the skin resulting in temporary or even permanent loss of both motor and sensory functions

Handtools which exploit sound physiological principles are less likely to create injury than those which do not.

Principles in handtool design

In order to minimise injuries arising from handtool use, they need to be designed with human capabilities and limitations in mind - this is the field of ergonomics.

The most important element in the system is the operator and all design should be centred around his or her own capabilities. Two aspects of this are work design and task demands. These are important areas and need to be addressed before examining the role of tool design.

Based on human anatomy, handtool design needs to meet a number of requirements. The musculoskeletal system operates like any mechanical system and produces the highest force and greatest efficiency when arranged optimally. For example, some joints work most efficiently when in a particular position. The wrist is a critical component in most manual activities. In the use of handtools it acts as a) a stabiliser for the hand in a particular position, b) a transmitter of force and c) a means of manipulating the hand. The wrist is most stable and transmits most force when it is in the 'normal' position ie. when the hand is in line with the forearm.

8% of the population are left handed. Tools should therefore be designed for left handed and right handed users. This can often be achieved by ensuring that the handtool has a 'flexible' grip which will suit both right and left handed users.

One of the most important human characteristics in handtool design is concerned with the dimensions of the hand. Critical hand dimensions in tool use include breadth, length and grip diameter. These dimensions differ widely between individuals and most significantly between males and females, although there is considerable overlap between the two groups. For a given tool size, hand size can significantly affect the amount of force that can be effectively exerted on the tool. There is a considerable difference in the force that can be applied between people with very small hands (mostly females) and those with large hands (mostly males). However, there are general guidelines for grip diameter which are suitable for the majority of both males and females.

Handtools need to be designed using the optimum type of grip for the task involved. The diffrenet types of grip and and their use for different tasks is well documented in the literature. However, specific grip configurations such as finger grooves should be avoided.

The strength capability between individuals also varies considerably. People with high and low strength use hand tools and as far as is possible, their capabilities should be taken into account in their design. This will often require that the handtool should be designed to give maximum mechanical advantage and thus reduce the need for high strength in for example, gripping or applying leverage.

The musculoskeletal system can be damaged if shock or certain forms of vibration are transmitted through a handtool to the bones and joints. Where there is the possibility of shock or vibration being transmitted, the design of the tool should be such that these transmitted forces are absorbed by the design of the tool itself.

The skin surface of the hand has very high frictional properties in relation to some materials. Soft surfaces with a matt finish give a very high friction against the skin. Tool handles therefore should be covered in smooth, non slip compressible materials.

Design check list

In summary, good tool design should meet the following criteria :

- distribute grip force
- avoid forces on the sides of the fingers
- ensure there is ample finger and hand room in the handle
- handles should be covered in smooth, non slip compressible materials
- to avoid the hand slipping off the tool, a protective flange should be provided for tools requiring high downward force
- tools should be well balanced in the hand
- any power and air cables for use with the tool should be flexible, easily manipulated and not interfere with the job
- avoid pinch grasp
- avoid sharp edges and corners
- avoid finger grooves in the handles
- tools should be designed for left and right handed users
- transmission of vibration should be minimised
- any adjustments of the tool e.g. reversing direction of rotation, wherever possible, should be facilitated by using one hand only
- specific tools should only be used for the job for which they are designed

Selecting the right tool

Obviously selecting the right tool is very important if injury is to be avoided. This may seem a difficult task when there are so many tools on the market many claiming to be 'ergonomic'. Selecting the most appropriate tool is not simple but involves looking at the whole work situation. This can be done systematically following several stages. These are described below :

1. Work analysis and rectification

- **analyse task** - task analysis is a commonly used approach in ergonomics. It involves a detailed analysis of all the actions the operator has to carry out in using the tool for different tasks. For more details of this approach, the reader is referred to standard ergonomic text books such as the Applied Ergonomics Handbook [4]. Such an analysis can identify the postures used, the extent of the forces that need to be applied through the hand, arm and shoulder and the level of performance or accuracy that needs to be achieved. The results of such an analysis can lead to the next stage namely, the identification of work design and work organisation issues.

- **identify work design and work organisation issues** - many difficulties which operators experience in carrying out tasks can be overcome by designing the work in a different way. By changing the design of the work so that the task is done in a way more convenient to the operator may avoid the need for poor posture when using a handtool. Changing the work organisation in terms of the sequence of tasks, the use of more automatic tools or the selection of operators more suited to the task. For a more detailed description of work design and work organisation approaches the reader is referred to a publication by Wilson et al [5].

- **make changes as necessary to optimise work design and work organisation** - such changes may require expert help, such as those qualified in ergonomics. However, although this may be beyond the competence of those who use or select tools, such a step is often worthy of consideration because of the economic benefits that might accrue in making changes to the design and organisation of the work. Again, readers are referred to ergonomics text books for a more detailed understanding of the approaches involved [5].

2. Identify tool use issues

These include :

- **operating forces** - are high forces involved in gripping, pushing or pulling?
- **repetitions per unit time** - are the hand or arm motions carried out many times per minute?
- **reach requirements** - does the task involve reaching beyond what might be described as comfortable reach?
- **awkward postures and joint movements** - is the wrist or arm involved in awkward postures ie bent or twisted?

3. Selecting the right tool

- **appraise tools available from different manufacturers** - this should be carried out for each task in terms of the design criteria given earlier. A good guide as to whether the tools have been properly designed is to ask the manufacturer whether they have been designed for particular tasks, and whether the tools have been designed from a usability point of view based on analysis of users. A further important question is whether the tools have been subjected to user trials. Of course it is necessary to have proof that such activities have been carried out in a methodical manner and access to reports demonstrating this would be essential. A good example of general ergonomic guidelines for appraising handtools is that provided by Caple [6] who gives guidleines for powered tools used in the automotive industry.
- **select a few alternative designs for evaluation** - attempt to make a selection of one or two examples for evaluation. The design check list given earlier will help.
- **evaluate tools with users** - this should be carried out over a period of time and involve all of the tasks for which the tool is intended to be used, using questionnaires, interviews or diary methods. Product evaluation with users is a well established ergonomics technique which can provide very detailed information on the users qualities of handtools. An excellent description on product assessment and user trials can be found in the publication 'Evaluation of human work' [7].
- **make final selection** - this will depend on two main factors. The first is the suitability of the tool for the tasks to be carried out and secondly, the suitability of the tool for the user. Both of these are interdependent and in the ideal tool optimise the task demands and the user capabilities. The cost of the tool may also be considered an important factor but in reality such a cost is often low compared with the cost gains in work quality.

References

[1]   Putz-Anderson, V. 1988. Cumulative trauma disorders : a manual for musculoskeletal diseases of the upper limbs. Taylor & Francis, London.

[2]   Health and Safety Executive. 1974. The UK Health and Safety at Work etc. Act of 1974. HMSO, UK.

[3]   Health and Safety Executive. 1994. Work related upper limb disorders - a guide to prevention. HMSO, UK.

[4]   Galer, I. 1987. Applied ergonomics handbook. Butterworths, London.

[5]   Wilson, J R., Corlett, E W. 1990. Evaluation of human work, Taylor & Francis, London.

[6]   Caple, D. 1991. Powered handtools - ergonomic guidelines to selection and use in the automotive industry. David Caple Associates, Australia.

[7]   McClelland, I. 1990. Product assessment and user trials. In : Evaluation of human work. Ed. Wilson, J R., Corlett, E N, Taylor & Francis, London.

Advances in Occupational Ergonomics and Safety II
Edited by Biman Das and Waldemar Karwowski
IOS Press and Ohmsha, 1997

The use of QFD and group technology methods in the safety function design and symbol allocation of machines

Hsien-Jung Wu

Department of Industrial Design

Tunghai University

Taichung, TAIWAN

ABSTRACT

The paper describes a novel approach to machine design, from a product designers' point of view. The approach assigns safety functions and allocates safety symbols on machines using QFD (quality function deployment) and GT (group technology) techniques. In an industrial machine, such as a milling machine or a lathe, certain safety functions and symbols are required. Generally, these are organized by the designer so that they provide necessary warning and control. For example a protruding button generally indicates an emergency stop. Most product designers, however, typically focus on the graphical imagery and visual features of safety symbols and thus ignore important safety functions. This paper, however, focuses on the machine operation ergonomic concerns and applies QFD techniques where ergonomics and safety matters are defined as the quality requirement. During the QFD stages, GT algorithms are used to supplement the classification of operation ergonomics and their overall relation to safety design.

1. Introduction

In an industrial machine, such as a milling machine, certain safety functions and symbols are required and commonly organized by the product designer to provide necessary warning and control. However, most product designers focus on the graphical imagery and visual effect of safety symbols which are characterized as the aesthetic issue of the industrial machine design and thus ignore important safety functions. The problem of this phenomenon is the unawareness of ergonomic concerns during the traditional design stage. Discussion of methods for the conventional product design process can be found in [1] and [2].

Generally speaking, most product designers stress the design parameters on the following factors: function, aesthetics and cost. Therefore, ergonomics issues are usually informed by the ergonomist and no integration is presented in product design.

Recently, considerable attention has been paid to the ergonomics issues in design of products and workplace. Through the concept of concurrent engineering (CE) and design for manufacturability (DFM), the viewpoint from the ergonomists and operators are pushed into and integrated with the design process. Various approaches for integrating ergonomics concerns in the product design stage, such as computer graphic simulation, object-oriented systems and participatory ergonomics team approach, are proposed by researchers[3], [4], [5],[6].

In the product design stage, relevant ergonomics issues can be found in the following areas: product usability, product safety, quality control, product assembly, maintenance and equipment reliability, and workstation design [2]. This paper particularly addresses product safety considerations in the design of industrial machines. This paper examines the safety function design and symbol allocation of machines that is different from the methods proposed by other researchers mentioned previously. In this paper, a novel approach to implement safety function design in industrial machines is proposed from a product designers' viewpoint. During the product design stage, this hybrid practice of quality function deployment (QFD) and group technology (GT) is applied to reflect operation ergonomics and their relation to safety design. Introduction to these two techniques are briefly described in the following section.

2. QFD and group technology

The QFD methodology was originally developed in Japan and subsequently adopted in other countries during mid-1980s. QFD is a structured tool of concurrent engineering to incorporate product attributes with customer requirements through mapping those requirements into specific design features[7]. This mapping is done by several translation matrices whose number of iteration is determined by the complexity of the product. Applying the QFD technique during the design stage can adequately reacting the needs of customer.

Group technology is generally considered to be a manufacturing concept which identifies the similarity of parts and processes in design and manufacturing. Group technology is broadly applied to production flow analysis, classification and coding systems, machine loading, scheduling and process planning. It aims mainly at increasing productivity and reducing production costs. Discussion and application of group technology can be found in [8] and [9]. Several methodologies developed for GT applications are: Single linkage cluster analysis, Bond energy method, Rank order cluster analysis, Direct cluster analysis, Multi-objective cluster analysis and fuzzy cluster analysis.

3. Safety function and product design

As mentioned in previous section, product safety is one of the ergonomic concerns in the design process and is the main focus in this paper. Product deficiencies due to inadequate design is the major cause of accidents for operators in the workshop. Since the product design is the first stage in the product development, it is reasonable to involve safety function in this process. In this paper, ergonomic concerns of industrial machines through safety function design and symbol allocation are illustrated.

For example, a protruding button and a sheltering door are usually used as safety devices in a numerical control milling machine. The former provides the function of emergency stop and the latter prevents operators from injury caused by abnormal machine operations. The designer should consider these safety functions and allocate appropriate symbols in the machine for operators to use with ease. Most product designers focus on visual features of safety symbols whose real safety function is ignored. To solve this problem, the combination of QFD and group technology is proposed in this paper.

This approach can be viewed as a two-step (QFD-GT) translation matrix and applied in iterative manner if required. The first step is to arrange elements in the matrix where ergonomic concerns (safety functions) of machines are collected as customer requirements (in raw) and their associated locations in the machine are viewed as design parameters (in column). The interrelationships between safety functions and location are then listed in the cross area of the matrix. The second step is to classify those relationships into groups with similarity and rearrange elements of raw and column in the matrix. In the example of a milling machine, emergency stop, safety symbols and sheltering door are all required safety functions. In addition to aesthetic concern, designers need to properly allocate these features. To deal with implementing machine ergonomics concerns, this design procedure is listed as follows:

1. list safety functions,
2. list possible locations,
3. deploy factors collected from 1 and 2,
4. identify interrelationships,
5. calculate the similarity with GT,
6. rearrange the matrix,
7. repeat 1-6, if required,
8. allocate design features in machine.

Through this design procedure, the real machine operation ergonomics, such as emergency button and door are integrated into the machine design at proper location based on the similarity of interrelationships calculated in the matrix. Users of this design procedure can apply any cluster analysis methods in group technology such as bond energy and rank order cluster method. The result of this application provides the designer with design advice to implement safety function and solve the conflict between issues of product functions and product aesthetics which usually distresses product designers.

4. Conclusions

A hybrid approach to machine design is presented from a product designer's point of view. This approach assigns and allocates required safety functions or safety symbols on machines using QFD and GT techniques. Ergonomic concerns in product design are defined as customer requirements in QFD and are then translated to associated design features represented as proper locations on machines by group technology. The result shows the integration between design and ergonomic concerns.

References

[1] M. Baxter, Product Design. Chapman & Hall, London, 1995.

[2] A. Mital and I. E. Morse, The Role of Ergonomics in Designing for Manufacturability. In: M. Helander and M. Nagamachi (ed.), Design for Manufacturability: A Systems Approach to Concurrent Engineering and Ergonomics. Taylor & Francis, London, 1992, pp. 147-159.

[3] R. Ortengren, Computer Graphic Simulation for Ergonomic Evaluation in Work Design. In: M. Helander and M. Nagamachi (ed.), Design for Manufacturability: A Systems Approach to Concurrent Engineering and Ergonomics. Taylor & Francis, London, 1992, pp. 107-124.

[4] M. Nagamachi and Y. Yamada, Design for Manufacturability through Participatory Ergonomics. In: M. Helander and M. Nagamachi (ed.), Design for Manufacturability: A Systems Approach to Concurrent Engineering and Ergonomics. Taylor & Francis, London, 1992, pp. 219-231.

[5] G.P. Mounihan, D.J. Fonseca, T.W. Merritt and P.S. Ray, An Object-Oriented System for Ergonomic Risk Assessment. Expert Systems, May 1995, Vol.12(2), pp. 149-155.

[6] F. Daniellou and A. Garrigou, Human Factors in Design: Sociotechnics or Ergonomics? In: M. Helander and M. Nagamachi (ed.), Design for Manufacturability: A Systems Approach to Concurrent Engineering and Ergonomics. Taylor & Francis, London, 1992, pp. 55-63.

[7] U. Menon, P.J. O'grady, J.Z. Gu and R.E. Young, Quality Function Deployment: an Overview. In: C.S. Syan and U. Menon (ed.), Concurrent Engineering. Chapman & Hall, London, 1994, pp. 91-99.

[8]H.M. Chan and D.A. Milner, Direct Clustering Algorithm for Group Formation in Cellular Manufacturing, Journal of Manufacturing Systems, Vol.1(1), 1982, pp. 65-74.

[9]I. Ham, Group Technology. In: Handbook of Industrial Engineering. John Wiely, New York, 1982, pp. 7.8.1-7.8.19.

Advances in Occupational Ergonomics and Safety II
Edited by Biman Das and Waldemar Karwowski
IOS Press and Ohmsha, 1997

Tacit knowledge. The basic source of information for design of ergonomic hand tools

O. Bobjer, R.J. Feeney, C. Jansson

Ergonomi Design Gruppen AB, Box 14021, S-161 14 Bromma, Sweden

Robert Feeney Associates, Somerset House, 26 Frederick Street, Loughborough LE11 3BJ, UK

AB Sandvik Bahco, S-745 82 Enköping, Sweden

Abstract

In conjunction with Sandvik Saws and Tools, a major European manufacturer of hand tools, an eleven-point programme has been developed for a research based approach to hand tool design.

This programme is based on sound ergonomics knowledge and techniques. It involves a team approach which includes both ergonomists, industrial designers and engineers. The programme follows a step by step approach. Starting with a basic analysis of the tasks, users and environment in which the tools are to be used. An important stage in the process is a detailed analysis of tools presently on the market and the basis for their design. The research and prototype design stages involve a significant involvement of professional users with the aim of exploiting their professional, and often tacit, knowledge. Users are involved to record their experiences with their existing hand tool and with new experimental models which take the shape of both basic conceptual models and more refined prototypes which both look and act as final tools.

The whole process takes about 2 years to complete and is carried out in close conjunction with the manufacturer. The outcome is hand tools which have proven ergonomic qualities and which meet the requirement of the task and the needs of the user. This approach has proved to be very successful in terms of user feedback on the qualities of the tools developed. It has also proved to be commercially successful.

1.   Introduction

Sound ergonomics knowledge and techniques is often asked for by hand tool designers. Sandvik Saws and Tools, a major European manufacturer of hand tools, has in close collaboration with ergonomists and industrial designers, developed an eleven-point programme for a research based approach to hand tool design.

Important in the process are involvement of a significant number of professional users with the aim of exploiting their professional, and often tacit, knowledge. In addition to recording their experiences with their existing hand tool, new experimental models are keys to their knowledge. They take the shape of both basic conceptual models and more refined prototypes which both look and act as final tools. The approach starts with a basic analysis of the tasks, users and environment in which the tools are used. The outcome is hand tools which have proven ergonomic qualities and which meet the requirement of the task and the needs of the user. This approach has proved to be very successful in terms of user feedback on the qualities of the tools developed. For many years the design of high quality tools for professional use in industry has been technology driven rather than operator oriented. Thus more attention has been paid to the composition of steel, life of the cutting edge, joints etc. The reason for that is often the fact that the quality of the tool-end of the hand tool is discussed, tested and specified in the criteria when purchasing tools.

By introducing ergonomists in the design process interest can be focused on the operator demands and thus the size and shape of the handle end of the hand tool as well as to the dynamics of the tool use.

2.   Preliminary specifications

The basis for the programme is the task analysis that will form the tool specification. Key questions are raised relating to the task, user, environment and the workstation. Answers are found by interviewing users and observing the way they work, and by drawing on experience from foremen and supervisors. Using this data, specifications are developed for the new tool on factors such as: What shapes are desirable? Suitable weight? Which materials are most appropriate and which are unsuitable? What are the performance parameters? What kind of force will the tool exert? In what direction? How will it affect the user? The risk factors for cumulative trauma disorders, force, frequency posture vibration and cold are of significant importance.

3.   Market analysis

Tools that are claimed to be the best in technical terms as ergonomically are examined. And those most often selected by professionals. Do these tools meet the specifications above?

Some key questions are:

Which tools are the right size in relation to the size of the operators hands?

Which tools actually reduce the risk of injury?

Which tools are easiest to handle?

Reduce the pressure exerted on user's hands?

How is the weight, centre of gravity, handle friction ?

Why do some tools perform better than others?

What characteristics do these tools share?

4.   Background research

What can we learn from user experience that has been documented elsewhere? Research papers, textbooks, reports and analytical reports are examined. Together with the study of international medical databases, particularly: What are the risks associated with this particular type of tool? Which factors increase the risk of work-related injuries? What are the statistics on accidents and injuries? Which injuries are reported? What can we learn from the technical performance tests that have been carried out? What experience have Sandvik Saws and Tools had with this type of tool? What can be learnt from it?

5.   Prototype design

A series of experimental prototypes are now developed. When using these access is gained to the users tacit knowledge and other information that is usually extremely difficult to find. Several experimental prototype tools are made out of similar materials and in the same colours, but with variations in shape or size. Several series of such experimental prototypes are often made to study discreet aspects of the tool.

6.   User test #1

Professionals are exposed to the experimental prototypes and the results are recorded. Users who rely heavily on the tools are chosen from different industrial sectors in several target countries in which the given tool is used. Measurements are then taken of each user's hands. The tests are performed using scientific methods. The users try each prototype under realistic circumstances. Information is collected on the way each user actually employs the experimental prototypes and what he or she thinks of it. Special attention is paid to the aspects known to contribute to cumulative trauma disorders e.g.

force, frequency, posture, pressure points, vibration and cold. A variety of methods are used to establish which aspect of the tool the users prefer. Ranking, individual rating and comparing pairs of tools are the most common by used methods. The performance of each operator and tool, is recorded with the help of video recordings, interviews and questionnaires. Also instrumental and calibrated methods such as goniometers, EMG, strain gauges and force platforms may be used. Both spontaneous reactions as well as considered opinions are noted. If a user feels pain, or unnecessarily high pressure at certain points of the hand or discomfort, these points are carefully noted e.g. on a sketch of the user's hand.

7.   Prototype evaluation and modification

Improvements are based on in-depth analysis of the preceding user tests. The user preferences in parallel with documented ergonomics theories give us the information we need. Modifications of the best prototypes are suggested which would make the tools even better. Questions concerning the range of products or special series of tools to meet specific demands, small, medium or large size tools with adjustable hand span are discussed.

8.   User test #2

New prototypes are prepared to be tested by a wider selection of users. They are made, as far as possible, to look as a finished manufactured product. A large number of users are involved to test them in a greater number of countries.

9.   Final design recommendations

The size, shape, and engineering of the tool are decided and decisions will be made whether to make the tool in several sizes, or whether the same tool should be suitable for use by hands of many different sizes. Decisions are made on precise design of the various parts of the tool. Materials, colours and graphics are specified in detail. Finally, a tool that is identical in every way to the product that will be sold to professional users world-wide is manufactured. A true-to-life prototype.

10.   Product specifications

Production of manufacturing specifications are prepared in close collaboration between the hand tool engineering designers and the industrial designers. Based on these specifications, a small series of "finished" tools is manufactured for our final user test. This includes the materials to be used and their characteristics. The type of technical tooling and its qualities. The new Ergo tool is frequently based on new ideas and existing manufacturing specifications can not simply be re-used. The designers and production engineers prepare all the necessary CAD definitions drawings and specifications for the new tool and its production process. Based on these specifications, a small series of "finished" tools is manufactured for our final user test.

11.   User test #3. Preparation for launch

User feedback on the tool's performance and handling over an extended period of time is evaluated. If this final test prove that the tool works as it should, the tool is approved for mass production and marked with the Sandvik Ergo symbol.

12.   Follow-up

It is not easy to prove scientifically that one hand tool is better than another. Even a tool that has been correctly and ergonomically designed can be used in the wrong way. If users often apply excessive force or adopt inefficient working postures, the inherent quality of the tool is negated and the risk of work-related injuries rises accordingly. Co-operation with qualified, independent, researchers is initiated at this stage, with the aim of checking the new tools, and their users, over a longer period of time and reporting the outcome, together with a plan of action, to the Sandvik Saws and Tools Ergo committee.

References

[1]   Armstrong, T.J., 1986, Ergonomics and cumulative trauma disorders. Hand Clinics, 2(3), 553-565

[2]   Bobjer, O., 1984, Screwdriver handles - design for power and precision. Proceedings of the 1984 International Conference on Occupational Ergonomics, pp. 4443-446.

[3]   Bobjer, O., Johansson, S-E. and Piguet, S., 1993, Friction between hand and handle. Effects of oil and lard on texture and non-textured surfaces; perception of discomfort. Applied Ergonomics, 24 (3), pp. 190-202.

[4]   Bobjer, O., Bergkvist, H. and Lohmiller, W. R., 1995, Development of prototype tools for field testing. Proceedings of the second International Scientific Conference on Prevention of Work related Musculoskeletal Disorders PREMUS 95, Montreal, Canada, Institute de research en santé en sécurité du travail du Québec.

[5]   Bobjer, O., Jansson, C., 1997, A research approach to the design of ergonomic hand tools. The 11-point program. Proceeding of the International Ergonomics Association Conference, Tampere, Finland 1997.

[6]   Silverstein, B.A., Fine, L. J. and Armstrong. T.J., 1987, Occupational factors and carpal tunnel syndrome. Am. J. Ind. Med., 11, pp 343-358.

Advances in Occupational Ergonomics and Safety II
Edited by Biman Das and Waldemar Karwowski
IOS Press and Ohmsha, 1997

" The Use of Cognitive Studies in Product Design; A Multimedia Design tool to aid in their application "

Catherine Grundy, *S. Lecturer, Alastair Patterson; University of Westminster; 115 New Cavendish St., London, W1M8JS.* in conjunction with:
Brian Smith; *Design Director, PDD Ltd, 286 Munster Rd., London SW6 6A*
Stephen Fraser; *Design Director, Fraser Designers, 6 Hampstead West, 224 Iverson Rd, NW 6 2HL, England.*

Abstract:

The object of the research was to find examples of product designs which communicate effectively with the user and also to collate case histories which demonstrate why this is very important. The initial findings from the studies are being used to develop a prototype Multimedia design tool that will aid designers to address these issues. The paper will, in itself be a call for contributions to the database.

Introduction:

In designing a product interface, we must allow the product to be visually clear and to be seen in a way which facilitates our mental processing. To develop the object without first studying how our brains percolate visual ideas could be unprofitable. Many have therefore recognised the need for a focus on how human beings understand objects to allow products to be successful within an increasingly sophisticated international market.

The idea of teaching Cognitive Studies in Product Design has become reasonably widespread within education as a result of this thinking. The difficulty, however, lies in presenting such a theoretical subject in a way that it will inspire ideas and lead to successful application. Young Product Designers are usually keen to get on with the business of designing an artifact and long theoretical introductions of any kind can seem like a distraction. It is in the practical realisation that often these ideals remain unfulfilled; it is the kind of subject where useful ideas are occasionally 'lost in the translation'.

There are a series of issues that need to be considered; ranging from how the physiology of the eye affects absorption of information to how we behave when we have absorbed and understood it. There are many principles to be found at each stage of this perception process that can provide interesting clues about how to improve designs. What appears to be needed is a way of presenting what would otherwise be long list of facts in a useful way.

Concept:

The conclusion was reached that a useful way to resolve these issues was via a computer package that consisted of two parts:

1. A Multimedia Study Guide where the information and case histories were provided about Cognitive theory, allowing the user to navigate through and learn at their own pace.

2. A Design and Modelling package, which performs in a similar way to existing 3 Dimensional modelling packages but which has filters and functions which apply chosen cognitive principles to the model. The tools and actions performed in the package can all be cross-referenced to the relevant part of the Study Guide to explain the purpose of their use.

The proposal for the Modelling package has not had software written to verify that the effects are possible, however, the operations performed are all similar to those existing in Macintosh programmes, for example: Freehand and Photoshop. The basic proposal should be understandable from the content of this paper, although admittedly a knowledge of the two packages mentioned and 3D modelling packages like Form Z would help in understanding how the idea could be realised. There is not space here to cover the principles of these packages, which require a manual to learn.

The best way to illustrate use is via a simple example that can be used to introduce ideas about Display and Control design. First it is neccessary to construct a shape, to do this we can use Visual Elements. The Modelling package is described as a 2D version to make the task of describing and considering it simpler. A description of the Visual Elements may appear in a text book as follows:

Basic Principles of Seeing: Visual Elements

Fig 1.

The visual elements are the basic building blocks from which all product forms are made, they include dots, lines, and basic geometric shapes. They are simply a way of categorising parts of forms for further useful analysis, We exert different amounts of physiological effort when we look at different shapes. When taking in a horizontal line, for example, our eyes simply move in one dimension; our main field of activity is along this dimension so we regard it as usual. When we take in a diagonal line, however, we are moving our eyes along two sets of coordinates and it is accepted that we make more effort to see it. This means that it is more visually provoking and can appear more interesting. Likewise when viewing a circle, we have maximum demand on our perceptive mechanism; because the ratio of two coordinates is continuously changing, this means that they can also have greater impact. These principles can be used to draw attention to particular aspects of a product or make an object eye-catching as a whole.

This text can be more easily absorbed and understood if broken down into smaller, more digestible sections allowing the user to move through at their own pace as part of the **Multimedia Study Guide.** E.g.s of the interface exist, but their is insufficient room to describe them here.

The screen related to creating and using Visual Elements for the **Modelling package** would appear as in Fig 5. and the actual tools used to produce shapes from the elements are on the top line of tools (1.) From the left, these include straight horizontal and vertical lines; diagonal lines; rectangles; circles and ellipses; curved lines. In each case, when the tool is selected, a dialogue box on the screen would allow the user to click on a button transferring them to the information given above in the **Multimedia Study Guide.**

Once created, the shapes can be selected, moved, re-sized, and altered in similar ways to existing packages. Once a Display and Control array has been created, basic rules can be applied, like applying a Visual Coding to certain buttons. A simple description may appear as follows:

Creating Common Themes.
To simplify our view of the world, we have a preference for reducing what we have to

understand by identifying common themes. We can facilitate understanding a product by creating visual links between parts of an object with similar function to indicate their common them. This coding can be done via their visual elements, colour or size, though they may be at different locations on the product.   For example on a telephone, the number buttons may all be elliptical while all the function buttons are square.Occasionally one can add tactile methods of coding and a similarity of distance away from the user.

Fig3.

Designing for children can call for radical ways of making a product clear and simple to use. PDD designed a 'Roamer robot' for valiant technology, designed for youngsters to experiment with programming. It is a self sufficient robot which can be programmed to do simple manoeuvres and make sounds, etc.The buttons for building up programmes are distinguished by shape, colour and grouping. The movement arrows are indicated separately, placed spatially in the directions of motion .

In the **Multimedia Study Guide** application the user would be able to navigate themselves through a series of screens at their leisure with examples and explanations of the above.

The **Modelling tool** would demonstrate these principles by applying on request some simple geometric changes for a chosen product interface layout. The row (2) of tools relate to changes which apply a visual coding. Tool 2.1 relates to colour changes in applying a coding. On selection by mouse click, the computer will request in the INSTRUCTIONS box (fig 5) that all the objects requiring a similar code be selected, again via mouse click. To indicate the last object, a double click is required. The INSPECTOR box would allow the user to pick their colours for shading the objects. This are all similar actions to those already found in Mackintosh programmes. Tool 2.2 applies coding by shape change. The user will be asked to select an object to copy the shape of and again to select the objects to apply it to. Tool 2.3 applies a spatial change and has a range of inbuilt options to choose from regarding the particular groups of buttons, which will again appear in the INSPECTOR box. Using these two boxes to give instructions and select choices for a particular tool gives a wide range of options to the user in modifying a basic model. Examples of the kind of finished appearance for a Mobile Phone example are given in Figs 6 and 7.

The next row of tools (3) provide a further example, they apply the principle of compatibility to a design. This may be described as follows:

Compatibility and principles of Mapping:
Another factor that helps human beings to understand a process is a high level of compatibility between the visual display and the controls affecting it. We have a good sense of space and often a simple rearrangement of objects can clearly provide a useful link between elements. This is the principle of mapping which is a mental activity that we engage in, again to simplify our understanding of events. It is a subset of the principle of providing conceptual models. The cooker in the next figure shows two methods of relating the controls to the ring they affect, the right hand one is preferred because it is spatially more compatible

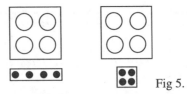

Fig 5.

The tools function by requesting that the user indicate the two items that require a relationship to be formed between them with the mouse. A choice is available between applying a spatial compatibility or creating a visual link between them. The programme introduces some preset layouts that will help the user brainstorm about designs. All these transformations can then be edited by selecting them and making changes like move, change size etc. found in typical Mackintosh programmes.

Summary.

The treatment of the **Modelling tool** in this paper has not been given as a rigorous analysis of the software involved, but in its proposal form should have nevertheless demonstrated a useful method of teaching and **promoting** the use of Cognitive Studies in design, in conjunction with the **Multimedia Study pack**. The transformations in the **Modelling tool** should be executable since they are all similar to those found in other Macintosh programmes, Freehand and Photoshop

The Modeller may have limited use as a precise 3D stand-alone package , due to the many other arrays of tools and functions already needed (there may be a clash of space and interests) but would provide a useful add-on device for other such programmes. It could be an excellent brainstorming tool where objects could be experimented on and at a basic level, it will at least provide a method by which to learn the principles.

Although only 2D layouts of controls have been covered here, other Cognitive Studies have been analogously treated, each set of tools can be related to a different item on a Menu at the top of the screen e.g. a set related to Display and Control design; one which covers transformations related to visual weight; 'morphing' functions etc.

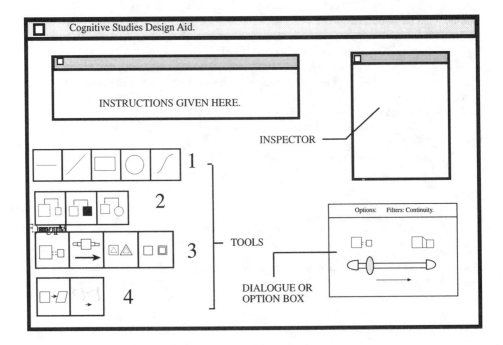

III. PHYSICAL ERGONOMICS

8.   Occupational Biomechanics

Advances in Occupational Ergonomics and Safety II
Edited by Biman Das and Waldemar Karwowski
IOS Press and Ohmsha, 1997

Obstacle Negotiation Characteristics During Dynamic Task Performance on Inclined Surfaces

A. Bagchee and A. Bhattacharya
*Biomechanics-Ergonomics Research Laboratory, Department of Environmental Health,
University of Cincinnati, Cincinnati, OH 45267-0056*

Abstract
Several of the falls occurring at the workplace occur at the same level due to tripping and/or slipping. Strategies used for avoiding trips may be further compromised when the walking surface is inclined and/or elevated in the form of a ramp or rooftop. This study aimed at evaluating the obstacle negotiation strategy between level ground and an inclined surface during normal gait. Kinematic analysis results from four subjects showed the average approach distance as well as the clearance distance of the foot to the obstacle were higher for trials involving carrying of the box than normal walk for both plane walk and ramp walk. This may be indicative of an overcompensation for the obstacle when direct vision of the immediate path of travel is interrupted by a large hand-held object. The approach distance and the clearance was found to be smallest for the upslope ramp walk.. Smaller clearance during the upslope ramp walk is indicative of an increased proximity of the subjects' foot to the obstacle thereby increasing the risk of trip and fall on a graded surface.

Introduction

Slips, trips, and falls at the workplace continue to be a major source of injury and fatality in United States. Falls from an elevation was the leading cause of fatality (25%) [1], and was 3.5 times the occupational fatality rate for all industries in the United States. The injuries resulting from fall are severe in nature and are often debilitating [1, 2]. A number of these falls occur due to slips and trips occurring at inclined surfaces found at workplaces and construction sites. A ramp is often used to facilitate transfer of material between different elevations. Ramp surfaces are also recommended for allowing access to physically disabled persons, and are a preferable alternative to stairs for aged people [3]. Though OSHA recommends strict guidelines for the design of such rampways (max. gradient of 20 degrees without handrails, 30 degrees with handrails)[4], rampways used at construction worksites may be temporary and may or may not comply with the recommendations.

The present study was performed to investigate the effect of inclination, environmental lighting, and carriage of a hand-held load on the obstacle negotiation characteristics of normal healthy males. While inclination changes the shear forces at the shoe surface inclination, carrying a large hand-held weight impedes the frontal vision causing an increased burden on the feed-forward mechanism essential for maintenance of balance during forward progression [5]. Environmental lighting further affects the afferent visual cues available to the subject.

Method

Four healthy males (average age = 29.5 ± 1.3 years, weight = 69.6 ± 10.6 kg, height = 173.3 ± 4.8 cm) participated in the study that required walking on a 7.5 m long walkway consisting of : (i) Level Surface (Level Walk), and (ii) Inclined Surface (Ramp Walk). The walkway was 90 cm wide, to which an inclined surface at 11° inclination was added for the Ramp

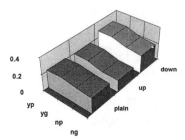

Figure 1 Toe Clearance (TC) above the obstacle

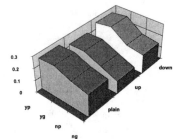

Figure 2 Approach Distance (AD) to the obstacle

Walk. An obstacle, with a rise of 10.5 cm and width of 3 cm, was placed in the middle of the walkway (in the middle of the ramp in Ramp Walk) spanning the entire width of the walkway. The treatment conditions were as follows - **a) Surface:** 1-Level, 2-Ramp; **b) Direction:** 1-Upslope, 2-Downslope; **c) Hand-held Weight:** 1-None, 2-Box (57x57x11.4 cm^3); **d) Environmental Lighting:** 1-Good (>45 footcandles), 2-Poor (< 1 footcandle). The subjects performed two repetition of each test condition. Retro-reflective markers were placed on the body of the subject at the following anatomical positions: Toe, Heel, Ankle, Knee, and Hip. A sagittal view of the subject was captured using a Burle (model TC351A) camera placed 3.7 m from the ramp. Digitized data was used to calculate the following spatial **clearance parameters** for the ipsilateral foot: (1) **Approach Distance** (AD) of the toe to the obstacle, (2) clearance of the toe above the obstacle - **Toe Clearance** (TC), (3) **Landing Distance** (LD) of the heel from the obstacle.

Results

The results are shown graphically in figures 1, 2, and 3 for the four subjects. The tasks are

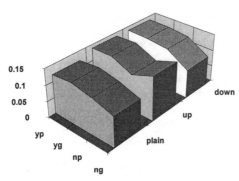

Figure 3 Landing Distance (LD) beyond the obstacle.

represented as (1) yg - With Weight, Good Light; (2) yp - With Weight, Poor Light; (3) ng - No Weight, Good Light; (4) np - No Weight, Poor Light. It is observed that all three clearance parameters decreased for tasks involving carrying of hand-held weight averaged over the level, upslope and downslope walks ($AD_{No\ Weight}$ = 24.9 and AD_{Weight} = 16.8; $TC_{No\ Weight}$ = 23.4 cm and TC_{Weight} = 19.0 cm; $LD_{No\ Weight}$ = 13.3 and LD_{Weight} = 11.3 cm).

Difference due to environmental lighting was found to be negligible for all three clearance parameters. The clearance parameters of AD and TC showed smaller values for upslope walk compared to the level and downslope walk ($AD_{level\ walk}$ = 26.3 cm; $AD_{UpSlope}$ = 21.8 cm; $AD_{DownSlope}$ = 26.8 cm; $TC_{level\ walk}$ = 20.7 cm; $TC_{UpSlope}$ = 17.1 cm; $TC_{DownSlope}$ = 25.8 cm)

Discussion

Walking on an inclined surface introduces additional demands on the body. It has been shown that the required coefficient of friction (COF) at the shoe surface interface increases significantly with increasing surface gradient [6]. The increase in the demand of the required COF created due to the inclination at the shoe surface interface introduces an additional demand on the postural balance maintenance that increases with the degree of inclination [6]. Stepping on a inclined surface introduces greater degree of plantar flexion/dorsiflexion (depending on the downslope vs. upslope gait) requiring further effort in the maintenance of dynamic balance. During upslope gait, the position of CG is dorsal, making the subject bend forward to bring the projected center of gravity (CG) closer to the supporting foot. This modified movement strategy causes the step length to decrease [6] and may be responsible for lower rise of the foot above the obstacle, resulting in lower values of clearance parameters of AD, TC, and LD for the upslope gait. The size of the hand-held load may contribute to blocking frontal vision that may compromise the subject's ability to receive a visual feedback during forward progression, essential in maintaining a continuous progression in gait. This may be reason for increased clearance parameters for tasks requiring the carrying of a hand-held weight that effectively impedes the forward vision of the impending step.

Results from this study indicate a need for a detailed study of the effect of both size and weight of a hand held load during manual material handling on inclined surfaces and ramps. Better criteria for required coefficients of friction between the shoe surface interface should be developed based on the results to prevent slips, trips, and falls during work on inclined surfaces.

References

[1]   C. F. Robinson, T. Alterman, and C. A. Burnett, Mortality Patterns among Construction Workers in the United States, *Occupational Med.,* **10**(2) (1995).

[2]   R. Pater, How to Reduce Falling Injuries, *Natl. Saf. Hlth. News,* **131**(10) (1985). 87-91.

[3]   National Bureau of Standards: Guidelines for Stairs Safety, by J. Archea, B. L. Collins, and F. Stahl [NBS Building Science Series 120] Wash. D.C., Govt. Printing Off. (1979).

[4]   Walking and Working Surfaces and Personal Protective Equipment (Fall Protection Systems):Notice of proposed rulemaking, *Fed Regis.,* (10 Apr., 1990): 13360.

[5]   A. E. Patla, in Search of Laws for the Visual Control of Locomotion: Some Observations, *J. Experimental Psychol,* **15**(3) (1989). 624-628.

[6]   E. J. McVay and M. S. Redfern, Rampway Safety: Foot Forces as a Function of Rampway Angle, *Am. Ind. Hyg. Assoc. J.,* **55**(7) (1994). 626-634.

Advances in Occupational Ergonomics and Safety II
Edited by Biman Das and Waldemar Karwowski
IOS Press and Ohmsha, 1997

Laboratory Environment and Biomechanical Modeling Tools for Ergonomic Assessment of Material Handling Devices

Maury A. Nussbaum and Don B. Chaffin*
Dept. of Industrial and Systems Eng., Virginia Polytechnic and State University
302 Whittemore Hall, Blacksburg, VA, 24061-0118
*Center for Ergonomics, The University of Michigan
1205 Beal Ave., Ann Arbor, MI 48109-2117

Numerous investigations have demonstrated the association between unassisted manual material handling (MMH) and increased risk of musculoskeletal injury. The potential benefits of partially assisting in the material handling process through use of Material Handling Devices (MHDs) is readily apparent. Traditional investigations and biomechanical modeling of material handling tasks have focused on the static component of lifting and handling. To allow for more realistic 3-dimensional dynamic evaluations of complex MHD tasks, a comprehensive experimental and computerized modeling environment was developed. Data were obtained from lab-based load transfer experiments, and were analyzed to compare manual and MHD-assisted load transfers. A variety of biomechanical measures and estimates are contrasted as a function of critical task parameters. Existing hardware and software technologies, in combination with well-developed biomechanical modeling methodologies are now available for detailed biomechanical analysis of load-handling activities. These technology should allow for quantitative evaluations and comparison of existing MHD designs, and contribute towards the development of ergonomics guidelines for successful MHD implementation.

1. Introduction

Unassisted manual material handling (MMH) as a risk factor for musculoskeletal injury has been demonstrated in numerous investigations. Notwithstanding the increased mechanization of contemporary manufacturing processes, manual methods of product transfer, palletizing/depalletizing operations, and assembly remain the common way of working in many sectors, and frequent manual handling of products or goods can be expected to continue. A wide variety of mechanized material handling devices (MHDs) have been developed and marketed as a means to alleviate biomechanical loads and reduce injury risks. However, there are increasing reports of situations where mechanized assist devices, while available, have not been used to advantage because of lack of information regarding their effectiveness in reducing musculoskeletal injury risk and lack of guidelines regarding ergonomically sound design and evaluation of these devices. Further, the complexity of many MMH tasks, and the paucity of comprehensive biomechanical investigations, suggests that MHDs may not be specifically designed to reduce musculoskeletal stresses (e.g. low-back loads).

The wide variety of application areas, combined with the broad availability of technologies, has combined to give a rapid increase in the availability of MHDs from commercial vendors. These devices cover an order of magnitude or more in price and may range in level of engineering complexity from simple 'pendulum' hoists to pneumatically controlled articulated arms with built in braking systems and adjustable force sensing capabilities. By reducing the magnitude of (gravitational) loads that the worker must handle, MHDs should lead to a reduction in musculoskeletal stresses.

Traditional investigations and biomechanical modeling of material handling tasks have focused on this static aspect [1,2] and static loads are employed as the basis of most manual handling limits. The potential benefits of MHDs may not be realized because of significant task dynamics and MHD inertia, and this can be compounded when allowances are not made for increased motion times using an MHD. Woldstad and Chaffin[2] reported that for moderately heavy loads, MHDs are often discarded after installation, and that   ᵛ workers do not always report perceived decreases in workload using MHDs. They suggested that the fatigue experienced by MHD users is related to dynamic forces resulting from large system inertias.

MHDs require significant expenditures in terms of time, training, and cost. The time factor is especially evident in jobs with relatively short cycles times. Here the added incremental times required for acquiring and placing objects may be sufficient to overturn, in the mind of the designer, any potential musculoskeletal benefits. Additional, non-productive time, may occur during the learning phase that is generally required for MHD use [3]. In the absence of appropriate research studies and results, a cost-benefit analysis for MHD use cannot be given in any detail to justify the substantial start-up costs for MHDs. This lack of information provides the primary motivation for the present study, the focus of which is to: 1) provide data to aid in the design and evaluation of alternate MHD types; and, 2) demonstrate whether, and to what extent, MHDs offer relief to the musculoskeletal system.

A comprehensive experimental and computerized modeling environment was developed with the intent of providing information to aid in MHD evaluation and design. This research program had several goals. Data were obtained from experiments designed to investigate critical aspects of load transfer activities, and were analyzed to quantitatively compare manual and MHD-assisted load transfers. A variety of biomechanical measures and estimates were contrasted as a function of critical task parameters. An overview of the experimental protocol, the biomechanical models, and some preliminary experimental results are presented here.

2.   Methods

Whereas MHDs can potentially be used in an infinite variety of tasks, this initial investigation focused on what were considered 'elemental' activities involved in load acquisition, transfer, and placement. Experimental tasks were created to allow for investigation of 'transitional' biomechanical loads, i.e. those occurring during initiation and termination of movement. This focus was justified because of the strong likelihood of peak musculoskeletal loads occurring at these times and arising from the requisite accelerations of body segments, objects being transferred, and the MHDs themselves.

A laboratory environment was constructed in the University of Michigan's Center for Ergonomics to allow for simulation of object transfers using manual methods and MHD assistance. Hardware and software consisted of 5 components: 1) surface markers placed over the major torso and upper extremity joints along with a 4-camera MacReflex™ system for marker tracking and 3-D reconstruction; 2) triaxial hand force transducers; 3) a 12-channel EMG recording system; 4) force plate and rigid fixation device for MVC acquisition; and 5) a National Instruments™ data collection system for acquiring, storing, and time-synchronizing data.

The set of experimental tasks encompassed the range of commonly adopted postures and load positions used in industrial MH tasks. Loads used in the experiment also cover a range for which MHDs are typically applied. Ten subjects participated in the experiment: 5 males and 5 females. All were undergraduate students and all completed an informed consent process. A partial factorial experimental design was performed with subjects treated as a blocking variable. Several independent variables were manipulated during the experiment:

1) **method**–objects were moved manually or using two types of MHD (hydraulically balanced articulated arm or an overhead hoist on a moveable overhead track).
2) **load mass**–boxes with mass equal to 10 and 20 kg were transferred using all three methods, and a 40 kg mass was transferred using the two MHDs.

2) **task**–5 basic transfer tasks were studied and consisted of either acquiring a load or placing a load at ankle, elbow, or shoulder height. The 'acquire' and 'place' tasks were combined into single experimental trials, which are further described below. All tasks were performed in the sagittal plane, with an additional frontal plane transfer that was done at elbow height.

3) **speed**–two pacing conditions were studies. A preferred, pace was simply that which the subject adopted, after practice, as 'comfortable'. The second, 'faster', pace was achieved by decreasing the allowable transfer time by ~20% using repeated tones, the interval between which was set by the experimenters and to which the subject was given several practice trials to accommodate.

For each object transfer, or experimental trial, subjects started from a relaxed standing position (Figure 1). The object (a wooden box with weights inside), sat on a small platform in front of the subject. For MHD assisted trials, the MHD end effector was bolted to identical boxes. A trial consisted of a small motion to grab and acquire the box, bring it to a comfortable carry position at approximately elbow height, a brief pause, and a small motion to return and place the box on the wooden platform. There were a total of 54 trials, which required 5-7s each for completion, and at least one minute of rest was given between each.

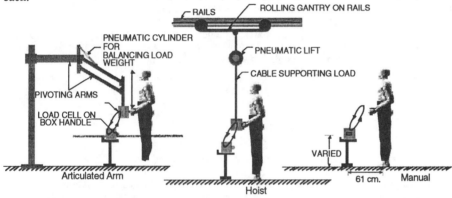

Figure 1. Illustration of three different load transfer methods used in experimental protocols

An inverse kinematic approach was used to obtain dynamic external joint moments and forces at the L3/L4 motion segment. A 'top-down' segmental analysis was performed, starting with hand forces (either measured directly or estimated from object accelerations) and including body segment kinematics obtained from differentiation of the positional data. Appropriate body segment data was obtained from a combination of literature values and anthropometric data taken for each subject.

A dynamic EMG-based torso model was employed to estimate both muscle forces and the associated spinal forces (at L3/L4) during the trials. Hardware and software filtering and normalization of the EMG data was performed to allow for muscle force estimation. A model similar to that presented by Cholewicki et al.[4] and Granata and Marras [5] was used for estimation of muscle force from normalized EMG (NEMG):

$$F_m = [G * NEMG_m * CSA_m * f(length)]^y + Fp_m$$

where the force in muscle m is an additive function of the active and passive (Fp) force components. The active component is a multiplicative function of a gain (G = force/unit area), normalized EMG, muscle cross sectional area (CSA) at resting length, and length and velocity modulators. In practice, CSA is not available and for the present analysis its product with G was considered constant and this value determined through calibration (strength) trials. The shape of the force-EMG relationship (linear or non-linear) was determined by the exponent y (the best performance was obtained with a value of 1.2). The length-tension relationship was quantified using equations derived from the literature and incorporated into a geometric model of the torso [6]. A velocity compensator was not included as pilot work showed this effect was negligible in the particular tasks being studied. From predicted muscle forces, the L3/L4 reactive moment and spine forces (compression, a-p and lat shear) were determined.

3 .   Results

The EMG-based model was validated by comparing predicted (internal) spinal moments with moments estimated using the inverse kinematics model. Coefficients of determination derived from linear regression were generally in the range 0.5-0.9 and the prediction error (rms[external - predicted]) was in the range from 10-40Nm.

There was a significant effect of subject, task, and mass on both peak and average sagittal plane moments at the L3/L4 level. The highest external moments were found during the manual tasks and the lowest when using the powered hoist. The effect of increasing load mass was largest during the manual tasks, whereas increasing mass had a much smaller effect when using either MHD. Speed, or any interactions with speed, did not significantly effect peak or average moments.

Significant effects on peak and average spinal forces were found for most independent measures and their interactions. Peak compression and shear forces were generally ~40% higher than the average values. Both peak and average spine forces were highest during manual tasks, averaging approximately 2000N across trials, followed by the articulated arm (1200N), and lowest when using the hoist (1000N). A large weight effect was found during the manual tasks, the effect being much reduced for both MHDs. A relatively consistent, albeit small, effect of speed was seen (100-200N) during the paced trials.

4 .   Summary

This study investigated biomechanical loads associated with MHD use during the 'transitional' phases of realistic load transfer tasks. Substantial effort was required to allow for fully 3-D dynamic experimentation and biomechanical model analysis. Although only in the initial phases of the investigation, the preliminary results suggest that both MHD scenarios substantially reduces musculoskeletal loads as evidenced by the external lumbar moments and predicted spinal forces. Nonetheless, high peak spinal loads were observed in some MHD tasks, particularly those performed at increase speed, higher weights, and at low elevations. The results support the use of MHDs as an intervention to control low back disability in MMH. Further analysis should yield specific information that will enable more comprehensive guidelines for the ergonomic evaluation and design specifications for MHDs.

5 .   **Acknowledgment:** This research was sponsored by Ford Motor Company.

6 .   References

[1]   M.L. Resnick and D.B. Chaffin, Kinematics, kinetics, and psychophysical perceptions in symmetric and twisting pushing and pulling tasks, *Human Factors* **38** (1996) 114-129.

[2]   J.C. Woldstad and D.B. Chaffin, Dynamic push and pull forces while using a manual material handling assist device, *IIE Trans.* **26** (1994) 77-88.

[3]   D.B. Chaffin *et al.*, Low back stresses when learning to use a materials handling device, *Ergonomics* (1997) submitted.

[4]   J. Cholewicki *et al.*, Comparison of muscle forces and joint load from an optimization and emg assisted lumbar spine model *J Biomechanics* **28** (1995) 321-331.

[5]   K.P. Granata and W.S. Marras, An EMG-assisted model of trunk loading during free-dynamic lifting *J Biomechanics* **28** (1995) 1309-1317.

[6]   M.A. Nussbaum and D.B. Chaffin, Development and evaluation of a geometric model of the human torso *Clinical Biomechanics* **11** (1996) 25-34.

Advances in Occupational Ergonomics and Safety II
Edited by Biman Das and Waldemar Karwowski
IOS Press and Ohmsha, 1997

PRELIMINARY ANALYSIS OF BIOMECHANICAL STRESSES DURING DRYWALL LIFTING

Christopher S. Pan, S. Sharon Chiou, and Hongwei Hsiao
National Institute for Occupational Safety and Health
Division of Safety Research
1095 Willowdale Rd., Morgantown, WV 26505

ABSTRACT

Constant lifting of massive and bulky drywall sheets presents overexertion hazards among drywall installers. According to the Bureau of Labor Statistics, overexertion (23.3%) was the leading traumatic injury cause among drywall installers in 1993 and 63.5% of them occurred while workers were performing lifting tasks. Computer simulations of four techniques for lifting drywall sheets of 60, 80, and 100 pounds were conducted to evaluate the biomechanical stresses involved. The University of Michigan Three Dimensional Static Strength Prediction Program (3DSSPP™) was used for the simulations. It was found that all four lifting techniques produced considerable biomechanical stresses at the drywall installers' shoulders, torsos, and hips. Only a limited percentage of the male population has sufficient strength capability to perform the task. The estimated L5/S1 disc compression forces were high, ranging from 645 to 1228 lbs for various loads and postures analyzed. One lifting method in particular put drywall installers at an increased potential of overexertion at the shoulders. It is estimated that only 36% of the U.S. male population has sufficient shoulder strength to lift a 100 lb drywall sheet when this lifting method is used. Results from this study provided preliminary evidence regarding the biomechanical stresses associated with drywall lifting. Further studies are recommended to identify proper drywall lifting methods and to develop safer assistant devices to reduce overexertion injuries.

1. Introduction

Lost-work-time injuries in construction rank among the highest in United States industries. Among all construction specialties, drywall installers are ranked as one of the top 10 occupations that are at increased risk of occupational injury, based on the workers' compensation data of 21 states [1]. In a focus-group study, drywall installation was considered to be one of the two most difficult carpentry specialties [2]. Lifting, carrying, and securing drywall sheets were reported as being "difficult" tasks [2]. In addition, according to the Bureau of Labor Statistics, the incidence rate of traumatic injury (6.8%) for drywall installers was higher than that of all construction workers (4.9%) in 1993 [3, 4]. Overexertion (23.3%) was the leading traumatic injury cause among drywall installers and 63.5% of the overexertion injuries occurred while workers were performing lifting tasks [3, 4].

Handling massive and bulky drywall sheets is a task that increases the risk of overexertion injuries during drywall installation. A typical drywall sheet weighs between 51 to 109 pounds. The standard size is 4-ft wide and 8- to 16-ft long. Therefore, some drywall installation tasks, such as lifting, carrying, or hanging the drywall sheets, require considerable muscle force and may force the worker to adopt awkward working postures. The high musculoskeletal load imposed on the worker may result in muscle fatigue, or over a longer time period, musculoskeletal trauma disorders and chronic muscle pain [5]. Although there is increased concern about work-related musculoskeletal injuries in the drywall industry, the overexertion hazards of manually handling drywall sheets and possible injury-reduction methods have not been well explored. The objective of this study is to gain preliminary understanding of the biomechanical stresses imposed on the worker while lifting drywall, and to determine strategies that would reduce the risk of injury for drywall installers.

2. Method

A video analysis of actual drywall installation was performed to identify current drywall lifting methods. The videotapes were obtained from four construction site visits in southern Ohio and Northern West Virginia, involving six drywall installers, for a total duration of 4 hours and 20 minutes. Four lifting methods employed in drywall handling were identified through video analysis (Figure 1). Lifting method 1 was the most common posture workers employed to adjust the drywall sheet in place before it was fastened to the wall. The remaining three methods were often used by the worker to load or unload drywall sheets onto a cart or dolly. The postures associated with each of the four identified lifting methods were reconstructed in the University of Michigan 3D Static Strength Prediction Program (3DSSPP™) to estimate the L5/S1 disc compression forces and the percentage strength limits. The analyses were performed under the assumption that the lifting motions were smooth. Computer-aided figures were manipulated until their postures closely matched the postures identified from the videos. The weight loads of 60, 80, and 100 pounds were analyzed. These loads represented typical drywall-sheet weights of 51 to 109 pounds. The worker anthropometry was set for a 50th percentile male with a weight of 165.6 pounds and a height of 69.7 inches. With the biomechanical stress information estimated by the computer program, the drywall lifting methods which imposed significant stress on the worker as well as on the individual body parts, were identified.

3. Results

Lifting method 1 was found to be the most commonly used drywall lifting technique among the subjects studied. Lifting methods 1 through 4 accounted for 50%, 6%, 17%, and 27% of the observed drywall lifts, respectively. Biomechanical analyses indicated that all four lifting techniques produced biomechanical stresses greater than the NIOSH Strength Design Limit (SDL) at drywall installers' shoulders, torso, and hips. Table 1 presents the percentages of the male population with sufficient strength to lift 60-, 80-, and 100-lb drywall sheets. Lifting a 100-lb drywall sheet using methods 3 and 4 placed excessive stresses on the worker's shoulders. Only 53% and 36% of the male population were estimated to have sufficient shoulder strength to perform lifting methods 3 and 4, respectively, with a 100-lb sheet. In contrast to other methods, lifting methods 1 and 2 created greater stresses on the workers' elbows and only about 60% to

Figure 1. Illustration of four drywall lifting methods

70% of the male population would have enough elbow strength to lift a 100-lb drywall sheet. The fraction of people capable of lifting a drywall sheet decreased with the increase in the weight of the drywall. It was estimated that more than 90% of males would be able to lift a 60-lb drywall sheet using methods 1, 2, and 3, but only 83% of the male population could perform the task using method 4, due to the stresses on the workers' hips. Over 50% of male adults were predicted to have enough strength to lift a 100-lb drywall sheet with methods 1, 2, and 3, but only 36% of the male population have enough shoulder strength to accomplish the task using method 4. In addition, in Table 1, it was found that all of the lifting methods placed considerable stresses on workers' backs. When a 100-lb drywall sheet is lifted, the worker low back loadings exceeded the Back Compression Design Limit (BCDL) of 770 pounds recommended by the NIOSH Work Practice Guide for Manual Lifting.

Table 1. Summary of the percentage of male population with sufficient strength capability to lift a 60, 80, or 100 lb drywall sheet and the associated L5/S1 disc compression forces as estimated by the University of Michigan 3DSSPP™ Model

Category	Method 1			Method 2			Method 3			Method 4		
	60lb	80lb	100lb	60lb	80lb	100lb	60lb	80lb	100lb	60lb	80lb	100lb
Elbow	94	80	62	98	84	70	99	96	88	99	94	84
Shoulder	97	91	77	95	83	60	93	79	53	93	71	36
Torso	95	91	84	96	93	88	97	95	93	94	91	86
Hip	93	89	84	94	91	87	92	89	85	83	75	65
Knee	99	99	99	99	99	99	98	98	98	97	97	98
Ankle	99	98	97	98	97	95	99	99	99	99	99	99
D.C.F.*	655	734	830	649	757	857	659	750	836	915	1072	1228

* L5/S1 disc compression force

4. Discussion

Results from this study (Table 1) indicate that the four lifting methods placed considerable stress on the worker's elbows, shoulders, torso, and hips — only a limited percentage of the general male population has sufficient upper extremity (i.e., elbow) and trunk strength to perform the task. It should be noted that shoulders, torso and hips were included in the trunk group in the BLS's part-of-body-affected classification. This finding of limited strength in the general male population is consistent with BLS traumatic injury data for drywall installers — of all body parts, the trunk was most frequently injured, accounting for 38.2% of the traumatic injuries, followed by upper extremity injuries (24.9%) [3].

Previous researchers have identified the L5/S1 disc as the weakest link of the body segments when performing heavy lifts [6]. Compared with the other three lifting methods, lifting method 4 resulted in higher L5/S1 disc compression forces. The L5/S1 disc compression forces in lifting method 4 exceed the BCDL (770 lbs), ranging from 915 to 1228 lb for the loads analyzed. The higher L5/S1 disc compression forces for lifting method 4 might be due to the fact that twisted and asymmetric postures were involved, resulting in an increase in the moment of loading on the trunk. Another interesting result of this study is that the L5/S1 disc compression forces were lower than the BCDL when lifting methods 1, 2, and 3 were involved and the loads were under 80 lb. This outcome may have resulted from the fact that the drywall sheets were held very close to body.

A small number of subjects was observed, so the study results may not be generalized to a large population. Another study limitation is that the biomechanical analysis [7] only accounts for the exposures of loads and postures. Other exposures such as frequency and duration [8, 9], as well as physiological factors, may have significant impact on drywall installation-related injuries. A survey of drywall installers and a BLS injury database analysis are also being conducted by NIOSH to increase the understanding of drywall installation-related injuries and help formulate injury prevention strategies. In addition, assistant devices or/and redesign of the size of drywall sheets may deserve consideration to reduce the risk of overexertion injury among drywall installers.

5. References

[1] H. Hsiao and R. L. Stanevich., Injuries and ergonomic applications in construction, In: A. Bhattacharya and J. McGlothlin (eds), Occupational Ergonomics - Theory and Application, Marcel Dekker, Inc, New York, 1996, pp. 545-567.
[2] J. Warren, A. Bhattacharya, G. Lemasters, H. Applegate, and R. Stinson, Focus Groups: An aid for ergonomics assessment of carpentry tasks, 1994, *Abstract of the Annual American Industrial Hygiene Conference and Exposition.*
[3] Bureau of Labor Statistics. Occupational Injuries and Illnesses: Counts, Rates, and Characteristics, 1992: Washington, DC: US Government Printing Office, 1995. US Department of Labor, Bulletin 2455.
[4] C. S. Pan and S. S. Chiou, Biomechanical stress control in drywall installation, 1997: National Institute for Occupational Safety and Health. *Unpublished Protocol.*
[5] A. Mital, A. S. Nicholson and M. M. Ayoub, 1993. *A Guide to Manual Materials Handling.* London, England: Taylor & Francis.
[6] M. M. Ayoub and A. Mital. 1989. *Manual Materials Handling.* London, England: Taylor & Francis.
[7] The University of Michigan. 1993. *3D Static Strength Predication Program*, Ver. 2.0, User's Manual. Ann Arbor, Mich.: The University of Michigan, Center for Ergonomics.
[8] Marras, W. S., Lavender, S. A., Leurgans, S. E., Fathallah, F. A., and Ferguson, S. A. (1995) 'Biomechanical risk factors for occupational related low back disorders', *Ergonomics*, 38(2), 377-410
[9] Bhattacharya, A., Greathouse L., Warren, J., Li Y., Dimov, M., Applegate, H., Stinson, R., and Lemasters, G. (In press). An ergonomic walkthrough observation of carpentry tasks: a pilot study, Applied Occupational and Environmental Hygiene Journal.

Advances in Occupational Ergonomics and Safety II
Edited by Biman Das and Waldemar Karwowski
IOS Press and Ohmsha, 1997

Postural and Load Effects on Lumbosacral Orientation

Yung-Hui Lee* and Yi-Lang Chen**
*Dept. of Industrial Management, National Taiwan Institute of Technology,
**Dept. of Industrial Engineering and Management, Mingchi Institute of Technology,
Taiwan, R.O.C.

Abstract. This study focused on static postural and load effects on lumbosacral orientation. Nonlinear first-order regression models of the torso angle and the pelvic angle versus the lumbosacral orientation were fit to the data with the resulting R-square values between 0.86 and 0.92 for the vertebral level of L1, L3, L5, and S1. Based on the external measurements of the torso and the pelvic angles, the vertebral orientation can easily be calculated.

1. Introduction

A realization of the lumbar and sacrum orientation is clinically relevant. The determination of lumbosacral rotation pattern in lifting is also of ergonomical implication. Documentation of the vertebral orientation is the required kinematic input for models to calculate moments and forces on the low back. The purpose of this study was to determine as well as quantitatively describe the relationship between the measurements of the torso angle, the knee angle, and load handling, with the lumbar spine in a lordotic or kyphotic position, to the measurement of lumbosacral angles.

2. Materials and Methods

Subjects Twelve healthy male subjects were recruited for the videographic experiment. The data of nine of the 12 subjects were used for predicting model development and the data of the other three subjects were used for model validation. These subjects' age ranged from 22 to 31 years (average 26.4 years).

Measurement Protocol The angles of the vertebral markers and the joint angles were recorded videographically as the subject held a load of 0, 10, or 20 kg; torso in angle of 90, 120, 150, or 180° to the horizontal; knee straight, bent 90°, or bent 135°; lumbar in posture of lordosis or kyphosis. The definitions of the lordotic and the kyphotic lumbar posture followed Delitto and Rose (1992). In the lordotic posture, the subject was requested to align his lumbar in normal lordosis and align his pelvis in an anterior tilt. In the kyphotic posture, the subject was requested to align his lumbar in kyphosis and align his pelvis in a posterior tilt, as illustrated in Figure 1. Lumbosacral angles were examined externally using vertebral markers in a total of 24 different postures that are also illustrated in Figure 1. There were two repetitions of each trial. As a result, a total of 1728 static lift trials (12 subjects x 3 loads x 4 trunk positions x 3 knee bends x 2 lumbar postures x 2 repetitions) were performed. A videograph was taken after the load was lifted. The subjects completed all experiments in six sessions. Within a two-hour session, all treatment combinations were performed in a random order. Minimum rest periods of two hours were required between any two adjacent sessions to avoid carry-over fatigue effects.

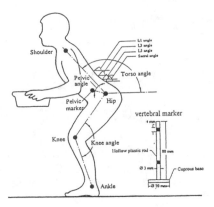

Fig 1 Vertebral markers and joint markers in the study

Model Development The externally measured vertebral angles were, firstly, transferred into internal vertebral angles (i.e., lumbosacral orientations) using the previously developed transformation models (Chen and Lee, 1997). The prediction models of the transferred internal vertebral angles were then developed using a stepwise regression technique. This was done by selecting joint angles as well as load handling as predictors. Only significant variable preselected by ANOVA (analysis of variance) were included in the prediction models. The significant level chosen was 0.001.

3. Results

Error of Remarking The position data were obtained based upon an average of three remarkings on radiographic films. The CV% of L1, L3, L5, and S1 were 3.42, 4.85, 6.02, and 6.97%, respectively. These variations demonstrated that the validity of the data of L1 and L3 were superior to those of L5 and S1. Previous study by the authors (Chen and Lee , 1997) had found that the CV% of remarking was about 5.5 times as much as that of redigitizing.

Posture Effects on Vertebral Orientations The result of the ANOVA analysis indicated that the effects of subject, lumbar posture, knee angle, torso angle, handling load, and some of two-term interactions significantly ($p < 0.01$) affect vertebral orientation. Among all, lumbar posture and torso angle contributed most. The difference in lumbar posture contributed 4.0 % to the variance at L1 level, and the contribution increased to 48.5 % at the S1 level. The contribution of the torso angle, however, decreased from 94.2 % at the L1 level to 47.6 % at the S1 level.

Predictive Models Development and Validation The significant variables selected by ANOVA were considered as candidate predictors for the determination of vertebral angles. Table 1 lists the variables selected by stepwise regression technique ($p < 0.15$) and their R-square values. Based on the fact that the variables of the torso and the pelvic angles appeared in all analyses and that these two variables together accounted for 92%, 92%, 90%, and 86% of the variance at the levels of L1, L3, L5, and S1, respectively, they were selected as the best predictors for the determination of lumbosacral angles. There were fewer variables in the models, with almost equal R-square values, than the models of Anderson et al (1986).

Table 1. The vertebral orientation prediction models and the R-square values

Vertebrae	Intercept	Torso angle	Pelvic angle	R^2
L1	-89.2730	0.9776	-0.2987	0.924
L3	-84.3439	0.9266	-0.4647	0.923
L5	-40.8083	0.6832	-0.5216	0.898
S1	-10.1442	0.5443	-0.4610	0.860

To validate the models, the authors used the torso and pelvic data of 3 different subjects as input for these models. The calculated vertebral angles were then compared with their corresponding measurements. The paired t-test showed that the differences are not statistically significant. The mean (SD) differences was ranged from -0.8°(6.5°) to 1.1°(5.9°) and were listed in Table 2. Since the data were averaged across four torso positions in the sagittal plane, there were large SD listed in the table .

Table 2. The comparison of the predicted vertebral angles and the measured ones. Data were averaged across four torso positions in the sagittal plane (data in degree)

Vertebrae	Measured angle[1] Mean (SD)	Predicted angles Mean (SD)	Difference	T value[2]
L1	33.4(28.1)	34.2(27.9)	-0.8(6.5)	-2.0959
L3	28.6(26.1)	27.8(25.3)	1.1(5.9)	2.5236
L5	40.0(18.4)	40.5(17.9)	-0.6(4.9)	-1.6042
S1	54.4(16.2)	53.8(14.2)	0.6(4.1)	2.1862

1. The measured angles were the measured vertebral angles after data transformation using previously developed transformation models.
2. Results of paired comparisons t-test showed no significant difference between the measured and the predicted vertebral angles (significance level = 0.001)

4. Discussion

The major finding in the model development was that lumbar posture had a statistically significant effect on the lumbosacral orientation by altering the extendibility of the soft tissues of the back. Effects of the lordortic and the kyphotic lumbar postures on sacral orientation in four trunk positions are illustrated in Figure 2. The difference ranged from 9.8° to 18.4°. In the lordotic lumbar posture, the sacral angle increased linearly with the increase of the torso flexion; while in the kyphotic lumbar posture the sacral angle increased only after the torso flexed over 120°. The sacral angles in the lordortic posture are larger than those in the kyphotic one. This can be explained by the fact that in the lordortic posture, the subject's trunk was held rigid so as to force all torso flexion to occur in the rotation of the sacrum about the hip joint rather than activities in the lumbar region. The increased inclination of sacrum in the lordotic posture implies that more shearing, rather than compressive, force acts on the endplate.

The development of the prediction models of lumbar/sacral angles did not include the knee angle as a predictor. This can be attributed to the tightness of the hamstring which plays an important role in restraining sacrum rotation as the knees bend. Our development of models, in which the combined data set (data of lordortic and kyphotic postures) was used, did not include the load handling as a predictor for lumbosacral orientation. This is consistent with the results of Anderson et al. (1986) They explained that the moment at L5/S1 increases as the torso was flexed due to the increasing moment arm for the upper body weight overrided the effect of a pre-set percent of maximum load in the hands. A significant effect of the load handling on lumbosacral orientation, however, was observed in the lordortic lumbar posture. One of possible reason can be attributed to the nature of the static posture adopted in this study. While maintaining a static posture with the lumbar in a kyphotic posture, the amount of effort to maintain stability is far larger than that of the effort to maintain the load in hand.

Quantitative models presented in this study took a novel approach to modeling the vertebral orientation of the lumbar/sacrum spine in different lumbar postures in the sagittal plane. The usefulness measure for providing a predictive function for other populations (e.g. female, elderly, Caucasian) is a matter for further investigations. In addition, vertebral rotation patterns in dynamic lift would also be an important subject for further studies.

5. References
Anderson CK; Chaffin DB, and Herrin GD, A study of lumbosacral orientation under varied static loads. Spine 11(1986) 456-462.
Chen, YY and Lee, YH, A noninvasive protocol for the determination of lumbosacral orientation, Clinical Biomechanics (1997) in press.
Delitto RS, Rose SJ: An electromyography analysis of two techniques for squat lifting and lowering. Phys Ther 1992;71: 438-448.

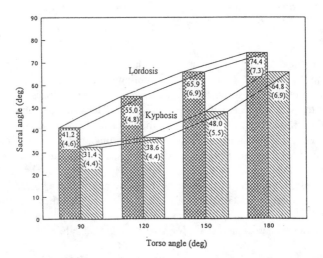

Fig 2. Comparison of sacral angles in the lordotic and kyphotic lumbar postures

Advances in Occupational Ergonomics and Safety II
Edited by Biman Das and Waldemar Karwowski
IOS Press and Ohmsha, 1997

Gender Differences in Model Estimates of Trunk Muscle Activity

Mark L. MCMULKIN[1], Jeffrey C. WOLDSTAD[2], and Richard E. HUGHES[3]

[1]*Industrial & Mfg. Engr. Dept., Wichita State University, Wichita, KS 67260-0035, USA*
[2]*Industrial Engineering Dept., Texas Tech University, Lubbock, TX 79409-3061, USA*
[3] *Dept. of Environmental Health, University of Washington, Seattle, WA, 98195 USA*

Abstract. The objective of this study was to determine if optimization-based biomechanical models predict torso muscular activity of males and females equally well. For each of two optimization models, two sets of muscle geometries (moment arms, lines of action, and cross-sectional areas) were used as inputs: one included data from male subjects, and one included data from female and male subjects. Six male and six female subjects performed isometric exertions to resist loads consisting of combinations of three moments while EMG activity was recorded. For five muscles (LRA, RRA, REO, LES, and RES), force estimates of the model combinations correlated significantly better with male normalized EMG muscle activity than with female muscle activity. Neither muscle geometry set nor model set significantly improved correlations for females.

1. INTRODUCTION

This study investigated the ability of optimization-based biomechanical models to estimate torso muscular activity of males and females. Two optimization models were considered: the Minimum Intensity Compression (MIC) model [1] and the Sum of the Cubed Intensities (SCI) model [2]. For both models, a free body diagram at the L3/L4 level of the torso is analyzed including relevant muscles to determine the moment equilibrium equations. The MIC model, a reformulation of an iterative linear programming model by Schultz *et al.* [3], minimizes the maximum intensity or tension that any one muscle can sustain, such that static equilibrium is maintained. A second step determines the muscle forces so that the compression force on the disc is minimized given the intensity determined in the first step. The SCI model determines the muscle forces by minimizing the sum of the cubed muscle intensities while maintaining static equilibrium. Each model requires inputs of muscle geometries which includes moment arms from the L3/L4 disc, the line of action in three dimensions, and the cross-sectional area.

The model estimates of muscle forces have been compared to electromyographic data to evaluate the accuracy of the models. The iterative linear programming model of Schultz *et al.* [3] has been compared to EMG values collected by surface electrodes [3,4,5] and to EMG values collected by wire electrodes [6]. Hughes *et al.* [7] and Hughes and Chaffin [8] reported the SCI model to be more consistent with surface EMG data that the MIC formulation. Only male subjects were used in experimentation in these studies [3,4,5,6,7,8]. Also, the muscle geometry inputs were limited to one set of data based on male subjects. For example, Hughes *et al.* used 10 muscles with moment arms taken from Tracy *et al.* [9], lines of action taken from Dumas *et al.* [10], and cross-sectional areas from Tracy *et al.* [9] with adjustments for fiber orientation made as in McGill *et al.* [11], and oblique area proportions taken from Chaffin *et al.* [12] which used female subjects.

In the current study, two sets of muscle geometries were used as inputs: one was a compilation of several studies as used by Hughes *et al.* [7] and one was reported by Han *et al.* [13]. The Han *et al.* muscle geometries included data from four females and six males. The four combinations of models and muscle geometries will be abbreviated as MIC-C (MIC model with compilation geometry), MIC-H (MIC model with Han et al. geometry), SCI-C (SCI model with compilation geometry), and SCI-H (SCI model with Han et al. geometry) for this paper.

The objective of this study was to test the hypothesis that combinations of optimization-based biomechanical trunk models and muscle geometries will estimate male and female muscle activity equally well.

2. METHOD

2.1 Subjects

Twelve healthy subjects, six of which were male and six of which were female, participated in this study. The mean height, mass, age of the male subjects was 174.3 cm (SD 4.4), 66.1 kg (SD 6.2), and 21.3 years (SD 3.6), respectively. The mean height, mass, age of the female subjects was 171.4 cm (SD 6.0), 64.0 kg (SD 6.58), and 21.0 years (SD 2.8), respectively

2.2 Materials and Apparatus

Static combinations of attempted flexion/extension, right and left lateral bending, and twisting were exerted by the subjects through hand loading techniques. Eighteen different combinations of flexion/extension and lateral bending moments, each with a 30 Nm resultant, were generated. Two levels of torsion were included at the 18 combinations of flexion/extension and lateral bending moments, resulting in 36 conditions. Weights were held by the subjects to generate the loading conditions and were computed to account for moments applied at the L3/L4 disc due to the weight of the arms during hand loading conditions. To aid the subjects in maintaining an upright posture while external loads were applied, separate light emitters were mounted in front and behind the subject with the light beams in planes parallel to the frontal plane.

The EMG activity of four muscle pairs were recorded: erector spinae (LES, RES); rectus abdominus (LRA, RRA), external oblique (LEO, REO), and latissimus dorsi (LLD, RLD). The raw EMG signals of the muscles under study were sampled at 500 Hz and then high-pass filtered using a 30 Hz cutoff [14]. The EMG data were processed by taking the root mean square (RMS) with a 60 ms time constant. The mean RMS values for each trial were normalized [15,16] to get percent muscle activity using the equation

$$EMG_{Normalized} = \frac{EMG_{Test\ Trial} - EMG_{Resting}}{EMG_{Max.} - EMG_{Resting}}$$

2.3 Protocol

The experiment was conducted over a two day period. Each day, six MVC trials described by McGill (1991) were performed, and the muscle resting EMG level was measured as the subject lay on a bench. The subjects completed a randomly ordered sequence of 18 hand loading trials each day. Subjects were required to resist the moments for three seconds while the EMG signals were collected. The subjects were given two minute rest breaks between trials.

To evaluate the accuracy of the four model and geometry combinations, the percent muscle activity ($EMG_{Normalized}$) was correlated with the model's muscle forces estimates. The muscle forces estimated by each model combination was used as the regressor variable to predict percent muscle activity measured in the experiment. A linear model was assumed between model muscle force and measured muscle activity. The regression models were developed for each combination of subject, muscle, and torsion moment so 18 observations were included in each regression equation. Model muscle force and measured muscle activity that have the same pattern of activity and inactivity will have higher R^2 values. The R^2 values were compared using an Analysis of Variance (ANOVA) with five factors, muscle, torsion, geometry, model, and gender. The results indicating significance ($p<0.05$) of factors associated gender were of interest.

3. RESULTS

A significant gender effect indicated male muscle activity was predicted better (mean $R^2 = 0.44$) than female muscle activity (mean $R^2 = 0.33$) by model force estimates. For individual muscles, male muscle activity was predicted significantly better than female muscle activity for the RRA, LRA, REO, LES, and RES by 8 to 25 %, whereas no muscles were predicted better for females (Figure 1).

For each model and muscle geometry, the difference in R^2 values remains constant between males and females at about 0.10, indicating no specific model and geometry combination led to equal predictions for males and females. However, overall the SCI model, mean R^2 equal 0.44, predicted percent muscle activity better than the MIC model, mean R^2 equal 0.33. The compilation geometry had a higher mean R^2 equal 0.41 than the Han geometry, mean R^2 equal 0.37.

4. DISCUSSION

The purpose of this study was to determine if different combinations of biomechanical optimization models and muscle geometries would predict muscle activity of males and females equally well. The results of this study indicate that the muscle activity of five muscles are predicted significantly better for males than females. None of the model or geometry combinations improved the prediction of female muscle activity to the level of male muscle activity predictions. The results of this study indicated model estimates of muscle forces correlated better with male muscle activity than female activity regardless of the two muscle geometry sets. Geometry sets need to be generated for females to indicate if there are differences in lines of action, cross-sectional, or moment arms.

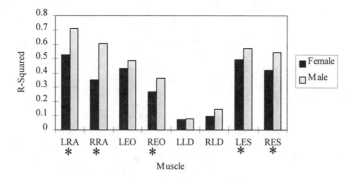

Figure 1.   Mean R^2 values for male and female muscle activity predicted by model estimates. Asterisks below muscles indicate significant differences between genders using LSD post-hoc test.

After determining that male and female muscle activities were not predicted equally, the goal was to identify specific muscle geometries or models which led to improved predictions. No improvements were found for female muscle activity predictions using the Han et al (1992) data although it includes data from four female subjects and six male subjects. Compilation muscle geometry based on male subjects is accepted as predicting female muscle activity equally well. The results for male and female muscle activity prediction do not imply that all model and muscle geometry combinations estimate muscle activity equally well. For males, the SCI and MIC models accounted for 49% and 38% of the variance respectively, and for females , the SCI and MIC models accounted for 38% and 28% of the variance respectively. The difference between genders for both models is the same (10%), but in both cases the absolute percent variance accounted for is better for males.

Several limitations exist in the model development and experimentation used in this study. First, 10 muscles were included in the model formulations to represent the internal force generating components of the lumbar region of the torso. Second, only young healthy male and female subjects were used in the study. Third, all model estimates and physical exertions were for isometric loading limiting the generalization to dynamic tasks. Fourth, flexion/extension and lateral bending moments were generated simultaneously by subjects holding weights in front and to the sides, 90 degrees apart.

REFERENCES

[1] J.C. Bean, D.B. Chaffin, and A.B. Schultz, Biomechanical model calculation of muscle contraction forces: a double linear programming method, *Journal of Biomechanics* **21** (1988), 59-66.

[2] R.D. Crowninshield and R.A. Brand, A physiologically based criterion of muscle force prediction in locomotion, *Journal of Biomechanics* **14** (1981) 793-801.

[3] A.B Schultz, K. Haderspeck, D. Warwick, and D. Portillo, Use of lumbar trunk muscles in isometric performance of mechanically complex standing tasks, *Journal of Orthopaedic Research* **1** (1983) 77-91.

[4] Z. Ladin, K.R. Murthy, and C.J. De Luca, Mechanical recruitment of low-back muscles: theoretical predictions and experimental validation, *Spine* **14** (1989) 927-938.

[5] A. Schultz, R. Cromwell, D. Warwick, and G. Andersson, Lumbar trunk muscle use in standing isometric heavy exertions. *Journal of Orthopaedic Research* **5** (1987) 320-329.

[6] C. Zetterberg, G.B.J. Andersson, and A.B. Schultz, The activity of individual trunk muscles during heavy physical loading, *Spine* **12** (1987) 1035-1040.

[7] R.E. Hughes, D.B. Chaffin, S.A. Lavender, and G.B.J. Andersson, Evaluation of muscle force prediction models of the lumbar trunk using surface electromyography, *Journal of Orthopaedic Research* **12** (1994) 689-698.

[8] R.E. Hughes and D.B. Chaffin, The effect of strict muscle stress limits on abdominal muscle force predictions for combined torsion and extension loadings, *Journal of Biomechanics* **28** (1995) 527-533.

[9] M.F. Tracy, M.J. Gibson, E.P. Szypryt, A. Rutherford, and E.N. Corlett, The geometry of the muscles of the lumbar spine determined by magnetic resonance imaging, *Spine* **14** (1989) 186-193.

[10] G.A. Dumas, M.J. Poulin, B. Roy, M. Gagnon, and M. Jovanovic, A three-dimensional digitization method to measure trunk muscle line of action, *Spine* **13** (1988) 532-541.

[11] S.M. McGill, N. Patt, and R.W. Norman, Measurement of the trunk musculature of active males using CT scan radiography: Implications for force and moment generating capacity about the L4/L5 joint, *Journal of Biomechanics* **21** (1988) 329-341.

[12] D.B. Chaffin, M.S. Redfern, M. Erig, and S.A. Goldstein, Lumbar muscle size and locations from CT scans of 96 women of age 40 to 63 years, *Clinical Biomechanics* **5** (1990) 9-16.

[13] J.S. Han, J.Y. Ahn, V.K. Goel, R. Takeuchi, and D. McGowan, CT-Based geometric data of human spine musculature. Part I. Japanese patients with chronic low back pain, *Journal of Spinal Disorders* **5** (1992) 448-458.

[14] M.S. Redfern, R.E. Hughes, and D.B. Chaffin, High-pass filtering to remove electrocardiographic interference from torso EMG recordings, *Clinical Biomechanics* **8** (1993) 44-48.

[15] S.A. Lavender, Y.H. Tsuang, A. Hafezi, G.B.J. Andersson, D.B. Chaffin, and R.E. Hughes, Coactivation of the trunk muscles during asymmetric loading of the torso, *Human Factors* **34** (1992) 239-247.

[16] G.A. Mirka, The quantification of EMG normalization error, *Ergonomics* **34** (1991) 343-352.

9. Manual Materials Handling

Advances in Occupational Ergonomics and Safety II
Edited by Biman Das and Waldemar Karwowski
IOS Press and Ohmsha, 1997

The Evaluation of Two Repetitive Lifting Activities

Tearesa Wegscheid, Tycho. K. Fredericks, and Dale DeWeese

Human Performance Institute, Department of Industrial and Manufacturing Engineering, Western Michigan University, Kalamazoo, MI 49008-5061 U.S.A.

A field study of repetitive packing operations within a Midwestern automotive parts manufacturing facility was conducted. Assembly and core setting operations were evaluated using the NIOSH (1991) lifting guidelines, oxygen consumption, and heart rate measurements. These two departments were chosen because of their similarities in terms of weight of parts and frequency of lifts. The major difference between the two departments was that the company had invested in material handling devices for the assembly department to reduce the risk of back injuries. With this in mind, the objectives of the study were to compare the two different departments with respect to the NIOSH Lifting Guidelines and physiological measures. A total of 17 lines, 15 assembly and two core setting lines were reviewed. Twelve company workers served as subjects. Steady-state oxygen consumption levels, heart rates, and anthropometric data were collected for each subject. Results indicated that both lines (100%) in the core setting department and 2 out of 15 (13.3%) lines within the assembly department did not comply with the NIOSH guidelines. The physiological findings supported the NIOSH guidelines as well as documented a reduction of physiological stress in the assembly department.

1.0 Introduction

Manual material handling can be the act of manually pulling, pushing, or lifting any object. Manual material handling activities have produced the largest number of worker compensation injuries in the industry. National Institute for Occupational Safety and Health (NIOSH) developed *Work Practices Guide to Manual Lifting* in 1981 (revised in 1991) to reduce the number of injuries contributed to manual material handling. The 1991 NIOSH equations were designed to provide lifting limits that safely accommodate 75% of the female population and 99% of the male population.

The current study is a field evaluation of two repetitive packing operations in a Midwestern automotive parts manufacturing facility. Although ergonomic changes were recently made in the assembly department, an immediate reduction in the injury rate was not observed which concerned management. With this in mind, the objectives of the study were to analyze both operations using the NIOSH lifting equation, determine the physical demands placed on employees, and determine if the previous changes reduced the risk of back injuries.

2.0 Method

2.1 Subjects

Twelve line workers (9 male and 3 female) were randomly selected from second and third shift operations for the study. Eight employees operated machines in the assembly area and four were core setters in the foundry area. The average age of the subjects was 37 years old with a standard deviation of 9.5 years and a range of 24 to 60 years. None of the subjects had a history of musculoskeletal disorders symptoms or upper extremity disorders. All the subjects were familiarized with the experimental procedures and equipment prior to the start of the data collection.

2.2 Equipment

The height and weight of each subject was measured and provided by the company's medical staff. Grip strengths were measured utilizing a JAMAR hydraulic hand dynamometer. A CosMed, Model K-2, portable oxygen consumption unit with a telemetric heart rate transmitting and receiving unit was used for all steady-state VO^2 consumption and heart rate measurements. Weights for brake caliper and sand castings were measured on a certified, electronic scale supplied by the company. Horizontal and vertical distances were measured utilizing a 25-foot Stanley tape measure. Frequency of the lift was determined by an on-site time study procedure with a calibrated Faehr electronic stop watch.

2.3 Procedure

Two processes were studied, an assembly operation and a core setting operation. The assembly task involved picking up a completed caliper assembly from a palletized fixture and placing it into a vacuum-formed shipping tray. The operator then retrieved a machined caliper casting from a supply basket, loaded the palletized fixture, and activated a palm switch to complete a production cycle. The core setting operation involved picking up two sand castings from a pallet and placing each sand casting into a mold form carried by a conveyer belt. The difference between the operations was the application of material handling devices. The assembly line used material handling devices to place the caliper castings and shipping trays at knuckle level for each operator. The core setting operation did not have material handling devices available, thus requiring the subject to consistently lift from a pallet on the floor.

The first phase of the study involved the collection of data pertaining to the operator's environment. The brake calipers and the sand castings manipulated by the operators were weighed, a time study for each operation was conducted to obtain line rates, and the dimensions for the NIOSH (1991) guidelines were measured. Fifteen assembly operations and two core setting operations were measured.

The second phase of the study involved the collection of background information on all subjects. Information included medical history, employment duration, personal hobbies and standard anthropometric measures.

The third phase of the study was to measure the subjects' steady-state resting heart rates and VO^2 consumption levels. Readings were measured prior to the start of their normal work shift. Steady-state working heart rates and VO^2 consumption measurements were taken while each subject worked at the normal production line pace. Readings were recorded at 15 second intervals and steady-state resting and working values were used for all subsequent calculations.

3.0 Results

The descriptive statistics for the subjects are shown in Table 1. The mean grip strength (45.6 +8.16 kg) was compared to estimates for U.S. male adults [4] to determine if the samples taken were a representative sample of the U.S. population. It was determined that there was not a significant difference between the sample used in this study and a much larger population. The results showed similar findings for the female sample population used in this study. In both cases, the samples used in this study could be considered representative of the U.S. population.

Table 1. Descriptive statistics of the subjects (n = 12)

Measure	Mean (SD) (Assembly Males)	Mean (SD) (Assembly Females)	Mean (SD) (Core Setter Males)
Age (years)	44.2(9.4)	32(8.5)	26.7(4.7)
Weight (kg)	94.9(22.6)	63(5.5)	96.7(6.9)
Stature (mm)	1816(75.7)	1685(26.4)	1740(77.3)
Grip Strength (kg)	487.3(9.5)	32(7.51)	42.7(4.8)

The average weight of the part before assembly was 6.99 pounds and the average weight of the part after assembly was 11.08 pounds. The weight of the parts prior to assembly ranged from 3.11 pounds to 17.59 pounds and the range of the parts after assembly was 5.17 pounds to 21.95 pounds. The average weight of the sand castings was 11.23 pounds with a range of 9.89 pound to 13.12 pounds. The results of a t-test showed no significant difference between the weight of the parts for the two departments.

The results of the time studies showed that the line rates varied from 62 to 300 pieces per hour. The average frequency of the lift was 3.5 lifts/minute, with the range of the lift frequency between 1.72 lifts/minute to 5 lifts/minute. The results of a t-test showed no significant difference between the lifting frequency for the two departments.

The results of applying the NIOSH 1991 equation to the assembly department indicated 2 of the 15 (13.3%) lines were considered hazardous (LI > 1). In the core setting department, it was determined that both lines (100%) were hazardous.

Several t-tests (at α = .05) were conducted to compare the male core setters to the male assembly workers. The results showed a significant difference between the age and height of the two groups. Furthermore, the results of the t-test comparing the females to the two male groups showed, as expected, significant differences between age, weight, height, and grip strength. Table 2 shows the physiological measures for heart rate and VO^2 consumption for each subject group. Two subjects were statistically found to be outliers and were not used in data analysis.

Further analysis was conducted to determine if there was a difference between the physiological measures of the female assembly workers, the male assembly workers, and the male core setters. The results of a t-test showed that there was not a significant difference in working VO^2 consumption between the three groups. Since there was a significant difference between the age of the assembly males, assembly females, and the male core setters, heart rates were normalized for each group with respect to their estimated maximum heart rate. The results of the t-test showed that there was a significant difference between the heart rate for the male assembly workers and the male core setters. It was determined that the male cores setters' heart rates were higher than the male assembly workers.

Table 2: Physiological measures (n = 10)

Department	Rest HR (bmp) Mean (SD)	Rest VO^2 (liters/min.) Mean (SD)	Normalized Working HR (bmp)* Mean (SD)	Working VO^2 (liters/min.) Mean (SD)
Assembly Male	87.6(9.14)	0.38(0.09)	12.8(9.8)	0.85(0.22)
Assembly Female	76.5(3.54)	0.28(0.05)	10.2(1.7)	0.7(0.11)
Core Setters Male	76.5(3.54)	0.44(0.14)	25.0(5.5)	0.92(0.29)

* Working heart rate was normalized to estimated maximum heart rate.

4.0 Discussion/Recommendations

Through the application of the NIOSH (1991) lifting equation, it was determined that 13.3% of the assembly lines exceeded the lifting index (LI). It was further determined that the horizontal multiplier was the driving factor in the elevated LI. Recommendations included the reduction of the horizontal distance by simply removing barriers between the employees and the work. The LI's for the core setting lines were hazardous in all cases (100%). The main contributors in this case were the horizontal multipliers and the vertical origin multipliers. Recommendations for the core setting lines included the uses of material handling devices to reduce the vertical origin multiplier (back flexion) and the reduction of the horizontal multiplier (remove constraints between the employee and the work). The difference between the assembly and core setting department was the extensive use of material handling devices in the assembly area. The LI reflects the reduction in physical demands.

The results of the physiological measures showed that there was a significant difference between the normalized heart rates of the core setters and the assembly workers. This would suggest that the physical demands were higher for the core setters as compared to the assembly workers. The use of material handling devices in the assembly area positioned materials no lower than knuckle height, eliminating asymmetrical lifting and lifting above the shoulder. These engineering changes successfully reduced the physiological demands placed on employees. This study successfully demonstrated to the company that the new material handling system does in fact reduce the physiological demands and the risk of back injuries.

References

[1]   Chaffin, Don B. and Andersson, Gunnar B. J., *Occupational Biomechanics*. New York: John Wiley & Sons, Inc, 1991.
[2]   Dempsey, Patrick G., Ayoub, M. M., Westfall, Peter H., The NIOSH Lifting Equations: A Closer Look. *Advances in Industrial Ergonomics and Safety VII*. Ed by A.C. Bittner and P. C. Champney. London: Taylor & Francis Ltd, 1995.
[3]   Kumar, S., A Conceptual Model of Oxerexertion, Safety, and Risk of Injury in Occupational Settings, *Human Factors*, 36(2), 1994, 197-209.
[4]   Pheasant, S., *Bodyspace: Anthropometry, Ergonomics and the Design of Work*, London: Taylor & Francis Ltd, 1996.
[5]   Waters, T. R., Putz-Anderson, V., Garg, A., Applications Manual for the Revised NIOSH Lifting Equation DHHS(NIOSH) pub. No. 94-110. Springfield, VA: National Technical Information Service, 1994.

Advances in Occupational Ergonomics and Safety II
Edited by Biman Das and Waldemar Karwowski
IOS Press and Ohmsha, 1997

Load Transfer Investigation During a 2-D Sagittal Plane Box Lift

Eger TR and Stevenson JM

Ergonomics Research Group Queen's University, Kingston, Ontario Canada

Abstract

In order to develop safe criteria for lifting, biomechanical link-segment models have been used to predict the loads experienced by the back. Link-segment models beginning with load calculations at the hand segment are often employed in industrial settings. The predictive power of this approach rests in the determination of the load transfer to the hands. Unless the "box" is instrumented, the transfer of the load to the hands can only be estimated. The purpose of this study was to compare the effects on lumbar moments of the actual load transfer (TRUE) from the forceplate with two estimation methods (SLOPE and INSTANT). The actual load transfer to the hands was measured using an AMTI ^{TM} forceplate. The SLOPE method estimated load transfer to the hands as the slope of the TRUE curve, with box load being applied to the hands in equal increments. The INSTANT method of load transfer applied the full box load to the hands at one point in time. Ten healthy male and ten healthy female subjects with no past history of low back pain completed 20 box lifts in the sagittal plane. Box loads were randomized between 5, 9, 13, and 18 kg. All box lifts began at the floor and finished at a shelf 15 cm below subject acromium height.. The L4/L5 moments predicted using the SLOPE method of estimating load transfer to the hands were superior to the INSTANT method.

1. Introduction

Manual materials handling is a regular requirement of many industrial, custodial and manufacturing occupations. Unfortunately lifting is also a major factor in the development, and reoccurrence of low back pain and injury. In fact, over 65 % of industrial workers report low back pain symptoms during their career [1]. In 1981 and 1991 the National Institute for Occupational Health and Safety published guidelines to help reduce the number and severity of low back injury and pain incidents. In the original guidelines, biomechanical and epidemiological data identified increased risk for low back pain and injury within the first few seconds when lifting from the floor [2]. In 1983, Garg and colleagues stressed the need to study the dynamics of lifting near the lift origin since this information could be a factor in low back injury [3].

Load transfer, defined as the period in which 0 % of the load to 100 % of the load is supported by the hands, needs to be considered carefully when utilizing link segment models that begin load calculations at the hand segment. The accuracy of this approach rests in the determination of the load in the hands. Actual hand load can be measured directly if the "box" being lifted is instrumented or a forcplate is available, but generally this is not a possibility in the majority of industrial settings. In the past, researchers have applied the full load of the box to the hands at one point in time [4]. This assumption is an oversimplification since peak accelerations and back moments occur near the start of the lift. This paper will evaluate the impact of two different methods of estimating load transfer to the hands. The resulting moments at the L4/L5 level will be compared to the moments calculated when the actual load in the hands is known.

Figure 1: 2-D sagittal plane box lift from the floor to a shelf 15 cm below shoulder height.
The picture on the left displays the forceplate (outlined in white) used to collect forces.

2. Methodology

2.1 Subject Selection

Ten healthy females and ten healthy males with no past history of low back pain volunteered to participate in this study. The mean age of the females and males were 24 and 25 years respectively. The females had an average height of 168 cm (std. 7.3) and an average weight of 64.9 kg (std. 10.2 kg), while the average height and weight of the males was 182 cm (std. 7.0 cm) and 80 kg (std. 7.6 kg) respectively.

2.2 Experimental Protocol

Each subject completed 5 sagittal plane box lifts from the floor to a shelf 15 cm below shoulder height at weights of 5, 9, 13, and 18 kg (Figure 1). Lifting order was randomized for all subjects. Light emitting diode markers were placed on the knuckle, wrist, elbow, shoulder and hip (top of anterior superior illiac spine of each subject). Kinematic data were then collected at 100 Hz using the OPTOTRACK ™, a 3D optoelectric motion tracking system. Kinematic data of upper body segment end points were also obtained by digitizing video. True load transfer to the hands was recorded using an AMTI ™ forceplate at a sampling rate of 100 Hz.

2.3 Load Transfer Models

Kinematic and load transfer data were then entered into a quasi-dynamic hands-down link segment model in order to predict moments at the L4/L5 level. The actual load transfer was measured by the forceplate with the assumption that any decrease in load as the box was lifted off the forceplate corresponded to an increase in load experienced by the hands. This method of determining load transfer is referred to as the "TRUE" method (Figure 2). Two load transfer methods were then used to estimate load transfer since a forceplate is generally not available outside a laboratory setting.

The first method termed the "INSTANT" method assumed load transfer to the hands occurred fully at one point in time. This point was defined as the video frame before the first frame in which the box could clearly be seen fully off the floor. Method 2, SLOPE, estimated hand load by calculating the linear slope of the TRUE load transfer curve (Figure 2). Load transfer with the SLOPE method was predict from a video image of the subject lifting. The start of load transfer was defined by the video frame in which the vertical displacement of the wrist is at its lowest value after the hands have made contact with the box. While the end of load transfer was defined by the video frame where separation between the box and the floor could first be seen clearly. Once the number of video frames (load transfer time) was known, the weight of the load was divided equally and applied over the number of load transfer frames until the full weight of the box was in the hands.

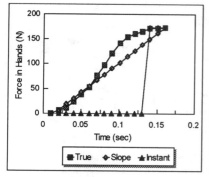

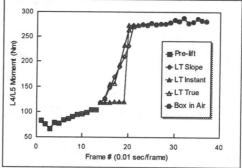

Figure 2: TRUE load transfer along with the SLOPE method and INSTANT method of predicting load transfer to the hands are shown.

Figure 3: L4/L5 predicted moments are shown for a complete lift. TRUE, SLOPE, and INSTANT values of moment predictions are shown for the load transfer region of the curve.

3. Results and Discussion

To have a clearer understanding of the role of load transfer in relation to a complete lift L4/L5 moments are shown for the complete lift from floor to shelf height for one subject trial (Figure 3). Predicted L4/L5 moments are shown using the TRUE, SLOPE, and INSTANT methods.

For all subjects at all weights the SLOPE method of predicting load transfer was more representative of the TRUE load transfer to the hands. If the area under the moment time curve was considered, the INSTANT method underestimates the TRUE which is not the case for the SLOPE.

The SLOPE method for predicting load transfer to the hands demonstrated three different effects on the L4/L5 moments relating to the style, and speed at which a subject lifted. Subjects who lifted very quickly had a steep load transfer slope as well as a steep load transfer curve as can be seen in Figure 4a. These subjects on average tended to be men with a load transfer time in the range of 0.07-0.15 seconds. For subjects who spent more time initiating the lifting of the box, the SLOPE method tended to overestimate the L4/L5 moment (Figure 4b). In situations where the subject "rolled" the box off the surface as they lifted the SLOPE method underestimated the L4/L5 moment (Figure 4c).

In essence, the effectiveness of the SLOPE method of estimating the load in the hands during load transfer is dependant on the lifting style one employs. If the true load in the hands can not be measured during load transfer than the slope method of predicting load transfer to the hands is preferred over the instant method. Moreover, the longer the load transfer time, the greater the need to estimate load in the hands more accurately since this is associated with longer loading time. This is especially important when calculating L4/L5 moments for heavy lifts and for women, since the average load transfer time at 18 kg is 0.16 seconds for women and 0.14 seconds for men while the average load transfer time at 5 kg is 0.12 seconds for women and 0.09 seconds for men.

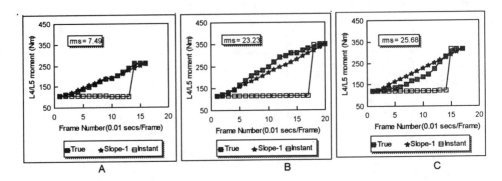

Figure 4: L4/L5 moments are predicted using the TRUE load transfer values, and Load transfer predicted from the SLOPE method and INSTANT method. RMS values are reported for the SLOPE compared to the TRUE. A) an example of a near perfect match between the TRUE method and SLOPE method. B) illustrates how L4/L5 moments can be slightly underestimated with the SLOPE method C) shows overestimation of L4/L5 moments using the SLOPE method.

4. Summary

Biomechanical link-segment models are often used to predict the moments experienced by the back during lifting. The quality of industrial applications are often limited by the kinematic and force collection equipment available for data collection. In situations where a load being lifted can not be instrumented to reveal the true load transfer to the hands, the SLOPE method is more accurate when compared to the INSTANT method in the estimation of load transfer. Therefore, L4/L5 predictions are improved with the slope method.

Future efforts will examine the characteristics of load transfer curves in detail to gain an understanding of the differences across gender, lifting style, strength, and fatigue. The literature reports greater risk for injury near the start of the lift hence further research needs to focus on the load transfer period in order to identify possible causes of injury.

References

1. Rodgers, Working with Backache. Perinton Press, United States of America, 1985.
2. National Technical Information Service. Scientific Support Documentation for the Revised 1991 NIOSH Lifting Equation, PB91-226274 (US Department of Commerce, Springfield, VA), 1991.
3. Garg, D., Sharma, D. B. Chaffin, and J. M. Schmidler. Biomechanical Stresses as Related to Motion Trajectory of Lifting. *Human Factors*, 25 (1983) 839-853.
4. W. Wheeler. Investigation of the Effect of Shoulder Joint Translation on the Lumbar Moments for Two-Dimensional Modelling Strategies. Unpublished Masters Thesis, Queen's University, 1994.

Advances in Occupational Ergonomics and Safety II
Edited by Biman Das and Waldemar Karwowski
IOS Press and Ohmsha, 1997

The Queen's-DuPont Longitudinal Low Back Pain Study: Initial Examination of the Physical Measures

Stevenson JM, Weber CL, Dumas GA, Smith JT, Albert WJ, Lapensée M
Ergonomics Research Group Queen's University, Kingston, Ontario Canada

Abstract

This longitudinal study followed 150 employees, who lifted 7,000 kg per day in 4-12 kg increments, for a two year period. The goal of the study was to determine potential risk factors which may predispose an individual to low back pain (LBP). The subjects comprised of workers who reported mild or no back pain prior to the study. Initial measures related to physical strength and endurance, lifting tasks and psycho-social and back pain status were collected at the beginning of the study period, with follow-up questionnaires administered every six months. The purpose of this paper is to introduce the physical measurement methodology developed for the study and to present the preliminary analysis from some of these measures. The data from the physical measures were compared across admission groups and no significant differences were found thus allowing data to be collapsed across sub-groups for future analysis.

1. Introduction

To date there exist five longitudinal studies [1,2,3,4,5] devoted to the understanding of the predisposing factors to low back pain (LBP). In the fall of 1994, through the collaborative efforts of the Ergonomics Research Group (ERG) at Queen's University and DuPont Canada (Kingston) Inc., the Queen's-DuPont Back Research Study was developed to determine risk factors that may predispose an individual to LBP. The study was conducted for a two year period with the goal to determine risk factors that may predispose an individual to LBP. This paper introduces the methodology adopted to achieve this goal.

2. Methodology

2.1 Participant Selection

In the summer of 1994 an 'Initial Back Pain Survey' was delivered to 585 employees, who lift over 7,000 kg per shift in 4-12 kg loads, in the spinning operations at DuPont. The goal of the initial survey was to determine those individuals who were willing to participate in the study as well as their history with LBP. The participation response was encouraging (77%); however only a quarter of this group indicated never having had back pain. Because only 20-25% of the sample was expected to develop LBP over the course of the two-year collection period, the sample was expanded to include individuals with minimum and mild prior experiences with LBP. Therefore, three types of subjects were included; those who: 1) had no history of LBP; 2) experienced LBP over the last year but had not sought medical treatment and had not altered activities at home or at work; and 3) experienced LBP two or more years ago but had not sought medical treatment, and may or may not have altered activities. The 150 volunteers were comprised of 77 individuals in group one, 43 in group two and 30 in group three.

2.2 Collection of Physical Measures

An initial battery of measures was collected for three separate areas relating to physical strength and endurance; lifting technique; and psycho-social status. The psycho-social measures were gathered through a questionnaire which focused on health, lifestyle and job satisfaction. Follow-up questionnaires measuring health, lifestyle and job satisfaction as well as back pain status were collected every six months for a period of two years. This paper focuses on the physical measures.

Scientific literature review and anatomical analysis led to the inclusion of the following six physical tests which have potential as predictors of predisposing factors to LBP: trunk velocity; spinal range of motion (ROM); quadriceps endurance; abdominal endurance; back muscle endurance; and hamstring flexibility.

To determine trunk velocity, spinal displacement was monitored with the FASTRAK (Polhemus, Inc.) electromagnetic motion analysis system. Motion sensors were placed on the vertebral spinous processes of T1, L1 and S1. Subjects stood erect, arms crossed over their chest and performed five full flexion and extension repetitions at maximum speed. Recent work by Marras and colleagues [6] provided evidence that the speed subjects are willing to move their trunk during a manual handling task is related to the degree and severity of LBP.

The FASTRAK was also employed to assess the spine ROM in full forward flexion, lateral bending and twisting. The subjects began in a comfortable standing posture for all three test. In the flexion test they were instructed to bend at the waist, reaching their arms as far back as possible, keeping them parallel to the floor. In the lateral flexion, subjects bent at the waist maximally to each side, keeping the upper body from flexing forward. The protocol was similar for twisting.

The quadriceps endurance test, implicated in an earlier study [7], required the employee to maintain a contraction of 50% of their maximal voluntary contraction until fatigue.

It has been documented [1] that discrepancies between the trunk flexor and extensor strength are associated with LBP. Abdominal endurance was assessed in accordance with the Canadian Standardized test [8], where the number of curl-ups are recorded when performed at a rate of 25 per minute.

Using a modified Biering-Sorensen test [1] with electromyography monitoring of erector spinae activity at the level of T10 and L3, the endurance of the musculature was assessed on both the right and left sides (figure 1).

With the subject lying supine, an angle elgon was used to measure the degree of hamstring flexibility during a straight leg raise test. Previous work has indicated that low hamstring flexibility demonstrated higher recurrence of LBP [1, 9].

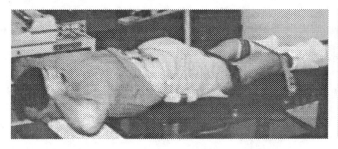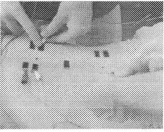

Figure 1: EMG collection during back endurance test.

3. Initial Analysis of Physical Measures

Due to the longitudinal nature of the project, the relationship between low back pain outcome and the physical, health and lifestyle and lifting measures has not been fully analyzed. The scores on hamstring flexibility, quadriceps endurance, abdominal endurance and back endurance were compared to determine if any statistical differences existed between the three groups of subjects. ANOVA was used to test the group differences and no significant differences were found in the four measures (Table 1).

Table 1: Mean Values (Standard Deviations) for Selected Physical Measures

Physical Measure	Overall Mean	Group 1 Mean	Group 2 Mean	Group 3 Mean
Right Hamstring Flexibility (degrees)	77.86 (12.71)	79.09 (11.91)	74.93 (14.13)	78.80 (13.55)
Quadriceps Endurance (seconds)	64.78 (12.02)	62.58 (26.36)	65.51 (32.97)	69.37 (24.58)
Abdominal Endurance (# or curl ups)	41.21 (22.77)	45.10 (22.41)	37.91 (22.68)	35.97 (22.77)
Back Endurance (seconds)	120.79 (57.21)	115.89 (53.05)	119.30 (64.27)	135.43 (56.28)

A further analysis was conducted to determine the differences in the three groups with respect to their muscular response. From the EMG data collected during the back endurance test the median frequency (MF) slopes, intercepts, percentage drops and endurance times were computed. Among the initial selection groups there were no significant differences between the aforementioned parameters. Through a repeated measures analysis there was a muscle main effect difference and a side main effect difference identified in the MF intercepts. This result indicates the importance of collecting EMG data on both sides of the spine as well as in both the thoracic and lumbar regions since their MF starting values were significantly different. There was also a significant ($p < 0.05$) gender difference in the percentage drops in the MF curves in three of the four muscle regions. The P-values of the left thoracic and the right and left lumbar regions were 0.014, 0.0004 and 0.004, respectively. The P-value for the right thoracic was 0.068. All muscles combined showed a P-value of 0.0013. Male subjects fatigued more quickly than the female subjects.

4. Summary

Results of selected physical measures including the EMG results have been evaluated to date to determine the differences among the three subject groups. It was determined that there were no significant differences between the groups on any of the physical measures at the onset of the study and therefore they can be collapsed for future analysis of the determinants of low back pain in this study.

Acknowledgements

This project was funded jointly by the Natural Science and Engineering Research Council - Collaborative Research Development Grant (#661-001/95), the University Research Incentive Fund (QU27-005) and DuPont Canada (Kingston) Inc.

References

1. Biering-Sorensen F. (1984). Physical measurements as risk indicators for low-back trouble over a one year period. **Spine, 9(2):**106-119.
2. Bigos S.J., Battié M.C., Spengler D.M., Fischer L.D., Fordyce W.E., Hansson T.H., Nachemson A.L. and Zeh J. (1992). A longitudinal, prospective study of industrial back injury reporting. **Clinical Orthopaedics and Related Research, 279:**21-34.
3. Cady L.D., Bischoff D.P., O'Connell E.R., Thomas P.C. and Allan J.H. (1979). Strength and fitness and subsequent back injuries in firefighters. **Journal of Occupational Medicine, 21(4):**269-272.
4. Chaffin D.B. and Park K.S. (1973). A longitudinal study of low-back pain as associated with occupational weight factors. **American Industrial Hygiene Association Journal, 34:**513-524.
5. Troup J.D.G., Foreman T.K., Baxter C.E., And Brown D. (1987). The perception of back pain and the role of psychophysical tests of lifting capacity. **Spine, 12:**645-657.
6. Marras W.S., Lavender S.A., Leurgans S.E., Rajulu S.L., Allread W.G., Fathallah F.A. and Ferguson S.A. (1993). The role of dynamic three-dimensional trunk motion in occupationally-related low back pain disorders. **Spine, 18(5):**617-628.
7. Trafimow J.L., Schipplein O.D. and Novak G.B.J. (1993). The effects of quadriceps fatigue on the technique of lifitng. **Spine, 18(3):**364-367.
8. Canadian Standardized Test of Fitness. (1986). Operations Manual (3rd ed.).
9. Battié M.C., Bigos S.J., Fischer L.D. , Spengler D.M., Hansson T.H., Nachemson A.L. and Wortley M.D. (1990). The role of spinal flexion in back pain complaints in industry: A prospective study. **Spine, 15:**768-773.
10. Schipplien O.D., Trafimow J.H., Andersson G.B.J. and Andriacchi T.P. (1990). Relationship between moments at the L5/S1 level, hip and knee joint when lifting. **Journal of Biomechanics, 23(9):**907-912.
11. Anderson C.K. and Chaffin D.B. (1986). A biomechanical evaluation of five lifting techniques. **Applied Ergonomics, 17(1):**2-8.
12. Frievalds A., Chaffin D.B., Garg A. and Lee K.S. (1984). A dynamic biomechanical evaluation of lifting maximal loads. **Journal of Biomechanics, 17:**251-262.
13. Dolan P. and Adams M.A. (1993). The influence of hip mobility on the bending moment acting on the lumbar spine. **Clinical Biomechanics, 8(4):** 185-192.
14. Potvin J.R., McGill S.M. and Norman R.W. (1991). Trunk muscle and lumbar ligament contributions to dynamic lifts with varying degrees of trunk flexion. **Spine, 16(9):**1099-1107.
15. Bigos S.J., Battié M.C., Spengler D.M., Fisher L.D., Fordyce W.E., Hansson T., Nachemson A.L. and Wortley M.D. (1991). A prospective study of work perceptions and psychosocial factors affecting the report of back injury. **Spine, 16(1):** 1-6.

Advances in Occupational Ergonomics and Safety II
Edited by Biman Das and Waldemar Karwowski
IOS Press and Ohmsha, 1997

Further Evaluations of a Revised Posture Prediction Algorithm for Static Lifting

Jeffrey C. WOLDSTAD
Institute for Ergonomics Research, Department of Industrial Engineering, Texas Tech University, Lubbock, Texas, USA 79409-3061

This paper presents a revised sagittal plane posture prediction computer algorithm. The model is intended to help ergonomists using computer-aided design (CAD) tools to analyze work places and working tasks. The revised model contains modifications including: the use of two new objective functions based on the sum-of-cubed muscle intensity and the sum of the squared joint torque; an additional link to predict the head and neck posture; an addition of a line-of-sight constraint that requires the posture to allow the subject to see the hands; and improvements to the optimization procedures. Predicted postures generated by the revised model are compared to the actual postures assumed by subjects holding a load in the laboratory. Results indicate that the revised model with the sum of squared joint torque objective function is substantially improved.

1. Introduction

Ergonomists are increasingly using computer tools to analyze work tasks and work environments. Programs are currently available to predict quantities such as reaches and clearances, line of sight and visual obstructions, external joint torques, internal joint forces, strength capabilities, and motion paths. Unfortunately, most of these computer tools require as an input an accurate depiction of the posture of the worker. To obtain this information analysts must either measure the posture of workers for the task of interest, or estimate the posture. The work presented in this paper is an attempt to provide more accurate methods to estimate working postures. Accurate posture prediction models have the potential to substantially reduce the time and effort involved in using computer tools by eliminating the need to measure and record body posture.

1.1 Original Model Formulation

The posture prediction models presented in this paper are revisions to models previously proposed [1,2,3]. They represent the body of the worker in the sagittal plane using five links; the forearm, upper arm, torso, thigh, and calf. Inputs to the models are the horizontal and vertical distances between the hand and ankle, the link lengths, the link weights, the link center-of-mass locations, the whole body weight, and the magnitude and direction of the force applied to the hands. Forward and inverse kinematic procedures are used to identify feasible body postures based on constraints requiring all of the joints to stay within a defined range of motion and the static posture to be stable or balanced. The resulting kinematic representation has three degrees of freedom that are specified as the hip position and the forearm angle relative to horizontal.

Given a set of feasible postures, nonlinear optimization is used to select the posture minimizing a desired objective. The three objective functions considered in the original formulation were: minimizing the sum of the individual joint torques, minimizing the maximum ration of joint torque to joint strength, and minimizing the distance from the body center-of-mass and the middle of the foot (see Table 1 below). Comparisons to the postures assumed by subjects in the laboratory indicated that the first objective (minimum sum of joint torques) was the most effective in predicting posture [1].

Table 1. Objective functions used for the optimization procedure. For each function, τ_{joint} is the torque at each of the 6 joints and s_{joint} is the estimated strength moment of that joint based on Chaffin and Andersson [4].

Label	Objective Function
Total Torque	$\text{Min}\left\{\left|\tau_{ankle}\right| + \left|\tau_{knee}\right| + \left|\tau_{hip}\right| + \left|\tau_{shoulder}\right| + \left|\tau_{elbow}\right| + \left|\tau_{neck}\right|\right\}$
Muscle Intensity	$\text{Min}\left\{\text{Max}\left[\dfrac{\tau_{ankle}}{s_{ankle}}, \dfrac{\tau_{knee}}{s_{knee}}, \dfrac{\tau_{hip}}{s_{hip}}, \dfrac{\tau_{shoulder}}{s_{shoulder}}, \dfrac{\tau_{elbow}}{s_{elbow}}, \dfrac{\tau_{neck}}{s_{neck}}\right]\right\}$
Balance	$\text{Min}\left\{\left|\tau_{ball} - \tau_{heel}\right|\right\}$
Squared Torque	$\text{Min}\left\{\tau_{ankle}^2 + \tau_{knee}^2 + \tau_{hip}^2 + \tau_{shoulder}^2 + \tau_{elbow}^2 + \tau_{neck}^2\right\}$
Cubed Intensity	$\text{Min}\left\{\left(\dfrac{\tau_{ankle}}{s_{ankle}}\right)^3 + \left(\dfrac{\tau_{knee}}{s_{knee}}\right)^3 + \left(\dfrac{\tau_{hip}}{s_{hip}}\right)^3 + \left(\dfrac{\tau_{shoulder}}{s_{shoulder}}\right)^3 + \left(\dfrac{\tau_{elbow}}{s_{elbow}}\right)^3 + \left(\dfrac{\tau_{neck}}{s_{neck}}\right)^3\right\}$

1.2   Revised Model

The revised model includes three major changes. First, the Nelder and Mead nonlinear search procedure [5] has been substantially improved. The method considers many more initial simplex alternatives and has a much stricter convergence criterion. As a result the method does a better job of identifying the global minima of the objective, although this is still not assured in the procedure.

The second improvement to the model was the inclusion of a head and neck link and line-of-sight vision constraints. The original model would often predict postures that made it impossible for the subject to see the load in the hands, or that would be fatiguing to the neck. To address this problem, a head link was added to the torso. Head and neck anthropometry are estimated from Webb Associates [6] and Drillis and Contini (as cited in [4]). Neck posture is determined by the algorithm to minimize the angular deviation of the neck from the torso, while keeping the hands within a 34 degree visual cone in front of the eyes. The visual cone for the eyes extends 10 degrees above the vector perpendicular to the neck and 24 degrees below this vector (Weston, 1953 as cited in [7]). To assure a reasonable posture, the neck posture is compared to range-of-motion data for the neck provided in Webb Associates [6] and Faust, Chaffin, Snyder, and Baum [8]. The neck is also included in moment and strength calculations for the objective functions.

A third modification to the model was the use of two new objective functions in the nonlinear optimization procedure. The first objective function was based on the sum-of-cubed intensity criterion function used previously by Crowninshield and Brand [9] to predict muscle forces. This objective minimizes the sum of the cubed ratio of joint torque to joint strength. The second objective function minimized the sum of the squared torque at joint. It was constructed to put a higher loading on the weaker upper torso joints. Both new objective functions as well as the three original objective functions are shown in Table 1.

2.   Method

Postures predicted by the revised model using each of the five objective functions shown in Table 1 were compared to observed postures measured in the laboratory. Eight male and eight female college students participated in the experiment. Male subjects averaged 23 years (sd. = 2.8) of age, 181 cm (sd. = 6.7) in height and 77 Kg (sd. = 6.8) in weight. Female subjects averaged 22 years (sd. = 4.0) of age, 165 cm (sd. = 5.0) in height and 57 Kg (sd. = 6.8) in weight. Each subject performed eight isometric sagittal exertions at each of four designated hand positions. Hand positions were specified in terms of the horizontal and vertical distance from the ankle. The four hand positions used were: (0.3 m, 0.5 m), (0.3 m,1.2 m), (max, 0.5 m), (max, 1.2 m), where "max" represents each subjects maximum reach distance. During each trial, subjects held a 4 kg weight attached to a wooden dowel (total weight of 4.6 kg).

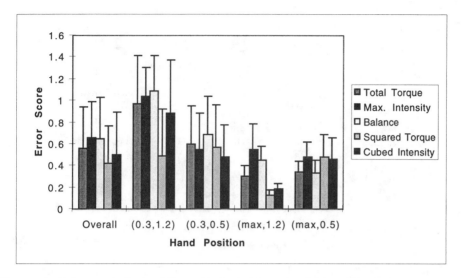

Figure 1. Prediction error for the five different objective functions using all data combined and separately for each hand position. Error bars indicate one standard deviation above the mean value.

The weight was held with two hands and both the dowel and the subjects heels were aligned with markers. Subjects were given no instruction on what posture to assume for a given condition, other than the specification of hand and foot position. Sagittal plane body postures were measured using a Watsmart three-dimensional motion analysis system at a sample rate of 20 Hz. The data set used in this comparison is the same data set used to evaluate the original model [1,2,3].

3.   Results

Prediction error for each model was defined as the Euclidean distance between the predicted and observed postures in the three-dimensional space defined by the unknown parameters of the model:

$$\varepsilon = \sqrt{\left(x_{hip(obs)} - x_{hip(pred)}\right)^2 + \left(y_{hip(obs)} - y_{hip(pred)}\right)^2 + \left(\phi_{(obs)} - \phi_{(pred)}\right)^2} \qquad (1),$$

where $(x_{hip(obs)}, y_{hip(obs)}, \phi_{(obs)})$ are the x and y hip position (in meters) and the forearm orientation (in radians) that define the observed posture, and $(x_{hip(pred)}, y_{hip(pred)}, \phi_{(pred)})$ are the same three variables that define the predicted posture. Predicted postures were estimated using each subjects individual anthropometry, the actual hand and foot positions measured during each experimental trial, and each of the five objective functions (2560 cases).

Prediction errors were analysed using a repeated measures analysis of variance (ANOVA). The ANOVA showed significant main effects for hand position ($F(3,45) = 22.03$, $p < 0.001$), and objective function ($F(4,60) = 15.81$, $p < 0.001$), and a significant Hand Position x Objective Function interaction ($F(12,180) = 7.67$, $p < 0.001$). The main effect of objective function and the Hand Position x Objective Function interaction are shown in Figure 1.

While the prediction error as defined above provides a good measure of the relative accuracy of the different models, it is difficult to determine using this measure how far the predicted postures are from the measured postures. Figure 2 shows the average deviation (in degrees) between the predicted posture and the observed posture for the five joints using the squared torque objective function. The figure indicates that even for the best objective function, the predicted posture is not as close as hoped to the observed. The model seems to have difficulty predicting the shoulder and knee joints, especially for the (0.3 m, 0.5 m) and the (max, 1.2 m) posture.

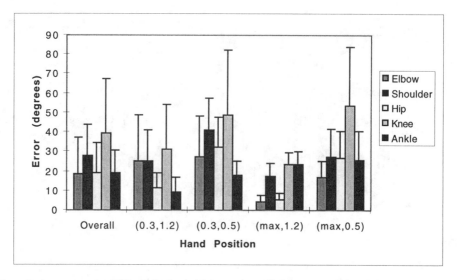

Figure 2. Average angular difference (in degrees) between the predicted posture and the observed posture using all data combined and separately for each hand position. Predicted postures were estimated using the squared torque objective function. Error bars indicate one standard deviation above the mean value .

4 . Discussion

The results indicate a substantial improvement in the accuracy of the revised model over the initial formulation. The model using the squared torque objective function was able to come reasonably close to the observed posture, especially for the two higher hand positions. One reason that the squared torque objective function was successful at the higher hand positions was that the four of the other objective functions tended to distribute the load moment throughout the body resulting in bent postures for the knee and hip joint. The squared torque objective weighted the joints lower in the linkage (with larger body weight above them) higher and loaded the upper body to a greater degree. All subjects assumed an upright posture that placed relatively high loads on the elbows and shoulders for this hand position.

Unfortunately, the model as currently formualted does not appear to be doing as well for lower hand positions. For the lower height lifts, many of the subjects seem to be reducing the moment at the knee by straightening the legs. This results in a larger moment at the torso and an overall larger value for the objective function. Current modeling efforts are directed at adding separate weighting functions to each joint.

5 . References

[1] M.J. Dysart, and J.C. Woldstad, Posture prediction for static sagittal-plane lifting, *Journal of Biomechanics*, 29 (1996), 1393-1397.
[2] M.J. Dysart, and J.C. Woldstad, Development and validation of a posture prediction algorithm for a static lifting task, *Proceeding of 12th Congress of the International Ergonomics Association*, Toronto, 1994.
[3] M.J. Dysart, *Development and Validation of a Posture Prediction Algorithm for a Static Lifting Task*. M.S. Thesis, Virginia Polytechnic Institute and State University, Blacksburg, VA.
[4] D.B. Chaffin, and G.B.J. Andersson, *Occupational Biomechanics*. Wiley, New York, 1991.
[5] M.S. Bazaraa *et al.*, *Nonlinear Programming*. Wiley, New York, 1993.
[6] Webb Associates (Eds.), *Anthropometric Source Book*, NASA Reference Publication 1024. National Aeronautics and Space Administration, Washington, D.C., 1978.
[7] S. Pheasant, *Bodyspace,* Taylor and Francis, London, 1986.
[8] D.R. Foust *et al.*, Cervical range of motion and dynamic response and strength of cervical muscles. *17th SAE Stapp Car Crash Conference Proceedings*, New York, 1973.
[9] R.D. Crowninshield and R.A. Brand, A physiologically based criterion of muscle forceprediction in locomotion, *Journal of Biomechanics*, 14 (1981), 793-801.

Advances in Occupational Ergonomics and Safety II
Edited by Biman Das and Waldemar Karwowski
IOS Press and Ohmsha, 1997

The Study of Work-Related Low-Back Disorders in Industry: Opportunities and Pitfalls

Patrick G. Dempsey
Liberty Mutual Research Center for Safety and Health
Hopkinton, Massachusetts, USA

Alex Burdorf
Erasmus University
Department of Public Health
Rotterdam, The Netherlands

The study of work-related low-back disorders in industry is less developed than the study of many other work-related injuries and illnesses. While this is unfortunate from the standpoint of our knowledge of the causes and prevention of low-back disorders, there are many opportunities for study for the same reason. An examination of both the pitfalls and opportunities associated with future studies is presented.

1. Introduction

Low-back disorders (LBDs) linked to work continue to represent one of the most significant sources of work-related injuries. In almost any industrial population, LBDs are among the top three causes of sickness absence and disability. Although an extensive amount of research has been dedicated to work-related causes of LBDs in the past few decades, the occurrence of back disorders among occupational populations seems to have remained largely unaffected. While laboratory studies can provide insight into the effect of various workplace and task variables on the acute responses of the cardiopulmonary and musculoskeletal systems -- and in some cases the psychological responses to various work designs -- such studies do not necessarily provide specific information concerning LBD risk associated with the variables. Epidemiological studies provide additional information that cannot be captured in the laboratory. The opportunities and needs for further studies in the workplace are tremendous. In the course of pursuing these studies, the investigators should be aware of both the opportunities and pitfalls that are present.

1.1 Opportunities

The magnitude of work-related LBDs and the lack of sufficient knowledge of the causes and prevention of these disorders present opportunities for future studies. Many additional studies are needed in a wide range of occupational settings. Unlike some occupationally-induced injuries and illnesses, LBDs are problematic for many diverse occupations such as health care, construction, manufacturing and service industries.

Some interesting opportunities arise when observational intervention studies are feasible. Due to changes in production processes, "natural experiments" take place in many companies. The impact of changes in workplace design, task parameters, and work organization on the occurrence of LBDs may be evaluated if historical information of sufficient quality on work processes, equipment, and activities is available. In-plant surveillance systems may provide sufficient and rapid information that enables an evaluation of the effectiveness of various deliberate and unintentional interventions at the workplace. While such studies lack some control over various variables and conditions, many of these natural experiments are taking place in workplaces around the globe. The low cost and large number of studies possible can alleviate some of the problems associated with less confident results associated with uncontrolled studies.

Job rotation is becoming an increasingly popular intervention to attempt to reduce the incidence of LBDs. Again, many natural experiments take place when job rotation is introduced into workplaces. Currently, there is insufficient epidemiological knowledge of the role of job rotation in reducing LBDs. However, there is some anecdotal, but unpublished, evidence to support these programs, as some companies have experienced a reduction in LBD incidence. These natural experiments could very well be formally studied to provide epidemiological knowledge of the effects of these interventions.

1.2 Pitfalls

The pitfalls associated with the study of work-related LBDs are rather extensive. Not only are LBDs an elusive class of disorders to study due to the multifactorial etiology and multitude of outcome measures, but exposure is very difficult to define and measure. The problems are exacerbated when exposure varies from workplace to workplace, from worker to worker, from day to day, and within the day. Seasonal production schedules and job rotation further compound the difficulties of measuring exposure. Exposure misclassification reduces power and certainty of the conclusions.

For work-related LBDs, the specificity of exposure at the workplace is low, i.e., a certain exposure, such as forceful lifting, does not result in a specific type of LBD. There are numerous classes of LBDs including prolapsed discs, strains, and sprains. Likewise, LBDs have a multifactorial etiology. Currently, little is known about whether certain exposures or risk factors differentially affect the various outcomes.

2. Scientific Challenges

2.1 Design Requirements vs. the Reality of the Workplace

It is not a particularly interesting observation that research goals may deviate from practical opportunities in the company or companies under study. These conflicts of interest can partly be dealt with by appropriate choices in designing the survey. Availability of the study population is a primary question to address; when workers are scattered over many facilities or do not perform their job in any well defined work area over the course of a day, the research efforts and costs to collect individual data are increased. Such challenges must be reflected in the design and execution of the study. For example, there is little available data on construction work, simply because construction workers are not a captive group. Ideal design choices are not always feasible when it is time to collect data at the workplace. In other industries, high turnover presents problems obtaining adequate exposure hours.

2.2 Exposure Assessment

During the past two decades, the attention to the specific role of exposure assessment in workplace surveys has significantly increased. Whereas in the past, job titles were regarded as a suitable characterization of strenuous tasks and activities within a group of workers, detailed workplace surveys have demonstrated that factors such as awkward postures, strenuous movements, and external loads vary considerably between and within workers in a similar job. Hence, exposure assessment should take into account all factors relevant to the exposure parameter of interest, given the purpose of the measurement program.

Basic considerations in establishing a measurement strategy for LBD risk factors pertain to the characterization of the risk factor, the measurement technique, the workers selected in the study, the working conditions, and the temporal variation in activities performed. Measurement techniques can be classified into three basic categories: 1) self-reports, (2) observations, and (3) direct instrumentation. In general, the level of detail and cost increases while moving from self-reports to direct instrumentation. Several reviews have been published that address aspect of reliability, accuracy, and precision of available measurement techniques in different assessment programs [1,4].

An important question in any measurement strategy is how to deal with the relevant determinants of exposure to risk factors. Sources of variation include factors such as shift patterns, variable production schedules, tasks performed, machinery and equipment used, materials handled, work techniques adopted, and anthropometric characteristics. Ideally, jobs selected for a study would be those with the fewest possible sources of variation, but this severely limits available observations and introduces certain biases. Analysis of variance techniques have been adopted to evaluate the contribution of these factors to the exposure patterns of individual workers and among workers in similar jobs.

2.3 Time/Accuracy Tradeoffs in Developing Data Collection Protocol

In order to study the relative contribution of risk factors to the occurrence of LBDs, comprehensive data at the *individual level* are needed. Appropriate allocation of resources to assessment of risk factors requires the measurement effort to be balanced. Estimates of risk factors at different levels of accuracy will strongly affect the results of the study. The required level of detail in exposure estimates should be set in advance rather than be the result of the application of particular measurement methods. When an exposure-oriented pilot survey is conducted prior to the large study, the performance of measurement instruments and the sources of variation in risk factors can be evaluated. Quantitative guidelines are available to evaluate several study designs according to the reliability of the measurement method, the optimum allocation of number of measurements to workers and groups, and the number of subjects needed in the study. When extended with cost considerations, one can make an educated decision whether it is better to measure 100 workers on two separate days or collect single measurements on 180 workers [1].

2.4 Defining Outcome Measures

In studies of the impact of work-related risk factors on the occurrence of LBDs, various outcome measures have been used. It is widely debated which definitions of health outcomes are preferred. Part of the confusion is that different health outcomes are needed in studies with different objectives and, thus, several terms have been coined such as back injury, back complaint, back claim, back pain and back disorder. It can be argued that the application of particular health endpoints in these studies is partly driven by the availability of data and the health system in place. Hence, results of these studies are difficult to compare since it is most likely that the interactions between the worker, the workplace requirements, and organizational aspects are different for different definitions of LBDs.

As an example, studies in companies based in the United States are inclined to rely on compensation claim data or OSHA 200 logs which may be biased towards acute and reasonably indisputable risk factors such as manual materials handling. In addition, defining a back disorder as work disability may focus on more severe cases of back disorders and, hence, also includes a strong psychosocial influence of subject behavior and the medical-social traits of the disability compensation system in place [3]. In contrast, in countries with a weaker link between sickness absence payments and cause of sickness, studies seem to focus more on the occurrence of back pain and associated symptoms. Hence, attention is less focused on the acute origin of disease and shifts to the contribution of long-term work-related risk factors such as exposure to whole-body vibration, awkward postures and strenuous movements. Characterization of back disorders by symptoms is likely to be less specific, more prone to complaint behavior, and influenced by determinants of reporting health status in general, such as age and education. It would be of interest to conduct international studies that encompass both types of health outcomes and establish their inter-relationships and the particular influence of the social security system on the occurrence of back disorders and underlying distribution of risk factors.

2.5 Statistical Analyses

Statistical methods present opportunities for dealing with the problems encountered during data collection and follow-up. Factors such as turnover during follow-up, confounding, and variable exposure during the study are factors that often must be dealt with. Dempsey and Westfall [2] discuss various modeling techniques to deal with some of these problems, such as unequal exposure times amongst subjects and non-linear exposure-response relationships. Ideally, well-designed experiments are fully crossed with respect to the predictor variables under study. This allows adequate estimation of interactions amongst variables. In field studies, such designs are impractical due to the difficulty of obtaining a sufficient number of workers to make such selection feasible. Again, the choice of an appropriate modelling technique can help to account for these problems. Thus, statistics can be one method for reducing the deleterious effects of some of the pitfalls mentioned.

3. Administrative and Logistic Challenges

3.1 Funding and Cooperation from Industry

A critical aspect of any field study is funding and cooperation from industry. Field studies are by their nature expensive. In the United States, funding for research is becoming increasingly competitive, and represents a significant barrier to such studies. Many industries are not interested in providing funding, perhaps due to the insufficient knowledge of the process required to garner an understanding of the causes and prevention of losses in the workplace.

Industry cooperation is also critical to the success of field study. Management must be willing to allow researchers into the facility to complete the measurements and employee interviews, which often involves workers' time. Further cooperation must be present during follow-up for determination of whether or not workers are still performing the same job. Access to injury and illness data is another necessity that industry may need to provide.

3.2 Obtaining Accurate Follow-up Data

Each longitudinal study requires a large effort to obtain information on changes in exposure to risk factors and the occurrence of LBDs over the course of the follow-up. In order to facilitate data collection at the workplace, researchers should investigate the possibilities of linking their data collection system to in-plant systems and business practices. In most plants, information systems available can provide useful insight into the use of equipment, allocation of personnel, production output, and personnel productivity. These routinely collected data may offer advantages when analyzing trends in risk factors and production processes.

There also may be inherent limitations in the injury and illness recording system. As mentioned earlier, outcome measures may include qualitative measures such as low-back pain or low-back disability, or specific diagnoses such as a prolapsed intervertebral disc. Some recording systems, such as the OSHA 200 log used in the United States, often do not provide specific diagnostic information, but are more likely to classify all LBDs into a fairly nebulous category that is not based upon a medical examination. Thus, increased cooperation by industry and even the compensation system may be aids to obtaining more accurate follow-up data. This will allow for investigations of the relationships between specific exposures and specific outcomes, rather than broader and less informative investigations.

4. Discussion and Conclusions

Throughout this paper, the various opportunities for and pitfalls to the studies of LBDs in industry have been discussed. The challenges presented by such studies are significant, and certainly outweigh the opportunities. However, as more of these studies are performed, more knowledge of the methods to deal with the pitfalls will be discovered. When reporting the results of field studies, investigators should consider reporting problems and how they were dealt with for the benefit of other researchers.

5. References

[1] A. Burdorf, Reducing random measurement error in assessing postural load on the back in epidemiologic surveys, *Scand J Work Environ Health* **21** (1995) 15-23.
[2] P.G. Dempsey and P.H. Westfall, Developing explicit risk models for predicting low-back disability: A statistical perspective, *International Journal of Industrial Ergonomics* (1997) in press.
[3] J.W. Frank, I.R. Pulcins, M.S. Kerr, et al., Occupational back pain - an unhelpful polemic, *Scand J Work Environ Health* **21** (1995) 3-14.
[4] A. Kilbom, Assessment of physical exposure in relation to work-related musculoskeletal disorders, *Scand J Work Environ Health* **20** (1994) 30-45.

Advances in Occupational Ergonomics and Safety II
Edited by Biman Das and Waldemar Karwowski
IOS Press and Ohmsha, 1997

Total Mechanical Energy Expenditure In Manual Lifting

Mohamed W. Fahmy[*], Shihab S. Asfour[*], and Ibrahim M. Jomoah[**]

[*]*Department of Industrial Engineering, University of Miami*
Coral Gables, FL 33124, USA
[**]*Department of Industrial Engineering, King Abdul Aziz University*
Jeddah, Saudi Arabia

Abstract

Most researchers focused on estimating the mechanical stresses at particular joints to determine the potential of injuries in manual lifting tasks. Mechanical energy expenditure (MEE) could be an effective tool combined with the mechanical stresses to compare different manual lifting tasks. A lifting experiment was conducted to study the effect of the load, posture, speed, and technique of lifting on the total MEE. Eight male college students participated in the experiment. Four independent variables were studied. These were: (1) load lifted (7 Kg, 14 Kg, and 21 Kg), (2) lifting technique (stoop and squat), (3) speed of lifting (fast and slow), (4) torso twisting angle (0 degree and 90 degrees). Analysis of variance was performed on the total MEE. Results showed that the load lifted, lifting technique, and the speed of lifting had a statistically significant effect on the total MEE($\alpha < 0.01$), while the torso twisting angle was not significant. The (torso twisting angle)*(speed of lifting) was the only significant interaction ($\alpha < 0.05$).

1. Introduction

Mechanical energy has been widely studied in gait analysis [1-4], running [5-8], and endurance sports [9,10] such as bicycling, rowing, and skating. Yet, it has rarely been employed in occupational biomechanics studies. Gagnon and Smyth [11] compared between lowering and lifting five different loads performed at five different heights. Gagnon and Smyth [12] studied the effect of movement on the total MEE and its distribution among the different joints for lifting two loads. Recently, Delisle and Gagnon [13] studied the effect of the involvement of multiple segments on energy transfers and economy using three different strategies in throwing a 7.5 kg load. De Looze et al. [14] evaluated the mechanical power during lifting a barbell using three different techniques.

In general, there are four methods for calculating MEE. In the first method, MEE is evaluated based on the joint power, in which the power at each individual joint is calculated as the product of joint moment and joint angular velocity, then, the absolute sum of the power is computed and finally multiplied by the time interval to evaluate the energy as the integration of the power over time [1,10-13]. In the second method, the mechanical energy is determined from the sum of the absolute changes of the mechanical energies of the body segments. The mechanical energy of each segment includes the translation, rotational, and potential energy [2,3]. Depending on the assumptions made, this method yields different results. These assumptions mainly affect transfer of energy between segments. In the third method, the total MEE is determined as the sum of external work and internal work [5]. The external work is defined as the absolute sum of the changes of the total energy of the center of mass of the body, while the internal work is defined as the absolute sum of the change in the kinetic energies of the segments in their movement relative to the center of mass of the body. In the early work by Fenn [5], he considered the external work and internal work as independent quantities and thus there is no energy transfer between adjacent segments. Aleshinsky [15] has shown that external and internal work are dependent and this method would lead to an overestimation of the energy. The fourth method was pioneered by Di Prampero [9,10]. This method is based on the flow of power from the body to the environment to overcome external forces such as friction force and gravity which then can be integrated to obtain the mechanical energy. This method has its implementation in endurance sports such as rowing, cycling, and skating.

2. Mechanical Energy Expenditure Computation

A three-dimensional biomechanical model was developed. The   human   body   was treated as a linkage system that consists of 10 segments and 13 joints. The segments are: lower legs, upper legs, lower back, upper back, upper arms, lower arms, and hands. The joints are: ankles, knees, hips ,L5/S1, shoulders, elbows, and wrists.   Details of the model are given elsewhere Jomoah [16]. At any time t during the motion, for segment i the static force$\{FS\}_i$ includes the weight of this segment. The inertial force vector $\{FI\}_{i,t}$ and inertial moment vector $\{MI\}_{i,t}$ for segment i, are calculated from

$$\{FI\}_{i,t} = - m_i * \{a\}_{i,t} \tag{1}$$

$$\{MI\}_{i,t} = - I_i * \{\alpha\}_{i,t} \tag{2}$$

where $\{a\}_{i,t}$ is the linear acceleration vector of center of the mass of segment i and m_i is the mass of segment i and $\{\alpha\}_{i,t}$ is the angular acceleration vector of segment i and I_i is the moment of inertia of segment i around its center of mass. The net moments and forces at each joint are calculated using inverse dynamic analysis as detailed in Jomoah [16]. For an inner joint j which connects two adjacent segments i and i+1 such as elbow, back, hip and knee, the power $P_{j,t}$ for this joint at any time t is calculated from

$$P_{j,t} = \{F\}^P_{i,t} \cdot \{V\}_{j,t} + \{M\}^P_{i,t} \cdot \{\omega\}_{i,t} + \{F\}^d_{i+1,t} \cdot \{V\}_{j,t} + \{M\}^d_{i+1,t} \cdot \{\omega\}_{i+1,t} \tag{3}$$

where $\{F\}^P_{i,t}$ and $\{M\}^P_{i,t}$ are the force and the moment vectors at the proximal end of segment i, and $\{F\}^d_{i+1,t}$ and $\{M\}^d_{i+1,t}$ are the force and the moment vectors at the distal end of segment i+1, and $\{\omega\}_{i,t}$ and $\{\omega\}_{i+1,t}$ are the angular velocity vectors at segment i, and i+1, respectively, and $\{V\}_{j,t}$ is the linear velocity vector of joint j. Applying Netown's third law at joint j results in

$$\{F\}^P_{i,t} = - \{F\}^d_{i+1,t} \tag{4}$$

$$\{M\}^P_{i,t} = - \{M\}^d_{i+1,t} \tag{5}$$

Substituting Equations (4) and (5) into Equation (3) gives

$$P_{j,t} = \{M\}^d_{i+1,t} \cdot [\{\omega\}_{i+1,t} - \{\omega\}_{i,t}] \tag{6}$$

In case of the most proximal or distal joint, which has one segment such as the wrist or the ankle in the current model. Equation (3) includes either the first two terms or the last two terms. It should be noted that in case of lifting as in the current study, the power at the ankle should have only the moment term since the linear velocity vector of the ankle is very close to zero, while the power at the wrist has only the force term, since no moment is generated at the wrist. Mechanical work at joint j is calculated from the fundamental equation

$$W_j = \int_{t_1}^{t_2} P_{j,t} * dt \tag{7}$$

where t_1 and t_2 are the times at the initial and the final motion. The mechanical work is numerically determined from

$$W_j = \sum_{t=1}^{M} P_{j,t} * \Delta t \qquad (8)$$

where M is the total number of frames during the activity and Δt is the time step during data collection, which is calculated from

$$\Delta t = \frac{t_2 - t_1}{M} \qquad (9)$$

The metabolic cost of negative work is significantly less than that for positive work as reported by Abbot et al. [17] and Davies and Barnes [18]. Willimas and Cavanagh [6] suggested the use of adjusted mechanical work (AMW) to account for this difference in efficiency.

$$AMW_j = W_j^+ + \frac{\left\| W_j^- \right\|}{d} \qquad (10)$$

where W_j^+ and W_j^- are the total positive and negative mechanical work at joint j during the activity, respectively, and (d) is the relative efficiency of negative to positive work. Several values have been suggested for (d) that range form one to infinity. For example, Zarrugh [3] assumed the metabolic cost of the negative energy is zero during walking. The AMW calculated in this case is considered as a lower limit for AMW. On the other hand, Eng and Winter [4] suggested equal efficiency between the negative and the positive work in calculating AMW which is considered as an upper limit for AMW. Gagnon and Smith [11,12], and Delisel and Gagnon [13]adopted 1.5 as an average value for (d) based on a study by Wells et al. [19]. This value was utilized in the current work. The total AMW (TAMW) for the body is determined by adding up AMW for each joint from

$$TAMW = \sum_{j=1}^{N} AMW_j \qquad (11)$$

where N is the total number of joints. The total adjusted mechanical work calculated from Equation (11) was considered the total mechanical energy expenditure.

3. Methods and Procedures

Eight male students participated in this study. Each subject was required to lift a box (38x38x25 cm) from floor level to table height (76 cm above the floor). Four independent variables were studied: These were: (1) load lifted (7 Kg, 14 Kg, and 21 Kg), (2) lifting technique (stoop and squat), (3) speed of lifting (fast and slow), (4) torso twisting angle (0 degrees and 90 degrees). The total MEE was chosen as the dependent variable. The Selspot system was used in this study to record the motion of the selected joints with respect to time. The Selspot system is an opto-electronic motion analysis system that utilizes active infrared light sources for determining actual positions of the joints. The sampling rate was 125 frames/second. Displacement data was collected for each joint. The data was smoothed using a polynomial of the 10th degree. The polynomial was then differentiated to obtain the velocity and acceleration.

4. Results and discussion

Results showed that load lifted, speed of lifting, and lifting technique had a statistically significant effect on the total MEE ($\alpha < 0.01$), while the torso twisting angle factor was not significant. The (torso twisting angle)*(speed of lifting) was the only significant interaction ($\alpha < 0.05$). The average ($\overline{X}$) and the standard deviation (SD) values of the total MEE for the overall experiment and for each independent variable are given in Table 1. From Table 1., it is clear that the total MEE increased as the load increased. The squat technique required more energy than the stoop one due to the utilization of a larger number of muscle groups during the motion. The total MEE for slow speed in lifting had an overall average that was higher than in case of fast speed. This is due to the fact that it requires longer time to perform the lift at slow speed. It is worth noting that fast speed lifting is always associated with higher stresses due to greater dynamic forces and moments. This suggests that there is an optimal speed in which a compromise between mechanical stresses and total MEE is achieved.

Table 1. The Average and the Standard Deviation Values for the Total MEE

	Overall	Load			Speed		Technique		Torso Angle	
		7 Kg	14 Kg	21 Kg	Slow	Fast	Squat	Stoop	0	90
$\bar{x}$ (J)	295	179	294	386	318	273	319	272	316	284
SD (J)	125	57	129	151	170	112	130	158	160	136

References

[1] A. Quanbury et al., Instantaneous Power & Power Flow in Body Segments During Walking, Journal of Human Movement Studies 1 (1975) 59-67.

[2] M. Pierrynowski et al., Transfers of Mechanical Energy Within the Total Body and Mechanical Efficiency During Treadmill Walking, Ergonomics 23 (1980) 147-156.

[3] M. Zarrugh, Power Requirements and Mechanical Efficiency of Treadmill Walking, J. Biomech. 14 (1980) 157-165.

[4] J. Eng. and D. Winter, Kinetic Analysis of the Lower Limbs During Walking: What Information Can Be Gained From a Three-Dimensional Model?, J. Biomech. 28 (1995) 753-758.

[5] W. Fenn, Work Against Gravity and Work During to Velocity Changes in Running, Am. J. Physiol. 93 (1930) 433-462.

[6] K. Williams and P. Cavanagh, A Model for the Calculation of Mechanical Power During Distance Running, J. Biomech. 16 (1983) 115-128.

[7] M. Kaneko, Mechanics and Energetics in Running with Special Reference To Efficiency, J. Biomech. 23 (1990) 57-63.

[8] D. Winter, Moments of Force and Mechanical Power in Jogging, J. Biomech. 16 (1983) 91-97.

[9] P. Di Prampero et al., Equation of Motion of a Cyclist. J. appl. Physiol. 47 (1976) 201-206.

[10] G. Schenau et al., Determination and Interpretation of Mechanical Power in Human Movement: Application to Ergometer Cycling, Eur. J. Appl. Physiol. 61 (1990) 11-19.

[11] M. Gagnon and G. Smyth, Muscular Mechanical Energy Expenditure as a Process for Detecting Potential Risks in Manual Materials Handling , J. Biomech. 24 (1991) 191-203.

[12] M. Gagnon and G. Smyth, Biomechanical Exploration on Dynamic Modes of Lifting, Ergonomics 35 (1992) 329-345.

[13] A. Delisle and M. Gagnon, Segmental Dynamic Analysis When Throwing Loads, International Journal of Industrial Ergonomics 16 (1995) 9-21.

[14] M. De Looze et al., Different Methods to Estimate Total Power and Its Components During Lifting, J. Biomech. 25 (1992) 1089-1095.

[15] S. Aleshinsky, An Energy 'Sources' and 'Fractions' Approach to the Mechanical Energy Expenditure Problem-II. Movement of the Multi-Link Chain Model. J. Biomech. 19 (1986) 295-300.

[16] I. Jomoah, A Comprehensive Study of Static and Dynamic Stresses for Symmetric And asymmetric Lifting Activities, Ph. D. Dissertation, University of Miami, Coral Gables, FL 33124.

[17] B. Abbot et al., The Physiological Cost of Negative Work. J. Physiol. 17 (1952) 380-390.

[18] C. Davies and C. Barnes, Negative (Eccentric) Work. II: Physiological Responses to Walking Uphill and Downhill on a Motor-Driven Treadmill, Ergonomics 15 (1972) 121-131.

[19] R. Wells et al., Internal and Physiological Responses During Concentric and Eccentric Cycle Ergometry, Eur. J. Appl. Physiol. 55 (1986) 295-301.

Advances in Occupational Ergonomics and Safety II
Edited by Biman Das and Waldemar Karwowski
IOS Press and Ohmsha, 1997

ASSESSMENT OF BALANCE IN MANUAL MATERIALS HANDLING

Alain DELISLE, Monique LORTIE and Marie AUTHIER
*Université du Québec à Montréal, Sciences Biologiques, C.P. 8888 Succ. Centre-Ville,
Montréal, Québec, H3C 3P8.*

Abstract. The management of balance during handling has rarely been studied, with most effort being focused on the floor - shoe interface. The goal of this study was to identify the factors involved in balance difficulties in manual handling by documenting the handlers' points of view. From two extensive series of previously conducted interviews, the comments related to balance were analyzed using thematic content analyses. Comments on balance involved 24 different themes which were grouped under 8 categories. The results emphasized that experts' view of balance is of a systemic nature, which explains the diversity of themes they discussed in relation to balance. Foot positioning and gait was the category most frequently discussed, revealing that more attention should be paid to its role in handling.

1. Introduction

Manual materials handling is the cause of many accidents, especially to the back [1]. Furthermore, an appreciable number of back injuries and manual materials handling accidents are related to a loss of balance [2,3]. Until recently, most research on balance problems has been focused on the floor - shoe interface. However, in manual materials handling, balance difficulties seem to correspond poorly to the normally retained triplet of slipping-tripping-falling, and the handling activity itself has rarely been studied for its inherent risks to balance. Lately, different studies conducted on handling have emphasized balance as an important parameter in handling. An accident analysis in a large transport industry has revealed that balance was an important risk factor [4]. Another study showed that when opting for a handling method, expert handlers considered balance as one of the three most important factors 33% of the time; however the level of agreement among handlers on the best method was more than 70% for only 2 out of 20 sequences shown [5]. Preliminary analysis also showed that simple handling strategies, such as the handgrip and tilt of the load handled, can affect the workers' stability [6]. Because incidents are frequent in manual materials handling [7], workers must adopt handling techniques that will ensure that they have proper stability in the event of any incident jeopardizing their balance. It therefore seems imperative to gain knowledge about how manual workers adopt their handling techniques to anticipate or to counteract balance disturbances. As a first step toward this goal, the present study aimed at identifying factors involved in balance difficulties while handling by assessing expert handlers' points of view.

2. Methods

2.1 Materials

Two extensive series of interviews were recently conducted with expert handlers and served as databases for the present study. All expert workers were from two large transportation firms; their duties consisted mainly in loading and unloading trailers. They were considered by both colleageues and management as the most competent handlers in the firms and had a remarkably low handling-accident incidence rate. The procedure used to select the handlers and its complete description are detailed in Authier and Lortie [5].

In the first series of interviews [5], 28 expert handlers were asked, at some point during the interview, to choose between two methods, for 20 videotaped sequences, the one was the best in terms of balance; they also had to briefly explain their choice. These explanations, generally expressed in one short sentence, were analyzed. The sequences filmed were performed by experienced workers in one of the two firms and the tasks were typical of what can be seen in these firms. The materials handled in each sequence varied from boxes to carpet bundles to washer/dryers. In the second series of interviews, five expert handlers were asked to comment on the handling modes of six novices videotaped while transferring 48 boxes of known weight in a laboratory setup (see Authier et al. [8], for a description of the subjects) and were also questioned about their own work activities [9]. The interviews were partly guided, registered and transcribed.   All comments related to balance, generally consisting of a few sentences, were identified.

2.2 *Analysis*

The explanations analyzed from the first series of interviews were first coded in order to facilitate their classification into distinctive themes; the frequency of appearence of these themes was determined.   Because some themes showed common aspects, they were reorganized into categories. Furthermore, from the answers to the questionnaire it was also possible to examine whether the experts, discussing a particular theme for a given sequence, chose the same method with respect to balance.

The comments on balance of the second series were always consisted of several sentences. The coding process was therefore more important than for the first series. Many themes could be discussed in the same comment. By reorganizing themes into categories, it was possible to determine associations between categories (i.e. the frequency of appearence of the same two or three categories in the comments was also determined).

3. Results

The comments or explanations related to balance involved 24 different themes (Table 1) which were grouped into 8 categories. Interestingly, the foot-gait category was the most frequently discussed in both series of interviews. Most of the themes were discussed in both series of interviews, with few exceptions: the level of weight supported as well as the footing were not mentioned in the second series, whereas the weight of the load was not discussed in the first series of interviews.

In the first series of interviews, the action on the load was the second most frequently discussed category, followed by the posture, and by handgrip-control and position categories. The theme most frequently discussed was gait, followed by the level of weight supported and trunk flexion/extension themes with similar frequencies. When different experts discussed the same theme as an explanation of their choice, their level of agreement ranged between 70% and 100% for the 20 sequences.

In experts' comments about novices' handling modes, the context and position categories were the second most frequently discussed, followed by the action on the load and handgrip-control categories, with similar frequencies (Table 1). The distance from the load was the single most frequently discussed theme. Some categories showed a strong association with others. For instance, when the context theme was discussed, the foot-gait category was also mentioned in the same comment for 85% of the cases. Similarly, when the position or action on the load categories were discussed, the foot-gait category was also mentioned for 74% of the cases in each category. Furthermore, when both the posture and position categories and the position and context categories were discussed in the same comment, the foot-gait category was also mentioned 83% of the time in each situation.

Table 1. Distribution of elements discussed by expert handlers in relation to balance.

Categories	Themes	1st series		2nd series	
Handgrip-control	Quality of handgrip	19		13	
	Control over the load	19		15	
	Load weight distribution	11	49	6	34
Action on the load	Level of weight supported	46			
	Dynamics of execution	22		9	
	Importance of effort	10		16	
	Others	20	98	11	36
Context	Weight of the load			8	
	When (at pickup or deposit)	8		24	
	Where (site of the load initially)	9		9	
	Others	6	23	6	47
Posture	Trunk flexion /extension	41		9	
	Trunk torsion	10		1	
	Trunk lateral bending	1			
	Knee flexion	5	57	15	25
Position	Orientation	14		17	
	Distance from the load	24	38	25	42
Foot - gait	Footing	16			
	Distance between the feet	4		12	
	Number of support	16		15	
	Gait	71		18	
	Weight distribution	7		20	
	Others	9	123	24	89
State of balance			17		9
Others			12		14
Total			417		296

4. Discussion

Although the tasks analyzed by the experts in both series of interviews were quite different and the procedures for the interviews also differed, it was interesting to observe that most of the themes discussed in the first series of interviews were also mentioned in the second series of interviews. Therefore, independently of the tasks analyzed, the experts' interpretation of balance was essentially based on the same themes, with only a few exceptions.

The fact that a theme was always discussed in relation to another and that strong associations were observed between categories, reveals that experts' view of balance is of a systemic nature. The load-worker interface (handgrip-control, action on the load categories), the worker himself (posture, position, foot-gait) as well as the context were components constantly found in experts' comments on balance, but also the relationship between these components. Associations between categories confirmed that the experts were concerned with the whole system (the worker in his environment and in relation to the load handled) and not just with isolated handling parameters. The systemic nature of balance can also explain the diversity of themes discussed by the experts, since each expert does not give the same priority to each theme. This diversity probably explains why expert handlers showed only poor agreement on the best method of handling in terms of balance, without regard to their explanations [5]. However, the results of the present study showed that when experts favored the same theme for justifying their choice, they also chose the same method most of the time.

The results revealed that expert handlers often considered foott positioning and gait (foot-gait theme) in their appreciation of balance in different handling activities. This is interesting because little importance is given to foot positioning and gait in training programs, and the foot position is almost always fixed in most biomechanical studies on manual materials handling. Recent studies have in fact shown the potential of foot mobility, during handling, to affect body joint loadings and asymmetry of posture as well as the handlers' stability [10,11,12]. Therefore, more interest should be paid to the role of foot mobility in manual materials handling. The results of the present study have further emphasized that the role of the feet is closely related to other themes. Combinations of handling parameters, such as foot mobility and the type of handgrip should also be studied for their impact on balance or joint loadings.

In conclusion, the information in the present study can be useful in training programs in handling by pointing out different ways of affecting balance. Interviews with expert handlers revealed that many strategies exist to prevent balance difficulties, and helped identify specific themes and relationships that should be used in orienting future research on balance during handling.

References

[1] J.D.G. Troup et al., A model for the investigation of back injuries and manual handling problems at work, Journal of Occupational Accidents 10 (1988) 107-119.

[2] D.P. Manning et al., The incidence of underfoot accidents during 1985 in a working population of 10,000 Meyerside people, Journal of Occupational Accidents 10 (1988) 121-130.

[3] M.H. Pope, Risk indicators in low back pain, Annals of Medicine 21 (1989) 387-392.

[4] M. Lortie et al., Analyse des accidents associés au travail de manutentionnaires sur les quais dans le secteur transport. Le Travail Humain 59 (1996) 187-205.

[5] M. Authier and M. Lortie, Assessment of factors considered to be important in handling tasks by expert handlers, International Journal of Industrial Ergonomics 11 (1993) 331-340.

[6] A. Delisle et al., Handgrip and box tilting strategies in handling: effect on stability and trunk and knee efforts, International Journal of Occupational Safety and Ergonomics 2 (1996) 109-118.

[7] M. Lortie and R. Pelletier, Incidents in manual handling activities, Safety Science 21 (1996) 223-237.

[8] M. Authier et al., Handling techniques: The influence of weight and height for experts and novices, International Journal of Occupational Safety and Ergonomics 1 (1995) 262-275.

[9] M. Authier, Analyse ergonomiques des stratégies de manutentionnaires experts et novices, Unpublished doctoral thesis, Université de Montréal, 1996.

[10] M. Gagnon et al., Pivoting with the load: an alternative for protecting the back in asymmetrical lifting, Spine 18 (1993) 1515-1524.

[11] A. Delisle et al., Feet mobility in asymmetrical handling : effect on stability and asymmetries of posture and efforts, submitted, 1996.

[12] A. Delisle et al., Load acceleration and footstep strategies in asymmetrical lifting and lowering. International Journal of Occupational Safety and Ergonomics (in press).

Advances in Occupational Ergonomics and Safety II
Edited by Biman Das and Waldemar Karwowski
IOS Press and Ohmsha, 1997

Analysis Of Kinematic Data: A Comparative Study Of Several Techniques

Mohamed W. Fahmy, Adham R. Ismail, and Shihab S. Asfour
*Department of Industrial Engineering, University of Miami,
Coral Gables, FL 33124, USA*

Abstract

Studying human movement has received considerable attention by various researchers. Motion analysis systems typically introduce noise to the displacement data recorded. This noise is amplified when the data is differentiated for the purpose of computing velocities and accelerations, which are in turn used for force and moment calculations.

Orthogonal polynomial functions, Cubic spline functions, and Digital filters are commonly used to process the displacement data. In this study, a comparison will be made among these techniques for data collected during a manual lifting activity using the 'Selspot' motion analysis system. The main objective of this paper is to investigate the effect of the above mentioned smoothing techniques on the same set of noisy data. A comparison of the techniques for processing displacement data, for a manual lifting task, is given.

1. Introduction

The accuracy of displacement data obtained from motion analysis systems, such as the "Selspot" system, depends greatly on the accuracy of tracking body markers attached to the subjects under study. Many problems are often encountered when using such systems to obtain velocities and accelerations necessary for force and moment calculations.

Noise of different sources is introduced to the displacement data recorded. This noise, which is inherent in even apparently smooth displacement curves, is amplified when data is differentiated, thus producing totally unacceptable under- and over-estimations of the first and second derivatives. The raw displacement data has to be initially smoothed in some manner.

Several investigations have been conducted for the purpose of identifying an optimal smoothing technique of the raw data. Winter et al. [1] analyzed the frequency spectrum of kinematic signals during human gait. They found that signal power, for a sampling frequency of 60 Hz, is concentrated in the first few harmonics and that 99.7% of the signal power was contained below the 8th harmonic for the trajectory data of 7 different body markers. They suggested the use of a digital low-pass filter with a cutoff frequency of 5 Hz. Pezzack et al. [2] used an instrumented aluminum arm to compare second order Butterworth digital filter, second order finite difference, and Chebychev least-square polynomial of degrees 6-16. The motion studied was the adduction/abduction of the arm. Results showed greater confidence in digital filtering combined with a first order finite difference scheme compared to other techniques. Zernicke et al. [3] also compared orthogonal polynomial techniques with spline techniques for a film of raw data for a kicking task. The degree of the polynomial was obtained based on a least square error formula. The vertical reaction forces recorded by the force platform were compared to the vertical reaction forces computed from the rigid body model. An over-smoothing by the orthogonal polynomial was observed. Cubic splines closely corresponded to the force platform data. However, they pointed out that the effects of certain cubic spline function's constraints need further investigation. McLaughlin et al. [4] used data obtained from cinematographical records to compare smoothing using cubic splines with a 5th degree polynomial for the angular acceleration of the lower leg during running. They also compared cubic splines to second order forward finite difference for computing angular velocity and acceleration of the forearm during elbow flexion. Results showed that the usage of cubic spline function was superior to the other two techniques. Yet, they pointed out the fact that investigators should exercise caution near the end points of the data when using cubic spline functions. Challis and Kerwin [5] used data generated from mathematical functions, to which noise was superimposed, to compare quintic spline function, truncated Fourier series, and second order Butterworth digital filter smoothing techniques. Their results showed that quintic spline functions provided better qualities and proved to be superior to the other investigated techniques. Burkholder and Lieber [6] compared polynomial regression, stepwise regression, and quintic spline smoothing techniques for a specific mathematical functions with increasing levels of white noise. Results showed that quintic spline and stepwise regression methods provided the best fit for the assumed noisy function. Woltring [7] and Wood and Jennings [8] suggested the use of quintic splines over cubic splines showing better boundary values for both velocity and acceleration.

The purpose of this paper is to compare acceleration curves obtained from after smoothing the raw displacement data using the three different techniques explained in the "Methods Section" of this paper.

2. Methods

Three different techniques were used to smooth the raw displacement data: (1) polynomial function, (2) cubic spline, and (3) second order Butterworth forward-backward low-pass filter. In the first technique, the data was approximated as a polynomial function of the nth degree, PF(n). The polynomial coefficients are typically obtained by minimizing the mean square error of the raw data. The polynomial function was modified from that typically used in literature by bringing the initial and final velocity and acceleration values close to zero. In the second technique, cubic spline function with smoothing factor P_k, CSF(P_k),was used. The spline technique breaks the curve to be fitted into sections each of which starts and ends with an inflection point with special fitting being done between adjacent sections. The cubic spline methods provide piecewise polynomials of some degree, n, joined together at points called knots in such a manner as to have (n-1) continuous derivatives. The spline approximation procedure employed in this paper is that of Reinsch [9,10], Anselone [11], and Spath [12]. Curves were developed for different values of P_k until a satisfactorily smooth curve appeared. The smoothing factor is defined as the ratio between jumps in the third derivatives at the knots, and the residuals resulting from differences between smoothed and raw displacement data at the same knots. In the third technique, a Butterworth digital filter with cutoff frequency f_c, BDF(f_c), was used. This is a low-pass filter which eliminates high frequency noise from the raw data. Velocity and acceleration were then obtained by differentiating raw data using a second order finite difference scheme. The details of this method is given in Winter [13].

Two experiments were conducted. In the first experiment, the coordinates of the center of a cubic wooden box, released from rest from a height of 1 meter, were recorded using the "Selspot" system at a sampling frequency of 125 frames/second. The displacement data was smoothed using PF(n=10), CSF(P_k=0.01) and BDF(f_c=12). These values were chosen because they resulted in acceleration values, in the vertical direction, that were close to the gravitational acceleration ($9.81 \, m/\sec^2$). A second experiment was conducted in which a subject was asked to manually lift a box, weighing 70 N, from floor to table height (76 cm). The wrist joint was monitored using the "Selspot" system.

3. Results and Conclusions

A comparison of vertical acceleration values computed using different smoothing techniques for the box drop experiment is given in Figure 1. The time interval depicted in this figure, 0.16 seconds, represents the time between the release and the impact of the box. It is clear from the figure that all three smoothing techniques reached the steady state value (-9.81 m/sec^2) after approximately 0.08 seconds. The polynomial function, PF(n=10), had the least fluctuations around the gravitational acceleration value while CSF(P$_k$) and BDF(f$_c$) resulted in higher fluctuations. Thus, it can be concluded that in the case of smooth and monotonic displacement data, polynomial functions result in acceleration values that are more accurate than those obtained by the other two techniques.

A comparison of vertical acceleration values computed using different smoothing techniques for wrist joint motion during manual lifting task is depicted in Figure 2. Since the BDF(f$_c$) is a second order low-pass filter, the first two frames were lost on the forward direction and the last two frames were lost on the backward direction. An additional four frames were lost due to the differentiation of the displacement data twice using a second order finite difference scheme. Thus, all acceleration curves were plotted starting at a time of 0.04 seconds rather than zero. The polynomial function seems to over-smooth the acceleration values and therefore failed to detect some of the expected acceleration peaks typical of a lifting task. The acceleration curves obtained using BDF(f$_c$=12) and CSF(P$_k$=0.01) were almost identical in both value and trend, and were of higher magnitude than those obtained by PF(n=10). It is felt that the true acceleration values should lie somewhere in between. Therefore, a comprehensive study is needed to be conducted to investigate which of these techniques would result in the most accurate acceleration values for manual lifting tasks. The use of accelerometers should aid in the selection of the most appropriate smoothing technique.

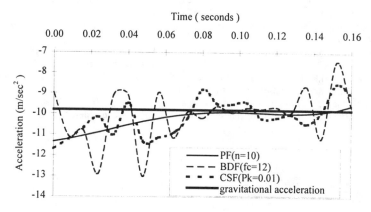

Figure 1. Comparison of vertical acceleration values computed using different smoothing techniques for the box drop experiment.

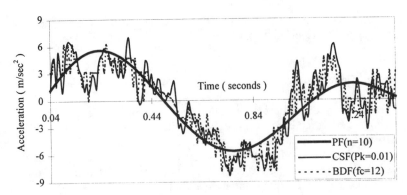

Figure2. Comparison of vertical acceleration values computed using different
smoothing techniques for wrist joint motion
during manual lifting task.

References

[1]   D.A.Winter et al., Measurement and reduction of noise in kinematics of locomotion, *J. Biomechanics* **7** (1974) 157-159.
[2]   J.C.Pezzack et al., An Assessment of derivative determining techniques used for motion analysis, *Technometrics* (1976) 377-382.
[3]   R.F.Zernicke et al., Fitting biomechanical data with cubic spline functions, *The Research Quarterly* **47** (1975) 9-19.
[4]   T.M.McLaughlin et al., Biomechanical analysis with cubic spline functions, *The Research Quarterly* **48** (1976) 569-582.
[5]   J.H.Challis and D.G.Kerwin, An evaluation of splines in biomechanical data analysis, In: G.H.Groot and H.P.Schenau (eds.), Biomechanics XI-B, Amsterdam, 1988, pp. 1057-1061.
[6]   T.J.Burkholder and R.L.Lieber, Stepwise regression is an alternative to splines for fitting noisy data, *J. Biomechanics* **29** (1996) 235-238.
[7]   H.J.Woltring, On optimal smoothing and derivative estimation from noisy displacement data in biomechanics, *Human Movement Science,* **4** (1985) 229-245.
[8]   G.A.Woods and L.S.Jennings, On the use of spline functions for data smoothing, *J. Biomechanics* **12** (1979) 477-479.
[9]   C.H.Reinsch, Smoothing by Spline functions, *Numerische Mathematik* **10** (1967), 177-183.
[10] C.H.Reinsch, Smoothing by spline functions II, *Numerische Mathematik* **16** (1970), 451-454.
[11] P.M.Anselone and P.J.Laurent, A general method for the construction of interpolating or smoothing spline-functions, *Numerische Mathematik* **12** (1968), 66-82.
[12] H.Spath, Spline algorithms for curves and surfaces., Utilitas Mathematica Inc., Winnipeg, 1974
[13] D. Winter, Biomechanics and motor control of human movement, John Wiley, New York, 1990.

Advances in Occupational Ergonomics and Safety II
Edited by Biman Das and Waldemar Karwowski
IOS Press and Ohmsha, 1997

Introducing Japanese Manufacturing Techniques Into A Parts Distribution Center - Ergonomic Problems And Opportunities

Robert O. Andres, Ph.D., CPE, and David D. Wood, MSIE, AEP
Ergonomic Engineering, Inc.
Pelham, MA 01002

Abstract

The goal of reducing waste, inventories, and non-value adding activities in the parts distribution operations of an automobile manufacturer is accomplished by just-in-time (JIT) principles. Whether the approach is termed Kanban or Genba Kanri, the corporation undergoes dramatic shifts in how it operates with a concommitant adjustment of corporate culture. The success of ergonomic programs often require shifts in corporate culture - so the opportunity to insinuate ergonomics into production modifications is obvious. However, there are trade-offs when it comes to material handling issues which this case study will elucidate.

1.0 Introduction

Inventory reduction can lead to warehouse shelf or slot stocking with less than unit loads (defined as a full pallet). Those employees stocking the shelves must manually handle materials that previously were slotted by forklift. Lifting considerations of frequency versus load level have to be controlled to minimize back stresses, but the bottom line is that lifting takes place where previously there was none. On the positive side, workers selecting orders from the slots do not have to reach to the back of partially emptied pallets to lift the part required, so there are advantages and disadvantages from inventory reduction. A quantitative example based on the NIOSH lifting equation will illustrate these trade-offs.

The greatest opportunity for ergonomic interventions comes from the development of standard operating procedures (SOPs) from worker teams on the floor. Specific instructions for load handling to minimize ergonomic stresses become part of the SOPs. The real opportunity here is to reinforce any ergonomic awareness training that workers have received - in an interactive team environment. The benefits are not simply biomechanical, but the psychosocial aspects of the warehouse are also improved. Examples of ergonomic principles integrated into the standard operating procedures at an auto parts distribution center will be presented.

2.0 Discussion

The first situation examined involved the kanban approach to inventory control which was contra-indicated by ergonomic analysis. Instead of stocking the bulk racks with full pallet loads, accomplished by fork lift, the bulk racks were filled by stockers who moved items from a stocking cart onto the racks. A previous analysis had been performed to evaluate the lifting performed by order pickers. Table 1 presents the distribution of lifts by average weight, vertical origin and destination for the order pickers. A histogram of item weights selected (Figure 1) reveals that 78% of items selected weigh less than 10 lbs. The computer program that slots products puts fast moving stock in the middle racks (Figure 2).

Table 1. Percentage of lifts and average weight lifted for each lifting task condition by origin and destination for bulk picking. Low was defined as an origin or destination below 30 inches while medium fell between 31-60 inches. An origin or destination was categorized as high if the bottom of the box was above 60 inches. A total of 64 lifts were observed.

| Origin | Destination | | | | | | Total |
| | Low | | Medium | | High | | |
	% lifts	Wt	% lifts	Wt	% lifts	Wt	% lifts
Low	15.6	3.2	10.9	5.2	3.1	17.5	29.6
Medium	10.9	5.9	39.1	6.0	6.3	15.4	56.3
High	3.1	0.7	9.3	2.05	1.6	21.3	14.0
Total	29.6		59.3		11		100

Figure 1. Number of lifts per weight for bulk picking (total lifts 64).

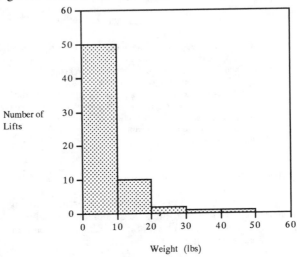

Weight (lbs)

Figure 2. Number of lifts per origin/destination category for bulk picking (total lifts 64).

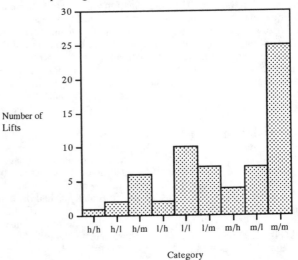

Category

The Lifting Advisor™ is an implementation of the 1991 revised NIOSH lifting equation developed by Ergonomic Engineering, Inc. The multitask option of the Lifting Advisor™ was used to model the entire cart loading operation including the 9 sub-task conditions. The horizontal distance was held constant at 20 inches to simulate a reach to the middle of a cart. The angle of asymmetry was fixed at 15 degrees and the hand coupling was deemed fair. A summary of the Lifting Advisor™ results is presented in Table 2. As seen in these results, bulk picking is not an extremely stressful job and administrative controls may be appropriate.

Table 2. Summary of the Lifting Advisor™ results for bulk picking (an average weight of 10 lbs was modeled). LI = lifting index, CRWL = combined recommended weight of the lift.

Ave LI		CRWL	
Origin	Destination	Origin	Destination
1.28	1.24	7.8	8.1

Under the kanban approach, the frequency of handling material would be higher for the stockers than for the pickers because they are more likely to move multiple items of the same part number into a bulk picking slot while their picking counterparts pick fewer multiples. Replicating the multi-task analysis for the stocking operation at higher frequencies yielded LIs greater than those in Table 2 but less than 2.0. The bottom line, ergonomically, is that more workers are exposed to lifting tasks than under the non-kanban approach of placing unit loads on the bulk racks. Cost/benefit analysis has to include the increased risk of low back incidents to be realistic.

The second Japanese management technique being implemented in this auto parts distribution center is called Genba Kanri. This involves systematic development of standard operating procedures (SOPs) for all jobs performed in the facility. Worker teams are trained to evaluate their jobs so that SOPs are streamlined for maximum efficiency. The main thrust is to break an operation into main steps, capture the key points of how the main steps are accomplished, and evaluate the reasons for the key points. This type of analysis reveals unnecessary steps and wasted materials. While the production value of such an approach is obvious, the opportunity to insert ergonomic procedures was ignored at first. Safety concerns were processed as exceptions instead of being interwoven in the key points. Given that the supervisors and employees had all received ergonomic awareness training, all it took was a suggestion from the consulting ergonomist that ergonomically sound techniques could be integrated into the SOPs for the original process to be improved. This integration has helped the company incorporate ergonomics into their corporate culture, and reinforces the ergonomics training down to the actual job task level.

3.0 Summary

Management techniques primarily focused on enhancing productivity can sometimes create more ergonomic challenges at a facility, as the example concerning kanban inventory control illustrated. However, some of the management techniques (such as Genba Kanri) offer excellent opportunities to interweave ergonomic considerations into daily operations at the most basic level.

Advances in Occupational Ergonomics and Safety II
Edited by Biman Das and Waldemar Karwowski
IOS Press and Ohmsha, 1997

Physiological Effects of Abdominal Belt Use During a Lifting Task

Deepak S. Madala, Robert E. Schlegel, and Jerry L. Purswell

School of Industrial Engineering, University of Oklahoma, Norman, Oklahoma 73019

Abdominal belts are widely used for manual material handling (MMH) tasks in industry despite the lack of any definitive research findings confirming their efficacy. The NIOSH back belt working group, in its review of research conducted on back belt usage, concluded that "the use of back belts may produce temporary strain on the cardiovascular system". The working group's conclusion is apparently based on the results of a single study which identified significant increases in heart rate during *aerobic exercise*, and in systolic blood pressure during both aerobic and isometric exercises, when the tasks were performed while wearing a *weight-lifting* belt. Many researchers have studied the effects of the weight training/lifting belt, which is usually a rigid belt as opposed to the *industrial abdominal* belt which is flexible and may or may not have a rigid support in the lumbar region. Few research studies have investigated the physiological effects of abdominal belts as measured by heart rate and blood pressure.

The current study investigated the physiological effects of a flexible abdominal belt in a MMH task. The task involved lifting and lowering a box from knuckle height to shoulder height for five 4-minute periods interspersed by rest periods determined by the subject's heart rate (HR). The weight lifted was 35% of the subject's maximum. The use of the belt did not affect systolic blood pressure. However, for subject's with lower absolute loads, an increase in heart rate was observed while wearing the belt, and, for subjects with higher loads, heart rate changes due to the task itself masked those caused by the belt. In conclusion, the theorized augmentative effect of the belt was not offset by an increased physiological cost at higher loads. These observations may lead one to hypothesize the existence of a critical weight (possibly within NIOSH limits) above which there is no physiological cost associated with wearing an abdominal belt.

1. INTRODUCTION

The NIOSH back belt working group, in its review of research conducted on back belt usage, concluded that "the use of back belts may produce temporary strain on the cardiovascular system" [1]. The working group's conclusion is apparently based on the results of a single study which identified significant increases in heart rate during aerobic activity, and in systolic blood pressure during both aerobic and isometric exercises, when the tasks were performed while wearing a *weight-lifting* belt. The *industrial abdominal* belt is usually flexible and with or without a rigid support in the lumbar region. Physiological effects of such abdominal belts as measured by heart rate and blood pressure have not been thoroughly investigated. In addition, investigation of the effects of abdominal belt use during dynamic tasks (e.g., the knuckle-to-shoulder lift) while using such physiological measures is inadequate.

Psychophysical studies [2] have shown that subjects tend to lift more weight when aided by an abdominal belt, but the physiological cost of wearing the belt is unknown. One of the first studies [3] that used physiological parameters to evaluate abdominal belts monitored blood pressure and heart rate while subjects performed various tasks with and without a 10 cm wide weight-lifting belt. Six healthy subjects performed three types of exercise. Mean systolic blood pressure was significantly higher with belt use for both aerobic and isometric activities, and a significant heart rate increase was obtained for the aerobic exercise. The authors concluded that "the use of a WLB (weight-lifting belt) can put an added strain on the cardiovascular system. Individuals that may have a compromised cardiovascular system are probably at greater risk when undertaking exercise with back support". Another study [4] investigated the impact of three types of semi-rigid abdominal belts on blood pressure, heart rate, body part discomfort rating and subjective ratings of belt support and comfort. Nine men and seven women lifted or lowered a 6.5 kg wooden box without handles at the rate of 4 lifts/lowers per minute. The authors concluded that there were no significant differences in systolic blood pressure, diastolic blood pressure or heart rate between the belt and no belt conditions. Also, there was no significant difference in body part discomfort.

2. METHODOLOGY

Eight male volunteers participated in the study. The task involved lifting and lowering a box weighing 35% of the subject's 1 RM (the maximum weight that a person can lift one time) from knuckle height to shoulder height. The task frequency was 6 lifts per minute performed for five 4-minute periods interspersed by rest periods determined by the subject's heart rate. All subjects performed the physical lifting task with the abdominal belt (WB) and without the belt (WOB). Abdominal belt tension was controlled individually for each subject. For each belt condition, the response variables heart rate (HR) and systolic blood pressure (SBP) were recorded across the five 4-minute work periods. Heart rate was recorded every 15 seconds and SBP was measured during rest periods. The weight lifted and the belt tension remained constant for each subject.

A Sunmark digital blood pressure monitor was used to measure systolic blood pressure. A Polar Vantage XL monitor was used to receive data transmitted by a Polar heart rate transmitter strapped to the subject's chest. The data collected by the monitor was downloaded to a PC using the Polar Interface and Polar Vantage XL software. The tension in the abdominal belt was measured (procedure described in [2]) using an Omega LCCB-300 load cell connected to an Ametek Series 6000 signal conditioner. The box used in the tasks measured 40.6 cm x 31.7 cm x 19.1 cm, with comfortable handles. To set the individual knuckle height and shoulder height for each subject, an adjustable height stool and table were used respectively. The abdominal belt used by all subjects was the OK 1 (Model 505).

3. RESULTS

The statistical model used in data analysis was a three-factor mixed effects ANOVA. The three independent variables included in the model were belt use, work period, and subject. The response variables were heart rate increase above resting HR (work pulse), and systolic blood pressure increase above resting SBP. Table 1 summarizes the results of the ANOVA conducted using the Statistical Analysis System (SAS).

TABLE 1 ANOVA Summary for All Response Variables.

Source	d. f.	Heart Rate Increase		Systolic Blood Pressure Increase	
		F value	Pr > F	F value	Pr > F
Belt (B)	1	3.62	0.0990	2.64	0.1485
Period (P)	4	19.92	0.0001	9.98	0.0001
Subject (S)	7	128.27	0.0001	20.73	0.0001
B * P	4	0.76	0.5619	0.51	0.7289
B * S	7	19.91	0.0001	1.58	0.1830
P * S	28	1.14	0.3686	0.68	0.8425

The belt condition produced a significantly greater HR increase than without the belt. The main effect of belt was not significant for systolic blood pressure. However, the subject by belt interaction was highly significant for heart rate. Averaged across all work periods, the increase in heart rate with the belt was higher than without the belt for Subjects 1, 2, 3, 4, 5, and 7. A Tukey multiple comparison procedure used to test the differences between the 16 subject-belt combinations (8 subjects x 2 belt conditions) demonstrated statistically reliable differences between belt conditions only for Subjects 1, 2, and 4. To further explain the subject differences, a regression equation was developed to predict the heart rate belt effect (work pulse with the belt minus work pulse without the belt) as a function of the actual weight lifted by the subject (Table 2).

TABLE 2 Data Used in the Regression Equation.

Subject	Mean Work Pulse WOB bpm	Mean Work Pulse WB bpm	Mean Work Pulse difference (WOB - WB) bpm	Weight Lifted (kg)
1	16.77	28.76	11.99	8.0
2	26.69	35.54	8.85	8.9
3	38.60	39.33	0.73	9.6
4	19.88	30.18	10.30	9.2
5	32.12	33.37	1.25	11.5
6	42.74	39.99	-2.75	14.2
7	38.43	42.35	3.92	12.6
8	37.07	33.85	-3.22	12.2

Regression equation:
Work Pulse Difference = 28.16 - 1.02*(weight lifted); $R^2 = 0.6738$

The R^2 for the work pulse difference regression equation implies that 67% of the work pulse differences between the WOB and WB conditions can be explained by the actual weight lifted (or alternatively by the subject's 1 RM capability). Subjects 1, 2, and 4, who had significant work pulse differences between the WOB and WB conditions, were also the subjects with the lowest 1 RM values. Subjects 5, 6, 7, and 8 with the highest overall heart rate increases (but with negligible work pulse differences between WOB and WB) were also the subjects with the highest 1 RM values.

To determine whether the current task was within acceptable NIOSH limits, the recommended weight limit (RWL) as defined by the revised NIOSH lifting equation was calculated. The obtained RWL was 15.33 kg which was above the weight lifted by any of the subjects. Hence, the lifting task studied was within the acceptable limit as suggested by NIOSH. However, the recommended weight obtained from the NIOSH equation is for a lifting task alone, whereas the current study involved both lifting and lowering. This may result in added strain and may reduce the RWL. Acceptability of a physical task may also be determined from the physiological stress caused by the task. Grandjean [5] suggested that the acceptable working heart rate limit for men should not exceed 35 beats per minute above the resting HR measured while the subject is seated. The average HR increase across the five 4-minute work-periods was 33.5 bpm. Therefore, the task considered in this study did not exceed Grandjean's recommended HR limit on the average. However, the maximum HR increase for some subjects did exceed this limit. HR increases for Subjects 2 (WB), 3, 6, 7 (both WOB and WB), and 8 (WOB) exceeded the 35 bpm limit. Subjects 6, 7, and 8 were the top three subjects in terms of the amount of weight lifted, and Subject 3 was ranked five.

4. CONCLUSIONS

In general, the abdominal belt had a minimal effect on the physiological measures obtained for the lifting task in this study. Systolic blood pressure did not differ significantly between the two belt conditions. The current study obtained a high correlation between work pulse differences between the WOB and WB conditions and the actual weight lifted. The higher the 1 RM value (and the corresponding weight lifted), the less likely it was to observe a significant effect of the belt on heart rate. This conclusion was based on the fact that work pulse differences between WOB and WB were significant for Subjects 1, 2, and 4 who also had the lowest 1 RM in the study. Subjects with the highest 1 RM were also the subjects with the smallest work pulse differences between WOB and WB. If the weight being lifted is low, then the belt itself may produce a significant work pulse increase. As the absolute weight being lifted increases, the work pulse increases accordingly. The additional work pulse increase due to the belt is relatively small in comparison. In other words, the belt effect is masked by the effect of the task itself. These observations may be extended cautiously to say that if the weight being lifted is very high (as with Subjects 6 and 8 with 1 RM ranks of 1 and 3), the belt may have an augmentative effect. This is based on the fact that lower mean heart rates, and lower mean SBP were observed when lifting was aided by the belt for Subjects 6 and 8. However, these differences were not statistically significant. These observations may lead one to hypothesize the existence of a critical weight (possibly within NIOSH limits) above which belts benefit lifting. Subjective data from questionnaires showed that the subjects would use abdominal belts, even when they were not totally convinced of the benefits of the belts. Most subjects entered the study with a strong pre-test impression about the positive benefits of the belt, and this impression was not altered by their participation. Subjects would rather use the belt as a precautionary measure than not use it. This situation is echoed in industry, where abdominal belts are being used even while the benefits remain uncertain.

REFERENCES

[1] NIOSH (National Institute for Occupational Safety and Health). Workplace Use of Back Belts: Review and Recommendations (DHHS NIOSH Publication No. 94-122), Cincinnati: Author, 1994.
[2] D.J. Bowen, J.L. Purswell, R.E. Schlegel, and J.P. Purswell. Preferred Tension and Psychophysical Lifting Limits With and Without Back Belts. In: A.C. Bittner and P.C. Champney, (Eds.), *Advances in Industrial Ergonomics and Safety VII*. Taylor & Francis, London, 1995, pp. 735-740.
[3] G.R. Hunter, J. McGuirk, N. Mitrano, P. Pearman, B. Thomas, and R. Arrington,. The Effects of a Weight Training Belt on Blood Pressure During Exercise, *Journal of Applied Sport Science Research* 3, (1989) 13-18.
[4] L.R. Contreras, M.J. Rys, and S.A. Konz. Back Support Belts in Lifting and Lowering Tasks. In: A.C. Bittner, and P.C. Champney, (Eds.), *Advances in Industrial Ergonomics and Safety VII*. Taylor & Francis, London, 1995, pp. 727-734.
[5] E. Grandjean. Fitting the Task to the Man: A Textbook of Occupational Ergonomics (4th ed). Taylor and Francis, London, 1988.

10. Human Strength and Measurement

Advances in Occupational Ergonomics and Safety II
Edited by Biman Das and Waldemar Karwowski
IOS Press and Ohmsha, 1997

Static and Dynamic Strengths of Males and Females in Seating and Standing Postures

Aghazadeh, F., Waly, S.M., and Nason, J.
Dept. of Industrial and Manufacturing Systems Engineering
Louisiana State University, Baton Rouge, LA 70808, USA

ABSTRACT

The purpose of this study was to investigate the differences in strengths of individuals on three strength tasks, a bicep lift, shoulder lift and shoulder pull. Nine male and twelve female subjects performed a series of exertions in static and dynamic conditions while either standing or seated. The effect of gender was as expected, female subjects recording, on average, 57.43% of that of male subjects in all conditions. The highest forces were generated for the shoulder lift strength task by male subjects in the static condition while standing (Mean = 130.55 kg, SD = 38.67 kg) and the lowest for the shoulder pull strength task for female subjects, also in the static condition while standing (Mean = 11.39 kg, SD = 3.99 kg). When expressed as a percentage of the force in the corresponding seated posture, female subjects recorded the largest change in force for the shoulder lift strength task in the static condition while standing (Mean = 167.78%). However, in the shoulder pull strength task, male subjects generated more relative force in the seated posture, static condition, the force in the standing posture being a small fraction of that while seated (Mean = 48.58%).

1. Introduction

Upper body strength is frequently required for performing manual tasks in both industrial and domestic environments. The strength data for grip, arm and shoulder have been collected by numerous researchers [1], [2], [3] and [4]. It was shown in these studies that strength varies with body posture. Furthermore, the angle at the elbow and at the shoulder play an important role in determining maximal exertions in various positions.

Two studies have investigated the effect of posture on rotational torque strength and push and pull strength. Results of a study by Rohmert [5] shows that as the elbow was extended, maximizing reach distance, rotational torque values decreased. The other study, conducted by Das and Wang [6], also varied the reach distance (elbow flexion) and height (shoulder flexion) but measured pull and push strength in each of the conditions. Contrary to data on rotational torque from the above study, the researchers found that maximum force production occurred at maximum reach distance for both pull and push tasks.

A similar finding was also shown in the work of Latif, Aghazadeh, Waikar and Lee [7] who set out to determine the optimal parachute rip-cord handle location for maximum force production. Of the many locations for the handle on the body the two that produced maximum force production were located on the thighs. Although not directly mentioned in the study, the two optimal locations required the arms to be fully extended.

Furthermore, t he study by Das and Wang [6] suggested that standing and seated posture result in different strength. It is the purpose of this paper to investigate the effect of standing and seated postures on three different strength tests for both static and dynamic strength.

2. Methods

Twenty-one students (9 males and 12 females) participated in the study. Average height was recorded as 1.78 m and 1.61 m for males and females, respectively. Each volunteer reported no musculoskeletal problems prior to commencing the test.

To measure static strength a handle and a load cell were attached to an adjustable metal arm so that it could be raised and lowered to match the height requirements of each subject. The maximum force was measured on a display unit. (Force Monitor ST-1, Dynadex Corp., MI). Dynamic strength was measured with the use of an MSR Super-2 500X (Misanron Health and Fitness Systems Inc., MO) and a hand held display unit (HSC-11, Ametek, PA). The seat height was 0.45 m and the distance from the seat to the top of the backrest was 0.45 m. There were no arm rests on the chair.

All subjects performed two exertions on each of three strength tasks while standing and while seated and completed these for both static and dynamic measurements. A two-handed grip was used in all trials. For static measurements the subject was instructed to begin exerting maximum force and hold for about three seconds. After a short rest they repeated the procedure. Following further recovery, the subject performed two more trials in the other condition (either standing or seated) not previously tested. The instruction to the subjects for dynamic strength measurements was to exert maximum force over the full range of motion for each posture.

In the static exertions the bicep lift was performed with the elbows flexed 90°, arms parallel to the trunk and palms facing upwards while in dynamic exertions the start position was with the elbows fully extended, hands in front of the thighs. Each subject then flexed the elbows until maximum flexion was reached. The shoulder lift required the arms to be fully extended in front of the body and an overhand grip taken on the handle. The dynamic exertions involved abduction of the shoulders and flexion of the elbows from this starting position until the handle reached the level of the neck. The final posture was the shoulder pull. With the shoulders flexed at 90°, an overhand grip was taken on the handle. The handle was brought to the chest by horizontally extending the shoulders and flexing the elbows in the dynamic exertions.

3. Results

In all conditions the female subjects scored lower in terms of absolute load (Table 1), on average recording loads 57.43% of the males. However, observation of the loads in the standing posture expressed as a percentage of the corresponding seated posture (Table 2) revealed there is no similar male dominance. Both genders showed a very slight decrease in the dynamic condition (99.16% and 98.11%, male and female, respectively). In the shoulder lift females recorded consistently higher percentage increases than the males from the seated to standing posture in both static (167.78%) and dynamic (117.72%) conditions while the opposite was true for the shoulder pull. In these trials males scored relatively lower in the standing posture than the females in both static (48.58%) and dynamic (75.57%) conditions.

In the static condition the mean load for males was 33.83 kg (standing posture) and 37.31 kg (seated posture) while the corresponding female scores were 21.22 kg and 18.38 kg, respectively. The scores for the two different postures in the dynamic condition were similar for males and also for females. The mean loads were 34.87 kg and 34.48 kg (male, standing and seated, respectively) and 24.38 kg and 25.37 kg (female, standing and seated, respectively). The loads for the standing condition, when expressed as a percentage of corresponding loads in the seated position (Table 2), ranged from 177.50% (female, static condition) to 40.29% (male, static condition) with mean values of 0.74% and 114.81% (male and female, static condition, respectively) and 99.16% and 98.11% (male and female, dynamic condition, respectively).

Table 1. Mean load and standard deviations (kg).

	Static Bicep Lift		Static Shoulder Lift		Static Shoulder Pull	
	Standing	Seated	Standing	Seated	Standing	Seated
Male	33.83	37.31	130.55	93.80	19.58	42.79
	12.16	9.18	38.67	39.90	5.32	5.86
Female	21.22	18.38	50.60	29.26	11.39	16.62
	12.93	5.35	26.14	16.06	3.99	3.91
	Dynamic Bicep Lift		Dynamic Shoulder Lift		Dynamic Shoulder Pull	
	Standing	Seated	Standing	Seated	Standing	Seated
Male	34.87	34.48	46.92	39.63	27.79	38.25
	12.35	15.57	12.56	6.66	21.29	18.05
Female	24.38	25.37	27.81	23.01	22.53	26.11
	14.46	17.41	9.43	4.54	17.81	18.39

Table 2. Maximum, minimum and mean standing posture loads expressed as a percentage of corresponding seated posture loads

	Static Bicep Lift			Static Shoulder Lift			Static Shoulder Pull		
	Max	Min	Mean	Max	Min	Mean	Max	Min	Mean
Male	109.41	40.29	90.74	211.78	72.66	138.65	60.00	30.70	48.58
Female	177.50	74.70	114.81	287.91	62.18	167.78	79.55	28.95	69.20
	Dynamic Bicep Lift			Dynamic Shoulder Lift			Dynamic Shoulder Pull		
	Max	Min	Mean	Max	Min	Mean	Max	Min	Mean
Male	113.04	77.78	99.16	140.48	89.63	110.24	100.87	50.61	75.57
Female	131.58	72.73	98.11	229.73	62.07	117.72	102.75	56.88	86.85

The mean loads for standing and seated postures in the static condition were 130.55 kg and 93.80 kg (males) and 50.60 kg and 29.26 kg (females), respectively. The dynamic condition scores followed similar trends, the mean loads for standing and seated postures being 46.92 kg and 39.63 kg (males) and 27.81 kg and 23.01 kg (females), respectively. The range of scores for the standing posture, expressed as a percentage of seated scores, was from 62.07% in the female dynamic condition to 287.91% in the female static condition. Mean values all indicate greater scores in the standing posture since they are above 100%, increases to 138.65% and 167.78% in the static condition (male and female, respectively) and to 110.24% and 117.72% in the dynamic condition (male and female, respectively).

Data for these trials are the reverse of those in the shoulder lift. Mean loads are greater in the seated posture (42.79 kg, males and 16.62 kg, females) than the standing posture (19.58 kg, males and 11.39 kg, females) (Figures 2 - 5). It follows that the mean percentage changes from seated to standing postures are all below 100%.

4. Discussion

As expected, the gender effect was visible in all conditions, postures and strength tasks when considering only absolute load scores. This result mirrors the findings of Latif et al [7] and Das and Wang [6] who recorded female strength as 61% and 56% that of males. It must be remembered, though, that the male subjects had larger body build and, therefore, advantage in absolute strength test. However, when designing for the 95th percentile of the population designers must be aware of the gender differences in absolute strength since it is a fact that in the general population women are of smaller build than men.

The bicep lift results showed no specific trend, the females recording an increase in load in the static condition from seated to standing posture while the males recorded decreases in the same condition. Neither males nor females showed any changes of note between the two postures in the dynamic condition. The variety of results from the bicep lift data indicates that there appears to be no advantageous posture for generating maximum lift force, either for males or females. However, the data show that for the shoulder lift females are able to record larger relative loads than the males in the standing posture while for the shoulder pull males can increase their force more than females in the seated posture. Again, these data can help in designing workstations where specifically women or men will be working, tasks involving lifting being easier in a standing posture (especially for women) while those involving pulling being easier in a seated posture (especially for men).

In the vertical shoulder lift the direction is directly upwards. In this position the body weight of the individual is bracing against the lift force. It follows that these forces will be larger than the pull forces since the body is more stable when pulling vertically upwards. Also, the standing posture will provide more resistance than the seated since, in the latter, the chair will take the majority of the body weight, the main force bracing the individual. In industrial settings this finding suggests that tasks involving heavy lifting should be done with the individual standing. Although, for prolonged tasks, standing is not recommended since fatigue can set in quickly, there will be less strain on the shoulder and arm muscles in this posture. It would be advantageous, therefore, to ensure that the weight of the object to be lifted be kept to a minimum so that a seated posture is possible.

6. References

[1] Hallbeck, M. S., Kamal, A. H., & Harmon, P. E. (1992). The effects of forearm posture, wrist posture, gender, and hand on three peak pinch force types. Proceedings of the Human Factors Society 36th Annual Meeting.

[2] Fredericks, T. K., Kattel, B., & Fernandez, J. E. (1995). Is grip strength maximum in the neutral posture? Advances in Industrial Ergonomics and Safety VII (eds. A. C. Bittner & P.C.Champney), Taylor & Francis.

[3] Hunsicker, P. A. (1955). Arm strength at selected degrees of elbow flexion. WADC Technical Report 54-548, United States Air Force, Project 7214.

[4] Kumar, S. (1991). Arm lift strength in work space. Applied Ergonomics, 22(5), 317-328.

[5] Rohmert, W. (1966). Maximalkräfter von Männern im Bewegungsraum der Arme and Beine. Westdeutscher Verlag, Cologne, Germany.

[6] Das, B. & Wang, Y. (1995). Determination of isometric push and pull strength profiles in work space reach envelopes. Advances in Industrial Ergonomics and Safety VII (eds., A. C. Bittner & P. C. Champney), Taylor & Francis.

[7] Latif, N. T., Aghazadeh, F., Waikar, A. M., & Lee, K. S. (1993). Determination of optimal location for parachute ripcord handle in a suspended position. Applied Ergonomics, 24(2), 119-124.

Advances in Occupational Ergonomics and Safety II
Edited by Biman Das and Waldemar Karwowski
IOS Press and Ohmsha, 1997

Grasp Control: Effect of Grasp Force

Grant A. Wilhelm and Ram R. Bishu

Department of Industrial and Management Systems Engineering
University of Nebraska-Lincoln
Lincoln, NE 68588-0518

Submaximal grasp force tests were performed by male and female subjects to
determine control over extended periods (2 minutes, 20 seconds). Subjects were
asked to grip a hand dynamometer and view grip force presented on a video display
terminal (VDT). Target grasp force levels were: maximum, 5, 10, 15, 20, and 25
lbs. Tests were conducted with both a bare hand and a gloved hand. Grasp control
was defined as variance around mean grasp force and was measured through standard
deviation. Data were broken into 5 sections: a 20-second stabilization period and
four 30-second intervals. Salient findings are: a) grasp control appears to decrease
with increasing target grasp force, b) males appear to have better control than
females, c) the ratio of grasp force to target grasp force decreases with increasing
target grasp force, and d) gloves do not affect grasp control. Implications of the
results for the practitioners are discussed.

1. Introduction

Almost all the human activities involve use of the hands and hence some form of grasp or
other prehension. It is also true that most of the grasping is at submaximal levels. Most of the
research attention on hand capabilities have focused on maximal strength capabilities while
very little attention has been given to capabilities at submaximal exertion levels. Typical daily
work includes hand exertions at submaximal levels for extended periods of time. Hand
capabilities for extended periods of time have been addressed through force endurance studies
[1, 2, 3]. Force endurance studies have looked at "how long a person can endure a level of
exertion". Stability of grasp and its control is equally important. The intent of this
investigation was to answer the question "How stable is grasp force?" The objective was to
determine the stability of grasp force at various levels of exertion and hand condition.

2. Method

2.1. Subjects

Ten male and ten female subjects, ranging in age from 18 to 45, voluntarily participated in this
study.

2.2. Experimental Conditions

Five levels of exertion (5, 10, 15, 20, and 25 lbs.) were combined with two levels of hand condition (bare hand, gloved hand) to yield 10 experimental conditions.

2.3. Apparatus

Grasp forces were measured using a Jamar A/D Hand Dynamometer (Model Number 5030PT) wired to an Analog Input Terminal Block, P/N 12871. Data were recorded using a direct sensor input card (UPC608®) and a 486 personal computer. UPC 'Easy Sense' software was used for data collection and real-time grasp force display/feedback. A Hewlett Packard 5-volt DC power supply was also used. A schematic of the apparatus is shown in Figure 1.

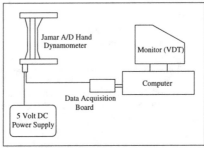

Figure 1. Experimental apparatus.

2.4. Procedure

Before each subject began, he/she was told to squeeze the Jamar with the right hand and watch the grip force displayed on the VDT in order to gain knowledge of how the system operated and responded. Each subject was instructed to keep his/her upper arm vertical and close to the body. The forearm was to be held parallel to the ground, forming a 90° bend at the elbow. The wrist was held in a neutral position.

The test order was randomized to insure there would not be an order effect present in the data.

Each test began by entering subject number and test number into the computer. The data acquisition began and the subject was instructed to begin grasp exertion at the instructor-specified target grasp force. Each test was 2 minutes 20 seconds in duration, after which time the subject ceased exertion.

3. Results

The data were first analyzed by computing the standard deviation and mean for each subject's data. The first 20 seconds of each trial was considered a "stabilization period" and therefore disregarded. The remainder of the trail data (2 minutes) were broken into four 30-second intervals. The standard deviation and mean of these intervals were computed. These values were then used in the statistical analysis.

3.1. Maximum

The average maximum grip force was found to be 107.9 lbs for males, 69.7 lbs for females. These results are consistent with published findings, which indicate a maximum grip force for university men of 108 lbs. and 73 lbs. for navy female personnel [4].

3.2. Statistical Analysis

Statistical Analysis System (SAS) was used to perform an analysis of variance (ANOVA) on the data. The ANOVA results for mean grasp force indicate that subject, gender, target grasp force, and time interval influence mean grasp force. However, hand condition (bare vs. gloved) and the interaction between hand condition and target grasp force were not statistically significant. See Table 1 for ANOVA results.

Table 1. ANOVA Results for Mean Grasp Force

Source	DF	F Value	Pr>F
Subject	19	22.91	0.0001
Gender	1	245.20	0.0001
Hand Condition	1	2.53	0.1118
Target Grasp Force	4	4217.30	0.0001
Time Interval	3	11.57	0.0001
Hand Condition X Target Grasp Force	4	1.96	0.0993

The ANOVA performed on standard deviation of grasp force indicate that subject, gender, and target grasp force significantly affect standard deviation of grasp force. Hand condition, time interval, and the interaction between hand condition and target grasp force were not significant. The ANOVA results are shown in Table 2.

Table 2. ANOVA Results for Standard Deviation of Grasp Force

Source	DF	F Value	Pr>F
Subject	19	36.34	0.0001
Gender	1	356.88	0.0001
Hand Condition	1	1.71	0.1910
Target Grasp Force	4	343.68	0.0001
Time Interval	3	0.92	0.4317
Hand Condition X Target Grasp Force	4	0.06	0.9936

Figure 2 shows a bar graph of target load versus measured force. It is surprising to note that mean measured force is lesser than target force for 25 lbs. This could be due to friction. Figure 3 shows the plot of standard deviation against target grasp force. It is seen that subjects exhibited better control at lower forces than at higher target grasp forces. Figure 4 shows the plot of standard deviation and gender. It is seen that males have greater control than females.

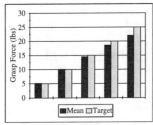

Figure 2. Comparison of mean grasp force to target grasp force.

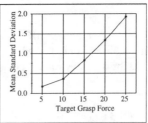

Figure 3. Mean standard deviation vs. target grasp force.

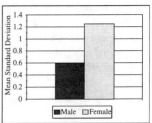

Figure 4. Comparison of mean standard deviation of grasp force for males and females.

4. Discussion

The results of this test indicate that males have greater control of grasp force than females, but only in the range of 15 to 25 lbs. Below this level, male and female grasp force control is similar. The reasons for this are most likely physiological and genetically based. However, there is a possibility that these results are also influenced by subject history. In other words, it is possible that a subject's occupation has a significant influence on grasp force control. A higher percentage of males perform occupational tasks which require and build grasp strength. This higher grasp strength could facilitate increased grasp force control, because the grasp forces tested would be a lower percentage of the maximum grasp force of that subject. Research into the occupational background of each subject would possibly clarify the influence of occupational tasks. In addition, further studies could be performed, using not two, but four types of subjects: males and females, and subjects with an occupational history of intense hand use and subjects without an occupational history of intense hand use.

5. References

[1] Rohmert, W. (1960). Ermittlung von Erholungspausen fur Statische Arbeit des Menschen. Int. Z. Angew. Physiol. Einsehl. Arbeitsphysiol., 18, 123-164.

[2] Monod, H., and Sherrer, J., (1965). The Work Capacity of a Synergic Muscular Group. Ergonomics, 8, 329-338.

[3] Bishu, R.R., Klute, G., and Byungjoon Kim (1994). Force endurance capabilities of extra vehicular activity gloves at different pressure levels. Proceedings of IEA 94, Volume 2: Occupational Health and Safety, Toronto, 80-82, August 1994.

[4] Ergobase, (1989). Biomechanics Corporation of America.

Advances in Occupational Ergonomics and Safety II
Edited by Biman Das and Waldemar Karwowski
IOS Press and Ohmsha, 1997

The Effects of Wrist Posture on the Force Exerted by Individual Fingers

Brandy A. FARRIS, Jeffrey E. FERNANDEZ, and Ramesh K. AGARWAL
College of Engineering, National Institute for Aviation Research
Wichita State University, Wichita, Kansas 67260 USA

Abstract. A study was conducted to determine the effect of wrist posture on individual finger strength. Ten females participated as subjects. The five postures studied were neutral, 1/3 maximum flexion, 1/3 maximum extension, 1/3 maximum ulnar deviation, and 1/3 maximum radial deviation. The results showed that fingers and postures had a statistically significant ($\alpha = 0.05$) effect on individual finger strength. Results also revealed that all fingers were significantly different from each other, with the highest contribution being the middle finger followed by the index, ring, and little fingers. In the design of work, the ergonomist needs to compensate for reduction in individual finger strength when working in non-neutral postures to possibly decrease the risk of CTD.

1.. Introduction

Occurrences of cumulative trauma disorders (CTD) have gradually increased over the last few years. The Bureau of Labor Statistics noted that in 1994 nearly 65 percent of illness cases were related to repetitive trauma [1]. Occupational risk factors leading to CTD are repetitive motion, forceful exertions with limited opportunity for recovery [2], poor and awkward postures [3], mechanical pressure, hand vibration [4], and exposure to cold. Continued exposure to these factors can cause pain, swelling, tingling sensations, and decreased strength and range of motion in the upper arm and wrist which may ultimately lead to injuries. One type of upper extremity CTD is carpal tunnel syndrome (CTS). A single case of CTS could cost (direct and indirect) up to $100,000 [5]. It was also noted that women are up to six times more likely to develop CTS than men [6].

Many hand tools used in industry require the application of high forces in awkward postures thus increasing the risk of a CTD. A survey of state and federal agencies found that hand tool use was associated with 9% of all work-related injuries [7]. The majority of workers were injured when they were struck by or struck against hand tools, or when they overexerted themselves [8]. In choosing an appropriate hand tool, the physical stressors such as posture, force, repetition, and contact stresses must be assessed [9]. In evaluating whether the posture and force are acceptable, it is necessary to determine the maximum forces an individual can apply in various wrist postures by each finger and compare it with the forces necessary to operate the hand tool.

Most previous studies to determine finger contribution were conducted in the neutral posture. Kinoshita *et al.* [10] noted that the contribution of static grip force to the total grip force for the index, middle, ring, and little fingers were 42.0%, 27.4%, 17.6%, and 12.9%, respectively. A study by Govindarajulu [11] examined the effect of grip span and posture on a multidigital gripping task using male subjects. The effect of wrist posture on a multidigital gripping task of males was also investigated in a study by Kattel *et al.* [12]. Results of both studies indicated that finger forces decreased as the wrist posture deviated from neutral. However, the contribution of individual finger forces had the same distribution irrespective of the wrist posture.

Most of the studies used male subjects and involved mainly the neutral wrist posture. Therefore, the objectives of this study were to determine the effects of wrist posture on individual finger strength, to determine the relationship between the individual finger strengths, and to determine the finger forces at different wrist postures using females.

2. Methods and Procedures

Subjects

Ten females volunteered to be subjects in this study. None of the subjects were experiencing any symptoms of a CTD. Range of motion, maximum voluntary grip strength, and Phalen's test were administered to determine the possible presence of a CTD. Prior to the data collection, written consent forms were completed by each subject and they were familiarized with the experimental procedures. The objective of the familiarization period was to allow the subjects to become familiar with the use of equipment and to increase cooperation and understanding between the subject and experimenter.

Apparatus

The equipment used in this study included a NK Hand Assessment System DIGITS-grip device interfaced with a personal computer. The NK System measures the individual force contribution of each finger. A Polar heart monitor, a Siber Hegner & Co., Inc. anthropometric kit, a Jamar hand grip dynamometer, a Jamar goniometer, a mechanical goniometer, and a pinch gauge were also used.

Procedure

Some anthropometric measurements of the subjects were taken. Maximum flexion and extension of the wrist in the transverse plane were recorded as well as maximum ulnar and radial deviation of the wrist in the sagittal plane. The five wrist postures investigated in this study were neutral, 1/3 maximum flexion, 1/3 maximum extension, 1/3 maximum ulnar deviation, and 1/3 maximum radial deviation. The grip span of the dynamometer was set at 51 mm, the first setting. The subjects were seated in an upright posture with the forearm at $90°$ to the upper arm using an adjustable height chair with adjustable height arm rests.

The five postures were randomized for each subject. Two to four exertions were performed (until measures were within 10 percent) for each posture using the Caldwell's protocol [13]. The subjects were asked to slowly attain their maximum force and maintain that force for 3 seconds. After each exertion the subject was relieved of the weight of the NK device and allowed to rest for two minutes. The grip force documented at each posture was the mean of two exertions of the dominant hand.

Experimental Design

This study uses a randomized block design with the subjects as blocks. The factors were wrist posture (five) and finger (four). The SAS statistical analysis software was used to statistically analyze the data on an IBM 3081 mainframe computer.

3. Results and Discussion

Table 1 displays the summary statistics of the subjects. When the height and weight of subjects in this study were compared with that of Ayoub *et al.* [14], no significant difference was found. This indicated that the subject population represented a typical US population. Table 2 presents the results of the index, middle, ring, little, and total finger forces in the five wrist postures.

Table 1. Descriptive statistics of the subjects

Measurement	Mean	Std Dev
Age (yrs)	24.60	6.95
Height (cm)	169.51	9.79
Weight (kg)	62.86	10.46
Hand length (cm)	17.5	1.02
Maximum Ulnar deviation (degrees)	31.00	4.43
Maximum Radial deviation (degrees)	19.05	3.76
Maximum Extension (degrees)	64.70	14.55
Maximum Flexion (degrees)	54.80	17.29
Jamar Maximum Grip Strength (kg)	19.0	5.37

Table 2. Summary of Finger Force in Different Postures (kg)

Position	Finger	Mean	Std Dev
Neutral	Index	5.69	1.81
	Middle	7.67	2.61
	Ring	6.29	2.20
	Little	2.61	1.08
	Total	22.29	7.00
1/3 Flexion	Index	5.16	2.46
	Middle	5.77	2.35
	Ring	3.72	1.53
	Little	1.79	0.71
	Total	16.40	5.49
1/3 Extension	Index	5.89	1.94
	Middle	6.88	2.97
	Ring	5.01	1.88
	Little	2.30	0.99
	Total	20.08	6.51

Position	Finger	Mean	Std Dev
1/3 Ulnar Deviation	Index	5.55	1.91
	Middle	6.19	2.19
	Ring	4.74	1.83
	Little	1.80	0.79
	Total	18.26	5.94
1/3 Radial Deviation	Index	5.31	1.52
	Middle	6.41	2.06
	Ring	4.28	1.70
	Little	1.54	0.97
	Total	17.71	4.52

An ANOVA was performed with subjects, fingers, and wrist postures. The results showed that subjects, fingers, and postures had a statistically significant ($\alpha = 0.05$) effect on individual finger strength. Results of the Duncan's Multiple Range Test revealed that all fingers were significantly different from each other, with the highest contribution being the middle followed by the index, ring, and little fingers, this was consistent with the results of both Govindarajulu's [11] and Kattel's [12] studies. The contribution of the force generated by the middle finger to the total force varied from 22% to 36%, for the ring finger from 23% to 28%, for the index finger from 26% to 31%, and for the little finger from 9% to 12%. The total force ratio of females to males in the neutral posture was 74%, the ratio with 1/3 wrist flexion was 78%, and the ratio with 1/3 ulnar deviation was 71% using results from this study and that of Kattel's study, respectively.

Duncan's Multiple Range results also showed that the three significant groupings of wrist postures were neutral and extension in group 1; extension, ulnar, and radial deviation in group 2; and ulnar deviation, radial deviation, and flexion in group 3. This would imply that the lowest risk group was the neutral posture and 1/3 maximum extension. The mean forces applied were maximum in the neutral posture followed by 1/3 maximum extension, 1/3 maximum ulnar deviation, 1/3 maximum radial deviation, and 1/3 maximum flexion, respectively. The total force generated in the neutral posture decreased by 27% at 1/3 maximum flexion, 21% at 1/3 maximum radial deviation, 18% at 1/3 maximum ulnar deviation, and 10% at 1/3 maximum extension. Consider an example of a hand tool that requires 9 kg of activation force. If the maximum force exerted in the neutral posture was 27 kg, the percent working force would be 9/27*100=33.33%. When working with the wrist in 1/3 maximum flexion the maximum force that can be applied would be 19.7 kg and the new percent working force would be 45.7%. Therefore, changing the posture from neutral to 1/3 maximum flexion caused a decrease in maximum force applied and a corresponding increase in percent working force. This increase relates to a possible increase in fatigue level (or onset of fatigue) and possible increase in the risk of CTD. Designers should be aware of the significant decreases in individual finger strength at non-neutral postures in the design of work in order to maintain a lower percent working force, decrease the level of fatigue, and possibly decrease the risk of CTD.

4. Conclusions

Based on the results of this study, it was concluded that the distribution pattern of individual finger forces for female subjects were middle, index, ring, and little, in descending order of force magnitude and that individual finger strength was wrist posture specific. In the design of work, the ergonomist needs to compensate for a reduction in individual finger strength when working in non-neutral postures in order to maintain a lower percent working force, decrease the level of fatigue, and possibly decrease the risk of CTD.

5. References

[1]   *Bureau of Labor Statistics Annual Occupational Injury/Illness Survey: Workplace Injuries and Illnesses in 1994* (http://tucker.mech.utah.edu/pub/info/bls.html).

[2]   R. Welch, The Causes of Tenosynovitis in Industry. *Industrial Medicine* **41** (1972) 16-19.

[3]   T. Hertzberg, Some Contributions of Applied Physical Anthropometry to Human Engineering. *Annals of the New York Academy of Science* **63** (1955) 616-629.

[4]   T. J. Armstrong, *et al.,* Hand Tools and Control of Cumulative Trauma Disorders of the Upper Limb. *International Occupational Ergonomics Symposium* (3rd), Yugoslavia: Taylor & Francis (1989) 43-50.

[5]   *CTD News,* Tallying the True Costs of On-the-Job CTDs (1993).

[6]   J.E. Fernandez, *et al.* A Study of Several Performance Measures of Workers with Carpal Tunnel Syndrome. In *Proceedings of the Human Factors Society 33rd Annual Meeting*, Human Factors Society: Denver, Colorado (1989) 265-271.

[7]   F. Agazadeh, and A. Mital, Injuries Due to Hand Tools, *Applied Ergonomics* **18** (1987) 273-278.

[8]   A. Mital, and A. Kilbom, Design, Selection and Use of Hand Tools to Alleviate Trauma of the Upper Extremities: Part II - the Scientific Bases (Knowledge Base) for the Guide. *International Journal of Industrial Ergonomics* **10** (1992) 7-21.

[9]   NIOSH, A Strategy for Industrial Power Hand Tool Ergonomic Research - Design, Selection, Installation, and Use in Automotive Manufacturing (1995) US Department of HHS.

[10]   H. Kinoshita, *et al.* Contributions and Co-Ordination of Individual Fingers in Multiple Finger Prehension, *Ergonomics* **38** (1995) 1212-1230.

[11]   S. Govindarajulu, Effect of Grip Span and Wrist Posture on a Multidigital Gripping Task. Unpublished MS Project (1996) Wichita State University, Wichita, Kansas.

[12]   B. Kattel, *et al.*, Evalutaion of the Force Exerted by Individual Fingers during a Multidigital Gripping Task, *Advances in Industrial Engineering Applications and Practice I*, Houston Texas (1996) 267- 272.

[13]   L. Caldwell, *et al.*, A Proposed Standard Procedure for Static Muscle Strength Testing. *American Industrial Hygiene Journal* **35** (1974) 206-210.

[14]   M. Ayoub, *et al.* Manual Material Handling in Unusual Postures Phase I, Institute for Ergonomics Research, Texas Tech University (1986) Lubbock, Texas.

Advances in Occupational Ergonomics and Safety II
Edited by Biman Das and Waldemar Karwowski
IOS Press and Ohmsha, 1997

The Effect of Grip Span on the Force Exerted by Individual Fingers

Kimberly M. DEVLIN, Jeffrey E. FERNANDEZ, and Ramesh K. AGARWAL
College of Engineering, National Institute for Aviation Research,
Wichita State University, Wichita, Kansas 67260-0035, USA

Abstract. The objective of this study was to determine the effects of different grip spans and wrist postures on forces exerted by individual fingers. Ten able-bodied females volunteered to be subjects for the study. The study consisted of measuring the maximum voluntary contraction of individual fingers at various combinations of two grip spans and two wrist postures. When working in the extended span and in the non-neutral posture, individual grip strength decreased significantly. Also, regardless of the grip span or wrist posture, the force distribution patterns of individual fingers, in descending order, were the middle, index and ring, and little fingers, respectively. It is concluded that modifications need to be made to tools consisting of different spans to help prevent an increase in percent working force, so as to reduce fatigue and possibly reduce the risk of cumulative trauma disorders.

1. Introduction

Gripping exertion is an important concept in redesign or design of hand tools. If the grip span of the hand tool is too large or too small for the individual, then the weaker muscles in the individual's hands are working at a disadvantage [1]. Force is one of the many risk factors that contribute to cumulative trauma disorders (CTD). Other occupational risk factors that contribute to CTD in the upper extremities are awkward postures, repetition, vibration, and low temperatures [1]. There are several integrated factors that could increase the risk of CTD: some factors are related to hand held tools (manual or powered), repetitive tasks and work pieces, design of the workstation, and the surrounding environment. Factors may be contributed by the task, the individual, or both [2]. Approximately 10% of all industrial injuries in the United States are contributed by the use of hand tools [3]. CTD have become a concern for all industries in today's society due to the rapid increase of assembly-line techniques, the increasing tempo of production, and the wide spread use of vibrating and air powered tools [4].

Costs of carpal tunnel syndrome (CTS), a specific type of CTD, vary widely across the United States. Approximately $3,500 was the estimated national average cost for a case involving CTS in 1985 [5]. Costs can range from $30,000 to $60,000 in more severe cases requiring surgery, compensation, and possible disability claims [6]. According to CTD News, the total cost of a CTS injury can total as much as $100,000, including direct and indirect costs [7].

The two main factors in the design of optimal hand tools on a hand grip task has been total grip strength and grip span. Several studies have focused on total grip strength and grip span. In a study by Eksioglu [8], it was concluded that maximum acceptable frequency, grip strength, and endurance time was affected by grip span, which could cause higher stress on the hand-arm system. Only a few studies have focused on the contribution of individual fingers to total grip strength. Govindarajulu [9] studied the effect of tool grip span and wrist posture of males. It was concluded that finger forces are considerably reduced when grip span was increased. Finger forces were also reduced when there was an increase from the neutral posture to 1/3 maximum flexion. Regardless of the grip span and wrist posture, the general pattern of finger and force distribution remained unchanged.

Therefore, the main goal of this study was to determine the effects of different grip spans and wrist postures on forces exerted by individual fingers of females.

2. Methods and Procedures

2.1 Subjects

Ten able-bodied females volunteered to be subjects for the study. The age range of the subjects was 19 to 41 years. A screening session was conducted to avoid potential subjects who have a history of CTD. Written consents were obtained from the subjects. The subjects were thoroughly familiarized with the experimental procedures prior to the commencement of data collection.

2.2 Equipment

The equipment used in this study included an anthropometric kit, a Jamar goniometer, an adjustable height chair with adjustable armrests, a Jamar hand dynamometer, a heart rate monitor, and the NK DIGITS-grip device and accessories. Accessories included an interfacing computer, loaded with the DIGITS-grip software program and other attachments. The NK DIGITS-grip device was developed by the NK Biotechnical Corporation. The device was used to determine individual finger strength and total hand grip strength.

2.3 Procedures

Standard anthropometric measures of the subjects' height, body weight, hand length, hand breadth at thumb, wrist thickness, wrist width, index finger, middle finger, ring finger, little finger, and thumb lengths, and width at first phalanges were collected [10]. Maximum flexion in the transverse plane was measured using a goniometer and recorded. Maximum grip strengths using the hand dynamometer were collected and recorded. All measurements were conducted for the subject's dominant hand only. The resting heart rate was obtained and recorded to ensure that the subjects were relaxed and in good physical condition.

The subjects were familiarized with the experimental conditions and procedures. The objectives of the familiarization period were (1) to allow the subjects to become familiar with the use of the equipment and (2) to increase cooperation and understanding between the subject and experimenter. The familiarization period also included the screening and introduction session.

The study consisted of measuring the maximum voluntary contraction of individual fingers at various combinations of two grip spans (physical positions 1 and 2 of the DIGITS-grip handle measuring 51 and 68.5 mm, respectively) and two wrist postures (neutral and 1/3rd maximum flexion). During the testing procedure, subjects were required to sit in a standard posture using armrests for support, while grip spans and wrist postures were set according to the randomly presented combination. Standard posture consists of the wrist at 0 degrees flexion, elbow at 90 degrees flexion, hip and knees at 90 degrees flexion, shoulder at 0 degrees abduction, and feet flat on the floor. Each subject was asked to slowly build up to her maximum voluntary contraction on the NK DIGITS-grip system and then sustain that force for three seconds according to the Caldwell Protocol [11]. The individual finger strength readings were obtained and noted from the NK DIGITS-grip software. A rest period of two minutes was given between each combination [11]. Two to four trials were administered to limit variations within 10% among readings. All data were collected within the same day. The subjects were not allowed to consume caffeine or dairy products 2 hours before the session and no intake of food 1 to 1.5 hours before the session.

2.4 Experimental Design

A randomized block design with subjects as blocks was used to analyze the collected data. The SAS statistical analysis package was used to analyze the data of the experiment on an IBM 3081 mainframe computer.

3. Results and Discussion

The descriptive statistics for the subjects are provided in Table 1. When the height and weight of this study were compared with that of Ayoub et al. [12] no statistical significant difference was found, this indicates that the sample population was a typical US population. Table 2 shows the summary of strength results of the four grip span-wrist posture combinations. As can be seen in the table, the general pattern of force distribution remained unchanged regardless of the span or wrist posture.

Table 1. Subjects descriptive statistics (n=10)

Measure	Mean (STD)	Measure	Mean (STD)
Age (yrs)	24.60 (6.95)	Middle finger length (cm)	7.65 (0.50)
Height (cm)	169.51 (9.79)	Ring finger length (cm)	6.89 (0.51)
Weight (kg)	62.82 (10.51)	Little finger length (cm)	5.72 (0.31)
Hand length (cm)	17.52 (1.02)	Thumb length (cm)	5.91 (0.54)
Wrist thickness (cm)	3.94 (0.65)	Width at first phalanges (cm)	6.37 (0.20)
Wrist width (cm)	5.05 (0.49)	Resting heart rate (bpm)	71.70 (11.22)
Hand breadth at thumb (cm)	7.75 (0.48)	Maximum flexion (deg)	54.80 (17.29)
Index finger length (cm)	7.02 (0.42)	Maximum grip strength (kg)	19.00 (5.38)

Table 2. Summary of strength in different grip span-wrist posture combinations (kg)

Finger	Neutral Posture			1/3 Maximum Flexion		
	51 mm span Mean (STD)	68.5 mm span Mean (STD)	Percent Decrement	51 mm span Mean (STD)	68.5 mm span Mean (STD)	Percent Decrement
Index	5.69 (1.81)	5.03 (2.01)	11.6%	5.17 (2.46)	5.17 (1.67)	0%
Middle	7.67 (2.61)	7.27 (2.57)	5.2%	5.78 (2.35)	5.34 (1.39)	7.6%
Ring	6.28 (2.20)	5.17 (1.24)	17.7%	3.71 (1.52)	3.50 (0.93)	5.7%
Little	2.60 (1.08)	2.2 (0.82)	15.4%	1.75 (0.72)	1.62 (0.82)	7.4%
Total	22.26 (6.94)	19.66 (5.39)	11.7%	16.39 (5.50)	15.63 (3.39)	4.6%

An ANOVA was performed with subjects, fingers, span, wrist postures, and the interaction between postures and fingers as factors. The results showed that subjects, fingers, span, wrist postures, and the interaction between postures and fingers had a statistical significant (α=0.5) effect on grip force. Results of the Duncan's Multiple Range Test showed that the contribution of forces by the fingers, in descending order, were middle, index and ring, and little fingers. These results are similar to the results of Govindarajulu (1996). When comparing total grip strengths of the four combinations of this study with that of Govindarajulu's, it was found that percentages of female/male ranged from 44% to 54%.

When working in extended span and non-neutral posture, individual grip strength decreased significantly. Table 2 shows that increasing the span from 51 mm to 68.5 mm caused a decrease of strength up to 17.7%. This would increase the percent working force, which in turn means an increase in fatigue (or onset of fatigue) and a possible increase in the risk of CTD. Percent working force is equal to the activation force needed divided by the maximum force multiplied by 100. If 10 kg was needed to activate a tool and the operator could contribute 40 kg of force in the 51 mm span position and 32.92 kg of force in the 68.5 mm span, then the percent working force for the 51 mm span and the 68.5 mm span would be 25% and 30.4%, respectively. Therefore, with an increase in span, there would be an increase in the percent working force causing an increase in the biomechanical stresses and possibly causing an increase in fatigue and risk of CTD. A greater decrease in grip force could be possible with a span larger than 68.5 mm. One of the goals of the designer should be to design hand tools taking into consideration span and making the appropriate adjustments needed to prevent an increase in percent working force, so as to reduce fatigue and the possible risk of CTD.

Previous studies, along with this study, consistently show that the middle finger contributes the greatest amount of force, regardless of span or posture. Therefore, future studies should be conducted to determine the advantages of the use of the middle finger in the design of hand tools, such as positioning the trigger where the middle finger could activate the tool.

Conclusions

When working in the extended span and in the non-neutral posture, individual grip strength decreased significantly. Also, regardless of the grip span or wrist posture, the force distribution patterns of individual fingers, in descending order, were the middle, index and ring, and little fingers, respectively. Therefore, while working with tools consisting of different spans, appropriate adjustments need to be made to prevent an increase in percent working force, so as to reduce fatigue and the possible risk of CTD.

References

[1]   V. Putz-Anderson, *Cumulative trauma disorders: A manual for musculoskeletal diseases of the upper limbs,* Taylor & Francis, London, 1988.
[2]   S. Taboun, Cumulative Trauma Disorders: An Ergonomic Intervention, In: B. Das (Ed.) *Advances in Industrial Ergonomics and Safety II,* Taylor & Francis, London, 1990.
[3]   A. Mital, Effect of body posture and common hand tools on peak torque exertion capabilities, *Applied Ergonomics* 17 (1986) 87-96.
[4]   V. Putz-Anderson, *Cumulative Trauma Disorders: A manual for musculoskeletal diseases of the upper limbs,* Taylor & Francis, London, 1988.
[5]   R. Hiltz, Fighting work-related injuries, *National Underwriter* 89 (1985) 15.
[6]   *Occupational Hazards,* Carpal tunnel syndrome: Getting a handle on hand trauma 42 (1987) 45.
[7]   Tallying the True Costs of On-the-Job CTDs, *CTD News,* 1993.
[8]   M. Eksioglu, *Determining the Optimum Grip Span and Modeling Work/Rest Cycles for Intermittent Gripping Tasks*, Unpublished PhD Dissertation, Wichita State University, Wichita, Kansas, 1996.
[9]   S. Govindarajulu, *Effect of Grip Span and Wrist Posture on a Multidigital Gripping Task*, Unpublished MS Project Report, Wichita State University, Wichita, Kansas, 1996.
[10] S. Pheasant, *Bodyspace - Anthropometry, Ergonomics and Design,* Taylor & Francis, London and Philadelphia, 1986.
[11] L. Caldwell *et al.*, A Proposed Standard Procedure for Static Muscle Strength Testing, *Amer. Ind. Hyg. J.* 35 (1974) 206-210.
[12] M. Ayoub *et al.*, *Manual Material Handling in Unusual Postures - Phase I,* Institute for Ergonomics Research, Texas Tech University, Lubbock, Texas, 1986.

Advances in Occupational Ergonomics and Safety II
Edited by Biman Das and Waldemar Karwowski
IOS Press and Ohmsha, 1997

The Effect of Handle Shape and Wrist Posture on Maximum Grip Strength

Tycho K. Fredericks

*Human Performance Institute, Department of Industrial and Manufacturing Engineering,
Western Michigan University, Kalamazoo, MI 49008-5061 U.S.A.*

The objective of this study was to determine the effect of handle shape and wrist posture on maximum grip strength. Fifteen Asian students from the University population volunteered to participate in the study. Three handle shapes and five wrist postures were tested in random order. Results indicated that both wrist posture and handle shape have a significant effect on grip strength. Decrements of up to 34% were observed in grip strength as the wrist deviated from the neutral posture. Decrements of up to 14% in grip strength due to the shape of the handle were observed. Implications of these results are discussed in the body of the paper.

1.0 Introduction

Musculoskeletal Disorders (MSD) pose major industrial problems in terms of increased medical costs, lost productivity, and degraded worker health and safety. According to the Bureau of Labor Statistics [1] nearly two-thirds of 1994's workplace illnesses were disorders associated with repeated trauma (332,000) such as carpal tunnel syndrome. Occupational risk factors leading to MSD are repetitive motion, forceful exertions with limited opportunity for recovery [2], poor and awkward postures [3], mechanical pressure, hand/arm vibration [4], and exposure to cold.

Since the force exerted on the hand or wrist while performing a task may be a contributing factor in the development of MSD, it has become imperative to design hand tools and tasks to minimize the risk of developing such illnesses/injuries. Several studies have independently reviewed the effects of handle shape [5] and deviated wrist posture on maximum grip strength [6], however, limited information is available on both. With this in mind, it was the intent of this study to determine the effects of handle shape and wrist posture on maximum grip strength for an Asian population.

2.0 Method and procedures

2.1 Subjects

Fifteen able-bodied male Asian students were selected from the student population at Western Michigan University. The mean age of the subjects was 30.07 years with a standard deviation of 4.59 and a range of 24 to 39 years. None of the subjects reported any MSD symptoms nor did they report any history of upper extremity disorders.

2.2 Equipment

Lafayette Instruments anthropometric measuring equipment was used to determine the anthropometric measurements of the dominant hand and stature of the subjects. An adjustable Jamar hydraulic hand dynamometer with three custom made handles was used to determine maximum grip strength. Handle shapes were fabricated out of wood and fit over the existing structure. The three handle shapes tested were rectangular (1:1.25 ratio of width to height), circular (with one side flat to be aligned with the existing handle), and triangular. The span of the hand dynamometer and length was held constant in all cases. A Jamar mechanical goniometer was used to measure the range of motion of the wrist (maximum flexion and extension in the transverse plane and maximum ulnar and radial deviation of the wrist in the sagittal plane).

2.3 Procedures

Standard anthropometric measurements of the subjects' stature, body weight, hand length, breadth at the metacarpals, and thickness at the metacarpals were collected. Maximum flexion, extension, ulnar deviation, and radial deviation of the wrist were measured using the goniometer.

A familiarization period was conducted prior to data collection. The intent of this period was to allow subjects to become familiar with the experimental conditions, equipment and procedures, as well as tone the muscles of the arm and hand. This period usually lasted 30 minutes and was conducted the day before data collection was to begin.

The study consisted of measuring the maximum grip strength at various combinations of wrist posture (neutral, 2/3 maximum flexion, 2/3 maximum extension, 2/3 ulnar deviation, and 2/3 radial deviation) with different handle shapes (rectangular, circular, and triangular). The neutral posture consisted of the wrist being at 0 degrees flexion, elbow at 90 degrees flexion, and the shoulder at 0 degrees abduction. All trials were presented to the subjects in random order. During the testing period, subjects were instructed to stand erect, while wrist postures and handle shapes were set according to the randomly selected combination. Readings were then collected in accordance with the Caldwell Regimen [7]. All grip strength measurements were taken with the dominate hand of the subject. Subjects were instructed not to consume any fluids or caffeine 4 hours prior to the experiment.

2.4 Experimental design

A randomized block design with subjects as blocks was used for analyzing the collected data. SAS statistical analysis package [8] was used to analyze the experiment.

3.0 Results and discussions

The descriptive statistics for the subjects are provided in Table 1. The mean height (1689.33 + 56.12 mm) and mean weight (30.07 + 4.59 kg) were compared to several different Asian populations to determine if the sample taken in this study could be considered representative of the Far East. It was determined that the average height and weight in this study were not significantly different than Hong Kong Chinese and Japanese populations respectively [9]. This indicates that the subjects used in this study could be representative of an Asian population.

Table 2 presents the summary data of the means (SD) for maximum grip strength for the five wrist postures and three handle shapes. Univariate analysis was performed on the data and the results indicated that the data were normally distributed. An ANOVA was performed to determine if wrist posture, handle shape, and the interaction of these two factors had a significant effect on grip strength. It was determined that both wrist posture and handle shape have a significant effect on grip strength. The interaction term was not significant and thus removed from the model. These results are presented in Table 3.

Table 1. Descriptive statistics of the subjects (n=15)

Measure	Mean (SD)
Age (years)	30.07 (4.59)
Weight (kg)	63.49 (6.95)
Stature (mm)	1689.33 (56.12)
Hand length (mm)	172.60 (10.92)
Breadth at the metacarpal (mm)	72.53 (5.34)
Thickness at metacarpal (mm)	23.73 (2.74)
Max. wrist flexion, transverse plane (degrees)	55.00 (8.59)
Max. wrist extension, transverse plane (degrees)	50.73 (8.32)
Max. wrist ulnar deviation, sagittal plane (degrees)	34.64 (7.58)
Max. wrist radial deviation, sagittal plane (degrees)	17.50 (5.89)

Table 2. Summary of grip strength (kg) for various combinations of handles and wrist postures, mean (SD)

	Handle Shape		
Wrist Posture	Rectangular	Circular	Triangular
Neutral	21.50	22.53	22.05
(Mid Pronated)	(2.37)	(2.30)	(2.48)
2/3 Maximum Flexion	15.03	15.67	16.30
(Transverse Plane)	(2.72)	(3.03)	(2.46)
2/3 Maximum Extension	17.03	18.33	17.85
(Transverse Plane)	(1.56)	(1.50)	(1.62)
2/3 Maximum Ulnar Dev.	14.29	16.54	16.19
(Sagittal Plane)	(2.15)	(3.42)	(3.25)
2/3 Maximum Radial Dev.	15.42	15.94	15.65
(Sagittal Plane)	(3.89)	(3.84)	(3.18)

Table 3. ANOVA for grip strength for handle, wrist posture, and the interaction term as factors

Source	df	Sum of squares	Mean square	F value	p > F
Subject	14	1242.16	88.73	2.81	0.0008
Handle	2	276.94	138.47	4.38	0.0139
Wrist Posture	4	6177.37	1544.34	48.85	0.0001
Handle * Wrist Posture	8	84.19	10.52	0.33	0.9524
Error	181	5722.37	31.62		
Corrected Total	209	13503.03			

Duncan's multiple range test was performed on wrist postures and handle shapes. Results for wrist posture indicated that grip strength values obtained in the neutral wrist posture were significantly higher than all wrist postures. It was also determined that 2/3 maximum extension was significantly different than all other wrist postures. Furthermore, it was determined that 2/3 radial deviation, 2/3 flexion, and 2/3 ulnar deviation of the wrist were not significantly different from each other. As for handle shape, Duncan's multiple range test determined that the grip strength data obtained from the circular and triangular shaped handles were not significantly different from each other. It was further determined that values obtained with the rectangular shape handle were significantly lower than the other two handles.

The results from the wrist posture segment of this study are similar to the findings of Kattel et al. [6]. In that study, it was determined that there was a 26% decrease in grip strength from the neutral wrist posture to 2/3 maximum flexion and a 25% decrease in grip strength from neutral wrist posture to 2/3 ulnar deviation. Although there is a significant difference in grip strength in the neutral posture between the two studies, the trends are similar. For the current study, a 29% decrease in grip strength was observed from the neutral wrist posture to 2/3 maximum flexion and a 29% decrease in grip strength was observed from the neutral posture to 2/3 ulnar deviation. A 34% decrement in grip strength was observed from the neutral wrist posture to 2/3 radial deviation with a rectangular handle.

The results of the handle shape segment of this study draw some similarities to a study done by Cochran and Riley [5]. In their orthogonal pull experiment, it was determined that rectangular handle shapes and triangular shapes were associated with significantly higher forces as compared with cylindrical which was associated with low forces. The current study also found that triangular handle shapes were also associated with higher force. As highlighted in their paper, this may be because a flat side of the triangular handle is placed against the hypothenar eminance of the palm and the fingers naturally wrap around and form to the opposite apex. This produces a good surface around which the fingers wrap and exert force. Contrary to Cochran and Riley [5] it was also determined that rectangular shapes were associated with lower grip strengths and cylindrical handles were associated with higher grip forces.

Reviewing decrements in grip strength due to handle shape, it was determined that there were reductions of up to 14% when the wrist was in 2/3 maximum ulnar deviation and a rectangular shaped handle was used instead of a cylindrical handle. This is especially interesting since ulnar deviation of the wrist is commonly seen in manufacturing when employees work with pistol grip tools on a horizontal worksurface.

4.0 Conclusions

The results of this experiment reveal that as the wrist posture deviated from the neutral to non-neutral postures (flexion, extension, ulnar, and radial deviation), grip strength decreased by up to 29%. Handle shape was also shown to have a significant effect on grip strength. Decrements of up to 14% could be seen due to handle shape. With this knowledge, tool handles and work design guidelines should be modified in order to decrease the risk of MSD in the upper extremities.

5.0 Acknowledgments

The author would like to thank Supanant Chandragholica, Jun-Seok Lee, and Hien M. Thach for their efforts in this endeavor.

6.0 References

[1] U.S. Department of Labor, Bureau of Labor Statistics, Occupational Injuries and Illnesses in the United States by Industry, Washington, D.C.: U.S. Government Printing Office, 1994.
[2] Welch, R., The causes of tenosynovitis in industry. *Industrial Medicine*, **41**, 1972, pp. 16-19.
[3] Hertzberg, T., Some contributions of applied physical anthropometry to human engineering. *Annals of the New York Academy of Science*, **63**, 1955, pp. 616-629.
[4] Armstrong, T.J., Ulin, S., and Ways, C., Hand tools and controls of cumulative trauma disorders of the upper limb. *International Occupational Ergonomics Symposium (3rd)*, Yugoslavia: Taylor and Francis, 1989, pp. 43-50.
[5] Cochran, D.J. and Riley, M.W., The Effect of Handle Shape and Size on Exerted Forces. *Human Factors*, **28(3)**, 1986, pp. 253-265.
[6] Kattel, B.P., Fredericks, T.K., Fernandez, J.E., and Lee, D.C., The effect of upper-extremity posture on maximum grip strength, *International Journal of Industrial Ergonomics*, **18**, 1996, pp. 423-429.
[7] Caldwell, L.S., Chaffin, D.B., Dules Du Bobos, F.N., Kroemer, K.H.E., Laubach, L.L., Snook, S.H., and Wasserman, D.E., A proposed standard procedure for static muscle strength, *American Industrial Hygiene Journal*, **35**, 1974, pp. 210-206.
[8] SAS, 1990, *SAS User's Guide*, Version 6.0 Edition, SAS Institute Inc., Cary, NC.
[9] Pheasant, Stephen, *Bodyspace: Anthropometry, Ergonomics and the Design of Work*, London: Taylor & Francis Ltd, 1996.

11. Workstation Design

Advances in Occupational Ergonomics and Safety II
Edited by Biman Das and Waldemar Karwowski
IOS Press and Ohmsha, 1997

The Determination of the Maximum Reach Envelope for Wheelchair Mobile Adults

John KOZEY and Biman DAS
Department of Industrial Engineering,
Technical University of Nova Scotia, Halifax, Nova Scotia

Both the concept and the determination of the maximum reach envelope (MRE) are important in the design of the industrial workstation. The published research regarding the MRE has been devoted to the design for the able-bodied worker. The present study determined the shape and dimensions of the 5th, 50th and 95th percentile MRE for a sample of wheelchair mobile adults.

1. Introduction

Conceptually the maximum reach envelope (MRE) defines a volume above the worksurface, immediately in front of the industrial operator. The MRE is achieved by movement of the upper extremity without any associated trunk motion. The application of the information about the MRE includes the design of consoles and control panels as well as, the placement of tools, other objects and the organization of material for the industrial workstation. The measurement of this volume in able-bodied individuals has been performed and presented in various forms in the past[1,2,3].

In light of the movement to design accessible workplaces the determination of both the normal reach area (NRA) and the MRE for individuals with physical disabilities is becoming increasing important. Kozey, Das and Kirby[4] have presented the NRA for individuals who require a wheelchair for mobility. While there has been some information published regarding maximum reaches to specific locations[5,6] little is known about the MRE for individuals who require a wheelchair. Therefore the purpose of this study was to determine the 5th, 50th and 95th percentile MRE for a sample of wheelchair mobile adults.

2. Methods

2.1. Subject Selection and Demographics: A representative sample of convenience consisting of 42 male and 20 female adults who required a wheelchair for mobility, were used in this study. Prior to the testing the subjects were briefed regarding the nature of the experiment and asked to sign a document of informed consent. The mean age of the male subjects was 39.2 (±12.1) years and the females were 37.3 (±12.7) years. The mean time of wheelchair use for the subjects was 11.2 (±8.7) and 12.7 (±13.2) years for the males and females, respectively. While there were differences among the subjects regarding the impairment which caused the use of the wheelchair, all of the subjects had full physical function of the upper extremities.

2.2. The Measurement System and Experimental Procedures: The subjects were positioned at an adjustable workstation specifically design for this study. The table surface was vertically adjustable and set to the proper work height for each subject. The subjects were positioned 2.5 cm from the front edge of the worksurface. The intersection of the body midline and the table edge was identified as the table reference point (TRP) and was used as the reference point for all subsequent reach measures. From this position the subjects moved a pointer which was part of a computerized potentiometric system for anthropometric measures (CPSAM). This system was design for 3-D anthropometric measures and has been described previously by Das et al.[7]

The data collection for each trial of the maximum reach motion occurred over a 60 second period at a sampling rate was 20 Hertz. During this period the subjects were asked to "paint" the inner surface of the MRE by continuously moving the pointer within the volume. At the end of the 60 second period the computer issued an auditory signal to signify the end of data collection. Three trials (3600 points) of the MRE were collected for each subject.

2.3. Determination of the Maximum Reach Envelope: The 5th, 50th and 95th percentile maximum reach envelope (MRE) were determined for the males and females separately. The MRE was determined by collecting the Cartesian coordinate values as the pointer of the CPSAM was displaced within the measurement volume. These data were converted into cylindrical coordinates (Θ_i, R_i, Z). In this coordinate system Θ_i represented the ith angular position in the horizontal plane between 10 and 130 degrees where, 0 degrees was along the table edge to the right of the body midline. The individual values were grouped into angular sectors of width 10 degrees and sorted by the Z Cartesian coordinate value. The data were then banded into horizontal bands (Z planes) above the worksurface. Each Z band was 100 mm in height centred about the 0, 150, 300, 450, 600, 750 and 900 mm Z values. R_i represented the radial length vector in the ith sector from the TRP to the pointer of the CPSAM. The mean and standard deviation value for the radial length of each sector for each subject was stored for statistical processing. The 5th and 95th percentile radial lengths for each sector were later calculated using a statistically based model verified in this research. The other statistical methods employed consisted of a linear multiple regression analysis to predict the radial length.

Using MINITAB the data for each percentile were regressed using a linear multiple regression in terms of Θ, Θ^2, Z and Z^2. The general form of the regression equation was:

$$Radial\ length = \beta_0 + \beta_1 \cdot \theta + \beta_2 \cdot \theta^2 + \beta_3 \cdot Z + \beta_4 \cdot Z^2 \tag{1}$$

where, the ß terms were the coefficients determined by the statistical regression. In all cases the ß terms were retained in the equation only when the t-Test for the coefficient was significant at $\alpha \leq 0.05$.

Using the predicted radial length value (R_i) for the groups at any value of Z and Θ_i the X and Y Cartesian coordinates for each sector on the table surface were calculated using: $X_i = R_i \cdot \cos \Theta_i$, and $Y_i = R_i \cdot \sin \Theta_i$

3. Results and Discussion

3.1. Determination of the Maximum Reach Envelope for Females and Males: Equations were derived which describe the radial length values of the 5th, 50th and 95th percentile MRE for the females and males. The respective regression coefficients for the predicted radial lengths are presented in Table 1. The calculated r^2 values for the females MRE were 93.1, 97.7 and 99.1% for the 5th, 50th and 95th percentile equations, respectively. The standard error of the estimate for the females MRE was 39, 20 and 12 mm for the 5th, 50th and 95th percentile MRE, respectively.

For the male MRE the calculated r^2 values were 95.6, 98.4 and 99.1% for the 5th, 50th and 95th percentile equations, respectively. The standard error of the estimate for the males MRE was 31, 18 and 13 mm for the 5th, 50th and 95th percentile MRE, respectively. Shown in Figures 1 and 2 are the maximum reach areas determined from the prediction ºquations for the Z = 0 mm band for females and males, respectively.

Table 1: Summary of the ß coefficients for the regression analysis of the MRE.

Sex	Percentile	β_0 (Constant)	β_1 (Θ)	β_2 (Θ^2)	β_3 (Z)	β_4 (Z^2)
	5th	562	-7.4332	0.0392	0.2340	-0.0007
Female	50th	651	-6.3400	0.0306	0.2328	-0.0006
	95th	741	-5.2500	0.0219	0.2320	-0.0006
	5th	586	-6.4562	0.0312	0.2754	-0.0006
Male	50th	714	-5.7610	0.0255	0.2827	-0.0006
	95th	842	-5.0681	0.0198	0.2894	-0.0006

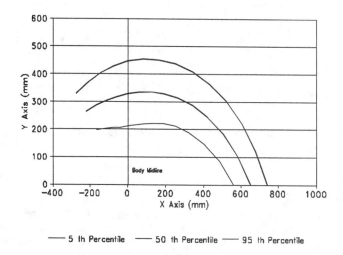

Figure 1: The 5th, 50th and 95th percentile maximum reach area for females on the Z=0 mm plane.

4. Conclusions

The purpose of this study was to determine the 5th, 50th and 95th percentile MRE adult females and males who require a wheelchair mobility. The MREs were measured using a CPSAM system developed for the determination of 3-D reach areas and envelopes. In conclusion, based upon the findings of this study:

(1)   A series of multiple linear regression analyses have been used to determine the equations which defined the boundaries of the maximum reach envelope (NRA) for a sample of 42 males and 20 females. This represents the first time the MRE has been directly determined for wheelchair mobile adults.

(2)   Using a Cylindrical coordinate system, the general form of the regression equation for the radial lengths of the MRE for males and females was: Radial length (R) =

$ß_0 + ß_1 \cdot \Theta + ß_2 \cdot \Theta^2 + ß_3 \cdot Z + ß_4 \cdot Z^2$, with the individual ß coefficients specific to the sex and percentile MRE. The Cartesian coordinate position for each reach vector can be determined trigonometrically.

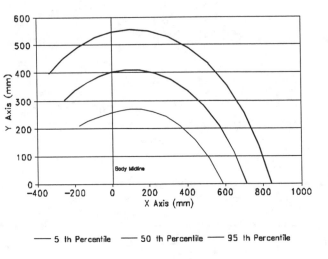

Figure 2: The 5th, 50th and 95th percentile maximum reach area for males on the Z=0 mm plane.

Acknowledgements

The authors wish to acknowledge the financial support of NSERC, the Canadian Department of Human Resources and the Rick Hansen Man-in-Motion Legacy Fund. We would also like to thank the Nova Scotia branch of the C.P.A. and the subjects for their co-operation.

References

[1] Kennedy, K.W., (1976), Reach capability of men and women: a three-dimensional analysis. published by the: National Technical Information Service, Springfield, Virginia.

[2] Behara, D.N., (1991), Determination and Modelling of Workspace for Industrial Workstation Design: An Engineering Anthropometry Approach. Ph.D. Dissertation, Department of Industrial Engineering, Technical University of Nova Scotia.

[3] Sengupta, A.K., (1995), Anthropometric Modeling and Evaluation of Workspace for Industrial Workstation Design, Ph.D. Dissertation, Department of Industrial Engineering, Technical University of Nova Scotia, Halifax, Nova Scotia.

[4] Kozey, J., B. Das, and R.L. Kirby, (1996), The Determination of the Normal Reach Area in the Horizontal Plane for Wheelchair Mobile Adults. In the proceedings of the 28th annual meeting of the Human Factors Association of Canada, 41-46.

[5] Floyd, W.F., L. Guttmann, C. Wycliffe-Noble, K.R. Parkes and J. Ward, (1966), A study of the Space Requirements of Wheelchair Users. *Paraplegia*, May, 24-37.

[6] Diffrient, N., A.D. Tilley and J.C. Bardagjy, (1974), *Humanscale 1-2-3*: Dreyfuss and Associates, M.I.T. Press.

[7] Das, B., J. Kozey and J. Tyson, (1994), A computerized potentiometric system for structural and functional anthropometric measurements, *Ergonomics*, 37(6), 1031-1046.

Advances in Occupational Ergonomics and Safety II
Edited by Biman Das and Waldemar Karwowski
IOS Press and Ohmsha, 1997

Reach Volume of Korean Population and Work Space Design

Jin Ho Kim, Jae Hee Park, Soo Chan Park, and Bong Kee Koh

Ergonomics Lab., Korea Research Institute of Standards and Science,
Deadeok Science Town, Taejon, Korea, 305-600

Abstract

The objective of this study is to provide the basic statistics of the measured data useful for ergonomic design. An anthropometric study of static measurements and grasping reaches was carried out. The 49 static measurements were selected to give general guidelines for layouts in workplaces. They were performed on a sample of Korean 179 males and 236 females, aged 18-50. Also, grasping reaches were made to a continuous series of horizontal planes at -10cm, 0cm, 30cm, 60cm, and 90cm above the seat reference point (SRP). The grasping reaches were measured on a sample of 29 males and 21 females. The results can be applied to give guidelines for product designs and layout of workplaces.

1. Introduction

Since work areas must comfortably accommodate workers while offering an arrangement for maximum human effectiveness, design of these areas is one of the major tasks of an industrial ergonomist. Reach measurements are essential for the product design and layout of workplaces. However, most of the existing data have been limited to a specific population, particularly, Caucasian population.

The main purpose of this study is to provide the basic statistics of the measured data useful for ergonomic design. An anthropometric study of 49 static measurements and grasping reaches was carried out to obtain information relevant to the design and layout of workplaces.

2. Static Anthropometric Measurements

The 49 static measurements were selected to give general guidelines for the layout in workplaces. All measurements were listed in Table 1. The measurements were made using a standard Martin-type anthropometer. We referred the standard definition and procedures of NASA (1978) (also see Kouchi, et. al., 1994).

The survey was performed on a sample of 179 males and 236 females, aged 18-50. Subjects were selected, using a random sequence, from the population at six sites in Korea. The data collected are presented in Table 1 together with the data from the United States of America and Japan.

3. Grasping Reach Measurements

We also measured the grasping reaches of 29 males and 21 females selected to be anthropometrically representatives of subjects for static anthropometric measurements. Table 2 shows the anthropometric characteristics of subjects.

A 3-D motion analysis system (VICON 140 ^{TM}) having 4 CCD cameras with infrared light was used to measure the reach volume. Grasping reaches were made to a continuous series of horizontal planes at -10cm, 0cm, 30cm, 60cm, and 90cm above the seat reference point (SRP). All measurements were taken with the subject on a seat with a backrest angle of 103° and a seat angle of 6°. The reach task was to grasp, with a right hand, a small knob between the thumb and forefinger at each level and to extend the arm fully, with the shoulders still in contact with the seat back. The horizontal distances from the seat reference vertical (SRV) through SRP were measured. The results are presented in Table 3 and Figure 1.

Table 1. Means and standard deviations for all measurements. Measurements are in cm or kg.

Item	Male						Female					
	Korean		Japanese[1]		USAF[2]		Korean		Japanese		USAF	
	Mean	S.D.	Mean	S.D.	Mean	S.D.	Mean	S.D.	Mean	S.D.	Mean	S.D.
Weight	69.32	8.81	63.30	8.28	78.74	9.72	54.64	7.32	52.60	6.22	57.73	7.52
Stature	171.55	5.45	171.40	6.26	177.3	6.2	158.25	5.12	159.13	5.30	162.1	6.0
Acromion height	139.27	4.92	138.01	5.67	145.2	5.8	128.47	4.63	127.77	4.86	131.9	5.5
Elbow height	104.86	5.09	104.26	4.42	112.3	4.6	96.54	3.79	96.46	3.65	NS	
Wrist height	83.48	3.25	82.33	3.82	86.6	3.9	77.16	3.40	77.01	3.21	NS	
Fingertip height	65.39	3.00	64.37	3.33	NS		60.03	3.15	60.54	2.78	NS	
Span	170.06	6.85	172.02	7.27	NS		156.28	10.94	157.39	6.57	NS	
Sitting height	93.32	2.68	92.60	3.39	93.2	3.2	85.93	2.93	86.76	2.74	85.6	3.2
Eye height, sitting	82.01	2.55	80.04	3.33	81.0	3.0	74.88	2.61	74.91	2.51	73.7	3.1
Acromion height,sitting	61.19	2.74	59.35	2.76	NS		56.18	2.42	55.42	2.24	NS	
Vertical arm reach,sitting	135.07	4.63	134.68	5.58	NS		124.61	5.23	124.02	4.74	NS	
Elbow height, sitting	26.69	2.53	25.42	2.51	25.2	2.6	24.53	2.39	24.37	2.23	22.7	2.5
Arm reach from back	79.26	3.23	81.99	3.63	NS		74.60	2.97	75.42	3.43	NS	
Functional reach from back	71.51	3.42	77.10	3.55	80.3	4.0	69.19	3.53	68.22	3.32	74.1	3.9
Grip reach from back	68.57	3.16	71.58	3.21	NS		64.75	2.89	65.77	3.10	NS	
Biacromial breadth	40.00	2.07	39.75	1.75	40.7	1.9	35.79	1.56	35.88	1.42	35.8	1.6
Upper arm length	30.32	1.60	31.30	1.49	36.0	1.7	28.16	1.42	28.87	1.50	NS	
Forearm length	24.28	1.40	25.16	1.25	NS		22.71	1.37	22.86	1.15	NS	
Acromion to fingertip length	73.03	2.94	73.53	3.10	NS		67.34	2.58	67.28	2.86	NS	
Acromion to olecranon length	33.99	1.74	34.06	1.57	NS		31.69	1.38	31.12	1.53	NS	
Olecranon to fingertip length	44.29	2.11	45.25	1.87	NS		41.04	1.90	41.35	1.67	NS	
Olecranon to grip length	33.93	1.42	33.37	1.52	NS		31.40	1.35	30.47	1.34	NS	
Wall to grip length	34.26	2.32	34.23	1.45	NS		31.47	1.56	30.67	1.38	NS	
Wall to wrist length	26.16	1.55	27.66	1.23	NS		24.15	1.34	24.37	1.27	NS	
Axillary arm circumference	31.15	2.63	29.89	2.38	NS		27.72	2.87	27.01	2.11	NS	
Upper arm circumference	29.27	2.35	28.08	2.50	30.8	2.3	26.37	2.82	25.36	2.08	25.6	2.3
Elbow circumference	25.87	1.47	NS		NS		22.93	1.60	NS		NS	
Forearm circumference	26.51	1.54	25.92	1.57	NS		23.06	1.65	22.81	1.23	NS	
Minimum forearm circumference	16.91	0.93	16.77	1.01	NS		15.52	1.18	15.38	0.97	NS	
Upper arm circumference, flexed	30.71	2.45	29.50	2.55	32.7	2.3	26.48	2.85	26.46	2.05	26.8	2.3
Elbow circumference, flexed	29.15	1.97	29.77	1.85	NS		25.19	1.67	27.79	2.33	NS	
Hand length	17.77	0.74	19.08	0.88	19.1	0.8	16.48	0.76	17.38	0.74	18.4	1.0
Palm length	9.92	0.48	11.30	0.58	NS		9.18	0.47	10.10	0.44	NS	
Finger I length	5.51	0.39	6.22	0.41	NS		5.04	0.39	5.85	0.34	NS	
Finger II length	6.54	0.38	7.11	0.40	NS		6.14	0.41	6.61	0.38	NS	
Finger III length	7.35	0.41	7.96	0.42	NS		6.85	0.41	7.28	0.39	NS	
Finger IV length	6.86	0.39	NS		NS		6.39	0.42	NS		NS	
Finger V length	5.36	0.40	NS		NS		4.98	0.42	NS		NS	
Hand circumference	20.60	0.87	20.15	1.04	21.6	0.9	18.46	0.99	18.34	0.89	18.3	0.9
Maximum hand circumference	25.13	1.05	24.89	1.14	NS		22.13	1.12	21.88	1.00	NS	
Index finger breadth, proximal	1.41	0.12	1.71	0.15	NS		1.18	0.16	1.57	0.08	NS	
Index finger breadth, distal	1.15	0.11	1.73	0.18	NS		0.94	0.18	1.32	0.07	NS	
Wrist circumference	16.95	0.73	16.74	0.77	NS		15.41	0.92	15.05	0.72	NS	
Metacarpal bone head thickness	2.64	0.22	2.75	0.27	NS		2.12	0.29	2.41	0.14	NS	
Maximum hand breadth	10.10	0.46	10.18	0.47	NS		8.68	0.57	9.00	0.42	NS	
Hand breadth	7.98	0.39	8.41	0.40	8.9	0.4	7.09	0.47	7.40	0.36	7.6	0.4
Fist circumference	27.85	1.29	26.70	1.18	NS		24.44	1.40	23.91	1.05	NS	
Grip diameter,inside, index finger	15.07	1.03	NS		NS		13.54	1.02	NS		NS	
Grip diameter,inside,middle finger	16.81	0.04	NS		NS		15.31	1.04	NS		NS	

1) Kouchi M. et al., 1994.

2) NASA, 1978.

Table 2. Anthropometric Data of subjects selected for measuring grasping reach

		n	Upper arm length	Forearm length	Acromion to fingertip length	Grip reach from back
Male	M ± S.D.	29	31.47 ± 5.13	23.25 ± 2.04	73.90 ± 13.77	71.30 ± 14.98
Female	M ± S.D.	21	29.29 ± 4.46	21.40 ± 1.17	66.78 ± 8.86	64.95 ± 7.20

Table 3. Right Hand Grasping Reach To A Horizontal Plane -10cm, 0cm, 30cm, 60cm, and 90cm Above The Seat Reference Point. Horizontal Distance From The SRV. All measurements are in mm.

angle	Man					Woman				
	90cm	60cm	30cm	0cm	-10cm	90cm	60cm	30cm	0cm	-10cm
135	244.0±53.4	280.1±37.1								
120	277.7±49.0	309.1±47.7				246.5±23.1	297.4±27.8			
105	295.6±47.4	361.0±60.1	380.3±67.6			274.1±21.7	354.2±40.8	360.1±54.5		
90	312.0±56.5	404.3±61.6	377.1±58.3			286.4±40.9	391.8±46.8	409.1±40.3		
75	333.0±58.9	444.6±60.9	414.5±60.4			297.3±46.9	429.7±48.2	439.3±48.3		
60	352.6±53.7	477.5±58.3	454.1±48.0			306.5±47.8	462.3±45.3	474.5±49.4		
45	372.9±51.7	506.5±47.3	488.0±43.9			304.7±51.8	479.5±41.3	495.5±46.1		
30	389.6±45.8	527.6±40.8	514.2±35.1			298.0±62.0	483.1±38.3	500.3±40.9		
15	400.1±47.7	538.0±35.6	529.2±28.2			292.4±70.8	477.2±43.5	496.8±42.4		
0	404.7±54.9	545.0±35.4	538.2±26.9			290.9±76.3	477.8±47.9	495.1±45.6		
-15	414.6±55.9	555.2±38.2	555.7±29.2			294.7±82.8	490.2±50.3	508.9±51.8		
-30	434.7±56.6	576.9±39.8	580.8±32.2	484.5±42.7	412.9±64.1	307.2±88.8	509.7±51.0	535.4±56.8	431.9±48.8	
-45	461.6±54.3	606.6±40.5	606.7±35.4	506.8±37.3	434.6±43.1	321.6±90.1	534.8±48.4	559.9±51.8	448.3±56.8	386.6±42.7
-60	495.9±54.3	642.3±41.6	636.5±39.0	529.6±37.8	455.4±39.9	340.8±90.5	562.4±45.3	588.9±57.5	466.4±68.3	399.6±58.5
-75	536.5±60.2	681.1±41.7	669.9±36.9	552.7±40.5	479.7±41.7	372.1±90.6	596.0±46.8	617.3±49.4	488.7±71.8	418.1±64.7
-90	582.5±59.4	719.4±39.1	699.2±34.1	572.9±41.7	499.9±47.6	404.1±87.7	628.2±46.6	644.0±47.8	513.1±73.8	442.5±68.9
-105	628.3±52.2	749.2±37.9	722.3±31.1	594.9±42.9	519.6±50.4	447.5±81.3	657.2±44.8	669.4±44.1	538.5±67.3	469.2±64.7
-120	658.0±52.1	770.0±38.1	739.0±31.7	605.4±39.8	547.8±60.2	489.9±74.0	686.3±41.4	686.8±39.8	553.5±51.4	478.4±59.8
-135	717.1±17.1	783.1±49.3	740.2±39.1	624.6±52.2		500.8±76.3	725.7±59.5	704.7±38.0	572.2±44.8	500.7±39.9
-150										

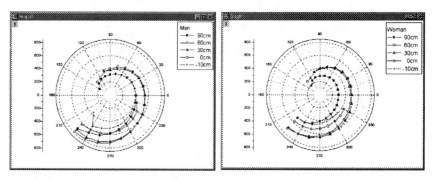

Figure 1. Grasping Reach To A Horizontal Plane A Horizontal Plane -10cm, 0cm, 30cm, 60cm, and 90cm Above The Seat Reference Point.

4. Conclusions and Discussions

Devices and controls should be placed within the operator's arm or foot to guarantee effective performances. Hence, reach measurements are essential for the product design and layout of workplaces. However, most of the existing data were limited to a specific population, particularly, Caucasian population. This study provided some information relevant to the design and layout of workplaces for Korean. The results can be applied to give general guidelines for industrial designs such as layouts of controls, designs of workspaces or workstations, and so on.

Reference

[1] Kouchi M., Yokoyama K., Yamashita J., Yokoi T., Ogi H., Yoshioka M., Atsumi H., and Hotta A., *Human Body Dimensions Data for Ergonomic Design*, ISSN OPIP-5351 Vol.2, No.1, 1994.

[2] Bullock, Margaret I., The Determination of Function Arm Reach Boundaries for Operation of Manual Controls, *Ergonomics*, 17(3), 1974.

[3] Kennedy, K. W., *Reach Capability of the USAF Population, Phase I, The Outer Boundaries of Grasping Reach Envelopes for the Shirt-Sleeved, Seated Operator.* AMRL-TDR-64-59, Aerospace Medical Research Lab., Wright-Patterson Air Force Base, Ohio, 1964.

[4] King, B. G., Morrow, D. J., and Vollmer, E. P., *Cockpit Studies - The Boundaries of the Maximum Area for the Operation of Manual Controls*, Report 3, Project X-651, National Naval Medical Center, Bethesda, Md., 1947.

[5] NASA Reference Publication 1024, Anthropometric Source Book Volume I: Anthropometric for Designers, N79-11734, 1978.

[6] NASA Reference Publication 1024, Anthropometric Source Book Volume II: A Handbook of Anthropometric Data, N79-13711, 1978.

[7] Woodson, W. E., *Human Factors Design Handbook*, McGraw-Hill Book Company, 1981.

Advances in Occupational Ergonomics and Safety II
Edited by Biman Das and Waldemar Karwowski
IOS Press and Ohmsha, 1997

Physiological cost of task performance in workspace reach envelopes

Arijit K. Sengupta
Department of Engineering Technology
New Jersey Institute of Technology
Newark, New Jersey, USA.
and
Biman Das
Department of Industrial Engineering
Technical University of Nova Scotia
Halifax, Nova Scotia, Canada.

The oxygen uptake (VO_2) and heart rate (HR) were determined for performing a repetitive horizontal lifting and moving task in the normal, maximum and extreme workspace reach envelopes. The VO_2 and HR increased significantly for the normal to the maximum to the extreme workspace conditions. The average increases in VO_2 in the maximum and the extreme workspaces when compared to the normal workspace were 19 and 52%, respectively. The corresponding average increases in the HR were 6 and 14% respectively. The results of this investigation objectively validated that worker physiological cost during task performance would increase significantly with the increase in workspace reach levels.

1. Introduction

In many industrial workstations, workers perform manual tasks involving repetitive arm motions. The tasks do not involve heavy exertion, but fatigue, pain and repetitive strain injuries in arm, shoulder and neck region are prevalent among the industrial workers [1,2,3,4]. The ergonomic design guidelines describe the performance of industrial tasks in the normal and maximum workspaces. These workspaces are defined by the reach levels and arm posture during manual work, and their dimensions are derived from the upper body anthropometry and the work surface height. The design guidelines are based on the notion that progressively more muscular effort is required to perform a handling task within the normal, maximum and beyond maximum (extreme) workspaces. This increased effort manifests in the form of worker fatigue, pain and diminished worker productivity. However, no experimental evidence is available which document the degree of the change in physiological cost due to performing the work in different workspaces. The objective of the research was to determine whether worker physiological cost during task performance would increase significantly with the increase in reach levels.

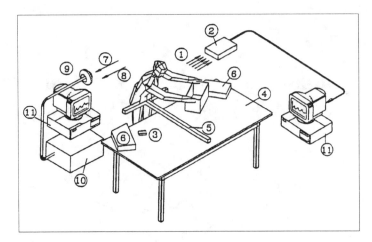

Legend:
1. EMG signals from
   preamplifier
2. Flexcomp digital encoder
3. Micro switch
4. Adjustable height table
5. Dividing bar
6. Fixed stops
7. Expired air from
   subjects
8. Heart rate signal
9. Flow meter
10. SM 5000 metabolic
    analyzer
11. Personal computers

Figure 1. Experimental setup for physiological evaluation of workspaces.

2. Experimental Methods

Eight male and eight female subjects with no history of musculoskeletal and cardiovascular problems participated in the study. The average age of the male and female subjects were 24.9 and 27.6 years, respectively. The mean height and weight of the male subjects were 177.6 cm and 80 kg, respectively. The corresponding values for the female subjects were 167.5 cm and 63.4 kg, respectively. The experimental setup is illustrated in Figure 1. The experimental task consisted of repetitive lifting and moving a box (30 cm length x 20 cm depth x 17.5 cm height, weighing 5 kg) from right to left, between two stops affixed at 150 cm apart in a standing working posture. The weight (limit) of the box was computed from the NIOSH guidelines of manual material handling [5]. The frequency of the lift was controlled by computer beeps at a rate of 10 lifts per minute. At the end of each lift the box was carried back to the starting position by an assistant. It should be noted EMG signal were also recorded in this investigation but not reported in this paper (Figure 1).

The table height was adjusted for each subject such that subject's elbow height corresponded to the height of the handholds of the box. In each experimental session the distance of the subject from the table edge was varied to simulate working within his or her normal, maximum and extreme workspaces. For lifts in normal workspace, the subjects stood close to the table edge such that subject's forearm remained horizontal while holding and moving the box between the two stops. For the maximum workspace, the subject was positioned away from the table edge, such that the elbow remained fully extended throughout the lift. For lifting in extreme workspace, the subject was asked to move back to the farthest possible distance from where he or she could lift the box and could maintain the lifting task at the specified frequency. This posture involved torso flexion in addition to the elbow extension. This position was determined by trial and error for each subject.

The lifting tasks were performed in three consecutive sessions of 15 minutes duration each for the three workspaces, and 15 minutes of rest were provided between two consecutive sessions. The sequence of the lifting task within normal, maximum and extreme workspaces was randomized for each subject. The SM5000 metabolic system was used to record and monitor oxygen uptake (VO_2) and heart rate (HR) throughout each lifting session. It took one and a half hour for each subject to complete the experimental procedure.

3. Experimental results

The VO_2 and HR for normal, maximum and extreme workspace sessions were plotted against time for each subject. The data included both the resting and recovery data. The plots showed a gradual increase of both VO_2 and HR from their resting levels and then stabilized to a steady working level value. At the end of the work cycle, the recovery period showed a gradual decline. Approximately a 5 minute interval near to the end of the cycle, where the data showed a stable trend, was selected for averaging the data. These average values for the individual sessions were used as a measure of VO_2 and HR for further analysis.

Considerable variation in the VO_2 was noticed among the subjects, however, except for one subject, the VO_2 of all subjects progressively increased while working in the normal, maximum and extreme workspaces. The average values of HR provided similar results. Except for two subjects, the HR of all subjects progressively increased with the increasing reach levels.

Table 1. Physiological cost of task performance in workspace reach envelopes.

Reach envelopes	VO$_2$ (l/min)			Heart rate (bpm)		
	Mean	Lower limit	Upper limit	Mean	Lower limit	Upper limit
Normal	0.52	0.49	0.56	95	92	97
Maximum	0.62	0.58	0.65	101	98	103
Extreme	0.79	0.76	0.82	108	105	110

Note: Lower and upper limit values are based on 95% confidence interval.

The means (n=16) of VO_2 for normal, maximum and extreme workspaces were 0.52, 0.62 and 0.79 l/min, respectively (Table 1). This represented an increase of 19% and 52% for the maximum and the extreme workspaces compared to the values obtained for the normal workspace. The means (n=16) of HR for normal, maximum and extreme workspaces were 97, 103, and 110 bpm (Table 1). This constitutes an increase of 6% for the maximum and 14% for the extreme workspace, compared to the normal workspace value. The magnitude of the increases in HR was not as dramatic as that in VO_2. One would expect more static loading in the case of working in the extreme workspace thus a higher rise in HR was expected. However, based on the relationship of the observed VO_2 and HR, this fact could not be ascertained.

Analysis of variance was performed separately for the dependent variables, VO_2 and HR. The two main factors were workspace and sex. A repeated measure design on the workspace factor was used as the same subjects performed the tasks in three different levels of the workspace factor [6]. The sex effect, and the interaction effect between workspace and sex, were not significant for both VO_2 and HR. The workspace effect was significant at 5% level for both VO_2 and HR. The 95% confidence intervals for the workspace factor level means (Table 1) provided non-overlapping intervals for both VO_2 and HR. Additionally, a pair-wise comparison of the workspace factor level means by Tukey's test [6] also established that the mean VO_2 and HR were significantly increasing from the normal to the maximum to the extreme workspaces.

4. Conclusions

The conclusions reached by this investigation were:
(a) For performing a repetitive horizontal lifting and moving task in the normal, maximum and extreme workspace reach envelopes, the phyiological cost in terms of oxygen uptake (VO_2) and heart rate (HR) were determined.
(b) The physiological cost of performing the task with the maximum workspace was significantly ($p<0.05$) higher than that in the normal workspace. The average increases in the VO_2 and HR were 19 and 6%, respectively.
(c) Similar statistically significant results were found for performing the task in the extreme workspace compared to working in the maximum workspace. The corresponding increases in the VO_2 and HR were 27 and 7%, respectively.
(d) It was proven objectively that worker physiological cost would increase singnificantly with the increase in workspace reach levels.

5. Research Implications

From the viewpoint of worker physiological cost, it is desirable to perform industrial tasks within the normal workspace whenever possible and failing that, work should be performed within the maximum workspace. Working within the extreme workspace must be avoided, if possible.

Acknowledgment

This research was funded by the National Sciences and Engineering Research Council of Canada (NSERC Research Grant 0GP0006746).

References

[1] S. Kvanrnström, Occurrence of musculoskeletal disorders in a manufacturing industry with special attention to occupational shoulder disorders, *Scandinavian Journal of Rehabilitation Medicine* (Suppl.) 8 (1983) 1-114.
[2] T. J. Armstrong *et al.*, Repetitive trauma disorders: Job evaluation and design, *Human Factors*, 28 (1986), 325-336.
[3] R. H. Westgaard, and A. Aras, Postural muscle strain as a causal factor in the development of musculo-skeletal illness, *Applied Ergonomics*, 15 (1988) 162-174.
[4] A. G. Ryan, The prevalence of musculoskeletal symptoms in supermarket workers, *Ergonomics*, 32-4 (1989) 359-371.
[5] T. R Waters *et al.*, Revised NIOSH equation for the design and evaluation of manual lifting tasks, *Ergonomics*, 36-7 (1994) 749-776.
[6] J. Neter *et al.*, *Applied linear statistical models*, 2nd edition, Richard D. Irwin, Inc. (1985) *pp.* 1021-1025.

Advances in Occupational Ergonomics and Safety II
Edited by Biman Das and Waldemar Karwowski
IOS Press and Ohmsha, 1997

Computerized Proactive Ergonomic System for Automotive Assembly Operations

Dr. Salem Taboun, Dr. Leo Oriet, and Dean C. Hsieh
Department of Industrial and Manufacturing Systems Engineering
University of Windsor, Windsor, Ontario

A proactive stance towards ergonomics and workstation design involves
problem detection and elimination at early stages. A representational
model of beneficial components for such an approach assists in
promoting this stance. The Proactive Workstation Design Model
(PWDM) is a computer based model that provides a practical and
theoretical union of current ergonomic design principles established by
industry and government. The model improves the speed and
suitability of industrial job and workstation design.

1. Introduction

Workstations consist of human and machine components embedded in a local
environment and involve "the three dimensional space in which work is carried out"[1].
Ergonomics aims to ensure that human needs for safe and efficient working are met in the
design of worksystems. In the past, companies usually designed job processes and
production facilities first and then forced workers to adapt to the set standards and
equipment. Workers were expected to fit to the job and work at predetermined levels that
were set for production effectiveness and efficiency and not the comfort and safety of the
worker. By improving worksystem designs for workers in terms of both physical design and
job content, companies would benefit in the form of safe and content workers and higher
productivity with lower lost time and compensation costs.

For these types of gains, a proactive stance towards ergonomic practices and
workstation design would be advantageous to adopt. In this context, a proactive stance
involves problem detection and elimination in early stages. This calls for action before the
occurrence of negative effects. Conversely, a reactive approach to job and workstation
design involves waiting and acting on problems after they have negatively effected the
worker and production. To implement a proactive stance, a company would need to look at
not only its own procedures but also those of other companies in the same industry and
outside. Furthermore, all the components of such an approach are not always cohesive in
the workplace and the connection between the parts may not always be easily identified.
Thus, it appears necessary to simplify this approach by using a representational model of the
components beneficial to any company wishing to take such an approach. This spurred the
development of a Proactive Workstation Design Model (PWDM) which would involve the

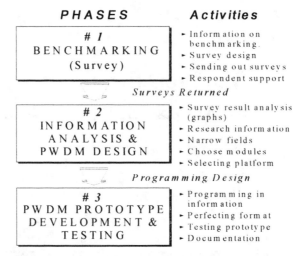

Figure 1: PWDM Development Phases

use of a computer created structure to provide a practical and theoretical union of current ergonomic design principles established by industry and government.

2. PWDM Development

The development procedure for the PWDM occurred over three distinct phases. The first phase involved the gathering of information to form the data storage area. This involved benchmarking and use of a survey. The second phase included the analysis of the benchmarking obtained material into a skeleton of the PWDM processor and information sorter. The second phase was also referred to as a design stage since the PWDM was planned and mapped out then.   The third phase involved the actual development of a PWDM prototype including testing and debugging. Figure 1 illustrates these phases.

3. Benchmarking

At the heart of the benchmarking phase of PWDM development was a survey. The survey was designed to solicit information from companies to PWDM development. It was the essential tool for data collection and basically consisted of six main sections. Survey questions ranged from asking about the company to questions about procedures used within the organization. Organizational commitment to safe workstation design and ergonomics were measured in terms of worker training and the existence of bodies within the organization to enforce the training and deal with problems as they arose were also inquired about. Yet, the most vital areas of the survey, with regards to PWDM development, involved questions that sought information about injuries and reviewed organizational health and safety tools.

4. Information Analysis and PWDM Design

Collected survey data was displayed using various statistical representational techniques such as histograms and Pareto charts. The use of histograms allowed the data to be grouped in a manner that indicated the frequency of responses to certain questions.

be grouped in a manner that indicated the frequency of responses to certain questions. Subjective questions that used rating scales regarding production of the organization would be well represented using histograms. Similarly, Pareto diagrams also assisted in studying frequency in a sample but at distinct traits in the sample. Pareto diagrams were useful in representing collected fill-in-the-box type questions.

In collecting and dissecting data, information and its relative use was categorized. Documents either yielded hard data or theoretical information useful in development of theory for the Model. In classifying information as hard data, the information usually contained formulas, equations, or quantitative information that produced finite results. The other category of theoretical information provided workstation defining material in a qualitative sense. The information falling into this group either aided in explaining how to configure the database or provided leads to more specific resources. In addition, preventive and corrective suggestions also fell into this category.

5. PWDM Prototype Development and Testing

The basic configuration of the Model involved the use of a pseudo object-oriented database and an interactive user area in a spreadsheet. Figure 2 shows a simplified version of the proposed model structure. The heart of the model resides in the data storage area. The object-oriented sense of the database was due to the fact that the data area was divided into modules that each pertained to specific aspects of job and workstation design. This was the inherent value of information gained from the survey since it not only provided guidance to data for the database but also the search parameters for the processor unit which would search the database with respect to user requested input by searching the different data modules in the PWDM.   Search parameters included ergonomic concerns such as static and dynamic muscle fatigue as well as job motion elements such as lifting, pushing, and pulling.

Further development of the PWDM consisted of mathematical models and equations discovered from research references. The quantitative information of this sort provided the basis of the processor unit. The processor basically became the formulas represented in the spreadsheet and the links that were made with the data modules. In essence, the PWDM processor unit exists within the software and computer through links and programmed formulas within and between the spreadsheet. The processor unit was set to provide the relay between Model user and the database. The user entered elemental data through an

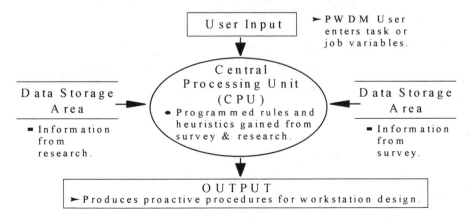

F igure 2: Proposed M odel Structure

interactive interface screen which would then be referenced by the processor unit contents with respect to the gathered data stored in the database. From this comparison, the optimal elements for a workstation or job design would be determined. The interface screen would also display the output from the Model.

There are nine modules in all. The two main sheets essential for user interface are named TASK and JOB. These two sheets served as the input and output sheets for the model. The names illustrated the strategy used to analyze workstations in PWDM. The physical traits of the worker and the attributes of the job the worker performs are both looked at. The physical traits include body dimensions, age, and gender. The attributes involved a breakdown of the job into its basic motions.

The other worksheet modules included job design analysis by observing the timing of job elements and their frequencies. In addition, physical activities were categorized. These included posture evaluation and motion types such as lifting, pushing, and pulling. This allowed for the PWDM to use its modules of biomechanics[2], the NIOSH Lifting Equation[3], anthropometry, and other design information. Finally, characteristics concerning the surroundings and facilities were evaluated as well including hand tools used, environmental temperature and work surfaces used.

The testing of the PWDM prototype basically consisted of making sure the mechanics of the spreadsheet structure worked properly and accurately. Furthermore, this included making sure that the solutions offered by the PWDM were not only adequate for job or workstation improvement but also fundamentally correct. In essence, testing involved comparing PWDM module results with existing models used in industry. The biomechanical module was evaluated in comparison to the University of Michigan Two Dimensional Model while the NIOSH module was compared to a manual calculation of the NIOSH lifting equation.

6. Conclusions

The completion of the prototype of the PWDM signaled the passing of all the three development phases. The benchmarking phase revealed that many companies ignore the proactive stance towards ergonomics and workstation design in their daily operations. Some of the factors for this were found to be due to unawareness and political reasons. Regardless, the survey phase aided in entering and completing the second phase of analysis and design. Information from the survey helped in directing the PWDM design which led to the final stage. The construction and testing of the PWDM proved to show that it was accurate and was designed appropriately for its use.

In conclusion, the PWDM proved to be more of a resource tool than originally envisioned. Although it referenced much information and offered plentiful advice, the Model would be limited in its proactive stance if not used properly. In a way, the PWDM became the ultimate, automated reference manual for use by a knowledgeable individual in the field of ergonomics.

References

[1] S. Bridger, *Introduction to Ergonomics*, McGraw-Hill., New York, 1995.
[2] B. Chaffin and G. B. Andersson, *Occupational Biomechanics*, John Wiley & Sons, New York, 1984.
[3] A. Garg, *User's Manual For The Revised NIOSH Guide Program For Manual Lifting*, National Institute of Occupational Safety and Health, Cincinnati, 1993.

Advances in Occupational Ergonomics and Safety II
Edited by Biman Das and Waldemar Karwowski
IOS Press and Ohmsha, 1997

An Ergonomics Workstation for the Undergraduate Human Factors Laboratory

Tanya Willis Magliulo
Great Dane Trailers, Savannah GA 31402

Kelly Weins
Phoenix Systems, Atlanta GA 30329

Stephanie Kimbell
Lucent Technologies, Atlanta GA

Laura Moody, Ph.D.
Mercer University, Macon GA 31207

The Industrial and Systems Engineering program at Mercer University includes two required courses in which human factors/ergonomics is taught - Work Measurement and Design, and Human Engineering. In both of these courses, students perform integrated laboratory experiments to demonstrate and explore issues of human performance and system design. To make the most of these laboratory exercises, the Human Factors Laboratory needed an ergonomic workstation that would allow students to perform experiments under a range of ergonomic conditions and test the effectiveness of possible workstation layout designs. The Mercer University School of Engineering curriculum also requires a two-quarter Senior Design Project which is interdisciplinary in nature. A senior design team consisting of students from industrial and mechanical engineering undertook a project to design, build, and test an ergonomic workstation for the Human Factors Lab. The Ergonomic Workstation provides several tilt angles, as well as height and depth adjustment that accommodate the size and reach of the first percentile woman through the ninety-ninth percentile man. A clear acrylic work surface allows for layout templates to be used for the different experiments and allows students to write or draw work areas, layouts, or other needed information directly onto the work surface. Four experiments using the workstation were also developed to demonstrate ergonomic principles to students taking human factors classes.

1. Introduction

The Industrial and Systems Engineering program at Mercer University includes two required courses in human factors/ergonomics. In the first, students learn principles and techniques of physical ergonomics, while in the second, they learn about the cognitive aspects of human-machine systems. Integrated within both of these courses are a series of laboratory experiments designed to illustrate key principles and techniques of ergonomic design. Until this year, however, students' ability to fully explore workstation design under a variety of ergonomic conditions was limited by the fixed position, standard size tables available in the Human Factors laboratory.

Mercer's School of Engineering curriculum also includes a two-term senior design project. The need for an adjustable ergonomic workstation that allows students to explore design under a range of conditions was presented to a senior design team consisting of one mechanical engineering and two industrial engineering students. This team met with the instructor to further define the project to include the workstation itself, along with a series of experiments using the workstation. Over the course of the two terms, the team defined the specific criteria for the workstation and experiments, explored several design options, defined a final design, implemented, and tested the workstation and accompanying experiments.

2. Workstation Design

We designed the Ergonomic Workstation to provide students Human Factors and Work Measurement and Design courses with a device to perform experiments under a wide range of work conditions such as variable work heights, variable tilt angles, and variable reach distances (see Figure 1). Using the workstation, students can evaluate a given task under specified conditions, then redesign the layout, height, tilt angle, and/or depth of the task in order to maximize both the ergonomic conditions and the efficiency of the task. In this way, students gain the hands on experience they need to truly understand ergonomic principles and their importance in design.

The Ergonomic Workstation provides height adjustment, depth adjustment, tilt adjustment, and an acrylic work surface. The height adjustment mechanism was designed and built to accommodate the first percentile woman through the ninety-ninth percentile man. This range allows students to perform the tasks both inside and outside the acceptable ergonomic range in order to demonstrate the effects on performance and the human body of performing taks under both favorable and unfavorable ergonomic conditions. To achieve the height range that was necessary, the landing gear from a tractor-trailer was used. This provided adjustment from the first percentile woman (33.6 in) to a height of 50.875 inches -- well beyond the 44.6 inches necessary to accommodate the ninety-ninth percentile man. A simple hand crank is used to raise and lower the workstation.

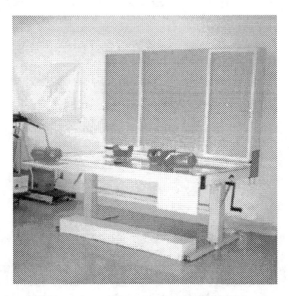

Figure 1. Ergonomic Workstation

To make the work surface adjustable with respect to tilt angle, we designed and built the tilt angle mechanism to provide tilt angles of 0, 5, 10, 15, and 20 degrees. The mechanism allows the freedom to experiment with different tilt angles to see the effects on the human body and on performance for a variety of tasks. The tilt angle design was modeled after a lounge chair that one would often use at a pool or a beach. Two iron bars placed on the under side of the workstation have grooves cut to provide all the possible tilt angles. When the workstation top is lifted, the grooves on the tilt angle bar slip onto an iron bar attached to the underside of the workstation.

We also designed the workstation to provide variable reach distance and vertical as well as horizontal work areas. We achieved both through the use of a Depth Adjustment Mechanism. This device works as a movable "wall" that can roll along the outside edge of the Ergonomic Workstation and be secured in place with eyebolts. This allows students to vary the reach distance to see its effects on the given task. The "wall" was built as a shelving unit with pegboard attached to the front. Various items such as small shelves, hangers, or control/display consoles can be attached to the pegboard and easily moved. The pegboard on the "wall" was attached in three sections so that the outside two sections could be angled in at a 45 degree angle.

The work area of the Ergonomic Workstation was also designed with flexibility in mind. The work area consists of a frame, a wood surface, and an acrylic surface. The acrylic surface is attached to the wood surface with hinges that allows templates to be placed beneath the acrylic. These templates are often used as the starting layout of an experiment. However, the acrylic work surface allows students to redesign their layout by drawing the new layout directly on the acrylic surface using dry-erase markers. When they are finished, the students can wipe the acrylic work area clean. The size of the work area was also designed to accommodate the reach and work areas of the first percentile woman through the ninety-ninth percentile man. In addition, side work areas on the workstation provide students with more flexibility in their design.

3. Laboratory Experiments

The design criteria for the experiments were as follows: each experiment must demonstrate ergonomic principles; each experiment must utilize the workstation; each experiment must offer a design element to the Human Factors students. With these criteria in mind, four experiments (The Ergonomic/Time Study, Assembly Line, Rapid Upper Limb Assessment Survey, and Control Panel) were developed to be used in conjunction with the workstation.

The Ergonomic/Time Study experiment requires students to design a layout for placing pegs in a pegboard and to determine his or her proper work area. The student must then perform the task in the preferred work area, outside the normal reach area, and within the overall work area. A time study is used to determine the effects of the work area on performance. The student is also to perform the task in the proper work area and vary the height of the workstation below the correct height, at the correct height, and above the correct height. Students must also use time studies to analyze the effects of varying work heights on performance. In addition, subjective evaluations of posture and body position are recorded by the students.

The Assembly Line experiment provides an existing layout and process for the task of packing small boxes in their appropriate places within a larger box. Students are required to perform a series of time studies to evaluate the layout, work method, and workstation settings. After completing a given number of trials, the students redesign the layout and work method, and make any necessary adjustments to workstation settings. Additional time studies are then conducted to evaluate the effectiveness of the new design.

The Rapid Upper Limb Assessment Survey (RULA) is a screening tool that evaluates the risk factors of posture, static muscle contraction, repetitive motion and force relative to a specific job [1]. In this experiment, students use the survey to evaluate these factors for the task of assembling a flashlight. Using the RULA survey, students evaluate body posture and angles of limbs to determine the hazard of cumulative trauma injuries associated with the task. The student then redesigns the workstation layout and work methods in an attempt to improve the RULA survey score.

The Control Panel experiment provides the students with a given layout for a control panel, and a scenario which briefly explains the process that is being controlled. As one student reads the scenario, the other student must listen for instructions and problems. The student must react promptly, adjusting the controls as necessary to alleviate the problems. A third student is responsible for recording response time and error rates. The students then redesign the control panel layout (move controls and labels, change the types of switches, etc.). The original scenario is repeated to demonstrate the effectiveness of a properly designed control panel.

Each of the experiments was tested by five teams of engineering students. During testing, the laboratory instructions were followed, and the required data was recorded. For each of the trials, at least one of the design team members was present to observe the students. By observing the students as they attempted each experiment, we determined which instructions were not being followed as intended and identified areas of confusion. In addition, students were encouraged to critique the experiments, the instructions, and the workstation itself. This student feedback was crucial in determining areas which needed clarification and led to significant improvements in the design of the experiments.

4. Conclusion - Using the Ergonomic Workstation

The Ergonomic Workstation was first used in the Human Factors laboratory in the fall quarter of 1996. The first three experiments described in the previous section were assigned to students in the Work Measurement and Design class. Using these experiments, students explored the effect of ergonomic design decisions on body posture, fatigue, and the time required to complete a task. The large work area allowed students to design and test layouts and work methods both inside and outside the normal and preferred work areas, while the adjustable work height and work angle allowed them to evaluate the effect of working under a variety of conditions. The workstation also proved useful to students as they completed their term projects, which involved designing an assembly process for a toy manufacturer. Using the workstation, student design teams were able to implement and test individual workstation designs for the assembly line, and perform time studies to determine how long each task in the assembly process should take.

In the future, we expect to expand our use of the Ergonomic Workstation in the Human Factors/Work Measurement laboratory. The four experiments designed as part of the senior design project form a good foundation for other explorations with respect to the design of workstations and work methods. In addition, the flexibility of the workstation will make it an excellent platform for experiments involving a variety of aspects of human-machine interaction, as illustrated by the control panel experiment described in the previous section.

Reference

[1] ErgoWeb, Inc. Demo Version: Introduction to the Rapid Upper Limb Assessment Survey (RULA). http://www.ergoweb.com/Pub/Demo/Rula.

12. Muscular Fatigue and Electromyography

Advances in Occupational Ergonomics and Safety II
Edited by Biman Das and Waldemar Karwowski
IOS Press and Ohmsha, 1997

Prediction of Localized Muscle Fatigue: I. Discriminant Analysis Approach

S. M. Waly[1] , S.S. Asfour[2], T.M. Khalil[2], and F. E. Garcia[1]

[1]*Department of Industrial & Manufacturing Systems Engineering*
Louisiana State University, Baton Rouge, Louisiana 70803
and
[2]*Department of Industrial Engineering, University of Miami*
Coral Gables, Florida 33124

ABSTRACT

The main objective of this study was to develop, test, and validate statistical models for the detection and prediction of muscle fatigue associated with sustained muscle contraction. Eighteen healthy male subjects participated in this study. The EMG signal was recorded from the onset of the load under investigation (rest) until the subject could not hold the load anymore (fatigue). Discriminant analysis was used successfully to develop a pattern classification model for the detection of local muscle fatigue. The models developed were tested and validated. The results of these validation procedures showed that the model performs well.

1. Introduction

Muscle fatigue has been associated with such external manifestations as the inability to maintain a desired force output, muscular tremor, and localized pain. Surface electromyography (EMG) has been extensively used to study and detect localized muscle fatigue. Many investigators studied the characteristics of the myoelectric signals (ME) to quantify localized muscle fatigue. Analysis of the ME signal, detected on the surface of the skin over a muscle, has been extensively employed. The frequency components of the surface myoelectric signal have been known to decrease when a contraction is sustained. Shift toward lower frequencies has been observed often and in a variety of muscles under different loading conditions. Many other investigators have also noted an increase in signal amplitude. Despite the noteworthy achievements in this area, more research is required to develop reliable techniques for the detection and prediction of muscle fatigue.

One of the major problems encountered in the application of surface electromyography as a non-invasive tool for monitoring muscle fatigue is relying on simple descriptive statistics to examine and report time and frequency domain parameters. The study reported by Houshmand and Herrin (1989) is the only attempt of a thorough examination of the statistical nature of the spectral components of the myoelectric signal. Statistical pattern recognition approach was used to classify the muscle condition into fatigued or rested states [1]. The relatively small sample size, the use of a fixed time rather than reaching the actual fatigued state, and fixing the amount of load held instead of a percentage of the maximum voluntary contraction for each individual are some of the problems that make it difficult to generalize the results of this study.

The main objective of the present study was to develop, test, and validate statistical models for the prediction of muscle fatigue associated with sustained muscle contraction. In this study, the effects of heavy isometric loading (maximum and 80% of the maximum) on the recorded EMG were investigated. Also, the effect of electrode orientation on the detection of muscle fatigue during heavy isometric loading was investigated.

2. EMG Signal Processing and Interpretation

The ME signal is an exceedingly complicated signal which is affected by the anatomical and physiological properties of muscles, the control scheme of the peripheral nervous system as well as the characteristics of instrumentation that is used to detect and observe it. In general, the utilization of the complicated EMG signals depends on the ability to extract useful features that describe the signal in both the time and frequency domains. In the present study, the recorded EMG signals were analyzed using MATLAB® numeric computation software and its signal processing toolbox developed by the MATH WORKS, Inc. Both time and frequency domain analyses were conducted. In this study, the full wave rectified integral (FWRI) and the root mean square (RMS) values were estimated in the time domain analysis. In the frequency domain analysis, the estimated power spectrum and its characteristic fractile frequencies were calculated. The characteristic frequencies used in this study were 1, 5, 10, 25, 50, 75, 90, 95, 99 fractile frequency, and the peak frequency.

3. Methods and Procedures

Eighteen healthy male subjects with no history of musculoskeletal injuries participated in this study. All subjects were selected on a voluntary basis from the student population or having sedentary life style. They represented a wide spectrum of body weights, heights, age, and muscle strengths. They ranged in age between 22 and 40 years with a mean value of 27.2 years. Subjects weights ranged from 53.2 kg to 105.9 kg (117 to 233 lbs) with a mean value of 75.86 kg (166.89 lbs). Heights ranged from 160 cm to 187.5 cm (5' 4" to 6' 3") with a mean value of 172.5 cm (5' 9"). All subjects volunteered to participate in this study and were informed about the experiment in advance.

All subjects were required to perform a static muscle effort corresponding to a predetermined load level. The load was applied to permit static contraction of the biceps brachii muscle. The load was placed in the dominant hand of each subject with the upper arm hanging freely in a neutral adducted position to the side of the body. The forearm was flexed at $90°$ at the elbow joint. The wrist was maintained in a straight neutral position with hand supinated to support the load. The load consisted of a bar and two balanced weights attached to both sides of the bar. Two levels of loading were studied. These loads were set to the maximum amount of weight the individual can hold for a few seconds (3-5 seconds) and 80% of the maximum weight. The maximum weight was determined on a separate day prior to the experimental sessions. Subjects were instructed to hold the weight, as described earlier, as long as possible. EMG was recorded from the biceps brachii muscle using two sets of electrodes simultaneously. One set was placed along the muscle fibers and the other across the muscle fibers. EMG was recorded from the onset of the load under investigation until the subject could not hold the load anymore.

Mainly two sets of dependent variables, obtained from time and frequency domain analyses, were used in this investigation. The routine use of a separate Analysis of Variance (ANOVA) for each dependent variable introduces the question of the effect(s) of multiple comparisons on statistical decision errors. The strategy outlined by Hummel and Sligo (1971) was used in the present study [2]. They demonstrated that routine use of ANOVA for each dependent variable, following a significant overall Multivariate Analysis of Variance (MANOVA), resulted in probability values that were close to the desired α levels. The statistical analysis system package (SAS®) was used to perform all needed analysis.

4. Results

As mentioned earlier, full wave rectified integral (FWRI) and root mean square (RMS) were the two parameters used for the time domain analysis. Load, electrode orientation and muscle condition (rest or fatigue) were the independent variables, while FWRI and RMS were the response variables of this experiment. MANOVA results showed lack of statistical significance at the 0.05 level for the all interactions and main effects of the three independent variables. It is worth noting that placing the electrodes along the muscle fibers resulted in higher amplitudes than placing the electrodes across the muscle fibers. However, these differences did not meet the significance level (p=0.0664).

The peak frequency and fractile frequencies of the estimated power spectrum were the response parameters used for the frequency domain analysis. MANOVA results showed no statistical significance at the 0.05 level for the all interactions of the three independent variables. Both electrode orientation and muscle condition showed statistical significance at the 0.01 level. No significant effect for the load was observed.

In view of the significant MANOVA findings of these main effects, univariate F tests were performed on the dependent variables separately. These ANOVAs showed that electrode orientation has a significant effect on the peak frequency, 1st, 5th, 10th, 25th, and 99th fractile frequencies. It is worth noting that electrode orientation has mainly a significant effect on the lower frequencies. The muscle condition (rest vs. fatigue) was found to be significant for all characteristic frequencies used in this study.

Discriminant analysis was used to develop a classification model of the muscle state of rest or fatigue. Only the characteristic frequencies were used in this analysis since the time domain parameters did not show significant change as a result of fatigue. Two separate models were developed for the two electrode orientation studied. Fifteen subjects were selected at random for the development of these models, while the remaining three subjects were used to validate the models. This validation approach was used to avoid an upward bias in the classification accuracy. Evaluation of the classification accuracy was based on the percentage of correct classification compared to those expected by chance. It has been recommended that classification accuracy should be at least 25% greater than classification chance [3]. In this study with a chance accuracy of 50%, the minimum acceptable classification accuracy should be at least 62.5%.

The two models obtained showed similar results in terms of their ability to classify the observations correctly. When the data set used for the development of the model was applied to the model, 83% and 77% correct classification was obtained for the model based on electrodes along and across the muscle fibers respectively. Using the validation data set, both models showed a correct classification rate of 83% (10 out of twelve). It is worth noting that these models were based on all characteristic frequencies used in the present study. Backward elimination stepwise discriminant analysis was conducted to eliminate variables that have little or no significant contribution to the discriminant model(s). The reduced model based on electrodes along the muscle fibers showed a better ability to classify the observations correctly. When the data set used for the development of the model was applied to the reduced model, 85% and 76.7% correct classification was obtained for the model based on electrodes along and across the muscle fibers respectively. Using the validation data set, these models showed a correct classification rate of 75% and 66.7% respectively. To further validate this model, the experiment was repeated (additional two trials for the two loads) and the model was applied to classify the muscle condition. The results of this second validation showed a correct classification rate of 85%.

5. Conclusions

(1)   The time domain parameters did not show statistical significance at the 0.05 level for the all interactions and main effects of the three independent variables (load, electrode orientation and muscle condition of rest or fatigue).

(2)   The effects of electrode orientation on the FWRI and RMS values showed that placing the electrodes along the muscle fibers resulted in higher amplitudes than placing the electrodes across the muscle fibers. However, these differences did not meet the significance level (p=0.0664). Further investigations are needed to study these effects.

(3)   The frequency domain parameters were significantly affected by the main effects of electrode orientation and muscle condition.

(4)   Electrodes placed across the muscle fibers showed lower fractile frequencies compared to electrodes along the muscle fibers. The effect of electrode orientation was only significant for the lower fractiles with the exception of the 99th fractile (peak frequency, 1, 5, 10, 25, and 99 fractile).

(5)   The effect of muscle fatigue was significant for all the characteristic frequencies used. The shift in these frequencies was not linear across the spectrum. Therefore, monitoring a single characteristic frequency may not be adequate for the quantification of the spectrum shift.

(6)   Discriminant analysis was used successfully to develop a pattern classification model for the detection of local muscle fatigue. The models developed were tested and validated. The results of these validation procedures showed that the model performs well.

(7)   The results obtained in this study showed that the median frequency decreases significantly with fatigue. Also, the median frequency was not significantly affected by electrode orientation (p=0.0532). However, the discriminant analysis results showed that the median frequency is not among the characteristic frequencies that can be used to classify the muscle condition into fatigue or rest conditions.

6. References

[1] Houshmand, A.A. and Herrin, G.D. Discriminant analysis of electromyographic signals for detection of local muscular fatigue. In: Advances in Industrial Ergonomics and Safety I, edited by A. Mital, London: Taylor & Francis, 1989

[2] Hummel, T.J. and Sligo, R.J. Empirical comparisons of univariate and multivariate analysis of variance procedures. Psychological Bulletin 76:49-57, 1971

[3] Hair, J.F., Anderson, R.E., Tatham, R.L. and Grablowsky, B.J. Multivariate Data Analysis, Oklahoma, Pertroleum Publishing Company, 1979

Advances in Occupational Ergonomics and Safety II
Edited by Biman Das and Waldemar Karwowski
IOS Press and Ohmsha, 1997

Prediction of Localized Muscle Fatigue:
II. A Learning Vector Quantization Approach

F. E. Garcia[1], S. M. Waly[1], S. S. Asfour[2], and T. M. Khalil[2]

[1]*Department of Industrial & Manufacturing Systems Engineering*
Louisiana State University, Baton Rouge, Louisiana 70803

and

[2]*Department of Industrial Engineering*
University of Miami, Coral Gables, Florida 33124

ABSTRACT

The main objective of the study was to develop, test, and validate a pattern classification method for the detection and prediction of muscle fatigue associated with sustained muscle contraction. To achieve the objectives of this research, a pattern classification method based on Learning Vector Quantization (LVQ) was used. This method allows for the clustering of the EMG signal into two muscles conditions: fatigue and rest. The LVQ was trained and tested using a data set containing the EMG signals of eighteen subjects. Classification features were based on nine fractiles of the power spectrum (1,5,10,25,50,75,90,95,99).

The results obtained showed that the LVQ model's performance was better with the electrode's orientation parallel to the muscle fibers. Furthermore, the LVQ's predictability did not suffer when compared across different subjects as well as different trials. In every case, the inclusion of both measurements of electrodes dramatically improved the performance of the LVQ.

1. Introduction

Eighteen healthy male subjects with history of musculoskeletal injuries participated in this study. All subjects were required to perform a static muscle effort corresponding to a predetermined load level. The load was applied to permit static contraction of the biceps brachii muscle. Two levels of loading were studied. These loads were set to the maximum amount of weight the individual can hold for a few seconds (3-5) seconds and 80% of the maximum weight. The EMG signal was recorded from the onset of the load under investigation until the subject could not hold the load anymore. Then, the nine fractiles of the power spectrum (1,5,10,25,50,75,90,95,99) were calculated at each muscle state (rest and fatigue) for the two electrodes' orientation across and along the muscle. A more detailed description of the data collection and analysis can be found elsewhere [1,2].

2. Learning Vector Quantization

Given four sets of data with known states, this paper attempts to classify EMG signals for the states: rest and fatigue. This attempt was aided through the use of neural nets. The specific algorithm was based on the Learning Vector Quantization (LVQ) approach. The LVQ was chosen as the method of analysis because data is clustered according to the similarity of the other data inputs. The layout of the algorithm utilized in this study is illustrated in Figure 1 [3].

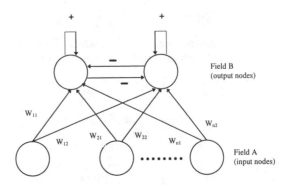

Figure 1. The LVQ layout (modified from Rao and Rao, 1995).
Field A has either 9 or 18 nodes.

In aiding the training of the LVQ, a 'conscious mechanism' was included in the algorithm (see steps 4 - 7 in the algorithm). For each state, the signal was broken down into nine percentiles per electrode with the frequency given as an average of that fractile. Each frequency was placed in a vector totaling 9 elements for each state. This vector was used as the input to the LVQ. The output node was two nodes having only two possible outcomes. The values for node 1 and node 2 were 1,0 for rest and 0,1 for fatigue respectively.

When training and testing for both electrodes combined, the input vector would have 18 nodes with the first nine nodes encompassing the fractiles for 'across' and the second nine for the electrode along the muscle.

LVQ Algorithm Nomenclature:

X	training vector $[X_1, \ldots, X_n]$.
T	correct category for the training vector.
W_{ij}	for the jth output unit and the ith
Z_j	category represented by the jth output.
i	index of input nodes
j	index of output nodes
J	the winning output node
m	number of output nodes
n	number of input nodes
γ	constant value
β	constant value
d_j	Euclidean distance between input and weight vector for j^{th} output vector.

Modified LVQ Algorithm: [3,4]

Step 0. Initialize: Weight vector W_{ij} to small random values.
Step 1. While stopping condition is false, do Steps 2-9.
Step 2. For each training vector X, do Steps 3-8.
Step 3. Find *J* so that $d_j = || X - W_{ij} ||$ is a minimum.
Step 4. Compute the outputs of the nodes.

        $Z_j = 1$ if output node is *J*
        $Z_j = 0$ if output node is not *J*

Step 5. For each node, compute a term representing the fraction of times that it wins the competition, where β is a positive constant: $f_j^{new} = f_j^{old} + \beta (Z_j - f_j^{old})$
Step 6. For each node, calculate a "guilt" value, where γ is a positive constant: $g_j = \gamma (1/m - f_j)$
Step 7. Hold a second competition among the nodes to determine which has the smallest value of ($d_j - g_j$). Declare the winning node with the minimum value as the new *J*.
Step 8. Update W_{iJ} as follows: if $T = Z_J$ then $W_{iJ}^{new} = W_{iJ}^{old} + \alpha [X - W_{iJ}^{old}]$
                                  if $T \neq Z_J$ then $W_{iJ}^{new} = W_{iJ}^{old} - \alpha [X - W_{iJ}^{old}]$
Step 9. Test stopping condition.

For the LVQs trained, the constant values were: $\gamma = 10$, $\beta = 0.0001$, m=2, and n=9 or 18. The learning rate α was set to 0.2, and the initial weights were randomized to values between 0.25 and 0.25. The stopping condition was convergence or oscillation.

3. Results

First, the neural net was trained with two sets : one with maximum load (Trials 1&2) and one with 80% (Trials 3&4) of maximum. It was tested with the remaining two sets. The LVQ was trained and tested with all the possible combinations of trials that contained maximum load and 80% of load. These are the results from the application of the LVQ:

Table 1. Training and testing across trials.

Electrode Orientation	Training Trials	Accuracy	Testing Trials	Accuracy
Across	1&3	70.83%	2&4	72.22%
Across	1&4	72.22%	2&3	70.83%
Across	2&3	70.83%	1&4	70.83%
Across	2&4	72.22%	1&3	70.83%
Along	1&3	83.33%	2&4	86.11%
Along	1&4	84.72%	2&3	79.17%
Along	2&3	79.17%	1&4	80.56%
Along	2&4	84.72%	1&3	77.78%
Both	1&3	100.00%	2&4	100.00%
Both	1&4	100.00%	2&3	100.00%
Both	2&3	100.00%	1&4	100.00%
Both	2&4	100.0 0%	1&3	100.00%

As expected, the electrode across the muscle predicted the worst, followed by the electrode along the muscle. Using both electrodes as input to the LVQ, results were expected to be better than either one by itself. However, 100% accuracy was not expected.

Next an attempt was made to determine if the LVQ model was capable of producing similar results (see Table 1) that were independent of subjects. To perform this task, 13 subjects' data was chosen at random to be used to train the LVQ. The remaining 5 subjects' data was used for testing. All trials performed by each subject was is used both training and testing the LVQ.

Table 2. Training and testing across subjects.

Electrode Orientation	Training Accuracy	Previous Average*	Testing Accuracy	Previous Average*
Across	71.15%	71.53%	72.50%	71.18%
Along	79.81%	82.99%	80.00%	80.91%
Both	100.00%	100.00%	100.00%	100.00%

Again, the best results were found using both electrodes; and, the electrode across the muscle predicted the worst, followed by the electrode along the muscle. Furthermore, this attempt produced similar results as the previous attempt as evidenced when comparing the average of the previous training and testing accuracy (see Table 2 denoted with a *).

4. Conclusion

The results obtained showed that the LVQ model's performance was better with the electrode parallel to the muscle fibers. Furthermore, the LVQ's predictability did not suffer when compared across different subjects as well as different trials. In every case, the inclusion of both measurements of electrodes dramatically improved the performance of the LVQ. In conclusion, the LVQ is effective for prediction of muscle fatigue.

5. References

[1] Waly, S. M., Analysis and Prediction of Localized Muscle Fatigue Isometric Muscle Contraction. Unpublished Ph. D. Dissertation U. of Miami, (1994).

[2] Waly, S. M., Asfour, S. S., Khalil, T. M., and Garcia, F. E., Prediction of Localized Muscle Fatigue: I. Discriminant Analysis Approach, *Advances in Occupational Ergonomics and Safety* II (1997).

[3] Rao, H. and Rao, V., C++ Neural Networks and Fuzzy Logic. ISBN: 1 55851552 6. MIS Press, N.Y, 1995, pp. 115-117, 302.

[4] Fausett, L., Fundamentals of Neural Networks: Architectures, Algorithms, and Applications. ISBN: 0 13 334186 0. Prentice-Hall, Englewood Cliffs, NJ, 1994, pp.187-195.

Advances in Occupational Ergonomics and Safety II
Edited by Biman Das and Waldemar Karwowski
IOS Press and Ohmsha, 1997

Electromyographic Assessment of Prehensile Hand Function and Muscle Control

Bryan BUCHHOLZ

Department of Work Environment, University of Massachusetts Lowell, One University Avenue, Lowell, MA 01854, USA

Abstract. The purpose of this study was to examine the effect of object size on the force-producing capabilities of the hand, in order that hand tools might be optimally designed. Fine-wire electromyography (EMG) was used to ascertain the activity of the muscles that move the long finger. An adjustable hand force dynamometer using strain gage applications was employed to directly measure phalangeal components of power grip force. Sub-maximal as well as maximal contractions were evaluated. Almost all of the subjects exerted about half of their total power grip force with their distal phalange. Flexor Digitorum Profundus was the primary active muscle throughout the prehensile tests, although Flexor Digitorum Superficialis was generally active as well. Both muscles' activities increased linearly with grip force. Extensor Digitorum Communis was, in general, not active until the grip force levels approached maximum. The Interossei were usually active at low levels that increased with grip force, with variability that may have been related to the control necessary to maintain a specified level of grip force.

1. Introduction

One of the most important functions of the hand is its ability to apply force to other objects. This is apparent in the many prehensile activities of daily living. The ability of the hand to produce force is related to its posture and also to the posture of the wrist. The postures of the hand and therefore its strength capabilities are in part determined by the size and shape of the object grasped and partly by the requirements of the task. There are two basic reasons for this: 1) Physiological - The change in contractile capabilities of the muscles as they change in length and 2) Biomechanical - The change in tendon moment arm length with changing hand posture, as well as the change in moment arm length of the grip forces.

The purpose of this study was to look at these phenomena by measuring the strength capabilities of the hand in different prehensile tasks using both strain gage applications and electromyographic (EMG) techniques. The major objective of this project was to quantify the relative contribution of each of the finger muscles to force production in various gripping functions.

Electromyography (EMG) has been used for over forty years to analyze muscular function. Early investigations [1,2,3] found that integrated EMGs (iEMG) increased in a nearly linear fashion with muscle tension. More recent work indicated that the relationship between iEMG and muscle tension is more curvilinear in shape [4] and often described using a power function or piece-wise linear regressions [5], though linear regression can be used to acceptably approximate a large portion of the sub-maximal range of this relationship [6].

Long *et al.* (1960, 1961, 1962 and 1964) [7,8,9,10] carried out detailed studies of the unloaded movements of the long finger using EMG. Long *et al.* (1970) [11] continued this work by using EMG to qualitatively study the activity of the muscles moving the fingers in both power grip and precision handling. They found that lexor digitorum profundus (FDP) is the primary flexor in free motion, with the interossei and flexor digitorum superficialis (FDS) activities increasing with grip force. Interossei activity increases for spherical grasps and when rotation of the finger joints is resisted. The lumbricals are not, in general, active when FDP is. They looked at squeeze grasps on three cylinders with diameters of 1.3, 2.5 and 5.0 cm for maximum and half-maximum contractions.

2. Methods

Nine (six male and three female) subjects participated in the study. Subjects ranged in age from 25 to 33 years.

Fine-wire electromyography (EMG) was used to simultaneously ascertain the activity of the muscles and their specific digitations that move the long finger. The muscles studied were: flexor digitorum profundus (FDP), flexor digitorum superficialis (FDS), extensor digitorum communis (EDC) and the second (RI, radial interosseous) and third (UI, ulnar interosseous) dorsal interossei. The second lumbricalis muscle was not included partly because of its small size and partly because previous research [11] indicated that it was not active in prehensile activities. Tests designed to elicit a response from both the desired muscle and muscles adjacent to the desired muscle were performed to confirm electrode placement. Similar tests were used to normalize the EMG data to percent of maximal voluntary contraction (%MVC).

A hand force dynamometer using strain gage applications was employed to directly measure phalangeal components of power grip force. This dynamometer was similar to ones used by other researchers [12,13]. The dynamometer had three separate sensing beams using strain gages as force transducers. The strain gage beams were mounted on a fixture for a specific cylinder diameter and the location of the beams were adjustable so that the contact pad could be centered on each of the three phalanges of a single finger. A solid cylinder of the desired diameter with a slot cut out of it for the phalangeal pads was also mounted on the fixture. The dynamometer was adjustable in size, so that it could represent circular cylinders with diameters of 3.18, 3.81, 4.45 and 7.62 cm. Subjects were given visual feedback on their grip force level and asked to hold a specified level of sub-maximal force for approximately one second, then to increase their force to a second specified level and hold it, continuing this process through two more force levels until finally they would exert a maximal contraction. The levels that were used were approximately 10, 20, 30, 50 and 100% of MVC.

The EMG signals were amplified using custom-built pre-amplifiers and then amplified and integrated using a RMS (root-mean-square) integrator with a 55 msec time constant in a custom-built amplifier. The signal from the amplifier was digitized using a twelve-bit analog-to-digital (A/D) converter (MetraByte DAS-16) and stored on a microcomputer. Both raw and RMS-integrated EMG signals were digitized and stored. External force data from the dynamometer was also digitized simultaneously with the EMG.

3. Results and Discussion

Data from the power grasp dynamometer for a typical trial are shown in Figure 1. Almost all of the subjects exerted a majority of their power grasp force with the distal phalange, the proximal phalange exerted the second most force, and the least force was generated by the distal phalange. Similar results have been found previously by other researchers [12, 13].

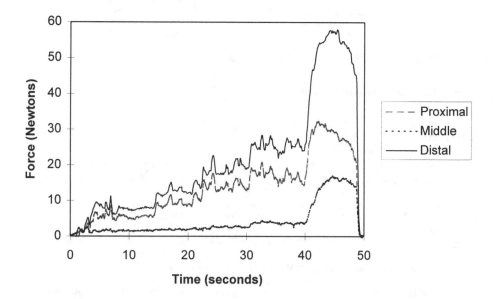

Figure 1 - Dynamometer data for a typical power grasp trial.

Electromyographic data for the same trial are shown in Figure 2. FDP was the primary active muscle throughout the prehensile tests, although FDS was generally active as well. The activity of FDP increased linearly with grip force, while FDS showed a linear increase for sub-maximal contractions and a greater increase as the maximum was approached. EDC was, in general, active only at low levels until the grip force levels approached maximum. Though the data in Figure 2 indicate a background activity of 5-10% MVC for EDC, this was not the usual case. The Interossei (RI and UI) were usually active at extremely low levels that increased with grip force. There was inter-subject variability for RI and UI that may have been related to the control necessary to maintain a specified level of grip force. These results confirm the work of Long et al. [11].

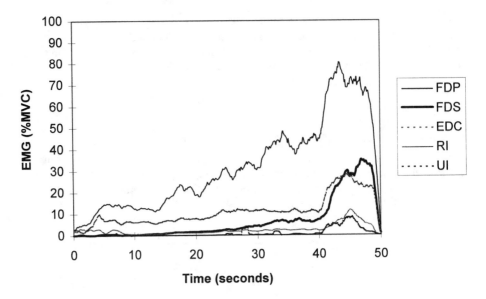

Figure 2 - Electromyographic data for a typical power grasp trial.

References

[1] H.J. Ralston, M.J. Polissar, V.T. Inman, J.R. Close and B. Feinstein, Dynamic features of human isolated voluntary muscle in isometric and free contractions, *Journal of Applied Physiology* 1 (1949) 526-533.

[2] V.T. Inman, H.J. Ralston, J.B. Saunders, B. Feinstein and E.W. Wright, Relation of human electromyogram to muscular tension, *Electroencephalography and Clinical Neurophysiology* 4 (1952) 187-194.

[3] O.C.J. Lippold, The relation between integrated action potentials in human muscle and its isometric tension, *Journal of Physiology* 117 (1952) 492-499.

[4] E.N. Zuniga and D.G. Simons, Nonlinear relationship between averaged electromyogram potential and muscle tension in normal subjects, *Archives of Physical Medicine and Rehabilitation* 50 (1969) 613-620.

[5] D.B. Chaffin, M. Lee and A. Freivalds, Muscle strength assessment for EMG analysis, *Medical Science in Sports and Exercise* 12 (1980) 205-211.

[6] T.J. Armstrong, D.B. Chaffin and J.A. Foulke, A methodology for documenting hand positions and forces during manual work, *Journal of Biomechanics* 12 (1979) 131-133.

[7] C. Long, M.E. Brown and G. Weiss, Electromyographic study of extrinsic-intrinsic kinesiology of the hand: Preliminary report, *Archives of Physical Medicine* 41 (1960) 175-181.

[8] C. Long, M.E. Brown and G. Weiss, Electromyographic kinesiology of the hand: Part II. Third dorsal interosseous and extensor digitorum of the long finger, *Archives of Physical Medicine* 42 (1961) 559-565.

[9] C. Long and M.E. Brown, Electromyographic kinesiology of the hand: Part III. Lumbricalis and flexor digitorum profundus to the long finger, *Archives of Physical Medicine* 43(1962) 450-460.

[10] C. Long and M.E. Brown, Electromyographic kinesiology of the hand: Muscles moving the long finger, *Journal of Bone and Joint Surgery* 46A (1964) 1683-1706.

[11] C. Long, P.W. Conrad, E.A. Hall and S.L. Furler, Intrinsic-extrinsic muscle control of the hand in power grip and precision handling, *Journal of Bone and Joint Surgery* 52A (1970) 853-867.

[12] A.A. Amis, Variation of finger forces in maximal isometric grasp tests on a range of cylinder diameters, *Journal of Biomedical Engineering* 9 (1987) 313-320.

[13] K.N. An, E.Y.S. Chao and L.J. Askew, Hand strength measurement instruments, *Archives of Physical Medicine and Rehabilitation* 61 (1980) 366-368.

Advances in Occupational Ergonomics and Safety II
Edited by Biman Das and Waldemar Karwowski
IOS Press and Ohmsha, 1997

Increase in Muscular Demand in Reponse to the Handling of Loads of Unpredictable Weight

Denis MARCHAND[1], Yves BEAUCHAMP[2], Marc BÉLANGER[1] and Beata MARSENZKA[1]

1. Université du Québec à Montréal
2. École de Technologie Supérieure
C.P. 8888, succursale Centre-Ville, Montréal, Canada, H3C 3P8

Abstract. In ergonomics, the problems associated with random tasks are seldom studied so as to enable to quantify the muscular costs entailed by such unpredictability. Bouisset and Zattara (1981, 1987) have shown that the performance of a movement likely to cause a postural imbalance is always accompanied by a preactivation of the axial muscles. The function of these anticipative postural adjustments is to reduce the disruption of the body's balance in intentional movements. The goal of our study was to establish and measure the variance level of muscular preactivation according to the unpredictable weight of the load to be handled. The subjects' task was to lift loads whose weight varied randomly at each trial. The subjects performed three series of tests comprised of three load levels [block 1 (2.3, 9.1, 15.9 kg); block 2 (4.5, 9.1, 13.6 kg); block 3 (6.8, 9.1, 11.4 kg)]. The muscles evaluated by EMG were the gastrocnemius, the biceps femoris, the sacrospinalis and the biceps brachii. Our results show that the lifter's uncertainty causes a superactivation of the axial muscles responsible for postural control. Moreover, uncertainty has the effect of increasing muscular activation when there are greater (random) differences in weight at each trial. This situation requires an increased expenditure of energy compared to the control situation where the weight is known before handling. Our results explain the importance of eliminating unpredictable situations.

Introduction

For problems related to repetitive load handling, traditional biomechanical studies have often been limited to impact of object's weight, the number of repetition and to different postures adopted within the environmental constraints (Armstrong et al., 1986, Zetterberg et al., 1987). This approach does not take into account the existence of anticipated control mechanisms which take place prior to the onset of load elevation. In this context, the notion of uncertainty refers to situations in which the available information does not allow for the adequate planning of an efficient movement execution. In fact, when the manipulated load is quite variable and unknown to the handler (e.g., garbage men, movers, etc...), these workers have some difficulties in adequately organizing the muscular activity for the intended movement. Consequently, if the load uncertainty increases the muscular demand, it becomes important to measure how this demand changes when the level of uncertainty is varied. Belinkii et al. (1967) were the first to demonstrate the existence of postural activity preceding and accompanying a voluntary movement such as a rapid elevation of the upper limbs. They noted that muscular activity responsible for stabilizing the posture began 40-60 ms before the onset of movement (i.e., muscular activity responsible for shoulder flexion). The role of these anticipated postural adjustments is to minimize the perturbation of the body's equilibrium which is linked to the intentional movements (Bouisset, et al., 1981, 1987). In general, the efficiency of the anticipated postural adjustments can be observed for intentional, well planned movements. However, certain work conditions can sometimes be difficult to predict (e.g., unexpected load, slippery floor, etc, ...). The stabilization during conditions which leads to postural instability is generally accomplished by the co-contraction of agonist and antagonist muscles. A study by Callaghan et McGill (1995) suggests that motor control of the trunk muscles (i.e., abdominal and dorsal) in not organized to allow for the reduction of the forces exerted on the lumbar segment of the spinal cord. The co-contraction of trunk muscles would principally serve to increase the rigidity of vertebral column and thus, prevent buckling (Crisco et al., 1992). These results demonstrate that uncertainty causes an overload of the axial muscles that are responsible for the postural control. This leads to an increase in muscular demand when the level of activation of the axial muscles (used to stabilize the posture) exceed the real demand required to do the task.

Methodology

Seven subjects participated in the experiment. The subject's task consisted of lifting loads which were randomly varied from one trial to another. The uncertainty in the load to be handled was created by different loading of the same container (i.e., box). Modification of the loads was obscured from the subjects. To measure the effect of the uncertainty level, subjects performed 3 blocks of 27 trials, each block consisting of 9 manipulations of 3 different loads. Blocks were randomly assigned for each subject in order to control for sequencing effects. Seven different load levels were used for each subject [block 1 (2.5, 10, 17.5 kg); block 2 (5, 10, 15 kg); block 3 (7.5, 10, 12.5 kg)]. Each block was preceded by control trials in which the subject had to perform 3 lifts of the loads presented in the block that followed. The onset of the lift was measured by strain gauges placed on the support handles of the load container (see the vertical dashed line at 100 ms in Figure 1). Surface electromyography (EMG) was used to measure the muscular demand for the postural control (Gastronemius Medialis - GM, Biceps Femoris - BF, and Sacrospinalis - SS) and for the load handling (Biceps brachii - BB). The skin overlying the muscle of interest was cleaned with alcohol swabs before the placement of the electrodes. The electrodes were placed place on the medial part of the muscle and followed the fiber orientation. The raw EMG signals were preamplified (35X) at the skin level followed by further amplification (Therapeutics Unlimited Inc., model 544) as needed. The trunk flexion angle was measured by electrogoniometers (Penny and Gyles). Signals were digitized at 1 Khz. The raw signals were verified before the onset of the recording for calibration purposes and then the linear envelope (rectified and low pass filtered at 6 Hz) of the signals was obtained. The EMG signals of the control and experimental trials were normalized as a percentage of the maximal EMG values obtained from the mean of 3 maximal isometric contractions. The EMG results presented in this study were obtained from a 100 ms window before the onset of the lift and were calculated as follows:

% of MVC net = [Mean of 3 experimental trials (block1, 2.5 kg and the preceding trial at 17.5 kg)] - [Mean of the 2.5 kg load control trials]

Results

Figure 1 illustrates how the uncertainty increases the contraction level compared to the conditions in which the weight of the load to be handled was already known. The increased muscular activation is seen mainly in the muscles responsible for postural control (e.g., GM, BF and SS) particularly before the onset of the lift (before 100 ms). GM appears to be the most affected by this uncertainty. Indeed, the uncertainty brought about a muscular pre-activation of this muscle with respect to the real demand of the task, which suggest that the control of the distal muscles must be preprogrammed. In this case, a bad anticipation of the load causes more force to be transferred on the load to be lifted. This exaggerated force can be seen in the strain gauges and BB EMG signals after the onset of the lift in Figure 1.

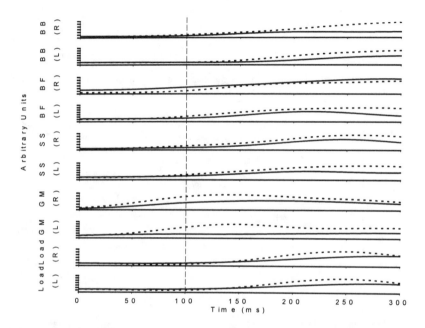

Figure 1. Linear envelope of EMG signals for an experimental trial (dotted line) and a control trial (full line).

The results of the ANOVA (Block X Load X Load on the preceding trial) indicate that the difference between the loads in block 1 leads to an significant increase in the real muscular demand in the GM, BF and SS ($p<0.05$), particulary for the small load. Figure 2 illustrates the percentage of over-activation of the postural muscles during the handling of the light load in each of the 3 blocks. These results suggest that for the situations in which there is a large difference between the loads to be handled, the subjects use neuro-muscular strategies similar to the mobilization of heavier loads. Moreover, when the block effect is combined to the that of the load of the preceding trial, there is an even greater muscular pre-activation level for the small load of each block. Figure 3 shows the effect of the preceding trial on the percentage of over-activation in the GM. In block 1, simply lifting the heaviest load just prior to handling the lightest load is enough to produce a significant increase in the mean level ($p<0.05$) of pre-activation compared to a situation in which the subject handled a similar load in the preceding trial.

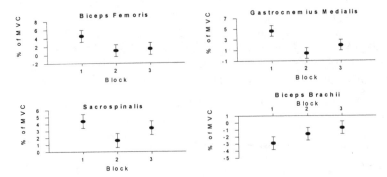

Figure 2.   Percentage of over-activation of the postural muscles during the handling of the light load in each of the 3 blocks

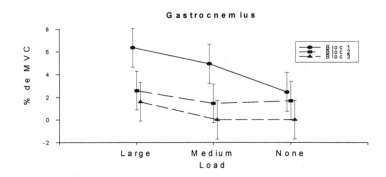

Figure 3.   The effect of the preceding trial on the percentage of over-activation. Items, large medium and none represents the difference between the small loads and that manipulated previously

Conclusion

The results of this study clearly demonstrate that the uncertainty in load handling leads to additional demands on the axial muscles responsible for the control of posture. However, the uncertainty effect is only significant for the conditions in which the difference between the loads is large and when the load in the preceding trial is high. For workers (load handlers), these results suggest that the load should be known or more easily visible before the onset of the movement.

References
[1]   T. Armstrong *et al.*, *Human factors* 28(3) : (1986) 325-336
[2]   V. Belenkii, *et al.*, *Biofizika* 12(1): (1967) 154-161
[3]   S. Bouisset, *et al.*, *Neurosci. Letters.* 22: (1981) 263-270
[4]   S. Bouisset, *et al.*, *Jour. Biomech.* 8: (1987) 735-742
[5]   J. Callaghan, *et al.*, *Spine*, 20(9): (1995) 992-998
[6]   J. Crisco *et al.*, *Clin. Biomech.* 7: (1992) 19-26
[7]   C. Zetterberg *et al.*, *Spine*, 12(10): (1987) 1035-1040

Advances in Occupational Ergonomics and Safety II
Edited by Biman Das and Waldemar Karwowski
IOS Press and Ohmsha, 1997

Evaluation and Management of Work Injuries Using Surface Electromyography

Elsayed Abdel-Moty, Ph.D., Tarek M. Khalil, Ph.D., P.E., Hubert L. Rosomoff, MD, D.Med.Sc
Soha Sadek, Ph.D., Roger Snider, PT, Martha Coya, OTR, Anthony Caputo, BS

University of Miami Comprehensive Pain and Rehabilitation Center
600 Alton Road, Miami Beach, Florida 33139
Phone: (305) 532-7246   Fax: (305) 534-3974
Internet: www.um-cprc.com   e-mail: cprc@um-cprc.com

1. ABSTRACT

Work-related injuries and the resulting soft-tissue changes and pain often produce compensatory changes in posture and in the manner by which workers perform job tasks. Our failure to treat work-related injuries effectively has been, in part, due to our inability to identify and treat the source of these altered motor patterns affecting patient's abilities to engage in useful activities at work or in daily living. A protocol was developed at the University of Miami Comprehensive Pain and Rehabilitation Center (CPRC) for the purpose evaluating this type of "hidden" imbalance in the function of the neuromuscular system using surface electromyography (EMG). Specifically, one protocol is for monitoring muscles involved in scapular rotation and stabilization during overhead lifting activities. The protocol can be generalized and its application can be transposed to most superficial muscle(s) or muscle group involved in complex functional maneuvers. This type of intervention proves useful in direct identification and management of problem areas thus enhancing rehabilitation outcome, reducing treatment time, and increasing patients awareness of compensatory activities due to pain and injury.

2. METHODS

The test set-up for multi-channel recording of EMG activity during dynamic tasks is illustrated in Figure 1. Equipment consist of: an 8-channel neurodata Grass™ unit for signal conditioning, the Ariel Performance Analysis System (Ariel Dynamics, CA) for digital signal processing, and the Multifunction Computerized Exercise System (CES, Ariel Dynamics, CA) for muscle output testing and evaluation. Peripheries include: surface electrodes, electrodes stand, and a color printer.

Patient are identified as candidates for this type of testing by the treating physician. Patients are also tested if the treating therapist concludes that more insight is needed to resolve a persisting painful condition. The following procedure is then followed:

1. Electrode placements for commonly involved superficial muscles were established with multidisciplinary insight to ascertain proper maneuvers for the muscle(s) chosen. An illustrative manual was developed for this purpose.
2. Following standard skin preparation techniques, electrodes are placed superficially close to the motor point of the target muscles and along muscle fibers.
3. Baseline EMG levels are recorded at rest prior to any activities.
4. Self-report of pain levels (scale of 0-no pain to 10-worst pain) related to the local areas involved in testing are noted.
5. The patient performs standardized maneuvers to determine: a) ability to activate a muscle compared to its contralateral; b) maneuver(s) producing best muscle fiber recruitment (higher EMG); and c) carryover to other maneuvers.

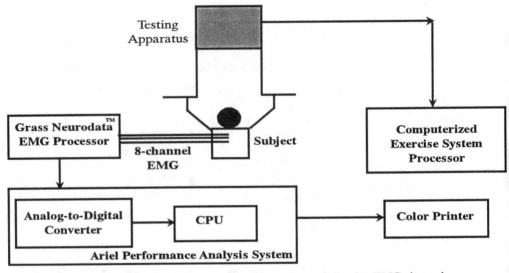

Figure 1. Motor Dysfunction Evaluation set-up. Following EMG electrodes placement for 8-channel recording, the patient is positioned at the computerized testing apparatus. On-line monitoring of muscle activity and of force output takes place while patient perform the task(s). The testing apparatus is then replaced by a functional task and procedure is repeated.

       At least 2 sets of maneuvers are performed. The first requires the patient to perform symmetrical, bilateral activity using the CES exercise apparatus. The patient then performs a "functional" activity such as moving weights in space. As needed, other maneuvers are added to investigate, say, static loading or fatigue.

6.   The time of the day, duration of each trial, and the corresponding EMG levels achieved as well as any other relevant observations related to EMG signal quality, noise and movement artifacts, etc. are recorded.

7.   The quality of all recorded EMG signals are checked via power (spectral) analysis of the EMG signals. Presence of low frequency movement artifacts, 60 Hz electrical interference, or high frequency noise provides rationale for re-testing.

8.   Noiseless EMG signals are then rectified (full-wave) and enveloped (T=0.5 sec).

9.   A graphical color print-out is obtained following computerized analysis of all recorded channels. The EMG signals of the various muscles are examined for: baseline activity, symmetry, magnitude / amplitude of the EMG signals, synchrony, timing of EMG activity patterns, relative response of various muscles, right-left symmetry, repetitiveness, and validity of the test. Patient's behaviors are also observed (especially compensatory movements, guarding, pain behaviors).

10.   EMG findings are then compared to relevant clinical findings. The multidisciplinary analysis determines the clinical significance of the findings, composes interpretations, and recommends treatment plans.

11.   Patient-specific, as well as condition-specific, multidisciplinary approaches are then generated to dea with the problems during patient rehabilitation. The overall objective is to decrease pain and improve functional capabilities in performing work tasks.

12.   EMG and other electrically-assisted methods (e.g. electrical stimulation and biofeedback) are used to

increase sensory perception (of muscles and joints); increase recruitment; increase strength and endurance; and re-establish synchrony, symmetry, pattern, and synergy of muscle activity specific to work capacities. Functional electric stimulation is used when muscle activity is minimal to improve recruitment and strength. It can be used passively and in conjunction with voluntary effort. Surface EMG is used during treatment to monitor recruitment ability. It helps improve patient's awareness of symmetry in muscle activity in order to ensure carry-over in work activities. The use of EMG assists the treating team to introduce new maneuvers as the patient progresses in work conditioning activities. When used in this manner, EMG can be a valuable tool in explaining compensatory motions to the patient. Therapeutic exercises are then used to increase strength, endurance and establish absent or diminished motor patterns (examples are: progressive resistive exercises, neuromuscular facilitation techniques, and neuro developmental techniques) .

CASE STUDY

This is a 37 years old male who sustained a lifting injury during fitness assignment as a Special Agent. He experienced immediate stabbing pain on the right side of the spine; medial to the scapula. He underwent several unsuccessful attempts to treat his condition. These included chiropractic manipulation, muscle relaxants, trigger point injections, traction, electrical stimulation, ultrasound, anterior cervical diskectomy, 6-7 fusion, and acupuncture. He was admitted to the CPRC for evaluation and treatment. Following 4 weeks of aggressive physical medicine and rehabilitation, he was discharged with full ranges of motion of the lower extremity and much improved ROM of the upper extremity. His functional tolerances also greatly improved. Three months later, he was re-admitted to the CPRC with several trigger points in the right upper trapezius and right infraspinatus muscles. At that time, the EMG protocol described above was carried-out to evaluate the source(s) of his continued painful condition. EMG activity of the upper trapezius, lower trapezius, serratus anterior, infraspinatus, and supraspinatus muscles were monitored during the "military press" maneuver. Findings (Table 1) assisted the treating team target problem areas. EMG biofeedback was used to enable the patient achieve symmetry and reduce muscle tension where applicable. The follow-up evaluation (Table 1) showed that this intervention was beneficial in achieving all objectives. Gains in muscle coordination translated in strength gains, restoration of ranges of motion, further pain reduction, and in his ability to return to work full duty. At 3 years follow-up, he continues to do well with the home maintenance program and to work full-time.

Table 1. Summary of EMG Evaluation Results for the Case Study

Target Muscle	Pre-Treatment Evaluation Results	Post-Treatment Evaluation Results
Lower Trapezius	▸ Right side higher than left at rest. ▸ Levels of firing asymmetrical	▸ Resting levels similar. ▸ Firing approached symmetry.
Upper Trapezius	▸ Right much higher than left at rest. ▸ Levels/pattern of firing asymmetrical	▸ Resting levels similar. ▸ Left side showed more activity (*over corrected*).
Serratus Anterior	▸ Slight compensation on left side.	▸ No compensation present.
Infraspinatus	▸ Asymmetrical levels of firing.	▸ Asymmetry remains.
Supraspinatus	▸ Asymmetry at rest and during activity	▸ Significantly higher firing. ▸ Slight asymmetry.
All Muscles	▸ Relative levels and patterns abnormal at rest and during activity.	▸ Patterns partially restored. ▸ Higher levels of firing.

4.   SUMMARY

On-line monitoring of muscle activity using surface EMG is used to identify and effectively treat motor dysfunction in workers with chronic pain conditions. This requires multidisciplinary evaluation / treatment approach to study multiple muscles involved in a chain of precise activities specific to recruiting these muscles.

The efficacy of using this approach for direct problem identification of motor dysfunction requires sophisticated EMG technology. Clinicians must be acquainted with available EMG systems especially with respect to their technical specifications as well as cost.

5.   REFERENCE

Khalil, T.M., Abdel-Moty, E., Steele-Rosomoff, R, Rosomoff, H, 1994. Ergonomics in Back Pain: Guide Prevention and rehabilitation. Van Nostrand Reinhold, NY.

13. Musculoskeletal Problems in Workplace

Advances in Occupational Ergonomics and Safety II
Edited by Biman Das and Waldemar Karwowski
IOS Press and Ohmsha, 1997

Procedure for the progressive assessment of risk of musculoskeletal problems of the upper limbs

Jacques MALCHAIRE and Bart INDESTEEGE
Unité Hygiène et Physiologie du Travail, Université catholique de Louvain,
Clos Chapelle-aux-Champs, 30-38, 1200 Bruxelles

Abstract: The paper presents a three steps procedure for the progressive assessment of the risk of musculoskeletal problems of the upper limbs.
The objective is to find solutions to these problems. The method involves:
- a screening step where the main constraints are identified and the first control measures taken by general practitioners
- a second step where ergonomists investigate more in details some specific operations
- a third step where specialists make measurements to optimize special control measures.

1. Position of the problem

Many methods have been described in the literature to assess the risk of musculoskeletal problems of the upper limbs (ULD), from check lists to sophisticated monitoring techniques. These methods of investigation have usually been developed and published by specialists trying to bring to the field what they consider necessary to assess the risk encountered at the workplace. This approach has two major drawbacks as:
. it does not usually correspond to the capacity and the competency of the people who have to analyze these working conditions in the field;
. the objective of these people is not to assess the risk as scientists do it for epidemiological purposes but to collect the information required to improve and possibly solve the problem.

The people in charge of risk prevention in industry therefore do not need methods defining a global index of stress but, on the opposite, a strategy for gathering information progressively as it is needed to define control measures.

The paper proposes a procedure in three steps of increasing complexity and accuracy, that can be used by different persons with different levels of competency and responsibility, to recognise, analyze and quantify the risk of ULD.

2. General scheme of the procedure

Level 1

This method must be
. simple to use in the field by the occupational health practitioners without any specific training;

. rapid, in order to be used systematically as soon as complaints arise at a workplace;
. inexpensive for the same reason.

The main objective is to determine
. on one side, the anatomical zone(s) of the upper limb, where there might be a risk of development of ULD and what risk factors are involved: force, angles, repetitivity, vibration, ... A checklist was developed for that purpose based on the proposal made by Keyserling [1];
. on the other hand: the characteristics of the worker population, their musculoskeletal history, their psychosocial main characteristics. A general questionnaire was developed for that purpose including some 50 questions. The Nordic questionnaire is included concerning the neck and upper limbs regions [2].

Level 2

Several improvements of the working conditions can be decided already based on simple observations. In some cases however, the task requires a combinaison of postures and actions and it is not possible to identify from the start which ones need attention in priority. A more sophisticated method is then needed, oriented toward the anatomical zone recognized at risk. It should remain rather simple and based essentially on observations and provide a semi-quantitative indication of the ULD risk involved.

The proposed method is an adaptation of the OWAS procedure making more than 100 instantaneous observations at regular interval during a representative work period. As in the OWAS procedure, the posture is compared to a set of reference situations, such as, for the wrist
. maximum flexion, neutral situation, maximum extension
. maximum ulnar deviation, neutral situation, maximum radial deviation
. the set of grip positions as defined by Armstrong [3].

The force is estimated using the opinion of the workers expressed on the Borg's scale for each elementary activity [4].

Repetitivity is expressed in terms of the number of variations in posture among the 100 observations.

Table 1 gives an example of the results in the case of a work involving 5 different operations. The results can be interpreted by comparison with threshold values recommended in the literature.

Clearly this level 2 method requires more competency from the user. It is also longer and more costly. It is justified only in cases where solutions cannot be readily found.

It is usually performed by ergonomists or other specialists with specific training about ULD.

Table 1:   Example of results from step 2 observation analysis

	OPERATIONS					Global	Limit
	1	2	3	4	5	100	
Duration (% time)	20	22	14	20	24	100	
Angles: Flexion > 45°	12	7	10	9	43	17	25%
Extension > 45°	23	33	19	6	36	24	25%
Radial deviation	9	6	10	3	29	12	25%
Ulnar deviation	42	17	28	14	11	21	25%
Grip: Pinch	49	11	46	17	62	37	
Grip	26	16	39	28	4	21	
Hammer	0	0	0	0	36	9	
Force	BORG'S SCORE						
	3	4	2	5	7	4.5	
Repetitivity index: Flexion/extension						0.27	
Deviation						0.47	
Grip						0.68	

Level 3

Still, more sophisticated working conditions might require further investigation for the adequate solutions to be found. This was the case of a windscreen wiper assembly line where the work was very rapid and complex and everything has already been done to improve the work[1].

The investigation is then based on direct measurements of angles, of EMG activity of the finger and hand flexors, of velocities, using sophisticated and costly transducers and data recorders carried on by a sample of workers, during representative work periods.

The results are expressed in terms of mean values of these parameters and/or percentage of the time during which threshold values are exceeded.

Again however, the main purpose is not to arrive at a quantitative estimation of the risk per se, but to identify analytically the movements, postures, operations that are systematically the most stressful and therefore need improvement.

This method requires sophisticated and highly specialized training for the collection and use of the data and can only be performed by specialists.

3. Conclusion

The procedure makes possible to organize the surveillance of the working conditions in a more efficient way. It relies on, mainly, occupational physicians to conduct the primary analysis (level 1), interview the workers, record the complaints of ULD and determine the upper limb zone which is the most at risk. Ergonomists are then required to observe the working conditions, record the times spent at high constraint levels and make suggestions for

---

[1] Unfortunately, the conclusion was for the company to automatize the job and the risk was eliminated for the worker on welfare.

improvement. The level 3 method will be needed only in special cases where observations are not possible and in order to detect smaller differences in the working procedure.

4. References

[1] W.M. Keyserling, D.S. Stetson, B.A. Silverstein and M.L. Brouwer, A checklist for evaluating ergonomic risk factors associated with upper extremity cumulative trauma disorders. *Ergonomics* **36** (1993) 807-831.

[2] I. Kuorinka, B. Jonsson, A. Kilbom, H. Vinterberg, F. Biering-Sorensen, G. Andersson and K. Jorgensen, Standardised Nordic questionnaires for the analysis of musculoskeletal symptoms. *Applied Ergonomics* **18** (1987) 233-237.

[3] T.J. Armstrong, J.A. Foulke, B.S. Joseph and S.A. Goldstein, Investigation of cumulative trauma disorders in a poultry processing plant. *American Industrial Hygiene Association Journal* **43** (1982) 103-116.

[4] G. Borg, Psychophysical scaling with applications in physical work and the perception of exertion. *Scandinavian Journal of Work and Environmental Health* **16** (1990) 55-58.

Advances in Occupational Ergonomics and Safety II
Edited by Biman Das and Waldemar Karwowski
IOS Press and Ohmsha, 1997

A Proactive Group Surveillance Protocol
For Musculoskeletal Disorders

R.J. Marley, A.J. Gebhardt, K.J. Stewart
Mechanical & Industrial Engineering Department,
Montana State University, Bozeman, MT 59717 (USA)

and

R. Nicholls
Montana Power Company, Butte, MT 59701 (USA)

Abstract. A self-report technique for categorizing an individual
worker's probability of seeking treatment for a musculoskeletal
disorder (MSD), referred to as the "BodyMap," had been previously
developed. This paper reports the use of the BodyMap for the
ongoing surveillance of MSDs in groups of workers, such as in
functional departments or by other job classifications. The tool was
administered to a group of 683 utility company workers in one of
twelve job classifications over a two year period. A protocol for
monitoring the self-report data was also established. Results indicate
that the ratings corresponded directly with changes is MSD rates as
well as the region of the body affected over the period examined.
Thus, it is suggested that the BodyMap may be used successfully as a
"leading indicator" of MSD risk to aid the ergonomist in identifying
potential concerns in departments and/or in helping to predict the
effects of work design interventions.

1. Introduction

Musculoskeletal disorders (MSDs) are an ever increasing concern for business and
industry in the U.S. and throughout the world as well. Industrial ergonomists, safety and
health care specialists may utilize several general approaches to assist them in assessing
concerns for work design and risk for MSDs. For example, assessment of known MSD risk
factors such as repetition, force, posture, mechanical stress, vibration, or temperature, may
provide insight into MSD potential and also lead to design/redesign recommendations. This
process can be time-intensive, however, and may often lead to difficulty of analysis when
multiple risk factors are present. Another approach is to track injury rate statistics. Such
statistics must be considered the benchmark data in terms of trend analysis and determination
of risk. Yet, as with any "trailing indicator," an interval of time is required for the data to be
compiled, analyzed, and interpreted. This can lead to frustration when trying to anticipate
the impact of work design changes, however.

Still another approach may be to utilize self-report data, often in the form of a
psychophysical scale. This approach has the advantage of being able to provide nearly
instant feedback on worker subjective ratings with respect to design changes or alternatives.
While ratings can be useful for intra- or inter-task comparisons, models for their relation to
actual injury statistics have not been well established. Therefore, the objective of this study

was to examine the use of a particular self-reporting discomfort assessment tool as a "leading indicator" for potential MSDs in groups of workers, such as in functional departments.

2. Methods

2.1. Instrument

A musculoskeletal discomfort assessment tool had been previously developed [1]. This instrument, referred to as the "BodyMap," relied upon a new approach which adapted useful features from earlier subjective methods [2-4]. Twenty five regions of the body were surveyed with respect to both frequency and level of discomfort. Figure 1 depicts the pictograph and recording scheme of the BodyMap. A data base of 797 employees from one of 14 job classifications at a utility company (data entry, operations, warehouse, maintenance, service crews, professional, etc.) was initially developed in 1993. Based upon the joint subjective ratings (frequency and level of discomfort), a statistical model was then developed which could reasonably predict whether the employee would seek treatment for a work-related discomfort according to their recent history (not a diagnosis tool, however). An interesting outcome of this analysis revealed that ratings of frequency and discomfort level are dependent upon one another [1]. Most subjective rating methods assess either one or the other.

The probability of a worker seeking treatment was, of course, dependent upon the joint score. These probabilities resulted in a classification scheme of high, medium, or low probability of seeking treatment. For convenience, outcome probabilities were labeled as the "red," "yellow," or "green" zones, respectively. The overall sensitivity of the BodyMap scores to identify those who are very likely to seek treatment (red zone) was 81.5%.

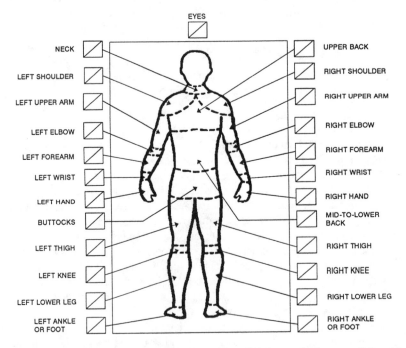

Figure 1. "BodyMap" pictograph and recording device. Subjects fill in boxes with frequency (0-3 scale) and level of discomfort (0-10 scale).

2.2. Current Application and Protocol

A follow-up BodyMap survey was readministered to 683 of the original group of 797 workers during 1995. Results from these surveys were also tabulated according to the red, yellow, green classification scheme. Rather than by individual outcome, however, results from both years were grouped by functional department. Subsequently, MSD related statistics were compiled for the two surveyed years, 1993 and 1995. The rates were then compared to trends in BodyMap scores according the corresponding bodily areas and injury types.

A protocol was developed in order to facilitate the comparison between ratings and injury rate. The protocol relied upon a simple, two-step function in which "risk" was considered high for a given department if one of the following conditions were met: 1) 10% or more individuals in the department were classified in the red zone of the BodyMap in a given bodily area; or 2) 15% or more individuals classified in either the red or yellow zones for a body area.

3. Results and Discussion

As indicated, MSD related injuries were compiled for both years, for each of 12 job classifications, and then related to a body part/area corresponding to one of the 25 regions of the BodyMap. For space considerations, a full summary of these "compartmentalized" data cannot be provided here. Most rates showed to significant change from 1993 to 1995 ($p <$ 0.05). Likewise, assignment to "high risk" or "low risk" according to the protocol described above also showed no significant change during the period examined.

However, several interesting trends appeared. For example, in those employees classified as "office" workers (data entry, clerical, etc.), the number of claims for lower back injuries dropped from four to zero from 1993 to 1995. Correspondingly, the percent of these workers classified in either red or yellow zones of the BodyMap ("high risk") fell from about 34% to 20% during the same period. This was significant according to the chi-square tests performed ($p < 0.05$). Though this department would be still classified as high risk according to the protocol, the relationship between real-time subjective ratings and subsequent statistics was considered strong.

In another example, statistics from the electric line service area showed a different trend. Claims for elbow related MSDs increased from one to four during the two year study period. Correspondingly, this department would have been reclassified by the protocol from low risk to high risk after the second survey with respect to the right elbow (6.7% to 22.6%). Figures 2 and 3 depict the BodyMap classifications for both departments illustrated here.

4. Conclusions

As ergonomists conduct analyses and perform design/redesign of work systems in an effort to reduce MSD risk, immediacy of feedback is important with regards to the outcome of their efforts. Subjective information from employees can play an important role in this process. This paper has reported a method to use an established self-reporting instrument to further help classify and track potential risk for MSDs for groups of workers. The protocol described was shown to be a useful "leading indicator" for actual injury statistics which followed. It is anticipated that this protocol can be a valuable addition to the ergonomists' "tool kit" by providing feedback regarding design interventions in a given department. The detailed feedback regarding specific bodily areas can also be valuable in detecting possible ergonomic concerns ahead of the trailing statistics.

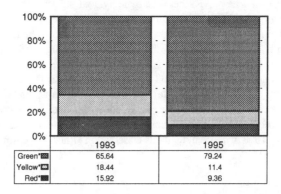

	1993	1995
Green*	65.64	79.24
Yellow*	18.44	11.4
Red*	15.92	9.36

Figure 2. Mid-lower back ratings on BodyMap for office workrers from 1993 to 1995.

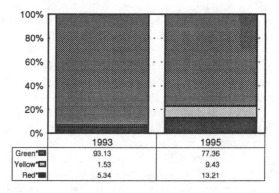

	1993	1995
Green*	93.13	77.36
Yellow*	1.53	9.43
Red*	5.34	13.21

Figure 3. Right elbow ratings on BodyMap for electric line workers from 1993 to 1995.

References

[1]   R.J. Marley and N. Kumar (1996), An improved musculoskeletal discomfort assessment tool. *International Journal of Industrial Ergonomics*, **17**(1), 21-27.

[2]   E.N. Corlett and R.P. Bishop (1976), A technique for assessing postural discomfort. *Ergonomics*, **19**, 175-182.

[3]   N. Saldana, G.D. Herrin, T.J. Armstrong, and A. Franzblau (1994), A computerized method for assessment of musculoskeletal discomfort in the workforce: A tool for surveillance. *Ergonomics*, **37**(6), 1097-1112.

[4]   S.L. Sauter, L.M. Schleifer, and S.J. Knutson (1991), Work posture, workstation design, and musculoskeletal discomfort in a VDT data entry task. *Human Factors*, **33**(2), 151-167.

Advances in Occupational Ergonomics and Safety II
Edited by Biman Das and Waldemar Karwowski
IOS Press and Ohmsha, 1997

Correlations of the Work ability index with individual and work related characteristics

Heikki SOININEN[1], Risto NORONEN [2] and Veikko LOUHEVAARA[3]

1) Medivire Occupational Health Services
Box 1739, FIN-70111 Kuopio, Finland
2) Oy Karl Fazer Ab, Helsinki, Finland
3) Finnish Institute of Occupational Health and University of Kuopio, Kuopio, Finland

1. Introduction

The majority of workers in physically demanding restaurant jobs such service, cleaning, kitchen and laundry works are women. They have a high number of work related mental, musculoskeletal and cardiovascular disorders and diseases reducing their ability to work. In the beginning of the 1990s one of the largest Finnish personnel restaurant chains started a program for maintaining and improving health, work ability and well-being of the entire personnel. For the selection and implementation of relevant actions within the program the work ability of the personnel was analysed. The aim of this study was to examine the relationships between the assessed work ability and individual and work related characteristics.

2. Material and methods

Work ability was determined with the Work ability index (WAI) [1]. It was based on a questionnaire, which was sent to 2600 women and men working in different restaurant jobs. Almost two thousand (1905) women and 111 men responded (78 %). The mean (±SD, range) age of the respondents was 39 (± 9, 16-63) years. About the half of them (52 %) aged 16-39 years. 35 % and 13 % of the respondents were in the age groups of 40-49 and 50-63 years, respectively.

The WAI includes subjective estimations on work ability taking into account job demands, psycho-physiological resources, diseases and work absenteeism. The index ranges from 7 to 49 points, and is divided into four categories: poor (7-27), moderate (28-35), good (36-43) and excellent (44-49) work ability [2]. The questionnaire also included questions on health habits, work related musculosceletal, stress and burnout disorders, work environment and work organization.

Chi-square test and analysis of variance were used for testing the differences between the groups. Correlations were calculated using Pearson's correlation test. The accepted level of significance was $p < 0.05$.

3. Results

The mean (±SD, range) of the WAI was 40 (± 6, 7-49). The male subjects had a higher WAI than the female ones ($p < 0.001$) (Tabel 1). Every tenth of the subjects (10 %) aged 50-63 years had poor work ability according to the classified WAI. The corresponding values were 2 % and 6 % in the age groups of 16-39 and 40-49 years, respectively (Fig.1).

Tabel 1. The values of the WAI for male and female respondents and in different age groups.

	Mean	SD	Range
All (n = 1956)	40	6	7-49
Men (n = 109)	42	6	17-49
Women (n = 1784)	40	6	7-49
16-39 years (n = 993)	41	5	13-49
40-49 years (n = 661)	39	6	11-49
50-63 years (n = 219)	37	7	7-49

The WAI correlated significantly with work satisfaction ($r=0.36$, $p<0.001$). Good education level of the respondents associated with the high WAI ($p<0.001$). There was also a systematic positive relationship between physical activity and the WAI ($p=0.05$).

The number of work related stress disorders ($r=-0.58$, $p<0.001$) and burnout disorders ($r=-0.47$, $p<0.001$) had the highest negative correlations with the WAI. Age correlated also significantly and negatively with the WAI ($r=-0.27$, $p<0.001$) but did not correlate significantly with the satisfaction te work conditions, the index of burnout disorders and the sum of work related stress disorders.

Obesity of the respondents correlated negatively with the WAI ($r=-0.19$, $p<0.001$). The WAI of the respondents working in physically demanding jobs was lower than that of the respondents having sedentary jobs ($p<0.001$). Significant ($p<0.001$) and negative associations were observed between the WAI and poor ergonomic work conditions such restless work environment, inadequate lightning noise, inconvenient temperature and increased risk for accidents.

Tabel 2. Correlations and significant interactions between the WAI and some individual and work related characteristics. WS = the satisfaction to work conditions, WRD = the sum of work related stress disorders and BUI = the burnout index.

	WAI, r and p value	WAI and significant interactions, p value
WS	0.36, <0.001	
Education level		<0.001, positive interaction
Physical activity		= 0.05, positive interaction
WRD	-0.58, <0.001	
BUI	-0.47, <0.001	
Age	-0.27, <0.001	
Obesity	-0.19, <0.001	
Job		<0.001 (physically demanding jobs, negative interaction)
Working years		<0.001, negative interaction

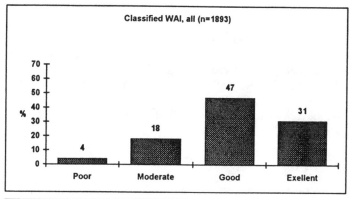

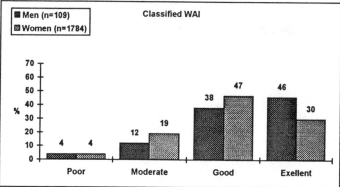

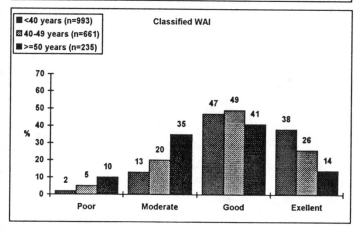

Figure 1. Classified work ability index (WAI). The values given are the percentages of the respondents in four WAI categories: poor (7-27), moderate (28-36), good (37-43) and excellent (44-49).

4. Discussion and conclusions

The results suggest that the maintenance of work ability of restaurant workers and particularly the ageing ones demands systematic actions which should be directed to work environment (ergonomics, safety, hygiene) work organisation (psychosocial and leadership issues) and individual workers (health promotion). The actions should be completed in the close cooperation of the personnel of enterprises and occupational health services. At the individual level it is important to identify as early as possible the workers with lowered work ability and carry out diverse health and fitness promotion programs.

Reference

[1] K. Tuomi *et al,* Prevalence and incidence rates of diseases and work ability in different
      work categories in municipal occupations. *Scandinavian Journal of Work, Environment
      and Health* 17 (suppl. 1) (1991) 67-74.
[2] K. Tuomi *et al,* Work ability index. Occupational Health Care 19. Finnish Institute of Occupational Health,
      Helsinki 1997.

Advances in Occupational Ergonomics and Safety II
Edited by Biman Das and Waldemar Karwowski
IOS Press and Ohmsha, 1997

Comparative Study of Low Back Pain Between Sedentary and Non-sedentary Workers

Mazzoni, Cláudia F., Marçal, Márcio A., and Couto, Hudson A.*

Ergonomic Research Group, Queen's University, Kingston, Ont, K7L 3N6 Canada, Phone: (613) 545-2658, Fax: (613) 543-2009
**ERGO- Occupational Health and Ergonomics Consultant, Av.Getulio Vargas 668/1306, Belo Horizonte, MG, Brasil Phone: (031) 226-3736*

Abstract

This study compared the incidence of low back pain (LBP) in two groups of 30 workers, one involved in heavy activity and the other involved in light activity. The groups were matched for gender, years of employment and age. Anthropometric data were collected and radiographic examinations and postural evaluations conducted. High incidence of low back pain was found in both groups and no significant difference occurred. Age, time in the activity and anthropometric data did not correlate with low back pain. An interesting finding was the higher incidence of degenerative processes among non-sedentary workers and higher rates of postural deviations in the sedentary workers.

1- Introduction

In the general population an estimated 80% of adults will have back pain that interferes with function at some point of their lives [1]. Sedentary or light activities and non-sedentary or heavy activities have been used to categorize different occupational population and work conditions. The high incidence of occupational LBP is also true for the Brazilian working population. In 1992, the Brazilian Department of Labour reported that back pain was responsible for 20% of the expenses associated with occupational injuries and it was the third cause of absenteeism in the workplace [2].

The purpose of this study was to compare the incidence of LBP between Brazilian workers involved in sedentary and non-sedentary activities. Various postural and anthropometric variables, and variables from radiographic examination were considered as potential risk factors for LBP.

2- Methods

Two groups of voluntary workers were established: group A consisting of warehouse employees responsible for carrying and lifting 60 kg bags; and group B consisting of office workers. Thirty subjects were randomly assigned to each group. Ages varied from 20 to 35 years old and the time performing the same activity varied from less than one year up to 20 years in both groups. Medical reports were used to determine the occurrence of LBP. The subjects were divided into 4 categories according to the presence and intensity of the problem. All subjects agreed to postural and X-ray examinations. Two physiotherapists (double-blinded) were responsible for collecting the postural and anthropometric data. The X-rays were analysed by a specialist who was blind to which group the subject belonged to. A chi square analysis (significance at $p< 0.05$) was performed to evaluate the differences between the two groups.

3 - Results

Considering the number of cases within the low intensity, medium intensity, and high intensity categories, the incidence of LBP was 83.3% among workers involved in heavy activities and 80.0% among those involved in light activity. No statistical difference was found between the two groups.

The time in the activity and age did not show correlation with LBP. The only aspect regarding the anthropometric data that was statistically different between groups was the girth, which was higher among sedentary workers.

The results for postural and radiographic examinations showed that all LBP workers involved in light activity presented some type of postural deviation. On the other hand, radiographic alterations, such as disc and vertebrae degenerations and foraminal narrowing, occurred 43% more in the LBP workers involved in heavy activity.

4 - Discussion

This study shows that both types of activities, heavy and light, are associated with high incidence of LBP. This result has also been observed in other studies [3,4]. However, no significant difference was found between the two groups. Such a finding is contradictory to the literature [1, 5, 6]. The small sample size in this study may explain the difference. Regarding age, no association with LBP was found. The range of 20 to 35 years seems to be low when compared to other studies. The maximal frequency of symptoms appears between 35 and 55 years [3, 7]. In the present study, the range of age was decided according to the subjects involved in the heavy activity. Thirty-five years was the highest age encountered in this group, a fact which may be explained as a natural selection for this type of activity. Different ways of perceiving pain and different attitudes could have influenced the final rates. The subjects in group A seemed to have higher threshold for pain, while the subjects in group B demonstrated less tolerance to pain and sought for medical attention as early as possible.

Years of employment in the activity did not correlate with incidence of LBP in both groups. A great number of symptoms of LBP have been reported within the first years of involvement in a new job [8].

In this study, the anthropometric data also did not show a significant difference between the two groups. This finding is consistent with other studies [8, 9].

An interesting finding is the high incidence of degenerative processes among non-sedentary workers and the high rates of postural deviations present in the sedentary workers. Different studies have shown that disc degeneration is more frequent in individuals with heavy activities, but the nature of the stress inducing the degenerative changes is not clear and there is controversy in correlating such alterations with LBP [9, 10]. Postural alterations are likely to be more common in workers with LBP, however it can not be stated whether poor posture leads to pain [7, 11]. Despite such controversies, the findings of this study may suggest that different processes might occur in the development of LBP, depending on the type of activity, in two groups matched for gender, years of employment, and age.

References

[1] L.H. Daytroy, M.G. Larson, E.A. Wright, S. Malspeis, A.H. Fossel, J. Rayan, C. Zwerling, and M.H. Liang, A Case-Control Study of Risk Factors for Industrial Low Back Injury: Implications for Primary and Secondary Prevention Programs, *American Journal of Industrial Medicine* **20** (1991) 505-515.

[2] H.A. Couto, Temas de Saude Ocupacional, ERGO LTDA, Brasil, 1987.

[3] V.H. Hildebrandt, Back Pain in the Working Population: PrevalenceRates in Dutch Trades and Professions, *Ergonomics* **38** (6) (1995) 1283-1298.

[4] H.O. Svenson, Low Back in Forty to Forty-Seven Years Old Men II: Socio-Economic Factors and Previous Sickness Absence, *Scandinavian Journal of Rehabilitation Medicine* **14** (1982) 55-60.

[5] G.B.J. Andersson, Low Back Pain in Industry: Epidemiological Aspects, *Scandinavian Journal of Rehabilitation Medicine* **11** (1979) 163-168.

[6] F. Larese and A. Fiorito, Musculoskeletal Disorders in Hospital Nurses: A Comparison Between Two Hospitals, *Ergonomics* **37** (7) (1994) 1205-1211.

[7] G.B. Anderson, Epidemiologic Aspects on Low Back Pain in Industry, *Spine* **6** (1) (1981) 53-60.

[8] J.L. Kelsey and A.L. Golden, Occupational and Workplace Factors Associated with Low Back Pain, *Occupational Medicine: State Art Rev.* **8** (1988) 7-16.

[9] J.L. Dales, E.B. Mac Donald, and R.W. Porter, Back Pain: The Risk Factors and its Prediction in Work People, *Clinical Biomechanics* **1** (1986) 216-221.

[10] G.B.J. Anderson and M.H. Pope, Occupational Low Back Pain: Assessment, Treatment and Prevention, Mosby Year Book, 1991.

[11] H.J. Christie, S. Kunar, and S.A. Warren, Postural Aberrations in Low Back Pain, *Arch. Phys. Med. Rehabil.* **76** (3) (1995) 218-224.

Advances in Occupational Ergonomics and Safety II
Edited by Biman Das and Waldemar Karwowski
IOS Press and Ohmsha, 1997

IDENTIFICATION OF RISK FACTORS ASSOCIATED WITH TRAUMATIC INJURY AMONG DRYWALL INSTALLERS

S. Sharon Chiou, Christopher S. Pan, and David E. Fosbroke
National Institute for Occupational Safety and Health
Division of Safety Research
1095 Willowdale Rd., Morgantown, WV 26505

ABSTRACT

The objective of this study was to gain preliminary understanding of the risk factors associated with drywall installation through the analysis of traumatic-injury characteristics. An analysis of traumatic injury with days away from work among wage and salary drywall installers in the construction industry was performed for 1992 through 1993. The estimated incident rates were 7.7 and 5.4 per 100 drywall installers for 1992 and 1993, respectively. These rates exceed the injury rates for all construction workers combined (5.2 and 4.9). Drywall installers were at a high risk of overexertion and falls to a lower level. Nearly half of the injured drywall installers suffered sprains, strains, and/or tears mostly to the back. About one third of the trunk injuries occurred while lifting solid building materials, mainly drywall. Falls from scaffolds resulted in the longest absence from work among all types of incident, with an average of about 21 days away from work. The leading causes of injury emphasize the need to focus efforts to prevent traumatic injuries on falls to lower levels and overexertion in lifting. Ergonomic and biomechanical studies are needed to develop proper work procedures involving drywall lifting and tasks performed on elevated surfaces.

1. Introduction

Construction workers face ergonomic and biomechanical risks due to the nature of their work. Many of the construction tasks require workers to maintain awkward postures and handle massive materials frequently. Drywall installation involves many aspects of material handling activity, which can be categorized into 4 major tasks: (1) hanging drywall on ceilings and walls; (2) applying tape to joints and corners; (3) applying skim coats of joint compound; and (4) sanding skimmed drywall. Because of the heavy weight (51-109 lb) and bulky size (4-feet wide, 8- to 16-feet long, 3/8- to 1/2-inch thick) of drywall sheets, handling sheets exposes drywall installers to potential hazards and injuries in every body part [1]. The incidence, severity, and frequency of drywall-handling injuries are associated with some of the high physical demands of this activity (e.g., a frequent combination of large forces and awkward postures) and worker characteristics (e.g., various handling methods). The objective of this study was to identify the risk factors involved with drywall installation, through the analyses of traumatic injury characteristics.

2. Method
2.1. Determination of Injury Frequencies

Traumatic injury data on drywall installers involving days away from work were derived from the Occupational Injury and Illness Survey conducted by the Bureau of Labor Statistics (BLS) for 1992 and 1993. These surveys provide estimates of the number and frequency of occupational injuries and illness based on a sample of approximately 250,000 OSHA logs kept by private-industry employers [2]. These data include four aspects of injuries and illness involving lost workdays: (1) the physical characteristics of the injury (nature of the injury); (2) which part of the body was affected; (3) how the incident occurred (type of event or exposure); and (4) what directly produced the condition (source of the injury) [2].

The current study focused on traumatic injuries associated with drywall installers (occupational code 573 based on the 1990 occupational classification structure developed by the Bureau of the Census) employed as wage and salary workers in the U.S. construction industry. An analysis of the nature, source, event, and body parts affected was conducted. In addition, two-way analyses were performed with the nature of the traumatic injury by the source of the traumatic injury, the injured body part, and the type of incident (event). These were done to identify the possible injury scenarios leading to high frequencies of injury. To determine the injury characteristics associated with specific body parts, the interactions of the injured body part by the event as well as the injured body part by the source of injury, were also examined.

2.2. Estimation of Traumatic Injury Rate for Drywall Installers

Due to the lack of exact numbers of wage-and-salary drywall installers in the construction industry, the denominator data were estimated based on the current population survey conducted by the Bureau of Census. The number of drywall installers employed as wage and salary workers in all private industries was 71,000 in 1992 and 89,000 in 1993. A reduction factor of 0.86 was used to estimate the number of wage-and-salary drywall installers in the construction industry. This reduction factor was approximated by the number of civilian drywall installers (including both self-employed and wage-and-salary workers) in the construction industry in 1992 (99,551) divided by the number of civilian drywall installers employed in all industries in 1992 (116,000). Therefore, the approximated number of wage and salary drywall installers in the construction industry was 61,060 = (71,000 x 0.86) and 76,540 = (89,000 x 0.86) for 1992 and 1993, respectively. The traumatic-injury rate was obtained by dividing the total number of injuries by the estimated number of drywall installers as described above.

2.3. Determination of Injury Severity

The severity of injury cases was assessed using the number of days away from work provided by the BLS. The BLS annual survey provided a list of the number of cases involving 1, 2, 3 to 5, 6 to 10, 11 to 20, 21 to 30, and more than 31 days away from work, tabulated by the characteristics of the injury (nature, parts of body affected, event or exposure, and source). The total number of days away from work (D_T) for a specific characteristic of injury was derived through the equation: $D_T = \sum (D_i \ x \ N_i)$ where,
D_T = total number of days away from work.

D_i = estimated average days away from work. D_i equals 1, 2, 4, 8, 15.5, 25.5, or 31 for cases involving 1, 2, 3 to 5, 6 to 10, 11 to 21, 21 to 31 or more than 31 days away from work, respectively.

N_i = number of injury cases for the corresponding D_i.

The average days away from work for a specific characteristic of injury was determined by dividing the total number of days away from work (D_T) by the total number of cases for the specific characteristic of injury. Due to the limited information available for injuries resulting in more than 31 days away from work, the method used in the current study may lead to the underestimation of total and average days away from work.

3. Results

3.1. Traumatic Injury Rate and Characteristics

Data from the 1992 and the 1993 BLS annual survey of occupational injuries and illness indicate that there were a total of 8,802 traumatic injuries, which resulted in 124,988 lost work days. The average lost work days per traumatic injury case was 14.2. The estimated lost workday traumatic incidence rates were 7.7 and 5.4 per 100 drywall installers for 1992 and 1993, respectively.

Nearly 66% of the traumatic injuries resulted from three natures of injury: sprains, strains, tears (42.9%); fractures (12.2%); and cuts, lacerations (11.1%). Among all body parts affected, the trunk, upper extremities, and lower extremities accounted for 36.0%, 26.0%, and 20.4% of all traumatic injuries, respectively. More specifically, the back (26.9%) was the most frequently injured body part followed by arms, wrists, hands, and fingers combined (25.1%). About 18.8% of the traumatic injuries to drywall installers happened to legs, ankles, and feet.

Four leading sources of injury constituted 45.2% of the total injuries: drywall (13.9%); the floor of the building (13.6%); bodily motion or position of injured, ill worker (12.5%); and the ground (5.2%). The leading events were overexertion (22.1%), falls to lower level (20.7%), bodily reaction (12.9%), struck by object (12.8%), and falls on the same level (10.2%). Together, overexertion and falls made up to more than half of all injuries (53%) occurring to drywall installers during the 2 years.

Forty-four percent of traumatic injuries to muscles, tendons, ligaments, and joints involved overexertion. Forty-three percent of traumatic injuries to bones, nerves, and spinal cord occurred when the workers fell to a lower level. More than half (57%) of the traumatic injuries to muscles, tendons, ligaments, and joints affected workers' trunks. Almost one third of trunk injuries (32.2%) were related to solid building material (e.g. wallboard, drywall) handling and 31.9% of injured trunks resulted from overexertion in lifting.

3.2. Injury Severity

Sprains, strains, and tears constituted 40.9% of drywall installers' total days away from work in 1992 through 1993 with an average of 13.6 lost work days per injury case. Fracture of bones accounted only for 21.9% of the injuries, but each fracture-injury case required more days away from work (25.2 days) than did the sprains, strains, and tears.

Injuries associated with floors, walkways, ground, and surfaces were responsible for 35.7% of total days away from work among all injury sources. In addition, injuries involving floor and ground resulted in the longest average absence from work (19.3 days) of all sources of injuries. More specifically, the number of injuries caused by the drywall (1214.8) was slightly higher than that caused by the floor (1207.1). However, the floor resulted in about 6,800 more days away from work (23309.7 days) than did the drywall (16461.2 days).

Falls, bodily reaction, and exertion accounted for 84% of the total days away from work among all incident types. Falls to lower level resulted in more total days away from work (35710.7 days) than falls on same level (13590 days). Of all types of falls, falls from scaffold required the longest average absence from work (20.7 days). Overexertion (25764.3 days) was responsible for less lost work days than falls to lower level, but more than falls on same level.

4. Discussion

Results from this study indicate that drywall installers in the construction industry had days-away-from-work traumatic injury rates of 7.7 and 5.4 per 100 workers for 1992 and 1993, respectively. These rates were higher than the injury rates for all construction workers combined (5.2% in 1992 and 4.9% in 1993). Drywall installers are at high risk for overexertion and falls to lower level. It was found that more overexertion cases occurred during lifting (13.8%) than carrying tasks (4.5%). This phenomenon might be attributed to the use of carts and dollies in transporting drywall sheets. Dollies that are designed for transporting drywall sheets are available and easy to use at construction sites [3]. However, drywall installers still have to lift the drywall sheets to load or unload the dolly. Moreover, installing ceiling drywall requires lifting sheets overhead in place until they are fastened, which produces considerable stress on the workers [3].

In contrast to overexertion injuries (average lost work days = 13.3), falls to lower level were quite severe with an average of 19.6 days away from work. Drywall installers are customarily required to stand on elevated surfaces (e.g. ladders, scaffolds, stilts, etc.) to hang and secure the drywall sheet to the ceiling or near the ceiling level. Once the drywall has been hung, the workers have to apply tape and joint compounds to the wall. This task is often done on stilts to reach the joints at the top of the wall [3]. These activities can place excessive demands on the postural stability of the worker and present a high risk of falls since the worker has reduced control over his/her ability to change stance to effectively compensate for momentary loss of balance.

The most frequently injured body part during drywall installation was the trunk (36%). Of all trunk segments, the back was the most vulnerable area, and accounted for about 27% of total traumatic injuries. Trunk injuries of drywall installers were most likely to be associated with the handling of solid building materials (32.2%), especially drywall. Furthermore, approximately one-third of the trunk injuries were the results of overexertion in lifting. These findings reaffirm that the handling of bulky and heavy drywall sheets placed inordinate stresses on drywall installers, particularly during drywall lifting.

Results from this study suggest that injury-prevention efforts for drywall installers should be directed toward tasks performed on the elevated and limited working areas as well as tasks requiring drywall lifting. A field study (e.g., survey) will be needed to determine how physical stress is related to the performance of drywall-installation tasks. Future laboratory studies are also needed to evaluate handling methods that reduce the risk factors for overexertion and falls during drywall installation.

5. References

[1] S. Schneider and P. Susie, Ergonomics and Construction: A Review of Potential Hazards in New Building Construction, *American Industrial Hygiene Association Journal* 55(7) (1994) 635-649.
[2] Bureau of Labor Statistics. Occupational Injuries and Illnesses: Counts, Rates, and Characteristics, 1992: Washington, DC: US Government Printing Office, 1995. US Department of Labor, Bulletin 2455.
[3] C. S. Pan and S. Chiou. Biomechanical Stress Control in Drywall Installation, 1997: National Institute for Occupational Safety and Health. *Unpublished Protocol.*

Advances in Occupational Ergonomics and Safety II
Edited by Biman Das and Waldemar Karwowski
IOS Press and Ohmsha, 1997

The Effect of Cognitive Load and Stress on the Musculoskeletal System during Typing Tasks

Liwana S. Bringelson , Tycho K. Fredericks, and Niki M. Thurkow

Human Performance Institute, Department of Industrial and Manufacturing Engineering
Western Michigan University, Kalamazoo, MI 49008-5061 U.S.A.

The objective of this study was to determine the effect of cognitive load and work stress on typing speed, errors, and finger forces. Previous research has studied the effect of mental load on lifting tasks; this study extends this work by studying the effect of cognitive factors, including mental load, in a keyboarding environment. Cognitive factors were manipulated using difficulty and duration of tasks to provide two levels of each cognitive factor. Proficient typists were selected as subjects to complete typing tasks under two levels of cognitive load and time conditions. Both subjective and objective data were collected as dependent variables. The keyboard was instrumented with force sensing resistors to collect forces from individual keys during the typing tasks. Results of the ANOVA indicate that cognitive demands had a significant effect on typing force. These results and the implications for musculoskeletal disorders in the office environment are discussed in the body of the paper.

1.0 Introduction

Traditionally, investigations of white-collar work environments (keyboarding and information processing tasks) have investigated the physical implications of different types of jobs, equipment design [1][2], or the implications of altering the cognitive load of the displays and/or controls [3]. Little has been done to provide an integrated perspective of the effects of cognitive stressors on the musculoskeletal system in these work environments.

Singh and Aghazadeh [4] investigated the interaction between human mental and physical capabilities in a study on lifting capacity. Through the use of a secondary cognitive task, it was determined that an the increased cognitive load affected various aspects of human lifting capacities. Other investigators have studied the effects of increased mental workload with respect to heart rate [5] and muscle activity [6].

The purpose of this study was to integrate the investigation of the effects of cognitive load and work stress on the musculoskeletal system. The experimental task was selected to be directly applicable to white-collar environments where these results may be applied to work and equipment design.

2.0 Methodology

2.1 Experimental Design

A 2 x 2 within-subject design was conducted with cognitive load and time stress as the two independent variables. Cognitive load was manipulated by using tasks that were written at two reading levels, as evaluated by the Flesch-Kincaid readability index; eighth-grade was designated as "low" and twelfth-grade was considered "high." The levels of the second independent variable, time stress, were introduced with the amount of time a subject had to complete the required typing task; 10 minute task time was the "low" condition, and

20-minute task time was "high."

There were three types of dependent variables collected: overall performance, subjective workload, and physiological. To measure overall performance both typing speed and number of corrections were recorded. Typing speed was calculated as words per minute (wpm) less one word per minute for each typographical error in the finished product. Number of corrections was the number of times the backspace key was used to delete a character or group of characters during the typing task. Subjective workload was measured using the NASA Task Load Index (TLX). Heart rate, blood pressure, and key force were collected as the dependent variables to measure the physiological responses to the different testing conditions.

2.2 Subjects

Six female students volunteered to participate in this study; they ranged in age from 20-25 years of age (mean=21.8 years, s.d.=1.7).) Baseline blood pressure (mean = 115.8/73.5, s.d.=6.0/5.7) and pulse (mean = 74.8, s.d.=9.0) were within normal range for all subjects. Prospective subjects were screened to be proficient typists if they could type without looking at their fingers, assessed by self-report.

2.3 Apparatus

Subjects typed tasks into WordPerfect 5.1 on a 486 computer. The macro function was used to record all keystrokes made to determine the number corrections that each subject made. The keyboard was placed on a desk so that the elbow of the subject was at a right angle and the wrist was in a neutral position. The position of the seat was adjustable for the comfort of the subject.

Forces were measured for 12 keys using force sensing resistors mounted on the keys on which subjects typed. The 12 keys in the middle of the standard QWERTY keyboard were selected to collect data across the range of motion of both the left (r,t,f,g,v,b) and right (y, u, h, j, n, m) index fingers. The force signals were recorded in a second computer (with a Pentium 200 MHz processor), in Labview v4.01. This computer was located next to the typing computer on the same desk. To calibrate the keyboard, weights were placed on each key and the force signal was recorded. A regression model was developed to relate the voltage to actual force.

2.4 Procedure

Before any of the typing tasks started, demographic data such as the age, occupation, gender, and education were collected. Prior to starting the typing tasks, physiological baseline data (blood pressure and heart rate) were collected. The first typing task was a practice task to get the subjects comfortable in the surroundings and to assess typing speed. Subjects were told that they were not given a time limit to complete the task, but that they should work as fast and as accurately as possible. For the four experimental typing tasks, subjects were told that they should try to complete as much as they could in the time limit and they should treat it as though it were an assignment that they had to turn in at the end of the task.

After each task, the subject's blood pressure and heart rate were taken. Also, subjects completed a subjective workload assessment using the computerized NASA Task Load Index (TLX) v1.0.

3.0 Results

Table 1 shows descriptive statistics for overall performance (typing speed and correction), subjective and physiological (systolic blood pressure, pulse rate, average force) variables.

Table 1 - Selected summary statistics, mean (standard deviation).

Read Level	Time Level	Typing speed (wpm)	Corrections (# per task)	Subjective Rating	Systolic Blood Pressure (mmHg)	Pulse Rate (bpm)	Average Force (mV)
Low	Low	39.7 (9.5)	80.5 (38.9)	50.5 (21.2)	106.7 (8.3)	73.2 (8.1)	0.18 (.04)
Low	High	25.5 (12.3)	120.4 (69.2)	47.0 (12.1)	114.3 (9.9)	73.5 (13.0)	0.18 (.04)
High	Low	33.7 (9.9)	69.2 (28.1)	64.2 (15.0)	117 (16.4)	68.7 (8.7)	0.17 (.05)
High	High	22.3 (9.9)	131.5 (59.2)	54.8 (24.4)	116.8 (18.1)	75.0 (16.0)	0.17 (0.5)

To evaluate overall performance, both typing speed and the number of corrections a subject made were recorded for all tasks. ANOVA results ($\alpha = 0.05$) revealed that typing speed decreased significantly as the reading level increased and as task time increased. The number of corrections was also significant for the task duration. The interaction between cognitive load and time stress was marginally significant ($\alpha = 0.10$).

The subjective workload data showed significant main effects for cognitive load and time stress. Perceived workload increased as reading level increased and as length of time decreased.

The reading level and task time had significant effects on the physiological data collected. Reading level, task duration and the interaction of the two showed significant effects on systolic blood pressure (Figure 1). Pulse rate showed significant effects for the task time and the interaction of task time and reading level (Figure 2). The average force on the keys, as recorded by the force sensing resistors, was marginally significant for only the cognitive load manipulation decreasing as reading level increased.

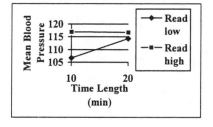

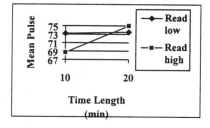

Figure 1 - Mean systolic blood pressure by reading level and task duration

Figure 2 - Mean pulse by reading level and task duration

4.0 Discussion and Conclusions

The subjective evaluation of the tasks indicated that subjects perceived two different levels of both of the independent variables. Therefore, the workload and time stress conditions both demonstrated high and low levels.

The results on overall performance indicated that the independent variables both reduced typing speed, as the cognitive load or time stress increased. The number of corrections were only affected by the increase in time stress, decreasing significantly under increased time stress. Although, the marginally significant interaction for corrections showed that when given more time, subjects made more corrections in the high reading level.

The physiological variables, blood pressure and pulse rate support the cognitive findings. As reading level increased, systolic blood pressure increased significantly. Pulse rate followed the same trend. The force data collected from the fingers typing on the keys indicated a result contrary to what was initially hypothesized; decreasing force with increasing cognitive load. This may be due to the extra time taken to type words and phrases that were not familiar to subjects, thereby decreasing the force used to activate the keys. These results, however, do not report the entire impact of these conditions on the musculoskeletal system; in future studies, EMG data will be analyzed to evaluate the fatigue and muscle effects of such tasks and work conditions.

In conclusion, this pilot study indicates that there are cognitive conditions that affect the physiological components of the human while performing keyboarding tasks. More extensive research will continue to provide an integrated perspective on these effects, including data on the muscles to provide a basis for how the task constraints in the white-collar environment may increase people's risk to musculoskeletal disorders.

5.0 References

[1]   B.J. Martin, T.J. Armstrong, J.A. Foulke, S. Natarajan, E. Klinenberg, E. Serina and D. Remple, Keyboard Reaction Force and Finger Flexor Electromyograms during Computer Keyboard Work, *Human Factors*, **38(4)** (1996) 654-664.

[2]   P. McAlindon and G.C. Lee, Perceived Workload between the Keybowl and the QWERTY Keyboard, *Proceedings of the Human Factors and Ergonomics Society 39th Annual Meeting*, (1995), 292-296.

[3]   P.A. Hancock, Effects of Control Order, Augmented Feedback, Input Device and Practice on Tracking Performance and Perceived Workload, *Human Factors*, **39(9)** (1996) 1146-1162.

[4]   S. Singh and F. Aghazadeh, Effect of Mental Load on Lifting Capacity, *Advances in Industrial Ergonomics and Safety VII*, Edited by A.C. Bitner and P.C. Champney, Taylor & Francis, 1995.

[5]   D.H. Lee and K.S. Park, Multivariate Analysis of Mental and Physical Load Components in Sinus Arrhythmia Scores, *Ergonomics*, **33(1)** (1990) 35-47.

[6]   R.W. Backs, A.M. Ryan and G.F. Wilson, Psychophysiological Measures of Workload during Continuous Manual Performance, *Human Factors*, **36(3)** (1994) 514-531.

[7]   F. E. Gomer, L.D. Silverstein, W.K. Berg and D.L. Lassiter, Changes in Electromyographic Activity Associates with Occupational Stress and Poor Performance in the Workplace, *Human Factors*, **29(2)** (1987) 131-143.

14.   Cumulative Trauma Disorders

Advances in Occupational Ergonomics and Safety II
Edited by Biman Das and Waldemar Karowski
IOS Press and Ohmsha, 1997

Predicting Tendon Damage Due to Repetitive Loading - a Proposed Model

Nancy E. Laurie MS, AEP

Department of Mechanical and Industrial Engineering
University of Massachusetts, Amherst, MA 01003

Cumulative trauma disorders (CTDs) are a group of chronic injuries that result from the body's inability to adapt to the demands of repetitive work. Attempts to model the occurrence of CTDs made up to this point suffer from their inability to assess the role of consecutive work periods over time. A model is proposed which predicts the stress and resulting strain experienced by primary wrist tendons during wrist flexion and extension motions and calculates a hypothetical level of damage.

1. Introduction

Cumulative trauma disorders (CTDs) such as tendinitis are a group of chronic injuries that result from the body's inability to adapt to the demands of repetitive work. At least four articles in the literature have attempted to develop models or methods to predict the occurrence of CTDs [1-4]. One common weakness is their inability to assess the role of consecutive work periods over time (with the possible exception of [1]). However, Goldstein [5] showed that cadaver tendons exhibit creep (become chronically stretched) when repetitively loaded under physiological conditions. Recently, Liao and Belkoff [6] modeled tendon failure as the sequential rupturing of individual tendon fibers while Wang et al. [7,8] developed models predicting tendon failure via creep and fatigue mechanisms. Results from these applied studies support Leadbetter [9] who suggests that degenerative pain in the tendon is caused by cyclic loading which induces molecular damage to tendon resulting in loss of tissue strength, increased deformation with loading and stimulation of mechanoceptors. Information from the above basic research studies may be utilized to develop a model of tendon cumulative microtrauma under repetitive loading conditions. This paper proposes a model which predicts the stress and resulting strain experienced by primary wrist tendons during motions and calculates a hypothetical level of damage.

2. Proposed Model

The goal of this model is to use subject specific anthropometric data and task specific kinematic data to predict the stress and resulting strain experienced by each primary wrist tendon and the resulting level of damage induced by repetitive wrist motion. The wrist is modeled as a universal joint with 2 degrees of freedom (flexion/extension, and radial/ulnar deviation). The following muscles are included to provide the necessary movement: flexor carpi radialis (FCR), flexor carpi ulnaris (FCU), extensor carpi ulnaris (ECU), extensor carpi radialis longus (ECRl), and extensor carpi radialis brevis (ECRb).

The model has seven modules or stages. Physical inputs to the model include: subject anthropometry, EMG muscle activity of the 5 muscles and external torque and wrist posture histories throughout the motion. The model outputs are muscle force, length and velocity profiles as well as tendon strain and level of damage. Figure 1 is a flow diagram of the model. The remainder of this paper explains each of the model's sub-components.

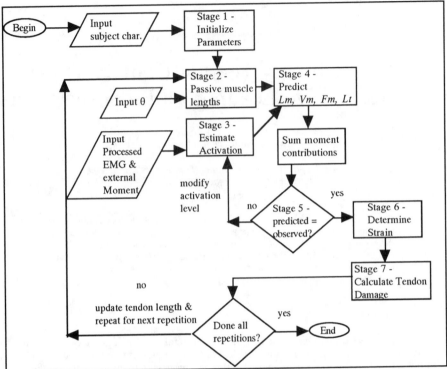

Figure 1. Model control structure.

2.1. Stage 1 - Initialize Parameters

Muscles can be distinguished by different anatomical and physiological characteristics which contribute to their force and moment producing capability about a joint. The first stage of the model accepts the subject's anthropometric measures and determines scale factors which are used to calculate the initial reference parameters of the 5 muscles. The parameters for each muscle are indexed as follows: muscle length, aponeurosis length, fiber length, PCSA, aponeurosis angle, fiber angle, pennation angle, number of sarcomeres in series, fraction of fast fibers, tendon length and tendon compliance coefficients. An original set of parameters were determined by dissection of cadaver specimens and adjusted to a biologically relevant position. This data was obtained through personal communications with Tom Burkholder of UCSD.

2.2. Stage 2 - Determine Passive Muscle Lengths for a Given Motion

This stage is responsible for taking the dynamic joint angle data and the reference muscle parameters as input and producing an array of passive muscle lengths evenly spaced with a constant time increment. Passive muscle lengths are determined using excursion versus joint angle equations for each of the primary wrist movers reported in [11]. These equations are a function of wrist angle only and since the FCR originates on the medial epicondyle of the humerus it has the ability to flex the forearm. In addition, FCU originates on the medial epicondyle, medial olecranon process and the posterior border of the ulna so it too has the ability to flex the forearm. However, if the elbow is held in a fixed position then it is only necessary to consider each primary wrist mover at the wrist joint.

2.3. Stage 3 - Estimate Activation Level

It is the goal of this stage to estimate the activation level of a muscle given its measured electromyograms (EMGs). The proposed model will incorporate the normalized dynamic pattern of each muscle's activity processed with a linear envelope. According to Winter [10] one can consider the output of activation as similar to a lightly filtered, rectified EMG (or linear envelope). He states that if the model input is an EMG, excitation dynamics are of no interest. Processed EMG will be used as the first pass to predicting individual muscle force levels. Four out of the five muscles modeled are superficial and can be detected using surface electromyography. ECRl is located underneath ECRb and the EMG signal measured will be a combination of the two muscles. This is not anticipated to be a problem because these muscles are synergistic. The combined signal will be used in the first pass to activate both muscles.

The only way to balance the predicted torque with the externally measured torque is to use the activation level as a scalar to "tweak" individual muscle forces so the difference between internal predictions and external measures are within an aceptable tolerence. Various methods have been used in the literature to accomplish this [12,13,14]. It is not clear at this time which method will work best for this model.

2.4. Stage 4 - Predict Muscle Force, Velocity, Length and Tendon Strain for One Cycle

At this stage in the model the goal is to use the passive muscle lengths array to predict muscle force, velocity, length and tendon strain for one repetition of the task. This is accomplished by implementing a modified version of the model used by Loren et al. [11]. Note that this module does not take into account the muscle activation level which acts as a scalar on the final predicted force output. The force that is predicted here is the maximum force capable of being generated given the length and velocity of the muscle.

A two component Hill-type muscle model is used to represent each of the muscles in the model. The muscle model consists of a contractile component (CC) in series with a passive elastic component (SEC). The CC is modeled as an amplified sarcomere and has the properties of force-length, force-velocity and force-activation. The SEC has a passive force-extension property.

This module uses an iterative process to step through each of the passive muscle lengths in the array. Note that the passive muscle length array is composed of passive muscle lengths for different wrist joint positions throughout a given movement. The size of the array is dependent on the duration of the movement and the number of samples taken per second. The movement may consist of wrist flexion/extension at any speed including 0 (static contraction). This was done so that the model could be applied in various working situations.

2.5. Stage 5 - Checking the Predicted Muscle Forces

Each muscle is capable of generating a given amount of torque about the wrist joint. Torque is the product of an individual muscle force and the muscle's moment arm. Each muscle is capable of creating either a flexion or extension moment and radial or ulnar moment. The individual moment contributions are summed to produce a model predicted resultant moment for each degree of freedom. The predicted moment is compared with the measured moment. If the difference is above a specified tolerance the activation level is modified (see stage 3) and input to stage 4 once again. This procedure is repeated until the predicted moments are within tolerance to the measured moments.

2.6. Stage 6 - Determine Tendon Creep

If we consider only one cycle of wrist motion then the above model would be adequate. However, if as Goldstein [5] suggests, tendon creep can occur well within the physiological range of forces generated during a typical task then the above model must be modified to account for this. Given inadequate rest, this creep can accumulate over the course of many repetitive cycles even though the other cycles of wrist motion are performed with identical kinematics. The pertinent output is tendon strain. After each repetition, depending on the force exerted by the muscle and duration of the exertion, this tendon strain or creep may increase over and above that predicted by the current model. Therefore, it must be modified by some factor *"C"*.

This increase in tendon length *"C"* changes the passive muscle length array. Muscle lengths would be slightly shorter for the same wrist angle resulting in a different sarcomere force output for the same joint angle. This could be either more or less force depending on the actual sarcomere length (due to the parabolic nature of the sarcomere force - length curve). By modifying the resulting passive muscle lengths one can account for the longer tendon without changing the mechanics of the model.

Therefore, the purpose of stage 6 is to determine the maximum tendon strain during the cycle, the force applied and the duration of the force and determine the amount of creep which developed as a result. The resulting output is used to modify the passive muscle length array for the next repetition and calculate the damage predicted to happen in the tendon.

The viscous strain model developed in [5] is utilized. For a detailed explanation of this model see [5]. To summarize, the total strain at any point in time t is the sum of the elastic strain induced by a given stress and the viscous strain that has accumulated up to this point minus any recovery strain due to a reduction in stress level. The elastic strain equations of [11] is used for each of the five muscles in the model.

2.7. Stage 7 - Calculate the Tendon "Damage" Function

The goal of this stage is to predict tendon damage *(D)* given the amount of strain accumulated. The damage function is of the same form used by [7,8] to model creep and fatigue damage in Wallaby tail tendons. Please see [7,8] for a detailed explanation. Damage is represented as 1 minus the stiffness ratio as defined in [7,8]. The stiffness ratio is a measure of the loss of tendon stiffness due to the accumulation of strain. Stiffness has been shown to be directly proportional to tendon strength. So as strain accumulates in the tendon it becomes less stiff and hence damaged.

3.   References

[1]   D.L. Fisher, R.O. Andres, D. Airth and S. Smith, Repetitive motion disorders: the design of optimal rate-rest profiles, Human Factors 35(2):283-304, 1993.

[2]   S.A. Miller, and A. Freivalds, A stress-strength interference model for predicting CTD probabilities, International Journal of Industrial Ergonomics 15:447-457, 1995.

[3]   A. Moore, R. Wells, and D. Ranney, Quantifying exposure in occupational manual tasks with cumulative trauma disorder potential, Ergonomics 34(12):1433-1453, 1991.

[4]   J. Moore and A. Garg, A job analysis method for predicting risk of upper extremity disorders at work: Preliminary results, In: R. Nielsen and K. Jorgensen (ed.), Advances in Industrial Ergonomics and Safety V, 1993.

[5]   S. A.Goldstein, Biomechanical aspects of cumulative trauma to tendons and tendon sheaths, Doctoral Dissertation University of Michigan, 1981.

[6]   H. Liao and S. M. Belkoff, A model to study the tensile failure of tendon, In Advances in Bioengineering ASME 26, (1993) 619-621.

[7]   X. Wang and R. Ker, Creep rupture of wallaby tail tendons, J. Experimental Biology. 198, (1995) 847-852.

[8]   X. Wang, R. Ker and R. Alexander, Fatigue rupture of wallaby tail tendons, J. Experimental Biology 198, (1995) 847-852.

[9]   W. Leadbetter, Cell-matrix response in tendon injury, Clinics in Sports Medicine 11(3), (1992) 533-579.

[10]   D. Winter, Biomechanics and Motor Control of Human Movement, (New York:John Wiley & Sons, Inc.), 1990 pp. 165-212.

[11]   G. Loren and R. Lieber, Tendon biomechanical properties enhance human wrist muscle specialization, J. Biomechanics 28(7), (1995) 791-799.

[12]   G.E. Caldwell and A.E. Chapman, The general distribution problem: a physiological solution which includes antagonism. Human Movement Science 10 1991, 355-392.

[13]   M. R. Pierrynowski and J.B. Morrison, A physiological model for the evaluation of muscular forces in human locomotion: theoretical aspects. Mathematical Biosciences 75 1985, 69-101.

[14]   R. Happee, Inverse dynamic optimization including muscular dynamics, a new simulation method applied to goal directed movements. Journal of Biomechanics. 27(7) 1994, 953-960.

Advances in Occupational Ergonomics and Safety II
Edited by Biman Das and Waldemar Karowski
IOS Press and Ohmsha, 1997

Prevalence of Tendinitis and Related Disorders among U.S. Workers Based on an Analysis of the 1988 National Health Interview Survey Data

Shiro Tanaka, Deanna K. Wild, Lorraine Cameron

Division of Surveillance, Hazard Evaluations, and Field Studies (DSHEFS)
National Institute for Occupational Safety and Health (NIOSH)
Centers for Disease Control and Prevention (CDC)
4676 Columbia Parkway, Cincinnati, Ohio 45226, U.S.A.

The Occupational Health Supplement Data of 1988 National Health Interview Survey were analyzed for tendinitis and related disorders by using the Survey Data Analysis (SUDAAN) software. Among the 30,090 respondents who had worked anytime during the previous 12 months, 0.26% (95% confidence interval: 0.18; 0.34) reported that they experienced a "prolonged hand discomfort" which was called tendinitis, synovitis, tenosynovitis, de Quervain's disease, or epicondylitis, by a medical person. By means of a statistical weighting scheme, this was extrapolated to a national estimate of approximately 335,000 persons (95% CI: 233,000; 439,000) reporting one of these disorders for that year. Of these, 44% or 147,000 reported that their medical person said that the condition was work-related. Combined with the previously estimated 356,000 cases of work-related carpal tunnel syndrome, we estimate that in 1988 there were approximately 503,000 cases of hand/wrist cumulative trauma disorders among 127 million U.S. workers (prevalence of 0.4%).

1. Introduction

Since the early 1980s, the U.S. Bureau of Labor Statistics (BLS) reported a steady increase of "Disorders associated with Repeated Trauma (DART)" or cumulative trauma disorders (CTDs) in many segments of American industry. Included in these categories are disorders such as carpal tunnel syndrome (CTS), tendinitis, synovitis, tenosynovitis, and bursitis [1]. In particular, CTS has in recent years received special attention by the news media as well as occupational health professionals probably due to its magnitude and specific symptomatology [2]. However, CTS is not the only disorder that afflicts the upper extremity as a result of repetitive and/or strenuous manual work [3,4,5,6]. To obtain a more complete scope and the magnitude of CTDs in the hand/wrist region, we have attempted to obtain a national estimates of CTDs other than CTS.

2. Materials and Method

Sample and Survey

The National Health Interview Survey (NHIS), conducted by the National Center for Health Statistics (NCHS), is a continuous survey designed to make national estimates of health characteristics for the civilian, non-institutionalized population of the United States. Households, which are the sampling unit of the survey design, are selected by a multistage probability sampling strategy [7]. Each year supplemental health surveys are added to the core survey. In 1988, the National Institute for Occupational Safety and Health (NIOSH) and Bureau of Labor Statistics (BLS) sponsored a supplement on occupational health. Questions related to hand discomfort and carpal tunnel syndrome were included in this Occupational Health Supplement (OHS) [8].

At each sampled household, one adult (18 years old or older) was randomly selected for the OHS interview without allowing a proxy. Altogether, 44,233 interviews were completed with an overall response rate of 87%. Non-responses, which were mostly due to refusal, absence on repeated visits, or mental incapacity, were adjusted for by the statistical weighting [7].

Measures and Definitions

The respondents who worked anytime during the 12 months prior to the survey were categorized as "recent workers" and included in the analysis. The respondents were next categorized by presence or absence of "prolonged hand discomfort," which was defined as hand discomfort which was felt for a total of 20 days or more, or 7 or more consecutive days during the past 12 months. If a "recent worker" saw a medical person (medical doctor, chiropractor, physical therapist or other medical person) for "prolonged hand discomfort," then the next question "What did the medical person call your hand discomfort?" was asked. If the response was "tendinitis, synovitis, tenosynovitis, de Quervain's disease, or epicondylitis," it was recorded as such without validation of the medical record. These diagnoses were lumped together in the final data set and could not be separated for each separate disorder. (DeQuervain's disease is tenosynovitis of abductor pollicis longus and extensor pollicis brevis at the radial styloid process. Although epicondylitis is a disorder at the elbow, it could not be segregated from disorders of hand/wrist in the 1988 NHIS/OHS data set.)

Analysis

The data tape provided by NCHS contained both the raw (unweighted) counts and the weights necessary to convert the raw counts to population-wide estimates. Each respondent was weighted to represent anywhere from 3,000 to 10,000 people in his/her demographic category, depending on such factors as the probability of selection and household nonresponse [7]. The population prevalence of tendinitis, synovitis, tenosynovitis, de Quervain's disease, or epicondylitis, were calculated as a group with their 95% confidence intervals (95% CI's) using Survey Data Analysis (SUDAAN) software [9].

3. Results

Among the 30,090 "recent workers" there were 94 (0.31%) who reported prolonged hand discomfort and one of medically-called disorders (tendinitis or related conditions). Of these 94 cases, 62 (66%) were females and 32 (34%) were males. Their prevalence (and 95% CI) in the corresponding population was 0.42% (95% CI: 0.30; 0.54) and 0.22% (0.14; 0.30), respectively. The difference between these values was statistically significant ($p < 0.0037$ by *chi*-square test).

The 94 cases could be grouped into 67 (71%) who reported having been exposed to bending/twisting of the hands and wrist at work and 27 (29%) who did not. Of these, 0.45% (95%CI: 0.31; 0.59) of the exposed reported one of the medically-called tendinitis or related conditions, while 0.18% (0.10; 0.26) of those not exposed reported one of those conditions. The difference was statistically significant ($p = 0.0003$).

After excluding 16 individuals who gave inconsistent responses from the initial 94, the remaining 78 respondents were used to derive a national estimate of people who had a prolonged hand discomfort and were told by a medical person that they had one of those conditions in 1988. This can be extrapolated to an estimated 335,000 cases nationally (95% CI: 233,000; 439,000). However, only 35 (44%) of the 78 cases were told by a medical person that the condition was work-related, which represent approximately 147,000 workers nationally who experienced prolonged hand discomfort considered to be work-related tendinitis or a related condition.

4. Discussion

Although their significance as occupational musculoskeletal disorders have been overshadowed by the recent surge of carpal tunnel syndrome cases, it still remains that tendinitis, tenosynovitis and other related disorders are important subgroups of CTDs or RSIs of occupational origin. While tendinitis can occur at any tendons in the body, the majority of work related tendinitis occurs in the upper extremities due to their usage in repetitive manual work. In this analysis, we focused on tendinitis of the hand/wrist area by the definitions and analytical procedures described in the method.

Whether it is called tendinitis, tenosynovitis or carpal tunnel syndrome, these disorders can be considered as a group, since their etiology is similar, i.e., repetitive and often forceful use of the body part without appropriate rest. CTS is only different in that, in addition to tenosynovial inflammation, or because of that, the median nerve is compressed within the tight structure of the carpal tunnel. Therefore, when we consider a national estimate of hand/wrist CTDs, it is necessary to combine all of these conditions, as it was done by BLS through the year 1992. BLS reported 115,400 cases of DART in 1988, while our estimate is about 4.4 times as many. This discrepancy can be traced to several reasons: (a) the BLS survey excluded the public sector, establishments with less than 11 employees, domestic household employees, and self-employed individuals, while NHIS/OHS covered the entire adult non-institutionalized working population; (b) case definitions are different between BLS' occupational illness and NHIS/OHS; (c) Data-generating surveillance (such as with use of questionnaire) tends to collect more cases than record-based surveillance (such as review of OSHA-200 logs).

5. Conclusion

Tendinitis and related disorders of the hand/wrist are an important subgroup of work-related cumulative trauma disorders. They deserve continued surveillance and future research for intervention and prevention.

6. References

[1] Bureau of Labor Statistics, Occupational Injuries and Illnesses in the United States by Industry, 1990, U.S. Department of Labor, Bulletin 2399, April 1992.

[2] S.Tanaka, D.K.Wild, P.J.Seligman, W.E.Halperin, V.J.Behrens, V.Putz-Anderson, Prevalence and Work-Relatedness of Self-Reported Carpal Tunnel Syndrome among U.S. Workers: Analysis of the Occupational Health Supplement Data of 1988 National Health Interview Survey, *American Journal of Industrial Medicine* 27(1995) 451-470.

[3] A.R.Thompson, L.W.Plewes, E.G.Shaw, Peritendinitis Crepitans and Simple Tenosynovitis: A Clinical Study of 544 Cases in Industry, *British Journal of Industrial Medicine* 8 (1951) 150-160.

[4] P.W.Lapidus, R.Fenton, Stenosing Tenovaginitis at the Wrist and Fingers, *Archives of Surgery* 64 (1952) 475-487.

[5] R.D.Muckart, Stenosing tendovaginitis of abductor pollicis longus and extensor pollicis brevis at the radial styloid process (de Quervain's disease), *Clinical Orthopedics* 33 (1964) 201-208.

[6] P.Roto, P.Kivi, Prevalence of Epicondylitis and Tenosynovitis among Meatcutters, *Scandinavian Journal of Work, Environment and Health* 10 (1984) 203-205.

[7] J.T.Massey, T.F.Moore, V.L.Persons, W.Tadros, Design and Estimation for the National Health Interview survey, 1985-1994. National Center for Health Statistics; Vital & Health Statistics Series 2, No.110. DHHS Publication No. (PHS) 89-1384. Washington, DC, 1989.

[8] C.Park, D.K.Wagener, D.M.Winn, J.Pierce, Health Conditions among the Currently Employed, United States 1988. National Center for Health Statistics; Vital & Health Statistics 10 (186). DHHS Publication No. (PHS) 93-1514. Hyattsville, MD, 1993.

[9] Research Triangle Institute (RTI), Survey Data Analysis (SUDAAN), Research Triangle Park, NC, 1990.

Advances in Occupational Ergonomics and Safety II
Edited by Biman Das and Waldemar Karwowski
IOS Press and Ohmsha, 1997

Psychosocial & Treatment Factors Impacting Carpal Tunnel Syndrome Outcomes

David Zehel, *University of Wisconsin-Madison, Department of Industrial Engineering.*

Abstract: This study proposed to investigate factors effecting the long term outcome (LTO) of workers with surgically treated Carpal Tunnel Syndrome (CTS). It was hypothesized that individuals more involved with their job situation, medical treatment and return to work would have shorter recovery times and better long term outcomes. It was thought that workers who understood the treatment process including what they could do to hasten it and were supported and encouraged to do so by their employer, and others in the system, would have the best outcomes.

An extensive literature review was conducted along with interviews of personnel involved in the worker care system to identify factors impacting CTS return to work issues. Job related factors include relationships with other employees, knowledge of ergonomics, ability to alter the physical workplace, understanding of the worker compensation system, return to work arrangements, and expectations and post surgical contact with employer. Medical factors include length of conservative treatment, understanding of CTS and the repair process, rehabilitation, surgical expectations, post surgery contact with employer and length of time away from work.

Hospital discharge records of all CTS surgeries performed in Wisconsin were the initial data base used for this study. Information was also gathered via a mailed questionnaire. Pre-existing physical conditions that could contribute to the development of CTS were used to remove cases from the study. Workman's compensation cases selected were matched on significant factors so that comparisons could be made. A logistical regression was planned to determine what combination of factors predicted the best outcomes.

1. Introduction:

Although many factors are thought to contribute to the development, progression and correction of CTS, the main focus of this research will be on surgical treatment of CTS and the workplace-worker-health care provider interaction regarding outcomes. Types of rehabilitation will be investigated along with possible changes in the workplace that confront a returning worker. Surprisingly there has been little research of this type despite its need being recognized [1,2].

The efficacy of surgery is an important factor in this research for several reasons. It is invasive and drastic in comparison to conservative medical treatments and its short-term success has been rated excellent for almost all cases to less than half the cases treated [3,4]. Surgery's long term success is even more varied [5]. Unfortunately the outcome measures used have little consistency and are often quite subjective, even to the point of appearing to be based solely on the treating physician's judgment.

Surgical treatment is of two types, the initially developed open technique or the much newer endoscopic technique. Both sever the Carpal Tunnel ligament to reduce pressure on the median nerve. The open procedure involves an incision at the base of the palm not generally extending into the wrist crease, exposing the ligament so that it can be cut through. The procedure is rather straight forward, routinely performed in somewhat less than an hour and often badly done in much less than that [6]. It is generally performed under local anesthetic and on an out-patient basis. Complications can involve increased sensitivity of the incision scar, infections and damaged tendons and nerves.

CTS surgery rehabilitation takes a variety of forms. Supervised physical therapy is not generally ordered with open hand surgery with patients expected to work at regaining hand function on their own [7]. Rehabilitation specialists recommend four to six weeks before workers can return to their jobs, but healing can take three months or even longer [8]. There are studies indicating workers' compensation CTS cases result in longer recovery times [3]. This might be an artifact of the workers' compensation system with cases challenged by management possibly exacerbating the recovery process or it might be a result of work related cases involving more damage than non-work related cases.

Recovery can be aided by early return to work if suitable work is available. Often referred to as light duty, this type of work can speed the recovery process by exercising the hand and getting the worker off workers' compensation sooner, a definite advantage for the employer [9]. But light duty work has often been challenged by both employers and physicians. Employers have generally done so for several reasons with claims of no light duty work available and administrative problems being commonly mentioned. One Wisconsin company tried bringing recovering workers back (from all types of injuries, not just CTS surgery) not to the plant but to a nearby sheltered workshop. This allowed the company to support a worthy community cause, encouraged the healing process with work under closely supervised conditions and got injured workers off their workers' compensation rolls sooner [10]. Physicians are more likely to use early return to work when they have some assurance that the work does not compromise their patient's recovery. This requires coordination between business and physicians regarding the patients status with both making their needs, expectations and capabilities known to the other [9,11,12].

There is wide variation in reported outcomes of CTS surgery. Most studies have not been explicit in surgical evaluation criteria. Others have used subjective treatment evaluations provided by the treating physician, certainly not the most objective judge of treatment result. It seems reasonable to suggest the best judge of surgical treatment efficacy to be the patient involved. Their CTS surgery expectations would obviously influence their satisfaction with the actual outcome but nothing apparently has been published on how CTS patients are, or should be, advised regarding their recovery limits. If a physician advises them as to their potential surgical outcome they have a puzzling range of 27% to 98.3% "excellent" results to quote from the literature [2,3,5,7,13,14,15]. Probably this wide range reflects the in-exactness of measures used.

2. Hypothesis:

2.1.) More directed medical care results in better long term outcomes than less directed.

This means all the participants in the treatment process, injured worker, employer and health care providers are working towards the same goals and with the same understandings of limiting conditions. This hypothesis was developed as a reaction to the observation of the compartmentalization of various aspects of the treatment and recovery process.

2.2.) Supported workers have better long term outcomes than those who aren't.

Workers who have the support of their fellow workers, family members, employers and health care providers are expected to have significantly better outcomes than those who lack this support.

3. Methodology:

The Wisconsin Division of Health has been accumulating information on all state CTS surgeries via hospital discharge reports since July 1990. Only subjects whose surgeries were covered by worker compensation and have no other existing physical conditions that could contribute to CTS will be used. The hospital discharge reports will also provide valuable demographic information.

A nine page, forty-plus, question survey instrument was developed to gather information in four areas, (timeline, health care, knowledge and interactions), believed necessary to test the research hypothesis. The questionnaire, a consent form and a letter outlining in general the purpose of the study will be sent to each potential subject.

A phone survey questionnaire based on a review of the returned surveys will be developed. It will focus on interactions in the worker-employer-health care provider relationship. A panel of physicians surgically treating CTS cases will review the initial survey data to provide additional insight into the CTS treatment process. The phone survey will be conducted by a survey research lab connected with the University.

Logistical regression will be used to analyze the data. The questionnaire was developed and structured with this in mind.

4. Results:

Unfortunately this research has been stalled. The main problem has been obtaining data from the state. Wisconsin's Division of Health has received CDC and Sentinel Event Notification System for Occupational Risks (SENSOR) grants for an occupational disease surveillance program. The program was developed to target specific health problems and through enhanced reporting efforts obtain a better understanding of potential causal factors. Although data has been collected on CTS surgeries, little has been done with this information. Challenges to other public health research here in Wisconsin have caused state agencies to become cautious in allowing collected data to be used in ways that might threaten litigation. This has resulted in extended review and discussion that was not anticipated or suggested when the research was proposed.

Only cursory analysis of the collected CTS data base has been done. Wisconsin had approximately 7,250 people per year undergoing CTS surgery in the early 1990's [16]. Approximately one-fourth were covered by the worker compensation system. If the state's experience is similar to Maine's (where a much smaller study was conducted) approximately one-fourth of the worker compensation cases will still be off of work 18 months after surgery [17].

At one time it appeared possible to link Wisconsin's CTS data base, worker compensation files, and this research's data base to gain a direct cost comparison of CTS long term outcomes but this has been put aside for future research. It could be that linking such records will not be possible due to the threat of legal action on the part of any of a wide number of participants, or near participants, in the process.

5. Discussion:

This research was prompted by the author's ten years of loss control work for a major insurance carrier. During this time widely different worker-management relationships were observed. Some companies treated an injured worker as someone who inexplicably failed them by developing a job related illness. They often did little in aiding the worker in finding qualified medical care nor were they generally willing to assist in their early return to work preferring instead to accept them back only when they were fully medically released. Other companies encouraged workers to come forward with their injuries as soon as symptoms were noticed so that they could be directed to medical help. These companies often worked with medical professionals to facilitate the return of injured workers both pre- and post treatment. Additionally they often made certain the worker was briefed on their worker compensation benefits and put in touch with a representative of the insurance carrier. It appeared that those companies who worked with all involved in the treatment process had better results then those who didn't. Testing these observations led to this research.

The anticipated outcome of this research is information useful to employers so that they can better deal with CTS injured workers and their attending health care professionals. The end result should be a reduction in the substantial direct and indirect costs of surgically treated CTS.

References:
[1] Rempel, D.M., Harrison, R.J., Barnharts, S. (1992) Work-related Cumulative Trauma Disorders of the Upper Extremity. JAMA, vol.267#6:838-842.
[2] Adams, M.L., Franklin, G.M. Barnhart, S. (1994). Outcome of Carpal Tunnel Surgery in Washington State Workers' Compensation. American Journal of Industrial Medicine, 25:527-536.
[3] Yu, G.Z., Firrell, J.C., Tsai, T.M. (1992) Preoperative factors and treatment outcome following carpal tunnel release, Journal of Hand Surgery-British Vol., 17(6):646-50.
[4] Cotton, P.(1991) Symptoms May Return After Carpal Tunnel Surgery. JAMA, 265(15):1922-23.
[5] Haupt, W.F., Wintzer, G., Schop, A., Lottgen, J., Pawlik, G. (1993) Long-term Results of Carpal Tunnel Decompression-Assessment of 60 Cases. Journal of Hand Surgery, vol.18B#4:471-474, August.
[6] Ashbell, T.S. (1992) Re: Two Devastating Complications of Carpal Tunnel Surgery. Annuals of Plastic Surgery, 28(6):380-381, June.
[7] Schenk, R.R. (1988) Keeping in touch with Pain, Safety and Health, December, pg. 40-42.
[8] Pagnanelli, D.M., M.D., (1989) Hands-on Approach To Avoiding Carpal Tunnel Syndrome, Risk Management, vol. 36, May, 20-23.
[9] Millender, L.H. (1992) Occupational Disorders of the Upper Extremity: Orthopedics, Psychosocial and legal Implications, Chapter 1, in Occupational Disorders of the Upper Extremity, Ed. by Millender, L.H., Louis, D.S., Simmons, B.P., Churchill Livingstone, New York, pg. 1-13.
[10] Smith, M.J., Zehel, D.J. (1990) Cumulative Trauma Injury Control Efforts in Select Wisconsin Manufacturing Plants, in Advances in Industrial Ergonomics and Safety II, Ed. By Biman Das, Taylor & Francis, pg. 259-264.
[11] Eversmann, W.W. (1992) Employers' Response to Occupational Disorders, Occupational Disorders of the Upper Extremity, Ed. by Millender, L.H., Louis, D.S., Simmons, B.P., Churchill Livingstone, New York, Chapter 6, pg. 69-78.
[12] Lynch, R.T., Leonard, J., Powers, J. (1997, In press) Vocational rehabilitation for injured workers, in Physical medicine and rehabilitation clinics of North America, Ed. By Johnson, K.L., and Haselkorn, J., Vovcational Rehabilitation, Philadelphia: W.B. Saunders.
[13] Rothfleisch, S. Sherman, D. (1978), Carpal Tunnel Syndrome, Biomechanical aspects of Occupational occurrence and Implication's Regarding Surgical Management,Orthopaedic Review, vol. 7#6, June.
[14] Langloh, N.D., Linscheid, R.L. (1972) Recurrent and Unrelieved Carpal-tunnel Syndrome, Clinical Orthopaedics and Related Research, #83, March-April, pgs. 41-47.
[15] Semple, J.C., Cargill A.O. (1969) Carpal Tunnel Syndrome: Results of Surgical Decompression, Lancet: 918-919.
[16] Hanrahan, L.P., Higgins, D., Anderson, H., Smith, M. (1993) Wisconsin Occupational carpal tunnel syndrome surveillance: the incidence of surgically treated cases. Wisconsin Medical Journal, Dec., pgs. 685-688.
[17] Katz, J. (1996) Occupational and Clinical Outcome Comparison of Workers' Compensation Carpal Tunnel Syndrome Cases Treated Surgically and Non-surgically, paper presented at the International Conference on Occupational Disorders of the Upper Extremities, Oct 24-25, Ann Arbor, Michigan.

Advances in Occupational Ergonomics and Safety II
Edited by Biman Das and Waldemar Karwowski
IOS Press and Ohmsha, 1997

A REVIEW OF THE ADVANCEMENTS IN CARPAL TUNNEL SYNDROME RESEARCH

Kari Babski and Lesia Crumpton, Ph.D.

Department of Industrial Engineering
P.O. Drawer 9542
Mississippi State University
Mississippi State, MS 39762

Abstract. Many research studies have been conducted in which ergonomic measures for preventing and controlling the development of cumulative trauma disorders (CTD's) in the workplace have been proposed. However, CTD's are still a major problem facing industry today. Carpal Tunnel Syndrome (CTS) is one such CTD whose occurrence is developing in epidemic proportions in the workplace. The medical costs, as well as the pain and suffering experienced by persons afflicted with this disorder are factors that provide the impetus for identifying measured to combat the occurrence of CTS. The objective of this paper was to review and briefly summarize the research literature available for preventing and controlling CTS.

1.0 INTRODUCTION

Carpal Tunnel Syndrome (CTS), a nerve disorder where the median nerve becomes compressed in the carpal canal area which results in pain, numbness, and tingling primarily in the first finger, second finger, and the palm of the hand, is one of the most common injuries in today's workplace. CTS accounts for one-third of all work related injuries [1]. Due to these staggering numbers, ergonomists and medical professionals have attempted to perform research studies aimed at understanding the development of this disorder as well as determining methods for the prevention and control of this illness. As a result of these efforts, many factors have been hypothesized to contribute to the development of CTS in the workplace including repetition, duration, force exertions required by the hand, vibration, and wrist posture.

Many of the methods developed to prevent and control the onset of CTS have focused on eliminating or reducing the occurrence of the aforementioned hypothesized factors in job tasks. While some of the developments have been successful in preventing and controlling the development of CTS some have not. A discussion of some common methods developed for preventing and controlling the development of CTS follows.

2.0 ERGONOMIC INTERVENTIONS

The main thrust for preventing and controlling CTS has been in the redesign of the workplace. Ergonomic interventions employed in the workplace to prevent and control the development of CTS include: workstation design changes, tool design changes, stretching exercises for the hands, and employee education awareness training.

2.1 Workstation Design

Workstation design interventions have primarily focused on eliminating or minimizing the awkward postures of the human operator while performing occupational tasks, specifically of the wrist and of the body. The use of adjustable work surfaces allows operators to position the work surface height to eliminate flexion, extension, or ulnar and radial deviation of the wrist. Similarly, the use of adjustable chairs also allows the operators to position themselves at the proper working height to ensure that the wrists are in a neutral position while performing job tasks.

The development of CTS is often associated with performing keyboarding operations. Several keyboards have been developed to reduce or eliminate the awkward postures induced by the standard QWERTY keyboard. The Kinesis keyboard has recessed keys and is designed to optimize the position of the hands and minimize the deviation of the wrist. Split keyboards allow operators to place the keyboard at various angles to allow for correct postures of the shoulder and elbow. Adjustable tilt keyboards are also available to reduce wrist deviations. Studies have shown each of these modifications to be effective in eliminating or reducing awkward postures of the wrists while performing keyboarding tasks.

One workstation design change that has received negative reviews is that of wrist rests [2]. Initially, wrist rests were developed to provide support for the wrists and reduce the amount of stress in the arms and wrists [2]. However, the use of wrist rests actually increase the pressure in the carpal tunnel area by placing force of the carpal bones covering the median nerve [2]. Forearm supports are used as an alternative design to wrist rests. They were also designed to reduce the amount of stress in the arms and wrists but without creating additional forces on the carpal canal. One study on the use of forearm supports showed promising results [2]. The study indicated that forearm supports allowed the operators to have freedom of movement while keeping the wrists straight and allowing the arms to relax.

2.2 Tool Design

The design of tools has become increasingly significant to efforts aimed at preventing and controlling CTS due to the application of force required by the hand to use/activate the tools. To combat the effects of poor tool design in the development of CTS, several guidelines have been generated for the design of manual and power tools. Important guidelines for the use of manual tools include the following[3]:

1. Use tools that distribute the grip forces over a large area;
2. Use tools in which the handles extend beyond the palm;

3. Do not use tools in which a pinch grip is necessary;
4. Do not use tools that create pressure on the sides of the fingers;
5. Tools with circle grips should accommodate a wide range of users;
6. Do not use tools with finger grooves;
7. Cover the handles of tools with soft, non-slip materials to cushion the hand and distribute the forces;
8. Use tools that allow the handle to be rotated to allow for their use while the wrists are in a neutral position.

The use of power tools can also contribute to the development of CTS mainly due to the weight of the tools and the amount of vibration experienced by the operators while using these tools. Guidelines for the use of power tools include the following [3]:

1. Minimize the amount of vibration from the tools through the use of rubber handles or gloves to absorb the vibration of the tools;
2. Provide flexible cords to allow the operators to use the tools in the correct position; and
3. Suspend the tools overhead on balancers to allow the operator to guide the tool without having to bear the weight of the tool in the hand.

Roberta Carson has identified four steps for selecting tools for job tasks [3]:

1. Use anthropometric data in the design of tools to accommodate a wide range of users.
2. Decrease the number of repetitions the workers must perform with the tool.
3. Reduce the amount of force required by the hand to use the tool.
4. Eliminate any awkward postures associated with tool use.

Redesigning tools can help to eliminate or minimize the occurrence of factors hypothesized to contribute to the onset of CTS, such as awkward postures, force, and vibration.

2.3 Exercises

Recently the use of exercises and stretches for the hands and wrists have become preventive measures for CTS. These exercises were developed to reduce the amount of pressure in the carpal tunnel area [4]. Studies of these exercises have shown that the use of these exercises can reduce the amount of pressure in the carpal tunnel area significantly and for extended periods of time [4]. Based on research, after performing these exercises the pressure in the carpal tunnel area remained lower for 10 minutes after the completion of the exercises [4]. It is recommended that the exercises be performed before, during, and after work.

2.4 Education

Education is an essential factor to preventing and controlling CTS, because it helps to ensure that operators perform operations correctly and actively assist in taking precautions needed to assist in combating this disorder. A change in the behavior of the operators will assist in successfully reducing the number of CTS cases. Education should involve all workers and members of an organization to create an awareness of CTS, it's symptoms, and precautions needed to avoid its occurrence.

Education is also important to ensure that the operators use the equipment correctly. Studies have shown that when individuals are given adjustable equipment with no training on how and why they need to use the equipment, the individuals will not use them [6]. Therefore, any benefit expected to be gained from the use of the equipment will go unrealized [6].

Education on the use of proper postures while working can increase the operators knowledge of awkward postures and how this impacts the development of CTS. Thus, they can identify when that are in a potentially dangerous work position. A study has shown that when operators were given training on what CTS was and were trained on the correct postures, these operators were able to maintain the correct positions while maintaining their performance [6].

Some education guidelines have been developed to help operators in minimizing their risk of developing CTS [7]:

1. Keep the wrists straight;
2. Avoid prolonged periods of repetitive movements;
3. Decrease the speed and force of all repetitive movements;
4. Take frequent breaks; and
5. Perform hand and arm exercises;

3.0 FUTURE CONSIDERATIONS

The repercussions of the occurrence of CTS in the workplace has sparked an enormous amount of research on ergonomic interventions that can be utilized to prevent and control the development of CTS. Although the use of these ergonomic interventions have been effective, more studies are needed to quantify the usefulness of these measures. Also, the development of more prediction models can be helpful in identifying what tasks or aspects of a task could contribute more significantly to the development of CTS. These forecasting models can be used to identify possible changes in the work task design to prevent the onset of CTS. The use of ergonomic interventions and prediction models coupled with periodic employee screening and monitoring programs will also help reduce the number of CTS cases.

REFERENCES

[1]   Editorial Review, Preventing Carpal Tunnel Syndrome, *HR Focus*, (July 1995) 23.
[2]   Alan Hedge and James Powers, Wrist postures while keyboarding: effects of a negative slope keyboard system and full motion forearm supports, *Ergonomics*, (March 1995) 508-517.
[3]   Roberta Carson, Ergonomically Designed Tools, *Occupational Hazards*, (September 1995) 49-54.
[4]   Editorial Review, Preventing CTS Through Exercise, Occupational Hazards, (May 1996) 14.
[5]   Tim Pottorff et al., Toward a Knowledge Based System of CTD's for Office Work, *Advances in Industrial Ergonomics and Safety Vol. IV*, (1992) 731-738.
[6]   Kathleen McCann and Beth Sulzer-Azaroff, Cumulative Trauma Disorders: Behavioral Injury Prevention at Work, *Journal of Applied Behavioral Science*, (September 1996) 277-291.
[7]   William Case, Carpal Tunnel Syndrome: Relief for a Common Wrist Problem, *The Physician and Sports Medicine*, (January 1995) 27-28.

Advances in Occupational Ergonomics and Safety II
Edited by Biman Das and Waldemar Karwowski
IOS Press and Ohmsha, 1997

Effect of Session Length and Time Between Sessions on the Reliability of Psychophysical Evaluations of Repetitive Hand Grasping

Eric E. Swensen, Robert E. Schlegel and Jerry L. Purswell
University of Oklahoma, School of Industrial Engineering, Norman, Oklahoma, 73019

Researchers have used the psychophysical method of adjustment to study various parameters of repetitive hand grasping work/rest cycles. However, these studies have often not reported the reliability of the measure used or the impact of session duration. The objectives of the current study were to determine (1) the stability of psychophysically-determined rest times across sessions separated by 1 to 14 days, (2) the difference in subject-determined rest times for a ten-minute vs. a twenty-minute test session, and (3) the extent of variation across sessions in the maximum voluntary contraction (MVC) hand grip.

Nine female subjects performed a simulated industrial hand grasping task in twenty-minute sessions conducted across four weeks. Each subject was required to exert a grasping force of 30% of her MVC for five seconds. Travel distance was 0.64 cm (0.25 inch) to simulate activating the trigger on a power tool. The subject then relaxed her grip for a rest period whose length could be adjusted at two-minute intervals. These subject-determined rest intervals were recorded at ten and twenty minutes into the task. Test sessions were conducted on Days 1, 2, 9 and 23.

Mean MVC values increased from Session 1 to Session 3, with no statistically significant difference among Sessions 2, 3, and 4. Mean rest times did not vary significantly among the sessions across the four-week period, indicating a reasonable level of stability in the psychophysical measure. However, the initial set-point of the rest time prior to subject adjustment did affect the final rest time value. There was no significant difference in the rest time selected at the end of ten minutes vs. twenty minutes. This study provides support for the use of psychophysical methods in setting work/rest cycle parameters for repetitive hand grasping, but also identifies areas where caution must be observed in establishing the test methodology.

1. Introduction

Cumulative trauma disorders (CTD) and carpal tunnel syndrome (CTS) have been described as the most common problems of the hand in the United States [1]. Over the last four decades, research has identified several occupational factors as contributing causes of CTS. These include repetitive movements, forceful exertions, sustained or constrained postures, vibration, low temperature, and mechanical stress [2, 3, 4, 5]. Silverstein [3] found that high force-high repetition jobs had a significantly greater risk for CTS than low force-low repetition jobs. In addition to these risk factors, task parameters such as exertion time and work duration have been reported as important occupational risk factors [6]. Several authors have used the psychophysical method in hand grasping research [6, 7, 8]. They used the method to investigate work-rest grasping cycles that were acceptable to subjects.

Researchers have used the psychophysical method of adjustment to study various parameters of repetitive hand grasping work/rest cycles. However, these studies have often not reported the reliability of the measure used or the impact of session duration. The objectives of the current study were to determine (1) the stability of psychophysically-determined rest times across sessions separated by 1 to 14 days, (2) the difference in subject-determined rest times for a ten-minute vs. a twenty-minute test session, and (3) the extent of variation across sessions in the maximum voluntary contraction (MVC) hand grip.

2. Literature Review

Psychophysical methodologies applied to physical exertion have been used primarily in manual material handling studies. Two of the first psychophysical frequency wrist posture studies investigated simulated sheet metal drilling tasks. These studies used different forces and wrist postures (wrist flexion and ulnar deviation). Both studies found that the maximum acceptable frequency (MAF) of grasping was significantly reduced during wrist flexion when compared to a neutral wrist posture [7, 8]. Grip strength decreased significantly with wrist flexion, although not with ulnar deviation. Both authors suggested that the psychophysical approach was valid and reliable for determining workload guidelines for hand/wrist work.

Abu-Ali [6] used the psychophysical adjustment method to investigate the effect of wrist posture, force, and exertion period on acceptable work cycle parameters of rest period, rest-to-work ratio (RWR) and duty cycle for females. The study identified a significant effect of force and wrist angle. The RWR was higher for 50% MVC compared to 25% MVC and for the 1-second exertion period compared to the 5-second exertion period. A direction-of-change effect was found that resulted from experimenter-induced rest time changes. When rest times were changed by the experimenter, the subject detected the change and the direction of change in rest time. Subjects then made the appropriate compensation. However, they returned to a value that was greater than or less than the pre-change value, depending on whether time was added or subtracted from the pre-change value, respectively.

The psychophysical method of adjustment was used by Marley and Ramalingam [9] to examine acceptable hand forces under dynamic grasping conditions. Twelve males were used to investigate a grasping task for a 25-minute psychophysical adjustment session. The study examined four combinations of grasp frequency and velocity of tool activation. The data showed that both grasp frequency and tool handle velocity were significant factors. When subjects were required to perform frequent grasps, the subjects selected less resistance compared to the value selected at the lower frequency.

3. Method

Nine female subjects were recruited to participate in this study. The mean age for this group was 26.7 years (range 20 to 45 years). All subjects were right-handed and were pre-screened for prior repetitive motion injury. All subjects tested negative for prior CTS symptoms and were cleared to participate. A series of five MVC measurements was recorded. The first two measurements were discarded and the final three were averaged to serve as the baseline MVC from which the individual load of 30% MVC was developed.

The experiment began with a dynamic hand dynamometer configured to record pre-trial MVC measurements. A load cell was wired to a computer and MVC measurements were collected using LABTECH Notebook software. MVC measurements were recorded with two-minute rest periods between exertions. The system was then configured for the dynamic grasping task. Weights were attached to the end of a cable attached to the movable handle. The weights pulled the handle into the rest position The entire system was attached to the experimental chair with drawer glides. This allowed the dynamic hand dynamometer to glide back and forth. To support the unit, a pair of outriggers with casters was attached to the pulley end of the unit.

The movable handle of the hand dynamometer allowed the subject to squeeze the handle and simulate the activation of a trigger lever or a trigger. The movable handle was fitted with a flange that activated micro-switches attached to a plate on the dynamometer. These switches recorded the position of the handle during the experiment. Subjects were instructed to squeeze the handle on cue (SQUEEZE light illuminated) and were required to squeeze the handle for a displacement of 0.64 cm (0.25 inch). This simulated the activation of a trigger on a power tool. When this position was reached, the GOOD light illuminated. Subjects were instructed to hold this position until the SQUEEZE light extinguished (a five-second exertion period). The subject then released the grasp and the handle returned to the resting position. The lights extinguished and the rest period began. At the end of the rest period, the SQUEEZE light illuminated and the cycle repeated. Every two minutes the subject had the opportunity to adjust the rest period. When the ADJUST light illuminated, the subject had five seconds in which to make any adjustments to the rest time. These adjustments were then used to update the rest period. This entire process continued for a total of twenty minutes. The subject was instructed to maximize the number of hand grasps while minimizing any discomfort.

The independent variables manipulated during the study were number of days between sessions and elapsed time into the session. Test sessions were conducted on Days 1, 2, 9 and 23, yielding intervals of 1, 7, and 14 days between sessions. Rest times were recorded at the end of 10 minutes and 20 minutes of elapsed session time.

4. Results

Mean MVC values ranged from 15.9 to 33.1 kg (35 to 73 lbs). On average, the mean pre-trial MVC values were greater than the post-trial MVC values. Post-trial MVC values were collected after the twenty-minute experimental session. Subjects rested for eight minutes after the session while the apparatus was changed to collect MVC data. Statistical analysis revealed that pre- vs. post-trial values differed significantly ($F(1,50) = 6.97$, $p < 0.0335$). Other researchers have determined that recovery times range from 40 to 80 minutes for 50% MVC hand grasps [6] and 120 minutes for maximal MVC hand grasps [10]. Neural muscular junction fatigue of the neural receptors and metabolic fatigue are likely causes for the difference in MVC values between observations. Mean pre-test MVC values increased from Session 1 to Session 3 ($F(3,50) = 4.09$, $p < 0.0197$), with no statistically significant difference among Sessions 2, 3, and 4. It is evident from the data that subjects continued to develop their grip strength as the sessions continued over the four-week period. The coefficient of variation for the pre-test MVC values averaged 0.06 with a range among the subjects of 0.03 to 0.10.

Mean rest times did not vary among the sessions across the four-week period, indicating a reasonable level of stability in the psychophysical measure. There was no significant difference in the rest times selected for the ten-minute vs. the twenty-minute durations. However, the initial set-point of the rest time prior to subject adjustment did affect the final rest time value. Comparison of the two initial set points showed a significant effect upon the ending rest time values ($F(1,35) = 9.74$, $p < 0.0168$). It was found that the initial rest time of two seconds resulted in a significant difference in rest time obtained at ten minutes vs. twenty minutes ($F(1,35) = 10.91$, $p < 0.0131$). The initial rest time of nine seconds did not produce a similar effect. When subjects were started at two seconds, they made adjustments after the ten-minute mark such that the concluding twenty-minute mark rest time was significantly greater than the ten-minute rest time value. This was not the case when subjects were started at nine seconds.

This effect confirms what Abu-Ali [6] found when changes were made to subject-established rest times. He found that the force applied (% MVC) and the direction of change influenced the establishment of a new subject-determined rest time. In general, he found that when time was added to the rest time, subjects detected the change and reduced their rest time. However, they did not return to the previously set value. Similar reactions were found when rest time was subtracted. In like fashion, the current study found that when started at two seconds, subjects approached the study's overall mean rest time of 4.90 sec, but they did not reach this value. When started at nine seconds, subjects adjusted the rest time downward, but again did not reach the mean rest time.

5. Conclusions

The objectives of this study were to determine (1) the stability of psychophysically-determined rest times across sessions separated by 1 to 14 days, (2) the difference in subject-determined rest times for a ten-minute vs. a twenty-minute test session, and (3) the extent of variation across sessions in the maximum voluntary contraction (MVC) hand grip. Mean rest times did not vary among the sessions over the four-week period. There was no significant difference in subject-determined rest times for a 10-minute vs. a 20-minute task. Mean MVC coefficient of variation values averaged 0.06. This is similar to values determined by Bishu et al. [10]. However, the initial set-point of the rest time prior to subject adjustment did affect the final rest time value. Experimenter-induced rest time starting points had an effect upon subjects that could be statistically measured. It is evident from the data that selecting the starting rest time is very important when using the psychophysical method of adjustment. This study showed that subjects could determine a comfortable work/rest cycle within a twenty minute session.

References

[1]   P.C. Amadio, Historical Review: The Mayo Clinic and Carpal Tunnel Syndrome. *Mayo Clinic Proceedings,* **67**(1) (1992) 42-48.

[2]   S.A. Goldstein, T.J. Armstrong, D.B. Chaffin, and L.S. Matthews, Analysis of Cumulative Strain in Tendons and Tendon Sheaths. *Journal of Biomechanics,* **20** (1987) 1-6.

[3]   B. Silverstein, L. Fine, and T. Armstrong, Occupational Factors and Carpal Tunnel Syndrome. *American Journal of Industrial Medicine,* **11** (1987) 343-358.

[4]   L. Cannon, E. Benacki, and S. Walter, Personal and Occupational Factors Associated with Carpal Tunnel Syndrome. *Journal of Occupational Medicine,* **23** (1981) 255-258.

[5]   Y. Lifshitz, and T. Armstrong, A Design Checklist for Control and Prediction of Cumulative Trauma Disorder in Intensive Manual Jobs. In *The Proceedings of the Human Factors Society 30th Annual Meeting.* Human Factors Society, Santa Monica, CA, 1989, 839-841.

[6]   M.A. Abu-Ali, *Maximum Acceptable Frequency of Grasping at Different Force, Wrist Angle, and Exertion Time Levels for Females, Using the Psycophysical Approach.* Unpublished doctoral dissertation, University of Oklahoma, Norman, OK, 1993.

[7]   R.J. Marley, *Psychophysical Frequency at Different Wrist Postures of Females for a Drilling Task.* Unpublished doctoral dissertation, Wichita State University, Wichita, KS, 1993.

[8]   C.H. Kim, *Psychophysical Frequency at Different Forces and Wrist Postures of Females for a Drilling Task.* Unpublished doctoral dissertation, Wichita State University, Wichita, KS, 1991.

[9]   R.J. Marley, and A.K. Ramalingam, Psychophysically Acceptable Dynamic Hand Force. In A. Bittner and P. Champney (Eds.). Advances in Industrial Ergonomics and Safety VII. Taylor and Francis, Bristol, PA, 1995, 539-543.

[10]   R.R. Bishu, M.S. Halbeck, R. King, and J. Kennedy, Is 100% MVC Truly a 100% Effort? In A. Bittner and P. Champney (Eds.). Advances in Industrial Ergonomics and Safety VII. Taylor and Francis, Bristol, PA, 1995, 544-552.

15. Human-Computer Interaction

Advances in Occupational Ergonomics and Safety II
Edited by Biman Das and Waldemar Karwowski
IOS Press and Ohmsha, 1997

The Effects of Icon Size and Layout Design Configuration on Time of Menu Selection Task in Human-Computer Interaction

J. Grobelny[1] and W. Karwowski[2]

[1]Institute of Organization and Management, Technical University of Wroclaw,
50-370 Wroclaw, Poland

[2]Center of Industrial Ergonomics, University of Louisville,
Louisville, Kentucky, 40292, USA

Abstract The main objective of this study was to investigate the effects of graphical icon size and icon layout configuration of a computer digitizing board on the effectiveness of user's choices in menu selection task. The results showed that during learning of the digitizing system, the icon layout significantly affects the novice users' performance as measured by task completion time. The results were also analyzed in terms of the Fitts' Law. It was shown that this law could be used for prediction of task time for menu selection with the condensed (square) layout configuration of graphical icons.

1. Introduction

Contemporary computer systems utilize graphical interfaces which allow to construct pictograms, icons, symbols for individual keys, etc. The graphical symbols are metaphors of real objects, instructions, or processes which take place in the computer system. Pointing, selection, and confirmation of objects through the use of computer mouse in the process of human-computer communication is common to many human-computer interaction design solutions. The fundamental elements of the human-computer dialogue, including the graphical ones, become more and more standardized regardless of the computer operation system.

Communication with a computer through the point-and-confirm mode (by clicking with a mouse) is utilized by the communication systems designed according to the "direct manipulation" (DM) mode [1]. Although the concept of DM is much broader, as it is concerned also with other aspects of computer systems, the human-computer interface and graphical objects are permanent features of such systems. In particular, the computer digitizing board allows for natural utilization of the DM concepts.

The main purpose of this study was to investigate the effect of geometrical layout configuration of graphical icons on the effectiveness of human-computer interaction while utilizing the digitizing board. Specifically, the study focused on the importance of icon's size and layout of icons. Such icons are typically selected by the user through the use of a mouse from different menus located on the control panel of the computer digitizing board.

Since the process of graphical icon's selection is similar to the classical problem of controlled (target directed) movement, it was postulated that the Fitts' law could be useful for analysis and description of study results. It was also noted that the search process for an icon located on the board, especially during the learning phase, is analogous to the classical problem of searching for signals in the field of vision. In this case, the selection process of should take into consideration the conditions of the searching phase, as well as the choice of target itself.

The selection of an icon with a mouse on a digitizing board is an exercise which involves the controlled, goal-oriented movement. The Fitts' law specifies the average time for such a movement based on the index of difficulty [2], according to the following formula:

$$MT = a + b \, (ID); \quad (ID = \log_2 (2A/W)) \tag{1}$$

where *ID* is the index of difficulty, *A* is the movement amplitude, and *W* is the target width (tolerance in movement precision).

Applications of the above model, which was originally developed based on investigation of the limited movements in one direction, under different experimental conditions were discussed by Hoffmann and Sheikh [3]. The authors pointed out the potential for broad applications of the Fitts' law, but also noted a need for experimental investigations that would determine the specific nature of the index of difficulty (ID). For example, Drury and Hoffman [4] discussed an application of the Fitts' law to the analysis of keyboards for data entry tasks.

2. Methods and Procedures

A series experimental trials were conducted utilizing the randomized complete block design with subjects as blocks. Twelve subjects (7 males and 5 females) participated in the study. All subjects were college students (21-23 years of age) familiar with computer systems, but none of the subjects had used the digitizing board before. The subjects were asked to search for and locate a specific icon on the control panel of the digitizing board, and to select the found icon with the help of a computer mouse by clicking on it.

Each subject performed two series of ten searches for each of the icon layout configurations. A total of nine geometrical configurations of graphical icons were investigated (see Table 1). A configuration was defined by the icon's size (small=10 mm; medium= 15 mm; big=20 mm), and the shape of their layout (horizontal, vertical, or square-shaped). Each subject worked with the same computer system, where instead of a standard keyboard, the Summagraphics digitizing board was used. A transparent template with a specific icon layout configuration was centrally placed on the board. A special purpose computer program generated different experimental search (trial) scenarios, and measured the task completion time. Whenever an error was made, the task was repeated.

Figure 1 shows an example of a typical layout configuration investigated in this study. The icon configurations were designed in such a way as to ensure that the size of a single element corresponded to the real size of icons which are typically utilized in a standard human-computer interface (for example in AutoCad applications). Each of the graphical icons was either a simple sign (a digit or a number) or a pictogram of the commonly known real objects. This way, the recognition time for the objects to be searched for during experimental trials was minimized, while the real characteristics and appearance of the objects, which are known to the casual computer users, were preserved.

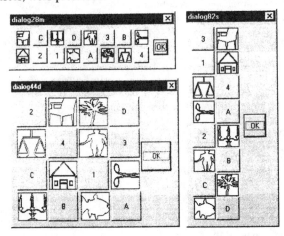

Figure 1. Horizontal, vertical, and square icon configurations.

3. Results

The results were analyzed using an analysis of variance. A two-factorial analysis with repetitions was utilized. All data were grouped with respect to the icon size and layout configuration used. The average icon selection (task performance) times for each of the nine configurations are shown in Table 1. There was a significant effect for icon configuration ($F(2,99)=3.84$, $p<0.05$). However, the effects of icon's size and the interaction between the icons configuration and icon size, were not significant. Figures 2 and 3 illustrate the effects of layout configuration and icon's size, respectively, on the observed selection times.

Table 1. Average selection times for each of the
nine icon configurations.

Icon size	Horizontal	Squared	Vertical
10 mm	1.82	1.66	1.76
15 mm	1.62	1.64	1.65
20 mm	1.74	1.56	1.70

For each of the icon configurations studied, the average index of difficulty was determined based on equation (1). The relationship between times of task performance and index of task difficulty was also determined (see Figure 4). It can be seen that Fitts' law, which describes this relationship using a linear form, does not apply here (Pearson r <0.01). In addition, a detailed analysis of the relationship between task performance (time) and index of difficulty for different icon configurations was made (see Figure 5). A linear relationship was only confirmed for a (4 x 4) or square icon configuration, while other configurations showed an optimum index of difficulty for which the (average) task time was minimized.

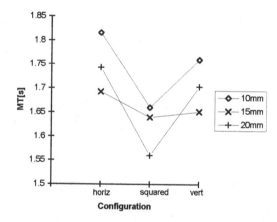

Figure 2. Average times for different icon configurations.

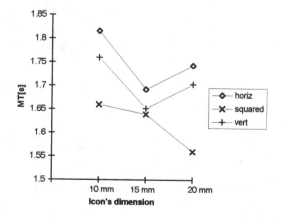

Figure 3. Average times for different icon dimensions.

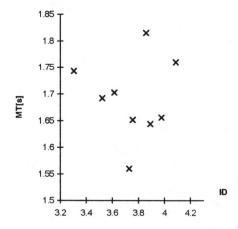

Figure 4. Average times and index of difficulty for all icon configurations.

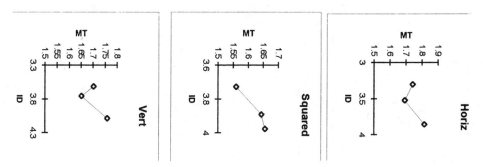

Figure 5. Average times for all icon configurations.

5.   Conclusions

The results of this study allow to formulate the following observations. Geometrical layout of the specific icon configuration on the computer digitizing board is important with respect to effectiveness in icon's task selection. The integrated (squared) icon layout is faster to use than the vertical of horizontal configurations. The Fitts' law can be applied for modeling of the relationship between time of task performance and index of task difficulty for compact icon layouts only, such as the square configuration.

Finally, this study also indicates a need for further investigations with respect to whether the reported relationships would apply to those icon configurations which are very well known to the subjects (e.g. were previously memorized by them), and whether the number of graphical icons in a given layout configuration would affect the results presented above.

References

[1] J. E. Ziegler and K. P. Fahnrich, Direct Manipulation. In: M. Helander (ed.), Handbook of Human-Computer Interaction. Elsevier Science Publishers B.V., North-Holland, 1988.
[2] P. M. Fitts and J. R. Peterson, Information Capacity of Discrete Motor Responses, Journal of Experimental Psychology 67 (1964) 103-112.
[3] E. R. Hoffmann and I. H.Sheikh, Effect of Varying Target Height in a Fitts' Movement Task, Ergonomics 36 (1994), 1071-1088.
[4] C. G. Drury and E. R. Hoffman, A Model for Movement Time on Data-Entry Keyboards, Ergonomics 35 (1992) 129-147.

Advances in Occupational Ergonomics and Safety II
Edited by Biman Das and Waldemar Karwowski
IOS Press and Ohmsha, 1997

BODY PART DISCOMFORT, ANTHROPOMETRIC MEASUREMENTS AND HEAD ANGLE ASSUMED DURING VDT INTERACTIVE ACTIVITIES AT A LAW OFFICE

Lawrence J. H. Schulze, Ph.D., PE., CPE, Department of Industrial Engineering, University of Houston, 4800 Calhoun Street, Houston, TX 77204-4812, Paul Phalen, and Frank Jeter, Compaq Computer Corporation, Houston, TX, U.S.A., Jacob Chen, Department of Industrial Engineering, University of Houston, 4800 Calhoun Street, Houston, TX, U.S.A., and Leonardo Quintana, Department of Industrial Engineering, Javeriana University, Santafé de Bogotá, Colombia, (S.A.)

Anthropometric measurements were collected from employees at a large multiple-site law firm. Head angles were also determined during VDT use. A body part discomfort survey form was completed by the same employees three times per day for five (5) consecutive days. Analysis of Variance and correlational analyses were conducted between body part discomfort and related anthropometric measurements. Correlations were very weak, at best, indicating that workplace designers would be better served by studying body part discomfort for relationships with factors other than anthropometry when interested in VDT interactive activities, save for the design ôf adjustable furniture. Analysis of Variance (ANOVA) was also conducted between operator head angle and reports of body part discomfort. The results indicate that there is an association between head angle and body part discomfort of the neck with -6º to -14º below the horizontal line of sight associated with the least discomfort. The overall impact of this research suggests that system integration (VDT and operator) are more important in determining operator comfort than specific anthropometric dimensions.

1. Introduction and Background

There are numerous anthropometry reference manuals available to workplace designers [1], whether these individuals are involved in designing a manufacturing line, a machine shop, or office environment. Designers typically use anthropometric data so that their designs (e.g.computer workstations) will accommodate the range of individuals intended to use that equipment [2].

Paluch and Tazor [3] indicated that anthropometric measurements contribute to reported discomfort only when individuals were performing tasks at a poorly designed or in an environmentally harsh working environment. Pederson, Pederson, and Staffelt [4], and Furguson [5] reported a lack of relationship between reported body part discomfort and anthropometry. Sauter and Schleifer [6] suggested that musculoskeletal discomfort is commonplace during work with visual display terminals (VDTs).

The purpose of this project was to assess any relationship between individual anthropometric measurements and body part discomfort reported by legal secretaries in a large international law firm. In addition, time of day, day of shift and head angle assumed by participants during VDT interactive activities were also assessed. A law firm was chosen based on the workload of performed by personnel Zapata, Chowdury, and Schulze [7].

2. Method

Thirty anthropometric measurements were recorded from more than 200 personnel within the law firm and included head angle during typing activities. Personnel were also asked to complete a body part discomfort survey. The form identified 16 individual body part locations and intensity ranged from just noticeable to intolerable pain on a 0 to 11 point scale. The survey was completed three times per day (before the work shift, at the meal break, and at the end of the work shift) for 5 consecutive work days. Of the 200 body part discomfort forms distributed, 133 were returned; 56 of these were complete for all shift days and were used for the analysis. Of the 56 personnel used in this study, 49 were female, 7 were male, 29 were legal secretaries, 8 were attorneys, 3 were accountants, 3 were legal aides, 2 were trainers, 2 were receptionists and 9 were various law firm support staff performing multiple functions.

Correlations were conducted between anthropometric measurements. and reported body part discomfort. The independent variables were workshift and job title. Correlational analysis was used in an attempt to draw inferences regarding the dependence and independence between the dependent variables of interest; the magnitude of the correlation between the variables would indicate the relatedness of the two dependent variables [Hays and Winkler, 1980].

An Analysis of Variance (ANOVA) was conducted to assess the impact of the time of day (beginning of shift, meal break, end of shift) and day of week (Monday through Friday). An overall body part discomfort score was used as the dependent measure in this analysis. A single factor ANOVA was also conducted on head angle and reported neck discomfort.

3. Results and Discussion

The results of the ANOVA conducted on overall body part discomfort and both day of week and VDT viewing angle are presented in Table 1. As can be seen from a review of Table 1, day of week was not a statistically significant effect ($p > 0.05$). However, viewing angle was statistically significant ($p < 0.0001$).

Table 1. ANOVA Summary Table of Day of Week and Head Angle

Source of Variation	df	Sum of Squares	Mean Square	F crit	F obs.	p
Day of Week (DOW)	4	1004	250.9	2.87	0.56	0.6000
Head Angle (HA)	5	46704	9341	2.71	20.9	0.0001
DOW * HA	20	8946	447.3			
Total	29	56653				

This main effect of head angle is illustrated in Figure 1. As can be seen, and results from the Duncan test confirmed, significantly less discomfort ($p < 0.05$) is associated with a head angle between -6º and 14º below the horizontal line of sight (HLOS) than with the other head angles. Further, no difference ($p > 0.05$) was found between the head angles of 15º - 30º above, 5º s above to 5º below, and greater than 18º below the HLOS. However these angles were associated with significantly greater ($p < 0.05$) discomfort than the range between 5º and 14º below the HLOS. Significantly greater discomfort ($p < 0.05$) was reported by personnel when head angels assumed were either 5º or 15º above or 15º o 19º below the HLOS. The number of participants sampled by head angle assumed is illustrated in Figure 2.

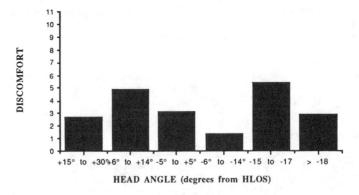

Figure 1. Mean discomfort values associated with the different head angles of participants.

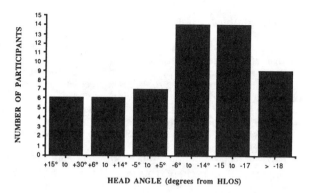

Figure 2. Frequency distribution of participants and measured head angles.

The results of the single factor ANOVA conducted for time of day indicated that there was a difference between reported neck discomfort by participants from the beginning of the shift to the middle of the shift ($p < 0.05$), the middle of the shift to the end of the shift ($p < 0.05$), and from the beginning of the shift to the end of the shift ($p < 0.05$). See Figure 3.

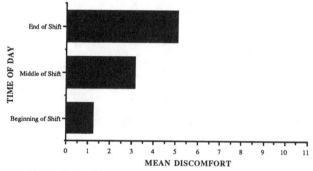

Figure 2.   Mean discomfort reported by time of day.

The correlation coefficients were consistently low in an attempt to associate anthropometric measuremetns with reported body part discomfort, with an average correlation coefficient of 0.03 and standard deviation of 0.12. None of the correlations were statistically significant ($p > 0.05$). Table 2 presents a sample of the highest correlations between dbody part discomfort and anthropometric dimension. As can be seen , there does not appear to be a relationship between anthropometric measurements and reported body part discomfort in this population of law firm personnel. These results support previous work in this area where little or no correlation was found between anthropometric dimensions of personnel and reported body part discomfort [3, 4, and 5].

Table 2.   Sample Correlation Coefficients Between Anthropometric Measurements and Reported Body Part Discomfort

Body Part	Anthropometric Measurement	Correlation Coefficient
Wrist	Hand Length	-0.11
Wrist	Wrist Circumference	-0.10
Wrist	Wrist Breadth	-0.04
Wrist	Wrist Thickness	-0.01
Lower Back	Sitting Height	+0.27
Shoulder	Shoulder Breadth	+0.03

4.   Conclusions and Recommendations

Design of the workplace will continue to present challenges for those involved in ergonomics and human factors engineering. The results of this study indicate that those individuals involved in workplace design, occupational health, human resources and risk management, would best be served by looking for other sources of body part discomfort other than personal anthropometric dimensions (e.g., wrist circumference, wrist thickness, etc.).

These results support the work of Grandjean, Hunting and Pidermann [9] and of Kroemer [10]. Specifically, these authors and this study found that the preferred inclination of the head during VDT tasks is from -5° to -15° below the HLOS (-6° to -14° in this study). As a result, such head angles should be recommended to VDT users as a starting point and their computer monitors adjusted to promote this viewing angle. However, individual differences and preferences of viewing angle are more important than blindly applying the results of this investigation. Further, since reported discomfort increased throughout the day, a focus on the workload distribution should be apllied during task performance.

5.   References

[1]   Weimer, J. (1993). Handbook of Ergonomics and Human Factors Tables. Englewood Cliffs, NJ: Prentice Hall.

[2]   Huchingson, R. D. (1981). New Horizons for Human Factors in Design. New York: McGraw-Hill.

[3]   Paluch, R., and Tazor, A. (1988). Influence of workload and anthropometric measures on musculoskeletal complaints. Trends in Ergonomics.Human Factors V. F. Aghezadeh (Ed.). Amsterdam: Elsevier Science Publishers B.V..

[4]   Pederson, O. F., Pederson, R., and Staffelt, E. S. (1975). Back pain and isometric back muscle strength of workers in a Danish factory. Scandinavian Journal of Rehabilitation Medicine. 7, 125-128.

[5]   Furguson, D. (1986). Posture, aching, and body build in telephonists. Journal of Human Ergology, 5, 183-186.

[6]   Sauter, S. L., and Schleifer, L. M. (1991). Work posture, workstation design, and musculoskeletal discomfort in a VDT data entry task. Human Factors, 33(2), 151-167.

[7]   Schulze, L. J. H., Zapata, M., and Chowdury, J. (1995). Ergonomic Evaluation of Bracewell & Patterson L.L.P Facilities. Houston, TX: Department of Industrial Engineering, University of Houston. Technical Reports.

[8]   Hays, W. L., and Winkler, R. L. (1970). Statistics: Probability, Inference and Decision. New York: Holt, Reinhart and Winston, Inc..

[9]   Granjean, E., Hunting, W., and Pidermann, M. (1983). VDT workstation design: Preferred settings and their effects. Human Factors, 25(2), 1261-175.

[10] Hill, S. G., and Kroemer, K. H. E. (1986). Preferred declination of the line of sight. Human Factors, 28(2), 127-134

Advances in Occupational Ergonomics and Safety II
Edited by Biman Das and Waldemar Karwowski
IOS Press and Ohmsha, 1997

Evaluation of Wrist Posture during the Operation of Four Electromechanical Mice

Pieter C. Kruithof Jr., AEP
Crown Equipment Corporation Design Center
14 West Monroe Street
New Bremen, OH
USA

Abstract. This research investigated the effect of mouse support height, mouse type, and hand size on the wrist posture of computer mouse operators. Twenty-four subjects were divided into three groups of eight according to hand length (small, medium, and large). Results showed that an increase in the mouse support height caused a decrease in the amount of wrist extension and an increase in the amount of ulnar deviation for both pointing and dragging tasks. There was also a significant interaction between mouse support height and hand size for wrist extension during pointing tasks. Mouse type and hand size were not found to have significant effects in either pointing or dragging tasks.

1. Introduction

The introduction of the Apple Macintosh in 1984 brought in the wide-spread acceptance of graphical user interfaces (GUI, or gooey) among computer users. Currently, graphical user interfaces such as Windows'95™ and MacOS™ are available on a large and increasing number of the 40 to 80 million video display terminals (VDT's) in the United States [1]. The majority of these GUI's utilize a mouse as the physical interface within these environments.

Until recently little research has been conducted on mice to identify specific biomechanical factors that may contribute to the development of musculoskeletal injuries. However, case studies [2] [3] have suggested that mouse users suffer from musculoskeletal impairments known as cumulative trauma disorders, or CTD's. This study investigated wrist posture and how it is affected by hand size, mouse type, and workstation height.

2. Methods

2.1 Subjects

Twenty-four right-handed subjects participated in the experiment. The subjects were divided into three groups according to their hand size; defined as the distance between the stylion landmark on the wrist to the tip of the middle finger [4]. Subjects in the small hand size group had lengths from 16.4-17.79 cm., subjects in the medium hand size group had lengths from 17.80-19.19 cm., and subjects in the large hand size group had lengths from 19.20-20.60 cm.

2.2 Apparatus

Wrist posture was collected using a measurement system developed at the Biodynamics Laboratory at Ohio State University [5]. The system was composed of two devices which consisted of a goniometer with a radial potentiometer attached to it's center of rotation. An adjustable workstation was used in the experiment to allow independent adjustment of the mouse support height and the monitor height. The Logitech MouseMan, Apple Desktop Bus Mouse, Apple Desktop Bus Mouse II, and the Kensington Thinking Mouse were selected for the study because of their differences in overall shape.

2.3   Experimental Design

The experimental design was a mixed factors design with one between-subject factor, Hand Size, and two within-subject factors: Mouse Type and Mouse Support Height. The order of presentation for the within-subject factors Mouse Type and Elbow Height was counterbalanced using a partial Latin square. The dependent measure was the average amount of wrist movement from neutral for flexion/extension and radial/ulnar deviation.

2.4   Procedure

Both pointing and dragging tasks were used in the experiment, as proposed by Johnson et al. [6]. The pointing task required the user to move the cursor over a target (a single half-inch square button) and "click" (quickly activate and deactivate) the mouse button. After being selected, the target moved to another random location on the screen.

The dragging task was composed of an "object" and "home" target at different locations on the screen. The user positioned the cursor over the "object" target and activated the mouse button. The object was then dragged over the "home" target and the mouse button was deactivated. Both targets immediately moved to different random locations within the screen and the sequence began again. Both tasks presented to the subjects were written in the Hypercard™ programming language.

Subjects completed twelve trials (Mouse Support Height x Mouse Type) per task, each lasting three minutes. Prior to the experimental trials, subjects were instructed on how to perform the experimental tasks and provided with an opportunity to practice each. In addition, each subject was asked to read a short brochure that informed them of proper ergonomic posture during the operation video display workstations according to ANSI/HFS 100 [7] standards.

3.   Results

A repeated-measures analysis of variance (ANOVA) on the flexion/extension values found that the main effect, Mouse Support Height was significant for both the pointing task (p=0.0001) and the dragging task (p=0.0001). The interaction of Mouse Support Height and Hand Size was also significant during pointing tasks (p=0.0052).

A Newman-Keuls post-hoc test showed that all three levels of Mouse Support Height were significantly different (p<0.05) from one another for both pointing and dragging tasks (Figure 1). The greatest average amount of extension occurred when the mouse surface level was set to 95% of elbow height. The smallest average amount of extension occurred when the mouse surface level was set to 105% of elbow height. For the interaction of Mouse Support Height and Hand Size, a Newman-Keuls post-hoc analysis found that both small and medium hand lengths had significantly greater (p<0.05) degrees of extension than large hand lengths for both 95% and 100% of elbow height (Figure 2). All three hand lengths were significantly different at 105% of elbow height.

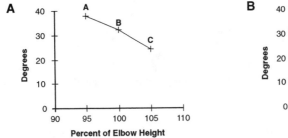 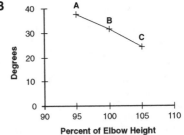

Figure 1 Main effect of Mouse Support Height on wrist flexion/extension during pointing (A) and dragging (B) tasks. Positive values indicate extension while negative values indicate flexion.

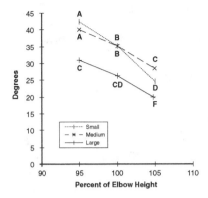

Figure 2 Main effects of Mouse Support Height and Hand Size on wrist flexion/extension during pointing tasks. Positive values indicate extension while negative values indicate flexion.

A similar ANOVA on the radial/ulnar deviations revealed that the main effect, Mouse Support Height was significant for both pointing tasks (p=.0001) and dragging tasks (p = .0001). The Newman-Keuls post-hoc showed that all three levels of Mouse Support Height were found to be significantly different (p<0.05) for both pointing and dragging tasks (Figure 3). The least average amount of ulnar deviation occurred when the mouse surface level was set to 95% of elbow height and the greatest average amount of ulnar deviation occurred when the mouse surface level was set to 105% of elbow height.

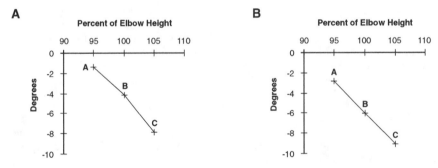

Figure 3 Main effect of Mouse Support Height on wrist radial/ulnar deviation during pointing (A) and dragging (B) tasks. Positive values indicate radial deviation while negative values indicate ulnar deviation.

4.   **Discussion**

Mouse Support Height was the only main effect found to be significant in any of the analyses and was a component in the one significant interaction that occurred. As Mouse Support Height was raised the degree of extension decreased. It is suggested that the angle of the lower arm to the horizontal plane decreased when the Mouse Support Height was raised.

For radial/ulnar deviation, increasing Mouse Support Height caused an increase in the level of ulnar deviation. It is likely that the increase was caused by the abduction of the upper arm as the hand (located on the mouse support) was raised. Assuming that the orientation of the mouse remained fairly constant, flexion at the elbow would be expected to occur as the arm abducts. For the cursor to react predictably to hand movement, both the hand and mouse must be aligned approximately perpendicular to the display. Consequently, ulnar deviation may occur as a result of the inability of the hand to deviate radially when the elbow becomes flexed.

deviation and flexion/extension are not possible because it has yet to be established that equal distances from neutral are similar in terms of their contribution to CTD's. Accordingly, caution should be exercised when comparing the costs and benefits of adjusting different variables that effect wrist posture. In addition, whole-body posture may also have an effect on wrist posture.

It was originally felt that subjects with small hand lengths would have significantly different posture because the mouse would be larger relative to the user's hand. However, Hand Size was not shown to be significant as a main effect in any of the analyses.

The main effect of Mouse Type was also not found to be significant in any of the ANOVA Summary Tables. A possible explanation is that the differences in physical dimensions of the mice were not great enough to affect the wrist and hand posture of the user. Unsolicited comments regarding preferences for specific mice had been made by subjects, but were inconsistent.

5.   Acknowledgments

This research was conducted in the Industrial Ergonomics Laboratory at Virginia Polytechnic Institute and State University.

6.   References

[1] Occupational Safety and Health Administration, Working Safely with Video Display Terminals. Department of Labor, Washington, DC, 1991.
[2] G. Franco et al., Tensinovite Posturale da uso Incongruo di un Dispositivo di Puntamento di un Elaborate. [Postural Tenosynovitis Caused by Misuse of a Computer Input Device]. Medicina Del Lavoro 4 (1992) pp. 352-355.
[3] C. Davie et al., "Mouse"-Trap or Personal Computer Palsy. The Lancet, 338 (8770), 1991 pp. 832.
[4] S. Donelson and C. Gordon, 1988 Anthropometric Survey of US Army Personnel: Pilot Summary Statistics. Tech. Report NATICK/TR-1/040). United States Army Natick Research, Development and Engineering Center, Natick, USA, (1991) pp. 180-181.
[5] R. Schoenmarklin and W. Marras, Quantification of Wrist Motion and Cumulative Trauma Disorders in Industry, Proceedings of the Human Factors Society 35th Annual Meeting. Human Factors Society, Santa Monica, USA, 1991.
[6] P. Johnson et al., Pinch Forces During Mouse Operations [Poster Presentation]. Human Factors and Ergonomics Societies 37th Annual Meeting. Human Factors and Ergonomics Society, Santa Monica, USA, 1993.
[7] Human Factors Society (ed.), American National Standard for Human Factors Engineering of Visual Display Terminal Workstations, ANSI/HFS 100-1988. Human Factors Society, Santa Monica, USA, 1988.

Advances in Occupational Ergonomics and Safety II
Edited by Biman Das and Waldemar Karwowski
IOS Press and Ohmsha, 1997

Using of Ergonomics of Working Place of Computers

Jerzy OLSZEWSKI
University of Economics Department of Labour and Social Policy
61-875 Poznań, Al. Niepodległości 10, Poland
e-mail: olszewsk@novci1.ae.poznan.pl

Abstract. In the first part of the paper the factors that have prompted the growth of the significance of computers as the common tools widely applied in many areas of life have been presented. The next section deals with the stressful conditions that computer users have to face, such as familiarization with computers in a short period of time, solitary work, supervision of the quality and efficiency of work, radiation of the screen. Basic principles are discussed that have to be taken into consideration while designing the ergonomic workplace for computer operators. Some undesirable consequences of working at a computer (radiation and electrostatic fileds) are considered. Also, methods of optimizing the microclimate as well as keeping the balance between negative and positive ions are presented. In the final section the economic aspects of ergonomic measures are discussed.

1. Introduction

Widespread and growing use of computers in almost every area of life, mainly in industry, office work, science, the service sector, transport etc., gave rise to a new workplace where the computer is extensively used. Therefore, the computer is becoming a common tool of the present, almost necessary in every plant and institution and in every family. The main reasons for this are relatively low cost, small dimensions, increasing reliability and durability combined with the capacity to collect and process information from all over the world. So Masara's plan whose cornstone was the origin of information society ceased to be something exceptional in the face of the efforts and success of other countries in this respect [1]. We witness a new electronic and integrated quality of ordinary work showing up based on three revolutionary inventions:

- computers,
- light guides,
- satellite communication.

To meet the challenge resulting from introduction of information technology it is necessary to speed up the process of adaptation of Polish society to life in information age.

In Poland computerization is showing up to a growing extent in many areas of socioeconomic life, in particular in production, the services industry, trade, transport, administration. Computers became an object of interest to many socioeconomic classes, especially young people, leading them to a kind of addiction. Computerisation exerts influence on social ties and socioeconomic structures, personal communication skills, leading in the case of many workers to unwillingness to work and anxiety about novelties.

The introduction of computer technology to social and private life has many not fully recognised and understood consequences.

Appreciating, both in theory and practice, the virtues of computerisation, one should consider its undesirable effects upon the human being concerned with some hazards to his physical and psychical life. The research aims at selecting and analysing factors most hazardous to human health and life which appear nowadays as a result of computerisation.

2. Physical strenuousness

Computerization results in strenuousness and hazards to the health of computer users. However the hazards are not fully recognised till now. The monitor together with additional equipment emits relatively high quantities of heat, thus rising locally the air temperature, decreasing   simultaneously its humidity. Furthermore, the monitor is the source of electromagnetic, electrostatic and X-ray radiation [2]. An important factor which should be taken into account are electromagnetic fields produced by the monitor while in operation, causing electrostatic potential between the operator and monitor to rise. The face of a computer operator attracts charged particles of dust like the monitor screen, making breathing difficult and impending the process of reading from the screen due to lack of distinctness. Dust and associated skin ionization may be the cause of allergic reactions and skin irritation. Electrostatic potential of the screen is neutralized by water particles contained in the air. In the case of high humidity that potential is significantly reduced. In the winter, when the low humidity level may persist in a room for many weeks, electrostatic potential of the screen may be significantly higher.

X-ray radiation produced by modern monitors has been significantly lowered in recent years. According to the data by Association of Technical Standards in Germany (TÜV-Rheinland) the radiation level produced by modern visual equipment is many times lower the background level (i.e. radiation caused by radioactive materials existing in nature), and is below the level which could be detected by measuring apparatus used to take measurements.

The aforementioned factors cause complaints reported by personnel working at a computer. The most frequent are: eye fatigue, mainly smartness of the eye, disturbed vision acuity and color perception, muscle and joint pains, wrist stiffness (pains), pain and stiffness in the neck and arms, numbness of the hands combined with cramps, anxiety, nervousness, weakness, smartness of the skin.

The presented health hazards justify the statement that jobs concerned with using computer monitors are counted as performed under strenuos conditions. It is worth mentioning here that the legislation in Poland classify these jobs as strenuous. For this reason the computer workplace should occupy at least 6 m^2 of the room at least 3.5 m high.

3. Spatial conditions and lighting

The width and length of a desk on which a computer, monitor and keyboard are placed constitute the essential elements of the spatial. conditions of the workplace. Professional branch organizations in Germany recommend in their safety rules the length of the desk, in the optimal working conditions, should be equal to at least 160 cm, its width - 80 cm. That means that the width of the table top should be enough to place a keyboard, a desk for auxiliary materials and monitor on it. Between a front edge of the desk and the keyboard a free space to support hands should be left, from 5 to 10 cm in width. For safety reasons the monitor should not stand out more than 1 cm from the back edge of the desk. The aforementioned requirements are met by tables at least 90 cm wide. The surface of the desk without a height regulator should be situated 72 cm above the floor level [3]. For approximately 80% of people that height dose not pose any problems and needs only height regulation of a chair. The characteristics of the optimal computer workplace are not limited to its dimensions. The desk is characterised not only but its dimensions, but a kind of surface which should be lusterless or half mat to prevent eye fatigue caused by light reflections coming from environment.

An important issue in the process of creating optimal working conditions is lighting. From the research conducted by the author follows that the most common mistakes are:

- placing the monitor against a background of the window whose high luminosity during a sunny day may limit the legibility while reading from the screen,
- using blinds or curtains which let too much light during a sunny day: reading from the screen may become difficult if the monitor screen is brightly illuminated,
- placing monitors in such a way they face windows: a bright picture is formed on the screen impeding reading,
- electrical lighting of the screen, not accurate in most cases.

It is recommended to keep the luminosity in a room where monitors are used at a level of 500-600 luxes.

4. Counteracting disadvantageous factors of work environment

In this section the ways of coping with the harmful effects of the described kinds of radiation are presented. For one thing there should be used such monitors whose radiation, electrostatic and electromagnetic fields are reduced thanks to some construction solutions (cowers preventing excessive emissions of radiation and electromagnetic fields). Monitors having such characteristics are marked with special signs, in Germany GS (Geprüfte Sicherheit), in Sweden SSI (awarded by Swedish Institute of Standardization) and SEK (awarded by Swedish Electrotechnic Committe) given to monitors meeting Swedish rigorous standards.

Apart from the aforementioned factors the microclimate plays an important role in creating the computer operator environment. The recommended indoor temperature should be between 21-22° C. Modern air conditioning systems are capable of adapting indoor temperature to outdoor temperatures preventing people working in the building from excessive temperature differences. Blinds and curtains should be used to protect equipment against excessive heating caused by direct sunlight. The relative air humidity in a room should be 50-60%. The higher the temperature, the lower the humidity level should be to prevent the air from getting close. The air humidity exceeding 50% prevents creation of excessive electrostatic fields close to the computer. The screen radiation causes lack of balance between positive and negative ions. As a result the air contains 200-300 ions per cm^3 instead of 2000-3000.

Installations for aeoions creation can be divided into two groups: high voltage ionizers and radioisotope ionizers. The most common are installations, where the source of ionizing rays is radioactive material. However, using that equipment needs special caution. The solution to attain high effectiveness of negative ionization applying safe voltages is a high voltage ionizer.

5. Economic premises of ergonomic undertakings

At the present time the problem of designing working conditions of computer operators and programmers is far from being solved. In the process of designing the computer workplace layout many mistakes are made. One of the reason is lack of appropriate furniture at the market meeting the aforementioned requirements. A second reason is a lack of knowledge of designers as well as limited financial resources. A third reason is lighting. One can very rarely come across a computer workplace properly designed in this respect. The fundamental reason is a lack of expertise of people involved in the process of designing correct, ergonomic lighting. Financial reasons are least important here.

Controling the microclimate parametrs is incorrect as well. Like in the case of lighting the most important reason is a lack of knowledge of personnel engaged in the design of working conditions of programmers and computer operators [4].

It should be stated that the most expensive undertaking is the design of the spatial environment. Its cost compared to that incurred in the case of the standard workplace is many times higher [5]. Proper design of lighting and microclimate conditions involves lesser financial problems.

Reference

[1] T. Kasprzak, Koncepcja przedsiębiorstwa XXI w., Ekonomista, nr 1, 1994, Key Text, Warszawa 1994,

[2] A.D.Bauman, Horwat.: The impact of natural radioactivity from a coal-fired power plant. Sci. Total. Environ.,1981,

[3] Komputer a zdrowie, pod red. Christy Lippmann, Poradnik dla osób korzystających z komputerów, Cedrus Publishing House, Warszawa 1992,

[4] Olszewski J.: Podstawy ergonomii i fizjologii pracy, Akademia Ekonomiczna, Poznań, 1993,

[5] J. Olszewski, Postęp techniczny a przemiany systemu pracy w przemyśle, z. 131, AE, Poznań 1993,

Advances in Occupational Ergonomics and Safety II
Edited by Biman Das and Waldemar Karwowski
IOS Press and Ohmsha, 1997

A Practical Evaluation of Ergonomic Keyboards

Johanna E. Thum, Eric Dawkins, Tim Krueger, and Tycho K. Fredericks, Ph.D.

Human Performance Institute, Department of Industrial and Manufacturing Engineering
Western Michigan University, Kalamazoo, Michigan 49008-5061 U.S.A.

The objective of this study was to evaluate the effectiveness of an ergonomic keyboard as compared with a standard QWERTY 101 style keyboard for hunt-and-peck typists. Five male students from the University population volunteered to participate in the study. The subjects performed two 45 minute typing sessions, one with each keyboard. Typing tests were administered using Typing Tutor 6 software. In order to compare the two keyboards, data was gathered for words-per-minute, error rates, subjective ratings of effort, and EMG values for the flexor and extensor muscles of the forearm. Results indicated that there were significant decreases in the words per minute and the subjective ratings of effort from the QWERTY to the ergonomic keyboard. While the means for EMG values were generally higher for the ergonomic keyboard as compared to the QWERTY keyboard, these results were not statistically significant.

1.0 Introduction

Cumulative trauma disorders (CTD's), are disorders of the hand and wrist that result from the strain of repetitive motions. In recent years, there has been a dramatic increase in occurrences of this type of disorder in the United States [1]. One of the most common CTD's is carpal tunnel syndrome (CTS), also called median nerve-compression syndrome, where repetitive manual exertions of the hand are believed to cause cumulative trauma to the wrist.

One of the tasks that has been linked to the development of CTS is keyboard use or typing. During typing tasks, increased pressure in the carpal tunnel appears to be caused by forces exerted by the tendons. These forces become greater as the wrist deviates into flexion or extension. During typing, the hand moves repeatedly through flexion and extension causing the compression forces on the median nerve to increase. These movements appear to pose the greatest risks for CTS during typing [2]. Furthermore, computer keyboard use may pose a particularly high risk for CTS because of the potential for significant overuse of the fingers [3].

Ergonomic keyboards are one of the new groups of products to enter the market, with suppliers offering many tempting choices that "will naturally improve efficiency" while being aesthetically pleasing. However, with the price for these keyboard ranging from $49 to over $2,000 [5], the question arises whether the ergonomic keyboard worth the extra costs? Furthermore, will these extra costs actually prove beneficial for the worker in providing a truly better keyboard?

Many studies have been performed to evaluate the effects of using an ergonomic computer keyboard to evaluate the typists comfort, speed, and ease of use, to investigate the possibility of reducing the risk of CTD's. However, the studies which have shown benefits for the user with these keyboards have limited their investigation to the benefits for touch typist [1] [6] [7] [8] [9] [10]. A considerable portion of the people that use computers today are not touch typists. These computer users are a considered hunt-and-peck typists, people who use fewer than 10 fingers and look at the keyboard while typing. With this in mind, an experiment was conducted to evaluate the effectiveness of an ergonomic keyboard as compared with a QWERTY keyboard when used by hunt-and-peck typists.

2.0 Methods and Procedures

2.1 Subjects

Five able-bodied male students were selected from the students population at Western Michigan University. The mean age of the subjects was 26.4 with a standard deviation of 5.50 and a range of 19 to 34. All the subjects were self-reported hunt-and peck typists of varying degrees of skill. These hunt-and-peck typists did not use all of their fingers while typing, and had to look at the keys during the task to find appropriate letters. None of the subjects reported any CTD symptoms, nor did they report any history of upper extremity dysfunction. All of the subjects were familiarized with experimental procedures prior to the commencement of the data collection

2.2 Equipment

A Microsoft Natural © Ergonomic keyboard and a standard QWERTY "101" style keyboard were used during this experiment. The typing tests were administered using Typing Tutor 6 © software from Kriya Systems, Inc. This software was installed on an IBM 80486 compatible computer. Data acquisition for EMG was obtained using an eight channel Telemyo transmitter and receiver and Noraxon Myosoft 3.4.o software from Noraxon USA, Inc.

2.3 Procedures

Each subject was required to complete an initial questionnaire including questions about age, race, occupation, CTD related illnesses and injuries, typing skills, and familiarity with ergonomic keyboards.

Prior to the actual tests, the subjects were familiarized with the experiment, including the Typing Tutor program and the keyboards. This period usually lasted 20 minutes and was conducted prior to the first experiment.

Typing Tutor 6 © software was used to administer standardized typing tests. An IBM compatible computer was set up to administer the test. The tests used were "book tests" where the typist was given continuous text to duplicate for the duration of the trial. The subjects were evaluated over two 45 minute sessions (one for each keyboard) with a minimum 30 minute break between the sessions. Subjects were seated comfortably in a chair with elbows at 90 degrees. The chair was adjusted for each subject to facilitate proper seating posture.

The Typing Tutor program displayed results in words-per-minute, characters typed, and mistakes. Due to a fundamental problem with the method the software records mistakes, the mistake rates had to be adjusted according to observations made during each session. The nature of the hunt-and-peck typist means that the typist is not monitoring the screen for errors since they need to see the keyboard in order to find the keys. The software evaluates the typing by tracking every keystroke. If the typist adds an additional space or letter in a word, every subsequent letter will be recorded as an error, even if the remainder of the typing is correct. This would inflate error rates for the tests. Other researchers investigated the differences between regular errors and what they called "chunk-errors" while using this software [12]. During each session, the "non-errors" (resulting from added letters and spaces not immediately identified by the typist) were recorded by hand during the entire session and subtracted from the total number of mistakes.

EMG values of the flexor and extensor muscles of the forearms were evaluated. Electrodes were placed on the appropriate muscles of the subject's forearms at a distance of 4.0 cm. EMG values were taken two times during each session for a duration of 5 minutes each. The first sample was taken between the 3rd and 9th minute after the session started, and the second sample was taken between the 30th and 36th minute into the session. For each 5 minute session, a 2 minute steady state period was chosen and analyzed.

Follow-up surveys were given to the subjects at the end of the experiment. This survey allowed subjective analysis concerning which keyboard the subjects preferred. Additionally, subjects reported their perceived exertion using the Borg scale [13]. Subjects were also asked to indicate which keyboard they would prefer to work with.

2.4 Experimental Design

A complete randomized block design, with subjects as blocks, was used for analyzing the collected data. Minitab statistical analysis software was used to analyze the data collected during the experiment.

3.0 Results and Discussion

A summary of the means and standard deviations for each of the response variables, separated by keyboard, is presented in Table 1. ANOVA results (Table 2) indicate that keyboard had a significant effect on words per minute and subjective ratings of effort. It was further determined that mistakes per character, and the EMG values for the flexor and extensor muscles of the forearm for the dominant hand, were not significantly different.

The mean words per minute decreased from 29.20 for the QWERTY keyboard to 26.00 for the ergonomic keyboard. However, the means of the mistakes per character were virtually the same between the two keyboards. According to the subjective rating, the subjects found the ergonomic keyboard more difficult to use. The Borg scale indicated that subjects rated their effort using the QWERTY keyboard at a mean of 1.80 and their effort using the ergonomic keyboard at a mean of 2.60.

The means for EMG values were generally higher for the ergonomic keyboard, indicating more muscle activity during these tests. The ANOVA results showed no significance differences for EMG values between the two keyboards. EMG's also indicated that the muscle activity tended to be higher at the beginning of the sessions than at the end, indicating a possible decrease in muscle activity over the duration of the test.

In general, the follow-up survey indicated mixed results. Two of the five subjects indicated a preference for the ergonomic keyboard. Furthermore, two subjects indicated that they typed "better" with the ergonomic keyboard. These findings could be due to the Hawthorne Effect [14]. Further studies would need to be conducted for a conclusive result.

4.0 Conclusions

While previous studies have indicated that ergonomic keyboards are better for the touch typist, this study indicates that they do not yield the same benefits for the hunt-and-peck typist. As fewer people are touch typists than hunt-and-peck typists, the purchase of an ergonomic keyboard for the "average individual" may not reduce the risks of CTD's for this population.

Table 1. Summary of Response Variables, mean(SD)   (n=5)

Response Variable	QWERTY Keyboard	Ergonomic Keyboard
Words per Minute	29.20 (3.77)	26.00 (3.61)
Mistakes per Character	0.021 (0.007)	0.022 (0.012)
Subjective Rating [13]	1.80 (0.84)	2.60 (0.89)
EMG Extensor Beginning (microvolts)	65.69 (21.24)	81.13 (54.27)
EMG Extensor End (microvolts)	67.55 (19.40)	66.52 (39.39)
EMG Flexor Beginning (microvolts)	70.69 (42.82)	99.86 (45.25)
EMG Flexor End (microvolts)	60.44 (41.34)	84.68 (42.01)

Table 2. Summary of ANOVA for response variables.

Response Variable	F-value	$p>F$
Words per Minute	13.84	0.020 *
Mistakes per Character	0.01	0.921
Subjective Rating [13]	16.00	0.016 *
EMG Extensor Beginning (microvolts)	0.03	0.599
EMG Extensor End (microvolts)	0.00	0.948
EMG Flexor Beginning (microvolts)	3.33	0.142
EMG Flexor End (microvolts)	1.45	0.294

*significant at $\alpha = 0.05$

5.0 Acknowledgments

The authors would like to thank Rajesh Krishnan, Steve Toner, Garett Rozek, Chong Wong, Vijay Krishnan, and Sadat Karim for their greatly appreciated help.

6.0 References

[1] C. Chen, P. Burastero, P. Tittiranonda, K. Hollerbach, M. Shih, and R. Denhoy, Quantitative evaluation of 4 computer keyboards: Wrist posture and typing performance. *Proceedings of the Human Factors and Ergonomics Society 38th Annual Meeting*, 1994, pp. 1094-1098.

[2] A. Hedge and J. R. Powers, Wrist postures while keyboarding: Effects of a negative slope keyboard system and full motion forearm supports. *Ergonomics, 38*, 1995, pp. 508-517.

[3] T. J.Armstrong, J. A. Foulke, B. J. Martin, and D. Rempel, An investigation of finger forces in alphanumeric keyboard work. *Designing for Everyone, Proceedings of the Eleventh Congress of the International Ergonomics Association, 1*, 1991, pp. 75-76.

[4] D. Rempel and J. Gerson, J., Fingertip forces while using three different keyboards. *Proceedings of the Human Factors and Ergonomics Society 35th Annual Meeting, 1991*, pp. 253-255.

[5] D. C. Churbuck, My aching hands!. *Forbes*, December 20, 1993, p. 246.

[6] P. J. McAlindon, Development and evaluation of the keybowl: A study on an ergonomically designed alphanumeric input device. *Proceedings of the Human Factors and Ergonomics Society 38th Annual Meeting*, 1994, pp. 320-324.

[7] C. M. Sommerich, Carpal tunnel pressure during typing: Effects of wrist posture and typing speed. *Proceedings of the Human Factors and Ergonomics Society 38th Annual Meeting*, 1994, pp. 611-615.

[8] M. Honan, E. Serina, R. Tal, D. and Rempel, D., Wrist postures while typing on a standard and split keyboard. *Proceedings of the Human Factors and Ergonomics Society 39th Annual Meeting, 1995*, pp. 366-368.

[9] W. J. Smith and D. T. Cronin, D. T., Ergonomics test of the kinesis keyboard. *Proceedings of the Human Factors and Ergonomics Society 37th Annual Meeting, 1993*, pp. 318-322.

[10] Gerard, M. J., Jones, S. K., Smith, L. A., Thomas, R. E., and Wang, T. (1994). An ergonomic evaluation of the kinesis ergonomic computer keyboard. *Ergonomics, 37*, pp. 1661-1668.

[11] A. Cakir, A., Acceptance of the adjustable keyboard. *Ergonomics, 38*, 1995, pp. 1728-1744.

[12] E. Matias, I. S. MacKenzie, and W. Buxton, W., One-handed touch typing on a QWERTY keyboard. *Human-Computer Interaction, 11*, 1996, pp. 1-27.

[13] G. A. V. Borg, Psychological bases of perceived exertion, *Medicine and Science in Sports and Exercise, 4*, 1982, pp. 377-381.

[14] F. J. Rothlisberger and W. J. Dickenson, Management and the Worker, 1939, Cambridge, MA: Harvard University Press.

Advances in Occupational Ergonomics and Safety II
Edited by Biman Das and Waldemar Karwowski
IOS Press and Ohmsha, 1997

Implementation of Arm Supports as an Aid to Computer Work in the Office

Dishayne T. GARCIA, Jeffrey E. FERNANDEZ, and Ramesh K. AGARWAL
College of Engineering, National Institute for Aviation Research,
Wichita State University, Wichita, Kansas 67260, USA

Abstract. This study compared four arm support systems during a computer typing task to investigate if an arm support system would affect the level of pain and/or discomfort. Ten healthy able bodied females participated in the study. The four arm support systems were no arm supports, Ergorest articulating arm supports, chair arm supports, and counter balance slings arm supports. Results indicated that arm supports had a significant effect on comfort, effort required and RPE, but had no significant effect on working or absolute heart rate. It was concluded that the Ergorest articulating arm support system would be recommended to minimize effort and RPE, and to maximize comfort. It is anticipated that the Ergorest articulating arm support system would decrease fatigue and possibly reduce the risk of CTDs for users of computers in tasks found in an office environment.

1. Introduction

Computer dominated jobs often require employees to work in constrained unsupported postures, at repetitive tasks and in precision work with hands, arms and fingers. A result of these requirements can be a variety of musculoskeletal conditions involving the entire upper limb, neck, and back, have approached the forefront of work related disorders. These conditions are commonly known as cumulative trauma disorders (CTDs) [1]. Nearly two-thirds (332,000) of the workplace illnesses were disorders caused by exposure to repeated trauma to workers' upper bodies (the wrist, elbow or shoulder), such as carpal tunnel syndrome. The number of CTD cases reported in 1994 was 10 percent higher than the corresponding 1993 figure (302,000) [2].

Occupational risk factors of CTDs include, but are not limited to, repetitive movements, forceful exertions, awkward postures, extended task durations, static muscle loads, cold temperatures, and vibration [1]. Changes in technology can be attributed to the increase in numbers and severity of CTDs. Technology in the computer office environment has increased efficiency with word processing packages where the stroke of a key can manipulate the text in any wanted fashion, yet it has decreased total upper extremity movements. Therefore, causing a sedentary work environment that encourages repetitive tasks for extended durations.

Computer users have widespread complaints of musculoskeletal discomfort due to the poor ergonomic design of work spaces. The most prevalent complaints involve aches and pain in the neck and shoulder regions. These complaints can be attributed to constrained postures and unsupported upper extremities during ordinary computer tasks [3]. Signs of physical discomfort can be an indication of worker and workstation incompatibility. Localized fatigue is associated with discomfort and/or pain which, if left untreated, leads to injury. Subjective assessments have shown employees prefer arm supports to alleviate pain and discomfort [4]. Objective measures such as electromyographic activity confirm this and have found that arm rests decrease EMG values by up to 57% [5]. Overexertion occurs when the level of effort, an indicator of physical fatigue, exceeds normal physiological and physical tolerance limits [6]. Therefore, by reducing the level of discomfort and/or fatigue at the end of a typical work day, the worker's quality of life can be improved and the risk of injury could be reduced.

It is expected by the year 2000 that 75% of all workers will use a computer and the number of home PCs will increase from the current 37% of all US households [7,8]. Therefore, the following study was conducted to investigate if an arm support system during a computer task affected the level of pain and/or discomfort.

2.0 Methods and Procedures

The task chosen for this study was a computer typing task. The objective response studied was heart rate. Comfort rating; effort required; rating of perceived exertion (RPE) of the fingers, wrist, forearm, upper arm, shoulders and whole body and overall choice of best arm support system were the subjective measures. Levels of discomfort and effort have been associated with fatigue, which leads to injury. RPE scales have been widely used due to the strong correlations between rating and physiological responses, especially when heart rate measure may be unreliable [6,9]. The subject performed the required task under four arm support conditions: no arm supports (NAS), ergorest articulating arm supports (EAS), arm supports attached to the chair (CAS), and counter balanced arm slings (CBAS).

2.1 Subjects

Ten female subjects were chosen from faculty and students at Wichita State University. The ages of the subjects ranged from 19-36 years of age. Subjects were screened for any history of CTDs.

2.2 Equipment

Anthropometric measurements were collected using the Siber Hegner Inc., anthropometric kit. An adjustable JAMAR hand grip dynamometer was used to measure grip strength. Heart rate was measured using a Polar CIC Inc., Vantage XL heart rate monitor. The CBAS used were a pair of Kromer zero gravity balancers (model 85720). The load range for this type of balancer was 3.0 to 5.0 kg with a cable travel of 200 cm, coupled to these balancers were Bauer and Black Therapeutic Arm Slings for full arm support. Two Ergorest articulating arm supports attached to the table were also used. These were height adjustable within a range of 7 cm. These supports also rotated about two joints.

The work station consisted of a table 71.1 cm high, computer, Expert Typing software for windows, monitor, keyboard, chair, footrest and the arm support system. Height of the chair and arm supports were adjusted so that the elbows of the subject were maintained at about 1.0 cm above the keyboard. The chair used in this study was an Eckadams® model 8011 without rolling casters to provide a fixed base. The arm rests on the chair were height adjustable within a range of 8.2 cm, but not rotatable.

2.3 Procedures

Anthropometric measurements were taken on the first session. Measurements for stature, popliteal height, buttock to knee length, sitting elbow height and sitting eye height were taken using the anthropometric kit. Resting heart rate was then taken at the beginning of each day with the subjects sitting down. The arm support system needed for the particular session was set up. The subject then practised typing on the computer keyboard using the software until 35 words per minute could be maintained.

The subject was then restricted to sit in a standard posture using the correct arm support condition for the particular session. A standard posture was confirmed when the elbows, hips, and knees were at 90 degrees, back was upright, and feet were supported.

According to the Expert Typing software the typing speed was set at 35 words per minute and at an intermediate level. Two computer typing tests were used so that a total of 20 minutes of typing could be accomplished. Working heart rate was taken at the 16th, 17th, 18th, 19th, and 20th minute.

At the end of each session RPE for fingers, wrist, forearm, upper arm, shoulders, and whole body using the Borg scale was administered along with total comfort and effort required surveys. The physical comfort survey was a five point scale where extremely comfortable, comfortable, neutral, uncomfortable, and extremely uncomfortable constituted the five anchors of the rating. Effort required was also a five point scale with the extremes being minimum effort and maximum effort.

The testing for each subject took two days. Each day two arm support systems were tested. A twenty minute rest between sessions was allocated to insure proper recovery. At the end of the fourth session the subject was asked to select the best overall arm support system. Sessions took place at very similar times of the day so that circadian rhythms could be similar.

2.4 Experimental Design

The experiment was designed as a Randomized Complete Block Design with subjects as the blocks. The data were analyzed using the SAS statistical package on an IBM 3081 main frame.

3.0 Results and Discussion

The descriptive statistics of the subjects are displayed in Table 1. Student t-test was performed on stature of this study with that of Ayoub's study [10]. No significant difference was found, hence, the sample population used could be considered a typical US population. Table 2 is a summary of the results of this experiment for the four different arm support system combinations. Information included are working heart rate, absolute heart rate and results from effort required, physical comfort, and perceived exertion surveys.

Results from the ANOVA indicate that types of arm supports had a statistical significant ($\alpha = 0.05$) effect on physical comfort, effort required, and RPE, but did not have a statistical effect on working or absolute heart rate. Results of the Duncan Multiple Range Test indicated two groupings for effort. CAS, CBAS and NAS made up group 1 and CBAS, NAS and EAS was group two. The two groups associated with comfort were EAS and the other three arm support systems. Results indicated three groupings for RPE. Group 1 consisted of the CAS and NAS, group two was the CBAS and group 3 was the EAS.

A survey administered at the end of the final session, asked the subjects to indicate which arm support system they thought was the overall best. Results showed 80% chose the EAS, while 10% chose the CAS and 10% chose NAS.

Table 1: Subject Descriptive Statistics

	Mean	Standard Deviation
Stature (cm)	162.7	8.3
Popliteal Height (cm)	41.7	2.1
Buttock to Knee Height (cm)	60.2	5.2
Sitting Elbow Height (cm)	63.3	3.2
Sitting Eye Height (cm)	112.8	5.4
Resting Heart Rate (bpm)	73.2	9.0

Table 2: Summary of Results of the Experiments in Mean (S.D.)

	NAS	EAS	CAS	CBAS
Working HR (bpm)	83.6 (8.9)	82.5 (7.1)	83.7 (7.9)	81.4 (9.4)
Absolute HR (bpm)	10.6 (3.9)	8.9 (4.9)	10.2 (3.2)	8.7 (3.6)
Effort Survey	3.0 (0.9)	2.3 (0.9)	3.6 (1.2)	3.0 (1.1)
Comfort Survey	3.5 (1.0)	2.5 (1.1)	3.9 (0.9)	3.6 (0.8)
RPE Fingers	2.3 (2.3)	1.4 (1.3)	2.1 (2.4)	1.9 (1.9)
RPE Wrist	2.6 (2.8)	1.6 (1.3)	3.3 (2.7)	1.6 (1.3)
RPE Forearm	3.0 (2.9)	1.1 (1.1)	3.4 (3.0)	3.4 (1.6)
RPE Upper	2.9 (3.0)	1.4 (1.5)	3.0 (3.5)	2.0 (2.0)
RPE Shoulders	3.2 (2.7)	1.6 (1.6)	3.5 (2.9)	1.7 (2.2)
RPE Whole Body	2.0 (2.3)	1.1 (1.3)	2.4 (3.0)	1.1 (1.6)

All previous results are typical to those found in a previous study where the same four arm support systems were studied during a light assembly task. Results in that study indicated the EAS system decreased EMG activity by 57% [5], which could help reduce the risk of CTDs. Other studies confirm that subjects prefer an arm support system over the NAS system [4]. Further studies with different computer tasks such as computer aided drafting and other office equipment should be conducted to understand the effects of arm supports in different office environments.

4.0 Concluding Remarks

Based on the results of this study the Ergorest articulating arm support system would be recommended to minimize effort and RPE, and to maximize comfort. It is anticipated that the Ergorest articulating arm support system would reduce fatigue and possibly reduce the risk of CTDs for users of computer work in the office environment.

5.0 References

[1] T.J. Armstrong et al. (1986). Repetitive Trauma Disorders: Job Evaluation and Design. Human Factors 28 (3) 325-336.
[2] U.S. Department of Labor, Bureau of Labor Statistics. (1996). Occupational Injuries and Illnesses in the States by Industry, 1994. Washington, D.C.: U.S. Government Printing Office.
[3] S.L. Sauter et al. (1991). Work Posture, Workstation Design and Musculoskeletal Discomfort in a VDT Data Entry Task. Human Factors 33 151-167.
[4] E. Keller and J. Strasser. (1996). Ergonomic Evaluation of an Armrest for Typing via Electromyographic and Subjective Assessment . Advances in Occupational Ergonomics and Safety I. Taylor and Francis, London/New York/Philadelphia. 838-845.
[5] M. Poonawala. (1996) Implementation of Arm Supports as an Aid to Light Assembly Work. Unpublished Master's Project, Wichita State University, Wichita, KS.
[6] S. Kumar. (1994). A Conceptual Model of Overexertion, Safety, and Risk of Injury in Occupational Settings. Human Factors 36 (2) 197-209.
[7] R. Wolkamir. (1994). When the Work You Do Ends Up Costing You and Arm and Leg. The Smithsonian Magazine. May 90-102.
[8] R. Fox. (1995). New Track. CACM 38 (5) 9.
[9] M.G. Klein, (1995) The effect of Posture, Force, and Duration on the Psychophysically Determined Frequency for a Pinching Task. PhD Thesis, Wichita State University, Wichita, KS.
[10] M.M. Ayoub et al. (1986). Manual Material Handling in Unusual Postures: Phase I. Institute for Ergonomics Research. Texas Tech University, Lubbock, TX.

Advances in Occupational Ergonomics and Safety II
Edited by Biman Das and Waldemar Karwowski
IOS Press and Ohmsha, 1997

Towards Multi-Dimensional Measurement and Improvement of VDU-Work

Chris STARY*, Thomas RIESENECKER-CABA,
Michael KALKHOFER, Jörg FLECKER

*WORKING LIFE RESEARCH CENTRE (WORC),
Aspernbrückengasse 4/5, 1020 Vienna, Austria*

*and Department for Business Information Systems,
Communications Engineering, University of Linz,
Freistädterstraße 315, 4040 Linz, Austria*

Abstract. VDU-work is a multi-dimensional process at the user interface. It forces software developers and usability engineers to tackle organizational, technical, cognitive, and social aspects. Unfortunately, techniques for development and measurement do not support the evaluation of user interfaces in a holistic way. The hindrances are caused by the diversification of disciplines involved in the design and measurement of user interfaces. We report on some analyses and a first solution that has been proposed to overcome existing deficiencies.

1. Introduction

Recent work in software ergonomics has shown a lack of multidimensional evaluation and design techniques for user interfaces, e.g. [1]. For instance, the suitability for tasks is considered to be one of the major criteria in software ergonomics (e.g., see the EU-directive on human-computer interaction [2], and ISO-standards [3]). Measurements either focus on cognitive, technical or organizational parameters. As a consequence, existing methodologies, such as MUSiC [4] do not integrate the concerned dimensions of the suitability for tasks, neither for measurement nor design.

A review analyzing 18 techniques for evaluation has led to the following results (for a detailed discussion see [5]):

- Some of the techniques, such as TCO [6], claim comprehensive measurement, but do not indicate the direction(s) for improvements. Practical redesign of user interfaces is not possible as long as it does not become evident in which direction changes have to be made. Do they concern the functionality of software, the organization of work, or cognitive parameters?

In addition, empirical tests have not been performed in the sense of test theory. As a consequence, the validity, objectivity, and reliability of the measurements is not known.

- A closer look to the type of techniques allows to categorize them according to their subject of measurement. This subject may either be the software product, such as in EVADIS II [7], the objectively determined conditions for task accomplishment, such as in KABA [8], or the individual perception of tasks, such as in MUSiC [4].

- Due to the diversification of computer science, occupational psychology, social and cognitive psychology, terms and methods are not defined in an uniform way: The terms and the methods may have different meanings. They have to be tuned mutually, in order to integrate them in common methodologies.

- In most of the cases, empirical experiences are missing. This fact makes it difficult to compare evaluation techniques, in particular, if they do not originate from occupational psychology.

In a second project the perspective from businesses as well as the requirements for the practical use of a comprehensive technique have been acquired. The results are summarized below, according to [9]:

- In enterprises where workplaces are evaluated according to particular classes of workplaces, such as offices, or software, such as text processing, often neglect user-oriented criteria.

- Due to the lack of techniques for the evaluation internal strategies and instruments are developed. These mostly ad-hoc approaches lack validation and reliability.

- The participation of employees in the course of evaluation is stressed out differently. Some companies claim users cannot be qualified to participate in evaluation, others rely on user participation for measurement and design.

- Enterprises are in particular interested in results of evaluation procedures that can be implemented in a straightforward way. Improvements are expected in the organization of work as well in technical belongings.

In the following we first give the design rationale for the development of a multi-dimensional technique based on the conceptual and empirical results. We then introduce a technique for evaluation that meets the listed requirements.

2. The Design Rationale and Concept for Multi-Dimensional Evaluation

Bridging the addressed conceptual gaps requires novel concepts, in order to support holistic measurement and adequate redesign of user interfaces:

- An additional phase enabling improvements has to be introduced: Any evaluation technique for comprehensive evaluation has to capture at least the following phases:
    (i) preparation of the evaluation,
    (ii) acquisition of data,
    (iii) evaluation and interpretation of results,
    (iv) controlled rework of user interface in case of identified deficiencies.

In particular, the last phase is not very common for evaluation and engineering techniques.

- A structured set of tools properly designed for each of the phases has to be provided and tuned for a smooth transition from evaluation to redesign. Again, most of the techniques for engineering or evaluation focus either on proposing design principles or on implementing measurements.

- Measurement and design cannot be performed independently of the tasks a user interface is supposed to support. Tasks have to be identified for the measurement. Usually it is assumed that one layer of granularity is sufficient to check task appropriateness. This strategy does not support the individual perception of tasks at the user interface.

- Evaluation should be supported in any application domain of software. Hence, the technique has to support the adaptation towards each case through particular mechanisms, such as the identification of tasks performed by the end users in a particular granularity as the initial activity.

Now we are going to sketch EU-CON (EU-CONform Evaluation and Engineering of VDU-Work) [9]. This technique has been developed for the integrated measurement and design of user interfaces to ensure compliance with the EU-directive on human-computer interaction [2]. EU-CON takes into account the social, organizational, technical, and cognitive dimension of human-computer interaction in a holistic way.

It starts out with a user-specific evaluation of a particular user interface. The users are enabled to give task-specific and individual answers. The second phase of the methodology involves the evaluator, i.e. an expert in cognitive ergonomics, that checks the indicative answers given by the users, in order to identify misconceptions, shortcomings and deficiencies. These may stem from the individual perception of tasks or interaction features, from the organizational or social setting the users are embedded in, or from the facilities provided by the user interface for task-specific interactions.

In order to support the work of the evaluator a handbook for engineering and design has been developed. It is based on the questionnaire the users have to answer in phase (i). It reflects the motivation of each question and give hints how to interpret possible answers. It then guides the evaluator along the identification of reasons for troublesome situations, as well as the removal of organizational, social, technical, and/or cognitive hindrances for effective and efficient VDU-work.

The novel methodology integrates measurement and (re)design in a way that

1. leads to an indication whether a particular user performing a particular task has particular difficulties, and
2. allows the identification of the organizational, social, technical, and/or cognitive deficiencies, and
3. guides the evaluator and/or user to remove the identified deficiencies.

First tests with the methodology have confirmed the benefits expected from the novel concepts. Overall, 70 people were involved in test cases. The test cases have been distributed equally over insurance companies, banks, production industries and trade companies. The tasks comprised office activities administration, management, software development and distribution, as well as trading.

3. Conclusions

The standards, directives, and the methodologies for evaluating workplaces providing computer support are more or less isolated. They focus either on technical features of interfaces, organizational constraints, or user characteristics, such as the mental workload. In case the development of an evaluation technique has been focused on the integration of different disciplines, such as computer science and cognitive psychology, several problems occur. These problems have been identified from a conceptual perspective (e.g., task-independent versus task-dependent measurement of task conformance) and the empirical perspective through structured interviews with responsibles from companies and government institutions, in to find out how they deal with ergonomic evaluation.

Based on these results, we have proposed a comprehensive evaluation and engineering technique that supports sufficient methodological and empirically valid input for evaluating and designing workplace equipped with interactive systems. The major improvement is the addition of a rework phase as part of the evaluation process, in order to enable continuous feedback/improvement cycles. Future activities will concentrate on checking the reliability, objectivity, and validity of this technique along further tests.

Acknowledgments

The work being reported has been funded by the Austrian Ministry for Science, Research and Culture under contract GZ 190.134/2-II/8/94, as well as the Austrian Ministry for Work and Social Affairs under contract GZ 120/19-GrA/95, as well as the European Commission in the Leonardo da Vinci-programme under contract 94/819/EG.

References

[1]   Stary, Ch.; Totter, A.: The Cognitive and Organizational Dimension of Task Appropriateness, in: Proceedings ECCE´8, European Conference on Cognitive Ergonomics, EACE, September 1996.
[2]   EU-Directive 90/270/EEC: Human-Computer Interaction, in EC-Bulletin, Vol. 33, L 156, p. 18, 21.6.1990.
[3]   ISO 9241 Part 10: Ergonomic Dialogue Design Criteria, Version 3, Committee Draft, December, Part 11: Usability Statements, Version 2.5, Committee Draft, July 1990.
[4]   Corbett, M.; Macleod, M.; Kelly, M.: Quantitative Usability Evaluation - The ESPRIT MUSiC Project, in: Human-Computer Interaction: Applications and Case Studies, Proceedings of the Fifth International Conference on Human-Computer Interaction, Orlando, Elsevier, Amsterdam, pp. 313 - 318, 1993.
[5]   Stary, Chr., Riesenecker-Caba, Th., Flecker J.: Evaluation of VDU-Workplaces - Steps Towards an Instrument according to the EC-Directive (in German), vdf, Zurich, 1995.
[6]   TCO: Swedish Confederation of Professional Employees: SOFTWARE CHECKER - An Aid to the Critical Examination of the Ergonomic Properties of Software, Handbook and Checklist, Sweden 1992.
[7]   Oppermann, R; Murchner, B.; Reiterer, H.; Koch, M.: Software-Ergonomic Evaluation. The Guide EVADIS II (in German), deGruyter, Berlin, 1992.
[8]   Dunckel, H. ; Volpert, W.; Zölch, M.; Kreutner, U.; Pleiss, C.; Hennes, K.: Contrastive Task Analysis (in German). The KABA-Guide: Fundamentals and Manual, Teubner, Stuttgart, 1993.
[9]   Stary, Chr., Riesenecker-Caba, Th., Kalkhofer, M.; Flecker J.: EU-CON - An EU-Conform Technique for Evaluating and Engineering VDU-Work (in German), vdf, Zurich, 1997.

16.   Participative Ergonomics

Participatory Ergonomics for Ergonomists

Cheryl L. Bennett
Lawrence Livermore National Laboratory
P.O. Box 808, L-309
Livermore, CA 94551

Abstract

This paper makes a case for the use of participatory ergonomics by and for ergonomists. A strategy for using participatory ergonomics in a conference workshop format is described. The process could be used as a tool for issues of common concern among ergonomists. It would also offer an experience of the participatory ergonomics process. An example workshop on quantifying costs and benefits of ergonomics is discussed.

1.0 Introduction

It is fitting that the concept of participatory ergonomics was identified and developed through collaboration. Discussions conducted by Drs. Noro, Kogi, and Imada at international conferences from 1983-1988 were instrumental in defining participatory methods for implementing ergonomics. [1] The term participatory ergonomics generally refers to a process whereby the "beneficiaries" of ergonomic improvements are "vitally involved in developing and implementing the technology."[2]

Participatory ergonomics has been successfully applied in widely diverse environments. Following relatively short (one day to four weeks) periods of training in participatory methods, participants from small enterprises in developing countries have made simple, low-cost solutions, improving both working conditions and productivity. [3] Participatory ergonomics has also complimented the quality-control-circle practices in some of the most technologically advanced Japanese companies. [4]

1.1 Expanding Participation Beyond Factories

The processes used in participatory ergonomics are intentionally adaptable and have been used in numerous ways as instruments for problem solving in industrial settings. However, Noro states that, "...one should not come to a hasty conclusion that participatory ergonomics is intended only for factory workers. Participatory ergonomics is a new medium in which everybody can participate for exchanging information on ergonomics." [4]

Ergonomic conferences offer another forum for participatory ergonomics, as demonstrated by the discussions that led to the inception of the concept. Certainly conferences foster interest in exchanging information on ergonomics. Conference workshops could provide a structure for ergonomists to work together on issues of common concern using the methods of participatory ergonomics. This paper will propose the use of participatory ergonomics methods at a conference workshop. As an example, a workshop on the issue of quantifying the costs and benefits of ergonomics will be discussed.

2.0 Participatory Ergonomics Workshops

2.1 Structure

Many conferences offer workshops. What is proposed here is using one-day workshops to allow ergonomists to focus together on a selected topic or problem. The participatory process is adept at engaging the participants and building upon their individual resources in developing approaches to solutions. Initial presentations of such a workshop would include a discussion of participatory ergonomics methods and process. This could be minimal in workshops with participants who were already familiarized. A facilitator experienced in participatory ergonomics would lead the discussion and prepare the participants for the second part of the workshop. It would also be advantageous to have topical experts present as technical facilitators. They could provide an orientation to the topic with a presentation on relevant research, methods or other information that could be used by the participants. During the next portion of the workshop, participants would work together in small groups assisted, as needed, by either type of facilitator. The conclusion of the workshop could be reserved for group discussion.

2.2 Attributes and Benefits

Using participatory ergonomics methods as a tool for ergonomists to work together offers many benefits (see Table 2.1).

A number of the methods used in participatory ergonomics are familiar and are used in other contexts (such as total quality management or accident investigation). Some of the techniques would be considered a logical approach to specific problems (such as having discipline or department representatives work together in a small group). Therefore, many ergonomists have previously used or been involved in activities that are considered part of participatory ergonomics. However, fewer have been through a step-by-step participatory ergonomics process. Even with an abbreviated session, much of what is learned through the experience will be highly transferable.

Having the workshop focus on a topic relevant to the participants and using participatory ergonomics rather than simply presenting a workshop on methods is important. Participants are more likely to integrate learning that is experienced and from which they receive immediate feedback. [5] Workshop topics that are relevant and of interest to participants can provide further motivation and potentially generate relevant products.

Differences among participants serve to enrich the participatory process. Variety in areas of expertise, academic background, and collective experience can substantiate the outcome. [6] This type of workshop provides a platform for collaboration among researchers and practitioners. The "gap" between researchers and practitioners is a common theme in comments made at conferences. [7] Working together in a participatory context offers opportunities for a different level of communication and mutual understanding.

Table 2.1

Benefits of Participatory Ergonomics Workshops for Ergonomists
• Training in participatory ergonomics methods included
• Workshops provide a transferable experience of the participatory ergonomics process
• Topics of focus selected for relevance and interest
• Products are of value to the participants
• Collaboration among diverse participants
• Researchers and practitioners benefit from working together

3.0 Example Workshop

3.1 Topic Background

Worldwide tightening of budgets is driving organizations to do more with less money. Decisions regarding ergonomic research, employing ergonomists, or intervention programs often have to be made without the information needed to analyze the costs and benefits. Part of the difficulty in projecting a rate of return for ergonomics is the paucity of methodology, but identifying the relevant costs or benefits is, at best, an inexact endeavor. [8] Intricately related psychosocial factors also make quantifying costs and benefits very challenging. [9]

Furthermore, as Noro points out, "There are many employers and managers who believe that the introduction of ergonomics decreases, rather than increases, productivity and does not bring about any profits to the companies." [4] Being able to identify costs and benefits would allow ergonomics investments to be evaluated more realistically when competing for limited resources. This is more important than ever with the significant cutbacks in government and military funding in addition to ongoing commercial sector cost-cutting. [10]

Within the usability faction of human factors professionals some great advances have been made in quantifying costs and benefits. This has been used primarily for software, but the general approach is applicable in other areas: "The first task in cost-benefit analysis of human factors work is to identify and quantify financially each of the expected costs (e.g., human factors and programming personnel, end user, walkthrough and testing) and the benefits (e.g., lower training costs, higher sales, increased productivity) of usability engineering. Estimates of all significant human factors cost and benefit variables in the project's life cycle are required for analyzing the relationship between the two." [11]

3.2 Workshop Process

The participants would determine the small group topics (see Table 3.1 for examples), the process to be used (see Table 3.2 for an example), and define the goal. The time would not be sufficient to thoroughly grasp the situation and analyze factors; identify the problem; or develop and improve measures to solve the problem. With the guidance of participatory ergonomics and financial facilitators, however, it is likely that substantial progress could be made in defining an approach to the identified problems. While confirming the "effect of the measure taken" would not be possible within the workshop, some participants might well become involved enough to have an interest in testing the results.

Table 3.1	Table 3.2
Potential Small Group Topics	**Potential Process Steps (from Noro) [4]**
Ergonomic research project	Select theme
Human Factors input in a product life cycle	Set goal
Ergonomic intervention programs	Grasp present situation and analyze factors
	Identify problem
	Develop and improve measures to solve problem
	Confirm effect of measure taken

4.0 References

[1]   Noro, K. and Imada, A. S., Preface, *Participatory Ergonomics,* edited by K. Noro and A. S. Imada, London: Taylor and Francis, Ltd., 1991, pp. vii-viii.

[2]   Imada, A. S., The Rationale and Tools of Participatory Ergonomics, in *Participatory Ergonomics,* edited by K. Noro and A. S. Imada, London: Taylor and Francis, 1991, Ltd., pp. 3-29.

[3]   Kogi, K. Participatory Training for Low-Cost Improvements in Small Enterprises in Developing Countries, *Participatory Ergonomics,* edited by K. Noro and A. S. Imada, London: Taylor and Francis, Ltd., 1991, pp. 73-480.

[4]   Noro, K., Concepts, Methods and People, *Participatory Ergonomics,* edited by K. Noro and A. S. Imada, London: Taylor and Francis, Ltd., 1991, pp. 30-49.

[5]   Paul, R., Understanding Individual Learning for Organizational Learning, in *Proceedings of the Human Factors and Ergonomics Society 40th Annual Meeting,* Santa Monica, CA, 1996, pp. 791-795.

[6]   Weick, K., 1987, Organizational Culture as a Source of High Reliability, *California Management Review,* 24, pp. 112-127.

[7]   Sind-Prunier, P. Bridging the Research/Practice Gap: Human Factors Practitioners' Opportunity for Input to Define Research for the Rest of the Decade, in *Proceedings of the Human Factors and Ergonomics Society 40th Annual Meeting,* Santa Monica, CA, 1996, pp. 865-867.

[8]   Riel, P. F., Justifying Investments in Industrial Ergonomics, *Advances in Industrial Ergonomics and Safety VII,* edited by A. C. Bittner and P. C. Champney, London: Taylor and Francis, Ltd., 1995, pp. 677-684.

[9]   Boden, L. I., Work Disability in an Economic Context, in *Beyond Biomechanics: Psychosocial Aspects of Musculoskeletal Disorders in Office Work,* edited by S. D. Moon and S. L. Sauter, London: Taylor and Francis, Ltd., 1996, pp. 287-294.

[10]   Griffith, D., Human Factors/Ergonomics: The state of the profession, in CybErg Conference Proceedings, edited by, L. Straker, Australia, 1996.

[11]   Karat, C., A Business Case Approach to Usability Cost Justification, in *Cost-Justifying Usability,* edited by R. G. Bias and D. J. Mayhew, New York: Academic Press, Inc., 1994, pp. 45-70.

Advances in Occupational Ergonomics and Safety II
Edited by Biman Das and Waldemar Karwowski
IOS Press and Ohmsha, 1997

A Participatory Ergonomic Training

Program for Preventing Low Back Pain

Marçal, Márcio A., and Mazzoni, Cláudia F.
Ergonomic Research Group, Queen's University, Kingston, Ont, K7L 3N6 Canada,
Phone: (613) 545-2658, Fax: (613) 543-2009

Abstract

A number of 158 employees including supervisors, managers and operators were involved in a participatory ergonomic training program. The one year follow up showed a decrease in the incidence of low back pain, absenteeism rate and job satisfaction. The increasing interest in the ergonomic aspects contributed to the creation of an Ergonomics Surveillance Group with participation from all levels of employment in the plant.

1 - Introduction

Many activities performed in industry might be potential risky for musculoskeletal injuries. In recent years many programs aimed at preventing low back injuries have become available. Different types of training and ergonomics approaches have been used such as: 1) back-school (lecture, physical exercises, practical lessons); 2) in-house versus on-site ergonomics training; 3) focusing on specific issues (proper lifting technique, for example); 4) audio-visual aids; 5) hand-outs. It is not surprising that with such a variety of methods, contradictory findings regarding the success of training programs are reported. Unclear definition of the training objectives may result in inefficient learning [1] and a lack of active involvement by managers and employees in training and in ergonomic interventions may also impact negatively on the final results [2,3,4]. However, participatory ergonomics training programs have been reported in the literature as an efficient method for the prevention of musculoskeletal problems [5,6,7]. This approach seeks to improve workplace issues through the continued involvement of both managers and workers [8].

The main purpose of this study was to verify the effectiveness of a participatory ergonomics training programme in reducing the incidence of low back complaints (53%) and the rate of absenteeism in a trunk and auto-parts industry.

2 - Methods

A number of 158 employees including supervisors, managers and operators were involved in this program. The first step was a meeting with managers and supervisors to get feedback about their expectations and their goals as well as set up clear objectives for the training. The second step was a meeting with the operators and informing them about the new approach that would be implemented and its purpose. At this time, their opinions and needs were discussed and incorporated into the training objectives. The operators also elected a total of 10 representatives, one for each sector, to work close with the consulting group.

To establish the training needs assessment a job analysis was performed in each sector to provide information about the main musculo-skeletal risk factors present. Supervisor and worker representatives participated in the analysis of the tasks, while the other workers responded to a short and informal interview, not only for furthering their understanding of the job, but also to motivate them to be involved in the program. The participatory ergonomic training was divided into lectures and practical interventions. Hand-outs containing the main concepts and points discussed were provided during the first and second sections of an eight hour lecture.

3 - Results

The usefulness of the training became clear during the follow up period. Within the first month, many cheap and efficient modifications were performed in the workplace such as a change in the workbench height, relocation of the storage area for heavy material, creating alternative ways to support the tools used during heavy material handling, etc. Changes in attitude also were reported by operators and supervisors. Some examples are improved technique during lifting, asking for help when the object was too heavy, and more use of mechanical aids, etc. Improvements in the communication among operators, supervisors and managers, and increases in motivation and job satisfaction were observed after 3 months. The one year follow up showed a decrease in the incidence of low back pain from 53% to 11%, as well as a decrease in the absenteeism rate. The level of involvement and interest in the ergonomics aspects of the workplace contributed to the creation of the Ergonomics Surveillance Group, with participation from all levels of employment in the plant.

4 - Discussion

The participatory training program applied at this industry had very good results, which were reflected in the decrease in the incidence of low back pain and in the absenteeism rate. Maciel and Barreira [9] also used a participatory intervention in the same type of industry and they report a 20% decrease in the visits to the medical service due to complaints of musculo-skeletal pain. Another study in an automotive seat assembly facility showed that the injury frequency was reduced by 18% and injury severity declined by 79%[10].

Worker participation has proved to be fundamental not only for identifying the risk factors in the workplace, but also in solving problems. Those employees who participated in the entire process (training design, job analysis and intervention ideas), were more committed to making the process work. In this study, worker participation improved employee satisfaction. It has been suggested that participation also allows workers to have some control over the job and the workplace [11]. In addition, managers and supervisors who demonstrated the same knowledge as the workers regarding the risk factors and basic ergonomics, provided to the workplace environment adequate support and motivation. Such actions enforced the real importance of the program not only for the industry, but also for the employees in general.

References

[1] J.E. Cohen, V. Goel, J.W. Frank, C. Bombardier, P. Peloso, F. Guillemin, Group Education Interventions for People with Low Back Pain: An Overview of the Literature, *Spain* **19**(11) (1994) 1214-1222

[2] S.L. Fitzier, Attitudinal change: The Chelsea Back Program, *Occupational Health & Safety* **51** (1982) 24-26

[3] A. Morris, Program Compliance Key to Preventing Low Back Injuries. *Occupational Health & Safety* (5) (1984) 44-47

[4] A.S. Imada, Participatory Ergonomics: Definitions and Recent Development, *Proceedings of the 12th Triennial Congress of the International Ergonomics Association* **3** (1994) 337-339

[5] A. Johansson, H. Shahnavaz, G. Westlander, Can Musculoskeletal Problems be Solved Through Worker's Participation? *Proceedings of the 12th Triennial Congress of the International Ergonomics Association* **2** (1994)

[6] P. Hasle, Participatory Training - A Method to Achieve Workplace Improvements, *Proceedings of the 12th Triennial Congress of the International Ergonomics Association* **5** (1994) 68-70

[7] K. Moro and A.S. Imada, Participatory Ergonomics, Taylor & Francis, London, 1991.

[8] P. Vink, Application of Guidelines in Participatory Ergonomic, *Proceedings of the 12th Triennial Congress of the International Ergonomics Association* **3** (1994) 331-334

[9] R.H. Maciel and T.H.C. Barreira, A Case Study on Participatory Ergonomics, *Proceedings of the 12th Triennial Congress of the International Ergonomics Association* **6** (1994) 117-119

[10] S. Fitch and C.T. Van Velzer, Participatory Ergonomics Works at a Seating Plant. Proceedings of the 28th Annual Conference of the Human Factors Association of Canada 105-110

[11] A.J. Marcotte, Analysing Work with Employee Participation, *Proceedings of the 12th Triennial Congress of the International Ergonomics Association* **3** (1994) 343-345

Advances in Occupational Ergonomics and Safety II
Edited by Biman Das and Waldemar Karwowski
IOS Press and Ohmsha, 1997

Quality Awards - The Chance for Ergonomics and Safety in Companies

H. Schnauber and C. Treier

Ruhr-Universität Bochum, Institut für Arbeitswissenschaft,

NB 1/69, Universitätsstraße 150, 44780 Bochum, Germany

More and more companies see that the realization of a quality management system after ISO 9000 - 9004 is only a first step to an effizient system. Quality strategies like Total Quality Management consequently leads to a broad „Integrative Company Management", but they are very complex for practice.

The Quality Awards look after the „best" quality management systems. For this they have reference models which are practical guides for Integrative Company Management respectively Total Quality Management (TQM).

Looking to the European Quality Management Model of the EFQM (European Foundation for Quality Management) the contribution demonstrates, that there are many criteria which consider important aspects of ergonomics and safety.

In practice ergonomics and safety is induced e. g. by laws. These Awards motivate companies to consider the working conditions „voluntary". They emphasis that the aspects of ergonomics and safety imply very important management functions. Therefore there is a big chance to realize the best solution of a work system.

1 TQM by the European Quality Management Model

A model which supports the realization of TQM must be a model with special functions:

    1.the real system is reduced for management decisions

    2.the broad aspects of the real system have to be considered by the model

Therefore the European Quality Management Modell is designed as a „Criteria Model" (figure 1).

Comparing the Model to typical work system models like TOP (Technik, Organisation, Personal that means Technology, Organization, Employee(s)) the European Quality Model is an enlarged work system model which considers the Customer and the Society (figure 2). The difference to the Quality Management System Model of DIN EN ISO 9001 can also be defined by the work system model TOP (figure 3). Allready this „theoretical" comparison of the models demonstrates that with the help of the European Quality Management Model all aspects of work design can be integrated regarding efficiency and humanity. The general potential of Quality Management for Ergonomics was presented in SCHNAUBER/TREIER, 1995.

2 Using the European Quality Management Model

The practice aspekts of a model has to be used to be transfered to activities. Therefore the using of the model is very important. The key word is called: Self Assessment. „Self Assessment is a comprehensive, systematic and regular review of an organisation´s activities and results referenced against a model of business exellence", like the European Quality Management Model. Self Assessment is no single work for managers - it is teamwork! So all important aspects of the company are considered and a strategie for improvement can be initiated. The model gets a „powerful diagnostic tool" for the manager, a compass for all employees of the company for going to „business excellence" that means efficiency and humanity - the gist aims of industrial science and ergonomics (compare ROHMERT, 1973). The model can be considered as a „ergonmic" tool for the manager to meet their mission, leading the company successful.

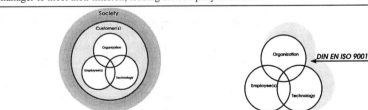

Figure 2 (left): The EQA-Model transfered to the elements of a work system
Figure 3 (right): The Quality Management Model of DIN EN ISO 9001 compared to the elements of a work system

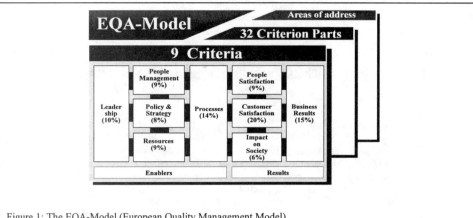

Figure 1: The EQA-Model (European Quality Management Model)

3 Ergonomic Aspects in the criteria - Some examples

Perhaps the best demonstration is by looking to the criteria from the point of view of a industrial engineer/manager. The model devides between two groups of criteria: the enablers and the results. These groups are connected to each other. With the help of criterion parts the European Quality Management Modell tries to transfer this complex correlation into a „simple" but broad checking system for assessment. In a third part practical hints are given to fulfill these criteria and their criterion parts. Of course it is not possible to present all criteria in this contribution. Therefore only for some cirteria exemplary comments are given. But these comments are sufficient to demonstrate the big and practical ergonomic dimension of the European Quality Management Model.

3.1 People Management and People Satisfaction

The demands of these criteria are, that the potential of the employees has to be activated by common values, by a company culture. For the criterion „People Management" following criterion parts are formulated: „Evidence is needed of how people

3a. resources are planned and improved.

3b. capabilities are sustained and developed.

3c. agree targets and continously review performance.

3d. are involved, empowered and recognised.

3e. and the organisation have an effective dialogue.

3f. cared for." (EFQM, Feb. 1997)

Looking at the areas of address, this criteria are „real" ergnomics and safety themes. In figure 4 the areas of address of the criterion part 3b. are summarized.

The criterion parts of the „People Satisfaction" measures and assesses from an ergnomic point of view. The criterion parts are mentioned following:

„Evidence is needed of

7a. the people´perception of the organisation.

7b. additional measurements relating to people satisfaction." (EFQM, Feb. 1997)

In figure 5 some of the interesting areas of address are listet.

The areas of address show that one very important aspect is the learning processes in companies. Hints of designing learning processes are given in SCHNAUBER/GRABOWSKI/SCHLÄGER/ZÜLCH, 1996.

3.2 Resources

Looking to this criterion and their parts (figure 6) the ergonomic dimension will be indirect. A good performance in this criterion leads to projects with big ergonomics and safety themes. For example the efficient use of the information resources is only possible by strategies which consider the needs of the workers. A information system is a part of the communication system! The connections to the supplier, can be only realized by cooperative forms (see REINHART/SCHNAUBER, 1997). This has consequences for the people management and the leadership because cooperative forms to the suppliers are more successful by cooperative forms in leadership in the company. The best improvement potential is the employee and his work place. So there are powerful connections to the criteria of People Management and People Satisfaction.

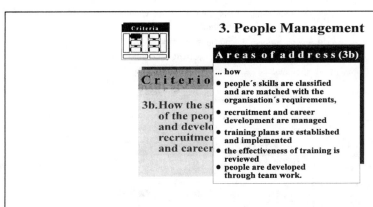

Figure 4: Areas of address to the criterion part 3b.

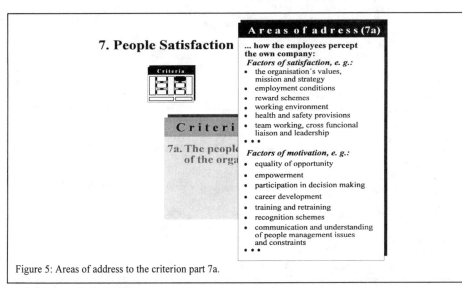

Figure 5: Areas of address to the criterion part 7a.

3.3 Impact of Society

In this criterion aspects of safety for employees and environment are integrated. The model says, that every organization has to satisfy the „needs and the expectations of loacal, national and international community at large (as appropriate)". The customer satisfaction is connected to this criterion. The fulfillment of this criterion will be very difficult because the values and culture of the company have to be harmonized. Society expectations are described by laws and norms. There are many examples that companies underestimate this criteria. The new german law „Arbeitsschutzgesetz" which is based on 89/391/EWG of European Community is one example for the dimension of this criterion. The ethical dimension of this criterion has a big correlation to the values and culture of the company. The European Quality Management Model has the potential power to grow in this direction. Especially by organization in health care or similar areas this criteria has fundamental importance. So the German CARITAS of the roman catholic church try to harmonize their christian values with the aspects of efficiency (=> total quality task). REHN (1997) shows that the European Quality Management Model can support this project.

4 Consequences

Of course this short contribution can be only a motivation to look to such models. There are many other quality prices, for example the Malcolm Baldrige National Quality Award of the USA. They are similar in the aims and criteria allthough the american quality award has different structure. Many companies look to such models. The number of organizations (500, the EFQM was founded 1988) in the EFQM is only one signal to this. The development of national (e. g. Ludwig Erhard Preis, Germany) and local quality prices (e. g. the Qualitätspreis of Nordrhein-Westfalen - a land of Germany) are further signals.

The Quality Prices are a chance and a theme for ergonomic and safety in three ways:

1. Convincing the Management that ergonomics and safety is important to be successful.
2. Influencing the development of the models and their areas of address by transfering practical knowledges.
3. In a way the models are „ergonmic" tools for the management to manage their complex mission to lead a company in direction of business excellence.

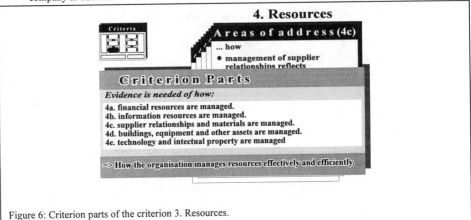

Figure 6: Criterion parts of the criterion 3. Resources.

5 References

Arbeitsschutzgesetz, 7. 8. 1996 (ArbSchG), Gesetz über die Durchführung von Maßnahmen des Arbeitsschutzes zur Verbesserung der Sicherheit und des Gesundheitsschutzes der Beschäftigten bei der Arbeit (Germany).

89/391/EWG (EG-Rahmenrichtlinie), 12. 6. 1989, EG-Rahmenrichtlinie über die Durchführung von Maßnahmen zur Verbesserung der Sicherheit und des Gesundheitsschutzes der Arbeitnehmer bei der Arbeit (European Community).

EFQM, Feb. 1997, Information table in the world wibe web (http://www.efqm.org)/ EFQM, 1996, Selbstbewertung 1997 - German - / EFQM, 1995, Selbstbewertung 1996 - English - (Brüssel in Belgium).

ISO 9000 - 9004 - DIN EN ISO 9000 - 9004, 1994, Standards for Quality Management Systems, May 1992 - August 1994.

Ludwig-Erhard-Preis, 1997, Auszeichnung für Spitzenleistungen im Wettbewerb. Bewertungsbroschüre. (Frankfurt: Deutsche Gesellschaft für Qualität or Düsseldorf: VDI).

Malcolm Baldrige National Quality Award, since 1987 (MBNQA), current informations see: http://www.nist.gov/director/quality-programm/.

Qualitätspreis Nordrhein-Westfalen, 1996, Der Qualitätspreis Nordrhein-Westfalen 1996 (Informationsbroschüre) (Düsseldorf: Ministerium für Wirtschaft, Mittelstand, Technologie und Verkehr des Landes Nordrhein-Westfalen).

REHN R., 1997, Ethik und Qualität. Qualitätsmanagement in beziehungsorientierten Dienstleistungsunternehmen - das Beispiel eines Caritasverbands. In: QZ. Qualität und Zuverlässigkeit. Qualitätsmanagement in Industrie und Dienstleistung (Ed. W. MASING). (München: C. Hanser), Vol. 42, No. 2, pp. 182 - 187.

REIHNHART, G. and SCHNAUBER, H., will be published 1997, Qualität durch Kooperation. (Berlin/Heidelberg/New York a. o., Springer).

ROHMERT, W., 1973, Formen menschlicher Arbeit. Kap. 2 In: Rutenfranz, J. and Rohmert, W. (Ed.), Praktische Arbeitsphysiologie (3rd edition, founded by Lehmann, G.). (Stuttgart/New York: Thieme)

SCHNAUBER, H. and TREIER, C., 1995, Ergonomic design as a basic for quality management. In: Bittner, A. C. and Champey, P. C., Advances in industrial ergonomics and safety VII. Proceedings of the tenth annual international industrial ergonomics and safety conference held in Seattle, Washington, USA, 13 - 16 June 1995 (London/Bristol: Taylor & Francis), pp. 673 - 676.

SCHNAUBER, H., GRABOWSKI, S./SCHLÄGER, S. and ZÜLCH, J., 1996, Total Quality Learning. (Berlin/Heidelberg/New York a. o., Springer).

Advances in Occupational Ergonomics and Safety II
Edited by Biman Das and Waldemar Karowski
IOS Press and Ohmsha, 1997

Effect of Source Attribution on Judgments of Warning Credibility and Compliance Likelihood

Michael S. WOGALTER[a], Michael J. KALSHER[b], and Raheel RASHID[a]

[a]Department of Psychology, North Carolina State University, Raleigh, NC 27695, USA

[b]Department of Philosophy, Psychology, and Cognitive Science, Rensselaer Polytechnic Institute, Troy, NY 12180, USA

Abstract. Communication models frequently include the source of a message as an important determinant of persuasion. However, research on the contribution of source characteristics to warning effectiveness is virtually non-existent. The present research investigated three types of sources: (1) specific regulatory governmental agencies (e.g., U.S. FOOD AND DRUG ADMINISTRATION), (2) specific scientific professional groups (e.g., AMERICAN MEDICAL ASSOCIATION), and (3) general statements in which an explicit source is not mentioned (e.g., IMPORTANT HEALTH WARNING). Participants rated 11 sources of the alcohol, cigarette, and iron supplement warnings on credibility and compliance likelihood. The results show that exemplars from the two types of specific sources made the warnings more credible and increased the compliance likelihood ratings compared to a signal word (WARNING) by itself. Having a signal word was better than no signal word. Implications for warning design are discussed.

1. Introduction

According to communication-persuasion theory [1], the effectiveness of a message depends in part on the source of that message (i.e., the entity from which the message derives). Warnings are a type of persuasion attempt intended to motivate people to comply with its directives. A warning that fails to persuade could lead to injury, death or property damage. Despite its potential importance, research on source effects in the warnings literature is virtually nonexistent except for two studies [2, 3]. For example, Lirtzman and Shuv-Ami [2] found that sources seen as content-domain experts enhance warning-message credibility.

In recent years, U.S. government has mandated warnings for various products. For two well-known products (cigarettes and beverage alcohol), the warnings include explicit sources as part of the message, i.e., SURGEON GENERAL and/or GOVERNMENT. Until recently, however, there has been no research on whether having an attributable source in the warning (in this case the government) affects warning effectiveness judgments. Recently, Wogalter, Kalsher and Rashid [3] examined the effectiveness of four types of signal word/source attributions: (1) WARNING, (2) GOVERNMENT WARNING, (3) U.S. GOVERNMENT WARNING, (4) U.S. FEDERAL GOVERNMENT WARNING on cigarette, alcohol, and iron warnings. The results showed that adding an attributable source (e.g., U.S. GOVERNMENT) significantly improved the perceived credibility of the warning and compliance likelihood as compared to the signal word alone (WARNING). In addition, the study showed that warnings with the signal word WARNING were given higher ratings than warnings without a signal word.

In this study, we examined three categories of sources: (1) specific regulatory governmental agencies (e.g., U.S. FOOD AND DRUG ADMINISTRATION), specific scientific professional groups (e.g., AMERICAN MEDICAL ASSOCIATION, AMERICAN PEDIATRIC ASSOCIATION), and general statements without a directly attributable source (e.g., IMPORTANT HEALTH WARNING). As in the Wogalter et al. [3] study, the effect of presence vs. absence of the signal word WARNING was also examined. The two dependent measures were perceived credibility and likelihood to comply with the warning. These measures have direct relevance to the communication-persuasion and warnings literatures, respectively.

2. Method

2.1. Participants

Fifty-seven undergraduates from Rensselaer Polytechnic Institute participated. This group had a mean age of 19.9 years (SD = 1.5). Thirty six were males. Forty-six were Caucasians.

2.2. Materials

Participants viewed warning messages for three products: They are shown below.

Alcohol warning

_____: (1) Women should not drink alcoholic beverages during pregnancy because of the risk of birth defects. (2) Consumption of alcoholic beverages impairs your ability to drive a car or operate machinery, and may cause health problems.

Cigarette warning

_____: Cigarette smoke contains carbon monoxide. Smoking causes lung cancer, heart disease, emphysema, and may complicate pregnancy. Smoking by pregnant women may result in fetal injury, premature birth, and low birth weight. Quitting smoking now greatly reduces serious risks to your health.

Iron supplement warning

_____: Keep away from children. Keep in original package until each use. Contains iron which can harm or cause death to a child. If a child accidentally swallows this product, call a doctor or poison control center.

The above alcohol warning message has been mandated since 1989 to be on all beverage alcohol containers sold in the U.S. The above cigarette warning message combined the four separate messages that have been on packages and advertising for cigarettes since the mid-1980s. The iron warning message was taken from one that the U.S. FDA was considering for iron supplement (e.g., multi-vitamin and mineral) labels..

The warning messages were printed on separate sheets and surrounded by a 4-point rectangular black border. Each had a blank space (underlined) followed by a colon to indicate the location of added prefix wording (if any). Below the warning were the 12 alternative prefixes. Two were controls. One lacked the prefix entirely; only a blank line was given (i.e., no source or signal word). The other control had just the signal word WARNING (but no attributable source). The other 10 alternatives consisted of either specific sources or general statements that were added before the signal word WARNING. There were three specific regulatory government agency prefixes: U.S. SURGEON GENERAL'S, U.S. CONSUMER PRODUCT SAFETY COMMISSION, and U.S. FOOD AND DRUG ADMINISTRATION. There were two specific scientific professional group prefixes: AMERICAN MEDICAL ASSOCIATION, and AMERICAN PEDIATRIC ASSOCIATION. There were six general statement prefixes: HEALTH, SAFETY AND HEALTH, U.S. PUBLIC HEALTH, MEDICAL HEALTH, and IMPORTANT HEALTH.

Credibility and compliance likelihood ratings were made on 9-point scales. The credibility scale was anchored at the even-numbered points with the following verbal descriptions: (0) not at all credible, (2) somewhat credible, (4) credible, (6) very credible, and (8) extremely credible. The compliance likelihood scale had the following anchors: (0) not at all likely, (2) somewhat likely, (4) likely, (6) very likely, (8) extremely likely.

2.3. Procedure

Initially participants were asked to read and sign a consent form. They were then told that the purpose of the study was to assess people's impressions of warnings that differed in their wording. After the ratings, participants were asked to complete a demographics questionnaire requesting age, gender, etc. Later, participants were debriefed and thanked.

3. Results

3.1. Credibility

A 3 (product warning: alcohol, cigarette, and iron supplement) X 12 (prefix) repeated measures analyses of variance (ANOVA) was applied to the credibility ratings. The effect

Table 1

Mean ratings of credibility as a function of product warning and prefix.

| Prefix | Warnings | | | |
	Alcohol	Cigarette	Iron	mean
__[blank]__:	2.81	2.95	3.07	2.94
WARNING:	3.51	4.00	4.09	3.87
U.S. SURGEON GENERAL'S WARNING:	5.25	5.72	5.61	5.53
U.S. CONSUMER PRODUCT SAFETY COMMISSION WARNING:	4.49	4.68	5.33	4.84
U.S. FOOD AND DRUG ADMINISTRATION WARNING:	5.25	5.32	5.54	5.37
AMERICAN MEDICAL ASSOCIATION WARNING:	5.53	5.56	5.46	5.51
AMERICAN PEDIATRIC ASSOCIATION WARNING:	5.02	4.95	5.67	5.21
HEALTH WARNING:	4.32	4.44	4.54	4.43
SAFETY AND HEALTH WARNING	4.54	4.56	4.89	4.67
U.S. PUBLIC HEALTH WARNING:	4.75	4.75	4.68	4.73
MEDICAL HEALTH WARNING:	4.74	5.00	4.82	4.85
IMPORTANT HEALTH WARNING:	4.72	4.67	4.72	4.70
mean	4.58	4.72	4.87	

of product warning was not significant, $F(2, 112) = 2.85, p > .05$. The ANOVA showed a significant main effect of prefix, $F(11, 616) = 25.61, p < .0001$. These means are shown in the right-most column of Table 1. Paired comparisons using the Tukey HSD test ($p < .05$) showed that participants gave higher credibility ratings when the signal word WARNING was present than when it was absent. Adding a general prefix (the words SAFETY AND HEALTH, IMPORTANT HEALTH, and MEDICAL HEALTH) to the signal word significantly increased credibility, although adding the prefix HEALTH to WARNING did not. The four highest rated prefixes (U.S. SURGEON GENEREAL'S, AMERICAN MEDICAL ASSOCIATION, U.S. FOOD AND DRUG ADMINISTRATION, and AMERICAN PEDIATRIC ASSOCIATION) were not statistically different from one another, but the two highest-rated sources (U.S. SURGEON GENERAL'S and AMERICAN MEDICAL ASSOCIATION) had significantly higher credibility than the U.S. CONSUMER PRODUCT SAFETY COMMISSION and the U.S. PUBLIC HEALTH prefixes.

The ANOVA also showed a significant interaction, $F(22, 1232) = 2.73, p < .0001$. Simple effects analysis showed that the pattern of means was consistent with the main effect of prefix described above except that the AMERICAN PEDIATRIC ASSOCIATION and U.S. CONSUMER PRODUCT SAFETY COMMISSION had significantly higher credibility ratings for the iron product warning than the other two product warnings.

3.2. Compliance Likelihood

A 3 (product warning: alcohol, cigarette, and iron supplement) X 12 (prefix) repeated measures ANOVA on the compliance likelihood ratings showed significant main effects of product warning, $F(2, 112) = 5.20, p < .01$, and prefix, $F(11, 616) = 19.09, p < .0001$. These means are shown on the bottom row and the right-most column of Table 2. The Tukey's test showed that compliance likelihood ratings were significantly higher for the iron than for the cigarette warning. Participants gave higher compliance likelihood ratings when the signal word WARNING was present than when it was absent. All of the source conditions had significantly higher compliance likelihood ratings than the signal word alone, except for the prefix HEALTH. The only other significant differences were between the highest-rated prefix AMERICAN MEDICAL ASSOCIATION and the general prefixes HEALTH, SAFETY AND HEALTH, and IMPORTANT HEALTH.

The ANOVA also showed a significant interaction, $F(22, 1232) = 2.32, p < .001$. Simple effects analysis followed by paired comparisons showed that the pattern of means

Table 2

Mean ratings of compliance likelihood as a function of product warning and prefix.

| | Warnings | | | |
Prefix	Alcohol	Cigarette	Iron	mean
__[blank]__:	3.53	3.16	3.91	3.53
WARNING:	4.23	3.88	4.79	4.30
U.S. SURGEON GENERAL'S WARNING:	5.33	5.12	5.54	5.33
U.S. CONSUMER PRODUCT SAFETY COMMISSION WARNING:	4.88	4.46	5.79	5.04
U.S. FOOD AND DRUG ADMINISTRATION WARNING:	5.40	5.09	5.51	5.33
AMERICAN MEDICAL ASSOCIATION WARNING:	5.51	5.30	5.84	5.55
AMERICAN PEDIATRIC ASSOCIATION WARNING:	5.16	4.86	5.89	5.30
HEALTH WARNING:	4.81	4.40	5.28	4.83
SAFETY AND HEALTH WARNING:	4.95	4.37	5.44	4.92
U.S. PUBLIC HEALTH WARNING:	5.07	4.53	5.40	5.00
MEDICAL HEALTH WARNING:	5.05	4.61	5.47	5.04
IMPORTANT HEALTH WARNING:	4.95	4.53	5.42	4.96
mean	4.91	4.52	5.36	

was consistent with the main of effects of warning and prefix described above except that the prefixes AMERICAN PEDIATRIC ASSOCIATION and U.S. CONSUMER PRODUCT SAFETY COMMISSION were rated higher for the iron warning than the other two product warnings. The three product warnings did not differ in compliance likelihood for the U.S. SURGEON GENERAL'S, U.S. FOOD AND DRUG ADMINISTRATION, and AMERICAN MEDICAL ASSOCIATION prefixes.

4. Discussion

The results show that a product warning with no source or signal word was rated less credible and produced lower compliance likelihood ratings compared to a warning with the signal word WARNING alone. However, the signal word alone was, in turn, rated less credible and produced lower compliance ratings compared to all of the specific source conditions. Non-attributable general statements produced intermediate ratings. These results are consistent with persuasion research showing that the effectiveness of messages is affected by attributes of the source. Attributing the warning to specific, reputable, expert sources such as the AMERICAN MEDICAL ASSOCIATION and the U.S. FOOD AND DRUG ADMINISTRATION makes the warning more credible and promotes greater compliance likelihood than no source. No significant differences between the scientific professional group sources and the governmental agency sources were found.

Thus, the results suggest that warnings with specific sources increase judged effectiveness. Because warnings are frequently limited in space/area, extra source-related words might preclude other useful information from being included, or it might require the use of smaller size print that could negatively impact legibility and noticeability. These tradeoffs should be considered in designing and evaluating warning content.

References

[1]   McGuire, W. J., The Communication-Persuasion Model and Health-Risk Labeling, in L.A. Morris, M.B. Mazis, and I. Barofsky, Cold Spring Harbor Laboratory, (1980), pp. 99-122.

[2]   I. S. Lirtzman and A. Shuv-Ami, Credibility of Sources of Communication on Product Safety Hazards. *Psychological Reports*, **58** (1986) 707-718.

[3]   M. S. Wogalter, Rashid, R. and Kalsher, M. J., Effect of Warning Signal Word and Source on Perceived Credibility and Compliance Likelihood. In *Proceedings of the 13th Triennial Congress International Ergonomics Association* (1997), in press.

Advances in Occupational Ergonomics and Safety II
Edited by Biman Das and Waldemar Karwowski
IOS Press and Ohmsha, 1997

Effects of Warning Border Color, Width, and Design on Perceived Effectiveness

Raheel RASHID and Michael S. WOGALTER
Ergonomics Program, Department of Psychology
North Carolina State University, Raleigh, NC 27695-7801 USA

Abstract. There is limited research on the effects of the presence and the types of border surrounding warning text. The present study tested 51 borders formed by combining different characteristics of color, design, and width. Seventy-two participants rated these borders on one of three dimensions: (1) attention-gettingness, (2) likelihood to read the warning, and (3) connoted hazard of the border. Results show that a warning with a surrounding border is rated more salient than one without a border. Borders in red were rated highest, followed by yellow, green, and blue respectively; black borders were rated lowest. The highest rated border designs were the thicker alternating stripe, saw tooth, and inward arrow patterns. The lowest rated border was a thin black line. These results have implications for enhancing warning noticeability.

1. Introduction

To be effective, warnings must attract attention, be understandable, and promote safe behavior [1]. The attention-getting stage is considered the crucial first step for subsequent processing and compliance, and consequently, aspects that enhance the attention-capture are among the most studied variables in warning research. Since the mid 1980s, a number of perceptual factors have been identified that enhance the noticeability of warnings, including size, color, pictorials, and icons. Another attribute that might increase warning noticeability is the presence of a border surrounding the warning message. The effects of warning borders have not received much attention in the empirical literature, and the research that exists is equivocal. Research has shown a negative effect [4], no effect [2,3], and a positive effect [5]. In the latter study, Edworthy and Adams [5] demonstrated that a thick red border surrounding a signal word (e.g., the term WARNING) significantly increases perceived salience.

The issue addressed in the present research was whether having a border around the entire warning text (not just the signal word) influences subjective measures of warning effectiveness. And if borders do make a difference, does it vary as function of the characteristics of the border? In the present study, 50 borders varying in color, design, and width plus one with no border were tested on perceived attention-gettingness, likelihood to read the warning, and connoted hazard.

Color was included because of its superior attention-gettingness characteristics [5], and its ability to convey hazard information [6]. Color can enhance warning salience, memory, connoted hazard, and compliance. Adams and Edworthy [5] showed that a red border surrounding the signal word is rated significantly more effective than a black border. In the present study, five colors are examined.

General perceptual principles suggest that a thick solid enclosure is preferable to a single line enclosure [7]. Adams and Edworthy [5] found a positive linear relationship between the border width around a signal word and perceived urgency. In the present study, the effect of three border widths are examined.

Previous research has shown that certain visual-spatial configurations in warnings (e.g., icons, shapes) vary in attention-attractingness and connoted hazard.[8]. However, border design has not been investigated before, and is examined in the present study.

2. Method

2.1. Participants

Seventy-two participants from North Carolina State University participated to fulfill the requirements of their introductory psychology course.

2.2. Design

A set of fifty-one warning stimuli was used. Fifty of the warnings had borders while one had no border (control). The set of borders were formed by combining different characteristics of color, width, and design. Five colors were used: red, yellow, green, blue, and black. Seven designs were used: single line, parallel lines, seven parallel lines, jagged lines, saw tooth, inward arrows, and alternating color stripes. Each design and width was crossed with all five colors. Three widths were used for the single line design (.07 cm, .35 cm, and .71 cm), two widths were used for alternating colored striped pattern (.35 cm, .71 cm), and only the thick width (.71 cm) was used for the inward arrow, sawtooth, jagged line, seven line and parallel line design. Examples of the borders are shown in Figure 1.

2.3. Materials

The stimuli were produced using an Epson Color Stylus II printer in 720 X 720 dpi on white paper. The warning message text was held constant. The text was printed in san serif font (Helvetica). The signal word WARNING was printed in 24-point bold capital letters on top followed by the main message in 18-point font: "Contains Methanol. Lung Disease Hazard. Avoid Breathing Fumes. Wear Respiratory Equipment and Protective Clothing When Handling." Each warning was printed and centered on separate sheets. In the 50 border conditions, a border surrounded the warning text (height by width was 10 X 15 cm). In the control condition, the warning text lacked a border. Each sheet was labeled with a number that was randomly assigned from 1 to 51. The stimuli were randomized for each participant and clipped to form a booklet. The response sheet contained 51 consecutively numbered blanks.

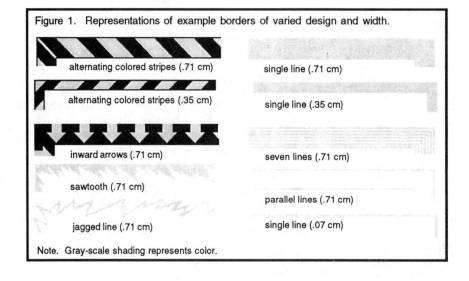

Figure 1. Representations of example borders of varied design and width.

alternating colored stripes (.71 cm)

single line (.71 cm)

alternating colored stripes (.35 cm)

single line (.35 cm)

inward arrows (.71 cm)

seven lines (.71 cm)

sawtooth (.71 cm)

parallel lines (.71 cm)

jagged line (.71 cm)

single line (.07 cm)

Note. Gray-scale shading represents color.

2.4. Procedure

Participants were instructed to examine each stimulus page and rate it on one of three dimensions: (1) "How *attention-getting* (or noticeable) would this warning be if it were on a product?" (2) "If you saw this warning on a product, how likely is it that you would *read* it?" (3) "To what extent does this border *communicates a hazard*?" There were 24 participants per question. Participants responded using Likert-type scales anchored at end points with (0) "not at all" and (8) "extremely."

3. Results and Discussion

Table 1 shows the mean ratings for each of the 51 conditions. Table 2 shows the means as a function of color, design, and width (collapsed across conditions). The ratings for the three dimensions were relatively consistent. The tables show that a warning with a border is rated more salient than one without a border. Borders in red were rated highest, followed by yellow, green, and blue respectively; black borders were rated lowest. Thicker width borders were rated more salient than thinner borders. The designs rated highest were colored stripes, inward arrows, and saw-tooth shape.

The present findings confirm earlier research [5] which showed that increased thickness increased salience.

Table 1. Means for 51 border combinations of color, width, and design.

Configuration	Width	Attention	Read	Hazard	Configuration	Width	Attention	Read	Hazard
No border	NA	0.50	1.33	NA	Black line	I	1.38	2.21	2.83
Yellow line	I	1.54	2.33	2.21	Black parallel lines	III	1.71	2.92	2.63
Yellow parallel lines	III	1.92	2.71	2.54	Green line	I	2.08	2.38	2.71
Blue line	I	2.29	2.54	2.13	Green parallel lines	III	2.42	2.83	2.54
Black line	II	2.58	3.33	3.33	Red line	I	2.58	3.13	3.50
Blue parallel lines	III	2.63	2.79	2.46	Red parallel lines	III	2.96	3.88	4.38
Black line	III	3.04	3.83	4.04	Blue line	II	3.08	3.42	3.08
Black jagged line	III	3.08	3.75	4.13	Yellow jagged line	III	3.08	3.13	3.67
Black/white stripes	II	3.08	3.83	4.00	Green line	II	3.17	3.50	3.25
Black 7 lines	III	3.25	3.33	3.54	Yellow line	II	3.33	3.79	3.63
Black/white stripes	III	3.58	4.25	5.04	Blue line	III	3.58	4.42	2.92
Blue 7 lines	III	3.58	3.88	3.21	Green jagged line	III	3.71	4.13	4.21
Yellow 7 lines	III	3.75	3.75	3.25	Black inward arrows	III	3.83	4.75	3.96
Blue jagged line	III	4.00	4.33	3.79	Green line	III	4.08	4.38	4.13
Red line	II	4.13	4.88	5.42	Yellow saw-tooth	III	4.17	4.08	4.83
Yellow line	III	4.20	4.46	4.13	Black saw-tooth	III	4.21	4.58	4.58
Green 7 lines	III	4.21	4.42	3.25	Black/green stripes	II	4.38	4.46	4.88
Black and blue stripes	II	4.46	4.46	4.38	Blue saw-tooth	III	4.46	5.17	4.67
Red 7 lines	III	4.58	5.13	5.54	Red jagged line	III	4.75	4.83	5.79
Black/red stripes	II	4.75	5.42	6.50	Black/blue stripes	III	4.92	5.29	4.71
Black/green stripes	III	5.04	5.50	5.17	Green inward arrows	III	5.08	5.13	4.54
Red line	III	5.13	6.04	6.13	Green saw-tooth	III	5.50	5.21	5.38
Yellow inward arrows	III	5.58	5.86	5.04	Blue inward arrows	III	5.58	5.13	4.25
Black/yellow stripes	II	5.63	5.63	5.88	Red inward arrows	III	5.83	5.83	6.00
Red saw-tooth	III	6.04	6.33	6.63	Black/red stripes	III	6.08	6.17	6.58
Black/yellow stripes	III	6.25	6.71	6.71					

Note.   I = .07 cm, II = .35 cm, and III = .71 cm widths. NA = Not applicable.

Table 2. Means of color, design, and width (collapsed across conditions).

Configuration	Attention	Read	Hazard	Configuration	Width	Attention	Read	Hazard
COLOR				*WIDTH and DESIGN*				
Red	4.68	5.16	5.64	No border	NA	0.50	1.33	NA
Yellow	3.95	4.25	4.19	single line	I	2.52	1.98	2.67
Green	3.97	4.19	4.00	single line	II	3.78	3.26	3.74
Blue	3.86	4.14	3.56	single line	III	4.62	4.01	4.27
Black	2.97	3.68	3.81	Parallel lines	III	3.03	2.32	2.90
				Seven lines	III	4.10	3.88	3.78
				Jagged line e	III	4.03	3.72	4.32
				Saw-tooth	III	5.01	4.88	5.22
				Inward arrows	III	5.34	5.18	4.76
				Colored stripes	II	4.46	4.76	5.13
				Colored stripes	III	5.58	5.12	5.64

Note.   Attention = attention-gettingness, Read = likelihood to read warning, and Hazard = conveys hazard.
I = .07 cm, II = .35 cm, and III = .71 cm widths. NA = Not applicable.

The findings suggest that borders influence warning salience and that the extent of this influence varies with the characteristics of the border (color, width and design). A thin plain line borders is less effective than a red thick design (e.g., stripes, arrows).

The failure to find an effect or a negative effect of a border surrounding a warning in previous work [3, 4] may be due to the methodology employed (e.g., reaction time). Lateral masking by the adjacent border might have degraded performance under the conditions employed in those studies.

An unexpected finding was that green was rated rather closely to yellow. While yellow is frequently used as a hazard color, green is not. Why this was found is not clear; further investigation is needed to provide an explanation.

In summary, this research indicates that a border around a warning can enhance salience, convey hazard information, and increase people's willingness to read the warning.

References

[1]   M. S. Wogalter and K. R. Laughery, Warning Sign and Label Effectiveness. *Current Directions in Psychological Science.* **5(2)** (1996) 33-37.
[2]   T. Barlow and M. S. Wogalter, Alcoholic Beverage Warnings in Magazine and Television Advertisements. *Journal of Consumer Research.* **20** (1993) 147-156.
[3]   S. L. Young, Increasing the Noticeability of Warnings: Effects of Pictorial, Color, Signal Icon, and Border. In *Proceedings of the Human Factors Society 35th Annual Meeting* (1991) 905-909. Santa Monica, CA: Human Factors Society.
[4]   K. R. Laughery and S. L. Young, Consumer Product Warnings: Design Factors that Influence Noticeability. In *Proceedings of the 11th Congress International Ergonomics Association.*
[5]   A. S. Adams and J. Edworthy, Quantifying and Predicting the Effects of Basic Text Display Variables on the Perceived Urgency of Warning Labels: Tradeoffs involving Font Size, Border Weight and Colour. *Ergonomics* **38** (1995) 2221-2237.
[6]   N. Olgyay, Safety Symbols Art: Camera-Ready and Disk Art for Designers. Van Nostrand Reinhold, New York, 1995.
[7]   M. S. Sanders and E. J. McCormick, Human Factors in Engineering and Design. McGraw Hill, 1993.
[8]   M. J. Kalsher et al., Hazard Level Perceptions of Current and Proposed Warning Sign and Label Panels. In *Proceedings of the Human Factors and Ergonomics Society 39th Annual Meeting* (1995) 351-355. Santa Monica, CA: Human Factors Society.

Advances in Occupational Ergonomics and Safety II
Edited by Biman Das and Waldemar Karwowski
IOS Press and Ohmsha, 1997

Improving Working Conditions And Work Performance In Temporary Work Sites

Juha SALMINEN[1] & Jorma SAARI[2]

[1] *Helsinki University of Technology, Construction
Economics and Management, Espoo, Finland*

[2] *Finnish Institute of Occupational Health, Laajaniityntie 1, 01620 Vantaa, Finland*

Abstract. Temporary work sites pose special problems to employees. Planning, material delivery and communication are critical factors for efficient and safe operation. Ten experiments were organized with three companies specializing in road maintenance, plumbing and installing ceiling elements. The goal of the intervention was to improve the performance of teams that continually move from site to site. Teams discussed past procedural problems, identified model work practices for planning future jobs, designed an auditing tool to measure their performance and conducted weekly audits for three months to ensure continued adherence to the new work practices. The work practices were related to various issues, such as safety, productivity, and quality. The results showed clear improvements in work performance. During the auditing period, all types of work practices improved significantly. The improvement process developed for this study was well accepted by the teams. A practical problem was, naturally, taking the time to carry out the new process.

1. Introduction

There are many jobs which are performed in continually changing locations. Road maintenance, roofing, plumbing, several construction jobs, landscaping, etc., are examples of jobs which might last from minutes to a few days or weeks in one location before moving to another one. Temporary work sites pose special problems to employees.

Continuous change presents a challenge as workers cannot easily develop mental maps of their working environment. Routines which would be easily established in stable work sites are lacking in continually changing locations. The worker's information processing capacity, normally freed through the use of routines, is taxed by the lack of routines. Using Rasmussen's [1] model, employees cannot simply operate on skill based level. They are required to operate at higher rule-based or knowledge-based levels which elevates the accident risk [2].

Under more stable conditions, such as in the manufacturing industry, feedback programs have been successful in accident prevention [4]. Those programs hinge upon measurements of conditions in the work environment over several weeks. When the work site changes all the time, the applicability of such an approach is questionable. The physical surroundings are less easily controlled by the workers and applicable checklists would be considerably different. However, it may be possible to identify and focus on some more stable factors. The goal of this study was to prepare and test a process utilizing the principles of feedback programs for mobile teams.

2. Materials and methods

The process is based on a participatory feedback program widely used in Finland, especially in the manufacturing industry [3]. In stable work environments, employee and management representatives work together to identify common goals and to define and evaluate progress. When applied to mobile jobs, this feedback program focuses on planning and on motivating model work practices which could be applicable to any work location. The process, known as Mobile, consists of the following steps:

1. Organizing and scheduling

2. Informing everybody

3. Identifying model work practices

Teams analyze their work process chronologically: planning and preparing, delivery of materials, flow of information, working and work environment, and finishing up. These practices refer both to measurable conditions and actions. (See Table 1 for an example)

4. Identifying problems with a permanent fix

These are one time actions, such as repairing a tool, modifying a work vehicle, or writing down each individual's responsibilities.

5. Preparing a self-auditing tool

The auditing tool consists of items which relate to model work practices and which can be answered on a "correct-incorrect" basis. The percentage of "correct" items gives a performance index.

6. Regular weekly auditing with feedback to the team by team members

7. Evaluation, and follow-up measures

Table 1. An example of model practices identified by a plumbing team

Safety
• The job is carried out without endangering safety .
Productivity
• The material and tool storage in the van is kept well stocked and in order.
• The jobs are scheduled so that the distances between jobs are minimized and moving during rush hours is avoided.
• When the job completed the materials used are accounted for and customer's signature is taken whenever possible.
Quality
• When receiving a job the address, schedule, description of the job, billing information and phone number are taken down accurately.
• The foreman, plumber and client are informed on deviations from plans immediately.
• The plumber is clean, polite and patient.
• The job is completed faultlessly and upon completion the site is tidied up.

The study involved ten teams of two to eight employees from three companies in the construction business. The companies participating in the study were a large construction company (roofing and road maintenance units), a plumbing company and a company installing ceiling elements.

The first author acted as a consultant for the teams, describing and facilitating the process. The teams made all decisions related to process content.

3. Results

Of the ten teams, six conducted weekly audits for the required 12 weeks. The remaining four teams had, for various reasons, gaps in their weekly audits. Only those teams with continuous measurements over the 12 week period are presented here. As shown in Table 1, the model work practices were related to different aspects of work, such as safety, productivity, or quality.

The self-audits of the six teams consisted of 33-39 items related to safety (16 % of all items), of 72 items related to productivity (27%), and of 30 - 35 items related to quality (13 %). Some items were job specific and could not be easily applied to other job sites, causing a fluctuation in the number of observed items per week.

Figure 1 presents the results of the weekly audits. The trend was towards improved compliance with suggested changes in all areas of work performance. The safety items seems to experience a slightly steeper rise than the other performance areas. The overall index also had a positive trend with most study groups.

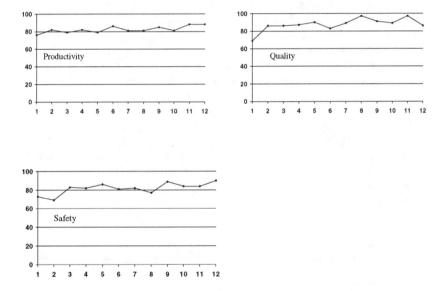

Figure 1. Aggregated performance indices for six teams which conducted all weekly audits for twelve consecutive weeks.

4. Discussion

One observation from this study is that the teams participating in this study accepted the process well. The acceptance of this process by workers who are otherwise primarily interested in getting the job done signifies the negotiation of a major hurdle in the improvement of working conditions. If workers believe that their concerns will be integrated into the process, it is easy to see how they are more likely to participate in the process.

Ultimately, the success of the process, though, is determined by the effect it has on the working environment and safety, particularly the items seen as priority issues by the working groups. Unfortunately, the audits were unable to capture all of the changes brought about by the process for two reasons. First, many of the changes were immediate and structural, such as fixing tools, and were implemented in the first stages of the process, i.e., before audits were started. Second, the audits, and these data presented here, show changes subsequent to the definition of model work practices. It is reasonable to expect that many of the changes defined as model work practices had also begun to change before the audits began, and therefore improvement in work conditions as seen through the audits would not be striking.

While four of the original teams did not complete all the required weekly audits over 12 consecutive weeks, this interruption was never brought about by team members. The supervisor had a critical role in the process, committing time and resources to facilitate its' success.

In stable industrial settings, these feedback models have been shown to reduce injuries [3,4]. However, it was not possible to verify the injury reduction potential of this process in mobile work settings given the varying nature of jobs, the ever changing risk factors and the relatively short time span of the study. However, anecdotal evidence supports the belief that safety was improved.

One weak point of the process lies in the identification of model practices. Peoples' perceptions about risks may lead them to under- or overestimate some risk factors. Likewise, small independent organizations may lack the scope of knowledge about injuries and hazards that larger organizations may have. Using a consultant to help identify model practices may prove helpful.

It is noteworthy that teams moving continuously from site to site have been so little studied. Yet, this format of work represents a network economy which seems to be increasing. Those safety problems encountered by subcontractors and other independent operators in various networks will continue to present more challenging safety problems in the future. Independent operators are compelled to regain some of their autonomy for injury reduction given the clear lack of work environment ownership or responsibility in mobile work situations.

Reference

[1] J. Rasmussen, Information processing and human-machine interaction. North-Holland, New York, 1986.

[2] J. Saari, Characteristics of tasks associated with the occurrance of accidents, *Journal of Occupational Accidents* **1** (1977) 273-279.

[3] J. Saari, participatory workplace improvement process. In: J. Stellman (ed.), ILO Encyclopedia of Occupational Health and Safety. International Labour Office, Geneva 1997, in press.

[4] B. Sulzer-Azaroff, T.C. Harris and K.B McCann, Beyond training: organizational performance management techniques, *Occupational Medicine: State of the Art Reviews* **9** (1994) 321-339.

17. Aging and Human Performance

Advances in Occupational Ergonomics and Safety II
Edited by Biman Das and Waldemar Karwowski
IOS Press and Ohmsha, 1997

The Effects of Job Task Demands on the Work Ability of Older Employees

Sabrina N. Williams and Lesia L. Crumpton, PhD

Department of Industrial Engineering
P.O. Box 9542
Mississippi State University
Mississippi State, MS 39762
sne1@ra.msstate.edu
crumpton@engr.msstate.edu

Abstract. To accurately determine the ability of older employees to safely and efficiently perform specific job tasks their mental and physical capabilities must be known. Information on work capabilities of employees can be determined using the work ability index. The Work Ability Index developed by the Finnish Institute of Occupational Health is a subjective index that estimates work ability based on health conditions, job demands, and psychological resources. To assess possible differences between the capabilities of younger and older employees, the work ability index values of older employees was compared to younger employees. The goal of this study was to determine the effect of job task requirements on work ability. Specifically, the effect of physical and mental demands of work on the impairment of work ability as employees age was assessed. The Work Ability Index was administered to 76 employees and the data was classified into categories such as mental, physical or both mental and physical based on the primary task demands of their occupations. Findings of this research project are presented in this paper as well as suggestions for improving the work ability of aging persons through job task modifications.

1.0 INTRODUCTION

The ability to perform a task is highly related to the demands of the work tasks and the functional capacity of the employee. Difficulties in job performance may occur if the employee's physical capabilities do not meet the job demands. Thus, it is extremely important for employers to recognize the specific abilities of employees to prevent the assignment of job tasks that exceed the employee's capabilities. To determine the extent to which employees, particularly older employees, are capable of performing specific job tasks, work capacity should be assessed and periodically monitored. Appropriate instruments to determine whether a person is physically or mentally capable of coping with the daily demands of work are often unavailable [1]. However, the Work Ability Index (WAI) developed by the Finnish Institute of Occupational Health, provides an instrument for the assessment of present and future expectations of an employee's ability to work, taking into account the demands of work and the physical and mental conditions of the employee [2].

2.0 MATERIAL AND METHODS

The participant group consisted of 76 participants (males and females). The ages of this group ranged from 23 to 68 years with a mean age of 44.8 years. Descriptive data on the participants is shown in Table 1. The jobs performed by the participants were classified into three work content categories according to a job analysis performed by the Finnish Institute of Occupational Health based on the German AET method [3]. Some examples of job classifications include: construction work, janitorial work, kitchen help and domestic work (physically demanding); technical supervision, teaching, clerical work, and administrative work (mentally demanding); and transport work, nursing, and dental work (mixed).

Table 1. Descriptive data on the participant group.

Work Content	Age < 50 years		Age ≥ 50 years	
	Males	Females	Males	Females
Mental	6	6	10	5
Physical	8	6	6	7
Mixed (Mental/Physical)	6	7	6	3

Data collection involved an individual interview with the participants. After receiving an explanation of the purpose of the study, the participants were asked to read an explanatory statement and sign a consent form. Work capability was assessed using the Work Ability Index (WAI) developed by the Finnish Institute of Occupational Health. This questionnaire was designed to be used as a comprehensive indicator of work ability on the basis of participants' response to queries about their physical, mental, and social capabilities. The sum of the scores for seven individual item gives a total WAI score ranging from 7 to 49 points. The value derived using the index is used to categorize the subject's work ability as either good (49-44 points), moderate (28-43 points) or poor (7-27 points). Items included in the work ability index are shown in Table 2.

Table 2. Items included in the work ability index.

Survey Item	Response Scale
1. Subjective estimation of current work ability	1-10
2. Subjective work ability in relation to job demands	2-10
3. Number of diagnosed	1-7
4. Work impairment due to disease	1-6
5. Sickness absence during the past year	1-5
6. Own prognosis of work ability after two years	1,4,7
7. Mental resources	1-4

3.0 RESULTS

3.1 Descriptive statistics on each group

Results of this study revealed that the mean work ability value was lowest in the participant group that performed physical work activities that were less than 50 years of age and highest in the participant group that performed job tasks involving a mixture of mental and physical demands who were 50 years of age or older. An ANOVA analysis was performed to assess significant statistical differences between the mean WAI values of the younger and older groups performing job tasks with similar demands as shown in Figure 1. This analysis revealed that there was no statistical significant difference in mean work ability of the two groups when evaluated at an alpha level of 0.05. Also, ANOVA analysis revealed no statistically significant difference in the work ability scores of persons performing similar primary work task demands when evaluated at an alpha level of 0.05.

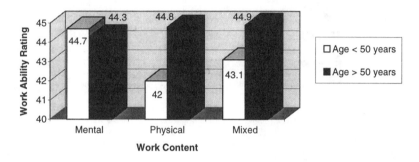

Figure 1. The mean work ability of each work group.

3.2 Effect of physical disorders and physical demands of work task on work ability

Responses to questions regarding physical disorders reported on the WAI by participants performing tasks consisting of physical or both mental/physical (mixed) work demands are shown in Figure 2. Although most participants from each group reported at least one physical disorder, the estimated impairment reported due to these physical disorders was minimal. The participants were also asked to rate their current work ability with respect to the physical demands of their jobs. Among the participants who performed job tasks consisting primarily of physical activities, 92.3 percent of the participants age 50 years or older rated their work ability very good while only 85.7 percent of the participants less than 50 years of age rated their work ability very good. Among the participants who performed job tasks consisting of both mental/physical (mixed) activities, 77.8 percent of the participants age 50 years or greater rated their work ability very good while only 46.2 percent of the participants less than 50 years of age rated their work ability very good.

3.3 Effect of mental demands on work ability

The participants were asked to rate their current work ability with respect to the mental demands of their jobs. Among the participants who performed job tasks consisting of mental work activities, 93 percent of the participants age 50 years or greater rated their work ability very good while only 58.3 percent of the participants less than 50 years of age rated their work ability very good. Among the participants who performed job tasks consisting of both mental/physical (mixed) work activities, 78 percent of the participants age 50 years or greater rated their work ability very good while only 30.8 percent of the participants less than 50 years of age rated their work ability very good.

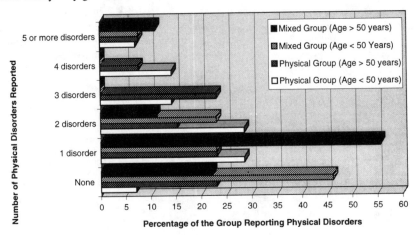

Figure 2. Physical disorders reported by participants in each work group.

4.0 DISCUSSION

The statistical analysis (ANOVA) on the data collected in this study did not reveal a statistical difference between the average work ability scores of persons performing jobs consisting of primarily mental, physical or those with both a mental and physical component. Research suggest employees experience a decline in work ability with age [2]. However, results of this study revealed a trend in the mean WAI values for the participants age 50 years or older in the groups performing primarily tasks with physical job demands and the group performing tasks with both physical/mental (mixed) job demands which suggest an increase in mean work ability with age. The differences between the mean WAI values of the younger and older groups can possibly be attributed to the experience of the older group and an increased period of acclimation.

REFERENCES

[1] W.J.A Goedhard *et al.*, Application of the Finnish Work Ability Index in the Netherlands, *Advances in Occupational Ergonomics and Safety I Vol 2*, (1996) 27-32.

[2] R. Cremer, Work ability of nurses in relation to age. In: Willem J. A. Goedhard (ed), Aging and Work 3. ISBN: 90 803145 1 X. Pasmans Offsetdrukkerij, Netherlands, (1996) pp. 49-58.

[3] J. Ilmarinen *et al.*, Classification of Municipal Occupations, *Journal of Work, Environment and Health* **17**: **1** (1991) 12-29.

Advances in Occupational Ergonomics and Safety II
Edited by Biman Das and Waldemar Karwowski
IOS Press and Ohmsha, 1997

AGE, WORK MODE AND ACCEPTABLE PHYSICAL WORK LOAD

T. Aminoff, J. Smolander, O. Korhonen, V. Louhevaara
Finnish Institute of Occupational Health, Laajaniityntie 1, FIN-01620 Vantaa, Finland

Abstract.
Ten young (aged 23-30 years) and nine older (aged 54-59 years) healthy men with a similar size of limb muscle mass performed 30 min arm crank and leg cycle ergometer exercises at relative work loads of 50 and 75 % of peak oxygen uptake (VO_2) for the corresponding muscle group. The measurements included heart rate (HR), gas exchange variables and ratings of perceived exertion (RPE). The physiological strain was similar between the age-groups. At both submaximal levels the work load, VO_2 and ventilation were significantly higher ($P < 0.01$) during leg work as compared to the arm work. HR and RPE increased with time during all tests. At the 50 % exercise level the increase in HR was significantly ($P < 0.001$) steeper and the RPE tended to be higher during arm-cranking compared to leg-cycling. The results indicate that the acceptable physical work load should be separately determined for each muscle group, and related to the peak capacity of the working muscle group. The acceptable physical work load, expressed as % of peak VO_2 for the corresponding muscle group, seems to be similar for different ages, but lower in work tasks using small muscle groups compared to work tasks using large muscle group.

1. Introduction

It has commonly been considered that physical work demands should decrease with increasing age because of the age-related decline of the maximal physical work capacity. The amount of decrease of work demands should follow the decline of work capacity [3]. However, we have recently reported that during one-arm and two-arm cranking the peak work capacity did not differ between healthy young and older men with a similar size of estimated limb muscle masses [1]. During two-leg cycling the peak work capacity of the older men was lower than that of the young men. These results suggest that the peak work capacity is dependent both on age and on muscular performance. A work load that is easy for one type of work may therefore be quite exhausting for another.

The purpose of the present study was to compare the acceptable physical work load for young and older men during prolonged arm or leg exercises. Furthermore, physiological indicators for the assessment of strain, which could be used uniformly for differing ages and work modes were evaluated.

2. Methods

Ten young (aged 23-30 years) and nine older (aged 54-59 years) healthy men with a similar size of limb muscle mass performed 30 min arm crank and leg cycle ergometer exercises at relative work loads of 50 and 75 % of peak oxygen uptake (VO_2) for the corresponding muscle group. The measurements included heart rate (HR), gas exchange variables and ratings of perceived exertion (RPE). During arm-cranking the absolute work load was similar for the young and older men because of similar peak values during arm-cranking. But during leg-cycling the absolute work load was higher for the young men than for the older men due to the difference in corresponding peak values [1].

The data was analyzed in two ways, (i) the effects of age and time and (ii) the effects of exercise mode and time were tested with two way analysis of variance with repeated measures on one factor (time mode). In the statistical analysis mean values of measurements made every minute in the beginning (5-10 min) of the tests and at the end (25-30 min) of the tests from all full-length (30 min) tests were used. The differences were considered significant if $P < 0.05$.

3. Results

For a given target relative load there were no significant differences in actual mean relative load among the exercise modes or age-groups.

During arm-cranking there were no significant differences in the physiological responses between the age-groups except that a higher ventilatory response was noted among the older men compared to the young men. During leg-cycling the HR values were higher among the young men compared to the older men. But, when the HR values were expressed as a % of peak HR in the corresponding maximal tests, no significant differences between the age-groups were found. [2]

Since the physiological responses during prolonged exercise were similar between the age-groups the results of the young and older men were combined in the analysis of the effect of exercise mode. At both submaximal levels the work load and the VO_2 were significantly higher ($P < 0.001$) during leg work as compared to the arm work due to the difference in corresponding peak values [1]. Also the ventilation was significantly higher ($P < 0.01$) during leg-cycling compared to arm-cranking. HR and RPE increased with time during all tests. At the 50 % exercise level the increase in HR was significantly ($P < 0.001$) steeper and the RPE tended to be higher during arm-cranking compared to leg-cycling. The HR (mean ± SD) increased during arm-cranking from 111 ± 10 to 122 ± 10 beats · min^{-1} and during leg-cycling from 115 ± 8 to 118 ± 8 beats · min^{-1}. The corresponding increases in RPE were from 11 to 14, and from 10 to 12, respectively. At the 75 % exercise level the HR increased during arm cranking from 146 ± 10 to 162 ± 12 beats · min^{-1} and during leg cycling from 149 ± 11 to 167 ± 13 beats · min^{-1}. The RPE increased from 13 to 17 during both exercise modes.

4. Conclusion

Physiological responses to prolonged exercise and age

The results indicate that a 30 min arm or leg exercise at the same relative submaximal work load produces a similar degree of physiological strain in healthy older men, with a well retained muscle mass, compared to young men. During arm-cranking, the young and the older men exercised at the same external work load, indicating a similar ability to perform prolonged work using smaller muscle groups expressed both in absolute and relative terms. [2]

Physiological responses to prolonged exercise and work mode

Differences in physiological responses between continuous dynamic arm and leg exercise are decreased when the work loads are determined relative to the peak capacity for the corresponding muscle group. However, the steeper increase in HR and RPE during arm cranking as compared to leg cycling at the 50 % exercise level indicated that the strain is higher when working with smaller muscle groups at same relative work loads.

Assessment of acceptable physical work load

The VO_2 is a measure of aerobic demands of work. In the literature, the acceptable physical work load has commonly been expressed as a percentage of maximal VO_2. However, the higher strain during arm-cranking compared to leg-cycling at the 50 % exercise level indicates that although the work load is related to the active muscle group, the acceptable physical work load, expressed as % of peak VO_2 for the corresponding muscle group, should be lower in work tasks requiring small muscle groups than in work tasks requiring large muscle groups.

The HR and RPE are easy to measure and seem according to the present study to be comparable indicators of the physical strain between arm and leg work. The HR expressed as a % of peak HR for the corresponding muscle group considers age-related differences in maximal HR during exercises using large muscle groups, and may therefore be adapted for different age-groups and types of exercises in the determination of physical strain.

Acceptable physical work load and age

A level of 50 % of maximal VO_2 has been suggested to be the upper limit of energy expenditure for dynamic work with rest pauses [4]. According to the present study the acceptable physical work load should, however, be separately determined for each muscle group, and related to the peak capacity of the working muscle group. The 50 % level [4] appears to be too high, especially during arm work.

The acceptable physical work load, expressed as % of peak capacity for the corresponding muscle group, seems to be similar for different ages. The acceptable absolute work load during leg work is, however, lower for older individuals compared to young individuals, while it during arm work could be similar for young and older individuals with a well retained muscular performance. Theoretically this would mean that older individuals could carry out the same work tasks requiring small muscle masses as young individuals with a similar degree of strain, while work demands requiring large muscle groups should be decreased with age.

5. References

[1] T. Aminoff, J. Smolander, O. Korhonen, V. Louhevaara, Physical work capacity in dynamic exercise with differing muscle masses in healthy young and older men, *Eur J Appl Physiol* **73** (1996) 180-185.

[2] T. Aminoff, J. Smolander, O. Korhonen, V. Louhevaara, Cardiorespiratory and subjective responses to prolonged arm and leg exercise in healthy young and older men, *Eur J Appl Physiol* (In press).

[3] J. Ilmarinen, Job design for the aged with regard to decline in their maximal aerobic capacity: Part II - The scientific basis for the guide, *International Journal of Industrial Ergonomics* **10** (1992) 65-77.

[4] J. Rutenfranz, J. Ilmarinen, F. Klimmer, H. Kylian, Work load and demanded physical performance capacity under different industrial working conditions. In: M. Kaneko (ed.), Fitness for the aged, disabled, and industrial worker. International Series on Sport Sciences, volume 20. Human Kinetics Books, Champaign. Illinois, 1990, pp. 217-238.

Advances in Occupational Ergonomics and Safety II
Edited by Biman Das and Waldemar Karwowski
IOS Press and Ohmsha, 1997

Effects of Muscular Exertion on Hand Steadiness - Part III

Nancy J. Mulvaney and Margaret J. Rys
Department of Industrial and Manufacturing Systems Engineering
Kansas State University
Manhattan, Kansas 66506, USA

Extensive research has shown that muscle exertion in the form of various types of exercise causes significant effects on hand steadiness. This study investigated the effect on hand tremor when subjects were required to perform various movement operations after muscle exertion. Seventeen subjects (twelve male and five female) were required to perform a series of exercises consisting of push-ups, bicycle, and rest. Hand steadiness was then measured by having the subjects move a 1.5 mm probe through a series of horizontal and vertical slots cut out of a metal plate for 30 second time periods. Two, four, and six inch slots were used. The results indicate that the only significant effects on hand steadiness due to exercise occurred one minute after muscle exertion in the horizontal orientation of the slots. The vertical slots produced no significant differences due to an overall poor performance on these slots. Also, as the length of the slots increased, the number of errors also increased.

1.0 Introduction

Extensive research has shown that muscle exertion in the form of various types of exercise causes significant effects on hand steadiness. Davis and Konz [1] found that immediately after muscular exertion was performed (push-ups), hand tremor increased over three times the initial amount. These effects on hand tremor continued to be significant for up to six hours after the initial exercise was performed. Further, Evans [2] found that exercise performed utilizing muscles other than the hand (subjects pedaled a stationary bicycle) also affected hand tremor. These results present some interesting considerations for those who perform precision work with their hands (i.e. doctors, dentists, electronic circuit builders).

These studies measured the effects on hand steadiness when the hand was held in a stationary position. Most operations that are performed by those who require precision work in their professions involve movement of the hand in some form (i.e. a doctor making a cut on the body during surgery). Therefore, the studies of Davis and Konz and Evans were recreated with the intention of examining what the level of effect on hand tremor would be when subjects were required to perform various movement operations after muscle exertion, and comparing this level to the previous studies.

2.0   Method

2.1   Task

Hand steadiness was measured by having the subjects move a 1.5 mm probe through a series of horizontal and vertical slots cut out of a metal plate for 30 second time periods. Three different lengths of slots were used: two, four, and six inches. Each slot had a width of approximately 4.7 mm (0.1875 inches). The plate was placed at a 45 degree angle for both the horizontal and vertical orientations. Each subject was seated during the testing, but was not allowed to rest his/her elbow on the table while performing the test. Each subject was tested once on each slot length in both the horizontal and vertical positions, for a total of six testing periods. The subjects returned after one hour, six hours, and twelve hours for further testing. Figure 1 depicts the hand steadiness testing apparatus and setup.

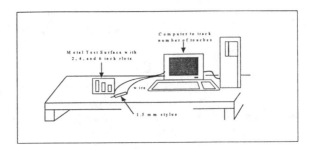

Figure 1. Hand Steadiness Testing Apparatus

2.2   Subjects

Seventeen subjects (twelve male and five female), with an average age of approximately 22 years were used in the experiment. The subjects received extra credit points in an undergraduate class.

2.3   Procedure and Experimental Design

Two-thirds of the subjects performed some type of exercise first; one-third did a series of push-ups to achieve muscle exertion, and the other one-third rode a stationary exercise bicycle. Specifically, those performing push-ups were required to complete the maximum amount of push-ups they could in a one minute period. Those riding the stationary bicycle were required to ride the bicycle for a five minute period at 20 km/h and a tension of 21 N for females and 26 N for males. The remaining one-third rested (sat quietly for a two minute period) during the first session. For those that performed exercise, a one minute resting period was allowed before testing occurred. One practice trial was allowed before each testing. After the initial session, the subjects returned for the next two weeks to perform the remaining two tasks. The task and slot sequences were assigned in a random fashion to each subject.

2.4   Measurement and Instrumentation

A computer was connected to the probe and the metal plate in order to measure the amount of times that a subject touched a side of the plate during the test period. The results for each subject were recorded on a standard data sheet.

3.0   Results

Analysis of Variance (ANOVA) procedures were performed to test for: 1) significant differences in performance within the individual exercises due to muscle exertion over time, 2) significant differences between exercises, 3) significant differences between slot lengths and orientations, and 4) significant differences between male and female subjects.

3.1   Significant Effects in Individual Exercises

The ANOVA tests found significant effects in performance in individual exercises over time for the two inch and six inch horizontal slots after push-ups (p-values of 0.036 and 0.038 respectively), and the six inch horizontal slot after bicycling (p-value of 0.017). The only significant effects in performance due to muscular exertion over time took place one minute after the exertion was performed.

3.2   Significant Effects Between Exercises

The ANOVA tests found significant effects in performance between exercises for the two and six inch horizontal slots one minute after exercise (p-values of 0.021 and 0.047 respectively), and the six inch vertical slot one minute after exercise (p-value of 0.017). Tables 1-3 summarize the multiple comparison tests for these procedures.

Table 1
Multiple Comparisons Showing Results of 95% Confidence Intervals for Means
Based on Standard Deviation: 2 Inch Horizontal Slot After 1 Minute

Comparisons		Level	N	Mean*	Std. Dev.
	A	Rest - 1 min. - 2 Inch Horizontal	17	3.647	2.914
B	A	Bicycle - 1 min. - 2 Inch Horizontal	17	5.059	3.944
B		Push-ups - 1 min. - 2 Inch Horizontal	17	7.529	4.810

Table 2
Multiple Comparisons Showing Results of 95% Confidence Intervals for Means
Based on Standard Deviation: 6 Inch Horizontal Slot After 1 Minute

Comparisons		Level	N	Mean*	Std. Dev.
	A	Rest - 1 min. - 6 Inch Horizontal	17	8.118	4.608
B	A	Bicycle - 1 min. - 6 Inch Horizontal	17	11.824	7.117
B		Push-ups - 1 min. - Inch Horizontal	17	13.176	5.982

Table 3
Multiple Comparisons Showing Results of 95% Confidence Intervals for Means
Based on Standard Deviation: 6 Inch Vertical Slot After 1 Minute

Comparisons		Level	N	Mean*	Std. Dev.
	A	Rest - 1 min. - 6 Inch Vertical	17	11.941	4.943
B	A	Bicycle - 1 min. - 6 Inch Vertical	17	15.824	8.033
B		Push-ups - 1 min. - 6 Inch Vertical	17	18.294	5.336

* Means with the same letter are not significantly different

It was found that for differences between exercises, performing push-ups always produced the greatest amount of performance errors, followed by bicycling, and then resting. There was never a significant difference between push-ups and bicycling or bicycling and resting, however there was a significant difference between push-ups and resting.

3.3   Significant Effects Between Slots

For all exercises and times, the differences in performance between the six slots were found to be significant at the 0.05 level (all had p-values of 0.000). In all instances, the vertical slots produced more errors than the horizontal slots. As the length of the slots increased, the number of errors also increased.

4.0   Discussion

The only significant effects on hand steadiness due to exercise occurred one minute after muscle exertion. This result is different from the previous studies by Davis, Konz, and Evans in that there was no significant effect found for any reasonable length of time after muscle exertion. Based on this result, it seems there is no reason for those who perform precision work with their hands to refrain from the type of muscle exertion performed in this study prior to conducting precision movement operations. It should be noted that the forms of muscle exertion used in this experiment are at the minimum level and longer exposures to muscle exertion may yield very different results.

The vertical slots produced no significant differences due to muscle exertion because of overall poor performance on these slots. For all exercises and all times, the vertical slots consistently produced higher numbers of performance errors than the horizontal slots. These results are believed to be due to the line of sight associated with the vertical tests. When one moves their hand in a vertical direction, the hand tends to block the center of the slot, which is the attempted target spot. The hand, therefore, acts as a barrier to making a straight movement in the vertical position. This is not true in the horizontal position, where the center of the slot (the target) is clearly visible during the duration of the horizontal movement.

As the length of the slots increased, the number of errors also increased. This is a logical result due to natural variability in hand steadiness over increasing lengths.

The six inch horizontal slot produced significant differences over time after both push-ups and bicycling. The two inch horizontal slot produced a significant difference over time after push-ups. It can be concluded that hand steadiness is affected by muscle exertion for extremely short or increasingly long horizontal movements. The effects due to the long movements are reasonable due to the increased variability in hand steadiness over increasing lengths. The effects due to the two inch movement were mostly likely increased by the difficulty to stop and reverse motions abruptly in a shorter slot. Most errors on the two inch slot occurred at either extreme end of the movement, rather than in the middle of the slot.

Hand steadiness is affected differently for different types of muscle exertion one minute after exercise on extremely short or increasingly long movements. This is logical due to the varying muscle groups that each exercise isolates.

From the results produced for significant differences between males and females, it was found that hand steadiness does differ in some way between the two genders. Although no apparent pattern was found in these results, men were found to have less variability in their hand steadiness over women. Therefore, overall hand steadiness seems greater for males than for females.

References

[1] Davis, R. and Konz, S.A. (1995) Effects of muscular exertion on hand steadiness. Advances in Industrial Ergonomics and Safety VII. Edited by A.C. Bittner and P.C. Champney, 533-535.

[2] Evans, M. (1996) Effects of Exercise on Hand Steadiness. Project performed for IMSE 850: Ergonomics. College of Engineering; Department of Industrial and Manufacturing Systems Engineering; Kansas State University.

Advances in Occupational Ergonomics and Safety II
Edited by Biman Das and Waldemar Karwowski
IOS Press and Ohmsha, 1997

Analyses of Glove Types and Pinch Forces in Windshield Glass Handling

Brian D. Lowe and Andris Freivalds, Ph.D.
Department of Industrial and Manufacturing Engineering
The Pennsylvania State University, University Park, PA 16802   USA

This field study investigated pinch forces required by employees for handling windshield glass in a warehouse. Pinch forces were measured with a Data Glove utilizing force sensitive resistors on the pulpar surfaces of the finger tips. The experimental conditions tested included three different gloves, three levels of shelf height, and different grip/handling strategies. Use of Spectra™ gloves was associated with 4% to 20% less grip force than was use of Nitrile™ gloves, depending upon the handling strategy. For glass on the lowest shelf level, a 'palm press' required the least amount of force because of additional support from the thighs. For middle shelf level glass retrieval, the 'over-under' pinch required significantly less grip force than the 'top edge' pinch. For the top shelf level retrieval (a two person operation) there was no significant difference in grip force between the passer and catcher.

1. Introduction

Employees at a warehouse distribution site for automotive glass handle hundreds of glass pieces daily, while lifting them from a shelf onto a motorized cart. The characteristics of windshield glass handling fit the profile of industrial jobs with high CTD risk, particularly high pinch forces. The company management has made effective ergonomic interventions to improve materials handling practices of the employees, including the use of gloves to increase the friction conditions between the hand and glass. Different handling strategies have also been suggested as a means of reducing the grip forces necessary to maneuver the glass. The purpose of this study was to analyze the efficacy of the gloves and handling strategies in terms of reducing pinch forces in glass handling.

2. Method

2.1 Apparatus

Glass pinch forces were measured with a glove constructed at the Center for Cumulative Trauma Disorders at Penn State. This technology has been used previously in evaluating grips on hand tools [1, 2]. The "Data Glove" consists of two baseball batting gloves between which force sensitive resistors (FSRs, Interlink Electronics™) are attached to the finger tip areas. The conductive polymer resistors are housed between the two gloves for protection. These sensors are sensitive to changes in resistance which results from increasing pressure on their surface. By applying a dome of epoxy on each sensor surface

TABLE 1. Description of pick types examined in field experimentation.

	LOW LEVEL	MIDDLE LEVEL	HIGH LEVEL
LAMINATED GLASS	thumbs forward (pinch top edge)	one hand over/one hand under grip (right hand up)	Passer (on ladder)
	thumbs back (pinch top edge)	one hand over/one hand under grip (left hand up)	Catcher (on ground)
	palm press against thigh	top edge pinch (thumbs back)	
TEMPERED GLASS	Edge forward	Edge forward	
	Front forward	Front forward	

the force which is applied to a single point is distributed over the entire surface of the FSR [3]. Analog output from the resistors was digitally converted with a Dash16-F (Metrabyte Corporation) A/D converter. The FSRs were sampled at 10 Hz for a duration dependent upon the type of handling maneuver. The low sampling rate was appropriate because of the static nature of the pinches and mean pinch force values were of interest.

2.2 Procedure

An experienced, right-handed, male glass handler volunteered as a subject for two, four-hour data collection sessions. The on-site data collection procedure involved actual glass handling tasks as performed in normal working procedures. Each trial consisted of the subject maneuvering a piece of glass from one of three shelf levels (low - 10 cm from floor, middle - 132 cm from floor, high - 254 cm from the floor) to the materials handling cart.

Three types of gloves were evaluated: Spectra™, Nitrile™, and a thick cotton glove. These gloves, which protect the hands as well as increase friction between the skin and glass, were donned over the Data Glove which was worn on the right hand of the subject. Several glass handling strategies were examined (described in Table 1). The combination of glass location (shelf height) and handling strategy constitute what is termed a glass *pick type* (refer to Table 1). Sensors on the index, middle, ring, and little fingers maintained a solid orientation on the glass surface in each handling maneuver. The sum of the forces measured at the four finger tips was used as the measure of pinch force in the analyses.

The results of the Data Glove analysis are segmented into two portions: analysis of laminated glass (auto and truck *windshields*) handling pinch forces and analysis of tempered glass (auto and truck *windows*) handling pinch forces. Laminated glass pieces are heavier and are oriented facing outward on the shelves; tempered glass pieces are smaller, lighter and are often oriented with the edge facing outward on the shelf. In both cases the analyses test whether the type of glove worn and the pick type affects the magnitude of the mean pinch force in handling the glass.

3. Results

3.1 Laminated Glass

Analysis of Gloves   The analysis of glove type on the mean pinch force for the second through fifth fingers (summed) is shown in Table 2. Glove Type had a statistically significant effect on mean pinch force ($p<0.05$). A Least Significant Difference (LSD) post hoc test revealed that the Spectra™ and Nitrile™ gloves were not significantly different from one another, while the thick glove resulted in significantly ($p<0.05$) lower mean pinch forces than these two.

Analysis of Pick Type   In this analysis the Spectra™ and Nitrile™ gloves were included as well as eight laminated glass pick conditions (Table 1) from all three shelf levels. Pick Type was shown to have a statistically significant effect on the mean pinch force (see Table 3). A grouping of pick types by statistical significance (Least Significant Difference post-hoc test) is also presented in Table 3.

TABLE 2. ANOVA for mean pinch force on laminated glass as a function Glove Type.

ANOVA summary table

Source	df	MS	F	p
GLOVE (G)	2	5.581	8.63	0.001*
PICK (P)	5	56.21	86.93	0.001*
G x P	10	3.764	5.82	0.001*
ERROR	36	0.647		
TOTAL	53			

Significance of GLOVE means

GLOVE type	n	Mean pinch force (N)
Spectra™	18	40.13 [a]
Nitrile™	18	42.85 [a]
Thick	18	32.37 [b]

a, b, and c means are significantly different

TABLE 3. ANOVA for mean pinch force on laminated glass as a function of Pick Type.

ANOVA summary table

Source	df	MS	F	p
GLOVE (G)	1	0.23	0.37	0.550
PICK (P)	7	38.31	59.51	0.001*
G x P	7	1.65	2.56	0.033*
ERROR	32	0.64		
TOTAL	47			

Significance of PICK Means

Pick Type	n	Pinch Force (N)
mid. - top edge pinch	6	77.54 [a]
low - thumbs forward	6	60.60 [b]
low - thumbs back	6	46.78 [c]
mid. - right hand up/left under	6	34.74 [d]
low - palm press against thigh	6	20.29 [e]
high - as catcher	6	15.61 [f]
high - as passer	6	14.14 [f]
mid. - left hand up/right under	6	9.10 [g]

LSD = 4.17, means with different letters (a-g) are significantly different at $\alpha = 0.05$

3.2 Tempered Glass

The analysis of tempered glass handling focused on the variables of: Glove Type (Spectra™, Nitrile™), shelf level (low, middle), and orientation (front facing out, edge facing out). The factor Pick Type is expressed with four levels - two shelf levels by two orientations. Table 4 shows the results of the ANOVA in which Glove Type has a significant effect on mean pinch force ($p < 0.05$), with the Spectra™ glove requiring 20% less grip force than the Nitrile™. Pick Type was also significant ($p < 0.05$) with the middle shelf picks requiring less pinch force than those from the low shelf (LSD = 0.739). See Table 4 for groupings of the Pick Type factor by statistical significance.

TABLE 4. ANOVA for mean pinch force on tempered glass as a function of Pick and Glove Type.

Source	df	MS	F	p
GLOVE (G)	1	1.612	6.92	0.018*
PICK (P)	3	1.667	7.16	0.003*
G x P	3	0.111	0.48	0.703
ERROR	16	0.233		
TOTAL	23			

Significance of PICK Means

Pick Type -- weight of glass (kg)	n	Mean Pinch Force (N)
Low shelf, Front facing -- 6.59 kg	6	30.37 [a]
Low shelf, Edge facing -- 3.86 kg	6	23.99 [b]
Middle shelf, Front facing -- 6.00 kg	6	20.78 [c]
Middle shelf, Edge facing -- 4.36 kg	6	18.46 [c]

Significance of GLOVE Means

Glove Type	n	Mean Pinch Force (N)
Spectra™	12	20.91
Nitrile™	12	26.00

LSD = 2.59, means with different letters are significantly different at $\alpha = 0.05$

4. Discussion

The Spectra™ gloves are preferred over the Nitrile™ because of their increased tackiness and associated lower grip force. Since both the Spectra™ and Nitrile™ gloves have tackier, higher friction surfaces it was surprising to see higher pinch forces with these gloves than with the thick, cotton glove in the laminated glass analysis. However, there are two reasonable explanations for this finding. First, the thick gloves, by virtue of their thickness and cushioning over the sensors may have distributed the applied force over a larger area than just the sensors and thus decreased the force applied directly on the sensors. Second, it has been shown that thick gloves can decrease the available grip force by up to 30% [4]. Thus, the subject may have generated equivalent pinch forces, but the thickness of the cotton glove may have reduced the amount of force transmitted to the sensors.

From the low shelf level the "palm press with no thumbs" required the least amount of force, most likely, because of the additional support from the thighs. Using this strategy, the pinch force can be "unloaded" as the glass face is rested on the thigh during transport from the low level shelf to the cart. Whole-body biomechanical factors should be considered before this method can be recommended for all workers, and, because of additional coordination skills, more training should be required by workers attempting this maneuver.

Although there is a statistically significant difference between a "thumbs forward" and "thumbs back", top edge pinch from the low shelf, this result should be interpreted cautiously based on the biomechanics of the grasp. In the "thumb forward" strategy, a greater loading is placed on the finger sensors which comprised the summed sensor force. In the "thumbs back" pick strategy more loading is placed on the thumbs (with no sensor) rather than the fingers. It was recommended that workers having difficulty with the "palm pinch" alternate between the thumbs forward and thumbs back pinches to distribute stresses over the hand.

For middle shelf level picks - the one hand over/one hand under pinch forces were significantly lower than the top edge pinch (thumbs back) forces. Furthermore, the latter requires greater upper body strength, therefore the one hand over/one hand under grip was recommended to the glass handlers for minimizing pinch forces. At the high shelf level there were no significant differences between pinch forces of the passer (who stands on a ladder) and catcher (who stands on the floor) positions. This is likely due to the fact that these maneuvers did not involve distinct grip types. Whole-body posture analyses should also be conducted on these handling maneuvers.

References

[1] Fellows, G.L. and Freivalds, A. (1991). Ergonomic evaluation of a foam rubber grip for tool handles. *Applied Ergonomics, 22* (4), 225-230.
[2] Yun, M.H., Kotani, K., and Ellis, R.D. (1992). Using force sensitive resistors to evaluate hand tool grip design. In *Proceedings of the 37th Annual Meeting of the Human Factors Society*, Santa Monica, CA.
[3] Jensen, T.R., Radwin, R.G., and Webster, J.G. (1991). A conductive polymer sensor for measuring external finger forces. *Journal of Biomechanics, 24* (9), 851-858.
[4] Wang, M.J., Bishu, R., and Rodgers, S. (1987). Grip strength changes when wearing three types of gloves. *Proceedings of* INTERFACE 87. Santa Monica, CA: Human Factors Society, pp. 349-354.

Advances in Occupational Ergonomics and Safety II
Edited by Biman Das and Waldemar Karwowski
IOS Press and Ohmsha, 1997

Productivity and Ergonomics - Are they compatible?

Marc L. Resnick

Industrial and Systems Engineering

Florida International University

Miami, FL 33199

Ergonomics and productivity have long been considered competing objectives in the
design of jobs. Changes that reduce repetitive trauma are often perceived as making
the process slower or less efficient as well. This incompatibility has led to a patent
distrust of ergonomics initiatives by representatives of government and industry.
This conflict is largely illusory, however, as ergonomics can be used to decrease
costs. Several strategies have been used to present ergonomics as a cost saver.
Previous strategies include promoting ergonomics as a way to decrease health and
safety costs and as a critical component of concurrent engineering. This paper
presents a third strategy. Ergonomics can be used directly to increase productivity.
Empirical research is presented that measures performance for jobs that are
ergonomically designed. The results show that within an ergonomically acceptable
envelope, layouts can be designed to maximize productivity. Considering both
ergonomic and productivity principles in the design of jobs can lead to reduced
labor costs as well as reduced risk of injury.

1.0 Background

One of the factors that hinders the widespread integration of ergonomics into
industry is the fear that ergonomic changes will have a negative effect on productivity.
This is especially true for small companies that do not have the economies of scale to
leverage their investment in ergonomics. It is a common belief that the implementation of
ergonomics increases the cost of labor due to slower work speeds, lower lifting limits, and
other changes designed to reduce musculoskeletal stresses. Unfortunately, the widespread
acceptance of this belief stems from the fact that it is often true. Many ergonomics
practitioners are not trained in methods engineering or do not utilize these techniques
when making ergonomic design changes, with the unfortunate consequences of increasing
labor costs. Lately, there has been an increased interest in research to evaluate the
relationship between ergonomics and economics. Several strategies have been used to
promote ergonomics as a way to reduce costs rather than increase them.

1.1 *Health and Safety Costs*

Several researchers [1-4] have approached this relationship as a way to reduce
health and safety costs. One [1] claims that ergonomics already reduces health and safety

costs, and the poor perception is largely due to a lack of information dissemination. Ergonomics has had a great deal of success, however people are unaware of the economic benefits of good ergonomic design. He cites many examples of reductions in work related musculoskeletal disorders (WRMDs) at several companies due to the implementation of ergonomics. The cost benefits of these interventions come from reduced workers' compensation and other medical related costs. Unfortunately, this argument is masked from plant manager level executives because of traditional accounting techniques in which many of these costs are paid from corporate rather than plant level budgets. Furthermore, the stochastic nature of workplace injuries prevents an ergonomist from explicitly predicting the number of injuries that are prevented for a given intervention. Much of the first problem can be alleviated through the introduction of activity based costing methods [5]. In general, the benefits of ergonomics in terms of reduced health and safety costs can only be proved with large sample sizes and over long periods of time, two luxuries that many companies cannot afford.

A similar argument is made regarding tool selection [2]. Bar code scanners, keyboards and other data entry devices can create high musculoskeletal stresses if they are not selected properly. These stresses can lead to injury and thus to increased health and safety costs. However, the benefits of selecting ergonomically appropriate tools are also better quantified with larger sample sizes.

1.2 *Management*

Another set of studies has evaluated the effect of institutionalizing ergonomics by incorporating it into the concurrent engineering process [6,7]. By implementing ergonomic evaluation tools (such as the NIOSH lifting guide or psychophysical analysis) during the original methods analysis when the job is being designed, the initial workplace layouts will not include any extreme postures or tasks that are ergonomically unsafe. This has the advantage of avoiding expensive modifications that may result from *post hoc* ergonomic analysis. The benefits of these interventions are also difficult to quantify. It is hard to establish a baseline for injury rates, and estimating the cost savings from not having to redesign the poor layouts that were avoided is not straightforward.

2.0 Productivity

A different avenue of investigation has been to empirically determine which combinations of workplace layout parameters maximize productivity while maintaining ergonomic safety. This approach has significant advantages over a focus on health and safety costs. The objective of this approach is to maximize productivity by establishing workplace layout specifications that allow workers to maximize the speed at which they do their work while insuring that postures are maintained within ergonomic guidelines. Thus in addition to reducing the risk of injury, labor costs are directly influenced. These costs are easily measurable and are associated with the individual job that is affected.

Two studies have investigated the effects of manipulating various job design parameters on performance time [8,9]. The first studied the effects of ergonomic workplace design changes on a repetitive manual assembly task. Subjects performed a manual assembly task under ninety workplace configurations. The parameters that were investigated included workplace height, part mass, line speed, and fatigue. The parameter combinations were fashioned to test the range that ergonomic evaluation would find acceptable. A linear regression model to evaluate the effects of the parameters on performance time was generated.

The results of this study were mixed. Reducing the mass of assembled parts from 1.2 to 0.3 kg improved productivity by 21%. Assembly time decreased by 17% as the line speed doubled from 15 per minute to 30 per minute. However, manipulating the height at which the assembly task was performed had no effect on productivity. This study concluded that even within the ergonomically acceptable movement envelope, performance time can vary widely depending on the specific layout of the workspace.

A similar study [9] investigated a tool handling task. Subjects performed a typical industrial task in twenty-seven conditions designed within an ergonomically acceptable work envelope. As in the previous study, a wide range within this envelope was tested. The effects of tool mass, work height, and movement distance on performance time were measured. Accuracy was also included by requiring subjects to complete at least 95% of the movements within a small tolerance, insuring that subjects did not achieve high performance by sacrificing the quality of the task.

All three variables had significant effects on performance time, even within the ergonomic work envelope, however the magnitudes of the effects varied. Here, mass had only a negligible effect on performance time. On the other hand, performance time was fastest when the movement height was 10 cm above elbow height compared to elbow height and 10 cm below elbow height. Movement distance had the greatest effect on performance time, increasing by 70% as the movement distance was extended from 20 to 120 cm. This study had similar conclusions to the first. Workplace layout within the ergonomic envelope had a significant effect on performance time.

Differences between the results of the two studies suggests that there are many factors that affect the relationship between workplace layout and performance. In the first study, mass had a significant effect on performance time, whereas in the second the effect was marginal. In the first study, movement height had no effect on performance time, whereas in the second, performance time was fastest at the highest point of the ergonomic envelope. The reasons for these discrepancies need to be investigated. However, the basic conclusion of both studies is that workplace design can significantly effect performance time. Optimizing both ergonomic and productivity parameters can decrease labor and health and safety costs simultaneously.

3.0 Conclusion

There have been several strategies used to prove that ergonomics has economic benefits. One focuses on reductions in health and safety costs. Conducting ergonomic evaluations on jobs with high injury rates and redesigning them to reduce musculoskeletal stresses can decrease these costs significantly. While most ergonomists will agree that ergonomics-based redesigns will have a net positive effect on costs, a weakness of this approach is that the benefits may be obscured due to the accounting techniques of indirect costs and the stochastic nature of WRMDs.

Another strategy has been to incorporate ergonomics into the concurrent engineering process. This is another positive step in improving workers' safety while also decreasing both health and safety costs and job construction costs. However, without empirical research to establish the specifications that maximize both objectives, they cannot be truly integrated. Furthermore, the economic benefits of this integration remain hard to quantify.

A promising new strategy is to use ergonomic criteria to narrow the work area to an acceptable envelope and then maximize productivity within this area. Because it influences performance time directly, this approach has a more evident effect on the bottom line of the specific activity, thus the economic argument to incorporate ergonomics into the job design process is more clear. The two studies summarized above provide evidence that ergonomics and productivity can be reconciled, however more empirical work remains to be completed. The discrepancies between the results of the two tasks need to be evaluated. Additional task types and more variables also remain to be investigated.

4.0 References

[1] H.W. Hendrick, The ergonomics of economics is the economics of ergonomics. *Proceedings of the Human Factors and Ergonomics Society 40th Annual Meeting*, 1996, pp. 1-10. Human Factors and Ergonomics Society, Santa Monica, CA.

[2] B. Moore, Ergonomics = Economics. *Materials Handling Engineering*, April, 1996, pp. 27.

[3] G.C. Simpson, Costs and benefits in occupational ergonomics, *Ergonomics,* 33(3), 1990, pp. 261-268.

[4] K.G. Parker, Why Ergonomics is good economics, *Industrial Engineering*, 27(2), 1995, pp. 41-47.

[5] P.G. Dahlen and S. Wernersson, Human Factors in the economic control of industry, *International Journal of Industrial Ergonomics*, 15, 1995, pp. 215-221.

[6] M.L. Resnick, Reconciling ergonomics and productivity, *Proceedings of the Institute of Industrial Engineers Conference and Expo.* 1996, Institute of Industrial Engineers, Atlanta, GA.

[7] M.L. Resnick, Concurrent ergonomics: A proactive approach, *Computer & Industrial Engineering,* 31(1/2), 1996, pp. 479-482.

[8] M.L. Resnick and I. Kaplan, An Empirical Model of Assembly Process Times for Design for Assembly and Operational Scheduling, *Proceedings of the Industrial Engineering Research Conference*, 1997, Institute of Industrial Engineers, Atlanta, GA.

[9] M.L. Resnick and A. Zanotti, Using Ergonomics To Target Productivity Improvements, *Computers & Industrial Engineering*, in press.

Advances in Occupational Ergonomics and Safety II
Edited by Biman Das and Waldemar Karwowski
IOS Press and Ohmsha, 1997

Is there any effect of workload on speech parameters of air traffic controllers?

Parimal Kopardekar[1] and Anil Mital[2]

[1]System Resources Corporation
5218 Atlantic Avenue, 3rd Floor
Mays Landing, NJ 08330

[2]Ergonomics and Engineering Controls Research Laboratory
Industrial Engineering
University of Cincinnati
Cincinnati, OH 45221-0116

Abstract. Air traffic control (ATC) operators routinely communicate with pilots using standard speech phrases. The objective of this research was to assess the utility of speech parameters for estimation of ATC workload. A simulation of Atlantic City Terminal Approach Control was used for the air traffic scenarios. Data from seventeen ATC operators were collected. The most commonly used speech phrase was analyzed for comparing the speech parameters under various workload levels. The workload level was based on the instantaneous count of aircraft handled. Eleven speech parameters, extracted from each speech segment, were considered as dependent variables. Controller, workload and replication were considered as independent variables. The results indicated that speech parameters were not significantly affected by the workload levels. However, individual differences among ATC operators were consistently observed.

1. Introduction

1.1 Air Traffic Control Operations

Air traffic control (ATC) operator has to constantly observe the air traffic, often under time pressure, to make sure that certain critical separations among aircraft are maintained. In the case of ATC operations, cognitive workload is more prevalent as the task imposes information gathering and processing demands. Since this task has severe safety repercussions, monitoring workload levels is imperative [1].

1.2 Speech Analysis

Speech analysis is concerned with the estimation, from the speech signal, of the parameters of a speech and its relationship with the possible sources of disturbances (e.g., workload). Speech analysis is an intuitively appealing tool for the estimation of workload because the controllers' task requires that they communicate with pilots using standard speech phrases, via radio, on a routine basis. Therefore, obtaining on-line speech data is very easy and completely non-intrusive.

1.3 Objective

None of these prior studies focused on air traffic control operations. Therefore, overall objective of this research was to examine the utility of speech analysis technique for assessing the workload of air traffic controllers.
The specific goals of this study were as follows:
1.   To examine the relationship of various speech parameters with workload levels; and
2.   To examine whether speech parameters differ among controllers.

2. Research Methodology
2.1 Participants

Seventeen active air traffic controllers from the Atlantic City Terminal Approach Control Center participated in this study. Their experience ranged from 1 to 20 years with mean as 7.66 years and standard deviation as 5.73 years.

2.2 Procedure

Atlantic City Terminal Approach Control Center was simulated for controlling the air traffic. The participant controller with his/her workstation was seated in one of the experimental rooms. In another room, two trained pseudo pilots were stationed. These pseudo pilots provided realistic voice feedback to controllers and operated software generated aircraft. Each scenario consisted of 8 arrivals, 8 departures, and 7 overflights for a total of 23 aircraft appearing during the 30 minute period.

2.3 Equipment

The experimental equipment consisted of a state-of-the art controller workstation, voice communication equipment, *ATCoach* simulation software, video and audio recording system, and video tapes. Data reduction and analysis equipment consisted of Media Vision's Pocket Recorder software, 486/DX-2 IBM compatible personal computer with a sound card, speech analysis software, and SPSS software.

2.4 Speech Segment or Phrase

Analysis of the most commonly used phrase "Altimeter 3000" is reported in this article.

2.5 Data Collection, Reduction and Analysis

Communications between controller and pseudo-pilots (simulating the role of pilots) and controller radar scope were recorded on video tapes. The number of aircraft, when the phrase was uttered, was also noted. Workload ratings (1-10 scale) were reported by controller at an every five-minute interval. Relevant speech segments were then recorded onto the Pocket Recorder software, developed by Media Vision, with a sampling rate of 22.5 KHz using 486/DX-2 IBM compatible personal computer. A 16 bit Analog to Digital sound card was used. Each of the speech segments was then analyzed using the speech analysis software to extract the eleven speech parameters.

2.6 Experimental Design
2.6.1 Dependent Variables

There were eleven dependent variables, as follows: Average fundamental frequency of a phrase in Hz, Standard deviation of the fundamental frequency of a phrase in Hz, Duration of a phrase in seconds, Average amplitude of a phrase in millivolts, Standard deviation of the amplitude of a phrase in millivolts, Average jitter of a phrase, Standard deviation of the jitter of a phrase, Average shimmer of a phrase, Standard deviation of the shimmer of a phrase, Average fundamental frequency of a phrase in semitones, and Standard deviation of the fundamental frequency of a phrase in semitones. These eleven variables were extracted from each of the recorded speech segments.

2.6.2 Independent Variables

There were three independent variables, which included Controller (17 controllers), Replication (2 replications), and Workload level (5 levels). Details of experimental design and analysis can be found in reference [2].

3. Results

A 5 X 2 X 17 MANOVA was performed with 11 dependent variables and three independent variables. The results of MANOVA indicated following significant effects:
1.   Three way interaction;
2.   Workload*controller interaction; and
3.   Main effect of controller.

In order to investigate which of the dependent variables were significant, univariate ANOVAs were performed. For the three-way interaction, only average amplitude and average fundamental frequency (Hz) were found to be significant. For the workload*controller interaction, only average fundamental frequencies (both in Hz and semitones) were significant. The main effect of controller was found to be significant for all of the eleven dependent variables indicating the presence of individual differences. The main effect of workload was found not to be significant indicating that none of the speech parameters were significantly affected by the workload level.

The main effect of replication was not found to be significant on any of the speech parameters indicating that the effect of timing or scenario run was absent and, therefore, validated the findings.

4. Discussion and Conclusions

None of the speech parameters were significantly affected by the workload factor. This indicated a general lack of sensitivity of these speech parameters with ATC workload. Interestingly, individual differences were observed. Replications were also consistent since the effect of replication was found not to be significant.

The previous literature suggests mixed results indicating the relationship between the speech parameters and workload. The only consistent finding among different researchers is that of an existence of the individual differences. Hecker *et al.* (1968) observed that some of the subjects were consistently soft spoken than others, with or without workload [3]. They also observed the similar differences for the fundamental frequency. Waskow (1966) [4] and Williams and Stevens (1972) [5] have reported similar observations about interindividual variability. Schneider and Alpert (1989) [6] and Schneider *et al.* (1989) [7] have also observed the individual differences in various speech parameters.

In general, the speech parameters did not indicate any effect of workload. This may imply a lack of sensitivity of the speech parameters to the ATC workload levels. This study, however, reiterated the findings of the presence individual differences. This finding cautions the researchers as the speaker independent voice recognition systems have to be robust enough to accommodate these differences among controllers.

5. References

[1] J. Rodgers, FAA forecast. In Thirteenth Annual FAA Aviation Forecast Conference Proceedings, Washington D.C.: Office of Aviation Policy and Plans, 1988.

[2] P. Kopardekar, Effect of workload on speech parameters of air traffic controllers, Unpublished doctoral dissertation, University of Cincinnati, Cincinnati, OH., 1995.

[3] M. Hecker, K. Stevens, G. Von-Bismarck, and C. Williams, Manifestations of task-induced stress in the acoustical speech signal, Journal of the Acoustical Society of America, 44, (1968) 993-1001.

[4] I. Waskow, The effects of drugs on speech: A review, Psychopharmacology Bulletin, 3, (1966) 1-20.

[5] C. Williams, and K. Stevens, Emotions and speech: some acoustical correlates, Journal of the Acoustical Society of America, 52 (4), (1972) 1238-1250.

[6] S. Schneider, and, M. Alpert, Voice measures of workload in the advanced flight deck: Additional studies (NASA Contractor Report 4258), 1989.

[7] S. Schneider *et al.*, Voice measures of workload in the advanced flight deck (NASA Contractor Report 4249), 1989.

Advances in Occupational Ergonomics and Safety II
Edited by Biman Das and Waldemar Karwowski
IOS Press and Ohmsha, 1997

Carrying Books - A Burden ?

Sheik N. Imrhan, Ph.D., P.E.
Dept. of Industrial and Manufacturing Systems Engineering
University of Texas at Arlington
Arlington, Texas 76019

This study examines the characteristics of book load carrying by students on a university campus. Two hundred and thirty eight students were asked to fill out a short questionnaire on carrying characteristics then their book loads were weighed. The data were analyzed to determine the relationships between various carrying characteristics and book load weight, exertion levels, frequency of carrying and amount of time load is carried.

1. Introduction

The interest on load carrying has been focused more on work situations and in the military [1,2] because of the grave potential consequences of injuries and cumulative trauma disorders to the body. Kroemer, Kroemer and Kroemer-Elbert (1994) provide a summary of the ergonomics of this activity. In general, loads should be carried near the mid-axis of the body as close to the body as possible, and at about the body's center of mass. Arm carrying is strenuous, especially one-handed carry. So is carrying loads that are asymmetrically distributed about the body in any way.

Over the last few decades the size and weight of books carried by elementary school, high school or college students seem to have increased considerably. Books may be carried in a variety of ways on the upper body, to and from school, but in each case the load acts on the spine The wrist, elbow and shoulder are also under strain when heavy book loads are carried in the hand. While the likelihood of suffering serious injuries among students are remote, except where carriers make sharp twists of the loaded spine or arms, anecdotal evidence indicates that muscular strain and discomfort are not uncommon. Students do complain of the burden of this activity. This is due mainly to the increase in size and weight of books being produced today. Ostensibly, for economic reasons, books are produced in single larger volumes than smaller multiple volumes, and in some cases a large proportion of a textbook is never used for a course because it covers material outside the course. This study was undertaken in an effort to understand the nature of book load carrying by college students and to elicit people's opinions on the physical severity of such carrying .

2. Methods

The study was conducted in two stages, four years apart, on an urban college campus of student population approximately 23,000. In each part, students walking along campus between classes were stopped, individually, and asked to participate voluntarily. They filled out a short questionnaire (taking about 1-2 minutes) requesting information such as age, height, weight, academic major, academic classification, and their book-load carrying habits. Certain characteristics about the load carrying were also recorded -- bag type, method of carrying, body part that is affected most, amount of time per day books are carried, and number of times per week books are carried.. Their book load was then weighed with a portable weighing scale (in increment of 0.1 lb) with their 'book bag' if one was used. In the first part of the study 132 subjects were investigated; in the second part, 106. The second part included two questions that were not included in the first part -- subject's rating of perceived exertion and indication of body parts affected by fatigue, discomfort or pain.

The data was analyzed using the Statistical Analysis System, PC version 6.11, on a desk top computer.

3. Results and Discussion

Table 1 shows the distribution of students carrying book loads according to various classifications.

Book load weights ranged from 0.5-24.8 lb (mean= 9.1 lb.; s.d.=4.4 lb). Ten % of the loads exceeded 14.2 lb and 25 % exceeded 11.5 lb. On the effect on the body overall, 5 % percent of students rated the load carrying as very hard or worse (RPE > 15), 25 % rated as somewhat hard or worse (RPE>13), and 50 % rated as fairly light or worse (RPE=11). On the effect on the part of the body normally carrying the load (right shoulder, left shoulder, back, etc.), 10 % of the students rated the load as having a very strong effect or worse (rating>7), 25 % as heavy or worse (rating> 5), and 50 % as somewhat strong or worse (rating >4).

Separate ANOVAs were performed using book load weight, RPE values, average time per day books are carried, and frequency of carrying as dependent variables, and sex and other variables as independent variables, but only where the sample size in the sex*variable subgroups were reasonably large. A 5 % level of significance was arbitrarily used in all tests.

Using book load (weight) as the dependent variable, the results indicate that for:
1. Sex and burden variables - only burden was statistically significant; that is, those who considered book load carrying a burden carried heavier loads (10.6 vs 8.0 lb), with no distinction between males and females.
2. Sex and type of book bag - book load did not differ according to the two types of bags analyzed (backpack and shoulder bags) nor between sexes.
3. Sex and transportation - transportation and the sex*transportation variables were significant.

Using the RPE as a continuous quantitative (dependent) variable, the results indicate the following for sex and burden, sex and type of bag, and method of carrying:

Table 1. Distribution of number of students carrying book loads according to various classifications

Carrying Characteristic

Sex	Male	Female			
	139 (58 %)	99 (42 %)			
Regular use of bag	209 (88 %)	29 (12 %)			
Type of Bag	Shoulder Strap	Back Pack	Briefcase, Handbag, and others	None	Non-response
	86 (36 %)	112 (47 %)	8 (3 %)	9 (4 %)	23 (10 %)
Considered a Burden	Yes	No			
	98 (41 %)	140 (58 %)			
Student Classification	Freshman	Sophomore	Junior	Senior	Graduate
	44 (18 %)	46 (19 %)	42 (15 %)	62 (26 %)	8.1 (3 %)
Mode of Transportation	Motor Vehicle	Walk	Motor Bike	Bicycle	
	61 (26 %)	30 (13 %)	13 (6 %)	28 (12 %)	
Academic Department	Natural Scienc	Liberal Arts	Business	Engineering	Other
	33 (14 %)	54 (23 %)	52 (22 %)	87 (37 %)	12 (5 %)

1. Sex and burden variables - only sex was significant. Females considered the load carrying more strenuous than males did (RPE = 12.3 vs 10.7) regardless of whether they considered it a burden or not.

2. Sex and type of bag - only sex was significant. Females found the carrying more strenuous (RPE = 12.3 vs 10.7 lb), regardless of the type of bag used.

3. Sex and method of carrying - females found carrying more strenuous, regardless of the method of carrying (RPE = 12.2 vs 10.8 lb).

4. Student classification did not affect the weight of books carried.

ANOVAs indicated that the amount of time students carried books per was not dependent on sex, whether the students considered carrying a burden, the method of carrying, nor the type of bag used for either sex. Finally ANOVAs also indicated that the frequency (days/week) with which books were carried did not depend on type of bag, method of transportation to campus or whether carrying was considered a burden for either sex but was dependent on the method of carrying. Books were carried more often on the shoulder compared to hand.

Even though females' carrying strength is about 2/3 that of males, they carried about the same weight as males. The difference in weight (0.6 lb) was not statistically significant and was obviously dictated by the academic courses in which they were enrolled..

The most preferred method of carrying the book load was on the right shoulder (by bag straps -- asymmetric loading) and the least preferred method was on the back, where the load distribution is known to be the best. The frequency of occurrence of discomfort, fatigue or pain was twice as great in the right shoulder as in the other body parts investigated. Backpacks were 10 times more common than briefcases which induce asymmetrical loading and concentrate strain in the arm

4. References

[1]   S.R. Datta and N.L. Ramanathan, Ergonomic Comparison of Seven Modes of Carrying Loads on the Horizontal Plane, *Ergonomics*, 14 (1971), 269-278.
[2] M. F. Haisman, Determinants of Load Carrying Ability, *Applied Ergonomics*, 19, (1988), 111-121.
[3] K. Kroemer, H. Kroemer and K. Kroemer-Elbert, *Ergonomics*, Prentice Hall, Englewood Cliffs, NJ, 1994.

5. Conclusions

These results of this study identify some of the factors associated with book load carrying. It seems that type of academic courses, the way one looks, and method of transportation play an important part; and there are a few important differences in carrying characteristics between males and females. The results are exploratory but they suggest that psychosocial factors tend to override biomechanical factors. The strength of these relationships can be enhanced with a larger sample size in future studies. Other factors also need to be investigated.

VI. WORKING ENVIRONMENT, HEALTH AND SAFETY

18. Noise and Vibration Effects

Advances in Occupational Ergonomics and Safety II
Edited by Biman Das and Waldemar Karwowski
IOS Press and Ohmsha, 1997

Objective Measurements and Subjective Evaluation of Reverberation Time in the Office — Development of Measures for the Improvement of Room Acoustics

Helmut **Strasser**, Prof. Dr.-Ing. habil.,
Kristina **Gruen**, Dipl.-Ing., and Werner **Koch**, Dipl.-Ing.
Institute of Production Engineering/Ergonomics Division
University of Siegen, Paul-Bonatz-Str. 9-11, D-57068 Siegen/Germany

Members of the design department in a medium-sized company were complaining to the management about the acoustic situation in new offices which adversely affected their personal well-being and their work performance. As a consequence, a work-scientific field study was conducted to analyze and evaluate the acoustic working conditions and, if necessary, to develop improvement suggestions. Objective criteria for the evaluation of communication disturbances, e.g. during meetings or telephone conversations, were gained from measuring the reverberation time in several rooms. Structured questioning via a specially developed questionnaire — with unipolar or bipolar 4-step scales — allowed a differentiated judgement of the current acoustic situation and its effects on the subjective condition. Furthermore, after recording the actual situation, suggestions for the improvement of the acoustics were developed and cost-utility prognoses were made. Finally, the potential solutions were discussed with the management; their prospective acceptance rate among the employees was assessed before they were realized.

1. Introduction

Annual statistical surveys of mutual industrial accident insurance associations show that noise induced hearing loss — as has always been the case — is the number one of the occupational diseases (e.g., to date there are more than fifty different known occupational diseases in Germany). Approximately 1/3 of all known cases originates from detrimental acoustic stress in the working environment. That is, however, only the tip of the iceberg of aural and extra-aural effects of noise, i.e. of acoustic stress that is unwanted, disturbing, aggravating, and frustrating; that impedes conversation; and that, in some circumstances, can cause damage to the hearing. Expenditures in the form of monetary compensation for the irreversible damage associated with technology are still relatively low in comparison with the damage to the economy of more than 20 billion US $ per year, as calculated by the German Association for Noise Control. For these reasons, "noise" is being attacked on various levels. The great variety of brochures, books, and journals (e.g. [1], [2], [3]) as well as technical regulations, guidelines, norms, and safety regulations (e.g. [4], [5], [6], [7]) reflects both the broad and deep knowledge of "noise" and the technical possibilities for noise control.

The acoustic situation, however, cannot solely be described in dB (which is a logarithmic measure for the intensity and pressure of sound, respectively), and a comparison between the rated value and the actual value with marginal tolerable levels is not always sufficiently expressive. Even if the permissible noise level according to Working Places Regulations (cp. [8]) is 70 dB(A) for simple office work and as low as only 55 dB(A) for mentally challenging work, these thresholds still cannot guarantee that no problems for the employees will arise, because in addition to the sound pressure levels also the acoustic situation in the room has to be "right." This room-acoustic situation is determined by the reflection or absorption properties of the floor, walls, and ceiling, and by the acoustic absorption of the materials in the room. In the case of multiple reflections together with acoustically inert, highly reflecting walls and ceilings, significant time lags between the "echo" and the speech signal (which reaches the point of immission directly) occur. These time lags are the reason for the interference with speech elements such as syllables and words. Thus, insufficient planning by architects, designers, and interior designers with respect to acoustics, especially together with acoustic transmission and amplifying systems, can have a detrimental effect on oral communication.

Concrete and glass, as well as linoleum or PVC coatings and smoothly varnished plastic or wood surfaces — i.e. highly reflecting materials which are, for manufacturing or economic reasons, often favored for walls and ceilings as well as inventory — are usually the reason for a distinct reverberation in a room. The reverberation time is defined as the time T, in which an exciting test sound after switching off has decreased by 60 dB. If a continuous noise, e.g. from a building acoustics analyzer, is utilized rather than the impulse noise of a starting pistol, it is possible to extrapolate the reverberation time (for a 60-dB decay) from the drop over small level differences.

2. Measuring the Reverberation Time

After the employees in the design department of a medium-sized company complained to the management about the acoustic situation in their new offices, the reverberation time in several open-plan offices and smaller single offices was measured with a building acoustics analyzer which simultaneously emits and receives noise signals in 1/3 octave bands. Because the situation on all floors was virtually the same, the study was limited to one floor. The reverberation time for various frequencies could be determined with sounds that were emitted with a high quality loudspeaker and were received (with a time lag) via a microphone in the acoustics analyzer.

One reverberation time measurement cannot be considered a fixed and secured value for a room. Even if the sound source and the microphone are positioned at the exact same spots, fluctuation may occur. As a consequence, an average of at least three measurements was computed. After the (pink noise) sound was switched off, the reverberation time was measured over a decay of 20 dB and was extrapolated for a 60-dB decay.

The upper part of Fig. 1 shows the results of two measurements at one test point in an open-plan office. The frequency-dependent reverberation times in this room with two glass walls was usually significantly below 0.5 s. From the results of the two series of measurements which were executed at different times, sufficient reliability can be concluded. In contrast to this "technical office" (which has reflecting walls, but also a number of cloth-covered partitions), measurements in a relatively "naked" open-plan office at comparable measuring points (9 and 10) led to distinctly higher reverberation times in a range of 0.5 to 1.0 s (see middle part of Fig. 1).

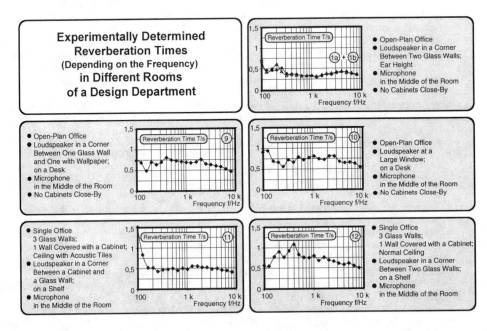

Figure 1: Reverberation times in different rooms of a design department

Rooms 11 and 12 were comparably equipped and of identical size, but the area of the glass surfaces (22 m² vs. 17 m²) as well as the ceilings were different. Again, the reverberation times were distinctly different (see lower part of Fig. 1). Special acoustic sheets on roughly 1/3 of the ceiling in room 11 already resulted in objectively observable lower values (ca. 0.5 s), at least for medium and high frequencies. The distinctly higher values from 0.5 to 1.0 s for room 12, which is of the same size but does not have noise-absorbing surfaces of significant area, must be considered as much more critical (due to the small volume of 53.50 m³) than the roughly equal values for the reverberation time in the much bigger room (approximately 450 m³) with measuring point 9.

When reverberation times in office buildings are evaluated, it can be assumed according to [9], [10], or [11] that the tolerable value for the reverberation time increases with room size and that the desirable level of reverberation time for "speech acoustics" is generally lower than that for "music acoustics." Usually, stipulations are valid only for the range from 500 to 1000 Hz. Decisive, frequency-dependent levels especially for smaller offices (smaller than 100 m³) do not exist. Desired levels that were empirically determined and evaluated are almost non-existent in work scientific/ergonomic literature.

3. Subjective Evaluation of the Acoustic Situation and Potential Improvements

The current acoustic situation and its effects on the subjective condition were evaluated by structured questioning of the employees with a bipolar 4-step scale for altogether 25 questions. Additionally, potential improvements for the acoustic situation were evaluated.

The graphs of Fig. 2 show answers to some of the questions; all answers (n ≤ 50) are included. It becomes clear from the histograms on the left-hand side that many employees felt that the acoustic situation was negative in general. At the beginning of the study, employees had pointed out that the person on the other end of the line during a telephone conversation had problems following the conversation when the employees talked in a normal tone of voice and at a normal volume. In the empirical study, roughly 40% are indifferent in their opinion (rating = 0); however, half of all persons that were questioned considered the situation unacceptable, with 10% rating the situation with "-4", which is the maximum (see upper left part of Fig. 2).

Since there are no runners or carpets in the office, it does not come as a surprise that the answers to a distinct question include impact noise in the "array of noises" (noise from office machines and high-heels, noise from conversations, ringing of telephones, etc.). The answers to another question prove that the current situation causes considerable general adverse effects on communication and speech intelligibility (see graph in the lower left part of Fig. 2).

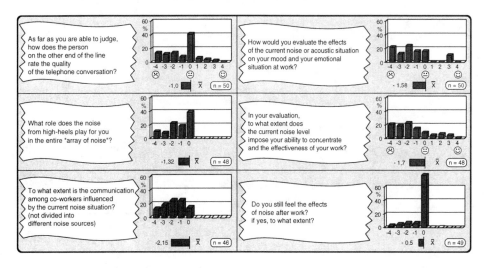

Figure 2:   Subjective evaluation of the acoustic situation and its effects on the condition with steps on a bipolar or unipolar scale with ratings from "-4" to "+4" and "0" to "-4" for positive and negative ratings

According to the answers to the question in the upper right-hand corner of Fig. 2, many employees (approximately 70%) feel that the acoustic situation negatively effects their mood; the rating ranges from "-1" ("slight") to "-4" ("very strong"). Twenty percent of the employees rated the effects as "very strong." Only a small fraction seems to not be irritated by the noise. It is remarkable that in the answers to the question about possible effects on the ability to concentrate, about ¾ of all persons that were questioned feel that their concentration suffers due to the acoustic situation. Roughly 60% of all employees even give ratings from "-2" ("considerable") to "-4" ("very strong"). Although it may be possible that in exceptional cases sound has a positive "wake-up-effect" and that it might increase vigilance (see positive ratings at the question with bipolar scale), in general the ratings are fairly negative. This has been backed up by a number of statements made by persons who were asked about effects of the noise on the general working situation and the working climate that had not been verbalized in the questionnaire. "Irritation" and "increased error rate" are examples.

Effects of the work noise or the "self-made array of noises" on the time after work does not seem to occur too often according to the histogram that represents the answers to the question in the right lower part of Fig. 2. However, it is questionable whether 18%, i.e. 9 persons, that rated the situation after work between "-1" and "-4" with an average of "-2.15" over that sample can be neglected.

Conversations (both in person and on the telephone) at the next desk are the disturbance that was by far mentioned most often. This holds true for specific (single) days as well as — slightly less distinct — for the weekly average. Noise from high-heels and office machines is of significantly less importance. They are less often rated with "-4", but the percentage of those people who feel a particularly strong negative influence on specific days — and that is still distinctly more than half of all people — should be reason enough to change the acoustic situation.

The acceptance of improvement suggestions had to be forecasted in the second part of the questionnaire. These suggestions had advocates as well as opponents (see Fig. 3); frustrating experiences that had been experienced in the past were one reason for this. According to the upper half of Fig. 3, the majority does not consider the replacement of all glass walls between two rooms with noise-absorbing material favorable (fairly balanced evaluation with a negative mean for this question on a bipolar scale), although roughly 20% consider that action very important (according to the lower left part of Fig. 3). The reduction of glass walls has about as

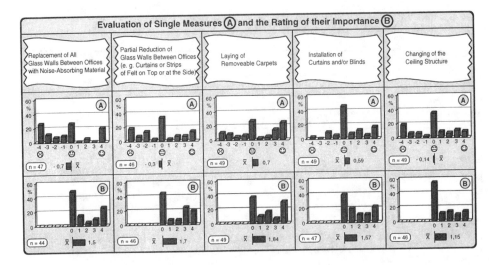

Figure 3: Evaluation of potential improvements for the acoustic situation on a bipolar scale (A) with ratings from "-4" (absolutely not desirable) to "+4" (very desirable) and evaluation of the improvements with regard to their importance (B) from a subjective viewpoint ("0" = unimportant; "1" = somewhat important; "2" = fairly important; "3" = important; "4" = very important)

many advocates as opponents, although this action is considered fairly important (average rating of the importance = "+1.7"). At least the laying of removable carpets or runners is considered positive in the mean. For hygienic reasons and due to the cost for the weekly cleaning, this action was not considered very desirable, but it was finally accepted as an alternative for unwanted non-removable carpet. The hanging of curtains and/or blinds instead of the present plastic slats at the window (they could be adjusted to the sun in order to avoid blinding) is not favored unanimously, but it is accepted on average. A change of the ceiling structure — a presumably expensive measure with little expected utility (based on selective and makeshift measures that were carried out to date) — is evaluated fairly equally both good and bad. Half of all persons questioned considers this action as not important (rating "0").

Although combined measures (which are not discussed here) are evaluated more favorably, it must be noticed that, surprisingly, the willingness of the affected people to accept concrete changes is not very high, even with the unacceptable acoustic situation.

4. Development of Concrete Suggestions for the Improvement of the Acoustic Situation in Rooms with Cost-utility Prognosis

From a work science point of view, there is — in spite of the various subjective reservations — no doubt that the acoustic situation can only be improved via a significant enlargement of the noise-absorbing areas. Because the absorption coefficient α of absorption materials depends greatly on the frequency, the effectiveness of the noise absorption is — depending on the spectrum of frequencies of the noises that have to be "fought" — highly varying. Thus, identical results cannot be expected for the noises from various sources such as "ringing of the telephone," "impact noise," and "conversations" or "noises from machinery."

The actual "equivalent absorption area" which consists of several materials and areas can be calculated according to the equation $A = \Sigma \alpha_i \cdot S_i$. Also the reverberation time as described before can be approximately determined according to Sabine's formula $T = 0.16 \cdot V/A$ (see [12]).

The absorption coefficients α_i of the various materials in a room as frequency-dependent values must be taken from the manufacturer's product information.

In room 12, two sides of the office consisted of windows to a considerable extent, and a third wall was covered mostly by a cabinet; the fourth wall consisted of glass and acted as a separation between two offices. For this office, the reverberation time for the actual situation and for two different plans was calculated.

The multiplication of the surface's size S_i (for example, area of floor and ceiling 16.20 m² each or area of glass surface 25.20 m²) with the frequency-dependent (very low) values of the absorption coefficient α_i leads to the (also frequency-dependent) individual absorption areas. Summation over all absorption areas leads to the "equivalent absorption area" A. With this data, the reverberation time ranges from 0.77 s (for 125 Hz) to 0.57 s (for 4000 Hz), which is in accordance with the results from the measurements (compare lower part of Fig. 1).

The fourth wall that consisted of glass and acted as a separation between two offices was very important to the employees and they did not want to give it up, mainly for the possibility of eye contact and the increased light. Thus, the complete coverage with noise-absorbing material (which would have been promising for acoustic reasons) could not be realized. After talks with the management, at least a substantial reduction of the glass area should be considered, for example in the form of cloth or cork tiles or special acoustic wallpaper.

An improvement of the noise absorption can also be expected from various alternations of the acoustic ceiling elements. The effects on the reverberation time were determined arithmetically for two of those elements. The elements were — according to the product information of different suppliers — available in different price ranges and could be attached (removable) or could be glued on.

The assumptions were that 2/3 of the glass wall (i.e. 16.80 m²) were covered with cloth tiles and that there were acoustic tiles of 16.20 m² each. These acoustic tiles boasted relatively high degrees of absorption already beginning with 500 Hz. As a result, almost identical reverberation times for versions I and II can be expected. Both versions lead to distinct improvements (as compared to the actual situation); yet, the costs for the two versions (according to the current price lists) are quite different. The total cost for version I (without fixing material and glue) is about 600 $, whereas the total cost for version II is only about one-third of that. Moreover, the less expensive version can be expected to lead to somewhat lower values of the reverberation time.

5. Discussion

Without doubt, noise as a typical stressor has a negative impact on speech intelligibility (see e.g. [13]), performance, and well-being at work, but also on regeneration possibilities after work. This is true not only for noise levels that people complain about, but also for an unfavorable acoustic situation with reverberation times that are felt as being too long.

If emphasis is placed on acoustic communication and a high level of attention and concentration is necessary for good performance, then the disturbances from bad acoustics — especially if the persons are under time pressure and pressure to perform well — have a significantly stronger effect than when mechanistical tasks and schematic thinking and acting are required. Slightly shorter values of the reverberation time can already have overproportionally positive effects on the subjective conditions.

All influences that interfere with the process of complex decision-making — after the registration of the work contents, after the planning, thinking, and discussing of alternatives, and after the repeated "processing" or "compression" of information, for example when a technical construction is developed — must be considered potentially negative for work performance. If someone's mood clearly is one of "irritation" and "oversensibility" instead of "calmness" and "balance," the processing time might actually decrease due to "risky" decisions, but it will usually result in a higher error rate or lower work quality. Thus, the realization of the results of an extensive acoustic study [14] which could only be presented in extracts in this paper is not only economically acceptable, but even an absolutely necessary investment in the required motivation and willingness to perform as well as the actual efficiency of the staff of a company's design departments. After all, a company's success not only depends on investments for technologies such as 3D-CAD equipment, but it also depends on its employees' innovation possibility. Well-considered measures can keep costs at an acceptable level, as the examples have demonstrated.

6. References

[1]   P. Schäfer, Lärm. Kap. 4.3 in H. Schmidtke (Hrsg.): *Ergonomie*. Hanser Verlag, München/Wien, 1993, 211-257.

[2]   H. Schmidt, *Schalltechnisches Taschenbuch* 4. Auflage. Düsseldorf: VDI-Verlag, 1989.

[3]   H. Strasser, Lärm. Kap. 2.5.1 in Th. Hettinger & G. Wobbe (Hrsg.): *Kompendium der Arbeitswissenschaft*. Kiel Verlag, Ludwigshafen, 1993, 243-274.

[4]   N.N., Emissionskennwerte technischer Schallquellen (ETS) — VDI-Richtlinien. *Beuth Verlag*, Berlin.

[5]   N.N., VDI-Handbuch "Lärmminderung" Hrsg.: Normenausschuß Akustik, Lärmminderung und Schwingungstechnik (NALS). *Beuth Verlag*, Berlin.

[6]   DIN 45 635, Geräuschmessungen an Maschinen — Luftschallemission; Hüllflächen-Verfahren. *Beuth Verlag*, Berlin, 1984.

[7]   N.N., Accident Prevention Regulation — Noise (APR-Noise): UVV-Lärm: Unfallverhütungsvorschrift der gewerblichen Berufsgenossenschaften. VBG 121. *Heymanns Verlag*, Köln, 1990.

[8]   N.N., German Working Places Regulation, *Verordnung über Arbeitsstätten — Arbeitsstättenverordnung vom 20. März 1975*. Schriftenreihe "Regelwerke Arbeitsschutz" im Auftrag des Bundesministers für Arbeit und Sozialordnung. Bundesanstalt für Arbeitsschutz und Unfallforschung, Dortmund, 1976.

[9]   N.N., *Measurements in Building Acoustics*, Booklet by Brüel & Kjaer, Naerum/Dänemark, 1989.

[10] W. Fasold und E. Sonntag, *Bau- und Raumakustik*, Müller Verlag, Köln/Braunsfeld, 1987.

[11] DIN 18 041, Hörsamkeit in kleinen bis mittelgroßen Räumen. *Beuth Verlag*, Berlin, 1968.

[12] L. Cremer und H.A. Müller, *Die wissenschaftlichen Grundlagen der Raumakustik*. 2. neubearbeitete Auflage. Hirzel Verlag, Stuttgart, 1987.

[13] H. Lazarus; G. Lazarus-Mainka, and M. Schubeius, *Sprachliche Kommunikation unter Lärm*, Kiel Verlag, Ludwigshafen, 1985.

[14] K. Gruen; W. Koch, and H. Strasser, *Analyse der akustischen Situation in Büroräumen und Ausarbeitung von Lösungsvorschlägen*. Forschungsbericht (117 Seiten) im Auftrag eines mittelständischen Betriebes, Fachgebiet Arbeitswissenschaft/Ergonomie, Universität-GH-Siegen, 1993.

Advances in Occupational Ergonomics and Safety II
Edited by Biman Das and Waldemar Karwowski
IOS Press and Ohmsha, 1997

Audiometric Objectification of the Influence of the Wearing Time on the Effectiveness of Personal Hearing Protectors

Hartmut **Irle**, Dipl.-Ing., Christian **Rosenthal**, Dipl.-Ing.,
and Helmut **Strasser**, Prof. Dr.-Ing. habil.
Institute of Production Engineering/Ergonomics Division
University of Siegen, Paul-Bonatz-Str. 9-11, D-57068 Siegen/Germany

Valuable recommendations for the choice, utilization, care, and maintenance of hearing-protective devices have been laid down in the international standard DIN EN 458. Yet, by considering the wearing time of a hearing protector, this standard assumes a scarcely understandable drastic reduction in the effective attenuation even when the device is not used for only a short time in a noise-filled area. A 30-dB sound attenuation of such a protective device would, e. g., decrease to 12 dB if it were unused for only 30 min of an 8-hour (h) shift. Thus, the actual influence of a shortened wearing time on the protection of earmuffs was tested in a laboratory study using audiometric measurements of the temporary threshold shift (TTS_2) and its recovery after exposure to noise. For that purpose, the effectiveness of a hearing-protective device depending on the amount of time worn as prognosticated by DIN EN 458 was compared with the actual physiological effect of the earmuffs. 10 test subjects (Ss) participated in 3 test series (TS), each. In the first of the TS, the Ss were exposed to pop music with an average sound pressure of 106 dB(A) for 1 h, during which the Ss wore noise-insulating earmuffs with a sound attenuation of 30 dB. The Ss were exposed to the same sound pressure in TS II; however, after 30 min, the earmuffs were removed for a duration of 3¾ min. Mathematically, this reduced the sound attenuation of the earmuffs to 12 dB; i. e., the average noise level over 1 h should be 94 dB, which would be equivalent to 85 dB(A) over 8 h. In order to evaluate the actual additional physiological cost of TS II, the Ss were exposed to 94 dB(A) for 1 h without earmuffs in a third TS. This acoustic load, which is energy equivalent to the load in TS II, is also equivalent to 85 dB(A) for 8 h. The results show that the continuous wearing of the earmuffs offers secure protection. However, the energetic approach and the levelling of differently structured noise loads according to the principle of energy equivalence leads to misconceiving results. The drastic reduction of the sound attenuation of the earmuffs predicted from the energetic point of view must be regarded as exaggerated. The TTS values show that TS II – which, according to the principle of energy-damage-equivalence, should result in the same effects as TS III – represents significantly less auditory fatigue. Thus, if the earmuffs are taken off briefly, a drastic reduction in the protection – as predicted in DIN EN 458 – does not result.

1. Introduction and Topic

Since 1994, valuable recommendations for the choice, utilization, care, and maintenance of hearing-protective devices have been laid down in the international standard DIN EN 458 [1]. Yet, when considering the wearing time of a hearing protector, this standard assumes a drastic reduction in the effective attenuation even when the device is not used for only a short time in a noise-filled area. A 30-dB sound attenuation of such a protective device would, e. g., decrease by 18 dB to 12 dB if it were unused for only ½ h of an 8-h shift. If the device went unused for just 4 min of a 480-min (8-h) shift, its noise insulation would decrease from 30 dB to only 21 dB, i. e., even then an insulation loss of 9 dB would result.

This loss is illustrated in Fig. 1. If hearing protection is worn continually, e. g., for 8 h in an area with a constant noise level of 105 dB(A), then – with an assumed attenuation value of 30 dB – the worker's hearing is subjected to only 75 dB (instead of 105 dB). If, however, the protective device is not worn for only ½ h – whether this occurs all at once or over several short periods of time is irrelevant – the worker is exposed to 105 dB for those 30 min. According to the 3-dB rule (which is generally used in acoustics), an assumed doubling of the exposure time corresponds with a 3-dB reduction of the noise level, i. e., 105 dB for ½ h are equivalent to 102 dB for 1 h, 99 dB for 2 h, as well as 96 dB for 4 h or, finally, 93 dB for 8 h (cp. middle part of Fig. 1). The 105 dB over ½ h therefore seem to be equivalent to 93 dB for 8 h. Energetically, this is completely correct since both exposures involve the same dose of noise.

Therefore, when the protective device is worn for 7½ h, the hearing is exposed to a noise of 75 dB + 93 dB over 8 h, each, the latter originating from the 105 dB for ½ h. Since 75 dB + 93 dB = 93 dB according to the rules of the rating level calculation, the protector seems to have substantially decreased in value due to the ½ h during which it was not worn. When the hearing is subjected to a noise of 93 dB rather than 75 dB, 18 dB (93 dB - 75 dB) are lost, i. e., a sound attenuation of only 12 dB (rather than 30 dB) results.

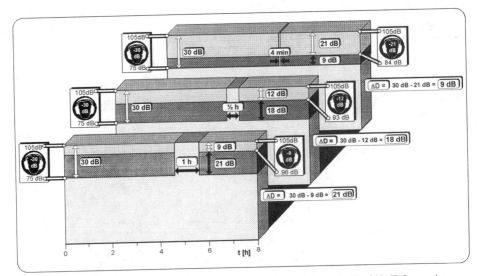

Figure 1: Reduced efficiency ΔD of a hearing protector with an insulation value D of 30 dB for a noise exposure of 105 dB / 8 h and a wearing time reduced by 1 h, ½ h, and 4 min when applying the energy equivalence principle

Even more curious is the case represented in the lower part of Fig. 1, where the hearing protection is not worn for a full hour. This results in a loss of 21 dB, which translates into a sound attenuation of only 9 dB compared to the original 30-dB attenuation.

Yet, even a short period of just 4 min without the protective device during an 8-h day presumably results in the loss of 9 dB. This all may seem plausible and reasonable according to the laws of energy equivalence, as shown in the upper part of Fig. 1. However, it seems as if such calculations according to DIN EN 458 are used to pressure the employees into continuously wearing hearing protection in order to avoid any risk to their hearing from detrimental noise. In this case, however, it seems that the energy equivalence which makes such calculations possible – as has repeatedly been shown (cp. [2], [3], [4]) – once again goes too far, since it is at least difficult to imagine and so far is an "open" question whether the aforementioned calculations are based on secured data of the actual sound attenuation of hearing protectors which are measured depending on the wearing time.

Therefore, the goal of this study was to shed some light on these speculations. It seemed reasonable to measure the actual effect of the hearing-protective devices via test exposures using relatively simple audiometric methods. The main idea was that the actual reduced protection which results when a noise-appropriate protective device is not worn for a limited amount of time during exposure to a high level of noise would be indicated by auditory fatigue, i. e., Temporary Threshold Shifts (TTS-values).

2. Methods

2.1 Test Set-up and Working Hypotheses

Due to pragmatical and especially ethical reasons, such tests are limited. Therefore, experiments on test persons involving exposures which exceed the noise limits for the workplace cannot be carried out. That is, exposures which are higher than the energy equivalent rating level of 85 dB(A) over an 8-h day (without hearing protection) cannot be utilized in the laboratory. Furthermore, experiments on groups of test subjects (Ss) involving 8-h exposures to noise would require an inappropriately high expense. Therefore, when the ethically still allowable limit of 85 dB(A) for 8 h is utilized as an orientation value, it should also be permissible to experiment using energy equivalent exposures of 88 dB / 4 h, 91 dB / 2 h, or 94 dB / 1 h.

As can be seen in the lower part of Fig. 2, an experimental, practicable exposure could also be chosen using this configuration – keeping in consideration the fact that, according to previous experiments (cp. [5], [6]), 94 dB for 1 h numerically result in approximately equal threshold shifts as 85 dB / 8 h. So, in one of three test series (TS III), 10 Ss were exposed to 94 dB / 1 h, after which the TTS_2 values and their recovery were measured. In a second test series TS I (cp. lower part of Fig. 2), the Ss were exposed again but now to 106 dB for 1 h according to a cross-over test design where they acted as their own control. However, in this case the Ss were protected by noise-insulating earmuffs with a Single Number Rating (SNR-) noise reduction (cp. [7]) of 30 dB, so that with 106 dB - 30 dB = 76 dB only very minimal threshold shifts could be expected. Whether or not the earmuffs actually provided the protection promised was also assessed using threshold measurements.

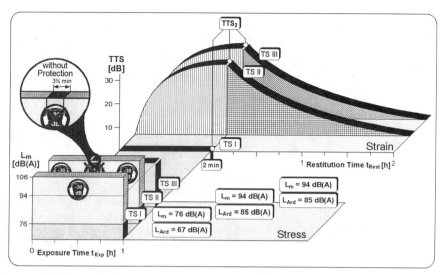

Figure 2:   Schematic representation of the 3 exposures and hypothetical physiological responses, i. e., growth and restitution of the temporary threshold shifts (TTS)

Finally, in TS II (cp. middle part of Fig. 2), the Ss removed the earmuffs for the short time of 3¾ min during a 1-h exposure to 106 dB, such that a sound exposure of 106 dB for that amount of time (taking into account the 3-dB rule) is equivalent to a continuous noise of 94 dB for 1 h, as described in the first exposure.

Therefore, one should expect the test series TS II and TS III to result in identical threshold shifts – as hypothetically represented in the upper part of Fig. 2 – which again can be interpreted as physiological cost brought upon the human organism by the energy-equivalent noise situations. However, if the test series in which the earmuffs were removed for a short period of time result in a significantly lower threshold shift than the shift resulting from 94 dB / 1 h, then it must be assumed that the loss of sound attenuation during shortened wearing times as propagated by DIN EN 458 and exemplarily described in the introduction is an exaggeration. Then it seems reasonable to assume that the scepticism reflected in DIN EN 458 is without scientific as well as practicable reasoning. Thus, it would have to be considered an over-subtle broad hint which is not conformable with the work-physiological human characteristics.

2.2 Noise Load and Hearing Protective Device

The Ss were exposed to noise in a soundproof cabin via loudspeakers; the exact desired sound pressure levels for both ears were achieved using an artificial head measurement system. Noise exposure in the form of music was chosen as the acoustic load for the experiment, since such an exposure seems at least as realistic and valid for the objectives of the study as White or Pink Noise which is usually utilized in laboratory experiments. The exposure during the "leak" time of 3¾ min, however, had to be comparable to the exposure during the remainder of the time with respect to dynamics (e. g., peak and average levels), frequency, and time structure. Thus, a music segment which is exactly 3¾ min long was selected; the selection was then copied and pasted together 16 times resulting in an uninterrupted, continuous hour of music. Furthermore, it had to be ensured that the level distribution of the exposure was as homogeneous as possible over the entire frequency range without distinct bass components and that it was not characterized by a specific content of impulses as is the case in heavy metal music.

The earmuff Optac Vario VOL SD was used which in a previous study [8] has proven – according to the suggested method of ISO 4869 and also according to measurements taken via an artificial head measurement system – a protective device with a SNR-value of 30 dB averaged over the frequency.

2.3 Test Subjects and Audiometric Methods of Selection and Evaluation

Only hearing-physiologically normal Ss were chosen for the experiments. The male Ss which were selected (age: 26 ± 6 years; height: 185 ± 5 cm; weight: 80 ± 10 kg) could – according to [9] – only exhibit hearing threshold shifts of no more than 15 dB as compared to persons with normal hearing for frequencies of up to 2 kHz and threshold shifts of no more than 25 dB for frequencies above 2 kHz. On each testing day, the resting thresholds before the exposures and the TTS_2 values after the exposures were determined for the Ss, whereby the frequency during which the highest threshold shifts occurred first always had to be determined. These threshold shifts usually occurred at 4 kHz or 6 kHz and were finally determined over the restitution time until recovery was completed.

3. Results

The upper part of Fig. 3 shows the measured values of the hearing threshold shifts (differences between the TTS values and the individual resting threshold at the respective frequency of maximal threshold shift) as determined for the 10 Ss for the test series with an exposure to 94 dB / 1 h. Furthermore, the arithmetic means and the regression line are shown. It is noticeable that significant threshold shifts occur after the exposure; the average of these shifts is approximately 20 dB and it takes up to 2 h for a full recovery. Thus, legally permissible exposures with a rating level of 85 dB(A) for 8 hours (cp. [10], [11]) lead to essential physiological cost to the hearing which may not be underestimated.

The middle part of Fig. 3 shows that the majority of the Ss experienced absolutely no threshold shift when exposed to 106 dB while wearing the protector. In the case of the Ss who did experience a hearing threshold shift, the shift was hardly objectifiable (usually less than 4 dB), and the Ss recovered fully within mere minutes. Thus, the earmuffs actually can be considered effective protection for exposures of up to 106 dB(A).

Finally, the lower part of Fig. 3 shows the results for the test series in which the Ss were exposed to 106 dB without hearing protection for a period of 3¾ min, which is energy equivalent to 94 dB for 1 h. On average, such an exposure results in threshold shifts of approximately only 10 dB; fortunately, recovery lasts approximately only 1h.

A simplified summary of the test results in Fig. 4 again shows that although the removal of the protective device is not without consequences, the effects are by no means as dramatic as the energy-equivalence principle upon which DIN EN 458 is based would have us believe. The physiological cost in TS II is significantly lower than in TS III. Finally, integration of the postexposure threshold shifts until their total disappearance results in significantly different values for the three test series. The Integrated Restitution Temporary Threshold Shift (IRTTS) value for TS I in which the device is continuously worn is only 3 dBmin. The exposure to 94 dB / 1 h in TS III, however, results in 503 dBmin. The brief removal of the earmuffs in TS II which is energy equivalent to 94 dB / 1 h resulted in 146 dBmin, i. e., the physiological cost is less than one-third of that in TS III.

4. Discussion and Final Conclusions

The dramatic decrease in protection of hearing protectors due to shortened wearing time – as it is stated in national and international standards – cannot be supported by these experimental results. Incidentally, the calculations of supposed losses in the insulation in DIN EN 458 are independent of the immission level and lead to losses that greatly vary in size between hearing protective devices whose effectiveness varies by nature. It can be calculated that the insulation of ear plugs with an insulation value of, e. g., 20 dB is reduced to 12 dB due to a "leak" of ½ h during an 8-h shift, i. e., it is reduced by 8 dB. Earmuffs whose insulation values of, e. g., 30 dB or 35 dB are also reduced to the same 12 dB are even more underrated. The loss of 18 dB or 23 dB simply makes no sense.

Finally, the point in time at which the hearing protector is removed is of significance for the protection. In this study, the midpoint of the exposure time was consciously chosen for removal of the device. Removal of the earmuffs towards the end of the exposure would certainly have resulted in higher threshold shifts which can be measured in the time after noise exposure. On the contrary, the removal or the delayed putting . on of the earmuffs at the beginning of the exposure should cause scarcely measurable threshold shifts after the exposure since possible hearing threshold shifts can almost disappear when the protective device ensures that the ears are exposed to noise immissions only below 70 dB(A).

In order to obtain information about the maximal magnitude of the threshold shift immediately after the hearing protective device was put on again or about the premature removal at the end of the exposure, a further study was carried out in which the hearing threshold shifts after a singular exposure of 106 dB for 3¾ min on the same Ss was measured as a control. The average of the TTS_2 values was 14.9 dB, i. e., they were objectively measurably lower than the values after the energy equivalent exposure to 94 dB / 1 h.

A short-term removal of a protector such as 3¾ min within 1 h, which is approximately equivalent to a ½-h removal within 8 h, does not end up in the prognosticated drastic reduction in protection. Instead of the essential auditory fatigue represented in an IRTTS value of 503 dB min, a reduction to 146 dB min, i. e., approximately one-third, resulted. Incidentally, this sum of threshold shifts can be considered a descriptive indicator for the physiological cost of work load, similar to the sum of work-related increases of heart rate above a resting level which still exist after a preceeding dynamic muscle work above the endurance level.

While it seems reasonable that the removal of the hearing protective device over an extended period of time should be avoided, the statistically secured results of this study show that "energy equivalence = strain equivalence" cannot be valid, just as it would be senseless to assume that the equation "energy equivalence = interference equivalence" is permissible in the context of the psychological (extra-aural) effects of noise. Thus, predictions such as the ones cited in the introduction should not be used to put pressure on the employees that are subjected to a noisy environment. However, greatest care should be exercised with respect to wearing comfort and sufficiently effective insulation values (cp. VDI 2560 [12]) when personal hearing protective devices are selected.

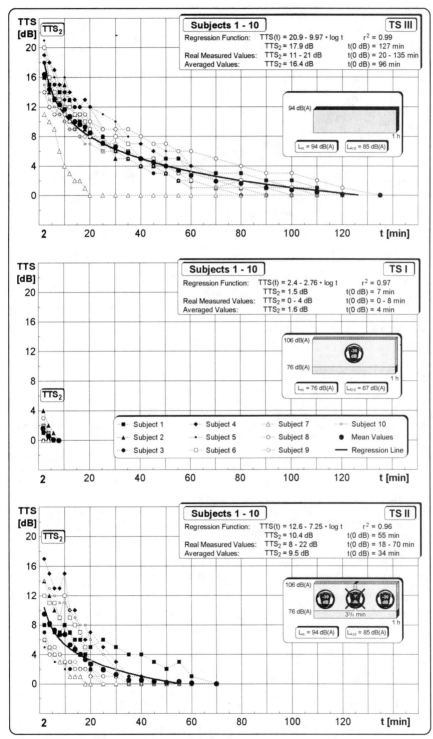

Figure 3: Individual and mean temporary threshold shifts and their restitution time course after the exposures of the test series TS I (middle), TS II (lower part), and TS III (upper part)

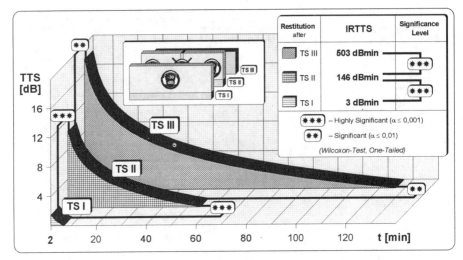

Figure 4: Restitution time course TTS(t) and physiological cost IRTTS with symbolic marking of the significance level of differences between the test series TS I, II, and III

Finally, if the earmuffs are taken off briefly, a drastic reduction in the protection – as predicted in DIN EN 458 – does not result. Again, this is a classic example that the standards and regulations for noise immission on man do not correspond with the actual physiological facts and, therefore, can only be used in a very limited manner. Utilization of the principle of energy equivalence has proven problematic in numerous studies (e. g., cp. [13], [14]); thus, the standards and regulations have been built upon an untrustworthy foundation.

5. References

[1]   DIN EN 458, *Hearing Protectors; Recommendations for Selection, Use, Care and Maintenance;* Guidance Document, 1993.

[2]   H. Strasser, Dosismaxime und Energie-Äquivalenz — Ein Kernproblem des präventiven Arbeitsschutzes bei der ergonomischen Beurteilung von Umgebungsbelastungen. In: H. Strasser (Hrsg.): *Arbeitswissenschaftliche Beurteilung von Umgebungsbelastungen — Anspruch und Wirklichkeit des präventiven Arbeitsschutzes.* 9-31. Ecomed Verlag, Landsberg/Lech, 1995.

[3]   H. Strasser, Curiosities of Conventional Noise Rating Procedures. In: A. Mital et al. (Eds.): *Advances in Occupational Ergonomics and Safety I.* ISOES, Cincinnati/Ohio, USA, 1996, pp. 619-626.

[4]   H. Strasser, and J. M. Hesse, The Equal Energy Hypothesis versus Physiological Cost of Environmental Work Load. *Archives of Complex Environmental Studies* 5 (1-2) (1993) 9-25.

[5]   J. D. Miller, Effects of Noise on People. *J. Acoustics Soc. Am.* 56 (3) (1974) 729-764.

[6]   H. Strasser; J. M. Hesse, and H. Irle, Hearing Threshold Shift after Energy Equivalent Exposure to Impulse and Continuous Noise. In: A. C. Bittner, and P. C. Champney (Eds.): *Advances in Industrial Ergonomics and Safety VII*, Taylor & Francis, 1995, pp. 241-248.

[7]   ISO 4869-2, *Acoustics; Hearing Protectors; Part 2: Estimation of Effective A-weighted Sound Pressure Levels when Hearing Protectors are Worn,*1994.

[8]   J. M. Hesse; H. Irle, and H. Strasser, Objective Measurement of Hearing Protection Provided by Earmuffs Versus Subjectively-Determined Sound Attenuation at the Hearing Threshold. In: A. Mital et al. (Eds.): *Advances in Occupational Ergonomics and Safety I.* ISOES, Cincinnati/Ohio, USA, 1996a, pp. 627-632.

[9]   ISO 4869-1, *Acoustics; Hearing Protectors; Part 1: Subjective Method for the Measurement of Sound Attenuation,* 1990.

[10] N. N., *German Working Places Regulations.* Arbeitsstätten – Vorschriften und Richtlinien, § 15 Schutz gegen Lärm, 1988.

[11] N. N., *Accident Prevention Regulation-Noise,* UVV-Lärm, Unfallverhütungsvorschrift der gewerblichen Berufsgenossenschaften (VBG 121), C. Heymanns Verlag, Köln, 1990.

[12] VDI 2560, *Persönlicher Schallschutz.* VDI-Verlag, Düsseldorf, 1983.

[13] J.M. Hesse; E. Vogt; H. Irle, and H. Strasser, Physiological Cost of Energy-Equivalent Noise Exposures with a Rating Level of 85 dB(A) — Restitution of a Continuous Noise-Induced Temporary Threshold Shift Under Resting Conditions and Under the Influence of an Energetically Negligible Continuous Noise Exposure of 70 dB(A). In: A. Mital et al. (Eds.): *Advances in Occupational Ergonomics and Safety I.* ISOES, Cincinnati/Ohio, USA, 1996b, pp. 639-644.

[14] H. Irle.; J. M. Hesse, and H. Strasser, Physiological Cost of Energy-Equivalent Noise Exposures with a Rating Level of 85 dB(A) — Hearing Threshold Shifts Associated with Energetically Negligible Continuous and Impulse Noise. *International Journal of Industrial Ergonomics*, in press, 1997.

Advances in Occupational Ergonomics and Safety II
Edited by Biman Das and Waldemar Karwowski
IOS Press and Ohmsha, 1997

Transmission of vibration from handle to hand, effect of biodynamic factors

Toppila, E. (1), Starck, J. (1), Pyykkö, I. (2)
(1) Finnish Institute of Occupational Health, Department of Physics,
Laajaniityntie 1, FIN-01620, Finland
(2) Helsinki University Central Hospital, Haartmaninkatu 2-4 E,
FIN-00290 Helsinki, Finland

The transmission of vibration from the handle of a vibrating tool to the hand is known to depend of the hand-grip force of the operator. We have developed a new method for the evaluation of the role of physiological factors in the transmission of vibration from the handle to the hand. The vibration of the handle was measured with an accelerometer mounted into the handle. The transmitted vibration was measured from the hand using laser-Doppler techniques. The evaluation method is based on the use of transfer function. A high coherence indicates a good transmission of vibration. This method was applied to forest workers in Suomussalmi county in northern Finland. A handle with a force transducer was mounted an a shaker and the transmission was measured using the method. The shaker measurements show that the transmission depends on the hand-grip force and the mass of the operator. The same experiment was repeated using a chain saw. During the experiment chain saw operators used the trained grip techniques allowing low hand-grip forces. In spite of this the measurements showed that relatively high hand-grip forces may occur when the blade is forced trough the wood. The experiment indicates that the highest risk of a vibration disease has a light weighted operator who is trying to force the saw.

1. Introduction

Workers' exposure to vibration is evaluated by measuring the magnitude of vibration at the handle of the tool [1]. Only the vibration transmitted to the hand can have an injurious effect on the worker. The procedures for the measurements from the hand or any part of the body when exposed to vibration have not been standardised. The dynamic response of the hand-arm system has been studied by several investigators. Most of the studies deal with the mechanical impedance of the hand which is determined by measuring simultaneously the velocity of the vibration and the dynamic force as close as possible to the contact surface of the hand and vibrating handle [2]. It seems, however, that the results of the impedance measurements reported by different authors are not in agreement [3]. This discrepancy may arise from the differences in measuring methods and measuring devices. Transmission of vibration can be described by analysing the frequency response function between the handle and the hand. This requires simultaneous vibration measurements in the vibrating handle and the hand. Generally an accelerometer has been used also for the measurements in the hand, but it presents limitations, especially in frequency range, due to the unsolid mounting of an accelerometer onto human tissue [4]. A new approach for the measurements is provided by applying the laser-Doppler technique which became commercially available some years ago. This techniques requires only a small piece of retroreflective tape on the surface of a vibrating object, thus minimising the loading effect of the measuring system at the point being measured. Recently Starck & al [4] has shown that the coherence function can be used as the sensitive measure of the transmission of vibration from tool handle to arm. They suggested that transmission depends, in addition to the hand-grip force, on the weight of the worker.

The aim of the present study was to evaluate the effect of the biological structure of the hand with different grip forces on the transmission of vibration from the handle to the hand.

2. Material and methods

The measurements were performed in Suomussalmi county in Northern Finland. 39 forest workers working for Metsähallitus were studied. The mean age was 46 and range 29 – 56. The mean weight of the subjects was 77 kg and range 53 – 103 (fig 1.).

The first measurement was performed in a small cottage equipped with the test system. A handle supplied with force measuring transducers on each side of the handle and an analogue display unit was mounted to the vibration exciter (Bruel & Kjaer 4813). The measurements were taken for different grip forces: 10, 20 N and at maximum grip forces which varied between 50 to 80 N. The handle was held in two different ways, in touch with the third digits of the hand, and in touch with the middle of the palm and thumb (fig 1). The shaker was excited with white noise at frequencies of 0 to 1.6 kHz generated by a random noise generator built in a 4-channel Dynamic Signal Analyser HP 35670A. The measurements were taken simultaneously from the handle by an accelerometer, from the wrist by fastening an accelerometer (B&K4375) with a tightener and plastic support (5) and from the distal end of the third metacarpal bone by a Laser Velocity Transducer (B&K 8323). The consistency of both transducers was controlled by simultaneous measurements from the same point. The frequency resolution in HP 35670A analyser was 4 Hz and the dynamic range 90 dB. The unweighted acceleration level was adjusted to 10 m/s^2.

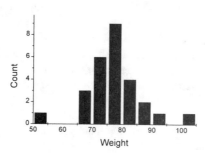

Figure 1. Distribution of test subject weights.

The coherence function measured for the acceleration signals [5]. If the coherence exceeded 0.7, the transmission of vibration was rated good at this frequency. As analysis function the total bandwidth with good transmission was used.

Figure 2. The positions of the handle during the measurements. A) grip with palm b) grip with fingers.

The second measurement was performed using a chainsaw (Husqvarna 162). A force measuring transducer on each side of the handle and an accelerometer (B&K4375) were mounted on the handle. The test subject was asked to cut slices from an about 30 cm diameter timber. The accelerometer and the sum output of the force transducer were connected to a 4-channel dynamic signal analyser (HP 35670A). The instrument was set to collect time history for 60 s with a 400 Hz bandwidth. Altogether 22 subjects performed both tests.

3. Results

When using forces 10 N and 20 N with finger grip the transmission bandwidths were low. No significant difference between 10 N and 20 N force was observed. When using maximum grip force the transmission bandwidth increased remarkably except for the heaviest subjects (over 90 kg).

With palm grip the results did not differ much with grip forces 10N and 20 N (fig 4). In both cases there were a group of men with low transmission bandwidth and a group with an elevated transmission bandwidth. In the latter group the weight of the person affected to the physiological dimensions have an important role in the transmission of vibration which may lead to the genesis of vibration hazards especially in work tasks where high grip forces are needed and the vibration contains high frequency and impulsive components.

The dependency of transmission bandwidth of the body weight was not as clear as in our previous study [4]. In the previous study only 6 test subjects were used. None of them was working daily with vibrating tools. Thus it is possible that they are more vulnerable to vibration than professionals used in the present study. Statistically 6 persons is a small sample which may also explain the differences in the results. Both studies confirmed that the body weight is an important parameter in the transmission of vibration from handle to arm.

All the forest workers were trained to use low hand-grip forces. Still during the chain saw operation 60 % of the subjects used handgrip forces exceeded 20 N. The high forces occurred when the engine was running at high speed and produced high vibration levels (fig. 5). The fact that 40 % of subjects used smaller forces show, that it is possible to work in a safer way.

The weight distribution of the test subjects disabled us to define the exact dependency of transmission bandwidth on body weight. Too many of the test subjects weighted 70-85 kg. Due to physical demands of the work it was not possible to find many light and heavy test subjects. Thus a quantitative analysis was not possible to perform.

6. Conclusions

High handgrip forces may occur if the saw is forced during the sawing operation. High handgrip force increases the transmission of vibration from handle to hand. The probability of high transmission depends on the weight of the operator.

References

[1] Taylor W, Brammer AJ. Vibration Effects of the Hand and Arm in Industry: An Introduction and Review. In: Brammer AJ, Taylor W. (eds) Vibration Effects on the Hand and Arm in Industry. New York , John Wiley&Sons,1982: 1-12.
[2] Burström L. Absorption of vibration energy in the human hand and arm. Luleå University of Technology 1990:87 D
[3] Hempstock TI, O'Connor DE. Accuracy of measuring impedance in the hand-arm system. Scand J Work Environ Health 12, 1986;4: 355-358.
[4] Starck J. Toppila E., influence of hand dimensions and grip force on vibration transmission into the hand, acute effects and symptoms of work with vibrating hand-help powered tools exposing with vibrating hand-help powered tools exposing the operator to impact and reactions forces, edeted by Steve Kihlberg. Arbete och Hälsa (1995:1).
[5] Bendat J., Piersol A. Random data, Analysis and measurement procedures. John Wiley & sons, New York, 1986
[6] Färkkilä M., Pyykkö I., Korhonen O., Starck J., Hand grip forces during chain saw operation and virbration white finger in lumberjacks, Br. J. Ind. Med. 36, 1979: 336-341.
[7] Starck J. Characteristics of vibration, hand grip force, and hearing loss in vibration syndrome. Publications of the University of Kuopio, Natural sciences, Original reports 4/84.

bandwidth. With maximum handgrip force there was a clear weight dependency. With test subjects over 90 kg the effect of handgrip force was minimal. The transmission of vibration was significantly greater in this case (table 1)

Table 1. The relative number of subjects with low transmission bandwidths.

Finger grip		Palm grip	
10 N /20 N	Max. force	10 N /20 N	Max. force
85	37	41	3

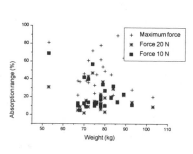

Figure 3. The transmission bandwidth of vibration in palm position with a grip-forces of 10 N, 20 N and maximum force

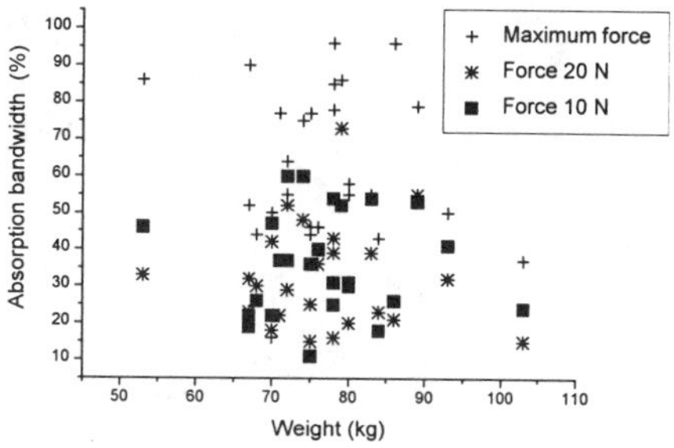

Figure 4. The transmission bandwidth of vibration in finger position with grip-forces of 10 N, 20 N and maximum force

A typical time history of the sawing test is shown in fig. 5. In all cases high grip forces occurred simultaneously with high vibration. In 60 % of the cases the mean grip force was over 20 N while the saw was running at high speed.

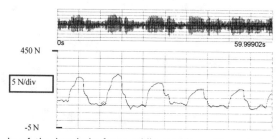

Figure 5. Example of the handgrip force while working with a chainsaw. The upper curve vibration level in the handle. The lower curve shows the handgrip force in the handle

5. Discussion

The present study confirmed earlier findings on the importance of grip force to the transmission of vibration (2,7). Among forest workers who suffered from vibration-induced white finger (VWF), the grip forces during operation with a chain saw were significantly higher than among those without any symptoms of VWF [6,7]. The results also showed that

Advances in Occupational Ergonomics and Safety II
Edited by Biman Das and Waldemar Karwowski
IOS Press and Ohmsha, 1997

Excessive Noise Levels that Enhance Special Effects, Are You Aware?

K. Osborne, R. Yearout and D. Lisnerski
Department of Management and Accountancy
The University of North Carolina at Asheville (UNCA)
Asheville, NC 28804-3299

Abstract. Entertainment special effects has been greatly enhanced by audio technology. Increasing sound levels and frequencies without a loss of clarity is now an effective tool for evoking audience response. Although the public may be aware of the hazards associated with power equipment and firearms, it rarely considers music or multi-media events as potentially hazardous. A recently released action film containing special effects with excessive noise levels was selected for investigation. Sixty-four percent of the variation approval rating could be explained by noise level. Although 70% of the subjects could recall specific scenes containing excessive levels, only 34% could recall quiet scenes. Appeal may be associated with the basic "flight or fight" instinct, thus audiences may accept excessive noise levels in an entertainment environment that otherwise might be unacceptable.

1. Introduction

Since the public is frequently unaware of hearing damage until it is acute, hazardous noise levels associated with leisure activities is of growing concern. Although the public may be aware of the risks associated with power equipment, concerts and firearms, it does not consider activities associated with amusement parks, such as simulation, or theater multi-media presentation as potentially hazardous. Previous investigations by Brown and Yearout [1] and Gray, Swaby and Schulze [3] showed that, with the exception of rock concerts, participants give very little thought to excessive leisure noise level exposure. These observations included professionals who were fully aware of the risks associated extended exposure but elected not to alter their behavior.

Meloni and Kruger [5] found that the annoyance of impulsive noise stemming from machine gun fire, was less than the annoyance of automatic cannon shots at a military training range. Subjects were exposed to both machine gun and cannon fire simulations in a home setting. Higher disapproval of the cannon volleys can be attributed to the type of environment relative to the expected noise tolerance. In the home, subjects do not accept the unexpected annoying sound of either weapon to exist. This study illustrates a lower approval rating and less tolerance for the annoying noise if it is foreign to the environment. Bubb [2] demonstrated recall and response effects in relationship to expected noise levels. Subjects responded to noise levels associated with a given task. Perceived acceleration of an automobile's motor and noise level of the motor were directly related. Brown and Yearout [1] illustrated that loudness equates to perceived power. This phenomena appears to be just as prevalent in film and amusement park activities such as racing simulation.

Misconceptions or lack of awareness concerning hearing loss risk creates a ethical issue for producers and promoters who are aware of the hazard. Producers and promoter should insure that noise level data for popular amusement activities are obtained. This management responsibility also should include disclosure of not only the noise levels of an activity but it's associated risk.

2. Experimental Protocol

Introduction: This paper focuses on whether or not a subject's recall and response to a multi-media event, specifically film, has a relationship with excessive and or unacceptable noise levels. Also examined was the ability of the subject to discern a specific event's noise level. Several recently released films were monitored. Of the potential candidates, the film that contained special effects and excessive noise levels (dBA) such as SLOW MAX(108.70), PEAK(119.60) and 3 dB SEL(119.01). This film was observed to locate several scenes that contained significant noise and scenes that contained noise levels that were within the acceptable range. Data collected by using a specially designed multi-item semantic differential scale.

Subjects: Sixty-five volunteer subjects (27 male, 38 female) were recruited from the University community. These were randomly assigned (based upon individual schedules) into four groups. Subjects' median age was between 20 to 25 years.

Laboratory: UNCA's multi-media classroom was chosen for the experiment. Although the noise levels could not exactly duplicate those of a typical theater, this high technology classroom had the capability to control noise within +/- 2 dBA. Speakers and screens were positioned to simulate an environment that was quite comparable to a contemporary multi-theater complex auditorium.

Experimental Design: The four selected groups were then randomly assigned to one of the two conditions, loud (PEAK dBA > 100 dBA) and not loud (PEAK dBA < 90 dBA). Average exposure time was 2.3 hours. Immediately after the conclusion of the film, subjects were administered the semantic differential scale survey.

3. Results

Analytical Techniques: To insure that the data was homogeneous, Levine's Test for Homogeneity of Variances was performed at the 0.05 significance level. When conditions for normality were met, Analysis of Variance (Type III Sums of Squares) and Least Significance Differences (LSD) Tests were used. When the data was determined to be non-parametric then Satterthwaite's Approximation with Bonferroni's Adjustment were used [6]. Frequency tables were used to determine significant variables for potential correlations. Once a variable was determined to be significant, further analysis which included correlation, General Linear Model (GLM) and regression analysis procedures were applied when appropriate.

Results: Preliminary analysis determined that there were no significant interrelationships between the two "loud" groups and the two "not loud" groups. Thus the investigator was allowed to pool the four groups into two groups, "loud" and a "not loud". Pooled significant statistics are in Table 1.

Table 1: Pooled Data for Significant Variables/Conditions

Loud Group (sample size = 30)

Variable	Mean or Rating	sd
PEAK	114 dBA	12
SMAX	104 dBA	10
3 db SEL	123 dBA	4

Not Loud Group (sample size = 35)

Variable	Mean or Rating	sd
PEAK	87 dBA	3
SMAX	80 DbA	3
3 db SEL	110 dBA	4

Other Variables/Perceptions
Film Approval Rating : 88% on a 100% scale
Median Perceived Noise Level: 105-110 dBA

Other Variables/Perceptions
Film Approval Rating : 69% on a 100% scale
Median Perceived Noise Level: 85-90 dBA

4. Analysis

General: There ware no significant age or gender effects. The two group means for all selected variables were statically significantly different at the 0.05 significance level. Variables of interest to the research question are addressed the following sub-paragraphs.

Recall: Subjects were queried to identify the loudest scene, next loudest scene and third loudest scene in the film. Seventy-seven percent of the subjects identified the previously selected scenes in order of loudness. When subjects were asked to identify quiet scenes, 34% could not recall any scene as being quiet. Of those that could recall a quiet event, no more than 6% identified the same scene. One specific scene that combined excessive noise with surprise was recalled by over 90%. Though this scene was not the film's loudest, it does typify the effective use of technology to evoke response through visual and audio stimulation.

Discomfort: Perceived noise levels were estimated by comfort discomfort votes on a semantic differential scale much like the Borg Vote for estimating heart rate. Votes for all responses are illustrated by percentage in Table 1.

Table 2: Estimate Film Noise Levels Based on Discomfort

vote (%)	(1)	(2)	(4)	(7)	(29)	(5)	(36)	(9)	(7)
	not loud		somewhat loud		loud		very loud		too loud
	+-----------+-----------+-----------+---------+---------+---------+---------+---------+								
noise (dBA)	75		85		95		105		>115
discomfort	none		not noticeable		some discomfort		ears ringing		hurt my ears

Approval Ratings: There was a significant correlation (0.801) between film approval ratings and perceived noise level. A regression model, 0.01 significance level and multiple correlation coefficient of 0.64, depicts that 64% of the variation in the approval rating could be explained by the perceived noise level. Figure 1 depicts this relationship between acceptance rating and perceived noise level.

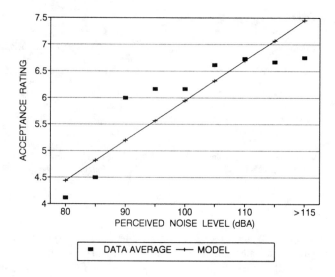

Figure 1: Film Approval Relationship with Noise Level

5. Conclusions

Based upon this exploratory research, it appears that film producers may be taking advantage of current technology to enhance special effects through noise levels that would be unacceptable in the workplace. An example is the just released "Star Wars" trilogy that touts an enhanced sound experience. Although audiences are aware the discomfort from excessive noise, this type of entertainment receives high acceptance. This appeal may be due to the basic "flight or fight" instinct, thus audiences accept these noise levels that under other circumstances might be unacceptable.

References

[1] P. Brown and R. Yearout, Impacts of Leisure Activity Noise Levels on Safety Procedures and Policy in the Industrial Environment, International Journal of Industrial Ergonomics, Vol. 7, Elsevier Science Publishers, Amsterdam, (1991) 341-346.

[2] H. Bubb, Experiments to the Contradiction, Noise as Strain or Noise as Feedback, Advances in Occupational Ergonomics and Safety I, Vol. 2, International Society for Occupational Ergonomics and Safety, Cincinnati, (1996) 650-659.

[3] D. Gray, M. Swaby and L. Schulze, The Use of Personal Stereo Equipment (PSE) in the Professional Engineering Office Environment, Advances in Industrial Ergonomics and Safety VII, Tylor and Francis, London, (1995) 259-264.

[4] J. Howe and R. Yearout, Music Style, Age and gender Relationships to Preferred Noise Levels for Headset Cassette Players, Advances in Industrial Ergonomics and Safety IV, Taylor and Francis, London, (1992) 1335-1340.

[5] T. Meloni and H. Krueger, Annoyance of Impulsive Noise Measured in the Laboratory, Advances in Occupational Ergonomics and Safety I, Vol. 2, International Society for Occupational Ergonomics and Safety, Cincinnati, (1996) 645-649.

[6] G. Milliken and D. Johnson, Analysis of Mess Data, Volume I: Designed Experiments, ISBN 0-534-02713-X (v.1), 1984.

Advances in Occupational Ergonomics and Safety II
Edited by Biman Das and Waldemar Karwowski
IOS Press and Ohmsha, 1997

SOUND PRESSURE LEVELS, USAGE, LISTENING PREFERENCE, SITUATION OF USE, AND HAZARD OF EXPOSURE KNOWLEDGE OF COLLEGE STUDENTS USING PERSONAL STEREO EQUIPMENT

Maria Hayne, Lawrence J. H. Schulze, Jacob Chen, Department of Industrial Engineering, University of Houston, Houston, TX 77204-4812, U.S.A., and Leonardo Quintana, Department of Industrial Engineering, Javeriana University, Santafé de Bogotá, Colombia (S.A.)

The sound pressure level (SPL) of personal stereo equipment (PSE) used by 100 college students was measured. Sixty-one percent listened to music at SPLs and durations associated with the risk of incurring hearing damage. No difference was found between female students. Studying was the activity associated with the greatest use followed by Other (jogging, exercising, etc.). Pop and Other (country & western, rap, etc.) music were listened most. Almost one half of the participants indicated that listening to PSE was not hazardous and they would not incur any hearing damage due to using PSE for long durations and/or at volume levels sampled.

1. Intoduction and Background

Noise exposure in the work place, has been known to produce hearing loss for a long time [1]. Within the last decade, light weight personal stereo equipment has proliferated in use in both recreational and work environments. Several studies have been conducted to determine the effects of personal stereos on hearing.

Brown and Yearout [2] measured leisure activity and workplace noise levels. Their results indicated that mean leisure activity noise levels (99 dB) were 10 dB higher than occupational noise levels. Fearn and Hanson [3] placed the microphone of a sound level meter against the earphone of a recorder playing pop music and found that the sound level (dBA) ranged from 66 dBA to 102 dBA at 1/4 and full volume levels. Hellstrom and Axelsson [4] measured the maximum output SPL from different types of portable cassette players. These authors found that the mean SPL was 112 dBA at the highest 'comfortable' level selected by the participants.

Howe and Yearout [5] sampled sound pressure levels of 100 participants. These authors found that males preferred mean SPL levels of 91.4 dBA versus 86.5 dBA for females. For supra-aural headphones, the mean dBA level was 89.7 while the mean dBA level was 79.7 for semi-aural. Further, the 15-19 year age group was associated with the greatest mean SPL level (95.3) followed, respectively, by <15 years (91.8), 50-59 (82.4), 30-39 (81.6), 40-49 (81.0), 20-29 (79.8), and <60 (77.1). Rap music was found to be associated with the highest mean SPL (96.3) followed, respectively, by Rock (88.3), Country Western (86.8), Jazz (85.5), New-age (84.8), Pop (83.1), and Classical (78.8).

Rice, Rossi, and Olina [6] studied the listening habits of personal cassette player (PCP) users. The results indicated that pop music was the predominant type of music listened to and PCP use most often occurred in the home. Further, 20% of PCP users admitted to symptoms of ringing or dullness of hearing following PCP use. Males tended to use their PCP for longer periods and at higher levels than female PCP users.

Skrainar, Royster, Berger, and Pearson [7] determined time-weighted average (TWA) sound levels of personnel using personal radios in a textile manufacturing facility. These researchers found that the mean TWA for workers not using personal radios was 86.6 dBA and 88.5 dBA for workers who did use personal radios during work activities.

Yearout, Lisnerski, Kwiatkowski, Locke, and Edwards [8] compared leisure noise level preferences of workers exposed to either 'loud' (above 85 dBA) and 'not loud' (below 85 dBA) work environments. Their results indicated that the 'loud' group preferred noise levels significantly higher than their pre-work levels.

Most recently, Hayn and Schulze [9] compared the SPL levels recorded for students using PSE and then listening to their car stereos. The results indicated that the mean SPL during PSE use was dBA while the mean SPL recorded when listening to the car stereos was 91 dBA.

The purpose of this study was to evaluate the PSE listening habits of college students and determine their attitudes toward the risk of listening to PSE for long durations and/or at high volume levels.

2. Method

2.1. Participants

100 randomly-selected college students (64 males and 36 females) participated in the study. The mean age of the participants was 22.6 years and ranged from 18-33 years of age. Business Administration, Natural Sciences, Engineering, Humanities and Fine Arts, Social Science and Education were the educational disciplines most represented. All classifications (Freshman, Sophomores, Juniors, Seniors, and Graduate Students) participated.

2.2. Apparatus

A Quest model 2800 integrating sound pressure level meter, calibrated before each measurement and set at the A weighting, was used to record the SPL emitted from the PSE headphones.

2.3. Procedure

Students walking on campus and visibly wearing headphones were asked to participate in the study. The students were asked to remove their headsets without changing the volume setting on the PSE and the SPL measurements were recorded by placing the microphone of the SPL meter against the left and right speakers of the headset. The peak and mean SPL measurements were recorded for a duration of 3.81 minutes, the mean song duration determined from a pilot study. A Student-t test was conducted to assess differences between and among levels of factors of interest.

3.   RESULTS

3.1. Gender

The percentage of male and female participants listening to PSE at given SPL levels is presented as Figure 1. As can be seen, the distributions are quite similar. However, the majority of the male participants (68%) listened to their PSE at levels over 85 dBA ($p < 0.05$).

3.2. Hours Used Per Week

Although the distributions of listening times (hours) throughout the listening week were different (Figure 2), the mean numbers of hours male and female students reported listening to their PSE were, essentially, equivalent (21.11 hours/week and 20.71 hours/week, respectively, $p > 0.05$).

3.3. Hours of Continuous Use and Listening Material

Separated by gender, females used their PSE for slightly longer periods of continuous use than did their male counterparts. However, these differences were not statistically significant ($p > 0.05$). The majority of the PSE users listened to Pop Music (25%) followed, respectively, by Other (24%), Speech (20%), Jazz (12%), Rock (11%), and Classical (8%). The Other category consisted of country, rap, gospel, etc. and was not specified by students in the questionnaire.

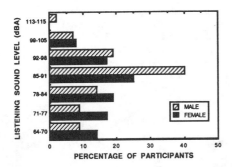

Figure 1. Distribution of listening sound levels (dBA) by gender.

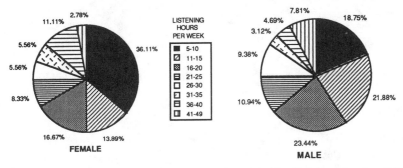

Figure 2. Distribution of listening hours per week reported by female and male participants.

3.4. Listening Situation

The majority of participants (41.94%) used their personal stereos while Studying, followed, respectively, by Other (35.48%), Work (8.60%), Everything (7.53%), and Car (6.45%). The Other category included jogging, exercising, walking between classes, etc..

3.5. Attitude Toward Personal Stereo Usage

As can be seen from Figure 3, over 41% of the participants indicated that the use of personal stereos does not cause any damage to hearing. Thirty-five percent had doubts about the damage that PSE could cause, and only 23% were aware of the risk of possible damage. A summary of the responses is presented in Figure 6 where: LONG = long duration of exposure; DON'T = use of PSE does not cause hearing loss; LOUD = exposure to high SPL may cause hearing loss; MAYBE = maybe PSE use is related to hearing loss risk; NO = PSE use is not related to risk of hearing loss; PROB = PSE use is probably related to the risk of hearing loss; and YES = PSE use is related to an increased risk of hearing loss.

4.   DISCUSSION

The mean SPL recorded across male and female participants was 85.5 dBA. Further, 61% of the participants were listening to sound levels which are considered high enough to increase the risk of incurring hearing loss. This percentage is fully 11% to 36% higher than that which has been previously estimated. In addition, 66% of the participants felt that either PSE use presented no risk or doubted that PSE presented any risk to incurring hearing loss. Obviously, these participants were oblivious to the risk of temporary and/or permanent hearing damage from listening to PSE for long durations and/or at high volume levels. Although these participants are seeking higher education, current and potential PSE users should be educated as to the potential risk of long-term hearing impairment as a result of PSE use. Amplitude limiting devices coupled with a visual display (light) should be incorporated into all PSE equipment to protect and warn users against sound levels that are potentially dangerous to hearing. Students should also be provided with health promotion information regarding threats to hearing loss due to high SPL exposure.

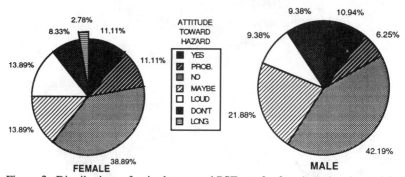

Figure 3. Distributions of attitudes toward PSE use for female and male participants.

5.   REFERENCES

[1]   Sataloff, R.T., and Sataloff, J. (1993). Occupational Hearing Loss (2nd ed.) New York: Marcel Dekker, Inc., 543-566.

[2]   Brown, P.J. and Yearout, R. D. (1991). Impacts of leisure activity noise levels on safety procedures and policy in the industrial environment. International Journal of Industrial Ergonomics. 7(4): 341-346.

[3]   Fearn, R.W. and Hanson, D.R. (1984). Hearing damage in young people using headphones to listen to por music. Journal of Sound and Vibration. 96(1), 147-149.

[4]   Hellstrom, P.A. and Axelsson, A. (1988). Sound levels, hearing habits and hazards of using portable cassette players. Journal of Sound and Vibration. 127(3), 521-528.

[5]   Howe, J.C. and Yearout, R. (1992). Music style, age and gender relationship to preferred noise levels for headset cassette players. Advances in Industrial Ergonomics and Safety IV . (S. Kumar, Ed). London: Taylor & Francis. 335-1340.

[6]   Rice, C.G. Rossi, G. and Olina, M. (1987). Damage risk from personal cassette players. British Journal of Audiology. 21, 279-288.

[7]   Skrainar, S.F., Royster, L.H., Berger, E.H. and Pearson, E.H. (1987). The contribution of personal radios to the noise exposure of employees at one industrial facility. American Industrial Hygiene Association Journal. 48(4), 390-395.

[8]   Yearout, R. Lisnerski, D.Kwiatkowski, C. Locke, J. and Edwards, D. (1994). The effects of a noisy work environment on preferred leisure noise levels. Advances in Industrial Ergonomics and Safety VI (F. Aghazadeh, Ed). London: Taylor & Francis. 271-274.   .

[9]   Hayn, M. and Schulze, L. J. H. (1997). Personal and car stereo volume levels: Hazards of leisure listening levels. Advances in Occupational Ergonomis and Safety II. In Press.

Advances in Occupational Ergonomics and Safety II
Edited by Biman Das and Waldemar Karwowski
IOS Press and Ohmsha, 1997

Effects of Individual Risk Factors in the Development of Noise-induced Hearing Loss

Starck, J. (1), Pyykkö, I. (2), Toppila, E. (1)
(1) Finnish Institute of Occupational Health, Department of Physics,
Laajaniityntie 1, FIN-01620 Vantaa, Finland
(2) Helsinki University Central Hospital, Haartmannink. 2-4 E, FIN-
00290 Helsinki, Finland

The present study investigates the role of individual risk factors in noise-induced hearing loss (NIHL) in order to explain the observed variation in NIHL. The study comprised 250 forest workers, 171 shipyard workers and 406 paper mill workers. Their total exposure to noise, taking into account the protection efficiency of hearing protectors, was evaluated by hygienic measurements and a questionnaire. Impulse noise performance was evaluated by the crest factor method. The medical examinations comprised audiometric measurements, determination of serum lipids and blood pressure. Smoking habits were queried. Comparison of the measured noise and audiometric data showed that for impulse noise the models underestimate hearing loss by 5 to 10 dB. Individual susceptibility to hearing loss could be explained by smoking, drugs, disturbances in peripheral blood circulation, elevated blood pressure, and serum cholesterol concentration, as well as heredity. The effect of the risk factors can be additive, indifferent or potentiative. Smoking alone seemed not to have any effect on hearing, but together with elevated blood pressure and vibration-induced white finger, smoking worsened hearing. Correspondingly, elevated blood pressure and cholesterol concentration had an additive effect on hearing loss. The analyses of these factors among forest workers, shipyard workers and paper mill workers explained 48 % of the variation in hearing loss, whereas age and noise explained only 25 % . During military service, the conscripts are exposed to extremely high impulse noise from different kinds of fire arms. Military service is responsible for a hearing loss of 5 dB which developed later in workers exposed to occupational noise. At present it seems that research should be targeted at the development of more comprehensive methods of risk assessment, considering all risk factors relevant to NIHL. The data can further be utilised even in an expert program aimed at the risk assessment of NIHL for the individual worker.

1. Introduction

For the risk assessment of noise-induced hearing loss (NIHL) the equal energy principle can be applied which, on average, is in good agreement with the observed hearing levels among the numerous subjects exposed to industrial noise [1]. It is not applicable for individual risk estimation. This is due to the great variability in the development of NIHL which the energy principle is not able to explain. Individual resistance and also vulnerability to occupational noise has been suggested to depend on heredity, diet, pigmentation, drugs, blood pressure and circulation, and at least to non-occupational exposure to noise [2-7]. The mechanism controlling the separate and especially combined effects of these factors is still unclear.

The present paper aims to reveal the possible association between NIHL and exposure to noise, serum lipids, blood pressure, and the protection efficiency of hearing protectors.

2. Methods and materials

The study comprised three different groups of workers: A follow-up study on forest workers (N = 118 - 205) during 1972 - 1995, a cross-sectional study on shipyard workers (N = 171) and a study on paper mill workers (N = 405).

The total occupational exposure to noise was evaluated by enquiring the occupational histories of the subjects and collecting the exposure data for the calculations as regards the usage of hearing protectors. The data were supplemented by hygienic measurements in different working conditions. In the measurements, a miniature microphone was placed at the entrance of the ear canal inside the earmuff [8]. Simultaneously another microphone measured the noise outside the hearing protector, thus allowing the calculation of the real attenuation of the hearing protectors. The data were utilised to calculate for each worker the A-weighted noise exposure level (L_{AEQ}) and noise immission level (L_{ANI}) which expresses the level of total noise energy entering the worker's ear. The impulse content of the noise was analyzed by applying the crest factor method [9]. The exposure of forest workers and shipyard workers to hand-arm vibration was analysed using the measurements [10].

The medical examinations comprised blood pressure measurements, total serum cholesterol and high density lipoproteins. Audiometry was taken at frequencies of 0.5, 1, 2, 4 and 8 kHz by a pure tone audiometer. A history of head injuries, noisy free-time activities, use of pain killers and antihypertensive drugs, and smoking habits were enquired. The presense of vibration-induced white finger (VWF) was evaluated among the workers exposed to hand-arm vibration from chain saws and work with hand-held power tools in the shipyard.

3. Results

The development of noise-induced hearing loss is dependent on exposure to noise, impulse content of the noise, protection efficiency of hearing protectors, factors causing individual susceptibility, and other possible exposure.

Exposure to noise can explain only 25 % of the observed variability in NIHL when the ISO 1999-1990 model is applied to the measurements. In our study groups there was a clear difference between the impulsiveness of the noise. Forest workers had very steady state exposure to noise, whereas shipyard workers were exposed to high impulse noise common in heavy metal industry. The results suggest that shipyard noise causes 5-10 dB greater hearing loss than the noise in forest work arising from the operation of chain saws. Exposure to shooting noise during free time and during military service promotes the development of NIHL. Among forest workers, shooting practices and hunting increased NIHL by 10 dB as compared to those forest workers with the same occupational exposure but no exposure to shooting noise.

Shooting practice during military service exposes the conscripts to extremely high level impulses from large calibre weapons, such as artillery firearms and antitank bazookas. The peak levels from such weapons may rise up to 180 dB. Due to the high level of low frequency components and nonlinear phenomena in the hearing protector device HPDs, the attenuation of hearing protectors remains very low. Our measurements have shown 4 dB attenuations for antitank bazooka impulses for the protectors that can be worn together with a military helmet. It is evident that exposure during military service may cause a considerable decrease in hearing if the person is later exposed to excessive occupational noise. Our analyses have revealed a 5 dB increase in NIHL due to military service.

The protection efficiency of hearing protectors was studied among paper mill workers. The average protection efficiency was 4 dB, even though the measured attenuation was 17 dB for the protectors used in the plant. The decreased protection was due to the lower usage rate which was on average 60%. In order to evaluate the importance of the usage rate on the development of NIHL, the workers were divided into three groups: never users, occasional users and full-time users. 50% of the never users had no NIHL and 15 % had modest or severe NIHL. Among the 50 % users, the cases of mild NIHL were more common than among the full-time users, but the number of severe cases was the same (Fig. 1).

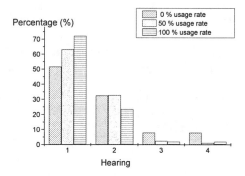

Figure 1. The effect of the usage rate of hearing protectors device's to hearing.
1 = normal hearing   2 = mild NIHL
3 = modest NIHL   4 = severe NIHL

Vibration-induced white finger syndrome was shown to be the most significant single risk factor for NIHL. The presence of VWF increased the NIHL by 10 dB on average at frequencies of 2 and 4 kHz.

Elevated blood pressure, cholesterol and smoking in combination had a stronger effect on hearing in combination than the sum of their separate effects would suggest. Especially smoking alone did not seem to be a risk factor at all, whereas in combination with the other factors it was.

Blood pressure and cholesterol level also had a stronger effect in combination together with noise. Among paper mill workers, the median values for noise exposure level (100 dB), total cholesterol (5.7 mmo/l) and systolic blood pressure (132 mmHg) and diastolic blood pressure (85 mmHg) were used as a criterion value for low risk and high risk groups. Thus altogether 16 groups were formed (Fig. 2). NIHL increases along with the number of risk factors. Blood pressure and cholesterol level in combination raise NIHL by 7 dB. In figure 2, there is a statistically significant difference between the four columns at the right and the left.

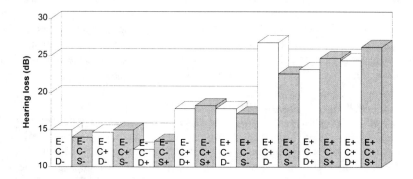

Figure 2. The effect of noise, blood pressure and cholesterol level on hearing at 4 kHz. E = exposure to noise, C = cholesterol, S = systolic blood pressure, D = diastolic blood pressure - below median value, + above median value

Other exposure. Forest workers and shipyard workers are exposed to hand-arm vibration from chain saws and hand-held power tools of different kinds [11]. The exposure levels in both groups are about the same. We could not show that exposure to hand-arm vibration augments NIHL, except that, if VWF symptoms had developed, then NIHL was even 10 dB more severe than in the symptomless workers.

Pain killers, such as salicylates, can promote the development of reversible NIHL. Among forest workers the effect was 1 dB on hearing if the consumption of salicylates was more than 50 tablets per year. The effect was not statistically significant, however.

4. Discussion

The great variation in the development of NIHL is a predominant feature. Age-related deterioration in hearing, so-called sosioacusis, together with noise explains 25% of the observed variability in NIHL. The constructional reasons are deficits in the functioning of the inner ear hair cells and their decreasing number. Metabolic disturbances may promote the development of these kinds of dysfunctions. The factors considered in to our study may reflect the symptoms and signs behind the metabolic disturbances in the course of several years.

When the ISO 1999 - 1990 model is applied to typical risk evaluation, as for example exposure level 100 dB and duration of exposure 25 years, the model will give a 60 dB range when expressed by the probability fractiles 90% and 10%. In our studies we have tried to explain this variation. At present, with our study material on about 800 workers, the rate of explanation on the variability has grown to 50% simply by considering the exposure parameters more comprehensively, by including protection efficiency of the hearing protectors to the exposure evaluation, by analysing the role of individual risk factors known or believed to influence the genesis of NIHL, and finally, by the effect of other exposures than noise. To proceed with the study, we must increase the study material and create a systematic method to do this in a consistent way. In order to do this we have already constructed a data base for collecting the data. Also new risk factors have to be included in the study. It seems evident that we have to pay more attention to the genetic factors. In the future it is should be possible by taking simple blood tests to screen for workers who pose the highest risk for the development of NIHL based on their hereditary factors. The continuation of the field studies will later facilitate the construction of a more applicable model for risk assessment purposes, and finally the development of an expert program to predict an individual's risk to develop NIHL.

References

[1] ISO 1999 (1990) Acoustics - Determination of occupational noise exposure and estimation of noise-induced hearing impairment. International Organization for   Standardization, Geneva
[2] Hinchcliffe R (1973) Epidemiology of sensorineural hearing loss. *Audiol.* 12: 446-   452.
[3] Hawkins JE. Comparative otopathology: ageing noise and ototoxic drugs. *Adv Oto - rhino - laryngol* 20: 125 - 141, 1971
[4] Chung DY, Willson GN, Cannon RP, Mason K. Individual susceptibity to noise. In: Hammernik RP, Henderson D, Salvi R, eds. New perspectives on noise-induced hearing loss. Raven Press, New York 1982. 511 -519.
[5] Pyykkö I, Pekkarinen J, Starck J (1986a) Sensory-neural hearing loss in forest workers. An analysis of risk factors. *Int arch occup environ health.* 59: 439-454.
[6] Pyykkö I, Starck J, Pekkarinen J. (1986b) Further evidence for the linkage between permanent hearing loss and digital vasospasm in subjects exposed to noise and vibration. *Am j otol.* 7: 391-398.
[7] Pyykkö, I, Starck J, Pekkarinen J, Färkkilä M (1988) Serum cholesterol and triglyceride in the etiology on sensorineural hearing loss. In: Vertigo, nausea, tinnitus and hypoacusia in metabolic disorders. C.F. Claussen, MV Kirtane, K Schlitter (ed). Elsevier Publishing Co., Biomedical Division. Amsterdam. 335-338.
[8] Pekkarinen J (1987) Industrial noise, crest factor and the effect of earmuffs. *Am ind hyg ass j.* 48: 861-866.
[9] Starck J, Pekkarinen J (1987) Industrial impulse noise: Crest factor as additional parameter in exposure measurements. *Appl acoustics.* 20: 263-274.
[10] ISO 5349 - 1986. Guide for the measurement and the assessment of human exposure to hand-transmitted vibration. Geneva 1986. 13 p.
[11] Starck J, Pekkarinen J, Pyykkö I. Impulse noise and hand-arm vibration in relation to sensory neural hearing loss. *Scand J Environ Health* 14 (1988) 265-271.

Advances in Occupational Ergonomics and Safety II
Edited by Biman Das and Waldemar Karwowski
IOS Press and Ohmsha, 1997

Data Base and Expert Program to Predict the Risk of Individual Hearing Loss

Starck, J. (1), Toppila, E. (1), Pyykkö, I. (2), Pihlström A (1)
(1) Finnish Institute of Occupational health, Department of Physics,
Laajaniityntie 1, FIN-01620 Vantaa
(2) Helsinki University Central Hospital, Haartmaninkatu 2-4E,
FIN-00290 Helsinki, Finland

A data base and analysis program for noise-induced hearing loss (NIHL) has been developed to predict the risk to develop of individual hearing loss. In addition to the workers' exposure to noise, it considers the factors behind the individual susceptibility and the exposure. The data on contributing factors influencing NIHL are stored in a relational data base. The exposure are based on the evaluation of the noise immission level, in which the, duration, frequency content, and the usage of hearing protectors are included. The input data can handle an unlimited number of exposure charts. If the noise level is not known, the program lists the noise levels of comparable conditions and provides an estimation of exposure. In addition to occupational noise, free-time and military noise are included in the total noise exposure calculations. The confounding factors for NIHL due to medical reasons, elevated serum cholesterol level, hypertension, and extensive use of pain killers, are also collected. Combined exposure, such as hand-arm vibration, tobacco smoking, aminoglycosides and solvents is inquired. The number or personal audiograms is unlimited. The program gives the predicted hearing loss with ISO 1999. In addition, these data are utilised with the NoiseScan model that estimates the effect of medical and other factors on NIHL. The NoiseScan program can explain about 50 % of the variation in NIHL, whereas the standard parameters, i.e. noise and age can explain less than 25 % of the variation. The main applications of the NoiseScan are: prediction of individual development of NIHL, development of individual hearing conservation program (HCP), planning of HCP actions, improvement of exposure estimations, and comparison of different efficiencies of hearing protector types. Finally, it will help to the control the confounding factors in NIHL.

1. Introduction

Noise-induced hearing loss (NIHL) is one of the most common health hazards in industrialized countries. The efforts to control industrial noise have succeeded only partly. The number of cases of severe hearing loss has decreased ,but the total number of cases with NIHL has remained stable. Although in large population the definition of risk is rather well established [1,2], several confounding factors make exact risk prediction in individual subjects difficult [3-5]. Although individual models for the development of NIHL have been provided [6,7] the studies have not, so far, been very successful. One reason may be the inaccuracies in the evaluation of the exposure data, in the usage rate of hearing protectors, in estimations of sosiocusis and in nosiocusis, especially in the detection of genetic factors.

The purpose of this work is to develop a data gathering program for NIHL, and further a model and an expert program that can handle the analyses and provide Hearing Conservation Program (HCP) data even on individual cases.

2. Study groups

For the evaluation of the data base collection program, we have gathered data from 406 paper mill workers, 176 shipyard workers and 200 forest workers. Individual work histories were collected, and the noise levels in different working conditions were measured. Special attention was paid to hearing protection by inquiring the types of hearing protectors used and the usage rate. The real ear attenuation of HPDs was measured by a miniature microphone method. The exposure data were used to calculate the A-weighted noise immission level (L_{ANI}) for each worker [8]. In addition to exposure to occupational noise, exposure to free- time and military noise was evaluated. The audiograms were collected. The medical histories of the workers were reviewed and their use of drugs was evaluated. Serum lipid levels and blood pressure measurements were analyzed. The work histories, together with the medical and nosiocusis histories were collected with a questionnaire.

3. Construction of the Program

Interface: When the database program is opened, several buttons are given on the computer screen (Fig. 1). The user can either add a new case or look at existing cases. After the selection, additional buttons are activated. The name of the subject is displayed at the top of the screen.

Exposure to noise: Under the "Noise exposure" button there are three buttons: work noise, free-time noise, and military noise.

Work noise: A data sheet is provided for each work task, noise exposure period, or occupation. A subject may have an unlimited number of noise exposure data sheets included in the total noise exposure calculation. Each data sheet begins with a statement on the duration of the work period. The noise exposure time is asked with an accuracy of hours per day and days per week. The frequency content of noise is divided into low-medium or high-medium frequency content. If the noise level is not measured or known, the program provides hints for noise level, based on occupation, work task, environment and machine type.

All certified protectors used in Western Europe are included in the database with their attenuation specifications. Thus, the attenuation is automatically given on the screen both for low and high frequency noise for the given HPD. In the final calculations, the protection efficiency depends on the usage rate of HPDs also by utilizing the HML - check method and energy principle [9].

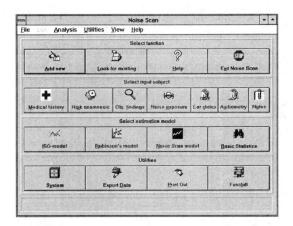

Figure 1. Main screen and buttons.

Free time noise: The exposure to free-time noise is collected with two screens. Special attention is paid to noise from shooting, from music and from work with noisy power tools. The usage rate of hearing protectors is queried. Noise from vehicles and from rock music is common in an urban society, and represents a different kind of free-time noise exposure.

Military noise: A separate data base file for military noise exposure collects the quality of the weapon and the number of shots separately for hand-held and large-caliber weapons Also the type and usage rate of hearing protectors is included in the evaluation of the exposure to military noise.

Medical history: Ear diseases and ear operations are asked separately on the same screen. If the answer to either of these questions is yes, a new screen is opened and the type of disease and operation or ear pathology is asked in detail. Neurological diseases and possible central nervous system infections are inquired, and if the history is positive, a screen with detailed questions is provided. Explosions or head trauma are asked as well.

Vertigo is an indication of inner ear disease that causes sensory neural hearing loss, mostly independently of NIHL. Tinnitus may or may not be present, and may increase the handicap of NIHL. A significant part of the unexplained hearing loss seems to be linked to genetic inheritance. The database therefore includes also a question on possible hearing deficiencies in the pedigree. Finally, exposure to aminoglycosides and the presence of vibration induced white finger is asked.

Risk anamnesis: From the main screen, a button "Risk anamnesis" opens the screen containing information on smoking habits, usage of pain killers, and exposure to solvents i.e. on factors which can increase the effects of noise on hearing.

Objective findings: Data on cholesterol and blood pressure can be stored in the objective findings screen by using the three latest observations. Weight, height and the color of the eyes can be stored here as well.

Audiometry: The audiometry screen is used for storing the audiograms. The number of audiograms is unlimited. When the pushbutton is selected, an empty audiogram sheet is displayed. The left button of the mouse is for the audiogram of the left ear, and the right button for the right ear. The year of examination, quality of the soundproof room, calibration of the audiometry, and type of audiometry are queried in the right-hand corner of the screen. Also the result of the speech audiometry can be input.

Estimated hearing loss: Our program gives the prediction for the hearing threshold level with the ISO 1999 by utilizing the collected data on the subjects exposure to noise. The probability fractiles with percentage values of 10 - 90 % are plotted, and for the comparison, the audiogram is plotted in the same figure.

3. Discussion

The interface between the computer program and the user must satisfy several demands: It must be user friendly, i.e. the content of the questions and input data must be easy to comprehend, and it must be self-controlling for input errors. It must be self-explanatory and, when needed, provide help for inputting or using the interface. The advantage of the graphical interface is that the item can be pointed easily by one hand, and interest can be focused constantly on the item on the screen. The objects on the screen can be self-explanatory and, accordingly, easy to understand.

The present data base for NIHL is used for data collection, teaching purposes and for providing simple and versatile information exchange between medical doctors, hygienists, and nurses working in the field of occupational medicine. It helps the staff to understand the variability of NIHL and to form a larger database or order to study the accuracy of the hearing conservation programs. It also provides an understanding of the benefits of protecting the ears with hearing protectors, by displaying the resulting hearing loss according to the ISO 1999 - 1990 standard model with and without the use of hearing protectors.

The Noise Scan expert program utilizes the data on the effects of different risk factors on the development of hearing loss. With the present data available we have been able to explain 50 % of the observed variation in the hearing levels when the exposure data explains only 25 % on the variation (Fig. 2). Thus the expert program has internal rules for handling and combining certain risk factors. It displays the present prediction for the audiogram and predictions for the future at five-year interval for the future. For comparison purposes the screen also shows the present audiograms and cumulative exposure data separately outside and inside the HPDs for the selected subject.

4. Conclusions

The aim in the development of an industrial database for hearing conservation is to warn about individual susceptibility, to warn about excessive noise pollution in selected working tasks or sites and, to allow comparison of various hearing conservation programs and finally to screen for the workers who are at risk the to develop hearing loss. In order to fulfill these demands, the database must have information on the relative distribution of the factors that affect the hearing loss. Such factors are audiometric testing methods, the testing environment, efficiency of the hearing protectors, exposure to military noise and to other non-occupational noise. It must provide accurate data on life-time noise exposure in various jobs or work tasks.

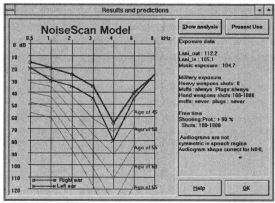

Figure 2. Predicted hearing lossaccording to Noise Scan.

Thus an unlimited number of working periods must be provided for each subject. The database must also include adequate data on the quality and usage rate of hearing protectors. Finally, the confounding factors must be controlled. These factors, such as elevated blood pressure, the presence of vibration-induced white finger syndrome, elevated serum cholesterol level, and use of various ototoxic drugs, can explain the significant variation in the extent of hearing loss in individual cases. In the present database we have tried to include the variables that are meaningful for the hearing conservation program.

References

[1] Robinson DW (1971) Estimating the risk of hearing loss due to continuousnoise. In: Robinson DW (ed). Occupational hearing loss. Academic Press, London
[2] ISO 1999 (1990) Acoustics - Determination of occupational noise exposure and estimation of noise induced hearing impairment. International Organization for Standardization, Geneva
[3] Humes LE (1984) Noise-induced hearing loss as influenced by other agents and by some physical characteristics of the individual. J ac soc Am. 76: 1318-1329.
[4] Pyykkö I, Pekkarinen J, Starck J (1986a) Sensory-neural hearing loss in forest workers. An analysis of risk factor. Int arch occup environ health. 59: 439-454.
[5] Borg A, Canlon B, Engström B (1992) Individual variability of noise-induced hearing loss. In: Noise-Induced hearing Loss. Dancer et al. (eds.), Mosby year Book, St. Louis. 467-475.
[6] Royster LH, Lilley LT, Thomas WG (1980) Recommended criteria for evaluating effectiveness of hearing conservation program. Am ind hyg assoc. 41: 40-48.
[7] Royster JD, Royster LH (1986) Using audiometric data base analysis. J occup med. 28: 1055-1068.
[8] Pyykkö I, Koskimies K, Starck J, Pekkarinen J, Inaba R (1989) Risk factors in the genesis of sensory neural hearing loss in Finnish forestry workers. Br j ind med. 46, 439-446.
[9] EN 452-1993. Hearing protectors - Recommendation for selection, use, care and maintenance - Guidance document. Brussels 1993.

Advances in Occupational Ergonomics and Safety II
Edited by Biman Das and Waldemar Karwowski
IOS Press and Ohmsha, 1997

Free Time and Military Noise in the Evaluation of Total Exposure to Noise

Esko Toppila[1], Jukka Starck[1], Ilmari Pyykkö[2], Anders Pihlström[1]

(1) Finnish Institute of Occupational Health, Department of Physics,

Laajaniityntie 1, FIN-01620, Finland

(2) Karolinska Institutet, Department of Otolaryngology, Stockholm,

Sweden

In the evaluation of noise induced hearing loss (NIHL) the equal energy principle is generally adopted. A properly made noise exposure evaluation must include the exposure to occupational noise, free time exposure and military service exposure. In all these cases the usage of hearing protectors may reduce the exposure significantly The reduction can be a source of a significant error, since it depends on the usage rate, the condition of protectors and goodness of the fitting of the protectors. The above mentioned factors may cancel almost all the attenuation provided by the protectors. Using proper techniques all the confounding factors can be recorded and the errors can be minimised. This leads to the use of questionnaires in conjunction with measurements. The most important sources of leisure time noise exposure are shooting and music. Exposure to music may exceed the occupational exposure among 5-20 % of young workers. As this exposure is almost impossible to measure, the evaluation must be based on questionnaires. By a proper design an accuracy of 5-20 dB can be achieved and the risk groups can be found. Target shooting is rarely a risk, because hearing protectors are usually worn. Hunters seldom use hearing protectors because of their need to hear the environment. On the other hand the number of shots is often quite low. The exposure can be evaluated rather accurately, but due to the highly impulsive character of the noise, there is no commonly accepted method for the combination of shooting noise with occupational noise. Military shooting can cause hearing loss by a single event. The total exposure can be measured with methods used for free-time shooting.

1. Introduction

The equal energy principle is widely the most widely accepted way to evaluate the exposure in the as risk assessment of noise-induced hearing loss (NIHL). The equal energy principle requires that all noise exposure is included independent of its origin. Practically all male persons in Finland are exposed to gun noise during their military service. Starck & al [1] has shown that the military service causes an extra 5 dB hearing loss to army recruits in Finland. Free-time noise becomes more and more important since its amount is increasing. The total amount of people exposed to a weekly dose exceeding 85 dB(A) during free time is at least of same order of magnitude than the amount of people exposed at work [2]. A hearing protection program (HCP) is a computer program intended to monitor and predict the risk of NIHL. Good predictions require reliable input data. Thus reliable evaluation of free-time exposure in addition to occupational exposure has become an important task in the evaluation of life time exposure. The evaluation of free-time noise is not easy. It is hardly possible to measure the noise levels or the duration of all noisy activities. Thus the evaluation must be made on the basis of questionnaires. The questionnaire must be designed in such a way that the results are as reliable as possible, but still it must be easy to fill and the results are independent of one who fills the form.

The purpose of this study is to analyse the role of free time exposure in the evaluation of total noise exposure by using three type cases. Also the accuracy of the evaluation is evaluated in the case when using the questionnaires which are used in our hearing conservation program called NoiseScan.

2. Methods

To develop and test the method three cases were created with known exposures to occupational, military and free-time noise . Case 1 corresponds to a man working on rural side. He works as a forest worker. His work exposure is a typical exposure found in a follow-up study 1972-1995. His free-time exposure is also typical for a habitant in the Suomussalmi county. It consists of shooting and in small extend of music. Case 2 and 3 correspond to typical shipyard workers [1]. The usage of hearing protectors for 2 corresponds to mean usage rate of protectors found in our studies. Case 3 is in this sense the ideal case. The music exposure is set to correspond to 75 % quartile exposure [3]. The levels in discos correspond to levels measured in a popular disco for young people in Finland. In all cases the music exposure is set to start at the age of 15 and to end at the age of 25. Working is supposed to start at the age of 20. These simulated results were fed in NoiseScan using the standard questionnaires. The results calculated by NoiseScan were compared to the true values.

3. Results

3.1 Exposure to work noise and music

The lifetime exposures of all three cases are shown in figures 1-3. The error caused by neglecting the music exposure is also shown. In case one where the level of work noise is 3 dB higher, the work noise becomes dominant 5 years after the exposure to music has ended.

Table 1. The exposure profiles of the example cases

	Case 1	Case 2	Case 3
Occupation	Forest worker	Welder	Plater
Noise emission level at work (dB(A))	101 dB	97 dB	97 dB
Usage of hearing protectors (% of time)	100 %	60	100
Attenuation of protectors	17	13	13
Noise immission level at work (dB(A))	84	93	84
Military service	Infantry	Artillery	Artillery
Shots with hand guns	300	50	50
Usage of hearing protectors	20 %	100 %	100%
Shots with heavy guns	2	50	50
Usage of hearing protectors	Always	Always	Always
Discos/concerts (h/week)	0.5	6	6
Disco emission level	100	102	102
Playing music (h/week)	-	-	5
Music emission level	-	-	92
Usage of protectors	-	-	Always
Total music exposure	81	94	94
Other noisy hobbies	Shooting	-	-
Exposure/year	50 shots		

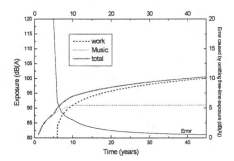

Figure 1. Lifetime exposure of case one

In case two work and free-time exposure have about the same level.   The work noise becomes dominant 10 years after the end free-time exposure. Case three differs from case two
only by the use of hearing protectors. 100 % use of hearing protectors cause music to become the major source of exposure during the whole working life.

3.2 NoiseScan results

The results of the NoiseScan evaluation are given in table 2. In case 1 NoiseScan evaluates,
that the music exposure is negligible and gives 0 dB as music exposure. This causes a 0.5
dB error in the total exposure evaluation. In case 2 and 3 NoiseScan makes a 4 dB error
music exposure. The effect is minor for total exposure evaluation because work noise is
dominant. In case three where music is dominant the error is 4 dB

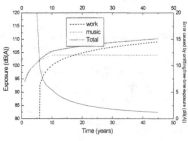
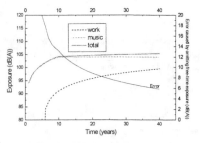

Figure 2. Lifetime exposure of case two   Fig 3. Lifetime exposure of case three

Table 2. the accuracy of NoiseScan evaluation in the example cases

	Case 1	Case 2	Case 3
True exposure to music (dB(A))	91	104	104
NoiseScan evaluation of music exposure (dB(A))	0 dB	100	100
Error in total exposure (dB(A))	0.5	1	4

3.3 Exposure to shooting noise

To evaluate the accuracy the peak levels which are used for risk assessment of various guns, must be used. The peak levels of military handguns are 155-165 dB, light cannons 160-165 dB and of heavy cannons and bazookas over 180 dB. The peak levels of salon pistols and rifles are below 140 dB and they need not be considered. The peak levels of all other guns varies from 155 to 165 dB(A)[4]. Thus the shots with handguns can be directly added. The number of shots is evaluated in order of magnitude in NoiseScan (table 3). This causes an error of 10 dB, if the logarithmic approach is accepted.

Table 3. The accuracy of NoiseScan evaluation for shooting noise

	Case 1	Case 2	Case 3
True number of shots with heavy arms	2	50	50
NoiseScan result	1-10	10-100	10-100
True number of shots with hand guns	2300	50	50
NoiseScan result	1000-10000	10-100	10-100

4. Discussion

In Finland there are about 250 000 people working in conditions where daily exposure exceed 85 dB. The amount of hunters is 300 000 and over 200 000 people are going often to musical events. Thus free time exposure is important in the evaluation of total exposure. However the accuracy of exposure is low because it is not possible to measure the levels. Also the evaluation of exposure times is very crude. Luckily for most people exposure to high levels end in the early thirties. However music exposure may be the dominant factor in total exposure if hearing protectors are properly worn at workplace. From epidemiological point of view this is not the case. Proper questioning techniques provides a reasonable evaluation of the music exposure. An accuracy of 5 dB is achievable. For shooting it is generally given only the maximum allowed value [5,6,7], although recently the concept has been criticised [8,9]. There is no commonly accepted method to combine shots of different intensity or a method to combine shots with steady state noise. If no shooting with heavy arms have occurred, all shots can be added together, since their peak levels are about the same. The designer of a module predicting the NIHL may either use the number of shots as one additional input parameter or may convert the shots into equivalent levels using a self-made model. The first approach requires only a method to combine shots from different sources and a way of taking into account the effect of hearing protectors. The latter approach requires also a model to be developed [10].

For hearing conservation purposes it is extremely important to identify the sources of exposure. It helps to direct the counter measures against the dominant noise sources. This task would be easier if valid models for combination of steady-state and impulse noise would be available.

5. Conclusions

A good hearing conservation program takes into account non-occupational exposure. This is done by the use of questionnaires. Properly designed questionnaires are easy to fill and still give reasonable accuracy. Taking into account the non-occupational exposure enables to direct the hearing conservation measures in appropriate directions.

References

[1] Starck J., Pekkarinen J., & Pyykkö I. Impulse noise and hand-arm vibration in relation to sensory neural hearing loss. Scand. J. Work Environm. Health. 14(1988):265-271

[2] Toppila E., Musiikki meluna,Akustiikkapäivä 1995, edited by, Järvinen A, Lahti T., Linjama J., Olkinuora P, Akustinen seura, 1995 (in Finnish)

[3] Mäkinen J., Björk E., Nuoret ja vapaa-ajan melu, Akustiikkapäivä 1995, toim., Järvinen A, Lahti T., Linjama J., Olkinuora P, Akustinen seura, 1995 (in finnish)

[4] Pekkarinen J, Ylikoski J, Starck J. Hearing protection against high level shooting impulses in relation to hearing damage risk criteria. J Acoust Soc Am 91;1, 196-202 (1992).

[5] Pfander F., Das Knalltrauma. Berlin, Heidelberg, New York Springer Verlag, 1975

[6] ACGIH, Threshold Limit Values for Chemical Substances and Physical Agents. American Conference of Governmental Industrial Hygienists. Cincinnati, 1992.

[7] 86/188/EEC Council directive on the protection of workers from the risks related to exposure to noise at work.

[8] Dancer AL, Franke R, Parmentier G, Buck K, Hearing protector performance and NIHL in externe Enrironments: Actual Performance of hearing protectors in Impulse Noise/Nonlinear behavoiur. in Scientific basis of Noise-induced hearing loss edited by Axelsson A, Borchgrevink H, Hamernik R Hellstrom PA, Henderson D, Salvi R, Thieme, New York 1996

[9] Patterson JH, Johnson DL, Temporary threshold shifts produced by high intensity free-field impulse noise in humans wearing hearing protection in Scientific basis of Noise-induced hearing loss edited by Axelsson A, Borchgrevink H, Hamernik R Hellstrom PA, Henderson D, Salvi R, Thieme, New York 1996

[10]Pekkarinen J, Iki M, Starck J, Pyykkö I. 1993. Hearing loss risk from exposure to shooting impulses in workers exposed to occupational noise. Brit. j. audiol. 27, 175-182.

Advances in Occupational Ergonomics and Safety II
Edited by Biman Das and Waldemar Karwowski
IOS Press and Ohmsha, 1997

Using Aurally-Equivalent Measurement Technique for the Determination of Noise Annoyance in Work Places

Genuit, HEAD acoustics GmbH, Germany; M. Burkhard, Sonic Perceptions, Inc., USA

Introduction

Binaural technology allows aurally-equivalent recording and monitoring of sound situations in work places. Its use means an improvement for the examination of annoyance effects in comparison to the conventional A-weighted sound pressure level measurements. The results of research studies as included in the presented paper prove that this may lead to an increase in work quality and safety. Also, the efficiency of noise reduction measures could be improved through more target-orientated noise diagnosis. In many work places the sound pressure levels are so high that the physical damage of human hearing is the most important issue. Here, the use of ear protectors is necessary. Several standardized measuring procedures permit the determination of their sound attenuation, but the resulting parameters do not describe adequately the subjective judgement. This is caused by the fact that the ISO head geometry does not reproduce the human head correctly and the effects occurring when the ear is closed are not considered. Here, the Artificial Head technology including the possibility of an aurally-equivalent monitoring of ear protector effectiveness offers an important improvement.

1. Noise annoyance at work places

Examinations of noise annoyance at work places normally are based on measurements of the A-weighted sound pressure level with one microphone and therefore are limited to the consideration of ear's physical damage. Such a procedure does not describe annoyance or sound quality in work places well. Furthermore, it does not consider that the negative effects of noise on workers in work places can be regarded as a multi-dimensional task that includes **physical, psychoacoustic** and **cognitive aspects.** For the understanding of these aspects the use of Artificial Head measuring technology is necessary /1/. It allows binaural, true-to-the-original recording and playback of noise pollution in the work place and subjective evaluation. The Artificial Head comprises simulations of the head, pinna, neck and shoulder. The relative dimensions and positioning of the individual simulation elements are based on mean data of test persons, the ear canal entrance serving as reference. The head simulation, a permissible simplification based on geometric figures, consists on two half sections as shown in figure 1.

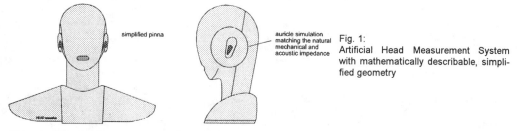

Fig. 1:
Artificial Head Measurement System with mathematically describable, simplified geometry

This simplification permits better reproducibility of measurement results and also makes standardization more straightforward. In compliance with CCITT P.58 the tolerances of these outer dimensions have been established on the basis of data contained in IEC Report 959 /2/.

The use of Artificial Head technology also includes a suitable analyzer and analysis: Due to the characteristics of human hearing the analyzer has to include a high resolution both in time and frequency. Additionally, it should have a dynamic range comparable to the human hearing. Only this ensures the necessary basis for an aurally-equivalent analysis of the measured binaural sound signals. For this purpose, not only the conventional psychoacoustic calculation procedures can be used, but also additional algorithms such as the hearing model of SOTTEK /3/.

The hitherto known methods for measuring loudness do not consider the binaural signal processing in the hearing. By aural evaluation of signals of two sound pick-ups in an Artificial Head the human hearing can select individual sounds from various signals and discriminate others with the help of the binaural signal processing. For complex sound situations with various sound sources the use of the binaural loudness in combination with Artificial Head technology provides an important improvement for the description of the subjective judgements. An application example of noise annoyance in work places dealing with the interior noise in an aircraft cockpit will be given in the following /4/: A comparative judgement of the noise measured inside of two different cockpits A and B using aircraft of the same brand and flown by the same pilots, revealed that cockpit A was rated significantly more annoying and louder than cockpit B by all pilots (see fig. 2a/b with included table).

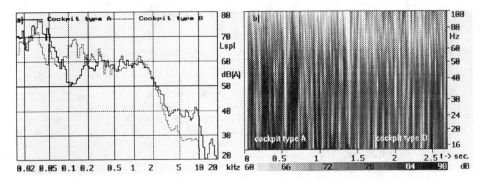

Fig. 2a: Noise inside cockpit
            height 24000 feet
            indicated airspeed 325, 0.758 mach
            a) type A b) type B

Fig. 2b: Low frequency analysis based on the
            hearing model /3/ with high resolution
            in the time and frequency domain:
            The low-frequent share in the noise of
            cockpit A becomes obvious.

Table 1	lin	A	B	C	sone	acum	subject.
A	79.8	75.5	76.9	78.6	29.6	1.8	-
B	78.7	69.5	75.2	78.1	21.8	1.2	o

A hearing-adapted investigation using the Artificial Head measurement technology in combination with objective analyses and subjective hearing tests yielded to the following results:

1. The sound pressure level of the cockpit interior noise is approximately the same for the two different types of aircraft.
2. The psychoacoustical value of loudness is insignificantly smaller for the type B cockpit in comparison to cockpit A.
3. In subjective hearing tests, the interior noise of cockpit A was judged significantly louder than type B cockpit.
4. The interior noise of cockpit A is clearly characterized by strong low-frequency beat-oscillations causing a feeling of pressure onto both ears (see fig. 2b).

An important element in the measurement chain of Artificial Head technology is the playback system. Research studies have shown the effect of binaural playback on physiological reactions of human being /10/. In these studies auditory tests were carried out in which the fingerpulse amplitude of the test persons was measured during exposure to industrial noise (circular saw and coupling device) from a single angle of incidence (unidirectional) and from two different angles of incidence (multi-directionally). Both noise situations produced the same SPL at the position of the listener. The results showed that the kind of playback influences the strength of the finger pulse reaction: The reaction to the multidirectional situation is higher than this to the unidirectional one by 4% in the case of loudspeaker playback and 10% in the case of headphone playback. This shows that monaural playback may not represent sufficiently the reaction of works on noise exposures in workers places /1/.

2.   Measuring the Characteristics of Ear protectors

The use of ear protectors is necessary in specific working conditions with high sound pressure levels to avoid damage of hearing. The sound attenuation performance of protectors is assessed according to standard measuring procedures. Up to now, standard tests of ear protectors have been mainly carried-out using test persons according to the hearing threshold procedure, whereby the protection is the difference of just audible sound level perceived by a subject with and without the protector on his or her ear. This procedure, also described as subjective, is very time intensive and costly, and it lacks reproducibility. It has been standardized in DIN ISO 4860, part 1 and ANSI S.12.6/1984 (R/1990). This method is subject to systematic error resulting from the deceptively high sound insulation values obtained at lower frequencies. A simplified procedure for measuring the quality of ear protectors and terms of their sound attenuation properties is, as a purely physical method independent of test persons. However, the acoustics properties of the head simulation used are quite different from those of an actual human head. For this, the Artificial Head Measurement System HMS II. 4 has been developed. It consists of a head and shoulder simulation and Artificial Head electronics. The first includes two pinna simulators which can both be fitted with ear simulators as given in IEC 711. The Artificial Head electronics integrates a preamplifier with an activatable highpass filter and test tone generator. Free-field equalization, making the system compatible with conventional measurement microphones, is also included. The ear simulation must be adequately sealed for the measurements. Sufficient structure-borne sound insulation is obtained by inserting the ear simulator in a larger mass. Great efforts have been made to achieve skin and flesh simulation of the outer ear, including the surface surrounding the external ear pinna. Basic investigation and measurements regarding the mechanical impedance around the pinna and in the auditory meatus have been carried out by SCHRÖTER /6/. Our own investigations suggested that a re-assessment of the question of flesh simulation was necessary, specifically relating to the circumaural parts, pinna and auditory meatus as separate elements.

The sound insulation of ear protectors has been measured with and without flesh simulation by FEDTKE /7/ using various head simulations. The results from this work indicate that the differences obtained could probably not be ascribed to the flesh simulation. Despite these results, simulation of the circumaural tissue was found to reduce variability of sound insulation observations for protectors enclosing the ear and measured on an HMS II. Thus flesh simulation in the vicinity of the external ear is part of the HMS II system.

In the pinna simulation the mechanical impedance of the plastic can almost be ignored. Plug-type ear protectors do not come into contact with the pinna, so that the acoustic impedance of the pinna cannot have any effect. However, the magnitude of this impedance is such that a completely rigid pinna would produce almost identical results. Also in the case of enclosing ear protectors measurement results might be affected by the mechanical contact between pinna and enclosure. In extreme cases, where the enclosure is of small volume, practical measurement is often hampered because the plastic pinna pushes the enclosure away from the head. This produces an acoustic leakage and an unrealistically drastic reduction in the sound insulation measured. For this reason the latest version of HMS II includes a pinna modification which allows more flexibility and compression.

The subjective procedure for measuring the sound insulation of ear protectors is subject to systematic error due to so-called physiological masking. This signifies the masking of exterior noises through internal physiological ones, such as blood pulsation. This leads to seemingly better sound insulation values for ear protectors than would otherwise result. Since this error is a subjective method one, calculation of it is only required where the two procedures are being compared. In the case of enclosing protectors, the noise produced by vibration of the resting head is significant. This noise enters the auditory meatus through the enclosing elements and is, therefore, a low-frequency effect. Thus, physiological noise is an essential factor at low frequencies in the case of enclosing protectors. Physiological masking provides a basic explanation for why, at low frequencies, sound insulation values found by the subjective method are larger than the values obtained by physical measurements. In the case of plug-type protectors the effects of physiological masking have been negligible in all Artificial Heads so far developed. This is because the unrealistic auditory meatae result in inaccurate measurement of sound insulation (when physiological masking is slight). In contrast, in the case of enclosing protectors at 63 Hz physiological masking frequently produces discrepancies.

According to PÖSSELT /8/, the closest estimate of the actual sound insulation value for an ear protector can be obtained by applying a correction algorithm to the value measured that considers the effect of bone-conduction. For an Artificial Head of infinitely good inherent sound insulation the bone-conducted sound component is not actually measurable. The finite bone-conducted sound insulation of a real head must be taken into account in the calculation. If, for the sake of simplification, it is assumed that the components due to air-borne and bone-conducted sound are in phase and superimposed, both components must be added.

Several methods for measurements of ear protectors were compared at the Physikalische Technische Bundesanstalt (PTB), /9/ Braunschweig. The investigation was limited to ear protectors for which subjectively obtained measurement data according to DIN ISO 4869 were available, so as to allow a comparison with those data obtained with the artificial head. The subjectively obtained data were taken from the "Ear Protector Specification" of the German Trade Institute. It was imperative to ensure that the ear protectors under examination were positioned optimally before measurement started. A test person would also re-position the ear protector to obtain the best possible sound insulation effect. During physical measurement, the optimum position was the one of various positions producing the highest insertion insulation. Fig. 4 shows the results for two enclosing ear protectors (Bilsom Viking 2421 and Bilsom blau 2450). Both curves generally correspond with the data measured subjectively according to DIN ISO 4869. Certain deviations occur at both low and high frequencies. The low frequency deviations can be easily explained in terms of physiological masking. The results show that it is possible to examine the characteristics of ear protectors by use of an Artificial HEAD if the above-mentioned issues are considered.

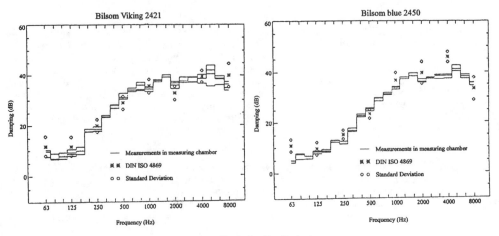

Fig. 4:   Sound Insulation Values measured for two Enclosing Ear Protectors

Summary

The objective determination of negative effects of noise in work places is only possible in a limited way by use of monaural microphone measurements. The involvement of expert knowledge is not only recommended but imperative. Artificial Head measuring technology, coupled with psychoacoustic evaluation, represents progress with respect to the objective determination of negative effects of noise. It still requires, however, the inclusion of cognitive aspects by experts. Advancements in Artificial Head measurement technology allow an aurally-equivalent determination of the insulating properties of ear protectors by using appropriate correction factors. Whereas in the case of enclosing ear protectors a very good correlation to results obtained in subjective procedures can be established, in the case of plug-type protectors insulation values obtained at low frequencies are higher than actual values. For plug-type protectors, therefore, further work is needed that leads to closer simulation of the auditory meatus and ultimately amendment to IEC 711.

Reference

/1/   K. Genuit, J. Blauert, M. Bodden, G. Jansen, V. Mellert, H. Remmers:
      Entwicklung einer Meßtechnik zur physiologischen Bewertung von Lärmeinwirkung unter Berücksichtigung der psychoakustischen Eigenschaften des Nachrichtenempfängers "Menschliches Gehör", Dortmund, Forschungsbericht (publication scheduled for 1997)

/2/   K. Genuit: **Development of a test setup for objective measurement of ear protectors,** Inter-Noise, 24.-26.08.1993, Leuven, Belgien

/3/   R. Sottek: **Modelle zur Signalverarbeitung im menschlichen Gehör,** Dissertation RWTH-Aachen 1992, Verlag M. Wehle

/4/   K. Genuit: **The binaural Analysis and Evaluation of Noise with consideration of the Human hearing** 8th FASE Symposium on Environmental Acoustics, 24.-28.04.89, Zaragoza, Spanien, p. 311-314

/5/   K. Genuit: **Instrumentation and Investigations for determining perception of noise annoyance** Noise-Con, 14. - 17.10.90 Texas, USA

/6/   H. Els, J. Schröter: **Die akustischen Eigenschaften des menschlichen Kopfes,** BAU, Dortmund, Forschungsbericht 239, 1980, ISBN 3-88314-122-4

/7/   Th. Fedke: **Messung der Schalldämmung von Gehörschützern mit verschiedenen Kopfnachbildungen,** Fortschritte der Akustik, DAGA'92, DPG-GmbH, Bad Honnef, p. 385-388

/8/   J. Schröter, C. Pösselt: **The use of acoustical text fixtures for the measurement of hearing protectors attenuation,** J. Acoustical Society of America 80 (2), August 1986, p. 505-527

/9/   Th. Fedtke, U. Richter: **Measurements of Sound Attenuation of Hearing Protectors at Artificial and Human Heads,** Inter-Noise'93, Leuven, Belgien

/10/ S. Schwarze, G. Notbohm, G. Jansen: **The influence of binaural hearing on physiological responses**

Advances in Occupational Ergonomics and Safety II
Edited by Biman Das and Waldemar Karwowski
IOS Press and Ohmsha, 1997

Integrating Noise Consideration Into Facility Location Analysis: An Analytical Approach

Suebsak NANTHAVANIJ

Department of Industrial Engineering, Sirindhorn International Institute of Technology
Thammasat University, Patumtanee, 12121, Thailand

Abstract. This paper shows that placing a new machine at its optimal location (as determined from a traditional facility location analysis technique) may intensify the noise hazard in the workplace. A new method which concurrently considers both noise and cost factors when solving facility location problems is introduced as an alternative approach. A numerical example also is given.

1. Introduction

Facility layout and location problems generally involve a consideration about where to locate a new facility by taking into account the interactions between the new and all existing facilities. Such problems can be approached using either a systematic layout planning (SLP) technique or an analytical method. Briefly, the systematic layout planning technique views the problems from a practitioner's viewpoint and provides guidelines and systematic methodology for solving the problems. The analytical approach, on the other hand, treats the facility location subject as the design problem and applies classical optimization techniques to formulate the mathematical models. There have been a number of textbooks written on these subjects. Some examples of these books are Love *et al* [1] and Francis *et al* [2].

Consider a situation in which there is an existing machine workstation on the factory floor and a new workstation is to be located. It is clear that placing the two machine workstations close together minimizes the total transportation cost which is the product of 'weight' and 'distance' in which the weight may consist of the transportation cost, the number of trips per time period, and travel speed. When the number of existing workstations increases, the location of a new unit tends to be close to those having greater 'relationships' with it in order to minimize the total cost. In a case which existing workstations generate very loud noise when they operate, locating the new unit near them will obviously intensify the workplace noise level.

In this paper, a traditional approach in solving facility location problems is reviewed. A drawback of the approach especially according to the ergonomic and safety consideration is pointed out. A new approach is suggested to minimize the adverse effect. Finally, an example is given to demonstrate the application of this new approach.

2. Facility Location Analysis

Prior to solving a facility location problem, it is essential to define the distance measurement system and the analysis technique which will be used. The following sections explain those which are used in the location example.

2.1 Rectilinear Distance System

Rectilinear distance may be called by different names such as rectangular distance, right-angle distance, or Manhattan distance. Letting (x_i, y_i) represent the (x, y) coordinates of the point, the rectilinear distance, d_r, between the two points can be determined from

$$d_r \quad = \quad |x_1 - x_2| + |y_1 - y_2|.$$

2.2 Minisum Location Problem

Most facility location problems are typically formulated as minisum problems. A minisum problem is a problem in which the objective function to be minimized is the total cost function. Assuming that there are m existing facilities and their locations are fixed at (x_i, y_i), $i = 1, ..., m$, and their interactions (weights, w_i's) with a new facility, to be located at (x, y) are known, the objective function can be written as

$$f(x, y) \quad = \quad \sum_{i=1}^{m} w_i \left[|x - x_i| + |y - y_i| \right].$$

It can be shown that by solving the two smaller and independent problems of minimizing the cost of transportation in the x-direction and minimizing the cost of transportation in the y-direction, the total cost of transportation, $f(x, y)$, can be minimized. Additionally, a cost contour map can be constructed using the technique discussed in Francis et al [2]. This map is particularly useful for selecting an alternative location should the optimal one be physically not feasible.

Since the minisum facility location technique does not account for the workplace noise level, it is possible that the obtained solution may result in enhancing the noise hazard in the workplace. This adverse effect can be investigated and minimized if both the noise level and the cost of transportation are concurrently considered during the determination of a location for the new machine workstation.

3. Analytical Determination of Noise Level at a Given Location

From the literature on the physics of sound [3], it can be shown that a combined sound intensity (watt/m^2), $\bar{I}$, at a given location when there are n noise sources is

$$\bar{I} \quad = \quad I_{ab} + \sum_{i=1}^{n} \frac{10^{\frac{L_i - 120}{10}}}{d_i^2},$$

where I_{ab} = ambient noise intensity (watt/m^2), and d_i = distance (in meters) between the ith noise source and the given location (measured using a Euclidean distance system).

4.   Using Noise Contour Map to Evaluate New Machine Location

From the above formula, the noise level at any location on the factory floor can be estimated. By drawing lines connecting those points having equal noise level, a noise contour map can be constructed. An analytical procedure for constructing a noise contour map is discussed in Nanthavanij *et al* [4].

By evaluating the noise contour map, it can be seen that the optimal location does not guarantee having the minimum combined noise level since while the minimum cost location is in the convex hull of all existing facilities, the minimum noise location is not. When changing the new workstation location, a new noise contour map can be analytically reconstructed and provides better insights to the workplace noise level. Placing the new workstation at a location which compromises between the cost and noise criteria is thus a better ergonomic alternative. This objective can be achieved by integrating the use of a cost contour map and the above combined noise formula.

Suppose that the alternative location for the new machine workstation is on a cost contour with a total cost value of G. The location which has the lowest combined noise level dominates other locations on that cost contour. The dominant location problem then becomes

$$\text{minimizing} \quad g(x, y) \;=\; I_{ab} + \sum_{i=1}^{n} \frac{10^{\frac{L_i - 120}{10}}}{d_i^2},$$

subject to

$$\sum_{i} w_i \left[|x - x_i| + |y - y_i| \right] \quad = \quad G,$$

By varying G, a set of dominant locations can be obtained. A plot of these dominant locations defines the search direction for the alternative locations of the new workstation.

5.   Example

Consider a factory floor with its width and length of 50 m and 30 m, respectively. Presently there are four existing machine workstations at (20, 12), (15, 20), (40, 18), and (22, 25). The ambient noise level is 70 dBA. Noise levels generated by these workstations are 110 dBA, 120 dBA, 95 dBA, and 100 dBA, respectively. The new workstation to be located has a noise level of 110 dBA and its relationships (weights) with the existing workstations are 1.3, 0.8, 1.7, and 1.2, respectively.

6.   Results and Conclusions

Figure 1 shows a noise contour map of the factory floor, existing machine workstations (represented by circles), the optimal (minimum cost) location of the new unit (represented by a square), and the dominant locations (represented by dots). The optimal location is at (18, 22) and the minimum objective value is 59.20. The combined noise levels at that location before and after placing the new workstation are 103.13 dBA and 110.81 dBA, respectively. The dotted line extended from the optimal location to the right of the figure indicates a set of dominant locations. In case that the chosen location is physically not feasible or a cost-noise compromised location is preferred, an alternate location can be selected from among these dominant locations. Each dominant location has a greater objective value than the optimal location but the noise level tends to be less. The further away the dominant location is from the optimal location, the greater the increase of the objective value.

With the above mathematical model and the preferred total cost (objective value), the analyst is able to determine the cost-noise compromised location for the new machine workstation.

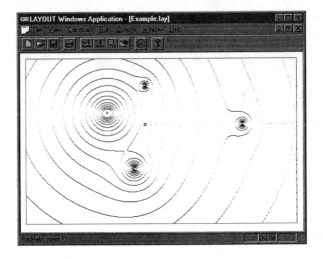

Figure 1: Factory Floor Layout

Acknowledgments

The author is indebted to the Fulbright Foundation for sponsoring his 4-month tenure as a Fulbright's senior visiting scholar at the Department of Industrial and Manufacturing Systems Engineering, New Jersey Institute of Technology, USA, where this research work was initiated.

References

[1]   R. F. Love et al., Facilities Location: Models & Methods. North-Holland, 1988.
[2]   R. L. Francis et al., Facility Layout and Location: An Analytical Approach. 2nd Edition, Prentice Hall, 1992.
[3]   C. M. Harris, Handbook of Noise Control. 2nd Edition, McGraw-Hill, 1979.
[4]   S. Nanthavanij et al., Analytical Procedure for Constructing Noise Contours, Proceedings of the 4th Pan Pacific Conference on Occupational Ergonomics, 1996, pp. 311-314.

19. Work Environment

Advances in Occupational Ergonomics and Safety II
Edited by Biman Das and Waldemar Karwowski
IOS Press and Ohmsha, 1997

Prediction of Thermal Stress in the Workplace with Natural Ventilation

S.M.Waly[1], S.S. Asfour[2], and H. Iridiastadi[1]

[1]*Department of Industrial and Manufacturing Systems Engineering*
Louisiana State University
Baton Rouge, Louisiana 70803

and

[2]*Department of Industrial Engineering, University of Miami*
Coral Gables, Florida 33124

ABSTRACT

It has been well established that extreme ambient temperature fluctuation can influence negatively the well being of industrial workers. Heat-induced occupational illnesses, injuries, and reduced productivity occur in situations in which the total heat load (environmental plus metabolic) exceeds the capacity of the body to maintain normal body functions without excessive strain. In the present study, the environmental component of the heat load was considered. The main objective of the proposed study was to develop a systematic method for relating outdoor climatic factors and the degree of heat stress in an industrial workplace with natural ventilation. The temperature and relative humidity inside a typical warehouse were monitored on a daily basis at 2:00 A.M., 8:00 A.M., 2:00 P.M., and 8:00 P.M. for 18 months period. Also the outdoor temperature (low and high) and relative humidity (at 7:00 A.M. and 7:00 P.M.) data reported by the weather bureau were recorded. Prediction models were developed to estimate the distribution of air temperature and heat stress throughout the year at locations within the workplace. Validation procedures showed that these models perform well.

1. Introduction

Thermal comfort is one environmental factor that can greatly affect worker's performance. It is the result of good control of temperature, humidity, and air distribution within the worker's vicinity. The aggregation of these environmental factors and physical work factors constitute heat stress -- the total heat load imposed on the body [1]. Exposure to heat stress might lead to heat strain which ranges from simple feeling of discomfort to complexities of heat stroke.

Heat stress indices are widely used to evaluate the amount of heat exposure to the workers. They can be measured directly by using particular apparatus that collects environmental conditions, such as temperature and relative humidity. A more comprehensive index incorporates actual physical work load into the calculation.

It has been demonstrated that the outdoor and indoor environmental conditions are related. It is logical to assume that in workplaces with natural ventilation, the meteorological conditions have a significant effect on the heat load imposed on the workers. Traditional monitoring of the climatic factors provides useful information on the level of heat stress at the place and time of measurement. Continuous observation of the climatic condition in the workplace is possible with modern instrumentation. However, its application and data handling at the work site are neither practical nor economical. An extensive review of the literature indicates that there are no easy and dependable means of predicting indoor heat stress as a function of local meteorological variables and building type and construction. Few attempts have been made to find applicable relationship between outdoor and indoor weather conditions. This is based on the assumption that indoor conditions are related with outdoor conditions, as shown in a study by Parmelee [2]. Furthermore, a study by Akbar-Khanzadeh and Ramsey [3] shows that the Wet Bulb Globe Temperature (WBGT) is correlated significantly with air temperature, and WBGT for different locations in the shop can be predicted accordingly.

Other studies have tried to incorporate factors other than outdoor weather conditions in predicting heat stress. Henschel and coworkers [4] conducted a study that included factors such as climatic environment, energy expenditure, and physiological responses to heat. In addition, a study by Dernedde [5] also offered another approach in assessing heat stress by the prediction of the wet bulb globe temperature in aluminum smelters.

The present study was conducted to see if there were relationships between temperature and relative humidity in a warehouse with natural ventilation and the outdoor weather conditions reported by weather bureau. This study also attempted to develop models that could be used to predict warehouse temperature and relative humidity at a different time of the day.

2. Methods

2.1 Data Collection

The data for this study were collected in Miami, Florida, for eighteen months. The workplace chosen was a warehouse without air conditioner; thus, the change in warehouse temperature and relative humidity were affected mainly by outside weather conditions. The first twelve month-data were used for constructing the models whereas the rests were used for validation process. The data collected included :

a. Warehouse temperature and relative humidity taken at 2:00 A.M., 8:00 A.M., 2:00 P.M., and 8:00 P.M.

b. Daily outdoor temperature and relative humidity reported by weather bureau, including high temperature, low temperature, humidity at 7:00 A.M., and humidity at 7:00 P.M.

2.2 Procedure

In the present study, five models to asses temperature values were developed. The first four models were developed to predict the warehouse temperature at 2:00 A.M., 8:00 A.M., 2:00 P.M., and 8:00 P.M. The fifth model incorporated the time as a factor in the model.. In addition to temperature models, five other models for predicting humidity were also developed by the same fashion.

All input variables (regressors) were the outdoor parameters reported by the weather bureau. All predicted values applied only to the corresponding time, except where time factor was used as the input variable.

3. Results and Discussion

Multiple regression analysis was performed in the study, resulting in ten models. These models and the corresponding R^2 values are summarized in Table 1. The first five models are for predicting warehouse temperature and the rests are for predicting warehouse humidity.

Table 1. Models for predicting temperatures (1-5) and humidity (6-10)

No	Model	R^2	Validation Correlation Coefficient [r]
1	T(2AM) = 19.273 + 0.393Thigh + 0.402Tlow - 0.003H7AM - 0.003H7PM	0.83	0.90
2	T(8AM) = 11.557 + 0.438Thigh + 0.423Tlow - 0.003H7AM - 0.025H7PM	0.87	0.92
3	T(2PM) = 17.090 + 0.765Thigh + 0.147Tlow - 0.044H7AM - 0.040H7PM	0.83	0.92
4	T(8PM) = 18.708 + 0.709Thigh + 0.170Tlow - 0.057H7AM - 0.041H7PM	0.86	0.91
5	T(t) = 13.877 + 0.576Thigh - 0.286Tlow - 0.027H7AM - 0.015H7PM + 0.253t	0.79	0.88
6	H(2AM) = 38.661 - 0.750Thigh + 0.753Tlow + 0.376H7AM + 0.083H7PM	0.42	0.56
7	H(8AM) = 23.527 - 0.476Thigh + 0.613Tlow + 0.409H7AM + 0.129H7PM	0.50	0.63
8	H(2PM) = 33.641 - 0.631Thigh + 0.555Tlow + 0.260H7AM + 0.302 H7PM	0.49	0.73
9	H(8PM) = 30.025 - 0.544Thigh + 0.500Tlow + 0.246H7AM + 0.344H7PM	0.55	0.74
10	H(t) = 33.834 - 0.600Thigh + 0.605Tlow + 0.323H7AM + 0.214H7PM - 0.216t	0.45	0.66

It is indicated that all models for predicting warehouse temperature are pretty good, in that the R^2 values are quite significant. This is true especially for the first four models. Further analysis by plotting the residuals showed that the models to predict temperature at 2:00 P.M. and 8:00 P.M. were better than the other three models.

In contrast with the temperature models, all models for predicting warehouse humidity had fairly low R^2 values that they might not be considered as adequate. Almost all R^2 are below 0.5. Note, however, that this does not mean that there is no relationship between outdoor parameters and warehouse humidity. This simply means that the relationship is not of a simple linear form. Further analysis are required to develop non linear models that are capable of predicting the indoor humidity values based on outdoor climatic conditions.

All models were validated by using the last six month-data which were not utilized for the development of these models. All the data provided by the weather bureau were applied to the models, resulting in predicted temperature or humidity values. These predicted values were compared with the recorded temperature or humidity values.

As can be seen from Table 1, the correlation coefficient between the predicted and observed values are relatively high, especially for temperature models (model 1-5). Except for model number five, the first four models have r values greater than or equal to 0.90. This indicates the adequacy of using temperature models for predicting warehouse temperatures. The humidity models, however, were obviously not good representatives of the actual conditions. All the correlation coefficients between the predicted and observed humidity are fairly low. This again suggests that the relationship may not be of a simple linear form.

4. Conclusions

Based on the results and analysis provided above, several conclusions can be drawn from the present study :
1. The warehouse temperature and humidity were related to the outdoor weather conditions. However, not all the relationships were of simple form.
2. Models for predicting warehouse temperature were considered adequate; however, none of the models for predicting humidity was representative.

5. References

[1]. Plog, Barbara A. ed., **Fundamentals of Industrial Hygiene**, 3rd ed., National Safety Council, 1988.
[2]. Parmelee, George V., **Applications of Meteorological Data to Indoor Climate in Buildings**, *Bulletin American Meteorological Society*, 36(6) : 256-264 (1955)
[3]. Khanzadeh, F. Akbar and Ramsey, J. D., **The Prediction of Temperatures and Heat Stress Limits in the Workplace with Natural Ventilation**, *American Industrial Hygiene Association Journal*, 48(4) : 396-399 (1977).
[4]. Henschel, A., Dukes-Dobos, F., Humphreys, C. M., Carlson, W., and Lee, D. H. K., **Assesment of Industrial Heat Stress**, *American Industrial Hygiene Association Journal*, January-February, 13-16, (1966).
[5]. Dernedde, Edgar, and Gilbert, Daniel, **Prediction of Wet Bulb Globe Temperatures in Aluminum Smelters**, *American Industrial Hygiene Association Journal*, (52), March, 120-126,(1991).

Advances in Occupational Ergonomics and Safety II
Edited by Biman Das and Waldemar Karwowski
IOS Press and Ohmsha, 1997

ENVIRONMENTAL ERGONOMIC STANDARDS: USA AND INTERNATIONAL

Jerry D. Ramsey
Texas Tech University
Lubbock, TX 79409-3061

1.   INTRODUCTION

Although the USA has not adopted regulatory standards, there are standards published by ANSI/ASHRAE, ASTM, ACGIH, and the US Military available for use by the employer/employee interested in addressing workplace thermal environment problems. On the international scene many countries, are adopting ISO standards for use in their respective country. This paper provides a better understanding of the family of environmental ergonomic standards by describing the scope and content of each of these sources of information and then evaluating their similarities and differences.

2.   USA STANDARDS

2.1   ANSI/ASHRAE

Thermal environmental conditions for human occupancy are presented in ANSI/ASHRAE 55 (1992) [1]. This consensus standard specifies combinations of indoor space and personal factors that will produce thermal conditions acceptable to 80% or more of the occupants within a space. Human comfort, as affected by clothing and metabolic rates, and the measurement/calculation of environmental variables are the major thrust of this standard. A thorough explanation of the fundamentals which serve as the basis for this standard can be found in the ASHRAE Handbook-Fundamentals (1993) [2].

2.2   ASTM

The annual book of ASTM standards, Volume 14.03 (1994) [3] includes standards relating to specifications, calibration, use, and test methods for temperature measurement. Although the primary emphasis of these standards is on measuring temperature of materials, there are ergonomically related ASTM standards for topics such as skin contact (C1057) [4], medical applications (E879) [5], psychrometry (E334, E337) [6, 7], and clothing insulation measurement (E1291) [8].

2.3   ACGIH

The ACGIH publishes on an annual basis adopted threshold limit values (TLV) for chemical substances, and biological and physical agents in the work environment including heat stress and cold stress (ACGIH, 1995) [9]. Heat stress TLVs are expressed in terms of WBGT values and levels of metabolic heat. Also presented in this document are methods for measuring and calculating WBGT, estimating metabolic rate, correction values for additional clothing, and work practices to ameliorate the heat. Cold stress is defined in terms of wind chill/equivalent chill temperatures, air temperatures and deep body/core temperatures. TLVs for work period and warm-up period schedules are presented, as are appropriate work practices for thermal conditions below -12°C.

2.4   Military Standards

Military Handbook 759 (1981) [10] concerns human factors engineering design for Army materiel and contains a section on thermal environments. Included are discussions of thermal measurements, heating, ventilation, and air conditioning of spaces, comfort and tolerance zones, use of WBGT and effective temperatures (ET), wind chill and contact temperature limits. Military Standard 1472 (1989) [11] contains general human engineering design criteria for military systems equipment and facilities. This standard extracts relevant limits, tables, and graphs from the environmental section of MIL-HDBK 759, and certain of them become standards in MIL-STD 1472. Prevention treatment and control of heat injury for US Armed

Forces personnel is a topic of a Tri-service Publication (1980) [12]. This publication presents information regarding the measurement of WBGT, estimating of metabolic heat and the use of physiological heat exposure limits (PHEL). More detail and current information on PHEL, including checklists, monitoring sheets, and reports, can be found in more recent Navy documents (1994) [13]. NASA also has a standard on man-systems integration with a section on the thermal environment (NASA, 1989) [14]. Emphasis of this standard is on design consideration and requirement for temperature, humidity, and air flow conditions that influence comfort and safety of the spacecraft crew. Several thermal indices are discussed as are the effect of clothing, heat illness, wind chill, metabolism, and combined stressors.

3.   ISO STANDARDS (GENERAL ENVIRONMENTAL ERGONOMICS)

3.1   ISO 7726 (Measuring physical environments)

Instruments and methods for measuring physical quantities (T_a, T_{wb}, T_{nwb}, humidity, velocity, mean radiant temperature, globe temperature) are presented in this standard (ISO 7726, 1996) [15]. Specifications for instruments in terms of response times, ranges, and accuracy are provided as an aid to users and manufacturers, but specific instruments are not exclusively required by the standard. Annexes include detailed discussions of measurement techniques, principles and calculations.

3.2   ISO 8996 (Metabolic heat)

Three methods for determining metabolic heat production are explained and compared in this document (ISO 8996, 1990) [16]. The first is use of tables to classify M according to activity or occupation. The second involves the use of heart rate which is linearly related to M during physical work (greater than 120 bpm). The third method represents the most accurate but requires more time and effort. It includes the measurement of oxygen consumption during work, or for very heavy work, during recovery as well.

3.3   ISO 9886 (Physiological measurements)

Evaluation of thermal strain by physiological measures is presented in this standard (ISO 9886, 1992) [17]. Typical strain measures covered include heart rate, body mass loss, skin temperature, and core temperature. Core temperature can be approximated by measuring rectal, esophageal, intra-abdominal, oral, tympanic, auditory canal, or urine temperatures. Techniques for each physiological measurement are discussed in terms of principles of the method, interpretation of results, and other considerations such as cost, convenience, annoyance, etc.

3.4   ISO 9920 (Clothing)

This standard specifies methods for estimating the thermal characteristics (resistance to dry heat loss and evaporative heat loss) in steady state conditions for a wide range of garments and clothing ensembles (ISO 9920, 1995) [18]. The document does not address the effects of water absorption (rain, snow, etc.), asymmetry of clothing ensembles, or special protective clothing/suits (water-cooled, ventilated, heated, etc.). Thermal insulation is calculated and tabulated in Clo units from values measured on standing thermal manikins. Extensive tables of data for clothing ensembles for male/female, and work/daily-wear clothing are included.

3.5   ISO 10551 (Subjective assessment)

This standard (ISO 10551, 1995) [19] covers the construction and use of judgment scales for use in providing data on the subjective assessment of thermal comfort or stress. Thermal assessment scales are provided for these types of judgments: perceptual (e.g., How do you feel?); affective evaluation (e.g., Do you find it uncomfortable?); thermal preference (e.g., Please state how you would prefer to be now.); personal acceptability (e.g., Do you judge this climate acceptable?); personal tolerance (e.g., Is it tolerable?). Examples of use of such scales are also presented.

3.6   ISO/CD 12894 (Medical supervision)

Currently under development is a standard concerning medical supervision of individuals exposed to extreme hot or cold environments (ISO/CD 12894, 1994) [20]. Its purpose is to provide advice to ergonomics investigations in either laboratory or field studies, concerning health screening and surveillance prior to and during such exposures. Depending upon the investigation the exposed persons may include the experimenter as well as the experimental subject. Information on the immediate treatment of exposure to extreme heat or cold is also provided.

4.   ISO STANDARDS (HOT, MODERATE AND COLD ENVIRONMENTS)

4.1   ISO 7243 (WBGT)

The estimation of the heat stress on working man, based on the WBGT-Index (Wet Bulb Globe Temperature) is covered in this standard (ISO 7243, 1989) [21]. It provides methods which can be used in an industrial environment for evaluating the heat stress to which an individual is subjected in a hot environment, and a method which allows a fast diagnosis. It applies to the evaluation of the mean effect of heat on man during representative activity, but does not apply to very short periods of work, nor to work in environments close to the zone of comfort. Specifications on the instruments and methods for measuring the environmental parameters (T_a, T_{nwb}, and T_g) are given.

4.2   ISO 7933 (Required sweat rate for hot environments)

This standard specifies a method of analytical evaluation and interpretation of the thermal stress experienced by a subject in a hot environment (ISO 7933, 1989) [22]. This is a rational method of calculating heat balance and the sweat rate the human body could produce to maintain this balance and equilibrium (i.e., required sweat rate). Different thermal stress and strain criteria are determined and compared with specified warning and danger levels. The criteria include maximum skin wettedness, maximum sweat rate, maximum heat storage, and maximum water loss. When the required sweat rate is greater than that which is physiological reasonable during an 8-hour work day, then an allowable exposure time can be calculated.

4.3   ISO 7730 (Moderate thermal environments)

Evaluating moderate thermal environments includes determination of the Predicted mean vote (PMV) and Predicted percentage of dissatisfied (PPD) indices, and the specification of conditions for thermal comfort (ISO 7730, 1994) [23]. The PMV value is a number on a 7 point scale that is calculated from the air temperature, mean radiant temperature, air velocity, humidity, metabolic rate and clothing insulation. The PPD calculated from this PMV index provides a predicted percentage of people who will be dissatisfied with the thermal conditions. Thermal discomfort caused by draughts is also discussed.

4.4   ISO/New Proposal (Contact surfaces)

The ISO is currently involved in new work item proposals concerning skin contact with hot, moderate and cold surfaces (ISO/TC 195/SC5 N79, 1993) [24]. A hot surface causes the sensation of pain or the damage of skin due to burning, and a cold surface causes the sensation of pain or the damage of frost bite. The moderate temperature surface does not cause these skin damages, but comfortable thermal touch is often required for elders and children in everyday life in surfaces such as handrails on stairs, handles of tools, furniture and floors. European standards in these areas will likely influence further development of this ISO standard.

4.5   ISO/TR 11079 (Cold environments)

Methods for evaluation of cold environments through the determination of required clothing insulation (IREQ) is covered in this standard (ISO/TR 11079, 1993) [25]. It is used primarily for those air temperatures at or below 10°C. The IREQ index uses the same general concepts of thermal equilibrium and its rational analysis as used in analysis of heat stress. It assumes a minimum cold tolerance level for skin temperature, and with these assumptions the amount of insulation required to obtain thermal balance can be calculated. To determine IREQ for a specific environment requires a measurement of various temperatures, air velocity, and estimate of metabolic heat. If available insulation is not adequate, methods for calculating maximum exposure times and required recovery times are presented.

5.   COMPARISON OF USA AND ISO STANDARDS

The environmental ergonomics standards found in the USA and internationally are very compatible. Environmental scientists from many nations have participated in development of the current understanding of how humans respond to their environment. Although political conditions differ widely, the technical content of standards used in most industrial nations is very similar. The ISO approach has been to develop specific standards for individual topics; each integrated with other standards, where appropriate, and individually updated. Thus international standards are available for clothing, metabolic heat, threshold limits, etc. Contrast this to the USA where individual groups, e.g., ASHRAE, ACGIH, US Military, etc., have developed documents which cover a broad range of thermal topics, and which overlap the content found in other documents. In those countries where ISO standards have been adopted, notably the European community, the management of environmental ergonomics is consistent with the principles found in most USA standards. In the USA where no regulatory standards for heat have been adopted, use of either the USA's voluntary/consensus standards or of those recommended by ISO should provide responsible protection and guidance for the worker exposed to thermal environments.

Reference

[1]   ANSI/ASHRAE 55: "Thermal Environmental Conditions for Human Occupancy," American Society of Heating, Refrigerating and Air-Conditioning Engineers, Inc., 1992.
[2]   ASHRAE Handbook--Fundamentals, "Physiological Principles for Comfort and Health," Chapter 8, pp. 8.1-8.29, American Society of Heating, Refrigerating and Air-Conditioning Engineers, Inc., 1993.
[3]   ASTM, "Annual Book of ASTM Standards," Volume 14.03 Temperature Measurement, 1994.
[4]   ASTM C1057, "Determination of Skin Contact Temperature from Heated Surfaces Using a Mathematical Model and Thermesthesiometer," 1990.
[5]   ASTM E879, "Thermistor Sensors for Clinical Laboratory Temperature Measurements," 1993.
[6]   ASTM E334, "Thermometry and Hydrometry," 1994.
[7]   ASTM E337, "Measuring Humidity with a Psychrometer," 1990.
[8]   ASTM E1291, "Measuring the Thermal Insulation of Clothing Using a Heated Manikin," 1990.
[9]   ACGIH, "Threshold Limit Values for Chemical Substances and Physical Agents and Biological Exposure Indices," 1995-1996.
[10]   MIL-HDBK-759A, "Human Factors Engineering Design for Army Materiel," March, 1981.
[11]   MIL-STD-1472D, "Human Engineering Design Criteria for Military Systems, Equipment and Facilities," May, 1989.
[12]   Tri-Service Publication, TB MED 507, NAVMED P-5052-5, AFP 160-1 "Prevention, Treatment and Control of Heat Injury," July, 1980.
[13]   Department of the Navy, "Navy Occupational Safety and Health (NAVOSH) Program Manual for Forces Afloat," OPNAVINST 5100.19C, January 19, 1994.
[14]   NASA, "Man-Systems Integration Standards," NASA-STD-3000, Volume I, page 5-117, October, 1989.
[15]   ISO 7726, "Thermal Environment -- Instruments for Measuring Physical Quantities," 1996.
[16]   ISO 8996, "Ergonomics -- Determination of Metabolic Heat Production," 1990.
[17]   ISO 9886, "Evaluation of Thermal Strain by Physiological Measurements," 1992.
[18]   ISO 9920, "Ergonomics of the Thermal Environment -- Estimation of the Thermal Insulation and Evaporative Resistance of a Clothing Ensemble," 1995.
[19]   ISO 10551, "Ergonomics of the Thermal Environment -- Assessment of the Influence of the Thermal Environment Using Subjective Judgment Scales," 1995.
[20]   ISO/CD 12894, "Ergonomics of the Thermal Environment: Medical Supervision of Individuals Exposed to Extreme Heat or Cold Environments," 1994.
[21]   ISO 7243, "Hot Environments -- Estimation of the Heat Stress on Working Man, Based on the WBGT-Index (Wet Bulb Globe Temperature)," 1989.
[22]   ISO 7933, "Hot Environments -- Analytical Determination and Interpretation of Thermal Stress Using Calculation of Required Sweat Rate." 1989.
[23]   ISO 7730, "Moderate Thermal Environments --Determination of the PMV and PPD Indices and Specification of the Conditions for Thermal Comfort," 1994.
[24]   ISO/TC 159/SC5 N79 "Ergonomics of the Thermal Environment: Comfortable Contact Surface Temperatures," 1993.
[25]   ISO/TR 11079, "Evaluation of Cold Environments -- Determination of Required Clothing Insulation (IREQ)," 1993.

Advances in Occupational Ergonomics and Safety II
Edited by Biman Das and Waldemar Karwowski
IOS Press and Ohmsha, 1997

AN ERGONOMICS MODEL TO ANALYZE WORKING CONDITIONS AND PROBLEMS OF DEVELOPING NATIONS

Bahador Ghahramani, Ph.D., P.E., CPE
206 Engineering Management Building
School of Engineering
University of Missouri - Rolla
Rolla, Missouri 65409 (USA)
E-mail: ghahrama@shuttle.cc.umr.edu

An ergonomics and safety model is described to assess and evaluate the most critical industrial improvement areas in a developing nation. This study was initiated and supported by a Fortune 500 Corporation interested in improving its global operations in developing nations. This initiative was also fully supported by an emerging nation that was concerned with its ergonomics and safety problems. The model was tested and validated in the emerging nation and the results were used to further enhance the model so that it can be implemented and adapted to other similar work environments. The model provides a practical methodology that analyzes and evaluates an emerging nation's current work environment, suggests practical solutions, and recommends effective remedies.

1. INTRODUCTION

A model was constructed to permit analysis of working conditions in developing countries. To help occupational ergonomists and safety practitioners, the paper follows a systems engineering approach that leads its readers through various stages of the model and analyzes each situation by example. The model was based on a check-list that incorporated eight groups of hazards or risks. The classification of the hazards was based on a comprehensive list of workstations and manufacturing environments commonly encountered in developing nations. E&S experts with various backgrounds were used to develop the model and to validate its effectiveness. The model was intended to be practical, easy to use, and simple to understand. The model prioritizes different hazard categories and provides intuitive tables, charts, and figures that enable E&S subject matter experts to remedy the problems. The model incorporates ratings of seven alternatives that were ranked with numerical values that ranged from zero (factor not known to be present) to six (imminent danger, immediate action required).

2. BACKGROUND AND METHODOLOGY

The objective of this initiative was to provide basic recognition for setting up priorities for the model. Another objective was to assist the targeted nation in solving its E&S problems using the priorities. The model was tested and validated using the targeted nation's E&S statistical data, surveys, questionnaires, qualitative and quantitative responses. Information was gathered from 80 industrial units covering about 40,000 employees.

The nation's statistics pertaining to E&S injuries were obtained from the country's Workmen's Compensation Fund Organization (WCFO) that was a branch of the government and supported by the United Nations and World Bank. Table 1 is a summary of the country's, industries with most common injuries, number of employees, industrial injuries, and percent frequency rate of the injuries for each industry for the past 10 years (1983 to 1993). Ranking of the table was based on an industry's importance to the country's economy and needs. The government bureau of statistics provided most of the information incorporated in this study.

Table 1, Industrial Injuries in the Targeted Country.

No.	Type of Industry	No. of Units	Employees	Industrial Injuries	Frequency rate*
1	Mining, quarry, gravel, sand and clay	65	31484	2478	32.794
2	Food, beverages and tobacco	420	159678	978	2.552
3	Textiles, and wearing apparel products	615	189657	678	1.489
4	Wood and wood products	302	43895	4523	42.934
5	Paper and paper products	195	634566	1678	1.102
6	Chemicals, and petroleum products	521	83145	4567	22.889
7	Non-metallic mineral products	156	27865	3467	51.843
8	Basic metal industries	167	24587	7345	124.473
9	Fabricated metal products, and machinery	609	67897	8935	54.831
10	Production and transportation equipment	170	35678	4562	53.278
11	Construction	156	35678	3412	39.847
12	Transportation and communications	2567	58956	3698	26.131
13	Trade, restaurants, and hotels	892	265789	897	1.406
14	Other manufacturing industries	12	26435	2346	36.978
15	Government industries	87	786	87	46.120
16	Other occupations	6895	126423	871	2.871
	TOTAL	13829	1812883	50522	

Note: * $F = \dfrac{(N)X(1,000,000)}{(E)X(2,400)}$ For 2, 400 working hours/employee/year.

Where: F (frequency rate of injuries); E(number of employees); and N(number of injuries).

The WCFO statistics covered more than 60% of the country's workforce. Small enterprises of less than 20 employees were not covered by WCFO and, therefore, were not used in this paper. The E&S injuries were available from WCFO covering more than 1,457,000 employees in 1994. During the 10 years duration, 45,658 enterprises were inspected that covered about 4,456 million employees. The statistics also revealed that, during the same 10 year period, government's E& S laws and policies resulted in: 4,674 warnings, 3,654 court orders requesting immediate improvements, and 79 court cases that resulted in severe fines and business closures. At the time of the study, the number of government inspectors enforcing E&S laws and regulations was 678 for the entire country.

The survey contained a checklist of workstation E&S requirements, and a database containing 12 different groups of hazards or risks.   The E&S   classification of certain hazards was taken from a comprehensive list of OSHA and NIOSH regulations, policies, practices, and guidelines.   Due to time and resource constraints only a limited number of the most common and critical hazards were identified and analyzed.

The data collected were from 82 enterprises.   The hazard ratings consisted of seven different alternatives.   The ratings ranged from 0 (factor not known to be present) to 6 (imminent danger, immediate action required).   UNIX was selected as the operating language due to broad capabilities and its scientific applications.   The E&S information gathered was further divided into two categories: establishments with less than 100 employees, and those with more than 100 employees.   To identify and prioritize E&S hazards, and to determine their associated risks, 7 different industry groups were analyzed and compared.

3.   ANALYSIS OF THE RESULTS

The priority rating used to analyze the E&S data consisted of: 0 (factor not known to be present); 1 (factor not observed, not expected); 2 (factor expected but not observed); 3 (factor observed but considered under control); 4 (factor is of concern, requires investigation); 5 (factor is serious, requires action in near future); and 6 (imminent danger, immediate action required to prevent accident).

Table 2 is also similar to the previous tables.   This table further categorizes the nation's serious hazards into its four primary industries.

Table 2, Hazard Factors Based on Industry Categories.

HAZARD NO.	FACTOR	TEXTILE	CHEMICAL	METAL	FOOD
10	Skin exposure	50	37	41	17
12	Cuts and bruises	41	39	38	21
4	Moving parts	42	36	37	21
7	Stumbling	38	35	38	18
14	Ejection	30	36	39	22
3	High level noise	48	30	32	15
8	Electricity	29	37	38	16
13	Labeling	27	39	36	13
5	Repetitive work	23	38	35	19
9	Unchanging position	39	37	22	16
6	Insufficient lighting	42	31	27	13
1	Personal protection	43	30	26	14
11	Workplace hygiene	41	29	30	12
15	Physical stress	44	28	28	11
2	Lack of knowledge	38	29	27	14

4.   DISCUSSION OF THE RESULTS

Figure 1 is a comparative analysis of the most commonly found hazards in four primary industries: textile, chemical, metal, and food.   The textile industry has had the most hazards, complaints, and injuries. This was primarily due to out-dated equipment and highly stressful work conditions.   In this industry, child labor was prevalent, underground, and mostly in remote locations.

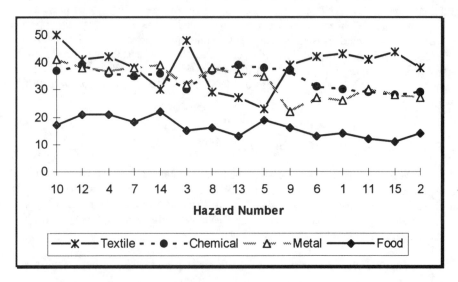

Figure 1, Prevalence of Most Common Hazards and Risks in Four Major Industries.

5.   CONCLUSIONS

This paper discussed an ergonomics model that analyzes working conditions and safety problems of developing nations.   The model was based on a check-list that incorporated nine E&S groups of hazards and risks. The check-list was used as a blue print and a foundation to evaluate E&S activities in most developing nations.   The model had two primary purposes: to help professional ergonomists and safety engineers in the developing nations to effectively address their E&S problems, and to initiate preventive measures that would eliminate root causes of the problems so that they would not occur again. The model was designed to be user friendly and practical.   The process incorporated ratings of seven alternatives that were ranked with numerical values and ranged from zero (factor not known to be present) to six (imminent danger, immediate action required).

REFERENCES

[1]   National Institute for Occupational Safety and Health, Health Hazard Evaluation Report
        (DHHS/NIOSH   Publications), Cincinnati, OH: US Department of Health and Human Services,
        National Institute for Occupational Safety and Health, April, 1993.

[2]   A. M. Colombia, D. Colombini, and E. Occhipinti, " Ergonomic Analysis and Redesign of
        Materials Handling Tasks in a Chemical Plant: a Field Study," The Ergonomics of Manual Work,
        Taylor and Francis, pp 667-670, 1993.

Advances in Occupational Ergonomics and Safety II
Edited by Biman Das and Waldemar Karwowski
IOS Press and Ohmsha, 1997

ERGONIMICS ANALYSIS OF TANKER OPERATIONS IN HUMID AREAS: CREATING HEALTHFUL WORK ENVIRONMENTS IN CONFINED SPACES

Bahador Ghahramani, Ph.D., P.E., CPE
206 Engineering Management Building
School of Engineering
University of Missouri - Rolla
Rolla, Missouri 65409 (USA)
E-mail: ghahrama@shuttle.cc.umr.edu

This paper analyzes the ergonomics and safety conditions of ocean-going ships, tankers, and barges hauling cargo and passengers on the lower reaches of the Mississippi River during warm and humid summer seasons. Annually, a great tonnage of goods is moved along the Mississippi, loading and unloading cargo at every major inland port. In the past decade, traffic passing on the river has tripled, resulting in congestion and injuries. Working conditions on board are poor due to the tropical environment, work stress, and hazards of the jobs. Evaluation of the medical data reveals that a large number of the crew was experiencing job related injuries, diseases, disorders, and exhaustion as the result of working conditions and environmental elements.

1. INTRODUCTION

The Mississippi river is known as the life line for commerce in the heart land of United States. It is one of the busiest rivers in the world, particularly in its lower reaches - ships of all sizes hauling cargo along the river. Due to high volume of commerce and trade, ocean going ships, tankers, and barges (all are referred to as tankers) have to operate these ports regularly loading and unloading goods and passengers. Unfortunately, most ships traveling in these humid areas have no proper safety guidelines or air circulation systems. Most of the crew have to work on the decks, the cargo areas bellow the deck, or the engine rooms that have poor ventilation systems. Medical data indicate that a large number of tanker crews suffer from exhaustion, injuries, and diseases that are directly related to improper air circulation and poor ventilation systems.

The primary purpose of this paper is to analyze the ergonomics and safety (E&S) accidents of these tankers during warm and humid summer seasons, and, to recommend requirements that can be adopted in the design of their work environments.

2.   BACKGROUND

E&S experts have stated that the existence of a vicious circle of work activities, extreme heat and humidity is the primary causes of reduction in physical working capacity (PWC) and low standard of work performance in tropical climates. Experience indicates that proper acclimation, physical training, and psychological preparedness of the crews may improve employee heat tolerance and PWC. E&S analysis indicates that an increase in temperature and humidity can reduce oxygen consumption, which can reduce PWC and increase the number of accidents. Subsequently, summer temperatures can also increase heart rate, body temperatures, perspiration rate, and change in the core temperature (rectal). PWC was measured through assessment of aerobic capacity by the Astrand-Rihming sub-maximal step up test and energy expenditure by the indirect time and motion study method. The tests revealed that PWC of the crew members also depended on age, body build, gender, duration, frequency of tasks, and their acclimation periods.

Most of the statistical data obtained in this study were obtained randomly from the crew performing varying tasks at different times and under different environmental conditions, and supported through a project assigned to AT&T Bell Laboratories. Measurement of physiological responses included oxygen intake (VO_2 max), and energy expenditure of the crews working on actual tasks at different time intervals. Besides oxygen intake (VO_2 max), other measurements were also obtained such as: pulse (heart) rate; rectal temperature; skin temperature; and perspiration rate (loss of body weight) at the beginning of, during, and after work. Table 1 is a presentation of number of injuries during one year of the study. As Table 1 indicates, most injuries happened during the warm and humid months of May, June, July, and August.

TABLE 1, MONTHLY INJURY REPORTS FOR 1994.

MONTH	CASES	%	DECK	%	ENGINE	%
January	10	6.5	6	6.5	4	6.6
February	8	5.2	5	5.4	3	11.5
March	7	4.6	4	4.3	3	4.9
April	8	5.2	5	5.4	3	14.8
May	19	12.4	10	10.9	9	8.2
June	17	11.1	12	13.0	5	4.9
July	29	19.0	18	19.6	11	18.0
August	18	11.8	11	12.0	7	4.9
September	7	4.6	4	4.3	3	6.6
October	8	5.2	4	4.3	4	4.9
November	8	5.2	5	5.4	3	6.6
December	14	9.2	8	8.7	6	9.8
TOTAL	153		92		61	

3.   ACCIDENT STATISTICS

In 1995, a descriptive study of 1994 accident data from tankers of all sizes was analyzed.   This study was carried out using medical reports sent to AT&T- Bell Laboratories.   It became evident that out of 256 documented accidents, only 123 cases happened on board, while the remaining 133 were traffic accidents during regular operations.   We further divided the statistical data into two categories: deck and engine room.   Table 2 is a presentation of the accidents on the decks, and the engine rooms.   This table shows that more accidents happened on the decks than in the engine rooms.

TABLE 2,   INJURIES BY PARTS OF THE BODY.

PART OF THE BODY	CASES	DECK	%	ENGINE	%
Head	31	13	14.1	18	29.5
Upper Extremities	28	17	18.5	11	18.0
Lower Extremities	37	29	31.5	8	13.1
Body	27	18	19.6	9	14.8
Eye	16	9	9.8	7	11.5
Other	14	6	6.5	8	13.1
TOTAL	153	92		61	

Table 3 categorizes accidents by their causes and job classifications.   As Table 3 indicates, slippery decks were the highest causes of injuries on the decks, while burns were the cause of the highest number of accidents in the engine rooms.

TABLE 3,   INJURIES BY CAUSE AND JOB CLASSIFICATION.

CAUSES	TOTAL CASES	DECK CASES	%	ENGINE CASES	%
Hitting by Lines	21	16	17.4	5	8.2
Burns	31	18	19.6	13	21.3
Dull Objects	7	4	4.3	3	4.9
Sharp Objects	8	5	6.5	3	3.3
Sandwich	18	12	13.0	6	9.8
Slippery	27	16	17.4	11	18.0
Electric Shock	8	5	5.4	3	4.9
Drowning	18	11	12.0	7	11.5
Noxious Gas	15	4	4.3	11	18.0
TOTAL	153	92		61	

4.   CONCLUSIONS

Accident study of tankers traveling through the lower reaches of the Mississippi indicates that more injuries happened during the hot and humid summer season than any other time of the year. Categorization of accidents indicates that lower extremity injuries were more prominent for both decks as well as engine rooms. Analysis of the data also revealed that more accidents happened on the decks than in the engine rooms of tankers. Figure 1 shows types of injuries in the tankers by fractures and concussions.

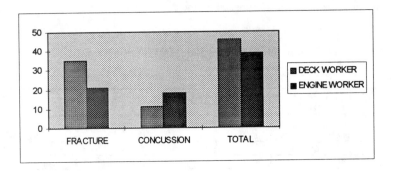

FIGURE 1,   INJURIES BY FRACTURE AND CONCUSSION.

REFERENCES

[1]   C. Fransson-Hall et al., A portable Ergonomic Observation Method (PEO) for Computerized On-line Recording of Postures and Manual Handling, *Applied Ergonomics* 26; 3 (1995) 199-221.

[2]   National Institute for Occupational Safety and Health, Health Hazard Evaluation Report (DHHS/NIOSH   Publications), Cincinnati, OH: US Department of Health and Human Services, National Institute for Occupational Safety and Health, April, 1993.

[3]   T. Backstrom and M. Doos, The Riv Method: A Participative Risk Analysis Method and It's Application, Accepted for Publication in the *New Solutions*, 1996.

[4]   R.L. Getty, " Physical Demands of Work are the Common Reference for an Integrated Ergonomics Program, " *Proceedings of the Human Factors & Ergonomics Society 38th Annual Meeting*, Santa Monica, CA: Human Factors Society, 1994.

[5]   K. Kemmlert, Preventive Effects of Work Place Investigations in Conditions and Employment Rate After an Occupational Musculo-Skeletal Injury, *Journal of Occupational Rehabilitation* 4;1 (1994) 11-21

Advances in Occupational Ergonomics and Safety II
Edited by Biman Das and Waldemar Karwowski
IOS Press and Ohmsha, 1997

Professional cleaning in the European Union: Ergonomics

Veikko LOUHEVAARA

Finnish Institute of Occupational Health and University of Kuopio, P.O.B. 93, 70701 Kuopio, Finland

Abstract. A professional cleaner is one of the most common occupations in the European Union (EU). With the economical support of the European Commission a multidisciplinary 3-year project "Prevention of health and safety risks in professional cleaning and the work environment" was established by the four member states of the EU: Denmark, Finland, Germany and Italy. During the first stage (1996-97) of the project review documents were prepared by three subjects groups: Ergonomics, Individual health and capacities and Environmental exposure. Ergonomics concentrated on physical and psychosocial stress factors associated with cleaners' work and work environment. Several studies indicate that cleaning work is strenuous both on the cardiorespiratory and musculoskeletal system as well as contains several psychosocial risk factors. Heavy muscular work and shortcomings in work organisations accelerate work disability particularly among ageing female cleaners. Ergonomic improvements at work sites are key measures for the reduction of work related risk factors and for the prevention of cleaners' musculoskeletal disorders and work disability.

1. Introduction

Cleaning is important work and necessary for all. It has positive effects on the productivity and quality of work as well as ergonomics and safety at work sites [1]. A professional cleaner is one of the most common occupations in the European Union (EU).The number of full or part-time cleaners is about 3 million in private, municipal and governmental sectors. The overwhelming majority of cleaners (about 95 %) are women. They are often ageing workers i.e., at the age of over 45 years [2] because in the EU the average age of the population and work force is rapidly increasing due to ageing of the large post-war age cohort born in 1945-50 [3]. Ageing cleaners have plenty of problems in their work ability and health resulting in a high incidence of sickness and a high frequency of early retirement [4, 5, 6, 7, 8]. This type of statistics is not available from the Southern Europe although, for instance, in Italy cleaning is a large and rapidly developing service branch [9].

With the economical support of the European Commission a multidisciplinary 3-year project "Prevention of health and safety risks in professional cleaning and the work environment" was established by the four member states of the EU: Denmark, Finland, Germany and Italy. During the first stage of the project (1996-97) three subjects groups (ergonomics, individual health and capacities and environmental exposure) gathered and disseminated information and each of them prepared a literature review on its topic.

Ergonomics was defined to mean a multidisciplinary field of science which is based on physiology, psychology and applications of technical sciences. It considers human capacities, needs and limitations in the interaction of technical and organisational work systems. The integrated knowledge of ergonomics aims to develop work contents and the environment with job design and redesign measures in order to prevent work-related diseases and work disability, and to improve the productivity and quality of work

The aim of this brief review on ergonomics of professional indoor cleaning jobs was to assess their physical work load and psychosocial stress factors, and to evaluate effects and feasibility of ergonomic interventions on work load and well-being.

2. Physical work load

The physical work load factors and strain responses associated with different tasks of professional cleaning have been studied in industry, shops, offices, schools and hospitals. The results were quite similar in various types of jobs and/or work tasks.

Absolute oxygen consumption which quantifies the amount of dynamic work load varied from 0.8 to 1.1 l/min. Peak load situations on the cardiorespiratory system were rare. The average relative aerobic strain for the 8-hour work shifts was often near the upper limit of acceptable cardiorespiratory strain i.e., about 40 % of the maximal oxygen consumption. Cardiac strain, which also reflects mostly dynamic work load when based on the measurements of heart rate, was highly individual depending on a cleaner's physical fitness level and occupational skills. The mean heart rates were 88-118 beats/min during the 8-hour work shifts and/or in specific work tasks. The cardiac strain was the highest during floor cleaning with the use of wet mopping and scrubbing work methods [4].

Poor work postures for the back and arms were common. The proportion of bent forward and/or twisted back postures was, on average, 50 % of working hours. The corresponding value for the work postures where one arm or both arms were above the shoulder level was 30 % of working hours. Also the cleaners spent about 10 % of working hours in a one-foot standing, squatting or kneeling position [4].

3. Psychosocial stress factors

Psychosocial stress factors at work include several large and problematic issues such human relationships, leadership and developmental aspects in work organisations. These factors are important with the respect of work ability as well as psychological and social needs of the workers.

The questionnaire studies in Finland, Denmark and Germany have revealed almost an equal profile of the psychosocial stress factors involved in professional cleaning [10, 11, 6, 7, 8]. Often every second of the cleaners (35-55 %) responded that they have little or not at all possibilities to influence on their work arrangements, tools and machines, division of labour or work partners. Almost all cleaners (75-90 %) stated that they had no possibilities to develop in their occupational career, to obtain any sort of advantages from the work or to regulate their work pace which resulted in experiences of continuous time pressure at work.

The high number of various psychosocial risk factors was often due to the false idea that professional cleaning is unskilled extra work which can be done by anyone without basic education or occupational training. Besides increased stress this concept is very expensive for taxpayers. It has been estimated, for instance, that within the EU the total costs of poor and unskilled cleaning are several billion ECUs just due to damages in materials and losses in productivity. Poor cleaning may also cause considerable expenses due to increased number of allergies.

3. Ergonomic interventions

Few ergonomic interventions with well-controlled designs have been carried out within professional cleaning. One of those was the Finnish study carried out by Hopsu et al. [6]. They applied the approach of participatory ergonomics which based on team work and learning by doing in habitual work units. Careful analyses of work load factors, developing and introducing redesign measures, ergonomic guidance and training and continuous providing of motivation were the main elements of the developmental learning process.

The aim of the intervention was to reduce and optimise acute load and strain at work with technical and organisational redesign measures regarding cleaners' individual characteristics and capacities. The subjects were 55 female cleaners aged 21-59 years. They were divided into the intervention (n=28) and control group (n=27). The intervention lasted for 12 months including questionnaire studies and work site assessments before and after the intervention.

After the ergonomic intervention harmful static postural load on the musculoskeletal system and cardiac strain according to the working heart rate were lower than before the intervention. Moreover, occupational knowledge and skills as well as satisfaction at work increased due to the intervention. The results and experiences of the intervention suggest that the key prerequisites for the successful interventions are the following: unreserved support of the top management, implementation of measures in habitual work units, measures are composed according to actual needs of cleaners, and quick feedback from the work site assessments which, particularly, enhance motivation and commitment of the cleaners.

The study indicated that the participatory ergonomics is an effective and feasible method for reducing physical work load and for improving work satisfaction among ageing professional cleaners.

4. Conclusions and recommendations

The studies referred in this review justified drawing the following conclusions and recommendations:
- Due to rapid ageing and a high amount of work disability among professional cleaners, an efficient strategy for the maintenance of work ability is needed in every cleaning company. Cleaning is changing rapidly but human capacities are changing slowly. Therefore, more individual and flexible solutions are urgently needed with advancing age at cleaning work sites.
- Ergonomics is an essential element for reducing physical load and improving well-being at cleaning work sites.
- In the near future, the increased quality requirements of the indoor climate will also set new challenges for cleaning.
- Cleaning work must not be divided into simple work tasks for the different groups of cleaners although this might save costs in a short run.
- Professional cleaning work will never disappear, and, therefore, it should be continuously studied and developed within the EU.
- The professional status of the cleaning jobs should be raised with continuous dissemination of relevant information of their positive effects on health, safety and productivity.

References

[1] J. Saari, Management of housekeeping by feedback. *Ergonomics* **30** (1987) 313-317.

[2] WHO (World Health Organization). Ageing and work capacity. Report of a WHO Expert Committee. WHO Technical Report Series 835, Geneva 1993.

[3] J. Ilmarinen, The aging worker. *Scandinavian Journal of Work, Environment & Health* **18** (1991) suppl. 2, 1-141.

[4] V. Louhevaara, Cleaning work. *Työ ja ihminen* **7** (1993) lisänumero 3, 169-175 (in Finnish).

[5] L. Hopsu, Working conditions in jobs where the majority of workers are women: Cleaning work: OECD panel group on women, work and health: National Report. Ministry of Social Affairs and Health. Helsinki 1993.

[6] L. Hopsu *et al.*, Feasibility of the ergonomic intervention and its effects on physical load and strain in professional cleaning. Rakennushallitus, raportti 3/1994. Helsinki 994 (in Finnish).

[7] J. Nielsen, Occupational health among cleaners. University of Copenhagen. National Institute of Occupational Health. Copenhagen 1995 (doctoral dissertation,in Danish with English summary).

[8] E. Huth *et al.*, Health promotion in hospital cleaning by improving job content and organisation. Fachhochschule Hamburg. Fachbereich, Ernährung und Hauswirtscaft. Hamburg 1995 (in German).

[9] G. Guzzi, Cleaning industry. MO.ED.CO. Milan 1995 (in Italian).

[10] Y. Engeström and R. Engeström, Mastering of cleaning work and qualified needs for occupational training. Servisystems Oy. Helsinki 1984 (in Finnish).

[11] T. Auto-Reivilä, Work load in cleaning - psychosocial work environment and measurement of work output. KTV Tutkimusosaston julkaisuja B-sarja 1. Vaasa 1988 (in Finnish).

Advances in Occupational Ergonomics and Safety II
Edited by Biman Das and Waldemar Karwowski
IOS Press and Ohmsha, 1997

A Case Study Examining Cumulative Trauma Exposure of Coal Mine Workers

Kim M. Cornelius and Fred C. Turin
National Institute for Occupational Safety and Health
Pittsburgh Research Center
P.O. Box 18070
Pittsburgh, PA USA 15236

A case study was conducted at an underground coal mine concerned about the increased frequency of aches and pains reported by their workers. In particular, they wanted to focus on the job of roof bolter operators and determine if something could be done to minimize their exposure to injury. Three primary forms of data were collected: accident, interview, and video taped observation. Data analysis identified roof bolting factors that posed risk to the development of cumulative trauma injuries. These issues included, materials handling, operator orientation in work space, vision obstruction, control bank design, and slipping and tripping hazards. Recommendations for reducing the cumulative trauma exposure were developed that should be useful to equipment manufacturers and to the management and workforce at underground coal mines.

1. Introduction

Although underground coal mining has become more mechanized, many jobs continue to be labor intensive and repetitive in nature. They entail tasks that, performed over time, can take a toll on the soft tissues and joints. The problem may be compounded by the fact that the mining industry has an aging workforce. As a person ages, the body's resilience to chronic wear and tear is reduced which may cause a worker to pay an increasingly higher health price for performing the same task [1],[2]. Mining companies are becoming more aware of the effects to the worker as the reports of injuries rise. One mine was concerned about early warning signs of cumulative trauma. In particular they were concerned about the increased frequency of aches and pains reported by roof bolter operators. Roof bolter operators spend a significant portion of their working day installing long bolts into the roof. This case study focused on roof bolter operators working in a high seam mine using a dual head, walk-through roof bolting machine.

2. Method

Three primary forms of data were collected and analyzed to identify problems. Before visiting the mine, researchers analyzed 43 lost time incident descriptions. It should be noted that those responsible for compiling incident descriptions usually identify the immediate activity as the cause of the injury. For cumulative trauma incidents there may be a combination of any number of factors which can lead to injuries. For this evaluation, researchers identified roof bolting activities and operator injuries having characteristics consistent with cumulative trauma exposure. Secondly, at the mine site, researchers conducted a series of interviews with the roof bolter operators. The objective of the interviews was to learn about bolting tasks and working conditions, to identify safety hazards, and to discuss the details of accidents and injuries. The interview data was analyzed to identify similarities in injuries and pains; tasks that may contribute to cumulative trauma; and aspects of the working environment that may contribute to cumulative trauma. Finally, bolter operators were observed performing tasks, bolting activities were video taped, and still photographs were taken of bolting equipment and mine conditions. An experienced bolter operator discussed the layout and operation of a roof bolting machine.

3. Results

After examining incident descriptions, 14 were selected as injuries which could have occurred from cumulative exposure and contained the following characteristics:
Five of the fourteen incidents involved pain in the back, neck, shoulder, or elbow.
▸ Two incidents occurred while putting a roof bolt in a drilled hole.
▸ Two incidents occurred while lifting bolting supplies.
▸ One incident occurred while torquing a roof bolt.
Nine of the fourteen incidents involved a strain or sprain injury to the ankle, knee, or hip resulting from a slip, trip or misstep.
▸ Seven incidents involved stepping or kneeling on uneven floor, loose materials on the floor, or equipment cable.
▸ Two incidents involved an operator stepping into or out of the bolting machine platform.
Twelve roof bolter operators were interviewed. The most common injuries cited were:
▸ lacerations and cuts to arms and face,
▸ shoulder, neck, and arm strains and pains,
▸ ankle sprains and twists, back pain and strains, and knee strains, and
▸ numbness in legs.
Operators said that roof bolting tasks require a lot of lifting, carrying, bending, reaching and stretching. Common activities cited as contributing to their pain and discomfort included: leg pains while leaning out to see the drill hole; hand and elbow pain from using the controls; sore knees, back, and shoulders from bending and twisting to install bolts or lift and position drill steels, wrenches, and bolts; shoulder and elbow aches from picking up and holding drill steels; and knee and back aches at the end of the shift from standing all day.
After reviewing observation notes, video tape, and still photographs, key items were identified and are listed in the table.

4. Discussion

Injuries to the musculoskeletal system are common in the workplace. However, many injuries such as muscle and ligament strains are not the result of a sudden mishap, but occur over time as a result of repeated microtraumas. This type of injury develops over weeks, months, or even years. There are three main risk factors that contribute to cumulative trauma disorders (CTDs): force, repetition, and awkward postures. Any one or combination of these contribute to development of CTDs.
It is necessary to examine the layout of the work area to help identify tasks which may contribute to cumulative trauma. Putz-Anderson [2] describes ergonomic concerns that, in general, should be minimized at the work area. These considerations were used

Table: Observations and issues concerning roof bolting machines.

Observation	Issue
Confined operator platform causes operators to twist and stretch to get drill steels, bolts, plates, and wrenches.	This places operator in awkward postures creating stress to the muscles and joints, particularly in the back and the knees.
Supply trays are positioned at heights well above the operators' waists.	Lifting and retrieving tools and bolts is stressful to the neck, arm, and shoulder.
Tops of control levers are positioned well above waist height.	The operator must work with the arm and wrist in awkward postures.
Operators lean against the back rail of operator compartment and out from under the canopy while performing drilling and bolting tasks.	This places the operators in awkward postures. Also, it is putting them at risk of being hit by falling rocks.
Operators shift their weight to the side of the body corresponding to the hand which places the drill steel into the drill chuck.	The muscles on the opposite side of the body, particularly the low back muscles, are stressed and may become fatigued.
Operators frequently extend their arm up and out to hold onto steels while drilling, and onto bolts while installing them.	This is stressful to the neck, arm, and shoulder muscles.
Drill steels are being inserted into the drill chuck usually at knee level or lower.	The operator must do more bending which stresses the low back muscles.
Transfer of supplies from the back of a bolting machine to supply trays involves frequent lifting, carrying, and twisting.	This places operator in awkward postures creating stress to the muscles and joints, particularly in the back and the knees.

as a guideline for the analysis. Analysis of data obtained from lost time incidence reports, interviews, and observations were used to identify roof bolting tasks which increase risk to the development of CTDs. These issues were arranged into the following categories: materials handling, operator orientation in work space, vision obstruction, control bank design, and slipping and tripping hazards.

Recommendations given below address three elements which define a system: human, equipment, and environment. Recommendations directed at the human element are intended to increase worker awareness of risk factors. This knowledge can then be motivation for workers to modify their behavior to reduce exposure. Equipment recommendations address modifications to existing equipment which can be performed at the mine site or retrofitted by the manufacturer and recommendations that would require more significant changes that should be addressed in the design of future roof bolting machines. Environmental factors play an important role in human-machine interfaces. The underground mining environment is particularly challenging for equipment designers.

Working environments in underground mines are dynamic and there can be large differences between mines. The recommendations provided are intended to be used as a guide for more comprehensive examinations of roof bolting activities. Each mine should conduct a mine specific evaluation due to varying conditions, equipment, and workforce. An evaluation team with diverse members including roof bolter operators, first line supervisors, engineers, and safety personnel is an effective approach for developing solutions [3],[4],[5]. Additionally, more specific information is available concerning human factors considerations for reducing roof bolting hazards [6] and for designing underground mobile mining equipment [7].

Evaluation teams formed at mines should take into consideration the following recommendations when more closely examining the roof bolting tasks.
- Increase worker awareness on the risk factors associated with developing CTDs.

▸ Examine activities which require high force, high repetition, and awkward postures to determine if the task or equipment can be modified.
▸ Modify materials handling tasks to carry supplies as close to the body as possible, restrict the size of the load, and minimize lifting distances.
▸ Eliminate barriers in the path which require operator to lift supplies up and over.
▸ Improve supply tray design and position, and method for stacking and retrieving supplies.
▸ Design bolter tasks and equipment to minimize shoulder abduction.
▸ Design operator work areas considering reach and visibility requirements.
▸ Reduce force required to activate controls.
▸ Increase spacing of controls to accommodate a gloved hand.
▸ Improve height of control bank in relation to operator.
▸ Consider a height adjustable, padded rail at back of operator platform.
▸ Evaluate the threshold between the HDDR walkway and the operator platform with special consideration given to slipping and tripping hazards.
▸ Improve housekeeping practices and implement an active program to evaluate.
▸ Increase worker awareness of slipping and tripping hazards.

5. Summary

The information presented is intended to provide the reader with an awareness of factors which may contribute to cumulative trauma injuries to roof bolter operators. The recommendations developed should be useful to equipment manufacturers and to the management and workforce at underground coal mines. Because there can be significant differences between mines in terms of environment, geology, workers, equipment, and processes, it would be useful to initiate an ergonomics committee to examine the issues described and tailor solutions to the conditions. It is apparent that the most effective long term solution would be for mine operators and manufacturers to work together to evaluate existing equipment and to develop future generations of mining equipment that incorporate sound ergonomic design principles.

References

[1] E. Grandjean, *Fitting the Task to the Man*. Philadelphia, PA: Taylor & Francis Inc., 4th edition, 1988.
[2] V. Putz-Anderson, *Cumulative trauma disorders: A manual for musculoskeletal diseases of the upper limbs*. Bristol, PA: Taylor & Francis Inc., 1988.
[3] C. Hamrick, Ergonomics in Mining: Ergonomic Intervention Strategies. *Applied Occupational Environmental Hygiene*, January 1992, pp. 14-16.
[4] J. O'Green, R. Peters, and A. Cecala, AEP Fuel Supply's Ergonomic Approach to Reducing Back Injuries. *Proceedings of 23rd Annual Institute on Mining Health, Safety and Research*, VPI, Blacksburg, VA, 1992, pp. 187-195.
[5] R. Carson, R. How to Start a Successful Ergonomics Program. *Occupational Hazards*, September 1993, pp. 122-127.
[6] F. Turin *et al.*, *Human Factors Analysis of Roof Bolting Hazards in Underground Coal Mines*. U. S. Bureau of Mines, RI 9568, 1995.
[7] *Human Factors Recommendations for Underground Mobile Mining Equipment*. Accessible through NIOSH-PRC World Wide Web page at www.usbm.gov, last modified October 7, 1996.

Advances in Occupational Ergonomics and Safety II
Edited by Biman Das and Waldemar Karwowski
IOS Press and Ohmsha, 1997

New Development Trends in the Application of Risk Theory of Man-Machine-Environment Systems

Juraj SINAY, Milan ORAVEC, Melichar KOPAS, Miroslav JURIS
*Technical University of Kosice, Faculty of Mechanical Engineering, Letna 9,
SK 041 87 Kosice, Slovakia*

Abstract. The place and the role of risk theory and their application in various technical systems are well-known. Machine systems are analyzed and judged mostly regardless of relations to man and to environment. For the future development must be taken into consideration the whole man-machine-environment system. Modern conceptions take into consideration also subsystem interactions, i.e. subsystem relations. In our contribution we speak about the pipe mill hall . This hall is a technological complex which is analyzed from the risk point of view. We point out at the possibility how to compute the level of technical risk with regard to man-machine-environment system.

1. Technical risk

The term risk is more then 200 years old. But the real application of technical risk started approximately 20 years ago. There are many new methods at the present time how to increase the production efficiency together with costs reduction according to international legislation.

Computer-oriented methods are widely-used means for the technical risk evaluation. Technical risk is usually defined as the product :

$$R = p \cdot f = \text{const.} \qquad (1)$$

where p is a probability of state occurrence

f is a range of technical damaging or health-injury. This parameter is also often called weight factor or consequence of risk situation.

2. Description of technological complex

In the next part we want to speak about the pipe mill hall. It is a big technological complex from the technical risk point of view. Products of this pipe mill are pipes with diameters from 500 to 1420 mm, with thickness from 5,6 to 12,5 mm and with length from 9 to 12 m. The arrangement of pipe mill hall is on Fig.1.

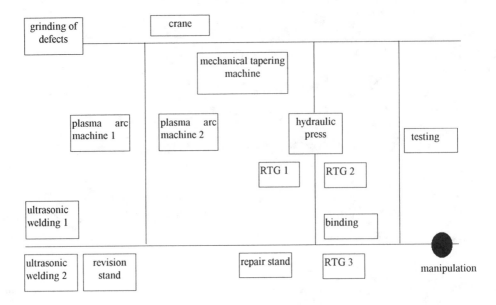

Fig.1

3. Risk level determination

If we want to obtain the values of technical risk levels in this technological complex so we need to know the values of probability **p** and consequence **f** . Number of failures or the frequency of failures equals to probability of risk state occurrence. Kind of accident equals to range of health-injury, i.e. equals to consequence or to weight factor. We can see all the important parts of pipe mill hall in the next table. For every one part are determined : the frequency of failures and the consequence of accident. Combination of these two parameters is the risk level. We operate with 3 levels of failures frequency : low, middle and high. We take into consideration 3 kinds of consequence : accident light, accident difficult and deadly accident. So we obtain also 3 risk levels : low, middle and high (see Tab.1). It is possible to determine from this table so-called weak-points in the whole technological complex. From the analysis of maintenance costs and from the analysis of technical risk is evident that the most important subject of our interest is the Ultrasonic welding 1. Therefore it is very useful to perform the technical risk analysis for all components of this machine for Ultrasonic welding 1. The result is in the next graph. In this graph the risk level equals to point evaluation : 1 - 5 unacceptable risk, 6 - 9 undesirable risk, 10 - 17 risk acceptable with control, 18 - 20 risk acceptable without control.

machine	frequency of failures	consequence	risk level
ultrasonic welding 1	middle	difficult accident	middle
ultrasonic welding 2	middle	difficult accident	middle
revision stand	low	deadly accident	middle
plasma arc tapering machine 1	middle	light accident	low
plasma arc tapering machine 2	middle	light accident	low
grinding of defects	low	light accident	low
crane	middle	deadly accident	high
mechanical tapering machine	high	light accident	low
hydraulic press	low	light accident	low
RTG 1	low	light accident	low
RTG 2	low	light accident	low
repair stand	high	light accident	low
RTG 3	low	light accident	low
testing	middle	light accident	low
binding	middle	light accident	low
manipulation	low	deadly accident	high

Tab.1

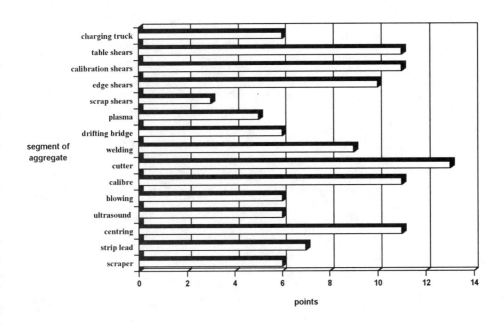

4. Conclusion

In our contribution we spoke about the technical risk evaluation for the complicated technological complex. It is necessary to take into consideration that during the process of risk determination we combined together two aspects : technical factor - frequency of failures and human factor - kind of accident. Therefore we obtained the technical-human combined risk values or levels. These levels are   only the primary and preliminary informations for designer. But these informations are very important for all the next steps of detailed technical risk analysis.

Reference

[1] MIL-STD 882C System safety program requirements, APR, 1993.

[2] STN EN 292.1 Bezpečnosť strojných zariadení, UNMS Bratislava, 11/96.

[3] EN IEC 56 410 Analyse des Risikos technischer Systeme, DIN Berlin, 4/95.

[4] J.Salanci and A. Sloboda and E.Kastelovič, Overovanie spoľahlivosti mobilných strojov preťažovaním v prevádzke. In: Spoľahlivosť v strojárstve a elektrotechnike, DT-ZSVTS, B.Bystrica, 1991, pp. 89-93.

Advances in Occupational Ergonomics and Safety II
Edited by Biman Das and Waldemar Karwowski
IOS Press and Ohmsha, 1997

Investigation of the Relationship Between Skin Vascular Reaction and Subjective Ratings of Comfort

Tycho K. Fredericks[1], Jim Tappel[2], Sadat Karim[1], Steve Toner[1], and Garett Rozek[1]

[1] *Human Performance Institute, Department of Industrial and Manufacturing Engineering, Western Michigan University, Kalamazoo, MI 49008-5061 U.S.A.*
[2] *Sierra Medical Systems, Inc., 7704 Sprinkle Road, Kalamazoo, MI 49001 U.S.A.*

Pressure ulcers are an inflammation or sore on the skin usually over a bony prominence resulting from prolonged external pressure. The blood supply to the affected area is compromised in relationship to the metabolic demands of the skin thus resulting in a progression of interrelated events that follow through ischemia and lead to tissue death. Thermography has been used as a reliable, non-invasive method of measuring regional blood flow. With this in mind, a study was conducted to determine the relationship between subjective ratings of comfort and reactive hyperemia (blood flow). Six male students from the University population served as subjects. Subjects were required to lie in the mid-prone position on 2 sleep surfaces (dynamic and static) for 2 periods of time (15 and 45 minutes). At the conclusion of the testing period, subjects rated their general level of comfort and were instructed to lie in a supine position while thermographic pictures of their greater trochanter were taken. Results of ANOVA revealed that surface had a significant effect on subjective rating of comfort. Although results of this pilot study did not show surface to have a significant effect on reactive hyperemia, there was a significant correlation between subjective ratings of comfort and reactive hyperemia. Implications of these findings are discussed in the body of the paper.

1.0 Introduction

Pressure ulcers are localized areas of cellular necrosis that develop when soft tissue is compressed for prolonged periods of time and blood perfusion is reduced. The extrinsic mechanical factors that contribute to this compression are pressure, shear, temperature, friction and moisture [1]. One popular method to measure the effects of bedding has been the use of interface pressure as a predictor of performance. At best, the interface pressure is a surrogate indicator of tissue ischemia. Thermography is a reliable, non-invasive method for the measurement of regional blood flow following periods of occlusion caused by normal weight bearing [2] and has been used as a predictive tool for pressure ulcers [3]. When the blood supply is compromised in relation to the metabolic demands of the skin, a progression of interrelated events may follow through ischemia, anoxia, cellular necrosis, and death. This occurs most commonly over bony prominence where the interface pressure has been reported as high as 100 to 150 mmHg in subjects lying on a regular mattress [4].

Even under the most ideal conditions, a soft static mattress cannot support the body to maintain sufficient blood perfusion in order to maintain homeostasis. Our body's physiological response is to change these pressure points periodically, even during periods of sleep. In situations where movement is not possible (during surgery), these pressure points are not relieved, increasing the possibility of ulcer formation. The subjective level of comfort is perhaps tied to this underlying mechanism of dynamic change. With this in mind, a study was conducted to determine the relationship between subjective comfort rating and reactive hyperemia on a static and dynamic mattress.

2.0 Method and Procedures

2.1 Subjects

A total of six able-bodied male college students with ages ranging between 20 and 22 years (mean 20.67 years and standard deviation 0.76), volunteered to participate in this experiment. Subjects were asked not to have consumed any form of alcohol, caffeine, or nicotine based products 24 hours prior to the experiment. Before the experimental data were collected, subjects were familiarized with the experimental procedures.

2.2 Equipment

An Inframetrics Model 760 infrared thermal imaging and measurement system was used to collect infrared images of the greater trochanter area of the subjects. ThermGRAM for Windows image processing software was used to analyze all infrared images. Lafayette Instruments anthropometric measuring equipment was used to determine anthropometric measurements of the subjects. A Marshall 97 automatic blood pressure and pulse monitor was used to take blood pressure and pulse readings. A Jamar mechanical goniometer was used to measure the angles between the lower and upper leg and between the upper extremities and upper leg.

2.3 Experimental Design

The experimental design for this study was a randomized complete block design with subjects as blocks. Surface type [regular static soft mattress and dynamic surface] and exposure time [15 and 45 minutes] were considered as fixed factors. Skin temperature around the trochanter area and the subjective comfort rating made by the subjects were considered as the response variables. SAS statistical analysis package [5] was used to analyze the experiment.

2.4 Procedures

Each subject was asked to attend a trial session where their anthropometric measurements were taken. The objective and various steps of the experiment were also described in this session. Each subject participated in four experimental trials. These four trials were performed at the same time to minimize the effects of circadian rhythms on body temperature. At the outset of an experiment, each subject was required to lay on their back for 15 minutes to allow their skin temperature to come to equilibrium with the room temperature. The initial blood pressure reading [systolic and diastolic] and pulse rate were taken at this time. A baseline infrared image of the greater trochanter area was then taken for subsequent analysis. Subjects were then instructed to lay on their right trochanter with a 120 degree angle between their upper and lower legs. The period of time required to be in the set position and the surface laid on, were presented to the subjects in random order. Upon completion of a testing episode, subjects rolled onto their backs exposing their trochanter region to the infrared camera and pictures were taken until the skin temperature returned to baseline. As soon as subjects rolled over, they were asked to rate their comfort according to a 11 point scale [6]. Lastly, the blood pressure and pulse rate were taken.

3.0 Results and Discussion

Descriptive statistics for the subjects are presented in Table 1. The mean height and weight of the subjects in this study were compared with those of the U.S. population [7]. Results indicated that there were no significant differences. This could mean the subject pool used in this experiment could be representative of the U.S. population.

Tables 2 and 3 present summary statistics for the subjective ratings of comfort and reactive hyperemia (change in temperature) of the greater trochanter for the various combinations of sleep surface and time spent on surface.

Table 4 presents the ANOVA results for subjective ratings of comfort. It was determined that surface had a significant effect on subjective comfort. However, testing time did not. Duncan's multiply range test revealed subjects were more comfortable on the dynamic surface as compared to the soft static surface.

ANOVA results for reactive hyperemia (or temperature change over the greater trochanter) indicated that testing time had a significant effect on reactive hyperemia and that surface did not. Duncan's multiply range test indicated that the longer the subject was required to lay on a surface, the greater the reactive hyperemia.

A Pearson correlation coefficients test indicated that there was as significant relationship between subjective rating of comfort and reactive hyperemia.

Table 1. Descriptive statistics of the subjects.

Measure	Mean (SD)
Age (years)	20.67(0.82)
Weight (kg)	87.59(12.61)
Stature (mm)	1800.23(76.71)
Hip height (mm)	937.26(66.22)
Buttock-knee length (mm)	645.16(51.82)
Buttock-popliteal length (mm)	538.48(24.64)
Hip breadth (mm)	367.08(14.34)

Table 2. Summary of subjective ratings for various combinations of time and surface, mean (SD)

Surface	Time	
	15 minutes	45 minutes
Dynamic Surface	2.00 (1.00)	2.17 (1.17)
Static Soft Surface	2.83 (0.75)	2.80 (1.10)

Table 3. Summary of temperature change (Celsius) of the greater trochanter area for various combinations of time and surface, mean (SD)

Surface	Time	
	15 minutes	45 minutes
Dynamic Surface	1.28 (0.61)	1.85 (0.57)
Static Soft Surface	1.13 (0.67)	2.20 (0.81)

Table 4. ANOVA summary for subjective ratings of comfort

Source	df	Sum of Squares	Mean Square	F value	Pr > F
Subject	5	10.455	2.091	3.88	0.019
Surface	1	2.909	2.909	5.39	0.035
Error	15	8.091	0.539		
Corrected Total	21	21.455			

This pilot study measured the thermal hyperemic responses on healthy young subjects lying on relatively soft surfaces for short periods of time provided meaningful but inclusive results. The subject rating gave insight into the level of comfort and anticipated differences between the static and dynamic surface. Antedocotal evidence shows that the body is constantly repositioning itself to maintain sufficient blood perfusion and alleviate areas of high pressure or low blood flow. The duration between this repositioning is related to the pressure or induced ischemia [4]. As seen in the results, time spent on the surface did not have a significant effect on comfort. This unexpected result is counter intuitive and leads to the conclusion that that the testing time needs to be increased. Increasing the time interval may reveal a difference in subjective comfort as well as reactive hyperemia. It may also provide a more realistic simulation of how sleep surfaces are professionally used.

In the surgical environment, it is not uncommon for orthopedic or cardiovascular surgeries to last over 4 hours, during which the pressure is not relieved. Total time spent on a firm surface in the supine position can easily double the actual surgical time. It is hypothesized that ischemia and cellular damage is initiated during surgery but is not noticed until 4-8 days afterward when a pressure ulcer develops. Further work needs to be done in the area of surface design and on geriatric populations where cardiovascular reserve is considerable lower.

4.0 Conclusions

The results of this pilot study revealed that time had a significant effect on reactive hyperemia. It was also determined that type of surface had a significant effect on comfort. The dynamic surface was subjectively superior to the soft static mattress. Additional studies of greater length of time need to be conducted in order rule out any Hawthorne effect the subjects might have experienced. Testing subjects for long periods of time would tax the physiological system greater and thus give a more conclusive picture of blood flow.

5.0 Acknowledgments

This material is based on work supported by Michigan State Research grant monies awarded this company/University by the Michigan Jobs Commission. Any opinions, findings, conclusions, or recommendations expressed in this publication are those of the authors and do not necessarily reflect the views of the Michigan Jobs Commission.

5.0 References

[1] Kosiak, M., Etiology of Decubitus Ulcers. *Archives of Physical Medicine and Rehabilitation*, **42(1)**, 1961, 19-29.

[2] Swain, I.D., and Grant, I.J., Methods of Measuring Skin Blood Flow, *Physics in Medicine and Biology*, **34**, 1989, 151-175.

[3] Newman, P., and Davis, N.H., Thermography as a Predictor of Sacral Pressure Sores. *Age and Aging* **10**, 1981, 14-18.

[4] Barnett, R. and Ablarde, J., Skin Vascular Reaction to Standard Positioning on a Hospital Mattress. *Advances in Wound Care*, Vol 7 No 1, 1994, p58-65

[5] SAS, *SAS User's Guide*, Version 5 Edition, Cary NC: SAS Institute, Inc.,1985

[6] Shackel, B., Chidsey, K.D., and Shipley, P., The assessment of chair comfort, *Ergonomics*, **12**, 1969, pp. 269-306.

[7] Pheasant, Stephen, *Body Space: Anthropometry, Ergonomics and the Design of Work.* London: Taylor & Francis Ltd., 1996.

Advances in Occupational Ergonomics and Safety II
Edited by Biman Das and Waldemar Karwowski
IOS Press and Ohmsha, 1997

PERSONAL AND CAR STEREO VOLUME LEVELS: HAZARDS OF LEISURE LISTENING ACTIVITIES

Maria Hayne, Lawrence J. H. Schulze, Department fof Industrial Engineeering, University of Houston, 4800 Calhoun Street, Houston, TX 77204-4812, U.S.A., and Leonardo Quintana, Department of Industrial Engineering, Javeriana University, Santafé de Bogotá, Colombia (S.A.)

This study compared measured sound pressure levels (noise) recorded from personal stereos and car stereos of college students. The study was divided into two parts. In the first part, the sound pressure level (SPL) emitted from the headphones of personal stereos used by college students was recorded at normal listening levels. In the second part, the same procedure was used to record the sound pressure level inside the automobiles of 10 college students. The average SPL level of students using personal stereos was 97 dBA; the average level inside the automobiles was 91 dBA. Each of these levels are above OSHA permissible levels for 8 hour noise exposure in the workplace. The average weekly exposure to these levels were 15 and 12 hours, respectively. These results indicate that noise exposure is significant in leisure listening activities and potential for permanent hearing damage exists for individuals exposed to these SPLs, as well as those individuals exposed to similar levels as these plus those to which they are exposed to in the work environments.

1. Introduction

The environment in which we live is filled with noise; from traffic to the roar of jet engines, from lawn maintenance equipment to the workplace. With the advent of personal stereos and sonic car stereos ('boom cars'), leisure listening levels have compounded our noise exposure.

Noise exposure associated with the workplace has long been know to produce hearing loss. The exposure to noise in the workplace is regulated by the Occupational Safety and Health Administration (OSHA). OSHA has set a limit for noise exposure at 90 dBA for 8 hours and allowable exposure is reduced by 2 hours for every 5 db increment above 90 dBA (1). However, these regulations to not consider exposure to noise during non-working hours and there are no regulations controlling personal noise exposure outside the workplace.

2. Method

A Quest Sound Pressure Level (SPL) meter (Model 2800) was used to sample the sound level exposures. For the personal stereos, the meter was positioned against the headphone (left and right) in an effort to simulate the contact of the headphone with the ear. For the car measurements, the meter was positioned at the ear level of the operator and measure for both right and left ear positions. The SPL meter was calibrated before each measurement. The sound pressure level emitted from the headphones of 15 randomly selected college students was sampled for personal stereos and 10 randomly selected college students for the car sound levels.

3. Results

The results of this investigation are presented in Figures 1 (SPL from personal stereos) and 2 (SPL from car stereos). The mean SPL (in dBA) recorded for the students listening to music on personal stereos was 97 dBA and ranged from 85 dBA to 119 dBA. The average weekly exposure was 15 hours per week and ranged from five to 23 hours. The listening hours were reported by the participants. The mean sound level recorded for students listening to music in their automobiles was 91 dBA and ranged form 80 dBA to 115 dBA. The average reported weekly exposure was 12 hours per week and ranged from five to 20 hours.

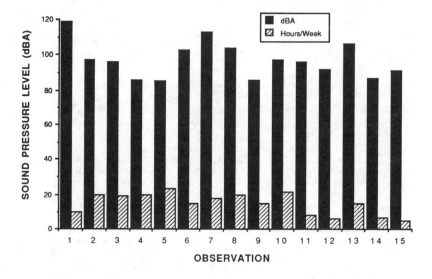

Figure 1.   Distribution of volume levels and weekly hours of exposure for students using personal stereos.

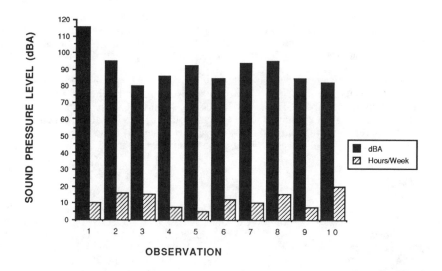

Figure 2.   Distribution of volume levels and weekly hours of exposure for students listening to music on car stereos.

4. Discussion

There was no correlation (association) between the volume levels recorded and the number of listening hours for either the personal stereos or car stereos listeners. However, it is not known if the students who have personal stereos also listen to music at the same levels in their cars, and vice versa. It would be safe to assume that it is possible that each group is also exposed to additional sound pressure levels from other sources. That is, students with personal stereos may listen to their car stereos and home stereos at comparable levels.

The mean levels found in this study were similar to those found in previous studies (2,3,4,5). However, the volume level was six dBA higher for those listening to the personal stereos than those listening to car stereos. This is an important consideration since the sound source is closer to the ear for individuals using personal stereos than individuals listening to music on car stereos. Therefore, the potential for permanent damage is greater for this type of exposure, coupled with the higher SPL recorded.

Recreational noise studies, such as those involving rock and roll music, have suggested that the cochlea can be damage by high-intensity music. Newer, smaller and interaural head sets (the speaker is positioned inside the ear canal) place the sound source even closer to the cochlea than conventional headsets or external speaker sources [3,6,7,8,9,10,11].

Stereos amplifiers with earphones can provide music at such intense level that damage to the hearing is possible. An equivalent continuous sound level in excess of 90 dBA is considered to be hazardous to the auditory mechanism. New technology has made headphone higher in quality and more modest in cost than previous components; therefore, allowing personal stereos to become widely used. Although the use of headphones with personal stereos have reduced environmental noise pollution, they have created potentially damaging consequences and may be delivering higher sound levels directly to more sensitive mechanisms of the inner ear.

Personal listening devices also tend to mask sound in the environment. The headphone renders the users deaf to warning sounds. Therefore, it is not wise to use headphones when operating any type of vehicle or equipment. Excessively loud sounds damag the innner ear and this damage cannot br repaired; The damage is irreversible damage. Further, hearing loss is cumulative; it takes 5 to 10 years to develop a hearing loss that you can notice yourself.

In regards to car stereos, the great wave is toward high-priced, high-wattage, and high-performance vehicle stereo systems. This focus is personified in car stereo sound off competitions. In these competitions, automobile audio enthusiasts compete on various levels, including, installation, sound quality, and loudness

4.1 *Warning Signs*

A number of warning signs or 'red flags' are presented below that identify conditions that are detrimental to healthy hearing.

- If, in a noisy environment, you cannot converse with others within three feet of you without having to yell, the exposure is potentially hazardous to your hearing.
- If someone has to yell at you in order to be understood while you are listening to music with headphones, the music is too loud.
- If you can hear the music on the personal stereo headsets while someone else is wearing them, the level is too loud
- If you can hear the music on the outside of the car with all the windows and doors closed, the music is too loud
- If your ear rings after exposure to high-level sound, it is likely that you have been overexposed. This ring in the ears is considered the inner ear's way of saying "ouch".
- If, after exposure to high-level sound, your hearing seems dulled, you probably are experiencing a temporary threshold shift. Your hearing will recover. However, repeated similar exposures can result in only partial recovery. Over time, you may end up in a permanent loss of hearing.

4.2 *Recommendations*

The following recommendations are presented regarding leisure listening to music via personal stereos and/or car stereos.

- Heed the warning signs of sound overexposure.
- Make sure you can hear sounds necessary for the operation of vehicles, hear on-coming traffic, and avoid distraction.
- Understand the danger of sound overexposure.
- Do not listen to personal stereos or loud music for more than one-half hour at a time.
- Turn the sound down if someone else can hear music from your headphones.
- Personal stereos manufactures should place warning labels or sound-level governors on their product indicating that hearing experts warn against extended use. This may require legislation.
- High visibility media campaigns are needed to develop public awareness of the effects of noise on hearing and the means for self-protection.
- A program of hearing conservation must be initiated whereby the dangers of excessive exposure to high intensity recreation environment sounds will be made clear to those participating in those activities.
- Education is the best means of empowering people to protect themselves from harmful conditions.

5. References

[1]   U.S. Department of Labor (1995). Code of Federal Regulations. Washington, D.C.: Office of the Federal Register, . 204-220

[2]   Brown PJ., Yearout RD. (1991). Impacts of leisure activity noise levels on safety procedures and policy in the industrial environment. International Journal of Industrial Ergonomics. 7(4): 341-346.

[3]   Fearn RW. , Hanson DR. (1984). Hearing damage in young people using headphones to listen to por music. Journal of Sound and Vibration 96(1): 147-149.

[4]   Howe JC., Yearout R. (1992). Music style, age and gender relationship to preferred noise levels for headset cassette players. Advance in Industrial Ergonomics and Safety IV . (S. Kumar, Ed). London: Taylor & Francis. 1335-1340.

[5]   Hayn M., Schulze LJH. (1997). Sound pressure levels, usage, listening preference, situation of use, and hazard of exposure knowledge of college students using personal stereo equipment in review. Advances in Occupational Ergonomics and Safety II. In Press.

[6]   Kuras JE., Findlay RC. (1974). Listening patterns of sef-identified rock music listeners to rock music presented via earphones. Journal of Audiology Research. 14, 51-56.

[7]   Clark WW. (1990). Amplified music from stereo headsets and its effect on hearing. Hearing Instution. 1(10):29-30

[8]   Rice CG., Rossi G., Olina M. (1987). Damage risk from personal cassette players. British Journal of Audiology. 21, 279-288.

[9]   Hellström P-A. Axelsson A. (1988). Sound levels, hearing habits and hazards of using portable cassette players. Journal of Sound and Vibration. 127(3), 521-528.

[10]   Medical Research Council Institute of Hearing Research. (1986). Damage to hearing arising from leisure noise. British Journal of Audiology. 20, 157-164.

[11]   Gallagher G. Hot music, high noise, & hurt ears. (1989). The Hearing Journal, . March, 7-10.

Advances in Occupational Ergonomics and Safety II
Edited by Biman Das and Waldemar Karwowski
IOS Press and Ohmsha, 1997

ON IDENTIFYING THE FACTORS INFLUENCING THE PERCEPTION OF WORK OF THE WORKERS ENGAGED IN REPETITION WORK

Dragan D. Milanović, Žarko Spasić
University of Mechanical Engineering, 27. marta 80, Belgrade, Yugoslavia

Abstract. The production line system represents a form of organizational technological solutions in the modern production work, resting upon the contradictions of technical solutions and socio-economical implications of this development. Particularly the developing countries are faced with the impossibilities of using the production line, functioning within the industrial system.

After a several year of the work on the production line, by using a multidisciplinary approach to the problem, important results have been obtained. The results that are numerous influential factors determine the worker's activity in repetition work.

1. Introduction

The ame of the present investigation has been to identify, out of a large number of the influential factors, a smaller number of those influencing the perception of work of those engaged in repetition work.

In this investigation, an ample questionnaire and recording documentation of research projects in the field has been utilized. By adapting the original questionnaire material, a matrix of the commencing data, as a basis for a multivatiant analysis has been formed.

The uniformity of data obtained through surveys so far is assured by the use of a Complex questionnaire. The Complex questionnaire, among others, contains a set of questions which make it possible to obtain information on how a worker experiences his job tasks being working on a production line. Due to the fact that the Complex questionnaire has not been pre-planned for the application of factor analysis, replies to some questions are modified.

2. Experimental Results

This survey applies the SPSS Package Program or say, that part of it, where data are processed by a factor analysis. SPSS - Statistical Package for the Social Science is an integrated system of computer programs used for statistical analyses of data.

Taking into account the adopted multiversion method, the best suited form of managing data is a matrix. In this matrix, the lines are examinees - the workers on the production lines and they number 1048, while the columns are variances and they number 108. From the total of 108 variances comprising all aspects of work on the production line, as many as 45 variances which substantially affect the work of a labourer on the production line are extracted. Thus the matrix 1048x45 is obtained as a basis for the application of factor analysis, Table 1.

Table 1. Data matrix

Examinees	Variable					
	P_1	P_2	P_3	...	....	P_{45}
I_1	Q_1	Q_{12}	Q_{12}	.	.	Q_{145}
I_2	Q_2	Q_{22}	Q_{23}	.	.	Q_{245}
I_3	Q_3	Q_{32}	Q_{33}	.	.	Q_{345}
.	.	.	.	.	.	.
.	.	.	.	.	.	.
.	.	.	.	.	.	.
I_{1048}	Q_{10481}	Q_{10482}	Q_{10483}	.	.	Q_{104845}

The data matrix is entered in the TRAKA database in " DBASE III plus" the structure of which is accepted and processed by the SPSS program.

The table 2 shows only a part of the result of VARIMAX rotation for TRAKA database. The complete survey results are given under the reference number [1].

In establishing this factor, only those variances take part which have factor load greater than 0.4. If the factor loads are less than 0.4, they are considered very low and negligible.

The factor analysis results obtained by dividing the base sample of workers for TRAKA database, by the values of certain variances into subsamples of workers, show that there is a certain number of invariant factors and a certain number of specific factors for each selected sub-sample of worker.

That means that there is no unique factor structure for all subsamples of workers, however there is an invariant factor substructure.

For some survey areas the essence lies in stable factors which should be as general as possible. Unstable factors are not interesting since they are related only to a particular situation or to a set of variances which are subject to analysis. Therefore, in further analysis, special attention will be paid to establishing invariant factors which determine the experience of work by the labourers engaged on the production line.

If we analyze and compare the results for TRAKA database and for the database obtained by dividing the base set of workers, the conclusion is that there is a certain number of factors which are stable and invariant. The following invariant factors are identified:

   -worker's interest in the work on line
   -psychophysical tiredness
   -work rhythm
   -measures for removing negative consequences of work on the line.

The factor "Worker's Interest in Work on Line" features all variant models obtained by dividing the base sample of workers into subsamples. Since in all variants of application it appears as the first extracted factor, it is considered to be the main factor. The main factor is the most significant factor since it explains the biggest part of the joint dispersion of variants.

Considering the structure of all variables which form this factor we can say it is very complex. All variables have a high-significance factor load, so it is difficult to single out the most-affecting variable.

Table 2. Results of factors analysis

Varimax Rotation 1, Extraction 1, Analysis 1 - Kaiser Normalization. Varimax converged in 10 iterations. Rotated Factor Matrix:					
	Factor 1	Factor 2	Factor 3	Factor 4	Factor 5
VARO01	0.06967	0.08299	-0.00206	-0.02357	0.08662
VARO02	0.04880	0.04864	-0.00214	0.04002	-0.02554
VARO03	0.02249	-0.00239	0.11157	-0.04430	0.06859
VARO04	0.12384	0.03181	0.10594	-0.06828	0.12904
VARO18	0.09306	0.57350	-0.03862	0.03810	-0.30244
VARO19	-0.05194	0.08516	0.03445	-0.00557	0.07109
VARO20	0.06011	0.23647	-0.09843	0.22220	0.05058
VARO21	-0.01906	-0.02301	-0.02623	0.04246	-0.02904
VARO22	0.01292	-0.09555	-0.04747	-0.02127	-0.05590
VARO23	0.02782	-0.17967	-0.05872	-0.07841	0.10347
VARO24	0.03553	0.11725	0.04517	0.01734	-0.07480
VARO25	-0.07701	-0.03831	0.01552	0.00576	0.07116
VARO26	0.16369	_0.81231_	-0.06987	0.05388	-0.01064
VARO27	0.20244	_0.72793_	-0.08455	0.07765	-0.01765
VARO28	0.09659	_0.76060_	-0.04707	-0.01024	0.08042
VARO29	0.10066	_0.75055_	-0.05921	0.02777	0.11598
VARO30	0.13246	_0.59467_	0.00070	0.00605	0.30265
VARO31	0.11525	0.13375	-0.02634	0.01177	_0.71903_
VARO32	0.04508	-0.02055	-0.01122	0.21304	_0.72960_
VARO33	0.11168	0.17845	-0.00852	0.12455	_0.66111_
VARO40	0.16363	_0.43871_	0.01053	0.08355	0.29347
VARO45	0.05548	_0.51791_	-0.02509	0.22501	0.21766
VARO53	0.05138	_0.49697_	0.21823	0.19278	-0.00064
VARO54	0.02800	_0.54100_	0.06483	0.27186	0.03808
VARO56	-0.00418	0.04782	-0.10026	_0.60671_	0.18574
VARO57	0.07028	0.06079	0.01465	_0.67372_	0.18110
VARO58	0.12727	0.09937	-0.02563	_0.66715_	0.05159
VARO61	0.06746	-0.02313	-0.03048	_0.68609_	-0.00077
VARO62	0.07347	0.16554	0.00861	_0.65732_	-0.04201
VARO63	0.03933	0.14313	0.09794	_0.44401_	0.11749
VARO64	0.04129	0.20156	-0.04539	_0.42713_	0.07593
VARO65	-0.01803	0.11995	-0.04689	-0.03566	0.01114
VARO79	_0.77156_	-0.01651	0.01032	0.11244	0.20419
VARO81	_0.73939_	0.38171	-0.06692	0.04914	-0.02012
VARO83	_0.76541_	0.37103	-0.04199	0.04512	0.02831
VARO84	_0.89053_	-0.08434	-0.03667	0.06112	0.01670
VARO85	_0.88064_	0.07788	-0.06787	0.05557	0.03203
VARO88	_0.81409_	0.33669	-0.06030	0.04029	-0.00622
VARO89	_0.89257_	-0.02433	-0.05080	0.06093	0.10010
VARO91	_0.84494_	0.22699	-0.08310	0.03729	0.04697
VARO96	-0.00250	-0.00114	_0.94843_	-0.04059	0.00237
VARO103	-0.06540	-0.03788	_-0.95329_	-0.03932	0.00766
VARO104	-0.10932	-0.00382	_0.96636_	0.00105	-0.03245
VARO105	-0.06944	-0.02287	_0.96763_	-0.01235	-0.00473
VARO106	-0.10088	-0.06170	_0.94503_	-0.00425	-0.02537

The joint feature of variables forming this factor is the worker's reaction to a simple and repeated work on the line. Doing repeatedly the same job over and over, the worker has no insight in the usefulness of the overall work process and therefoo.re looses the feeling that he has invested his work into something really worth.

Doing simple operations, the workers have no opportunity to participate intellectually in such operations and to express their initiatives. Simple tasks require modest skill, sometimes none at all, which in a longer period of time creates the feeling of limitedness and dissatisfaction in workers. The workers consider that their job can just be done by anyone which also has a nonincentive impact on workers.

A reliable sign of deep reactions of workers to negative consequences of the production line work are increased absenteeism and fluctuation.

The second factor points out the significance of physical and psychic tiredness of workers. It is featured as "Psychophysical Tiredness of Workers".

The investigations so far show that the majority of workers feel tiredness after the work on the production line. Conditionally, adopted expression "psychophysical tiredness" is used to determine hard-determinable types of causes which create the decline of work ability. Thus, monotony, indifference, repeatedness, etc., may speed up the occurrence of tiredness, even though no significant consumption of energy is required.

The third factor is the rhythm of work. The rhythm of work is the basic feature of work on the line and the most significant determinant in the workers, behavior. The consequence of such work is the apparent resistance of a worker who could feel all the difficulty of alienation at work.

The forth invariant factor is defined as the "Removal of Negative Consequences of Work on the Line". Common for all variables forming this factor with a significant factor load is that they make a set of measures for removing negative consequences of work on the production line. They comprise the variances which refer to the rotation of workers on the line, improvement of work, extension of work contents and method of communication.

3. Conclusions

By applying factor analysis and by establishing factors we can, knowing and measuring changes in one variance, foresee the changes that are going to happen in another variance. The factors which are determined during the course of factor analysis have a fundamental meaning compared to the variances observed.

The results obtained indicate that, by means of the factor analysis, it is possible to identify the factors determining the behavior of the workers engaged in repetition work. The factors formed posses, to a considerable extent, the same character as the relevant influencing factors established in the investigations carried out previously.

In addition to the results stated, the significance of the analysis can be seen in its ability to specify the factors characterizing certain projected data bases. Their diversity enriches a complex perception of the personality of the workers engaged in repetition work.

Refernce

[1] D. Milanović, Prilog istraživanju relevantnih uticajnih činilaca koji utiču na radni učinak na priozvodnim trakama, Dissertation, University of MechanicalEngineering, Belgrade, 1991.

Advances in Occupational Ergonomics and Safety II
Edited by Biman Das and Waldemar Karwowski
IOS Press and Ohmsha, 1997

Vection, Compensatory Sway, and Simulator Sickness

Younghak Yoo, Gene C. H. Lee, & Sherrie Jones
University of Central Florida
Orlando, Florida
USA

Abstract. A global model of simulator sickness is outlined that suggests the sequence of events leading to the development of simulator aftereffects. The model attempts to link control inputs, visual kinematics, illusory self-motion (vection), and compensatory postural sway to the origin of simulator sickness. A pilot study was conducted in support of a research program that will investigate the proposed model. Seven males and four females participated in a 5-min session in a fixed-base automobile simulator. Due to restricted sample size, descriptive statistics are presented for measures of simulator sickness, lateral sway velocity, driving performance, control inputs, and vection ratings. Although potential trends are discussed, no statistical conclusions can be drawn. Measurement issues for the next phase of research include increasing the sensitivity of vection ratings, and examination of the timecourse for development of compensatory sway.

1. *Introduction*

Motion sickness can occur in the absence of imposed inertial motion, when self motion is suggested by only visual stimulation [1]. Although symptoms are similar to those of motion sickness, this visually-induced motion sickness (VIMS) occurs without any vestibular stimulation. VIMS occurs in fixed-base simulators and is referred to as "Simulator Sickness." Concern for potentially negative training effects, as well as user's safety following simulator exposure, has stimulated much attention to the topic.

Research at the University of Central Florida (UCF) is addressing the etiology of simulator sickness in a fixed-base driving simulator. Our working model, based on the premise that simulator sickness is a form of VIMS, induced by viewing dynamic visual scenes, is as follows: Driver-generated control inputs dictate the frequency and magnitude of visual kinematics. The optical flow patterns conveyed by visual kinematics can produce illusory sensations of self-motion (vection), postural instability, and simulator sickness, although the specific relationship between these outcomes has not been empirically established. We believe that vection is a stimulus for compensatory sway in visually-based simulators, as observers attempt to maintain postural upright with respect to perceived forces of gravity implied by uniform motion of the visual field. In a fixed-base (i.e., non-moving) simulator, compensatory adjustments are not opposed by true gravito-inertial force, as would occur in the real world, when rounding a corner, for instance. From infancy, our learning experiences dictate expectations regarding the relationship between motion conditions and required strategies for maintaining postural control. When these anticipated relationships are not met, postural instability may result. According to a recent theory of motion sickness [2], postural instability is the source of motion-induced malaise, including VIMS. With respect to the proposed model, this paper presents: (1) supporting logic; (2) methodology and dependent measures from a pilot study to support research that will test the model; (3) preliminary (decriptive) data as a function of gender; and (4) lessons learned.

Among the most severe manifestations of VIMS are cases where users experience a strong sensation of vection [1,3]. The vection phenomenon is based primarily on the motion detection capabilities of the peripheral retina and relies upon multi-contrat objects moving at uniform velocity [1]. In a study of vection and simulator sickness, Hettinger et al., [4] concluded that vection is a necessary precondition for VIMS.

There is a strong neural linkage between the visual induction of vection and the vestibular apparatus: Specifically, the optokinetically-induced perception of self-motion is neurophysiologically-based upon visual-vestibular convergence in sub-cortical and cortical pathways and centers [5]. The primary function of the vestibular system is the transduction of linear and angular acceleration and to provide information about the orientation and movement of the head relative to forces of gravity. This information is used for subcortical control of posture and motor activity including maintaining the head in an upright position. The neural link between visual and vestibular afferents has consequences for postural control: Postural imbalance may result from misperception of the postural vertical, induced by a visual stimulus.

Helmholtz [6] was probably were the first to observe an influence of linear vection on postural balance. Lestienne, Soechting, and Berthoz [7] demonstrated that when subjects felt the sensation of forward motion through divergent horizontal motion of vertical stripes, the subjects showed a considerable tendency to fall backward. Dichgans and Brandt [1] report that the compelling sensation of body movement can affect postural balance in a vection drum and concluded that the postural imbalance may be the reaction to a misperception of postural vertical, induced by the moving visual stimulus.

Observers make compensatory postural adjustments in opposition to changes in perceived gravito-inertial force [2]. For example, when cornering a vehicle, all occupants (including the dog) lean into the turn to counteract the change in forces impinging upon the vehicle. Such postural control strategies are learned, in response to gravito-inertial force, but also corresponding information specified by the optic array. In a fixed-base simulator, changes in the optical array imply conditions that would normally be accompanied by changes in the gravito-inertial force vector in the real world, however, such forces are not present. Thus, when participants make compensatory postural adjustments, there is no gravito-inertial resistance. The lack of opposition disrupts the perception/action cycle, which can lead to postural instability. Riccio and Stoffregen [2] propose that postural instability is the cause of motion sickness, although they do not concur that vection is a necessary precursor to postural sway or sickness.

The subjective nature of vection presents a challenging measurement issue [8]. We believe that measurement of compensatory sway DURING exposure may provide a reliable, objective measure of susceptibility to vection and a predictor of both simulator sickness and postural instability following exposure. Our pilot study, described below, was conducted to establish experimental protocol, ascertain the range and variance of dependent measures, and identify remaining measurement issues.

2. Method

Eleven subjects (four females and seven males) between the ages of 19 and 28 years old drove a fixed-base driver training simulator located in the Interactive Driving Simulator Lab at UCF. The simulator presents a visual roadway environment projected on a 7' (v) x 10' (h) flat screen, and the subject responds with appropriate actions involving the steering wheel, accelerator, and brake to control the vehicle's position and heading. Subjects were instructed to maintain position within the center of the driving lane at a speed of 30 miles per hour while performing a 5-min driving course that included 40 turns (20 left and 20 right turns with straight-aways inbetween). The driving course was specifically designed to induce both circular and linear vection.

Dependent Measures

A. Vection. Prior to simulator exposure, the concept of vection was described as the illusion of self-motion, and examples of vection experiences in everyday life (e.g., in cars, movie theaters and amusement park rides) were provided. Upon exiting the simulator, subjects were asked if they experienced vection at any time during their simulator exposure. Vection was treated as a dichotomous variable (i.e., yes or no).

B. Postural Stability. An automated postural stability measure was used to record lateral sway velocity before, during, and after simulator exposure. A video camera mounted on a tripod was used to record a high-contrast 3" by 3" target reticle (attached to a headband) worn on the back of the subject's head. The image of the target reticle was then processed using software developed to permit frame by frame analysis of changes in reticle displacement in the lateral (Y) axis [9]. The psychometric stability and reliability of the automated measure was validated by Kennedy and Stanney [9]. Two 30 sec trials of static standing stability (heel-to-toe, arms folded) were videotaped before and after simulator exposure. Y velocity scores for the two trials were averaged to provide a single index for each of the pre and post-exposure measures and pre/post difference scores were computed for the aggravated means, and is referred to herein as "postural instability." Seated postural sway was recorded continuously during the 5-min simulated driving task and is referred to herein as "compensatory sway."

C. Simulator Sickness. The sixteen-symptom checklist of the Simulator Sickness Questionnaire was administed pre- and post-exposure to assess sickness (see [10], for checklist and scoring procedures).

D. Driving Performance. Control inputs (number of braking inputs and number of steering wheel reversals greater than 2 degrees and 5 degrees, respectively) and performance (yaw deviation from the front center of the car to the yellow centerline of the roadway) were logged by the host computer.

3. Results

One male subject requested nonparticipation following two and a half minutes of exposure due to dizziness and nausea; his data are included in the data analysis. Nine of the eleven subjects (six males and three females) reported vection experiences. Eight out of nine subjects who reported vection also reported sickness, whereas one of the two subjects who reported no vection reported sickness.

Table 1 displays the means and standard deviations (STDev) for total severity of simulator sickness (TSS), compensatory sway during simulator exposure (ComSway), postural instability following simulator exposure (pre-post difference scores [Instability]), driving performance (mean deviation from centerline [MeanDev]) and driver control inputs (number of braking inputs [#Brakes] and number of steering wheel reversals greater than 2 degrees [SWR>2] and 5 degrees[SWR>5], respectively) by gender.

Due to the small sample size, no statistical conclusions can be drawn from our pilot data, and it is not possible to make comparisons for the dependent measures in terms of "sick" vs. "Not sick". However, there appear to be some potential trends as a function of gender that warrant discussion. As can be seen in Table 1, males tended to report more simulator sickness symptoms, of greater severity, than did females, although there appears to be greater variability of symptoms among females. Y velocity scores for compensatory sway during simulator exposure tended to be higher for males, with twice the variability amongst subjects. It also appears that males exhibited greater post-exposure postural instability than did females, again, with much greater variability amongst scores for the males. The driving performance data suggest that females performed the task better than males in terms of deviation from the centerline, and again, the males tended to exhibit greater performance variability. In terms of control inputs, it appears that females tended to make more inputs than males.

Table 1. Means and Standard Deviations for Dependent Measures as a Function of Gender

Gender	TSS	ComSway	Instability	MeanDev	#Brakes	SWR>2	SWR>5
FEMALES							
Mean	55.17	6.85	0.73	4.86	24.00	232.75	199.75
STDev	35.27	2.27	1.50	1.51	7.87	18.75	41.92
MALES							
Mean	66.78	8.95	3.12	7.89	16.00	205.86	169.00
STDev	22.08	4.56	4.34	3.71	8.68	53.68	35.93

4. *Conclusions and Discussion*

The dichotomous nature of our vection measure (i.e., yes or no) did not yield the sensitivity required to relate perceptual differences between individuals with magnitude of compensatory sway and simulator sickness. Thus, scaling issues must be addressed that will yield a sufficient range of vection scores. The fact that ten of eleven subjects reported moderate to severe symptoms of simulator sickness suggests a ceiling effect, and the stimulus intensity must be reduced (via reduced exposure duration, number of turns, or both) to permit meaningful comparisons between "sick" vs. "not-sick" in future experiments.

The tendency for males to exhibit greater compensatory sway during simulator exposure as well as greater post-exposure instability than females, is consistent with males' tendency to report greater sickness. With increased sample size, these data may support our hypothesis that compensatory sway during simulator exposure is related to post-exposure instability and reports of sickness. Athough the data suggest that females tended to make greater control inputs, it looks as though males exhibited more eratic driving performance (in terms of deviation from the centerline), which could have resulted in males' tendency toward greater compensatory sway and sickness, which again, may lend support to our hypotheses. Driving speed may influence the dependent measures and will be examined in future studies.

References

[1] Dichgans, J. & Brandt, T. (1978). Visual vestibular interactions: Effects on self-motion perception and postural control. In: R. Held, H. Leibowitz, & H. L. Teuber, (Eds.), Handbook of Sensory Physiology, 8, 755-804. Berlin: Springer Verlag.

[2] Riccio, G. E. & Stoffregen, T. A. (1991). An ecological theory of motion sickness and postural instability. Ecological Psychology, 3(3), 195-240.

[3] Hettinger, L. J. & Riccio, G. E. (1992). Visually induced motion sickness in virtual environments. Presence 1(3), 308-318.

[4] Hettinger, L. J., Berbaum, K. S., Kennedy, R. S., Dunlop, W. P., & Nolan, M. D. (1990). Vection and simulator sickness. Military Psychology, 2, 171-181.

[5] Straube A. & Brandt, T. (1987). Importance of the visual and vestibular cortex for self-motion perception in man (circular vection). Human Neurobiology, 6, 211-218.

[6] Helmholtz, H. (1896) Von: Handbuch der physiologischen Optik. Hamburg-Leipzig: L. Voss.

[7] Lestienne, F. G., Soechting, J., & Berthoz, A. (1977). Postural readjustments induced by linear motion of visual scenes. Experimental Brain Research, 28, 363-384.

[8] Kennedy, R. S., Hettinger, L. J., Harm, D.L., Ordy, J. M., & Dunlap, W. P. (1996). Psychophysical scaling of circularvection (CV) produced by optokinetic (OKN) motion: Individual differences and effects of practice. Journal of Vestibular Research, 6(4), 1-11.

[9] Kennedy, R. S. & Stanney, K. M. (1996). Postural instability induced by virtual reality exposure: Development of a certification protocol. Int'l Journal of Human-Computer Interaction 8(1), 25-47.

[10] Kennedy, R. S., Lane, N. E., Lilienthal, M. G., Berbaum, K. S., & Hettinger, L. J. (1992). Profile analysis of simulator sickness symptoms. Presence, 1(3), 295-301.

20. Occupational Health and Safety

Advances in Occupational Ergonomics and Safety II
Edited by Biman Das and Waldemar Karwowski
IOS Press and Ohmsha, 1997

Investigation of occupational injuries in a meat processing plant

Krzysztof SWAT and Grzegorz KRZYCHOWICZ
Nofer Institute of Occupational Medicine
90-950 Lodz, P.O. Box 199, Poland

Abstract. A new method of occupational injury events analysis was used to identify sources of accidents in a meat processing plant in Lodz. The frequency of accidents reported in this plant was high and constantly growing during the last few years. Data on 77 accidents reported in 1993-1995 were analyzed. The analysis included also minor injuries which happened in the plant. As a result of analysis of the injuries, the main sources of accidents in the plant were detected and suitable remedies were proposed.

1. Introduction

Analysis of injury events occurring in industrial plants is not sufficiently employed as the source of information on the risk of accidents which may occur there.

In Poland, use of the information on accident events which had occurred in the past for accident prevention purposes is rather ineffective. In general, the information is limited to the accidents only and does not include minor incidents. Even elementary analyses intended to identify accident sources are prepared by few plants only. Even simple causes are not reviewed nor consistently reported. A situation like that makes that, in many instances, reasonable accident prevention is not possible.

Accidents and accident types are specific for each plant. Determination of the repeatability of accident circumstances is a key issue for accident prevention [1]. Our paper discusses the results of occupational injury events analysis performed in the meat-processing plant in Lodz. The number of accidents in that plant rose rapidly in 1993 - 1995 (frequency rates 2.8, 3.5, 4.6 accidents per 100 employees, respectively). The plant processes beef and pork from slaughter to the final product such as meat portions, cured product and preserves. In 1995, the plant employed 668 people.

2. Method

The number of reported injuries constitutes a natural direct source of information on accident risk. The number of accidents is the most common source of information on the risk involved. In our study, accident means a case formally reported as an accident by the safety supervisor of the plant. It means a sudden undesired work-related event, resulting in impairment of worker health. Practically only accidents resulting in sick leave days and death cases are reported in Poland. Our analysis of accidents was based on collective accident reports provided by safety supervisors of the meat processing plant and our own investigation of individual accident protocols. The second source of information on the risk of accidents in industrial plants are minor incidents which happen there. Therefore, the analysis performed for the plant included also minor injuries which had occurred there. In our study we attempted to assess the total number of injuries in the meat processing plant. Data on all first-aid cases noted by the plant's outpatient clinic were analyzed. Also sampling interviews with the workers were conducted to supplement the data on the number of injuries and working conditions.

A new method of accident event classification was applied [2]. The method entails classification of accident events into; falls and slips, accidents related to manual work, accidents due to contact with moving parts of machinery, accidents due to contact with sources of energy, and other.

3. Results

In 1993-1995, there were 77 occupational injuries with lost work days in the plant. According to the method, the accidents were classified into 'fall and slip', 'manual', 'machinery', 'energy' and 'other' accident types. Figure 1 shows the changes of the total frequency rate and frequency rates for particular types of accidents in the plant during the analyzed period.

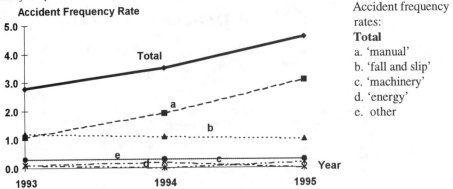

Figure 1. Accident frequency rates (number of accidents per 100 employees) for various types of accidents and the total accident frequency rate in the meat processing plant (1993-1995)

The data indicate that the most frequent types in 1993 were 'fall an slip' accidents, for which the frequency rate was 1.2 and 'manual' accidents, frequency rate 1.1. Higher total accident frequency observed in the subsequent years was attributable to the increase in the number of the 'manual' accidents, since the rates for the falls and slips and for the remaining accidents were almost unchanged.

To get a more detailed picture of the sources of the accidents in the plant, data obtained from the plant's outpatient clinic on all injuries requiring medical or pre-medical aid were analyzed. There were in total 254 such injuries in 1994, including 23 reported accidents. Thus, only every eleventh injury was reported as an accident. From the interviews with the workers, the total number of injuries in 1994 was estimated at 520.

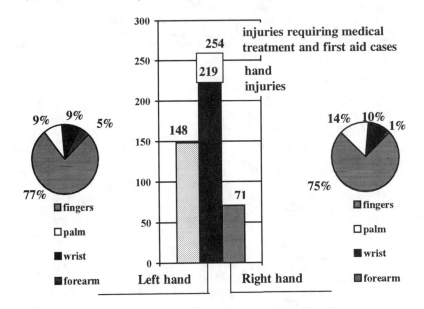

Figure 2. Hand injuries in meat processing plant vs. all noted injuries.

Among 254 reported injuries requiring first aid, 204 (80%) were wounds (cut, chafed or pierced skin); other injuries were remarkably less frequent . There were also 14 scalds, 11 bruises, 9 sprains, 6 breakages of extremities and 5 other injuries.

The majority of wounds were cut skin cases resulting from the use of knives. Injuries of the upper extremities (219 cases) dominated (Figure 2) The left hand was more frequently injured (148 cases) than the right hand (71 injuries). Fingers were the most frequently injured parts of the upper extremities (over 75% cases). 'Manual' injuries (218 cases) constituted the bulk of the injuries. There were also 17 'fall and slip', 14 'energy' and 5 other injuries.

An analysis of the types of injuries suffered by the employees during the accidents indicates that wounds were the major problem (16 cases in the total of 31 reported accidents in 1995). Figure 3 presents the changes in the accident frequency rate for the different types of injuries.

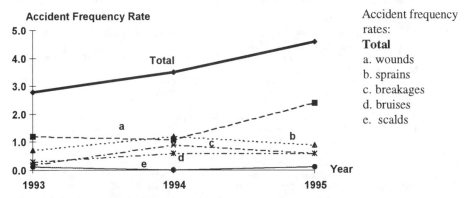

Figure 3. Accident frequency rates (number of accidents per 100 employees) for various types of injury and the total accident frequency rate in meat processing plant (1993-1995)

A sharp increase in the frequency of 'wound' accidents, rate 1.1 in 1994 to 2.4 in 1995, is the major trend visible in the graph. The analysis of all noted injury incidents in 1995 also shows that as much as 80.8% of injuries were wounds. Other injury types, such as sprains, breakages, and scalds were much less frequent. The majority of the production workers used knives, often without protective gloves on their hands because, when the gloves became wet (and this happens very often with that job), they no longer sufficiently protected the hands of the workers. The workers sharpened their knives themselves and, to make their job easier, they usually did it too much and too often, and in a relatively short time the blades received the form of narrow, sharp skewers. As a consequence, each contact of worker body with such knife blade resulted in injury.

After the plant had been privatized in 1993, work pace became higher. The nominal value of goods produced per one employee increased in 1993-1995 by about 40%. Interviews with line managers and workers revealed that production pace in 1995 fluctuated remarkably. Sometimes the pace was very high. At the moments of considerable work demand it often happened that workers were assigned jobs in which they were not skilled. As much as 70.9% accidents (22 cases of 31) occurred in the plant during four months of 1995.

Falls and slips constituted another accident problem in the plant (Fig. 1). Those accident types resulted from excessive wear of floor and staircase surfaces, where numerous pits and protrusions were present. The floors were slippery as they were soiled with the animal fat, and it was evident that they were cleaned too seldom. In addition, the shoes of the workers were in a poor condition, with soles sticked with fat. Besides, the workers stumbled on product-filled containers which were not removed on time from the walkways. The problems discussed above were related with poor housekeeping, the impact of which for work safety was strongly stressed by Saari [3].

4. Conclusions

The results of the study lead us to several important conclusions on the preventive measures which ought to be taken in the plant.

1. Knife wounds were the most important problem for accident prevention in the plant:
   - correct shape of knife blades should be determined and maintained by ensuring that blunt knives are sharpened in plant's tool shop only;
   - the workers should be provided with suitable protective gloves;
   - steps should be taken to ensure that workers always work with the protective gloves on their hands.
2. Slips and falls were the second most important problem. They resulted from poor maintenance of floors, stairs, and blocked passageways:
   - floor surfaces should be repaired;
   - housekeeping should be improved;
   - suitable housekeeping procedures should be developed and implemented.
3. The observed increase in the number of accidents was probably due to higher work pace, therefore: optimum work pace standards should be prepared for individual jobs and the work should be so scheduled that the relevant standards are not exceeded.

Some general conclusions can also be made:
A. At least several abnormalities were common to almost all studied accidents. We distinguished four essential causes of accidents;
1. insufficient supervision (inadequate control of whether the worker has followed the correct code of practice),
2. poor workplace organization (faults in the determination of workplace organization system, e.g. inadequate personal protection, too high work pace, incorrect work procedures, failure to nominate a person responsible for group tasks),
3. technical factor (defect of technical object, failure to meet the predetermined technical requirements),
4. worker inadvertence (individual error of the worker difficult to predict by the supervisor, resulting e.g. from an inadvertent action).
As the result of frequent coincidence of several sources contributing to a single accident, the above classification could not be easily employed for accident monitoring. It seems that the classification of accident types proposed in our study 'fall and slip', 'manual', 'machinery', 'energy' and 'other' accidents could be much more effective for successful preventive action. The classification makes it possible to observe trends in the changes of accident risk at different periods of time and indicate major safety problems to the management.
B. Collection of information on minor injuries in the meat processing plant made it possible to determine how many dangerous events happen in the plant before accident occurs. Incident studies constitute excellent material for accident prevention. There is a surprising repeatability of those events and their sources; this provides more abundant data for work safety analyses than the statistically small number of serious accidents.
Unfortunately, generally acceptable criteria for collecting information on minor incidents are not available in Poland, while e.g. in USA the OSH Act requires in Recordkeeping Form OSHA No. 200, also information on injuries without lost days if the injury resulted in 'loss of consciousness', 'restriction of work or motion', or 'transfer to another job' [4].
C. There was a relatively large number of accidents recorded in the studied plant, in which poor housekeeping was an important factor; this refers not only to 'fall and slip' accidents, and that encourages us to suggest the necessity of reporting separately all housekeeping-related accidents in a plant.
Our research in the meat processing plant has confirmed that well-designed analysis of injuries may highlight most important accident risk areas in an industrial plant and enables efficient accident prevention.

References

1. H.W.Heinrich, D. Petersen, N. Roos, Industrial Accident Prevention.. V-th edition, McGraw Hill Book Company, New York, 1980.
2. K. Swat, Accident-causation model for monitoring the risk of accidents in industrial plants. In: Advances in Industrial Ergonomics and Safety VII. Ed. by A.C. Bittner and P.C. Champney. Taylor and Francis, 1995 pp. 895-899.
3. J. Saari, M. Nasanen, The effect of positive feedback on industrial housekeeping and accidents - a long term study at ship-yard, International Journal of Industrial Ergonomics **4** (1989) pp. 201-209.
4. Recordkeeping Guidelines for Occupational Injuries and Ilnesses. U.S. Department of Labor. Bureau of Labor Statistics. Washington, September 1986.

Advances in Occupational Ergonomics and Safety II
Edited by Biman Das and Waldemar Karwowski
IOS Press and Ohmsha, 1997

Determinants of Lost Work Time: A Survival Analysis of Workplace Accidents.

E. Andrew Kapp, MS

Department of Industrial Engineering
University of Wisconsin - Madison
Madison, Wisconsin, USA

Abstract: The identification of the factors associated with accidents resulting in lower rates of return to work over time represents a first step in identifying those areas where intensified safety practices can be most beneficial in reducing costs. Survival analysis presents itself as a unique statistical tool for analyzing the factors effecting the rate of return to work for injured employees. A retrospective study of 238 worker's compensation cases from a large Midwestern university were examined using survival analysis to demonstrate its application.

1. Background

Although efforts to reduce all workplace accidents are important, reducing those accidents that result in lower rates of return to work over time represent the greatest potential for cost reductions. The identification of the workplace factors associated with these injuries represent a first step in determining those areas where intensified safety practices can be most beneficial in reducing the costs associated with personnel injuries. Previous research on variables affecting duration of lost work time found significant relationships between increased age and years of employment and lower rates of return to work following accidents [1] and lower rates of return to work for females and older employees [2].

2. Methods

This is a retrospective study of the 238 cases of employees who experienced accidents requiring one or more days of lost work time for recovery before returning to work. . The cases are from a large Midwestern university employing over 20,000 people. Information on the cases came from the University's Worker's Compensation Claims database. All the cases examined involved injury dates between May 1, 1994 and April 30, 1995. Data collected includes: the date of injury, age, gender, duration of employment, job category, the accident classification, and days lost due to injury. Descriptive statistics and survival analysis techniques were used for data analysis.

2.1 Survival Analysis

A Cox regression [3] was used to model the duration of lost work time following an accident as a function of the independent variables: age, gender, years of employment, job category, and accident classification. Specifically, the regression models the effects of the covariates and their coefficients on the cumulative survival function, i.e. the proportion of individuals surviving or remaining away from work at a particular point in time following the occurrence of an accident. The relative rate at which injured workers return to work over time (defined as the hazard for this study) is a closely related function and is also derived from the Cox regression.

The Cox regression models the hazard function on two quantities: the baseline hazard function which is dependent only on time, and the covariate dependent hazard function which is not dependent on time but on the values of the covariates and their coefficients. The Cox proportional hazards model allows the modeling of non-constant hazard rates, without any assumption about the underlying distribution of the base line hazard rate. The only assumption is the proportionality of the hazard rate over time. To verify the proportionality of hazards assumption, a graphical assessment of the proportionality of hazards was conducted. This involved plotting the log-minus-log survival plot for each of the independent variables included in the model [3]. All covariates included in the final model met the proportionality assumption.

Figure 1:

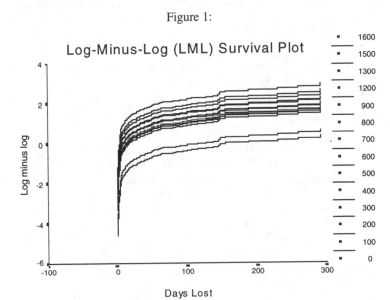

Key: 100: *Encounters with Animals*; 200: *Encounters with Machinery*; 300: *Encounters with Motorized Equipment*; 400: *Encounters with Object*; 500: *Encounters with Person(s)*; 600: *Encounters with Vehicle*; 700: *Exposures Due to Sharps injury*; 800: *Exposure to Hazardous Substances*; 900 *Exposure to Physical Hazards*; 1200: *Lifting, Moving, or Restraining Load*; 1300: *Motion of Individual*; 1500: *Slip, Trip, or Fall*; 1600: *Physiological Event (allergic reactions or seizures)*

3. Results and Discussion

Figure 2 displays the survival function for the sample. The survival function gives us a approximation of the probability of worker remaining away from work up to a certain point in time following an accident.

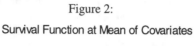

Figure 2:

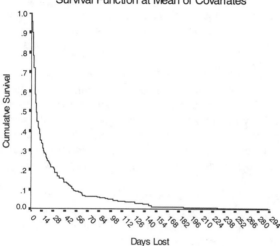

The survival functon provides a useful indication of the likelihood of the duration of lost work time for a member of the population, but does not differentiate according to any of the covariates. A more detailed, covariate dependent analysis of rate of return to work is provided by the results of the proportional hazards model (Table 1.).

Table 1: Summary of Results

Incident Classification	Frequency	Percent	Mean	$e^{\beta x}$	95% CI
0: Not classified	14	5.9	4.2	2.84*	1.61, 4.99
100: Encounter with animal	6	2.5	24.2	1.10	0.50, 2.42
200: Encounter with machinery	3	1.3	21.0	0.76	0.26, 2.25
300: Encounter with motorized equipment	2	0.8	119.5	0.29	0.08, 1.08
400: Encounter with object	10	4.2	15.0	1.41	0.75, 2.67
500: Encounter with person(s)	7	2.9	16.0	1.16	0.56, 2.42
600: Encounter with vehicle	3	1.3	6.3	1.83	0.62, 5.42
700: Exposure due to sharps injury	6	2.5	19.8	0.95	0.43, 2.09
800: Exposure to hazardous substance	4	1.7	7.3	2.12	0.82, 5.47
900: Exposure to physical hazard	3	1.3	10.7	1.48	0.50, 4.38
1200: Lifting, moving, or restraining load	87	36.6	29.5	0.85	0.61, 1.18
1300: Motion of individual	22	9.2	16.9	0.96	0.60, 1.53
1500: Slip, trip, or fall	70	29.4	27.3	0.90	0.64, 1.26
1600: Physiological event (allergic reaction or seizure)	1	0.4	188.0	0.22	0.03, 1.39

* indicates relative risk significant at P = .05

For each category of the variable the frequency, percentage, mean duration of lost work time, relative risk ($e^{\beta x}$), and its confidence interval are given. None of the demographic covariates were meaningful predictors for the rate at which injured workers returned to work. These findings are in opposition to those reported by Tate [1] and Cheadle et. al. [2]. It must be noted however, that both studies looked at a greater range of injuries (including cumulative trauma disorders), and a greater number of cases.

Incident Classification was the only variable found significant, and only one incident category was a significant predictor of the rate of return to work. Those experiencing accidents that were coded Not Classified experienced a significantly greater rate of return to work than workers involved in other types of accidents (exp β_x = 2.84, p < .01). This indicates that individuals experiencing this category of accident are 2.84 times more likely to return to work at any given time than workers recovering from the other types of accidents.

Although not statistically significant, accidents involving encounters with machinery displayed a much smaller likelihood of returning to work at any given time (exp β_x = .29, p <.07), indicating that workers recovering from these types of incidents are .29 times less likely to return to work at any given time than workers recovering from the other types of accidents. Encounters with motorized equipment includes any injury due to the action or motion of a piece of motorized equipment, such as a forklift, bulldozer, tractor or other heavy equipment not used primarily for transportation.

The extremely low rate of return to work for individuals experiencing accidents involving encounters with machinery may indicate an area where increased safety interventions are needed. Although the results were not statistically significant, a hazard rate of this magnitude may warrant attention.

With few assumptions, and the ability to estimate the hazard function and express the results in the form the relative risk, survival analysis presents itself as a useful method for the analysis of workplace factors and their effects on the rate at which injured workers return to work.

References

[1] Tate, G. (1992). Workers' disability and return to work, *American Journal Of Physical Medicine & Rehabilitation, 71*(2), 92-96.
[2] Cheadle, A., Franklin, G., Wolfhagen, C., Savarino, J., Liu, P., Salley, C., and Weaver, M. (1994). Factors influencing the duration of work-related disability, *American Journal of Public Health 84*, 190-196.
[3] Norusis, M./SPSS Inc. (1994) *SPSS Advanced Statistics 6.1,* Chicago: SPSS Inc.

Advances in Occupational Ergonomics and Safety II
Edited by Biman Das and Waldemar Karwowski
IOS Press and Ohmsha, 1997

A Method for Evaluating System Interactions in a Dynamic Work Environment

L. Steiner, F. Turin, and K. Cornelius
National Institute for Occupational Safety and Health
Pittsburgh Research Center
P.O. Box 18070
Cochrans Mill Road
Pittsburgh, PA USA 15236

As technology evolves, accidents may occur because human-system interactions were not considered adequately in the process. A systematic methodology can be used to evaluate the causes of mishaps and to develop recommendations that will enhance safety. A recent trend observed in underground coal mining is used to illustrate this principle because an underground mine is a dynamic work environment. Mining is characterized not only by frequent geologic changes but by technological evolution that can seriously degrade human performance and compromise worker health and safety. The case exemplified in this paper involves implementation of remotely controlled equipment for extended cut mining. Extended cut mining technology evolved with minimal ergonomic consideration even though the change from on-board to remote machine operation dramatically modified the role of the human component. In response to concern that system interactions should be examined more closely, a methodology was developed to identify hazards.

1. Introduction

Almost every process has a predecessor, and studying the predecessor helps to define needs and shortcomings to be addressed in the new design. It also suggests what information is needed by the users in order for them to be able to operate safely and effectively. The end users of a system can provide important feedback to better evaluate current and proposed designs. When new technology is introduced into a system, accidents may occur before it is realized that human-system interactions were not considered adequately in the design process. A systematic methodology to evaluate the causes of these mishaps and to develop remedial recommendations can enhance safety. This paper illustrates how such an approach was used to assess remote machine operation in underground coal mines.

The dynamic work environment of underground mining with its unpredictable geologic anomalies can result in numerous hazards. Most of these hazards, including mine roof collapse, occur near the working face where coal is being extracted. The face area is also where the most intricate interactions of people and equipment occur. For these reasons, a high priority has been placed upon minimizing hazards to the workers at the face. During the past decade remote control technology has been introduced to provide the safer environment. Now, machine operators are not required to be on the equipment, but can position themselves back and behind the machine. Because of that innovation, however, the technology has also provided a way for mines to take longer lengths of cuts, thus increasing production and leading to widespread adoption.

Once remote control technology began to be widely used, new issues became evident. Operator positioning was the primary human factors' concern expressed by industry personnel, but there were many technical questions involving ventilation and ground control during increased cut depths. From a researcher's perspective, the ability to answer these questions is confounded by the fact that each mine is very different in terms of geological characteristics, management and mine planning, equipment, seam height, and geographical area. Solutions are difficult to generalize. Nevertheless, it is essential to develop mechanisms for mines to evaluate new systems in order to predict and reduce accidents.

Extraction methods and equipment changes must allow for the ability of workers to adapt to changes in their dynamic mining environment. Consideration should be given to how the worker will use familiar information to make decisions in now unfamiliar situations. There will be both intended and unintended consequences. Robert Merton [1] denoted the impact these "functions" have on systems. Manifest functions are "intended and recognized by participants in the system" and latent functions are "those which are neither intended nor recognized." Merton's notion reiterates the need to provide comprehensive information for workers transitioning to a new system. Designers try to anticipate and eliminate surprises, but it is impossible to eliminate them all. How, then, will the new system affect the tasks the workers are currently used to? As suggested below, this question may be addressed and more "latent functions" predicted with a planned design process which includes strong ergonomics input to determine interactions and behaviors of participants.

2. Approach

A simple system or product design process involves several stages proceeding from general to specific. It starts with the definition of a need and a plan to produce a solution, and ends with a final product to monitor and evaluate. The process is iterative and each stage can be revisited at any time to improve the design of the system. It is critical to integrate ergonomics into *each* stage of the process [2]. Injuries can be reduced or avoided through proper consideration, planning, testing and retesting. Effort should be given to the human-machine-methods-environment interface from the onset. Regarding extended cut mining, the authors have investigated changes to interfaces in order to determine what impact the new process has on the worker's ability to adapt in the dynamic work environment. The following questions needed to be answered: What effect does the equipment change have on the operator and other workers in the face area? How do work methods change due to equipment change and relocation of the operator?

Several analytical methods were used to answer these questions. The methods were used interactively at different stages of the investigation.

2.1 *Literature Review*

An examination of the literature about new mining equipment and methods revealed that most concerns with implementation of the extended cut method lay in the areas of ground control and ventilation. These discussions centered upon regulatory compliance and production enhancements. There was little evident concern for specific operator needs. This review led to a better understanding of the system and guided development of methods that could be used to target human factors problem areas.

2.2 *Accident Analysis*

An important aspect of research to assess the safety of extended cut mining has been examination of accident data compiled by the Mine Safety and Health Administration (MSHA). The results of evaluations for 1990 and 1991 are provided by Bauer [3] and

Steiner [4]. Accident data of mines that had MSHA approval to take extended cuts were compared to accident data of mines which did not have extended cut approval. It was hoped that a comparison of injury incidence rates would offer insight into whether extended cut mining introduced new hazards or exacerbated existing hazards. Injury rates at mines with approval were higher than those at mines without approval, but fatality rates were lower. Mines with extended cut approval had higher injury incident rates for accidents that involved a worker being struck by or against something, accidents related to the handling of materials, and accidents involving a slip or fall. However, it was not possible to relate safety issues directly to extended cut mining activities. It would have been desirable to compare characteristics of accidents that occurred when an extended cut was being taken to those of shorter standard cuts; however, this information could not be derived from MSHA accident records. The implication to be drawn from this is that reporting methodologies should be changed to reflect changes in technology.

As a corollary, an exploratory study was initiated at two mines following the occurrence of fatal accidents to machine operators working within an intersection during extended cut mining. This study included a review of MSHA accident reports, interviews with face crew members, and meetings with representatives of MSHA, the United Mine Workers of America (UMWA), and the US Bureau of Mines (USBM). Safety concerns specific to worker activities within an intersection were identified. Although the accident data analysis had significant limitations, the results of those efforts combined with findings from the exploratory study provided insights that were used to develop more specific mine site evaluation strategies.

2.3 *Interviews*

An interview guide was developed to identify general safety issues. In particular, the goal was to determine what aspects of this technology were problematic to the mining industry. Topics included mining experience, work methods and procedures used, accidents and injuries, manual materials handling, control layout and design of equipment, visibility, ventilation, operator protection, maintenance, and general safety. Overall, workers had a positive attitude toward this technology. However, visibility of continuous miner operators and some aspects of maintenance were identified as common problems. It was learned that major differences exist in the specific type of problems encountered at each mine. A generalized solution approach would be an ineffective way to deal with diverse miner problems. Instead, data obtained from the interview guide was used to identify what areas needed further examination and to devise a systematic approach to analyze this technology.

A subsequent questionnaire was administered at mines in a particular geographical area in order to more narrowly focus some problem areas. The physical location of the operator during the turning task was an evident concern. The questionnaire also revealed a less than optimal illumination scheme on the continuous mining machine. Further research found that no changes had been made to the lighting systems on the machines since remote control was introduced.

2.4 *Activity Analysis/Structured Observations*

More information was required to determine the needs of workers doing specific tasks in the mining cycle. Work sampling techniques are frequently employed to provide information on the proportion of time spent by a worker on various activities. Ideally, collecting and analyzing information *prior* to implementing new technology would help to address potential problems. Mines that had not yet implemented extended cut technology, but were preparing to start, were identified. It was determined that useful information could be collected using work sampling techniques by examining mines both before and after implementing the longer cuts.

Operators and other mine personnel are faced with the question of where they should position themselves while remotely operating machinery. The most important factors are visibility, roof condition, ventilation and avoidance of moving machinery. The optimum location for an operator to stand may differ depending on length of cut and a number of other variables. The goal of the work sampling method was to identify differences in operator positioning in standard versus extended cuts. In particular, it was necessary to determine what cues and information were used. The locations of workers and equipment at the face area were recorded along with the direction the operators were looking and at what stage they were in the mining process. There did not appear to be a large difference between the before and after conditions. However, continuous miner operators would sometimes stand in an unsafe area in order to observe the longer cuts. Turning a crosscut appears to be the most variable and difficult task for operators regardless of length of cut. In addition to operator position and direction of view data, efforts continue to identify specific cues used to operate equipment remotely. Further research and analysis will determine the effects these changes have had on the continuous miner operator's ability to safely operate with new work methods and equipment changes.

2.5 *Analysis of Proposed Recommendations*

Once the human factors problem areas were more specifically defined, the next step was to investigate several alternative solutions and to study their impact on the technical aspects of the system. Work is underway to determine how to increase operator visibility through alternative mining plans and angled crosscuts. These changes rely heavily on ground control and ventilation analysis of the proposed systems. It is essential to attempt to determine the effects of these possible solutions prior to their implementation and continuously evaluate the solution after implementation.

3. Discussion

When changing from on-board operation to remote operation, the continuous miner operators were not the only ones impacted. Other mobile equipment operators in the face area were affected by this change as well. Before remote control, other face crew workers always knew the miner operator was on the mining machine. Now, the operator could be in several locations, presenting problems for everyone. Though work is progressing to resolve existing problems through the methods outlined, many of these concerns could already have been dealt with if a design team had integrated human factors methods in the development stages. Extended cut technology is just one example of a process that could have benefitted by early ergonomic intervention. Many industries other than mining can use this approach to evaluate current and new designs. If human factors issues are ignored, and major design decisions have been made, it is difficult to make more than minor changes after the fact. Simply put, the earlier human factors becomes involved in a design process, the better [2].

References

[1] Robert K. Merton, Social Theory and Social Structure, Glencoe, IL, Free Press, 1949.
[2] A. Chapanis, Human Factors in Systems Engineering. John Wiley & Sons, Inc., 1996.
[3] E. Bauer, L. Steiner, and C. Hamrick, Extended Cut Mining and Worker Safety in Underground Coal Mines. SME preprint 95-60, 1994.
[4] L. Steiner, F. Turin, and C. Hamrick, An Ergonomic and Statistical Assessment of Safety in Deep Cut Mining. In: Improving Safety at Small Underground Mines. Special Publication 18-94, United States Department of Interior, Bureau of Mines, 1994.

Advances in Occupational Ergonomics and Safety II
Edited by Biman Das and Waldemar Karwowski
IOS Press and Ohmsha, 1997

On the Relationship of Color and Risk Perception

S. David Leonard

University of Georgia, Athens, Georgia 30602, USA

Abstract. Colors are used in warning messages in combination with signal words to attract attention of users and to communicate the hazards associated with a product. The effectiveness of color as a signal has only recently been examined. Standards associating with colors with different levels of hazards have not been based on empirical study. Three experiments reported here obtained responses regarding the relative risks associated with colors. Colors combinations with signal words suggested by various standards organizations were not well supported by the data. Only the color red is highly related to the seriousness of the risk. The results are discussed in terms of strategies for warnings.

1. Introduction.

The field of ergonomics has been publicized extensively in recent years, but publicity has been largely confined to advertising the anthropometric measures some manufacturers have taken with respect to their products. A highly important aspect of ergonomic practice has often been ignored, that is the concern with the safe use of the products. Producing safe use in some cases may necessitate redesign of products to eliminate hazards. In other cases guards may keep the user from contacting the hazard. However, if neither of these is feasible, warning about the hazard is necessary. How the warning is presented is clearly relevant to the usefulness of it. It must be located where the user can have access to it; it must be clear and understandable to potential users whatever their backgrounds may be; and it must attract the user's attention. The importance of attention to warning cannot be emphasized too much. An unattended warning is equivalent to having no warning. The present studies were conducted to evaluate one aspect of the attention getting process, that is, the colors associated with the warnings. Colors are used in many cases to attract attention. Thus, it is reasonable that they be used with warnings. How they can be used with warnings is an important question. It would be advantageous that the color itself suggest a warning is present. Given the variety of objects of different colors in the environment, it is unlikely that it would be possible to select unique colors for this purpose, but it has been suggested that the colors be associated with the level of risk for a hazard.

Several standards for warnings associate particular colors with specific signal words [1,2]. Some investigators [3,4] have questioned the usefulness of these standards because they were not based on empirical data. A study to examine how individuals respond with signal words to colors and with colors to signal words indicated that the primary association of warning signal words was to the color red [4]. A criticism of this approach was that there was no similarity to the warnings on which the signal words were presented and responses were to words not colors. The present studies were performed to control for those possible confounds and to evaluate the relationship of color to perception of risk. Experiment 1 examine the perception of risk for color words and signal words.

Table 1

Mean Ratings of Signal Words and Colors in Experiment 1

Term	Current Rating	Leonard et al Rating	Color	Rating
Fatal	6.83		Red	6.24
Deadly	6.76	4.95	Orange	4.66
Danger	5.54	3.45	Black	4.49
Warning	4.02	2.53	Yellow	3.76
Caution	3.39	2.21	Green	2.51
Attention	2.41	1.77	Blue	2.51
Notice	1.83		White	1.78

2. Experiment 1

The survey was completed by 10 men and 31 women whose ages ranged from 20 to 68, with a median of 26 years. The questionnaire included two lists, one of words and the other of colors. Respondents rated each item on a seven point scale in terms of the seriousness of the risk that they associated with each color and with each word.

As seen in Table 1, the words *deadly* and *fatal* were most highly rated. This ordering of terms is consistent with that previously obtained by Leonard et al. [5]. The color ratings are also consistent with the findings of other studies, except for the color orange which has generally been rated lower than yellow [4]. One question about the color terms was the extent to which they represent the colors themselves. This was addressed in Experiment 2.

3. Experiment 2

Although color terms are used freely in conversation and in descriptions of various objects, it is possible that the visual impact of the colors themselves could produce different (possibly stronger) responses than the color words. Thus, in this experiment individuals were asked to respond to the colors themselves.

A total of 34 respondents were presented with two sets of color patterns and asked to rate them on the seven point scale used in Experiment 1. The first set of color patterns were drawn to be similar to the patterns used on many warnings with a box outline containing an oval color patch and a blank space below. The respondents were asked to indicate how serious they thought the message that would occupy the blank space would be. The six colors were *red, orange, black, yellow, green,* and *blue*. The second set of colors used the same patterns as the first but only one color was presented. For 16 of the respondents the color was red and 18 of them it was green. These colors were drawn over the words *fatal, deadly, danger, warning, caution, attention,* and *notice* typed in the ovals. The orders of colors and words were randomly determined.

The results displayed in Table 2 for colors are consistent with those of presentation of words only, except for the reversal of *yellow* and *orange*. This order is more consistent with that obtained previously [4]. The correlation of the results was $r = .96$.

The ratings of signal words in this procedure is highly similar to that obtained with the words alone. An interesting result, however, is the significant difference between the words embedded in the different colors ($t_{32} = 2.23, p < .01$). Because the color patches

Table 2

Mean Ratings for Colors and Signal Words Embedded in Red and Green

Color	Rating	Signal Word	With Red	With Green	Total
Red	6.41	Fatal	6.81	6.22	6.50
Orange	3.88	Deadly	6.81	6.28	6.53
Black	4.65	Danger	5.50	5.06	5.26
Yellow	4.18	Warning	4.88	3.83	4.32
Green	2.24	Caution	3.75	3.39	3.53
Blue	2.15	Attention	2.50	2.11	2.29
Total	3.92	Notice	2.72	1.67	2.16
		Total	4.71	4.08	4.38

were shown prior to the presentation of the separate color conditions, those data were not shown separately. Examination of the means for those who later received either the red or the green color-word combinations showed no significant difference. If anything, the group receiving the green color later rated the risks slightly higher. Therefore, it is unlikely the difference between the red and green color groups arose from a greater propensity of those in the red group to rate items as risky. The difference in ratings for the two groups was similar to the differences in the red and green color ratings. It seemed reasonable, therefore, to investigate this phenomenon further.

4. Experiment 3

The difference obtained between the colors in the color and signal word combinations suggested that there might be some association of colors with the perception of risk. If so, it would be relevant to determine if a pattern of color-risk perceptions existed. Thus, it was decided to include the color *yellow* in the combinations with signal words.

A total of 72 respondents who volunteered in psychology classes completed the ratings. The procedure followed was similar to that of Experiment 2. The respondents first rated the color patches in the diagrams simulating warning patterns. Then they rated the same set words, each of which was on one of the three colors *red, yellow,* or *green*. To improve the visibility of the words they were laid over the color patches using transfer letters of 24 point Helvetica medium type. Both the colors and the color-word combinations were rated on the same seven point scale used in the previous experiments.

The results of the color ratings are very similar to those obtained in Experiments 1 and 2 as shown in Table 3. The red patches were rated as involving the most serious risk. Again the orange patches were lower than the yellow and black in mean ratings. This is not in accord with the standards prescribed by the Westinghouse [2] and ANSI [1] publications.

Ratings of signal words were also similar to those of Experiments 1 and 2 in terms of order. However, contrary to the results of Experiment 2, there were no effects of the colors on which the words were presented. As seen in Table 3, the difference among the groups was small and was not significant ($F_{2,69} = 1.63, p > .10$). A possible basis for failure to find a difference in this case is that the signal words were more prominent in the color patches. If the signal word is obvious, little attention may be paid to the color. In Experiment 2 the signal words appeared engulfed in the colors, and more attention may have been directed toward the colors.

Table 3

Mean Ratings for Colors and for Signal Words Embedded in Red, Yellow, and Green.

Color	Rating	Signal Word	With Red	With Yellow	With Green	Total
Red	6.44	Fatal	6.75	6.92	6.88	6.85
Orange	3.42	Deadly	6.83	6.75	6.79	6.79
Black	4.21	Danger	5.58	5.83	5.08	5.47
Yellow	4.36	Warning	4.42	4.33	4.25	4.33
Green	2.07	Caution	3.67	3.46	3.08	3.40
Blue	2.11	Attention	2.38	2.71	2.46	2.51
Total	3.77	Notice	2.12	1.96	1.88	1.99
		Total	4.54	4.57	4.35	4.48

5. Discussion

These results indicate that people can evaluate color words as though they were the colors themselves. Further, different colors connote some differences in risks. However, there are two difficulties associated with the use of colors in warnings as in some common standards. The relative risk associated with these colors does not correspond to the patterns presented in the standards which associate *red* with *danger*, *orange* with *warning*, and *yellow* with *caution*. Fortunately, as the results of Experiment 3 indicate, if the signal word is prominent little attention is paid to the color in terms of its relation to risk.

Another feature of these studies is the large distance in scale value between the color red and other colors in terms of amount of risk connoted. This agrees with several other findings [4,6,7]. Indeed, the consensus is that the only color on warnings that is well associated with the risk is red. Although one might presume that using red on all warnings could dilute the effect on more serious warnings, it seems reasonable that its attention getting characteristic is useful for all warnings. Inasmuch as the verbal information is likely not affected by the color when the verbal information is prominent, serious consideration should be given to using only red as the color associated with warnings.

References

[1] American National Standards Institute Product safety signs and labels, National Electrical Manufacturers Association, Washington, DC, 1991.
[2] Westinghouse Electric Corporation, *Product Safety Label Handbook*, Westinghouse Printing Division, Trafford, PA, 1981.
[3] deTurck, M. A., Goldhaber, G. M., and Richetto, G., Uncertainty Reduction in Product Warnings: Effects of Fear and Color. *Journal of Products Liability*, **13,** (1991) 339-346.
[4] Griffith, L. J., and Leonard, S. D., Association of Colors with Warning Signal Words, *International Journal of Industrial Ergonomics*, in press.
[5] Leonard, S. D., Karnes, E. W., and Schneider, T., Scale values for warning symbols and words. In F. Aghazadeh (Ed.) *Trends in Ergonomics/Human Factors V*, Elsevier, Amsterdam, 1988, pp. 669-674.
[6] Braun, C. C., and Silver, N. C., Interaction of Warning Label Features: Determining the Contributions of Three Warning Characteristics, in *Proceedings of the Human Factors and Ergonomics Society, 39th Annual Meeting* Human Factors Society, Santa Monica, CA, 1955, pp. 984-988.
[7] Chapanis, A., Hazards associated with three signal words and four colours on warning signs, *Ergonomics*, **37 (2)**, (1994), 265-275.

Advances in Occupational Ergonomics and Safety II
Edited by Biman Das and Waldemar Karwowski
IOS Press and Ohmsha, 1997

Exploring The Link Between Housekeeping And Occupational Injuries

VINCENT DUFORT

Joint Departments of Epidemiology and Biostatistics

and Occupational Health, McGill University, 1130 Pine Avenue, Montréal, Canada H3A 1A3

Abstract. The association between levels of housekeeping and company safety (occupational injury and days lost due to injuries) was investigated using a 15 month prospective cohort study. Fifty-seven companies manufacturing transportation equipment and machinery in the province of Quebec, Canada, took part in this study. Housekeeping levels were assessed throughout the study period. Information on injury rates and other factors was obtained through the companies at the end of the study period. Associations between housekeeping and injury or days lost due to injuries were found. When controlling for confounding, obstructions remained significantly associated with injury and days lost, though no clear trends were seen across different levels of obstructions. Adjusted incidence rate ratios ranged from 1.81 to 2.39 for injuries and 1.97 to 3.38 for days lost when compared to companies with the best obstruction scores. While overall housekeeping is shown significantly correlated to company safety, this is not true for all aspects of housekeeping after adjusting for confounders.

1. Introduction

Injury, and occupational injury have been identified as substantial public health problems in North America [1,2,3,4]. Understanding injury etiology is an essential component in answering this problem. Theoretical models that describe plausible pathways to injury causation serve as one way to promote this understanding. Many models have been proposed to explain occupational injury genesis, however, some assumptions that are at the foundation of these models remain essentially untested. This is one of the challenges facing occupational injury epidemiology today.

According to safety experts, the state of housekeeping is one aspect of the work environment influencing injury rates [5,6,7]. This has, to some extent, been shown through injury taxonomy [7]. While obstacles or safety hazards are detected through injury taxonomy, it is not easy to verify the contribution of subtler factors, such as organization or aesthetics. Because of the inadequacy of injury taxonomy in identifying subtler antecedents, the possible connection between the aesthetic side of housekeeping and injury has still not been ruled out [8].

2. Objectives

The objective of this study was to test the hypothesis that there is a link between good housekeeping practices and occupational safety while controlling for other factors that may influence outcome. In this study, occupational safety was defined as injury rates and rates of days lost due to injuries.

3. Methods

This was a cohort study conducted among 57 of 78 eligible mid-sized companies (20-60 workers) in the transportation equipment and machinery manufacturing sector from the four most densely popolated regions of Quebec, Canada. Non-participants were either companies that refused to participate (16) or closed before the end of the study (5). Companies were visited an average of four times during the study period, each company was visited on at least two different occasions. One observer was used for the entire study.

Housekeeping covered obstructions, organization and cleanliness. The evaluation of housekeeping was performed during walk-through surveys of the companies using a checklist designed for this study. Two main features of the checklist were that 1) the attributes were easily observable without measurement apparatus and 2) subjective evaluations were avoided.

The level of housekeeping was calculated for each visit as the percentage of correct observations among all items observed during a visit. Test-retest reliability of the checklist showed reasonable agreement (Intra Class Correlation 0.73, 95% CI 0.68-0.78)

The outcomes of interest for this study were injury rate (injuries per million person-hours worked) and rate of days lost due to injuries (days lost per million hours worked). At the end of the study, information was abstracted from compensation claim forms used to signal injuries to Quebec's workers compensation board on all injuries occurring during the study period. Seven companies were unable to provide copies of compensation claims, but authorised the release of the information directly from the statistics branch of the Commission. The nature of the injury, date of the event, number of lost days, external cause of the injury, location of the event, job title, employment status, age and seniority of the worker were also abstracted. Information was also collected during the final visit on certain company/workforce characteristics which could be seen as potential confounders for the study.

4. Results

Unadjusted housekeeping scores were significantly correlated with both injury rate and rate of days lost due to injuries (p < 0.05). The correlation showed decreased injury rates with higher (better) housekeeping scores.

Mean age and mean seniority of workers were correlated with injury rates, but not with any of the housekeeping scores (p < 0.10). None of the other control variables were significantly correlated with either housekeeping measures or outcomes.

Adjusting for potential confounders (mean age and seniority of workers, age of factory, work station stability, presence of health and safety association, size of production pieces) housekeeping remains significantly associated with injury rate (p=0.03).

5. Discussion

While housekeeping was found to be associated with both injuries and days lost due to injuries in the studied companies, not all aspects of housekeeping showed significant associations. This could be due to two factors. First, it must be accepted that obstructions would be more closely associated to injuries than either cleanliness or organization. Second, the association for other aspects of housekeeping were weaker than with obstructions, and this study was not powerful enough to demonstrate the weaker associations. As well, the apparent associations between cleanliness and organization may be due to their close correlations to obstructions.

When housekeeping was categorised, trends in injuries and days lost were not apparent, though they may be expected. A possible explanation for this lack of trend may be the relatively narrow span of housekeeping levels measured. This may also be indicative of a threshold for housekeeping which was quickly reached by the poor performers.

Unlike previous studies, this study attempted to extensively control for potential confounders. This was done both by selection of companies from a narrowly defined industrial sector, as well as in the analysis which took into consideration other factors which were potential confounders.

Different properties of the work environment have historically been classified under the heading of housekeeping. In one textbook written for safety professionals, housekeeping includes:

> *"Cluttered and poorly arranged areas. Untidy and dangerous piling of materials. Items that are excess, obsolete or no longer needed. Blocked aisles. Material stuffed in corners, on overcrowded shelves, in overflowing bins and containers. Tools and equipment left in work areas instead of being returned to tool rooms, racks, cribs or chests. Broken containers and damaged material. Materials gathering dirt and rust from disuse. Excessive quantities of items. Waste scrap and excess materials that congest work areas. Spills, leaks and hazardous materials creating safety and health hazards." [5].*

Attributes which were measured in past studies included aesthetic, organizational as well as hazardous aspects of housekeeping. Some studies even went so far as to include subjective evaluations of lighting and noise levels in their assessment of general housekeeping. While most of the components of housekeeping were significantly associated with injury rates and rates of days lost due to injuries in the univariate models, once confounders were considered in the models this association dissapeared in all but the models including obstructions. These findings underscore a main weakness of previous studies which looked at injury etiology using univariate models -- While it is possible to find associations between a variable of interest and a certain outcome, it is imperative that possible confounders also be considered.

This study was not without limitations. Low sample size limits the power of the study yet it must also be recognized that it is difficult to improve power and maintain a feasible study. Working within these constraints, it was possible to show how previously relied upon univariate testing failed to control adequately for confounding. While only one sector of activity is addressed by this study, it was nevertheless helpful in demonstrating how similar studies in other sectors may help shed further light on the association between housekeeping and safety.

Given that the association between housekeeping and injury seems to persist with controlling for other potential confounders, it would be interesting to further explore the effect of improving housekeeping on the existing injury rates in industry. Some early studies have shown that injury rates may fall dramatically after the implementation of housekeeping improvement programs [8]. It remains to be seen if this reduction is a result of the improvement in housekeeping levels, or perhaps a result of the new dynamics established in companies with the introduction of these interventions.

References

[1] Baker SP (1989): Injury science comes of age. JAMA 262(16):2284-5
[2] CDC; Division of Injury Control, Center for Environmental Health and Injury Control, Centers for Disease Control (1990). Childhood injuries in the United States. AJDC 144:627-46

[3] Rice DP, MacKenzie EJ, and Associates (1989): Cost of Injury in the United States. A Report to Congress 282pp

[4] Rivara FP, Grossman DC (1996): Prevention of traumatic deaths to children in the United States: How far have we come and where do we need to go? Pediatrics 97:791-7

[5] Bird FE Jr, Germain GL (1990). Practical Loss Control Leadership. Institute Publishing, ILCI. HWY 78 PO box345 Loganville, Georgia 30249

[6] WHO (1982). World Health Organization. Psychological factors in injury prevention. Report of a meeting held in Geneva July 1982 31pp

[7] McDonald G (1989). Developing an on-site safety program. Journal of Occupational Health and Safety - Aust NZ 5(1);53-67

[8] Saari J, Näsänen M (1989) The effect of positive feedback on industrial housekeeping and accidents; A long-term study at a shipyard. International Journal of Industrial Ergonomics 4;201- 211.

[9] ILCI (International Loss Control Institute) (1991). TUTTAVA: A Performance System for Measuring and Motivating Good Housekeeping and Order; Implementation Team Handbook. 72pp

Advances in Occupational Ergonomics and Safety II
Edited by Biman Das and Waldemar Karwowski
IOS Press and Ohmsha, 1997

System of Psychophysiological Maintenance of Mental Labour: The main Direction of Ergonomics in Following Decade?

Alexander Burov

Infocenter ALIAS Ltd. Post Box 3, 254214. Kyiv. Ukraine

Abstract. The valuation of tendency of intellectualization of labour increase of numbers of problems connected with cognitive ergonomics is given. It is marked the complexity of valuation and prediction of mental fitness to work, necessity of account of psychophysiological "price of activity" which depends on the individual features of person. It is assumed, that the interest increases to macroergonomics aspects of labour which take into account the dynamics of interaction of human with environmental technogenious world. The systems of psychophysiological maintenance of mental labour will become tool means of such approach. They are based on individual approach and enabling enough precisely to evaluate three psychophysiological components of human's fitness to work: constant (genetic), trend (changes of some parameters of life) and oscillatory (parameters, varying day by day, during day and on more short intervals of time).

1. Introduction

The prediction of development of science and its directions is a macroeconomic means, as permits to plan the investments of financial and human resources in future economy as of the whole world, as of every country. The most obviously it relates to ergonomics - science, fast developing in last decades, which covers more and more the wide range of questions of human's interaction with the environmental world, first of all, with the technogenious one.

Ergonomics could be regarded as a scientific discipline (area of knowledge) which studies a human, instruments and means of activity, as well as an environment during their interaction with the purpose of maintenance of efficiency, safety and comfort of this interaction.

It is especially urgent for countries with the unstable economic system, developing countries, as far as they have to solve the problem not only of reorganization of internal development, but also integration in the world economic system. As an example, it could be Ukraine, economy and ergonomics of which were specialized as a part of the former USSR, and which are forced at present during relatively short period to be transformed in really independent systems. As far as given work considers the questions of development of ergonomics, main purpose is analysis of priority interests of ergonomist in the present time and in the near future, as well as possible priorities in the near future, that allows to predict the requirement in experts of some occupationals and in costs on development of theoretical and applied scientific problems.

2. Nature of labour and priorities of ergonomics

In the former USSR, as in the USA, engineering psychology developed from military problems. Ergonomics has its origin in experimental psychology and systems engineering. The purpose was to enhance systems performance, to develope the system methodology for design of complex technic and industrial processes. Besides, there was a greater tendency to use manual labor in many other countries and the ergonomics problems were focused on biomechanics, heat stress and work physiology, focus of ergonomics was specific to the need of the country.

However, with the introduction of computers in the most countries, a radical change came over the interest and the problems of usability of complex systems, which are now universal. The last decades are characterized by intensive process of change from manual labour to a mental one. The important significance is acquired not only by the task of designing of such human interactions as human-machine, human-environment, human-human [1], but also a reorganization of particular person's work process itself. This reorganization is based on conformity of the general professional requirements and his individual features (physical, psychophysiological, social and capacity for adaptation) in dynamics of his whole professional biography from start in occupation, through occupation mastering, maximization of his efficiency and up to leaving his occupation owing to loss of ability to be adapted to varying working conditions [2].

The necessity of individual features' adaptation to the general requirements affects the dynamics of human work functional structure during his life. The ergonomical approach to optimization of human interaction with working tools and means, as well as environment consists in mutual adaptation between human work functional structure and work environment [3]. And mechanisms of such adaptation can be differ in dependence on conditions, locations and time of human work, that is, they depend not only from interactions of the human-machine, human-environment, human-human, but also from dynamics of these interactions during all human's occupation. Hence, the improvements of human working conditions needs in taking into account the requirements as macroergonomics (space aspect of human interaction with environmental industrial world), as requirement ergodynamics (time aspect).

Apparently, this is a cause the most important current application of ergonomics in 25 ergonomics societies, which are members of the IEA, is the safety, and the most important emerging area around the world is methodology to change work organization and design [4]. Cognitive ergonomics, usability studies, human reliability, and human-computer interaction became new top priorities, as well as the organizational design and the study of industrial change processes.

3. The role of psychophysiology in ergonomics

The analysis of tendencies of ergonomics development and areas of its priority interest shows, that it is happened the shift in direction of intellectualization of labour and account its "cost" from the poin t of view of human's health. In other words, the speech goes about further labour humanization as concerning to conditions of activity, as its influence on further life of particular person.

If the area of greatest interests of ergonomists in 1980's was a human-computer interaction, in 1990's - cognitive ergonomics and organization ergonomics [4], as appear, the next century begin by the interest to psychophysiological aspects of work, that is, to psychophysiological maintenance of work, first of all, to reduction of damage for human health and to increasing of his fitness to work.

The today's feature is a further increase of share of mental labour and respective change of methodical base of ergonomical researches. But if today the main attention is paid to conformity of mental and physiological component of activity, as well as to classifications of this conformity, the natural following step should be the valuation of dynamics of this conformity and its prediction.

It has a more and more significance because if at physical labour of infringement of human's fitness to work are more or less obvious (subjective and objective impossibility to continue the work), at mental labour this bound is not so visible and human can continue to work (process of labour proceeds), but results of such activity become useless or even dangerous ones. Especially it is true concerning to critical occupations: the dispatchers, operators of treansportation, operators of power-generating systems, chemical enterprises etc.

The control of professional human's fitness to work becomes necessary not only on the basis of valuation of his qualification, but also of his psychophysiological abilities to execute the particular work on all stages of the professional biography from arrival in occupation to retire from the occupation. According to each stage they are used methods of valuation and prediction enabling to describe person as the complex system, which is dynamically varied day by day and year by year.

The description of system "the human" should be based on individual approach and evaluates three psychophysiological components of the human's fitness to work:

(a) constant, generically inherent to each person since birth and practically not varying with age (for example, mobility of nervous processes),

(b) trend, which is described by some parameters during human's life (for example, rate of decision making, reaction on the socially important factors),

(c) oscillatory, which is related to professionally important psychophysiological qualities change of human day by day, during day and on more short intervals of time (psychomotor reaction, stability of the heart rate and etc.).

The set of these components (their sums) determines the psychophysiological status of person, his ability to realize the professional knowledge, level of his health.

4. Systems of psychophysiological maintenance of labour

The methodologically adequate means for such approaches are the adaptive and self-adjusting systems of psychophysiological support and control, which permit for person to evaluate his state and his fitness to work, as well as indicate, when and in what way it is necessary to him to make correction of his state for the support of the health on the necessary level.

As it is known the psychophysiological parameters' fluctuation can be considerable in consequence of both endogenuos and exogenuos resons that can lead to the human's professional fitness to work reduction below the critical level, although functional deviations in the initial state could be insignificant yet. At the same time operator's fitness to work must always answer the required level during the necessary time.

The influence of each mentioned component of the human's fitness to work can be appreciated on various stages of his (including, professional) with help of following types of tool systems:

(a) for a psychophysiological initial professional selection,

(b) for a periodical check,

(c) for a daily check.

Each of systems permits to evaluate the reliability and efficiency of human work, as well as to construct the prognosis of changes of these parameters pursuant to estimated period of his professional biography . Each of these cases uses the psychophysiological criteria and parameters, ensuring the most the high accuracy of valuation and forecast of professional serviceability. The results of valuation and forecast permit to accept the measures not to admit of unreliable person to work or to increase his reliability and serviceability, as the duly and exact information concerning to significances of these parameters permits to operate reliability of human link of socio-technical system and to accept the preventive measures for preventions of accidents, increase of efficiency of work of person and improvement of his health.

Each of systems permits to evaluate the reliability and efficiency of work of operator, as well as to construct the prognosis of changes of these parameters pursuant in relation to the period of his professional biography [5]. Each of these cases they are used the psychophysiological criteria and parameters, ensuring the most high accuracy of valuation and prediction of operator's professional fitness to work. The results of valuation and prognosis permit to make arrangements not to admit of unreliable human to work or to increase his reliability and fitness to work, as the duly and exact information concerning to significances of these parameters permits to operate reliability of a human as an element of a socio-technical system and to accept the preventive measures for accident precautions, increase of efficiency of humqan work and improvement of his health.

References

[1] H.W.Hendrick, Human Factors in Organizational Design and Management. *Ergonomics.* N 34, 1991.
[2] A.Yu.Burov, Macroergonomics aspects of the psychophysiological maintenance of operators' reliability Human Factors in Organizational Design and Management V. Breckenridge, Colorado, USA. 1996.
[3] V. Venda and Y. Venda Dynamics in Ergonomics, Psychology, and Decisions: Introduction to Ergodynamics, Ablex, Norwood, N.J., 1995.
[4] M.Helander, The Changing Nature of Ergonomics around the World. In: IEA News. No 1. 1996.
[5] A.Yu.Burov, Yu.V.Chetvernya, Methodological Principles of Psychophysiological Forecasting of Operators' Reliability. In: Advances in Occupational Ergonomics and Safety I. In Proceedings of the XIth Annual International Occupational Ergonomics and Safety Conference held in Zurich , Switzerland, 8-11 July 1996, Int.Soc. For Occup.Erg.and Safety, Ohio, U.S.A. 1996, Vol.2, pp.729-731.

Advances in Occupational Ergonomics and Safety II
Edited by Biman Das and Waldemar Karwowski
IOS Press and Ohmsha, 1997

Effect of Creatine Supplementation on Upper-Extremity Work in Females

K. Hamilton-Ward,[1] M.C. Meyers,[2] R.J. Marley,[3] and W.A. Skelly,[4]

[1]*Exercise and Sport Sciences Dept., University of Florida, Gainesville, FL 32611*
[2]*Health & Human Performance Dept., University of Houston, Houston, TX 77204*
[3]*Mechanical & Industrial Engineering Dept., Montana State University, Bozeman, MT 59717*
[4]*Health & Human Development Dept., Montana State University, Bozeman, MT 59717*

Abstract. Creatine monohydrate (CrH_2O) is a nutritional supplement marketed with claims of increasing muscular strength and endurance. The purpose of this study was to investigate the influence of standard doses of oral CrH_2O on muscular performance during elbow flexion (EF) in females. Subjects were pair-matched on lean body mass, % body fat, weight, height, and age criteria, and then randomly assigned to either placebo (P) (n=13) or CrH_2O (n=11) treatment groups. Peak concentric (CON) and eccentric (ECC) isokinetic (IK) torque, one repetition maximum (1RM) utilizing a variable isotonic (IT) resistance, and muscular fatigue (FAT) during EF were evaluated. Subjects consumed either P or 25 g CrH_2O/day for a 7-day dietary phase. MANOVA revealed a significant treatment by trial interaction ($p<0.05$). Post hoc univariate analysis indicated a significantly greater change in EF_{FAT} following CrH_2O than following P ($p<0.01$). No significant differences existed for peak CON or ECC IK torque or for 1RM. Results suggest CrH_2O increased EF work capacity but did not influence peak IK or IT EF strength in females. Therefore, CrH_2O supplementation may be of benefit for enhancing upper extremity work capacity. While inference can be made only to strength-trained females, further investigation of the efficacy of CrH_2O for increasing work capacity and/or productivity, or perhaps reducing risk of overexertion injuries in industrial workers is warranted.

1. Background

Production and sales of ergogenic aids has become a lucrative industry with a steady increase in the number and variety of new products marketed annually. One such product is creatine monohydrate (CrH_2O). When taken orally during training, CrH_2O is purported to enhance fuel supply for working muscles, ultimately resulting in improved strength, endurance, and fat-free mass. The majority of research conducted on the efficacy of CrH_2O, though somewhat equivocal, includes compelling findings with regard to improved lower extremity strength and anaerobic capacity primarily in males [1-4]. Supplementation with CrH_2O appears to alter muscle energetics possibly resulting in more efficient use of metabolic fuels and a delay in muscle fatigue [1-4]. It appears that supplementation with 25-30 g of CrH_2O daily for five to seven days may improve performance of high-intensity, short-term, anaerobic work utilizing large muscle groups [1-4]. There is little scientific evidence, however, that supplementation with CrH_2O has any buffering effect during anaerobic activities. Furthermore, information on the effects of CrH_2O on upper body strength and anaerobic power is limited. To date, no research has been published regarding the effect of oral CrH_2O on explosive, upper body, sport or occupational movements. In addition, the majority of existing studies regarding CrH_2O have focused primarily on work response of males with limited comparison between gender. While research on gender-specific effects of Cr supplementation on work performance is lacking, there is evidence of higher total muscle Cr/phosphocreatine (PC) content in females versus males [5]. It is unknown, however, whether the relative quantity of PC stored in muscle relates to efficacy of CrH_2O supercompensation. Because of inherent gender differences in lean body mass and the possible gender difference in Cr/PC muscle content relative to tissue weight, the efficacy of Cr supplementation on the exercise response of females should be quantified. Therefore, the purpose of this investigation was to determine the effects of CrH_2O supplementation on upper extremity anaerobic response in females.

2. Methods

Following written informed consent, 24 college-aged females, who met the inclusion criteria of participation in upper extremity strength training, took part in this study. All testing was conducted at the Montana State University-Bozeman Human Performance and Ergonomics Laboratory.

2.1. Testing

Prior to initiation of testing, 12-lead EKG recordings, heart rate, and blood pressure were obtained from each subject to identify any contraindications to participation according to The American College of Sports Medicine Guidelines. Height (Ht) and weight (Wt) were determined and body composition (percent body fat; BF and lean body mass; LBM) were evaluated via skinfolds [6].

The first three of five total testing sessions were designed to obtain proper equipment settings, familiarize subjects with the procedures for testing and supplementation, and promote biomechanical efficiency. The last two testing sessions constituted data collection. Elbow flexion (EF) was selected as it is commonly used to evaluate concentric (CON) and eccentric (ECC) strength of elbow flexors including the biceps brachii, brachioradialis, and brachialis muscles. At each session, peak isotonic (IT) strength during EF was evaluated using the one repetition maximum (1RM) and expressed as the IT resistance at which each subject could only complete one repetition. Strength was also evaluated as the total number of repetitions that could be completed at 70% of 1RM. All testing was conducted using a LIDO WorkSET™ dynamometer (Loredan Biomedical, Inc., West Sacramento, CA) which has a reported test-retest reliability of 0.82-0.96 for torque readings and a high degree of internal validity ($R^2=1$) with regards to torque, power, and work [7]. The LIDO was interfaced with a personal computer via a A/D board and position and torque data were sampled at 150 Hz.

Subjects began each of the five testing sessions by warming-up with three EF IK CON/ECC contractions at approximately 50% of maximal voluntary contraction (MVC) on the dominant side at 90°/s. Range for EF testing was from maximum flexion to maximum extension. Subjects completed one MVC and the peak CON and ECC torques were recorded as EF IK_{CON} (Nm) and EF IK_{ECC} (Nm), respectively. Evaluation of EF_{1RM} began with a warm-up of three CON contractions at 50 percent of the estimated EF_{1RM}. Approximation of EF_{1RM} was made based on the linear relationship between the intensity and the number of repetitions performed. Load adjustments were made as necessary, until EF_{1RM} (Nm) was determined. Subjects then completed successive EF repetitions in the IT mode at 70% of 1RM until volitional fatigue (FAT). The number of repetitions was recorded as EF_{FAT}. All EF tests were separated by standard two-minute rest periods.

Throughout data collection, subjects maintained upper extremity strength conditioning without progressing the resistance to facilitate accurate evaluation of treatment effects without the positive influence of progressive resistance exercise. Each subject's physical activity was quantified by the investigator (average estimated METS per day) using a 7-day physical activity recall.

2.2. Treatment

Because the time course of Cr degradation following supplementation, suspected to be longer than one month, remains unknown, a cross-over design was contraindicated. Therefore, subjects were pair-matched based on Ht, Wt, BF, LBM, and age, and randomly assigned to receive either CrH_2O (25 g CrH_2O + 2 g sucrose; n=11) or P (2.12 g Polycose®; n=13) for seven days. Each treatment dosage was dissolved in approximately 6 oz of warm-to-hot caffeine-free herbal tea to facilitate dissolution without formation of creatinine [8].

Food frequency questionnaires were analyzed to quantify meat, fish, and poultry consumption (kg/wk) for estimation of dietary Cr intake (g/wk). Vegetarians were excluded from the study due to reports of increased Cr uptake by skeletal muscle in subjects with lower initial muscular Cr concentration, and lower normal serum Cr reference values reported for vegetarians [8].

3. Results

Multivariate analysis was performed on pair-matching variables, to verify efficacy of matching procedures, and on EF variables using the General Linear Model (GLM) procedure of SAS^R (ver. 6.08). An experiment-wise type I error rate of 0.05 was established a priori and the Bonferroni adjustment for multiple comparisons was used where appropriate. Subjects were stratified according to anthropometric variables and age, and treated statistically as a random effect. Wilks' criterion was used to identify significant effects and, when significant effects were observed, univariate F-statistics were examined to identify the importance of individual variables.

No significant differences existed between groups with respect to initial Wt, LBM, BF, Ht, or age ($p>0.05$). Mean Wt, Ht, and BF for the sample were consistent with United States averages for females in this age group. No significant differences ($p>0.05$) existed between the groups with respect to estimated average Cr intake from meat (kg/wk; 1 kg providing approximately 5 g Cr; $F_{1,22}=1.254$, $p=0.29$), or estimated average physical activity (METS/wk; $F_{1,22}=.06$, $p=0.81$) during the treatment phase.

Pre- and post-treatment Wt and muscle response are summarized in Table 1. With respect to Wt, CrH$_2$O supplementation resulted in no significant treatment effect ($F_{1,22}=.72$, $p=0.41$), a significant trial effect ($F_{1,22}=5.75$, $p=0.03$), and no significant treatment by trial interaction ($F_{1,22}=0.66$, $p=0.43$). These findings indicate that while Wt did change over time, the change did not differ significantly between treatment groups. Weight increased by 0.6% and 1.2% from pre- to post-treatment in P and CrH$_2$O groups respectively.

Table 1: Mean Weight and Muscular Response

Variable	P ^{a}: Pre	Post	CrH$_2$O ^{a}: Pre	Post
Wt (kg)	65.3 ± 3.5	65.7 ± 3.5	64.9 ± 2.2	65.7 ± 2.2
EF IK $_{CON}$ (Nm)	42.9 ± 2.9	42.1 ± 2.5	44.2 ± 2.0	46.6 ± 1.6
EF IK $_{ECC}$ (Nm)	55.2 ± 3.5	56.3 ± 4.2	62.0 ± 2.7	64.8 ± 5.1
EF$_{1RM}$ (Nm)	34.4 ± 2.5	35.0 ± 2.6	36.2 ± 1.8	37.8 ± 1.7
EF$_{FAT}$ (reps)^b	17.0 ± 1.5	15.0 ± 0.8	12.8 ± 1.0	16.4 ± 1.5

^{a} Mean ± SEM ^{b} Pre- to post-treatment difference significant between treatments ($p<0.05$)

Analysis of EF using Wilks' criterion revealed a significant treatment by trial interaction ($F_{4,19}=5.30$, $p<0.01$), a significant treatment effect ($F_{4,19}=6.71$, $p<0.01$), and no significant trial effects. In the absence of interaction, significant univariate treatment effects for EF IK$_{CON}$ ($F_{1,22}=13.39$, $p<0.01$), EF IK$_{ECC}$ ($F_{1,22}=16.76$, $p<0.01$), and EF$_{1RM}$ ($F_{1,22}=18.08$, $p<0.01$) are not indicative of significant differences between treatment group responses. Treatment effects may be reflective of pre-existing strength differences and/or similar changes in strength between the groups following treatment. However, a significant treatment by trial interaction for EF$_{FAT}$ ($F_{1,22}=9.42$, $p<0.01$) indicates that the increase in the number of repetitions completed prior to volitional fatigue following CrH$_2$O supplementation was significantly greater than that following P ingestion.

4. Discussion and Summary

The purpose of this study was to quantify the effects of oral Cr supplementation on upper extremity anaerobic response in females. An examination of four EF variables revealed a significant gain only in IT work to fatigue. Average peak IK and IT EF torque observed in this investigation exceeded expected values. The results of this study suggest a role for CrH$_2$O supplementation in enhancing IT work to fatigue in females during upper extremity physical conditioning or work activities. This finding is in agreement with previous findings applicable to lower body anaerobic work efforts and upper body strength training [1-4].

Both EF IK$_{CON}$ and EF IK$_{ECC}$ increased to a greater extent in the CrH$_2$O group than in the P group (EF IK$_{CON}$ decreased 1.9% and increased 5.4% in P and CrH$_2$O groups respectively; EF IK$_{ECC}$ increased 1.1% and 4.5% in P and CrH$_2$O groups respectively). Therefore, while no significant interaction existed for IK peak CON and ECC torque during EF, the significant treatment effects for these variables may lend credence to an effect of Cr supplementation in increasing peak IK strength. Limited information in the literature exists concerning the effect of CrH_2O on IK performance.

In summary, Cr is important in regulation of skeletal muscle metabolism. While the roles of endogenous Cr are reasonably well defined, the influence of supplemental CrH_2O is not. It is generally accepted that both muscle and plasma Cr concentrations can be elevated by providing exogenous Cr without any apparent ill effects. Beyond this point, however, both biochemical and performance effects resulting from exogenous Cr supercompensation become less definitive. The exact mechanisms by which exogenous Cr invades skeletal muscle, in addition to the course of action that ensues once intracellular Cr concentrations are elevated, remain unknown. The value of CrH_2O supplementation for the industrial worker is currently limited to possible enhancement of short-duration, high-intensity, intermittent physical activity including powerful activities of both the lower and upper extremities. The practical application of CrH_2O for enhancing productivity or minimizing overexertion injury is yet ill-defined.

Future research efforts should be focused on determining the exact mechanism(s) by which supplemental Cr may increase PC resynthesis and/or delay fatigue. In addition to elucidating mechanisms of action, the time course of supplemental Cr degradation must be discovered. Until more conclusive insight into the half-life of supplemental Cr is gained, experimental design will continue to be a concern in CrH_2O research. The influence of CrH_2O on repeated intermittent bouts of upper-extremity work should be further investigated. Additionally, well designed, highly controlled training studies that explore the relationship between CrH_2O efficacy and training volume could provide valuable information regarding the practical application of this potential ergogen. As the mechanisms by which CrH_2O may exert ergogenic effects are still unclear, efforts to discover whether other substances (e.g., insulin, glucose, vitamin E, chromium, vanadyl sulfate) may further enhance any ergogenic capabilities of CrH_2O are being pursued.

Further investigation into biochemical and performance effects of long-term CrH_2O supplementation should also continue to be pursued. As the mechanisms by which CrH_2O acts may be related to the extent of muscle uptake which may, in turn, be related to LBM and physical training, investigation into the appropriate dosage and timing of supplementation may be of value. This value may extend beyond the traditional sporting environment into other settings such as in the treatment of atrophy-related disease. In addition, the use of this supplementation to increase occupational work capacity (in generally lower intensity environments)   should be examimed with respect to potential impact upon overexertion discomfort.

References

[1] Balsom, P.D., K. Soderlund, and B. Ekblom, Creatine in humans with special reference to creatine supplementation. *Sports Medicine* **18** (1994) 268-280.
[2] Greenhaff, P.L., Creatine and it's application as an ergogenic aid. *International Journal of Sport Nutrition* **5** (1989) S100-S110.
[3] Maughan, R.J., Creatine supplementation and exercise performance. *International Journal Sport Nutrition* **5** (1995) 94-101.
[4] Volek, J.S., and W.J. Kraemer, Creatine supplementation: Its effect on human muscular performance and body composition. *Journal of Strength and Conditioning Research* **10**(3) (1996) 200-210.
[5] Forsberg, A.M., E. Nilsson, J. Werneman, J. Bergstrom, and E. Hultman, Muscle composition in relation to age and sex. *Clinical Science* **81** (1991) 249-256.
[6] Jackson, A.S., and M.L. Pollock, Prediction of body density, lean body weight, and total body volume equations. *Medicine and Science in Sports* **9** (1977) 197-210.
[7] Matheson, L.N., G. Mangseth, J.H. Segal, J.E. Grant, K. Comisso, and S. Westing, Validity and   reliability of a new device to simulate upper extremity work demands. *Journal of Occupational Rehabilitation* **2** (1992) 109-122.
[8] Harris, R.C., K. Soderlund, and E. Hultman, Elevation of creatine in resting and exercised muscle of   normal subjects by creatine supplementation. *Clinical Science* **83** (1992) 367-374.

AUTHOR INDEX

Author Index